OREGON
TITLE 16
CRIMES AND
PUNISHMENTS

2018 EDITION

Oregon Penal Code 2018
TITLE 16 CRIMES AND PUNISHMENTS

Table of Contents

PRINCIPLES

161.005 Short title. ORS 161.005 to 161.055, 161.085 to 161.125, 161.150 to 161.175, 161.190 to 161.275, 161.290 to 161.370, 161.405 to 161.485, 161.505 to 161.585, 161.605, 161.615 to 161.685, 161.705 to 161.737, 162.005, 162.015 to 162.035, 162.055 to 162.115, 162.135 to 162.205, 162.225 to 162.375, 162.405 to 162.425, 162.465, 163.005, 163.115, 163.125 to 163.145, 163.149, 163.160 to 163.208, 163.196, 163.215 to 163.257, 163.261, 163.263, 163.264, 163.266, 163.275, 163.285, 163.305 to 163.467, 163.432, 163.433, 163.472, 163.505 to 163.575, 163.665 to 163.693, 163.700, 163.701, 163.715, 164.005, 164.015 to 164.135, 164.138, 164.140, 164.205 to 164.270, 164.305 to 164.377, 164.395 to 164.415, 164.805, 164.857, 164.886, 165.002 to 165.102, 165.109, 165.118, 165.805, 165.815, 166.005 to 166.095, 166.350, 166.382, 166.384, 166.660, 167.002 to 167.027, 167.057, 167.060 to 167.100, 167.117, 167.122 to 167.162, 167.203 to 167.252, 167.310 to 167.340, 167.350, 167.810 and 167.820 shall be known and may be cited as Oregon Criminal Code of 1971. [1971 c.743 §1; 1979 c.476 §1; 1983 c.740 §25; 1983 c.792 §1; 1985 c.366 §2; 1985 c.557 §9; 1985 c.662 §10; 1985 c.755 §1; 1989 c.982 §3; 1989 c.1003 §5; 2003 c.383 §3; 2007 c.475 §4; 2007 c.684 §2; 2007 c.811 §6; 2007 c.867 §16; 2007 c.869 §5; 2007 c.876 §5; 2009 c.783 §6; 2009 c.811 §15; 2011 c.681 §5; 2015 c.321 §2; 2015 c.379 §2; 2015 c.645 §9; 2016 c.22 §4; 2017 c.649 §2]

161.010 [Repealed by 1971 c.743 §432]

161.015 General definitions. As used in chapter 743, Oregon Laws 1971, and ORS 166.635, unless the context requires otherwise:
(1) "Dangerous weapon" means any weapon, device, instrument, material or substance which under the circumstances in which it is used, attempted to be used or threatened to be used, is readily capable of causing death or serious physical injury.
(2) "Deadly weapon" means any instrument, article or substance specifically designed for and presently capable of causing death or serious physical injury.
(3) "Deadly physical force" means physical force that under the circumstances in which it is used is readily capable of causing death or serious physical injury.
(4) "Peace officer" means:
(a) A member of the Oregon State Police;
(b) A sheriff, constable, marshal, municipal police officer or reserve officer as defined in ORS 133.005, or a police officer commissioned by a university under ORS 352.121 or 353.125;
(c) An investigator of the Criminal Justice Division of the Department of Justice or investigator of a district attorney's office;
(d) A humane special agent as defined in ORS 181A.345;
(e) A regulatory specialist exercising authority described in ORS 471.775 (2);
(f) An authorized tribal police officer as defined in ORS 181A.680; and
(g) Any other person designated by law as a peace officer.
(5) "Person" means a human being and, where appropriate, a public or private corporation, an unincorporated association, a partnership, a government or a governmental instrumentality.
(6) "Physical force" includes, but is not limited to, the use of an electrical stun gun, tear gas or mace.
(7) "Physical injury" means impairment of physical condition or substantial pain.
(8) "Serious physical injury" means physical injury which creates a substantial risk of death or which causes serious and protracted disfigurement, protracted impairment of health or protracted loss or impairment of the function of any bodily organ.
(9) "Possess" means to have physical possession or otherwise to exercise dominion or control over property.
(10) "Public place" means a place to which the general public has access and includes, but is not limited to, hallways, lobbies and other parts of apartment houses and hotels not constituting rooms or apartments designed for actual residence, and highways, streets, schools, places of amusement, parks, playgrounds and premises used in connection with public passenger transportation. [1971 c.743 §3; 1973 c.139 §1; 1979 c.656 §3; 1991 c.67 §33; 1993 c.625 §4; 1995 c.651 §5; 2011 c.506 §22; 2011 c.641 §2; 2011 c.644 §§23,46; 2012 c.54 §§16,17; 2012 c.67 §§9,10; 2013 c.180 §§23,24; 2015 c.174 §11; 2015 c.614 §§147,148]

Note: Legislative Counsel has substituted "chapter 743, Oregon Laws 1971," for the words "this Act" in sections 2, 3, 4, 5, 6, 7, 19, 20, 21 and 36, chapter 743, Oregon Laws 1971, compiled as 161.015, 161.025, 161.035, 161.045, 161.055, 161.085, 161.195, 161.200, 161.205 and 161.295. Specific ORS references have not been substituted, pursuant to 173.160. These sections may be determined by referring to the 1971 Comparative Section Table located in Volume 20 of ORS.

161.020 [Amended by 1967 c.372 §9; repealed by 1971 c.743 §432]

161.025 Purposes; principles of construction. (1) The general purposes of chapter 743, Oregon Laws 1971, are:

(a) To insure the public safety by preventing the commission of offenses through the deterrent influence of the sentences authorized, the correction and rehabilitation of those convicted, and their confinement when required in the interests of public protection.

(b) To forbid and prevent conduct that unjustifiably and inexcusably inflicts or threatens substantial harm to individual or public interests.

(c) To give fair warning of the nature of the conduct declared to constitute an offense and of the sentences authorized upon conviction.

(d) To define the act or omission and the accompanying mental state that constitute each offense and limit the condemnation of conduct as criminal when it is without fault.

(e) To differentiate on reasonable grounds between serious and minor offenses.

(f) To prescribe penalties which are proportionate to the seriousness of offenses and which permit recognition of differences in rehabilitation possibilities among individual offenders.

(g) To safeguard offenders against excessive, disproportionate or arbitrary punishment.

(2) The rule that a penal statute is to be strictly construed shall not apply to chapter 743, Oregon Laws 1971, or any of its provisions. Chapter 743, Oregon Laws 1971, shall be construed according to the fair import of its terms, to promote justice and to effect the purposes stated in subsection (1) of this section. [1971 c.743 §2]

Note: See note under 161.015.

161.030 [Amended by 1955 c.660 §20; 1967 c.372 §10; repealed by 1971 c.743 §432]

161.035 Application of Criminal Code. (1) Chapter 743, Oregon Laws 1971, shall govern the construction of and punishment for any offense defined in chapter 743, Oregon Laws 1971, and committed after January 1, 1972, as well as the construction and application of any defense to a prosecution for such an offense.

(2) Except as otherwise expressly provided, or unless the context requires otherwise, the provisions of chapter 743, Oregon Laws 1971, shall govern the construction of and punishment for any offense defined outside chapter 743, Oregon Laws 1971, and committed after January 1, 1972, as well as the construction and application of any defense to a prosecution for such an offense.

(3) Chapter 743, Oregon Laws 1971, shall not apply to or govern the construction of and punishment for any offense committed before January 1, 1972, or the construction and application of any defense to a prosecution for such an offense. Such an offense shall be construed and punished according to the law existing at the time of the commission of the offense in the same manner as if chapter 743, Oregon Laws 1971, had not been enacted.

(4) When all or part of a criminal statute is amended or repealed, the criminal statute or part thereof so amended or repealed remains in force for the purpose of authorizing the accusation, prosecution, conviction and punishment of a person who violated the statute or part thereof before the effective date of the amending or repealing Act. [1971 c.743 §5]

Note: See note under 161.015.

161.040 [Repealed by 1971 c.743 §432]

161.045 Limits on application. (1) Except as otherwise expressly provided, the procedure governing the accusation, prosecution, conviction and punishment of offenders and offenses is not regulated by chapter 743, Oregon Laws 1971, but by the criminal procedure statutes.

(2) Chapter 743, Oregon Laws 1971, does not affect any power conferred by law upon a court-martial or other military authority or officer to prosecute and punish conduct and offenders violating military codes or laws.

(3) Chapter 743, Oregon Laws 1971, does not bar, suspend or otherwise affect any right or liability to damages, penalty, forfeiture or other remedy authorized by law to be recovered or enforced in a civil action, regardless of whether the conduct involved in the proceeding constitutes an offense defined in chapter 743, Oregon Laws 1971.

(4) No conviction of a person for an offense works a forfeiture of the property of the person, except in cases where a forfeiture is expressly provided by law. [1971 c.743 §6]

Note: See note under 161.015.

161.050 [Repealed by 1971 c.743 §432]

161.055 Burden of proof as to defenses. (1) When a "defense," other than an "affirmative defense" as defined in subsection (2) of this section, is raised at a trial, the state has the burden of disproving the defense beyond a reasonable doubt.

(2) When a defense, declared to be an "affirmative defense" by chapter 743, Oregon Laws 1971, is raised at a trial, the defendant has the burden of proving the defense by a preponderance of the evidence.

(3) The state is not required to negate a defense as defined in subsection (1) of this section unless it is raised by the defendant. "Raised by the defendant" means either notice in writing to the state before commencement of trial or affirmative evidence by a defense witness in the defendant's case in chief. [1971 c.743 §4]

Note: See note under 161.015.

161.060 [Repealed by 1971 c.743 §432]

161.062 [1985 c.722 §4; 1991 c.386 §8; repealed by 1999 c.136 §1]

161.067 Determining punishable offenses for violation of multiple statutory provisions, multiple victims or repeated violations. (1) When the same conduct or criminal episode violates two or more statutory provisions and each provision requires proof of an element that the others do not, there are as many separately punishable offenses as there are separate statutory violations.

(2) When the same conduct or criminal episode, though violating only one statutory provision involves two or more victims, there are as many separately punishable offenses as there are victims. However, two or more persons owning joint interests in real or personal property shall be considered a single victim for purposes of determining the number of separately punishable offenses if the property is the subject of one of the following crimes:

(a) Theft as defined in ORS 164.015.

(b) Unauthorized use of a vehicle as defined in ORS 164.135.

(c) Criminal possession of rented or leased personal property as defined in ORS 164.140.

(d) Criminal possession of a rented or leased motor vehicle as defined in ORS 164.138.

(e) Burglary as defined in ORS 164.215 or 164.225.

(f) Criminal trespass as defined in ORS 164.243, 164.245, 164.255, 164.265 or 164.278.

(g) Arson and related offenses as defined in ORS 164.315, 164.325 or 164.335.

(h) Forgery and related offenses as defined in ORS 165.002 to 165.070.

(3) When the same conduct or criminal episode violates only one statutory provision and involves only one victim, but nevertheless involves repeated violations of the same statutory provision against the same victim, there are as many separately punishable offenses as there are violations, except that each violation, to be separately punishable under this subsection, must be separated from other such violations by a sufficient pause in the defendant's criminal conduct to afford the defendant an opportunity to renounce the criminal intent. Each method of engaging in oral or anal sexual intercourse as defined in ORS 163.305, and each method of engaging in unlawful sexual penetration as defined in ORS 163.408 and 163.411 shall constitute separate violations of their respective statutory provisions for purposes of determining the number of statutory violations. [1987 c.2 §13; 1991 c.386 §9; 2003 c.629 §4; 2007 c.684 §3; 2017 c.318 §1]

161.070 [Repealed by 1971 c.743 §432]

161.075 [1965 c.516 §1; repealed by 1971 c.743 §432]

161.080 [Repealed by 1971 c.743 §432]

CRIMINAL LIABILITY

161.085 Definitions with respect to culpability. As used in chapter 743, Oregon Laws 1971, and ORS 166.635, unless the context requires otherwise:

(1) "Act" means a bodily movement.

(2) "Voluntary act" means a bodily movement performed consciously and includes the conscious possession or control of property.

(3) "Omission" means a failure to perform an act the performance of which is required by law.

(4) "Conduct" means an act or omission and its accompanying mental state.

(5) "To act" means either to perform an act or to omit to perform an act.

(6) "Culpable mental state" means intentionally, knowingly, recklessly or with criminal negligence as these terms are defined in subsections (7), (8), (9) and (10) of this section.

(7) "Intentionally" or "with intent," when used with respect to a result or to conduct described by a statute defining an offense, means that a person acts with a conscious objective to cause the result or to engage in the conduct so described.

(8) "Knowingly" or "with knowledge," when used with respect to conduct or to a circumstance described by a statute defining an offense, means that a person acts with an awareness that the conduct of the person is of a nature so described or that a circumstance so described exists.

(9) "Recklessly," when used with respect to a result or to a circumstance described by a statute defining an offense, means that a person is aware of and consciously disregards a substantial and unjustifiable risk that the result will occur or that the circumstance exists. The risk must be of such nature and degree that disregard thereof constitutes a gross deviation from the standard of care that a reasonable person would observe in the situation.

(10) "Criminal negligence" or "criminally negligent," when used with respect to a result or to a circumstance described by a statute defining an offense, means that a person fails to be aware of a substantial and unjustifiable risk that the result will occur or that the circumstance exists. The risk must be of such nature and degree that the failure to be aware of it constitutes a gross deviation from the standard of care that a reasonable person would observe in the situation. [1971 c.743 §7; 1973 c.139 §2]

Note: See note under 161.015.

161.090 [Amended by 1967 c.372 §11; repealed by 1971 c.743 §432]

161.095 Requirements for criminal liability. (1) The minimal requirement for criminal liability is the performance by a person of conduct which includes a voluntary act or the omission to perform an act which the person is capable of performing.

(2) Except as provided in ORS 161.105, a person is not guilty of an offense unless the person acts with a culpable mental state with respect to each material element of the offense that necessarily requires a culpable mental state. [1971 c.743 §8]

161.100 [Repealed by 1971 c.743 §432]

161.105 Culpability requirement inapplicable to certain violations and offenses. (1) Notwithstanding ORS 161.095, a culpable mental state is not required if:

(a) The offense constitutes a violation, unless a culpable mental state is expressly included in the definition of the offense; or

(b) An offense defined by a statute outside the Oregon Criminal Code clearly indicates a legislative intent to dispense with any culpable mental state requirement for the offense or for any material element thereof.

(2) Notwithstanding any other existing law, and unless a statute enacted after January 1, 1972, otherwise provides, an offense defined by a statute outside the Oregon Criminal Code that requires no culpable mental state constitutes a violation.

(3) Although an offense defined by a statute outside the Oregon Criminal Code requires no culpable mental state with respect to one or more of its material elements, the culpable commission of the offense may be alleged and proved, in which case criminal negligence constitutes sufficient culpability, and the classification of the offense and the authorized sentence shall be determined by ORS 161.505 to 161.605 and 161.615 to 161.655. [1971 c.743 §9]

161.110 [Repealed by 1971 c.743 §432]

161.115 Construction of statutes with respect to culpability. (1) If a statute defining an offense prescribes a culpable mental state but does not specify the element to which it applies, the prescribed culpable mental state applies to each material element of the offense that necessarily requires a culpable mental state.

(2) Except as provided in ORS 161.105, if a statute defining an offense does not prescribe a culpable mental state, culpability is nonetheless required and is established only if a person acts intentionally, knowingly, recklessly or with criminal negligence.

(3) If the definition of an offense prescribes criminal negligence as the culpable mental state, it is also established if a person acts intentionally, knowingly or recklessly. When recklessness suffices to establish a culpable mental state, it is also established if a person acts intentionally or knowingly. When acting knowingly suffices to establish a culpable mental state, it is also established if a person acts intentionally.

(4) Knowledge that conduct constitutes an offense, or knowledge of the existence, meaning or application of the statute defining an offense, is not an element of an offense unless the statute clearly so provides. [1971 c.743 §10]

161.120 [Repealed by 1971 c.743 §432]

161.125 Drug or controlled substance use or dependence or intoxication as defense. (1) The use of drugs or controlled substances, dependence on drugs or controlled substances or voluntary intoxication shall not, as such, constitute a defense to a criminal charge, but in any prosecution for an offense, evidence that the defendant used drugs or controlled substances, or was dependent on drugs or controlled substances, or was intoxicated may be offered by the defendant whenever it is relevant to negative an element of the crime charged.

(2) When recklessness establishes an element of the offense, if the defendant, due to the use of drugs or controlled substances, dependence on drugs or controlled substances or voluntary intoxication, is unaware of a risk of which the defendant would have been aware had the defendant been not intoxicated, not using drugs or controlled

substances, or not dependent on drugs or controlled substances, such unawareness is immaterial. [1971 c.743 §11; 1973 c.697 §13; 1979 c.744 §6]

PARTIES TO CRIME

161.150 Criminal liability described. A person is guilty of a crime if it is committed by the person's own conduct or by the conduct of another for which the person is criminally liable, or both. [1971 c.743 §12]

161.155 Criminal liability for conduct of another. A person is criminally liable for the conduct of another person constituting a crime if:
(1) The person is made criminally liable by the statute defining the crime; or
(2) With the intent to promote or facilitate the commission of the crime the person:
(a) Solicits or commands such other person to commit the crime; or
(b) Aids or abets or agrees or attempts to aid or abet such other person in planning or committing the crime; or
(c) Having a legal duty to prevent the commission of the crime, fails to make an effort the person is legally required to make. [1971 c.743 §13]

161.160 Exclusion of defenses to criminal liability for conduct of another. In any prosecution for a crime in which criminal liability is based upon the conduct of another person pursuant to ORS 161.155, it is no defense that:
(1) Such other person has not been prosecuted for or convicted of any crime based upon the conduct in question or has been convicted of a different crime or degree of crime; or
(2) The crime, as defined, can be committed only by a particular class or classes of persons to which the defendant does not belong, and the defendant is for that reason legally incapable of committing the crime in an individual capacity. [1971 c.743 §14]

161.165 Exemptions to criminal liability for conduct of another. Except as otherwise provided by the statute defining the crime, a person is not criminally liable for conduct of another constituting a crime if:
(1) The person is a victim of that crime; or
(2) The crime is so defined that the conduct of the person is necessarily incidental thereto. [1971 c.743 §15]

161.170 Criminal liability of corporations. (1) A corporation is guilty of an offense if:
(a) The conduct constituting the offense is engaged in by an agent of the corporation while acting within the scope of employment and in behalf of the corporation and the offense is a misdemeanor or a violation, or the offense is one defined by a statute that clearly indicates a legislative intent to impose criminal liability on a corporation; or
(b) The conduct constituting the offense consists of an omission to discharge a specific duty of affirmative performance imposed on corporations by law; or
(c) The conduct constituting the offense is engaged in, authorized, solicited, requested, commanded or knowingly tolerated by the board of directors or by a high managerial agent acting within the scope of employment and in behalf of the corporation.
(2) As used in this section:
(a) "Agent" means any director, officer or employee of a corporation, or any other person who is authorized to act in behalf of the corporation.
(b) "High managerial agent" means an officer of a corporation who exercises authority with respect to the formulation of corporate policy or the supervision in a managerial capacity of subordinate employees, or any other agent in a position of comparable authority. [1971 c.743 §16]

161.175 Criminal liability of an individual for corporate conduct. A person is criminally liable for conduct constituting an offense which the person performs or causes to be performed in the name of or in behalf of a corporation to the same extent as if such conduct were performed in the person's own name or behalf. [1971 c.743 §17]

JUSTIFICATION

161.190 Justification as a defense. In any prosecution for an offense, justification, as defined in ORS 161.195 to 161.275, is a defense. [1971 c.743 §18]

161.195 "Justification" described. (1) Unless inconsistent with other provisions of chapter 743, Oregon Laws 1971, defining justifiable use of physical force, or with some other provision of law, conduct which would otherwise constitute an offense is justifiable and not criminal when it is required or authorized by law or by a judicial decree or is performed by a public servant in the reasonable exercise of official powers, duties or functions.
(2) As used in subsection (1) of this section, "laws and judicial decrees" include but are not limited to:
(a) Laws defining duties and functions of public servants;

(b) Laws defining duties of private citizens to assist public servants in the performance of certain of their functions;

(c) Laws governing the execution of legal process;

(d) Laws governing the military services and conduct of war; and

(e) Judgments and orders of courts. [1971 c.743 §19]

Note: See note under 161.015.

161.200 Choice of evils. (1) Unless inconsistent with other provisions of chapter 743, Oregon Laws 1971, defining justifiable use of physical force, or with some other provision of law, conduct which would otherwise constitute an offense is justifiable and not criminal when:

(a) That conduct is necessary as an emergency measure to avoid an imminent public or private injury; and

(b) The threatened injury is of such gravity that, according to ordinary standards of intelligence and morality, the desirability and urgency of avoiding the injury clearly outweigh the desirability of avoiding the injury sought to be prevented by the statute defining the offense in issue.

(2) The necessity and justifiability of conduct under subsection (1) of this section shall not rest upon considerations pertaining only to the morality and advisability of the statute, either in its general application or with respect to its application to a particular class of cases arising thereunder. [1971 c.743 §20]

Note: See note under 161.015.

161.205 Use of physical force generally. The use of physical force upon another person that would otherwise constitute an offense is justifiable and not criminal under any of the following circumstances:

(1)(a) A parent, guardian or other person entrusted with the care and supervision of a minor or an incompetent person may use reasonable physical force upon such minor or incompetent person when and to the extent the person reasonably believes it necessary to maintain discipline or to promote the welfare of the minor or incompetent person.

(b) Personnel of a public education program, as that term is defined in ORS 339.285, may use reasonable physical force upon a student when and to the extent the application of force is consistent with ORS 339.291.

(2) An authorized official of a jail, prison or correctional facility may use physical force when and to the extent that the official reasonably believes it necessary to maintain order and discipline or as is authorized by law.

(3) A person responsible for the maintenance of order in a common carrier of passengers, or a person acting under the direction of the person, may use physical force when and to the extent that the person reasonably believes it necessary to maintain order, but the person may use deadly physical force only when the person reasonably believes it necessary to prevent death or serious physical injury.

(4) A person acting under a reasonable belief that another person is about to commit suicide or to inflict serious physical self-injury may use physical force upon that person to the extent that the person reasonably believes it necessary to thwart the result.

(5) A person may use physical force upon another person in self-defense or in defending a third person, in defending property, in making an arrest or in preventing an escape, as hereafter prescribed in chapter 743, Oregon Laws 1971. [1971 c.743 §21; 1981 c.246 §1; 2011 c.665 §§10,11; 2013 c.133 §4; 2013 c.267 §4]

Note: See note under 161.015.

161.209 Use of physical force in defense of a person. Except as provided in ORS 161.215 and 161.219, a person is justified in using physical force upon another person for self-defense or to defend a third person from what the person reasonably believes to be the use or imminent use of unlawful physical force, and the person may use a degree of force which the person reasonably believes to be necessary for the purpose. [1971 c.743 §22]

161.210 [Repealed by 1971 c.743 §432]

161.215 Limitations on use of physical force in defense of a person. Notwithstanding ORS 161.209, a person is not justified in using physical force upon another person if:

(1) With intent to cause physical injury or death to another person, the person provokes the use of unlawful physical force by that person; or

(2) The person is the initial aggressor, except that the use of physical force upon another person under such circumstances is justifiable if the person withdraws from the encounter and effectively communicates to the other person the intent to do so, but the latter nevertheless continues or threatens to continue the use of unlawful physical force; or

(3) The physical force involved is the product of a combat by agreement not specifically authorized by law. [1971 c.743 §24]

9

161.219 Limitations on use of deadly physical force in defense of a person. Notwithstanding the provisions of ORS 161.209, a person is not justified in using deadly physical force upon another person unless the person reasonably believes that the other person is:

(1) Committing or attempting to commit a felony involving the use or threatened imminent use of physical force against a person; or

(2) Committing or attempting to commit a burglary in a dwelling; or

(3) Using or about to use unlawful deadly physical force against a person. [1971 c.743 §23]

161.220 [Repealed by 1971 c.743 §432]

161.225 Use of physical force in defense of premises. (1) A person in lawful possession or control of premises is justified in using physical force upon another person when and to the extent that the person reasonably believes it necessary to prevent or terminate what the person reasonably believes to be the commission or attempted commission of a criminal trespass by the other person in or upon the premises.

(2) A person may use deadly physical force under the circumstances set forth in subsection (1) of this section only:

(a) In defense of a person as provided in ORS 161.219; or

(b) When the person reasonably believes it necessary to prevent the commission of arson or a felony by force and violence by the trespasser.

(3) As used in subsection (1) and subsection (2)(a) of this section, "premises" includes any building as defined in ORS 164.205 and any real property. As used in subsection (2)(b) of this section, "premises" includes any building. [1971 c.743 §25]

161.229 Use of physical force in defense of property. A person is justified in using physical force, other than deadly physical force, upon another person when and to the extent that the person reasonably believes it to be necessary to prevent or terminate the commission or attempted commission by the other person of theft or criminal mischief of property. [1971 c.743 §26]

161.230 [Repealed by 1971 c.743 §432]

161.235 Use of physical force in making an arrest or in preventing an escape. Except as provided in ORS 161.239, a peace officer is justified in using physical force upon another person only when and to the extent that the peace officer reasonably believes it necessary:

(1) To make an arrest or to prevent the escape from custody of an arrested person unless the peace officer knows that the arrest is unlawful; or

(2) For self-defense or to defend a third person from what the peace officer reasonably believes to be the use or imminent use of physical force while making or attempting to make an arrest or while preventing or attempting to prevent an escape. [1971 c.743 §27]

161.239 Use of deadly physical force in making an arrest or in preventing an escape. (1) Notwithstanding the provisions of ORS 161.235, a peace officer may use deadly physical force only when the peace officer reasonably believes that:

(a) The crime committed by the person was a felony or an attempt to commit a felony involving the use or threatened imminent use of physical force against a person; or

(b) The crime committed by the person was kidnapping, arson, escape in the first degree, burglary in the first degree or any attempt to commit such a crime; or

(c) Regardless of the particular offense which is the subject of the arrest or attempted escape, the use of deadly physical force is necessary to defend the peace officer or another person from the use or threatened imminent use of deadly physical force; or

(d) The crime committed by the person was a felony or an attempt to commit a felony and under the totality of the circumstances existing at the time and place, the use of such force is necessary; or

(e) The officer's life or personal safety is endangered in the particular circumstances involved.

(2) Nothing in subsection (1) of this section constitutes justification for reckless or criminally negligent conduct by a peace officer amounting to an offense against or with respect to innocent persons whom the peace officer is not seeking to arrest or retain in custody. [1971 c.743 §28]

161.240 [Repealed by 1971 c.743 §432]

161.245 "Reasonable belief" described; status of unlawful arrest. (1) For the purposes of ORS 161.235 and 161.239, a reasonable belief that a person has committed an offense means a reasonable belief in facts or circumstances which if true would in law constitute an offense. If the believed facts or circumstances would not in law constitute an offense, an erroneous though not unreasonable belief that the law is otherwise does not render justifiable the use of force to make an arrest or to prevent an escape from custody.

(2) A peace officer who is making an arrest is justified in using the physical force prescribed in ORS 161.235 and 161.239 unless the arrest is unlawful and is known by the officer to be unlawful. [1971 c.743 §29]

161.249 Use of physical force by private person assisting an arrest. (1) Except as provided in subsection (2) of this section, a person who has been directed by a peace officer to assist the peace officer to make an arrest or to prevent an escape from custody is justified in using physical force when and to the extent that the person reasonably believes that force to be necessary to carry out the peace officer's direction.

(2) A person who has been directed to assist a peace officer under circumstances specified in subsection (1) of this section may use deadly physical force to make an arrest or to prevent an escape only when:

(a) The person reasonably believes that force to be necessary for self-defense or to defend a third person from what the person reasonably believes to be the use or imminent use of deadly physical force; or

(b) The person is directed or authorized by the peace officer to use deadly physical force unless the person knows that the peace officer is not authorized to use deadly physical force under the circumstances. [1971 c.743 §30]

161.250 [Repealed by 1971 c.743 §432]

161.255 Use of physical force by private person making citizen's arrest. (1) Except as provided in subsection (2) of this section, a private person acting on the person's own account is justified in using physical force upon another person when and to the extent that the person reasonably believes it necessary to make an arrest or to prevent the escape from custody of an arrested person whom the person has arrested under ORS 133.225.

(2) A private person acting under the circumstances prescribed in subsection (1) of this section is justified in using deadly physical force only when the person reasonably believes it necessary for self-defense or to defend a third person from what the person reasonably believes to be the use or imminent use of deadly physical force. [1971 c.743 §31; 1973 c.836 §339]

161.260 Use of physical force in resisting arrest prohibited. A person may not use physical force to resist an arrest by a peace officer who is known or reasonably appears to be a peace officer, whether the arrest is lawful or unlawful. [1971 c.743 §32]

161.265 Use of physical force to prevent escape. (1) A guard or other peace officer employed in a correctional facility, as that term is defined in ORS 162.135, is justified in using physical force, including deadly physical force, when and to the extent that the guard or peace officer reasonably believes it necessary to prevent the escape of a prisoner from a correctional facility.

(2) Notwithstanding subsection (1) of this section, a guard or other peace officer employed by the Department of Corrections may not use deadly physical force in the circumstances described in ORS 161.267 (3). [1971 c.743 §33; 2005 c.431 §3]

161.267 Use of physical force by corrections officer or official employed by Department of Corrections. (1) As used in this section:

(a) "Colocated minimum security facility" means a Department of Corrections institution that has been designated by the Department of Corrections as a minimum security facility and has been located by the department on the grounds of a medium or higher security Department of Corrections institution.

(b) "Department of Corrections institution" has the meaning given that term in ORS 421.005.

(c) "Stand-alone minimum security facility" means a Department of Corrections institution that has been designated by the department as a minimum security facility and that has been located by the department separate and apart from other Department of Corrections institutions.

(2) A corrections officer or other official employed by the Department of Corrections is justified in using physical force, including deadly physical force, when and to the extent that the officer or official reasonably believes it necessary to:

(a) Prevent the escape of an inmate from a Department of Corrections institution, including the grounds of the institution, or from custody;

(b) Maintain or restore order and discipline in a Department of Corrections institution, or any part of the institution, in the event of a riot, disturbance or other occurrence that threatens the safety of inmates, department employees or other persons; or

(c) Prevent serious physical injury to or the death of the officer, official or another person.

(3) Notwithstanding subsection (2)(a) of this section, a corrections officer or other official employed by the department may not use deadly physical force to prevent the escape of an inmate from:

(a) A stand-alone minimum security facility;

(b) A colocated minimum security facility, if the corrections officer or other official knows that the inmate has been classified by the department as minimum custody; or

11

(c) Custody outside of a Department of Corrections institution:

(A) While the inmate is assigned to an inmate work crew; or

(B) During transport or other supervised activity, if the inmate is classified by the department as minimum custody and the inmate is not being transported or supervised with an inmate who has been classified by the department as medium or higher custody.

(4) Nothing in this section limits the authority of a person to use physical force under ORS 161.205 (2) or 161.265. [2005 c.431 §2]

161.270 Duress. (1) The commission of acts which would otherwise constitute an offense, other than murder, is not criminal if the actor engaged in the proscribed conduct because the actor was coerced to do so by the use or threatened use of unlawful physical force upon the actor or a third person, which force or threatened force was of such nature or degree to overcome earnest resistance.

(2) Duress is not a defense for one who intentionally or recklessly places oneself in a situation in which it is probable that one will be subjected to duress.

(3) It is not a defense that a spouse acted on the command of the other spouse, unless the spouse acted under such coercion as would establish a defense under subsection (1) of this section. [1971 c.743 §34; 1987 c.158 §22]

161.275 Entrapment. (1) The commission of acts which would otherwise constitute an offense is not criminal if the actor engaged in the proscribed conduct because the actor was induced to do so by a law enforcement official, or by a person acting in cooperation with a law enforcement official, for the purpose of obtaining evidence to be used against the actor in a criminal prosecution.

(2) As used in this section, "induced" means that the actor did not contemplate and would not otherwise have engaged in the proscribed conduct. Merely affording the actor an opportunity to commit an offense does not constitute entrapment. [1971 c.743 §35]

RESPONSIBILITY

161.290 Incapacity due to immaturity. (1) A person who is tried as an adult in a court of criminal jurisdiction is not criminally responsible for any conduct which occurred when the person was under 12 years of age.

(2) Incapacity due to immaturity, as defined in subsection (1) of this section, is a defense. [Formerly 161.380; 1995 c.422 §58]

161.295 Effect of qualifying mental disorder; guilty except for insanity. (1) A person is guilty except for insanity if, as a result of a qualifying mental disorder at the time of engaging in criminal conduct, the person lacks substantial capacity either to appreciate the criminality of the conduct or to conform the conduct to the requirements of law.

(2) As used in chapter 743, Oregon Laws 1971, the term "qualifying mental disorder" does not include an abnormality manifested only by repeated criminal or otherwise antisocial conduct, nor does the term include any abnormality constituting solely a personality disorder. [1971 c.743 §36; 1983 c.800 §1; 2017 c.634 §3]

Note: See note under 161.015.

161.300 Evidence of qualifying mental disorder admissible as to intent. Evidence that the actor suffered from a qualifying mental disorder is admissible whenever it is relevant to the issue of whether the actor did or did not have the intent which is an element of the crime. [1971 c.743 §37; 2017 c.634 §4]

161.305 Qualifying mental disorder as affirmative defense. Qualifying mental disorder constituting insanity under ORS 161.295 is an affirmative defense. [1971 c.743 §38; 1983 c.800 §2; 2017 c.634 §5]

161.309 Notice and report prerequisite to defense; content. (1) The defendant may not introduce evidence on the issue of insanity under ORS 161.295, unless the defendant:

(a) Gives notice of intent to do so in the manner provided in subsection (3) of this section; and

(b) Files with the court a report of a psychiatric or psychological evaluation, conducted by a certified evaluator, in the manner provided in subsection (4) of this section.

(2) The defendant may not introduce in the case in chief expert testimony regarding partial responsibility or diminished capacity under ORS 161.300 unless the defendant gives notice of intent to do so in the manner provided in subsection (3) of this section.

(3) A defendant who is required under subsection (1) or (2) of this section to give notice shall file a written notice of purpose at the time the defendant pleads not guilty. The defendant may file the notice at any time after the plea but before trial when just cause for failure to file the notice at the time of making the plea is shown. If the defendant fails to file notice, the defendant may not introduce evidence for the establishment of a defense under ORS 161.295 or

161.300 unless the court, in its discretion, permits the evidence to be introduced where just cause for failure to file the notice is shown.

(4) A defendant who is required under subsection (1) of this section to file a report of a psychiatric or psychological evaluation shall file the report before trial. The report must be based on an evaluation conducted after the date of the alleged offense and must address the issue of insanity under ORS 161.295 and the dispositional determination described in ORS 161.325. If the defendant fails to file a complete report before trial, the defendant may not introduce evidence for the establishment of a defense under ORS 161.295 unless:

(a) The court, in its discretion, permits the evidence to be introduced when just cause for failure to file the report is shown; and

(b) If the defendant is charged with a felony, the defendant is tried by a jury.

(5)(a) A court may not accept a plea of guilty except for insanity to a felony unless a report described in subsection (4) of this section is filed with the court. If the report has not been filed, the court may order that a psychiatric or psychological evaluation of the defendant be conducted by a certified evaluator and a report of the evaluation be filed with the court.

(b) When the court orders an evaluation of a financially eligible person under this subsection, the court shall order the public defense services executive director to pay a reasonable fee for the evaluation from funds available for that purpose.

(c) A certified evaluator performing an evaluation of a defendant on the issue of insanity under this subsection is not obligated to evaluate the defendant for fitness to proceed unless, during the evaluation, the certified evaluator determines that the defendant's fitness to proceed is drawn in question.

(6) As used in this section, "certified evaluator" means a psychiatrist or psychologist who holds a valid certification under the provisions of ORS 161.392. [1971 c.743 §§39,40,41; 1983 c.800 §3; 2003 c.127 §2; 2011 c.724 §1; 2017 c.48 §1]

161.310 [Repealed by 1971 c.743 §432]

161.313 Jury instructions; insanity. When the issue of insanity under ORS 161.295 is submitted to be determined by a jury in the trial court, the court shall instruct the jury in accordance with ORS 161.327. [1983 c.800 §16]

161.315 Right of state to obtain mental examination of defendant; limitations. (1) Upon filing of notice or the introduction of evidence by the defendant as provided in ORS 161.309, the state shall have the right to have at least one psychiatrist or licensed psychologist of its selection examine the defendant. The state shall file notice with the court of its intention to have the defendant examined.

(2)(a) Upon filing of the notice, the court, in its discretion, may order the defendant committed to a state institution or any other suitable facility, if the defendant is 18 years of age or older, for observation and examination as the court may designate for a period not to exceed 30 days.

(b) If the defendant is under 18 years of age, upon filing of the notice, the court, in its discretion, may order the defendant committed to a secure intensive community inpatient facility designated by the Oregon Health Authority for observation and examination as the court may designate for a period not to exceed 30 days.

(3) If the defendant objects to the examiner chosen by the state, the court for good cause shown may direct the state to select a different examiner.

(4) An examiner performing an examination on the issue of insanity of a defendant under this section is not obligated to examine the defendant for fitness to proceed unless, during the examination, the examiner determines that the defendant's fitness to proceed is drawn in question. [1971 c.743 §42; 1977 c.380 §3; 2007 c.14 §5; 2009 c.595 §101; 2011 c.724 §10; 2017 c.48 §2]

161.319 Form of verdict on guilty except for insanity. When the defendant is found guilty except for insanity under ORS 161.295, the verdict and judgment shall so state. [1971 c.743 §43; 1977 c.380 §4; 1983 c.800 §4]

161.320 [Repealed by 1971 c.743 §432]

161.325 Entry of judgment of guilty except for insanity; dispositional order. (1) After entry of judgment of guilty except for insanity, the court shall, on the basis of the evidence given at the trial or at a separate hearing, if requested by either party, enter an order as provided in ORS 161.327, 161.328 or 161.329, whichever is appropriate.

(2) If the court enters an order as provided in ORS 161.327, it shall also:

(a) Determine on the record the offense of which the person otherwise would have been convicted;

(b) State on the record the qualifying mental disorder on which the defendant relied for the guilty except for insanity defense; and

(c) Make specific findings on whether there is a victim of the crime for which the defendant has been found guilty except for insanity and, if so, whether the victim wishes to be notified, under ORS 161.326, of any hearings and orders concerning the defendant and of any conditional release, discharge or escape of the defendant.

(3) The court shall include any such findings in its order.

(4) Except under circumstances described in ORS 137.076 (4), whenever a defendant charged with any offense listed in ORS 137.076 (1) has been found guilty of that offense except for insanity, the court shall, in any order entered under ORS 161.327, 161.328 or 161.329, direct the defendant to submit to the obtaining of a blood or buccal sample in the manner provided in ORS 137.076. [1971 c.743 §44; 1977 c.380 §5; 1979 c.885 §1; 1981 c.711 §1; 1983 c.800 §5; 1991 c.669 §8; 1999 c.97 §2; 2005 c.337 §1; 2010 c.89 §9; 2011 c.708 §40; 2011 c.724 §2; 2017 c.634 §6]

161.326 Notice to victim. (1) If the trial court or the Psychiatric Security Review Board determines that a victim desires notification as described in ORS 161.325 (2), the board shall make a reasonable effort to notify the victim of hearings and orders, conditional release, discharge or escape. Nothing in this subsection authorizes the board to disseminate information that is otherwise privileged by law.

(2) When the board conducts a hearing involving a person found guilty except for insanity of a crime for which there is a victim, the board shall afford the victim an opportunity to be heard, either orally or in writing, at the hearing.

(3)(a) If the board fails to make a reasonable effort to notify the victim of a hearing under subsection (1) of this section or fails to afford the victim an opportunity to be heard at the hearing under subsection (2) of this section, the victim may request that the board reconsider the order of the board.

(b) If the board determines that the board failed to make a reasonable effort to notify the victim or failed to afford the victim an opportunity to be heard, except as provided in paragraph (c) of this subsection, the board shall grant the request for reconsideration. Upon reconsideration, the board shall consider the statement of the victim and may consider any other information that was not available to the board at the previous hearing.

(c) The board may not grant a request for reconsideration that is made:

(A) After the person has been discharged from the jurisdiction of the board;

(B) After the board has held a subsequent hearing involving the person; or

(C) If the board failed to make a reasonable effort to notify the victim of a hearing, more than 30 days after the victim knew or reasonably should have known of the hearing. [1981 c.711 §9; 2010 c.89 §6; 2011 c.708 §6; 2017 c.442 §7]

Note: The amendments to 161.326 by section 7, chapter 442, Oregon Laws 2017, become operative July 1, 2018. See section 36, chapter 442, Oregon Laws 2017. The text that is operative until July 1, 2018, is set forth for the user's convenience.

161.326. (1) If the trial court, the Psychiatric Security Review Board or the Oregon Health Authority determines that a victim desires notification as described in ORS 161.325 (2), the agency having jurisdiction over the person shall make a reasonable effort to notify the victim of hearings and orders, conditional release, discharge or escape. Nothing in this subsection authorizes the agency to disseminate information that is otherwise privileged by law.

(2) When the agency conducts a hearing involving a person found guilty except for insanity of a crime for which there is a victim, the agency shall afford the victim an opportunity to be heard, either orally or in writing, at the hearing.

(3)(a) If the agency fails to make a reasonable effort to notify the victim of a hearing under subsection (1) of this section or fails to afford the victim an opportunity to be heard at the hearing under subsection (2) of this section, the victim may request that the agency reconsider the order of the agency.

(b) If the agency determines that the agency failed to make a reasonable effort to notify the victim or failed to afford the victim an opportunity to be heard, except as provided in paragraph (c) of this subsection, the agency shall grant the request for reconsideration. Upon reconsideration, the agency shall consider the statement of the victim and may consider any other information that was not available to the agency at the previous hearing.

(c) The agency may not grant a request for reconsideration that is made:

(A) After the person has been discharged from the jurisdiction of the board and the authority;

(B) After the board or the authority has held a subsequent hearing involving the person; or

(C) If the agency failed to make a reasonable effort to notify the victim of a hearing, more than 30 days after the victim knew or reasonably should have known of the hearing.

Note: 161.326 was enacted into law by the Legislative Assembly but was not added to or made a part of 161.290 to 161.370 or any series therein by legislative action. See Preface to Oregon Revised Statutes for further explanation.

161.327 Commitment or conditional release of person found guilty except for insanity of felony; appeal. (1) Following the entry of a judgment pursuant to ORS 161.319, if the court finds by a preponderance of the evidence that a person found guilty except for insanity of a felony is affected by a qualifying mental disorder and presents a substantial danger to others, the court shall enter an order as follows:

(a) If the court finds that the person is not a proper subject for conditional release, the court shall order the person committed to a state hospital or, if the person is under 18 years of age, to a secure intensive community inpatient facility for custody, care and treatment. When the court orders a person committed under this paragraph, the court shall place the person under the jurisdiction of the Psychiatric Security Review Board.

(b) If the court finds that the person can be adequately controlled with supervision and treatment if conditionally released and that necessary supervision and treatment are available, the court shall order the person conditionally released.

(2) When a person is conditionally released under this section, the person is subject to those supervisory orders of the court as are in the best interests of justice, the protection of society and the welfare of the person. The court shall designate a person or state, county or local agency to supervise the person upon release, subject to those conditions as the court directs in the order for conditional release. Prior to the designation, the court shall notify the person or agency to whom conditional release is contemplated and provide the person or agency an opportunity to be heard before the court. After receiving an order entered under subsection (1)(b) of this section, the person or agency designated shall assume supervision of the person pursuant to the direction of the Psychiatric Security Review Board. The person or agency designated as supervisor shall be required to report in writing no less than once per month to the board concerning the supervised person's compliance with the conditions of release.

(3) In determining whether a person should be conditionally released, the court:

(a) May order evaluations, examinations and compliance as provided in ORS 161.336 (3) and 161.346 (2);

(b) Shall order that the person be examined by a local mental health program designated by the board and a report of the examination be provided to the court if each felony for which the defendant was found guilty except for insanity is a Class C felony; and

(c) Shall have as its primary concern the protection of society.

(4) Upon placing a person on conditional release, the court shall notify the board in writing of the court's conditional release order, the supervisor appointed and all other conditions of release, and the person shall be on conditional release pending hearing before the board. Upon compliance with this section, the court's jurisdiction over the person is terminated.

(5) The total period of commitment or conditional release under ORS 161.315 to 161.351 may not exceed the maximum sentence provided by statute for the crime for which the person was found guilty except for insanity.

(6) An order of the court under this section is a final order appealable by the person found guilty except for insanity in accordance with ORS 19.205 (5). Notwithstanding ORS 19.255, notice of an appeal under this section shall be served and filed within 90 days after the order appealed from is entered in the register. The person shall be entitled on appeal to suitable counsel possessing skills and experience commensurate with the nature and complexity of the case. If the person is financially eligible, suitable counsel shall be appointed in the manner provided in ORS 138.500 (1), and the compensation for counsel and costs and expenses of the person necessary to the appeal shall be determined and paid as provided in ORS 138.500.

(7) Following the entry of an order described in subsection (1) of this section, the court shall notify the person of the right to appeal and the right to a hearing before the board in accordance with ORS 161.336 (5) and 161.341 (3). [1979 c.867 §5; 1979 c.885 §2; 1981 c.711 §2; 1981 s.s. c.3 §129; 1983 c.800 §6; 1989 c.790 §48; 1995 c.208 §1; 2001 c.962 §89; 2003 c.576 §§578,579; 2005 c.685 §§1,1a; 2009 c.595 §102; 2011 c.708 §36; 2011 c.724 §3; 2013 c.1 §9; 2017 c.442 §12; 2017 c.634 §7]

Note: The amendments to 161.327 by section 12, chapter 442, Oregon Laws 2017, become operative July 1, 2018. See section 36, chapter 442, Oregon Laws 2017. The text that is operative until July 1, 2018, including amendments by section 7, chapter 634, Oregon Laws 2017, is set forth for the user's convenience.

161.327. (1) Following the entry of a judgment pursuant to ORS 161.319, if the court finds by a preponderance of the evidence that a person found guilty except for insanity of a felony is affected by a qualifying mental disorder and presents a substantial danger to others, the court shall enter an order as follows:

(a) If the court finds that the person is not a proper subject for conditional release, the court shall order the person committed to a state hospital or, if the person is under 18 years of age, to a secure intensive community inpatient facility for custody, care and treatment. When the court orders a person committed under this paragraph, the court shall place the person under the jurisdiction of:

(A) The Psychiatric Security Review Board, if the person is a tier one offender.

(B) The Oregon Health Authority, if the person is a tier two offender.

(b) If the court finds that the person can be adequately controlled with supervision and treatment if conditionally released and that necessary supervision and treatment are available, the court shall order the person conditionally released.

(2) When a person is conditionally released under this section, the person is subject to those supervisory orders of the court as are in the best interests of justice, the protection of society and the welfare of the person. The court shall designate a person or state, county or local agency to supervise the person upon release, subject to those conditions as the court directs in the order for conditional release. Prior to the designation, the court shall notify the person or agency to whom conditional release is contemplated and provide the person or agency an opportunity to be heard before the court. After receiving an order entered under subsection (1)(b) of this section, the person or agency designated shall assume supervision of the person pursuant to the direction of the Psychiatric Security Review Board. The person or agency designated as supervisor shall be required to report in writing no less than once per month to the board concerning the supervised person's compliance with the conditions of release.

(3) In determining whether a person should be conditionally released, the court:

(a) May order evaluations, examinations and compliance as provided in ORS 161.336 (3) and 161.346 (3);

(b) Shall order that the person be examined by a local mental health program designated by the board and a report of the examination be provided to the court if each felony for which the defendant was found guilty except for insanity is a Class C felony; and

(c) Shall have as its primary concern the protection of society.

(4) Upon placing a person on conditional release, the court shall notify the board in writing of the court's conditional release order, the supervisor appointed and all other conditions of release, and the person shall be on conditional release pending hearing before the board. Upon compliance with this section, the court's jurisdiction over the person is terminated.

(5) The total period of commitment or conditional release under ORS 161.315 to 161.351 may not exceed the maximum sentence provided by statute for the crime for which the person was found guilty except for insanity.

(6) An order of the court under this section is a final order appealable by the person found guilty except for insanity in accordance with ORS 19.205 (5). Notwithstanding ORS 19.255, notice of an appeal under this section shall be served and filed within 90 days after the order appealed from is entered in the register. The person shall be entitled on appeal to suitable counsel possessing skills and experience commensurate with the nature and complexity of the case. If the person is financially eligible, suitable counsel shall be appointed in the manner provided in ORS 138.500 (1), and the compensation for counsel and costs and expenses of the person necessary to the appeal shall be determined and paid as provided in ORS 138.500.

(7) Following the entry of an order described in subsection (1) of this section, the court shall notify the person of the right to appeal and the right to a hearing before the agency exercising jurisdiction over the person in accordance with ORS 161.336 (5) and 161.341 (3).

161.328 Commitment of person found guilty except for insanity of misdemeanor. (1) Following the entry of a judgment pursuant to ORS 161.319, the court shall order a person committed to a state mental hospital or other facility designated by the Oregon Health Authority if:

(a) Each offense for which the person is found guilty except for insanity is a misdemeanor; and

(b) The court finds that the person is affected by a qualifying mental disorder and presents a substantial danger to others that requires commitment.

(2) The total period of commitment under this section may not exceed the maximum sentence provided by statute for the crime for which the person was found guilty except for insanity.

(3) If the superintendent of the state mental hospital or the director of the facility to which the person is committed determines that a person committed under this section is no longer affected by a qualifying mental disorder or, if so affected, no longer presents a substantial danger to others that requires commitment, the superintendent or director shall file notice of that determination with the committing court. Upon filing of the notice, the superintendent or director shall discharge the person from custody. [1981 c.711 §3; 1983 c.800 §7; 1987 c.903 §36; 1995 c.529 §1; 2011 c.708 §37; 2011 c.724 §4; 2017 c.634 §8]

161.329 Order of discharge. Following the entry of a judgment pursuant to ORS 161.319, the court shall order that the person be discharged from custody if:

(1) The court finds that the person is no longer affected by a qualifying mental disorder, or, if so affected, no longer presents a substantial danger to others and is not in need of care, supervision or treatment; or

(2)(a) Each offense for which the person is found guilty except for insanity is a misdemeanor; and

(b) The court finds that the person does not present a substantial danger to others that requires commitment. [1971 c.743 §45; 1977 c.380 §6; 1981 c.711 §4; 2011 c.724 §5; 2017 c.634 §9]

161.330 [Repealed by 1971 c.743 §432]

161.332 "Conditional release" defined. As used in ORS 161.315 to 161.351 and 161.385 to 161.395, "conditional release" includes, but is not limited to, the monitoring of mental and physical health treatment. [1977 c.380 §1; 1983 c.800 §8; 2011 c.708 §11a; 2017 c.442 §11]

Note: The amendments to 161.332 by section 11, chapter 442, Oregon Laws 2017, become operative July 1, 2018. See section 36, chapter 442, Oregon Laws 2017. The text that is operative until July 1, 2018, is set forth for the user's convenience.

161.332. As used in ORS 161.315 to 161.351 and 161.385 to 161.395:

(1) "Conditional release" includes, but is not limited to, the monitoring of mental and physical health treatment.

(2) "Tier one offender" means a person who has been found guilty except for insanity of a tier one offense.

(3) "Tier one offense" means:

(a) Aggravated murder as defined in ORS 163.095;

(b) Attempt or conspiracy to commit aggravated murder as defined in ORS 163.095;

(c) Murder as defined in ORS 163.115;

(d) Attempt or conspiracy to commit murder as defined in ORS 163.115;

(e) Manslaughter in the first degree as defined in ORS 163.118;

(f) Manslaughter in the second degree as defined in ORS 163.125;

(g) Assault in the first degree as defined in ORS 163.185;

(h) Assault in the second degree as defined in ORS 163.175;

(i) Kidnapping in the first degree as defined in ORS 163.235;

(j) Kidnapping in the second degree as defined in ORS 163.225;

(k) Rape in the first degree as defined ORS 163.375;

(L) Rape in the second degree as defined in ORS 163.365;

(m) Sodomy in the first degree as defined in ORS 163.405;

(n) Sodomy in the second degree as defined in ORS 163.395;

(o) Unlawful sexual penetration in the first degree as defined ORS 163.411;

(p) Unlawful sexual penetration in the second degree as defined ORS 163.408;

(q) Sexual abuse in the first degree as defined in ORS 163.427;

(r) Robbery in the first degree as defined in ORS 164.415;

(s) Robbery in the second degree as defined in ORS 164.405;

(t) Arson in the first degree as defined in ORS 164.325;

(u) Using a child in a display of sexually explicit conduct as defined in ORS 163.670;

(v) Compelling prostitution as defined in ORS 167.017; or

(w) Aggravated vehicular homicide as defined in ORS 163.149.

(4) "Tier two offender" means a person who has been found guilty except for insanity only of offenses that are not tier one offenses.

161.335 [1971 c.743 §46; 1973 c.137 §1; 1975 c.380 §1; repealed by 1977 c.380 §10 (161.336 enacted in lieu of 161.335)]

161.336 Conditional release by board; termination or modification of conditional release; hearing. (1)(a) When a person is conditionally released under ORS 161.315 to 161.351, the person is subject to those supervisory orders of the Psychiatric Security Review Board as are in the best interests of justice, the protection of society and the welfare of the person.

(b) An order of conditional release entered by the board may designate any person or state, county or local agency capable of supervising the person upon release, subject to the conditions described in the order of conditional release.

(c) Prior to the designation, the board shall notify the person or state, county or local agency to whom conditional release is contemplated and provide the person or state, county or local agency an opportunity to be heard.

(d) After receiving an order entered under this section, the person or state, county or local agency designated in the order shall assume supervision of the person in accordance with the conditions described in the order and any modifications of the conditions ordered by the board.

(2) Conditions of release contained in orders entered under this section may be modified from time to time and conditional releases may be terminated as provided in ORS 161.351.

(3)(a) As a condition of release, the person may be required to report to any state or local mental health facility for evaluation. Whenever medical, psychiatric or psychological treatment is recommended, the order may require the person, as a condition of release, to cooperate with and accept the treatment from the facility.

(b) The facility to which the person has been referred for evaluation shall perform the evaluation and submit a written report of its findings to the board. If the facility finds that treatment of the person is appropriate, it shall include its recommendations for treatment in the report to the board.

(c) Whenever treatment is provided by the facility, it shall furnish reports to the board on a regular basis concerning the progress of the person.

(d) Copies of all reports submitted to the board pursuant to this section shall be furnished to the person and the person's counsel. The confidentiality of these reports is determined pursuant to ORS 192.338, 192.345 and 192.355.

(e) The facility shall comply with the conditional release order and any modifications of the conditions ordered by the board.

(4)(a) If at any time while the person is under the jurisdiction of the board it appears to the board or its chairperson that the person has violated the terms of the conditional release or that the mental health of the individual has changed, the board or its chairperson may order the person returned for evaluation or treatment to a state hospital or, if the person is under 18 years of age, to a secure intensive community inpatient facility. A written order of the board, or its chairperson on behalf of the board, is sufficient warrant for any law enforcement officer to take into custody such person and transport the person accordingly. A sheriff, municipal police officer, constable, parole and probation officer, prison official or other peace officer shall execute the order, and the person shall be returned as soon as practicable to the state hospital or secure intensive community inpatient facility designated in the order.

(b) The community mental health program director, the director of the facility providing treatment to a person on conditional release, any peace officer or any person responsible for the supervision of a person on conditional release may take a person on conditional release into custody or request that the person be taken into custody if there is reasonable cause to believe the person is a substantial danger to others because of a qualifying mental disorder and that the person is in need of immediate care, custody or treatment. Any person taken into custody pursuant to this subsection shall be transported as soon as practicable to a state hospital or, if the person is under 18 years of age, to a secure intensive community inpatient facility.

(c) Within 20 days following the return of the person to a state hospital or secure intensive community inpatient facility under this subsection, the board shall conduct a hearing. The board shall provide notice of the hearing to the person, the attorney representing the person and the Attorney General. The state must prove by a preponderance of the evidence the person's unfitness for conditional release. The hearing shall be conducted in accordance with ORS 161.346.

(5)(a) Any person conditionally released under this section may apply to the board for discharge from or modification of an order of conditional release on the ground that the person is no longer affected by a qualifying mental disorder or, if still so affected, no longer presents a substantial danger to others and no longer requires supervision, medication, care or treatment. Notice of the hearing on an application for discharge or modification of an order of conditional release shall be made to the Attorney General. The applicant, at the hearing pursuant to this subsection, must prove by a preponderance of the evidence the applicant's fitness for discharge or modification of the order of conditional release. Applications by the person for discharge or modification of conditional release may not be filed more often than once every six months.

(b) Upon application by any person or agency responsible for supervision or treatment pursuant to an order of conditional release, the board shall conduct a hearing to determine if the conditions of release shall be continued, modified or terminated. The application shall be accompanied by a report setting forth the facts supporting the application.

(6) A person who has spent five years on conditional release shall be brought before the board for hearing within 30 days before the expiration of the five-year period. The board shall review the person's status and determine whether the person should be discharged from the jurisdiction of the board. [1977 c.380 §11 (enacted in lieu of 161.335); 1979 c.885 §3; 1981 c.711 §5; 1983 c.800 §9; 1987 c.140 §1; 1989 c.790 §49; 2001 c.326 §1; 2005 c.264 §14; 2005 c.685 §2; 2009 c.595 §103; 2011 c.708 §2; 2017 c.442 §3; 2017 c.634 §10]

Note: The amendments to 161.336 by section 3, chapter 442, Oregon Laws 2017, become operative July 1, 2018. See section 36, chapter 442, Oregon Laws 2017. The text that is operative until July 1, 2018, including amendments by section 10, chapter 634, Oregon Laws 2017, is set forth for the user's convenience.

161.336. (1)(a) When a person is conditionally released under ORS 161.315 to 161.351, the person is subject to those supervisory orders of the Psychiatric Security Review Board as are in the best interests of justice, the protection of society and the welfare of the person.

(b) An order of conditional release entered by the board or the Oregon Health Authority may designate any person or state, county or local agency capable of supervising the person upon release, subject to the conditions described in the order of conditional release.

(c) Prior to the designation, the agency conducting the hearing shall notify the person or state, county or local agency to whom conditional release is contemplated and provide the person or state, county or local agency an opportunity to be heard.

(d) After receiving an order entered under this section, the person or state, county or local agency designated in the order shall assume supervision of the person in accordance with the conditions described in the order and any modifications of the conditions ordered by the board.

(2) Conditions of release contained in orders entered under this section may be modified from time to time and conditional releases may be terminated as provided in ORS 161.351.

(3)(a) As a condition of release, the person may be required to report to any state or local mental health facility for evaluation. Whenever medical, psychiatric or psychological treatment is recommended, the order may require the person, as a condition of release, to cooperate with and accept the treatment from the facility.

(b) The facility to which the person has been referred for evaluation shall perform the evaluation and submit a written report of its findings to the board. If the facility finds that treatment of the person is appropriate, it shall include its recommendations for treatment in the report to the board.

(c) Whenever treatment is provided by the facility, it shall furnish reports to the board on a regular basis concerning the progress of the person.

(d) Copies of all reports submitted to the board pursuant to this section shall be furnished to the person and the person's counsel. The confidentiality of these reports is determined pursuant to ORS 192.338, 192.345 and 192.355.

(e) The facility shall comply with the conditional release order and any modifications of the conditions ordered by the board.

(4)(a) If at any time while the person is under the jurisdiction of the board it appears to the board or its chairperson that the person has violated the terms of the conditional release or that the mental health of the individual has changed, the board or its chairperson may order the person returned for evaluation or treatment to a state hospital or, if the person is under 18 years of age, to a secure intensive community inpatient facility. A written order of the board, or its chairperson on behalf of the board, is sufficient warrant for any law enforcement officer to take into custody such person and transport the person accordingly. A sheriff, municipal police officer, constable, parole and probation officer, prison official or other peace officer shall execute the order, and the person shall be returned as soon as practicable to the state hospital or secure intensive community inpatient facility designated in the order.

(b) The community mental health program director, the director of the facility providing treatment to a person on conditional release, any peace officer or any person responsible for the supervision of a person on conditional release may take a person on conditional release into custody or request that the person be taken into custody if there is reasonable cause to believe the person is a substantial danger to others because of a qualifying mental disorder and that the person is in need of immediate care, custody or treatment. Any person taken into custody pursuant to this subsection shall be transported as soon as practicable to a state hospital or, if the person is under 18 years of age, to a secure intensive community inpatient facility.

(c) Within 20 days following the return of the person to a state hospital or secure intensive community inpatient facility under this subsection, the agency having jurisdiction over the person shall conduct a hearing. The agency shall provide notice of the hearing to the person, the attorney representing the person and the Attorney General. The state must prove by a preponderance of the evidence the person's unfitness for conditional release. The hearing shall be conducted in accordance with ORS 161.346.

(5)(a) Any person conditionally released under this section may apply to the board for discharge from or modification of an order of conditional release on the ground that the person is no longer affected by a qualifying mental disorder or, if still so affected, no longer presents a substantial danger to others and no longer requires supervision, medication, care or treatment. Notice of the hearing on an application for discharge or modification of an order of conditional release shall be made to the Attorney General. The applicant, at the hearing pursuant to this subsection, must prove by a preponderance of the evidence the applicant's fitness for discharge or modification of the order of conditional release. Applications by the person for discharge or modification of conditional release may not be filed more often than once every six months.

(b) Upon application by any person or agency responsible for supervision or treatment pursuant to an order of conditional release, the board shall conduct a hearing to determine if the conditions of release shall be continued, modified or terminated. The application shall be accompanied by a report setting forth the facts supporting the application.

(6) A person who has spent five years on conditional release shall be brought before the board for hearing within 30 days before the expiration of the five-year period. The board shall review the person's status and determine whether the person should be discharged from the jurisdiction of the board.

161.340 [1971 c.743 §47; 1975 c.380 §2; repealed by 1977 c.380 §12 (161.341 enacted in lieu of 161.340)]

161.341 Application for discharge or conditional release; release plan; examination; right to hearing. (1) If at any time after a person is committed under ORS 161.315 to 161.351 to a state hospital or a secure intensive community inpatient facility, the superintendent of the hospital or the director of the secure intensive community inpatient facility is of the opinion that the person is no longer affected by a qualifying mental disorder, or, if so affected, no longer presents a substantial danger to others or that the person continues to be affected by a qualifying mental disorder and continues to be a danger to others, but that the person can be controlled with proper care, medication, supervision and treatment if conditionally released, the superintendent or director shall apply to the Psychiatric Security Review Board for an order of discharge or conditional release. The application shall be accompanied by a report setting forth the facts supporting the opinion of the superintendent or director. If the application is for conditional release, the application must be accompanied by a verified conditional release plan. The board shall hold a hearing on the application within 60 days of its receipt. Not less than 20 days prior to the hearing before the board, copies of the report shall be sent to the Attorney General.

(2) The attorney representing the state may choose a psychiatrist or licensed psychologist to examine the person prior to the initial or any later decision by the board on discharge or conditional release. The results of the examination shall be in writing and filed with the board, and shall include, but need not be limited to, an opinion as to the mental condition of the person, whether the person presents a substantial danger to others and whether the person could be adequately controlled with treatment as a condition of release.

(3) Any person who has been committed to a state hospital, or to a secure intensive community inpatient facility, for custody, care and treatment under ORS 161.315 to 161.351, or another person acting on the person's behalf, may apply to the board for an order of discharge or conditional release upon the grounds:

(a) That the person is no longer affected by a qualifying mental disorder;

(b) That the person, if so affected, no longer presents a substantial danger to others; or

(c) That the person continues to be affected by a qualifying mental disorder and would continue to be a danger to others without treatment, but that the person can be adequately controlled and given proper care and treatment if placed on conditional release.

(4) When application is made under subsection (3) of this section, the board shall require that a report from the superintendent of the hospital or the director of the secure intensive community inpatient facility be prepared and transmitted as provided in subsection (1) of this section. The applicant must prove by a preponderance of the evidence the applicant's fitness for discharge or conditional release under the standards of subsection (3) of this section, unless more than two years has passed since the state had the burden of proof on that issue, in which case

the state shall have the burden of proving by a preponderance of the evidence the applicant's lack of fitness for discharge or conditional release. Applications for discharge or conditional release under subsection (3) of this section may not be filed more often than once every six months commencing with the date of the initial board hearing.

(5) The board is not required to hold a hearing on a first application under subsection (3) of this section any sooner than 90 days after the initial hearing. Hearings resulting from any subsequent requests shall be held within 60 days of the filing of the application.

(6)(a) In no case shall a person committed by the court under ORS 161.327 to a state hospital, or to a secure intensive community inpatient facility, be held in the hospital or facility for more than 90 days from the date of the court's commitment order without an initial hearing before the board to determine whether the person should be conditionally released or discharged.

(b) In no case shall a person be held pursuant to this section for a period of time exceeding two years without a hearing before the board to determine whether the person should be conditionally released or discharged. [1977 c.380 §13 (enacted in lieu of 161.340); 1979 c.885 §4; 1981 c.711 §6; 1983 c.800 §10; 1985 c.192 §3; 1989 c.790 §50; 1991 c.244 §1; 2005 c.685 §3; 2009 c.595 §104; 2011 c.708 §3; 2017 c.442 §4; 2017 c.634 §11]

Note: The amendments to 161.341 by section 4, chapter 442, Oregon Laws 2017, become operative July 1, 2018. See section 36, chapter 442, Oregon Laws 2017. The text that is operative until July 1, 2018, including amendments by section 11, chapter 634, Oregon Laws 2017, is set forth for the user's convenience.

161.341. (1) If at any time after a person is committed under ORS 161.315 to 161.351 to a state hospital or a secure intensive community inpatient facility, the superintendent of the hospital or the director of the secure intensive community inpatient facility is of the opinion that the person is no longer affected by a qualifying mental disorder, or, if so affected, no longer presents a substantial danger to others or that the person continues to be affected by a qualifying mental disorder and continues to be a danger to others, but that the person can be controlled with proper care, medication, supervision and treatment if conditionally released, the superintendent or director shall apply to the agency having jurisdiction over the person for an order of discharge or conditional release. The application shall be accompanied by a report setting forth the facts supporting the opinion of the superintendent or director. If the application is for conditional release, the application must be accompanied by a verified conditional release plan. The agency shall hold a hearing on the application within 60 days of its receipt. Not less than 20 days prior to the hearing before the agency, copies of the report shall be sent to the Attorney General.

(2) The attorney representing the state may choose a psychiatrist or licensed psychologist to examine the person prior to the initial or any later decision by the agency having jurisdiction over the person on discharge or conditional release. The results of the examination shall be in writing and filed with the agency, and shall include, but need not be limited to, an opinion as to the mental condition of the person, whether the person presents a substantial danger to others and whether the person could be adequately controlled with treatment as a condition of release.

(3) Any person who has been committed to a state hospital, or to a secure intensive community inpatient facility, for custody, care and treatment under ORS 161.315 to 161.351, or another person acting on the person's behalf, may apply to the agency having jurisdiction over the person for an order of discharge or conditional release upon the grounds:

(a) That the person is no longer affected by a qualifying mental disorder;

(b) That the person, if so affected, no longer presents a substantial danger to others; or

(c) That the person continues to be affected by a qualifying mental disorder and would continue to be a danger to others without treatment, but that the person can be adequately controlled and given proper care and treatment if placed on conditional release.

(4) When application is made under subsection (3) of this section, the agency having jurisdiction over the person shall require that a report from the superintendent of the hospital or the director of the secure intensive community inpatient facility be prepared and transmitted as provided in subsection (1) of this section. The applicant must prove by a preponderance of the evidence the applicant's fitness for discharge or conditional release under the standards of subsection (3) of this section, unless more than two years has passed since the state had the burden of proof on that issue, in which case the state shall have the burden of proving by a preponderance of the evidence the applicant's lack of fitness for discharge or conditional release. Applications for discharge or conditional release under subsection (3) of this section may not be filed more often than once every six months commencing with the date of the initial agency hearing.

(5) The agency having jurisdiction over the person is not required to hold a hearing on a first application under subsection (3) of this section any sooner than 90 days after the initial hearing. Hearings resulting from any subsequent requests shall be held within 60 days of the filing of the application.

(6)(a) In no case shall a person committed by the court under ORS 161.327 to a state hospital, or to a secure intensive community inpatient facility, be held in the hospital or facility for more than 90 days from the date of the court's commitment order without an initial hearing before the agency having jurisdiction over the person to determine whether the person should be conditionally released or discharged.

(b) In no case shall a person be held pursuant to this section for a period of time exceeding two years without a hearing before the agency to determine whether the person should be conditionally released or discharged.

161.345 [1971 c.743 §48; repealed by 1977 c.380 §14 (161.346 enacted in lieu of 161.345)]

161.346 Hearings on discharge, conditional release, commitment or modification; psychiatric reports; notice of hearing. (1) When the Psychiatric Security Review Board conducts a hearing under ORS 161.315 to 161.351, the board shall enter an order and make findings in support of the order. If the board finds that a person under the jurisdiction of the board:

(a) Is no longer affected by a qualifying mental disorder, or, if so affected, no longer presents a substantial danger to others, the board shall order the person discharged from commitment and conditional release.

(b) Is still affected by a qualifying mental disorder and is a substantial danger to others, but can be controlled adequately if conditionally released with treatment as a condition of release, the board shall order the person conditionally released as provided in ORS 161.336.

(c) Has not recovered from the qualifying mental disorder, is a substantial danger to others and cannot adequately be controlled if conditionally released on supervision, the board shall order the person committed to, or retained in, a state hospital, or if the person is under 18 years of age, a secure intensive community inpatient facility, for care, custody and treatment.

(2) To assist the board in making the determination described in subsection (1) of this section, the board may, at any time, appoint a psychiatrist or licensed psychologist to examine the person and to submit a report to the board. The report must include an opinion as to the mental condition of the person, whether the person presents a substantial danger to others and whether the person could be adequately controlled with treatment as a condition of release.

(3) The board may make the determination regarding discharge or conditional release based upon the written reports submitted pursuant to this section. If any member of the board desires further information from the examining psychiatrist or licensed psychologist who submitted the report, the board shall summon the person to give testimony. The board shall consider all evidence available to it that is material, relevant and reliable regarding the issues before the board. The evidence may include but is not limited to the record of trial, the information supplied by the attorney representing the state or by any other interested party, including the person, and information concerning the person's mental condition and the entire psychiatric and criminal history of the person. All evidence of a type commonly relied upon by reasonably prudent persons in the conduct of their serious affairs shall be admissible at hearings. Testimony shall be taken upon oath or affirmation of the witness from whom received. The officer presiding at the hearing shall administer oaths or affirmations to witnesses.

(4) The board shall furnish to the person about whom the hearing is being conducted, the attorney representing the person, the Attorney General and the district attorney of the county from which the person was committed written notice of any hearing pending under this section within a reasonable time prior to the hearing. The notice shall include:

(a) The time, place and location of the hearing.

(b) The nature of the hearing and the specific action for which a hearing has been requested, the issues to be considered at the hearing and a reference to the particular sections of the statutes and rules involved.

(c) A statement of the legal authority and jurisdiction under which the hearing is to be held.

(d) A statement of all rights under subsection (6) of this section.

(5) Prior to the commencement of the hearing, the board shall serve personally or by mail a written notice to each party as provided in ORS 183.413 (2).

(6) At the hearing, the person about whom the hearing is being held shall have the right:

(a) To appear at all proceedings held pursuant to this section, except for deliberations.

(b) To cross-examine all witnesses appearing to testify at the hearing.

(c) To subpoena witnesses and documents as provided in ORS 161.395.

(d) To be represented by suitable legal counsel possessing skills and experience commensurate with the nature and complexity of the case, to consult with counsel prior to the hearing and, if financially eligible, to have suitable counsel appointed at state expense.

(e) To examine all information, documents and reports that the board considers. If then available to the board, the information, documents and reports shall be disclosed to the person so as to allow examination prior to the hearing.

(7) A record shall be kept of all hearings conducted under ORS 161.315 to 161.351, except for deliberations.

(8) Upon request of any party, or on motion of the board, the hearing may be continued for a reasonable period not to exceed 60 days to obtain additional information or testimony or for other good cause shown.

(9) Within 30 days following the conclusion of the hearing, the board shall provide to the person, the attorney representing the person, the Attorney General or other attorney representing the state, if any, written notice of the order entered by the board.

(10) The burden of proof on all issues at hearings under ORS 161.315 to 161.351 shall be by a preponderance of the evidence.

(11) If the board determines that the person about whom the hearing is being held is financially eligible, the board shall appoint suitable counsel to represent the person. Counsel so appointed shall be an attorney who satisfies the professional qualifications established by the Public Defense Services Commission under ORS 151.216. The public defense services executive director shall determine and allow fair compensation for counsel appointed under this subsection and the reasonable expenses of the person in respect to the hearing. Compensation payable to appointed

counsel shall not be less than the applicable compensation level established under ORS 151.216. The compensation and expenses so allowed shall be paid by the public defense services executive director from funds available for the purpose.

(12) The Attorney General may represent the state at contested hearings under ORS 161.315 to 161.351 unless the district attorney of the county from which the person was committed elects to represent the state. The district attorney of the county from which the person was committed shall cooperate with the Attorney General in securing the material necessary for presenting a contested hearing. If the district attorney elects to represent the state, the district attorney shall give timely written notice of such election to the Attorney General, the board and the attorney representing the person. [1977 c.380 §15 (enacted in lieu of 161.345); 1979 c.867 §6; 1979 c.885 §5; 1981 c.711 §7; 1981 s.s. c.3 §130; 1983 c.430 §1; 1985 c.502 §23; 1987 c.803 §19; 1991 c.827 §3; 2001 c.962 §40; 2003 c.449 §32; 2005 c.685 §4; 2007 c.288 §7; 2009 c.595 §105; 2011 c.708 §1; 2017 c.232 §1; 2017 c.442 §2; 2017 c.634 §12]

Note: The amendments to 161.346 by section 2, chapter 442, Oregon Laws 2017, become operative July 1, 2018. See section 36, chapter 442, Oregon Laws 2017. The text that is operative until July 1, 2018, including amendments by section 1, chapter 232, Oregon Laws 2017, and section 12, chapter 634, Oregon Laws 2017, is set forth for the user's convenience.

161.346. (1) When the Psychiatric Security Review Board or the Oregon Health Authority conducts a hearing under ORS 161.315 to 161.351, the agency conducting the hearing shall enter an order and make findings in support of the order. If the agency finds that a person under the jurisdiction of the agency:

(a) Is no longer affected by a qualifying mental disorder, or, if so affected, no longer presents a substantial danger to others, the agency shall order the person discharged from commitment and conditional release.

(b) Is still affected by a qualifying mental disorder and is a substantial danger to others, but can be controlled adequately if conditionally released with treatment as a condition of release, the agency shall order the person conditionally released as provided in ORS 161.336.

(c) Has not recovered from the qualifying mental disorder, is a substantial danger to others and cannot adequately be controlled if conditionally released on supervision, the agency shall order the person committed to, or retained in, a state hospital, or if the person is under 18 years of age, a secure intensive community inpatient facility, for care, custody and treatment.

(2)(a) Except as otherwise provided in ORS 161.349, the Psychiatric Security Review Board shall exercise exclusive jurisdiction over a tier one offender until the board discharges the person from the jurisdiction of the board or the maximum period of jurisdiction expires.

(b) When the board orders a tier two offender committed to a state hospital, or a secure intensive community inpatient facility, under ORS 161.315 to 161.351, the order shall transfer jurisdiction over the person to the Oregon Health Authority.

(c) When the authority orders a tier two offender conditionally released under ORS 161.315 to 161.351, the order shall transfer jurisdiction over the person to the board.

(d) The authority shall assume jurisdiction over a tier two offender when the person is returned to a state hospital, or to a secure intensive community inpatient facility, under ORS 161.336 (4).

(3) To assist the agency in making the determination described in subsection (1) of this section, the agency exercising jurisdiction over the person may, at any time, appoint a psychiatrist or licensed psychologist to examine the person and to submit a report to the agency. The report must include an opinion as to the mental condition of the person, whether the person presents a substantial danger to others and whether the person could be adequately controlled with treatment as a condition of release.

(4) The agency exercising jurisdiction over the person may make the determination regarding discharge or conditional release based upon the written reports submitted pursuant to this section. If the authority or any member of the board desires further information from the examining psychiatrist or licensed psychologist who submitted the report, the agency shall summon the person to give testimony. The agency shall consider all evidence available to it that is material, relevant and reliable regarding the issues before the agency. The evidence may include but is not limited to the record of trial, the information supplied by the attorney representing the state or by any other interested party, including the person, and information concerning the person's mental condition and the entire psychiatric and criminal history of the person. All evidence of a type commonly relied upon by reasonably prudent persons in the conduct of their serious affairs shall be admissible at hearings. Testimony shall be taken upon oath or affirmation of the witness from whom received. The officer presiding at the hearing shall administer oaths or affirmations to witnesses.

(5) The agency exercising jurisdiction over the person shall furnish to the person about whom the hearing is being conducted, the attorney representing the person, the Attorney General and the district attorney of the county from which the person was committed written notice of any hearing pending under this section within a reasonable time prior to the hearing. The notice shall include:

(a) The time, place and location of the hearing.

(b) The nature of the hearing and the specific action for which a hearing has been requested, the issues to be considered at the hearing and a reference to the particular sections of the statutes and rules involved.

(c) A statement of the legal authority and jurisdiction under which the hearing is to be held.

(d) A statement of all rights under subsection (7) of this section.

(6) Prior to the commencement of the hearing, the agency shall serve personally or by mail a written notice to each party as provided in ORS 183.413 (2).

(7) At the hearing, the person about whom the hearing is being held shall have the right:

(a) To appear at all proceedings held pursuant to this section, except for deliberations.

(b) To cross-examine all witnesses appearing to testify at the hearing.

(c) To subpoena witnesses and documents as provided in ORS 161.395.

(d) To be represented by suitable legal counsel possessing skills and experience commensurate with the nature and complexity of the case, to consult with counsel prior to the hearing and, if financially eligible, to have suitable counsel appointed at state expense.

(e) To examine all information, documents and reports that the agency considers. If then available to the agency, the information, documents and reports shall be disclosed to the person so as to allow examination prior to the hearing.

(8) A record shall be kept of all hearings conducted under ORS 161.315 to 161.351, except for deliberations.

(9) Upon request of any party, or on motion of the agency conducting the hearing, the hearing may be continued for a reasonable period not to exceed 60 days to obtain additional information or testimony or for other good cause shown.

(10) Within 30 days following the conclusion of the hearing, the agency shall provide to the person, the attorney representing the person, the Attorney General or other attorney representing the state, if any, written notice of the order entered by the agency.

(11) The burden of proof on all issues at hearings under ORS 161.315 to 161.351 shall be by a preponderance of the evidence.

(12) If the agency conducting the hearing determines that the person about whom the hearing is being held is financially eligible, the agency shall appoint suitable counsel to represent the person. Counsel so appointed shall be an attorney who satisfies the professional qualifications established by the Public Defense Services Commission under ORS 151.216. The public defense services executive director shall determine and allow fair compensation for counsel appointed under this subsection and the reasonable expenses of the person in respect to the hearing. Compensation payable to appointed counsel shall not be less than the applicable compensation level established under ORS 151.216. The compensation and expenses so allowed shall be paid by the public defense services executive director from funds available for the purpose.

(13) The Attorney General may represent the state at contested hearings under ORS 161.315 to 161.351 unless the district attorney of the county from which the person was committed elects to represent the state. The district attorney of the county from which the person was committed shall cooperate with the Attorney General in securing the material necessary for presenting a contested hearing. If the district attorney elects to represent the state, the district attorney shall give timely written notice of such election to the Attorney General, the agency conducting the hearing and the attorney representing the person.

161.348 Judicial review. (1) When a person over whom the Psychiatric Security Review Board exercises jurisdiction under ORS 161.315 to 161.351 or 419C.544 is adversely affected or aggrieved by a final order of the board, the person is entitled to judicial review of the final order. The person is entitled on judicial review to suitable counsel possessing skills and experience commensurate with the nature and complexity of the case. If the person is financially eligible, suitable counsel shall be appointed by the reviewing court in the manner provided in ORS 138.500 (1). If the person is financially eligible, the public defense services executive director shall determine and pay, as provided in ORS 138.500, the cost of briefs, any other expenses of the person necessary to the review and compensation for counsel appointed for the person. The costs, expenses and compensation so allowed shall be paid as provided in ORS 138.500.

(2) The order and the proceedings underlying the order are subject to review by the Court of Appeals upon petition to that court filed within 60 days of the order for which review is sought. The board shall submit to the court the record of the proceeding or, if the person agrees, a shortened record. The record may include a certified true copy of a tape recording of the proceedings at a hearing in accordance with ORS 161.346. A copy of the record transmitted shall be delivered to the person by the board.

(3) The court may affirm, reverse or remand the order on the same basis as provided in ORS 183.482 (8).

(4) The filing of the petition does not stay the order of the board, but the board or the Court of Appeals may order a stay upon application on such terms as are deemed proper. [2011 c.708 §9; 2017 c.442 §8]

Note: The amendments to 161.348 by section 8, chapter 442, Oregon Laws 2017, become operative July 1, 2018. See section 36, chapter 442, Oregon Laws 2017. The text that is operative until July 1, 2018, is set forth for the user's convenience.

161.348. (1) When a person over whom the Psychiatric Security Review Board or the Oregon Health Authority exercises jurisdiction under ORS 161.315 to 161.351 or 419C.544 is adversely affected or aggrieved by a final order of the board or authority, the person is entitled to judicial review of the final order. The person is entitled on judicial review to suitable counsel possessing skills and experience commensurate with the nature and complexity of the case. If the person is financially eligible, suitable counsel shall be appointed by the reviewing court in the manner provided in ORS 138.500 (1). If the person is financially eligible, the public defense services executive director shall determine and pay, as provided in ORS 138.500, the cost of briefs, any other expenses of the person necessary to the review and compensation for counsel appointed for the person. The costs, expenses and compensation so allowed shall be paid as provided in ORS 138.500.

(2) The order and the proceedings underlying the order are subject to review by the Court of Appeals upon petition to that court filed within 60 days of the order for which review is sought. The agency that conducted the hearing shall submit to the court the record of the proceeding or, if the person agrees, a shortened record. The record may include a certified true copy of a tape recording of the proceedings at a hearing in accordance with ORS 161.346. A copy of the record transmitted shall be delivered to the person by the agency.

(3) The court may affirm, reverse or remand the order on the same basis as provided in ORS 183.482 (8).

(4) The filing of the petition does not stay the order of the agency, but the agency or the Court of Appeals may order a stay upon application on such terms as are deemed proper.

161.349 Person committed under ORS 161.315 to 161.351 sentenced to term of incarceration. (1) When a person who is committed to a state hospital or a secure intensive community inpatient facility under ORS 161.315 to 161.351 is convicted of a crime and sentenced to a term of incarceration and when the person is sentenced to a term of incarceration as a sanction for violating the conditions of probation, parole or post-prison supervision, the sentencing court shall stay execution of the sentence pending the conditional release or discharge of the person or the expiration of the period of time described in ORS 161.327 (5). When the person is conditionally released or discharged by the Psychiatric Security Review Board under ORS 161.315 to 161.351, or when the maximum period of jurisdiction described in ORS 161.327 (5) expires, the stay shall be lifted by operation of law and the person shall be delivered to the custody of the Department of Corrections or the supervisory authority to begin service of the sentence imposed.

(2) When a person described in subsection (1) of this section is delivered to the custody of the department or the supervisory authority as described in this section, the board shall notify the department or the supervisory authority when the period of time described in ORS 161.327 (5) will expire.

(3) The department or supervisory authority shall notify the board when the person has served the term of incarceration imposed by the court and the board shall resume exercising active jurisdiction over the person in accordance with ORS 161.315 to 161.351.

(4) As used in this section, "supervisory authority" has the meaning given that term in ORS 144.087. [2011 c.708 §15; 2011 c.708 §39; 2017 c.442 §13]

Note: The amendments to 161.349 by section 13, chapter 442, Oregon Laws 2017, become operative July 1, 2018. See section 36, chapter 442, Oregon Laws 2017. The text that is operative until July 1, 2018, is set forth for the user's convenience.

161.349. (1) When a person who is committed to a state hospital or a secure intensive community inpatient facility under ORS 161.315 to 161.351 is convicted of a crime and sentenced to a term of incarceration and when the person is sentenced to a term of incarceration as a sanction for violating the conditions of probation, parole or post-prison supervision, the sentencing court shall stay execution of the sentence pending the conditional release or discharge of the person or the expiration of the period of time described in ORS 161.327 (5). When the person is conditionally released or discharged by the agency having jurisdiction over the person under ORS 161.315 to 161.351, or when the maximum period of jurisdiction described in ORS 161.327 (5) expires, the stay shall be lifted by operation of law and the person shall be delivered to the custody of the Department of Corrections or the supervisory authority to begin service of the sentence imposed.

(2) When a person described in subsection (1) of this section is delivered to the custody of the department or the supervisory authority as described in this section, the agency having jurisdiction over the person while the person was committed to a state hospital or a secure intensive community inpatient facility shall notify the department or the supervisory authority when the period of time described in ORS 161.327 (5) will expire.

(3) The department or supervisory authority shall notify the Psychiatric Security Review Board when the person has served the term of incarceration imposed by the court and the board shall resume exercising active jurisdiction over the person in accordance with ORS 161.315 to 161.351.

(4) As used in this section, "supervisory authority" has the meaning given that term in ORS 144.087.

161.350 [1971 c.743 §49; 1975 c.380 §3; repealed by 1977 c.380 §16 (161.351 enacted in lieu of 161.350)]

161.351 Discharge by board; effect of remission; protection of society. (1) Any person placed under the jurisdiction of the Psychiatric Security Review Board under ORS 161.315 to 161.351 shall be discharged at such time as the board, upon a hearing, finds by a preponderance of the evidence that the person is no longer affected by a qualifying mental disorder or, if so affected, no longer presents a substantial danger to others that requires regular medical care, medication, supervision or treatment.

(2) For purposes of ORS 161.315 to 161.351, a person affected by a qualifying mental disorder in a state of remission is considered to have a qualifying mental disorder. A person whose qualifying mental disorder may, with reasonable medical probability, occasionally become active and when it becomes active will render the person a danger to others may not be discharged. The person shall continue under supervision and treatment necessary to protect the person and others.

(3) In determining whether a person should be committed to a state hospital or secure intensive community inpatient facility, conditionally released or discharged, the board shall have as its primary concern the protection of society. [1977 c.380 §17 (enacted in lieu of 161.350); 1981 c.711 §13; 1985 c.192 §4; 1989 c.49 §1; 2011 c.708 §4; 2017 c.442 §5; 2017 c.634 §13]

Note: The amendments to 161.351 by section 5, chapter 442, Oregon Laws 2017, become operative July 1, 2018. See section 36, chapter 442, Oregon Laws 2017. The text that is operative until July 1, 2018, including amendments by section 13, chapter 634, Oregon Laws 2017, is set forth for the user's convenience.

161.351. (1) Any person placed under the jurisdiction of the Psychiatric Security Review Board or the Oregon Health Authority under ORS 161.315 to 161.351 shall be discharged at such time as the agency having jurisdiction over the person, upon a hearing, finds by a preponderance of the evidence that the person is no longer affected by a qualifying mental disorder or, if so affected, no longer presents a substantial danger to others that requires regular medical care, medication, supervision or treatment.

(2) For purposes of ORS 161.315 to 161.351, a person affected by a qualifying mental disorder in a state of remission is considered to have a qualifying mental disorder. A person whose qualifying mental disorder may, with reasonable medical probability, occasionally become active and when it becomes active will render the person a danger to others may not be discharged. The person shall continue under supervision and treatment necessary to protect the person and others.

(3) In determining whether a person should be committed to a state hospital or secure intensive community inpatient facility, conditionally released or discharged, the board and the authority shall have as their primary concern the protection of society.

161.360 Qualifying mental disorder affecting fitness to proceed. (1) If, before or during the trial in any criminal case, the court has reason to doubt the defendant's fitness to proceed by reason of incapacity, the court may order an examination in the manner provided in ORS 161.365.

(2) A defendant may be found incapacitated if, as a result of a qualifying mental disorder, the defendant is unable:

(a) To understand the nature of the proceedings against the defendant; or

(b) To assist and cooperate with the counsel of the defendant; or

(c) To participate in the defense of the defendant. [1971 c.743 §50; 1993 c.238 §1; 2017 c.634 §14]

161.365 Procedure for determining issue of fitness to proceed; rules. (1) When the court has reason to doubt the defendant's fitness to proceed by reason of incapacity as described in ORS 161.360, the court may call any witness to its assistance in reaching its decision and shall order that a community mental health program director or the director's designee consult with the defendant to determine whether services and supervision necessary to safely restore the defendant's fitness to proceed are available in the community. After the consultation, the program director or the director's designee shall provide to the court a copy of the findings resulting from the consultation. If the court determines the assistance of a psychiatrist or psychologist would be helpful, the court may:

(a) Order that a psychiatric or psychological examination of the defendant be conducted by a certified evaluator as defined in ORS 161.309 and a report of the examination be prepared; or

(b) Order the defendant to be committed for the purpose of an examination for a period not exceeding 30 days to a state mental hospital or other facility designated by the Oregon Health Authority if the defendant is at least 18 years of age, or to a secure intensive community inpatient facility designated by the authority if the defendant is under 18 years of age.

(2) The report of an examination described in this section must include, but is not necessarily limited to, the following:

(a) A description of the nature of the examination;

(b) A statement of the mental condition of the defendant;

(c) If the defendant suffers from a qualifying mental disorder, an opinion as to whether the defendant is incapacitated within the description set out in ORS 161.360; and

(d) If the defendant is incapacitated within the description set out in ORS 161.360, a recommendation of treatment and services necessary to restore capacity.

(3) Except when the defendant and the court both request to the contrary, the report may not contain any findings or conclusions as to whether the defendant as a result of a qualifying mental disorder was subject to the provisions of ORS 161.295 or 161.300 at the time of the criminal act charged.

(4) If the examination by the psychiatrist or psychologist cannot be conducted by reason of the unwillingness of the defendant to participate in the examination, the report must so state and must include, if possible, an opinion as

to whether the unwillingness of the defendant was the result of a qualifying mental disorder affecting capacity to proceed.

(5) The report must be filed with the clerk of the court, who shall cause copies to be delivered to the district attorney and to counsel for defendant.

(6)(a) When upon motion of the court or a financially eligible defendant, the court has ordered a psychiatric or psychological examination of the defendant, a county or justice court shall order the county to pay, and a circuit court shall order the public defense services executive director to pay from funds available for the purpose:

(A) A reasonable fee if the examination of the defendant is conducted by a psychiatrist or psychologist in private practice; and

(B) All costs including transportation of the defendant if the examination is conducted by a psychiatrist or psychologist in the employ of the Oregon Health Authority or a community mental health program established under ORS 430.610 to 430.670.

(b) When an examination is ordered at the request or with the acquiescence of a defendant who is determined not to be financially eligible, the examination shall be performed at the defendant's expense. When an examination is ordered at the request of the prosecution, the county shall pay for the expense of the examination.

(7) The Oregon Health Authority shall establish by rule standards for the consultation described in subsection (1) of this section. [1971 c.743 §51; 1975 c.380 §4; 1981 s.s. c.3 §131; 1983 c.800 §11; 1987 c.803 §18; 1993 c.238 §2; 2001 c.962 §90; 2005 c.685 §5; 2009 c.595 §106; 2011 c.724 §7; 2015 c.130 §1; 2017 c.252 §25; 2017 c.634 §15]

161.370 Determination of fitness; effect of finding of unfitness; proceedings if fitness gained or regained; pretrial objections by defense counsel. (1) When the defendant's fitness to proceed is drawn in question, the issue shall be determined by the court. If neither the prosecuting attorney nor counsel for the defendant contests the finding of the report filed under ORS 161.365, the court may make the determination on the basis of the report. If the finding is contested, the court shall hold a hearing on the issue. If the report is received in evidence in the hearing, the party who contests the finding has the right to summon and to cross-examine any psychiatrist or psychologist who submitted the report and to offer evidence upon the issue. Other evidence regarding the defendant's fitness to proceed may be introduced by either party.

(2) If the court determines that the defendant lacks fitness to proceed, the criminal proceeding against the defendant shall be suspended and:

(a) If the court finds that the defendant is dangerous to self or others as a result of a qualifying mental disorder, or that, based on the findings resulting from the consultation described in ORS 161.365 (1), the services and supervision necessary to restore the defendant's fitness to proceed are not available in the community, the court shall commit the defendant to the custody of the superintendent of a state mental hospital or director of a facility, designated by the Oregon Health Authority, if the defendant is at least 18 years of age, or to the custody of the director of a secure intensive community inpatient facility designated by the authority if the defendant is under 18 years of age; or

(b) If the court does not make a finding described in paragraph (a) of this subsection, or if the court determines that care other than commitment for incapacity to stand trial would better serve the defendant and the community, the court shall release the defendant on supervision for as long as the unfitness endures.

(3) When a defendant is released on supervision under subsection (2)(b) of this section, the court may place conditions that the court deems appropriate on the release, including the requirement that the defendant regularly report to the authority or a community mental health program for examination to determine if the defendant has gained or regained capacity to stand trial.

(4) When the court, on its own motion or upon the application of the superintendent of the hospital or director of the facility in which the defendant is committed, a person examining the defendant as a condition of release on supervision, or either party, determines, after a hearing, if a hearing is requested, that the defendant has gained or regained fitness to proceed, the criminal proceeding shall be resumed. If, however, the court is of the view that so much time has elapsed since the commitment or release of the defendant on supervision that it would be unjust to resume the criminal proceeding, the court on motion of either party may dismiss the charge and may order the defendant to be discharged or cause a proceeding to be commenced forthwith under ORS 426.070 to 426.170 or 427.235 to 427.290.

(5) The superintendent of a state hospital or director of a facility to which the defendant is committed shall cause the defendant to be evaluated within 60 days from the defendant's delivery into the superintendent's or director's custody, for the purpose of determining whether there is a substantial probability that, in the foreseeable future, the defendant will have the capacity to stand trial. In addition, the superintendent or director shall:

(a) Immediately notify the committing court if the defendant, at any time, gains or regains the capacity to stand trial or will never have the capacity to stand trial.

(b) Within 90 days of the defendant's delivery into the superintendent's or director's custody, notify the committing court that:

(A) The defendant has the present capacity to stand trial;

(B) There is no substantial probability that, in the foreseeable future, the defendant will gain or regain the capacity to stand trial; or

(C) There is a substantial probability that, in the foreseeable future, the defendant will gain or regain the capacity to stand trial. If the probability exists, the superintendent or director shall give the court an estimate of the time in which the defendant, with appropriate treatment, is expected to gain or regain capacity.

(6)(a) If the superintendent or director determines that there is a substantial probability that, in the foreseeable future, the defendant will gain or regain the capacity to stand trial, unless the court otherwise orders, the defendant shall remain in the superintendent's or director's custody where the defendant shall receive treatment designed for the purpose of enabling the defendant to gain or regain capacity. In keeping with the notice requirement under subsection (5)(b) of this section, the superintendent or director shall, for the duration of the defendant's period of commitment, submit a progress report to the committing court, concerning the defendant's capacity or incapacity, at least once every 180 days as measured from the date of the defendant's delivery into the superintendent's or director's custody.

(b) Notwithstanding paragraph (a) of this subsection, if the superintendent or director determines that a defendant committed under this section is no longer dangerous to self or others as a result of a qualifying mental disorder, or that the services and supervision necessary to restore the defendant's fitness to proceed are available in the community, the superintendent or director shall file notice of that determination with the court. Upon receipt of the notice, the court shall order the person released on supervision as described in subsection (3) of this section.

(c) A progress report described in paragraph (a) of this subsection may consist of an update to:

(A) The original examination report conducted under ORS 161.365; or

(B) An evaluation conducted under subsection (5) of this section, if the defendant did not receive an examination under ORS 161.365.

(7)(a) A defendant who remains committed under subsection (6) of this section shall be discharged within a period of time that is reasonable for making a determination concerning whether or not, and when, the defendant may gain or regain capacity. However, regardless of the number of charges with which the defendant is accused, in no event shall the defendant be committed for longer than whichever of the following, measured from the defendant's initial custody date, is shorter:

(A) Three years; or

(B) A period of time equal to the maximum sentence the court could have imposed if the defendant had been convicted.

(b) For purposes of calculating the maximum period of commitment described in paragraph (a) of this subsection:

(A) The initial custody date is the date on which the defendant is first committed under this section on any charge alleged in the accusatory instrument; and

(B) The defendant shall be given credit against each charge alleged in the accusatory instrument:

(i) For each day the defendant is committed under this section, whether the days are consecutive or are interrupted by a period of time during which the defendant has gained or regained fitness to proceed; and

(ii) Unless the defendant is charged with aggravated murder or a crime listed in ORS 137.700 (2), for each day the defendant is held in jail, whether the days are consecutive or are interrupted by a period of time during which the defendant lacks fitness to proceed.

(8) The superintendent or director shall notify the committing court of the defendant's impending discharge 30 days before the date on which the superintendent or director is required to discharge the defendant under subsection (7) of this section.

(9) When the committing court receives a notice from the superintendent or director under subsection (5) or (8) of this section concerning the defendant's progress or lack thereof, the committing court shall determine, after a hearing, if a hearing is requested, whether the defendant presently has the capacity to stand trial.

(10) If at any time the court determines that the defendant lacks the capacity to stand trial, the court shall further determine whether there is a substantial probability that the defendant, in the foreseeable future, will gain or regain the capacity to stand trial and whether the defendant is entitled to discharge under subsection (7) of this section. If the court determines that there is no substantial probability that the defendant, in the foreseeable future, will gain or regain the capacity to stand trial or that the defendant is entitled to discharge under subsection (7) of this section, the court shall dismiss, without prejudice, all charges against the defendant and:

(a) Order that the defendant be discharged; or

(b) Initiate commitment proceedings under ORS 426.070 or 427.235 to 427.290.

(11) All notices required under this section shall be filed with the clerk of the court and delivered to both the district attorney and the counsel for the defendant.

(12) If the defendant gains or regains fitness to proceed, the term of any sentence received by the defendant for conviction of the crime charged shall be reduced by the amount of time the defendant was committed under this section to the custody of a state mental hospital, or to the custody of a secure intensive community inpatient facility, designated by the Oregon Health Authority.

(13) Notwithstanding the suspension of the criminal proceeding under subsection (2) of this section, the fact that the defendant is unfit to proceed does not preclude any objection through counsel and without the personal participation of the defendant on the grounds that the indictment is insufficient, that the statute of limitations has run, that double jeopardy principles apply or upon any other ground at the discretion of the court which the court deems susceptible of fair determination prior to trial.

(14) At the time that the court determines that the defendant lacks fitness to proceed under subsection (2) of this section, the court shall notify the defendant that federal law prohibits the defendant from purchasing or possessing a firearm unless the person obtains relief from the prohibition under federal law. The court shall again notify the defendant of the prohibition if the court finds that the defendant has gained or regained fitness to proceed under subsection (4) of this section. [1971 c.743 §52; 1975 c.380 §5; 1993 c.238 §3; 1999 c.931 §§1,2; 2005 c.685 §6; 2009 c.595 §107; 2011 c.508 §1; 2011 c.724 §8; 2015 c.130 §2; 2017 c.49 §1; 2017 c.233 §3; 2017 c.628 §1; 2017 c.634 §16]

161.375 Escape of person placed at hospital or facility; authority to order arrest. (1) When a patient, who has been placed at a state hospital for evaluation, care, custody and treatment under ORS 161.315 to 161.351 or by court order under ORS 161.315, 161.365 or 161.370, has escaped or is absent without authorization from the hospital or from the custody of any person in whose charge the superintendent has placed the patient, the superintendent may order the arrest and detention of the patient.

(2) When a patient, who has been placed at a secure intensive community inpatient facility for evaluation, care, custody and treatment under ORS 161.315 to 161.351 or by court order under ORS 161.315, 161.365, 161.370 or 419C.527, has escaped or is absent without authorization from the facility or from the custody of any person in whose charge the director of the facility has placed the patient, the director of the facility shall notify the Director of the Oregon Health Authority. The Director of the Oregon Health Authority may order the arrest and detention of the patient.

(3) The superintendent or the Director of the Oregon Health Authority may issue an order under this section based upon a reasonable belief that grounds exist for issuing the order. When reasonable, the superintendent or the Director of the Oregon Health Authority shall investigate to ascertain whether such grounds exist.

(4) Any order issued by the superintendent or the Director of the Oregon Health Authority as authorized by this section constitutes full authority for the arrest and detention of the patient and all laws applicable to warrant or arrest apply to the order. An order issued by the superintendent or the Director of the Oregon Health Authority under this section expires 72 hours after being signed by the superintendent or the Director of the Oregon Health Authority.

(5) As used in this section, "superintendent" means the superintendent of the state hospital to which the person was committed or the superintendent's authorized representative. [1997 c.423 §1; 2005 c.685 §7; 2005 c.843 §24a; 2009 c.595 §108; 2011 c.708 §7]

161.380 [1971 c.743 §53; renumbered 161.290]

161.385 Psychiatric Security Review Board; composition, term, qualifications, compensation, appointment, confirmation and meetings. (1) There is hereby created a Psychiatric Security Review Board consisting of 10 members appointed by the Governor and subject to confirmation by the Senate under section 4, Article III of the Oregon Constitution.

(2) The membership of the board may not include any district attorney, deputy district attorney or public defender. The Governor shall appoint:

(a) A psychiatrist experienced in the criminal justice system and not otherwise employed on a full-time basis by the Oregon Health Authority or a community mental health program;

(b) A licensed psychologist experienced in the criminal justice system and not otherwise employed on a full-time basis by the authority or a community mental health program;

(c) A member with substantial experience in the processes of parole and probation;

(d) A lawyer with substantial experience in criminal trial practice;

(e) A psychiatrist certified, or eligible to be certified, by the Oregon Medical Board in child psychiatry who is experienced in the juvenile justice system and not employed on a full-time basis by the authority or a community mental health program;

(f) A licensed psychologist who is experienced in child psychology and the juvenile justice system and not employed on a full-time basis by the authority or a community mental health program;

(g) A member with substantial experience in the processes of juvenile parole and probation;

(h) A lawyer with substantial experience in juvenile law practice; and

(i) Two members of the general public.

(3) The term of office of each member is four years. The Governor at any time may remove any member for inefficiency, neglect of duty or malfeasance in office. Before the expiration of the term of a member, the Governor shall appoint a successor whose term begins on July 1 next following. A member is eligible for reappointment. If there is a vacancy for any cause, the Governor shall make an appointment to become immediately effective for the unexpired term.

(4) A member of the board not otherwise employed full-time by the state shall be paid on a per diem basis an amount equal to $289.22, adjusted according to the executive pay plan for the biennium, for each day during which the member is engaged in the performance of official duties, including necessary travel time. In addition, subject to ORS 292.220 to 292.250 regulating travel and other expenses of state officers and employees, the member shall be reimbursed for actual and necessary travel and other expenses incurred in the performance of official duties.

(5) Subject to any applicable provision of the State Personnel Relations Law, the board may hire employees to aid it in performing its duties.

(6) The board consists of two five-member panels. The adult panel is responsible for persons placed under the board's jurisdiction under ORS 161.315 to 161.351 and 419C.544 and consists of those members appointed under subsection (2)(a) to (d) of this section and one of the public members. The juvenile panel is responsible for young persons placed under the board's jurisdiction under ORS 419C.529 and consists of those members appointed under subsection (2)(e) to (h) of this section and the other public member.

(7)(a) Each panel shall select one of its members as chairperson to serve for a one-year term with such duties and powers as the panel determines.

(b) A majority of the voting members of a panel constitutes a quorum for the transaction of business of the panel.

(8) Each panel shall meet at least twice every month, unless the chairperson determines that there is not sufficient business before the panel to warrant a meeting at the scheduled time. The panel shall also meet at other times and places specified by the call of the chairperson or of a majority of the members of the panel. [1977 c.380 §8; 1979 c.867 §7; 1979 c.885 §6; 1981 c.711 §15; 1981 s.s. c.3 §132; 1983 c.740 §26; 1983 c.800 §12; 1987 c.133 §1; 2001 c.962 §70; 2005 c.843 §20; 2009 c.595 §109; 2011 c.708 §8]

161.387 Board to implement policies; rulemaking. (1) The Psychiatric Security Review Board, by rule pursuant to ORS 183.325 to 183.410 and not inconsistent with law, may implement its policies and set out its procedure and practice requirements and may promulgate such interpretive rules as the board deems necessary or appropriate to carry out its statutory responsibilities.

(2) Administrative meetings of the board are not deliberations for the purposes of ORS 192.690. [1981 c.711 §§10,11; 2011 c.708 §11b]

Note: 161.387 was enacted into law by the Legislative Assembly but was not added to or made a part of 161.385 to 161.395 or any series therein by legislative action. See Preface to Oregon Revised Statutes for further explanation.

161.390 Rules for assignment of persons to state mental hospitals or secure intensive community inpatient facilities; release plan prepared by Oregon Health Authority. (1) The Oregon Health Authority shall adopt rules for the assignment of persons to state mental hospitals or secure intensive community inpatient facilities under ORS 161.365 and 161.370 and for establishing standards for evaluation and treatment of persons committed to a state hospital or a secure intensive community inpatient facility or ordered to a community mental health program under ORS 161.315 to 161.351.

(2) When the Psychiatric Security Review Board requires the preparation of a predischarge or preconditional release plan before a hearing or as a condition of granting discharge or conditional release for a person committed under ORS 161.315 to 161.351 to a state hospital or a secure intensive community inpatient facility for custody, care and treatment, the authority is responsible for and shall prepare the plan.

(3) In carrying out a conditional release plan prepared under subsection (2) of this section, the authority may contract with a community mental health program, other public agency or private corporation or an individual to provide supervision and treatment for the conditionally released person.

(4) The board shall maintain and keep current the medical, social and criminal history of all persons committed to its jurisdiction. The confidentiality of records maintained by the board shall be determined pursuant to ORS 192.338, 192.345 and 192.355.

(5) The evidentiary phase of a hearing conducted by the board under ORS 161.315 to 161.351 is not a deliberation for purposes of ORS 192.690. [1975 c.380 §7; 1977 c.380 §18; 1981 c.711 §14; 1993 c.680 §18; 2005 c.22 §109; 2005 c.685 §8; 2009 c.595 §110; 2011 c.708 §5; 2017 c.442 §6]

Note: The amendments to 161.390 by section 6, chapter 442, Oregon Laws 2017, become operative July 1, 2018. See section 36, chapter 442, Oregon Laws 2017. The text that is operative until July 1, 2018, is set forth for the user's convenience.

161.390. (1) The Oregon Health Authority shall adopt rules for the assignment of persons to state mental hospitals or secure intensive community inpatient facilities under ORS 161.315 to 161.351, 161.365 and 161.370 and for establishing standards for evaluation and treatment of persons committed to a state hospital or a secure intensive community inpatient facility or ordered to a community mental health program under ORS 161.315 to 161.351.

(2) When the Psychiatric Security Review Board or the authority requires the preparation of a predischarge or preconditional release plan before a hearing or as a condition of granting discharge or conditional release for a person committed under ORS 161.315 to 161.351 to a state hospital or a secure intensive community inpatient facility for custody, care and treatment, the authority is responsible for and shall prepare the plan.

(3) In carrying out a conditional release plan prepared under subsection (2) of this section, the authority may contract with a community mental health program, other public agency or private corporation or an individual to provide supervision and treatment for the conditionally released person.

(4) Before the authority conducts a hearing under ORS 161.315 to 161.351, the authority shall notify the board. The board may provide the authority with conditions of release that the board determines are advisable. If the authority orders the person conditionally released, the authority shall include the conditions of release in the order.

(5) The board and the authority shall maintain and keep current the medical, social and criminal history of all persons committed to their respective jurisdiction. The confidentiality of records maintained by the board shall be determined pursuant to ORS 192.338, 192.345 and 192.355.

(6) The evidentiary phase of a hearing conducted by the board or the authority under ORS 161.315 to 161.351 is not a deliberation for purposes of ORS 192.690.

161.392 Certification of psychiatrists and licensed psychologists; rules; fees. (1) The Oregon Health Authority shall adopt rules necessary to certify psychiatrists and licensed psychologists for the purpose of performing evaluations and examinations described in ORS 161.309, 161.365 and 419C.524. The rules must include a description of the standards and qualifications necessary for certification. The authority may charge a fee for certification under this section in an amount determined by rule.

(2) The authority shall consult with the Psychiatric Security Review Board about proposed rules described in subsection (1) of this section before issuing the proposed rules for public comment and before adopting the rules. [2011 c.724 §9]

Note: 161.392 was enacted into law by the Legislative Assembly but was not added to or made a part of ORS chapter 161 or any series therein by legislative action. See Preface to Oregon Revised Statutes for further explanation.

161.395 Subpoena power. (1) Upon request of any party to a hearing before the Psychiatric Security Review Board under ORS 161.315 to 161.351, the board shall issue, or on its own motion may issue, subpoenas requiring the attendance and testimony of witnesses.

(2) Upon request of any party to the hearing before the board and upon a proper showing of the general relevance and reasonable scope of the documentary or physical evidence sought, the board shall issue, or on its own motion may issue, subpoenas duces tecum.

(3) Witnesses appearing under subpoenas, other than the parties or state officers or employees, shall receive fees and mileage as prescribed by law for witnesses in ORS 44.415 (2). If the board certifies that the testimony of a witness was relevant and material, any person who has paid fees and mileage to that witness shall be reimbursed by the board.

(4) If any person fails to comply with a subpoena issued under subsections (1) or (2) of this section or any party or witness refuses to testify regarding any matter on which the party or witness may be lawfully interrogated, the judge of the circuit court of any county, on the application of the board or of the party requesting the issuance of the subpoena, shall compel obedience by proceedings for contempt as in the case of disobedience of the requirements of a subpoena issued by the court.

(5) If any person, agency or facility fails to comply with an order of the board issued pursuant to subsection (2) of this section, the judge of a circuit court of any county, on application of the board, shall compel obedience by proceedings for contempt as in the case of disobedience of the requirements of an order issued by the court. Contempt for disobedience of an order of the board shall be punishable by a fine of $100. [1977 c.380 §9; 1989 c.980 §8; 2011 c.708 §10; 2017 c.442 §9]

Note: The amendments to 161.395 by section 9, chapter 442, Oregon Laws 2017, become operative July 1, 2018. See section 36, chapter 442, Oregon Laws 2017. The text that is operative until July 1, 2018, is set forth for the user's convenience.

161.395. (1) Upon request of any party to a hearing before the Psychiatric Security Review Board or the Oregon Health Authority under ORS 161.315 to 161.351, the agency conducting the hearing shall issue, or on its own motion may issue, subpoenas requiring the attendance and testimony of witnesses.

(2) Upon request of any party to the hearing before the agency and upon a proper showing of the general relevance and reasonable scope of the documentary or physical evidence sought, the agency shall issue, or on its own motion may issue, subpoenas duces tecum.

(3) Witnesses appearing under subpoenas, other than the parties or state officers or employees, shall receive fees and mileage as prescribed by law for witnesses in ORS 44.415 (2). If the agency certifies that the testimony of a witness was relevant and material, any person who has paid fees and mileage to that witness shall be reimbursed by the agency.

(4) If any person fails to comply with a subpoena issued under subsections (1) or (2) of this section or any party or witness refuses to testify regarding any matter on which the party or witness may be lawfully interrogated, the judge of the circuit court of any county, on the application of the agency that issued the subpoena or of the party requesting the issuance of the subpoena, shall compel obedience by proceedings for contempt as in the case of disobedience of the requirements of a subpoena issued by the court.

(5) If any person, agency or facility fails to comply with an order of the board or authority issued pursuant to subsection (2) of this section, the judge of a circuit court of any county, on application of the agency that issued the order, shall compel obedience by proceedings for contempt as in the case of disobedience of the requirements of an order issued by the court. Contempt for disobedience of an order of the board or authority shall be punishable by a fine of $100.

161.397 Psychiatric Security Review Board Account. The Psychiatric Security Review Board Account is established separate and distinct from the General Fund. All moneys received by the Psychiatric Security Review Board, other than appropriations from the General Fund, shall be deposited into the account and are continuously appropriated to the board to carry out the duties, functions and powers of the board. [2001 c.716 §3]

161.398 Restorative justice program; rules. (1)(a) The Psychiatric Security Review Board may develop a restorative justice program to assist the recovery of crime victims when a person is found guilty except for insanity of a crime or responsible except for insanity for an act.

(b) The board may enter into a contract with a nonprofit educational institution or other nonprofit organization that provides for the administration of the restorative justice program by the institution or organization.

(2) Any documents or oral communications created, submitted or provided for use in the restorative justice program are confidential, exempt from public disclosure and:

(a) May not be disclosed to or used by board members.

(b) May not be used or disclosed by restorative justice program staff, volunteers or participants for any purpose unrelated to the program.

(c) Are not admissible as evidence in any subsequent administrative or judicial proceeding, including board proceedings and deliberations.

(3) The board may adopt rules to carry out the provisions of this section. [2017 c.442 §1]

161.400 Leave of absence; notice to board. If, at any time after the commitment of a person to a state hospital or a secure intensive community inpatient facility under ORS 161.315 to 161.351, the superintendent of the hospital or the director of the facility is of the opinion that a leave of absence from the hospital or facility would be therapeutic for the person and that such leave would pose no substantial danger to others, the superintendent or director may authorize such leave for up to 48 hours in accordance with rules adopted by the Psychiatric Security Review Board. However, the superintendent or director, before authorizing the leave of absence, shall first notify the board for the purposes of ORS 161.326. [1981 c.711 §12; 2005 c.685 §9; 2011 c.708 §11; 2017 c.442 §10]

Note: The amendments to 161.400 by section 10, chapter 442, Oregon Laws 2017, become operative July 1, 2018. See section 36, chapter 442, Oregon Laws 2017. The text that is operative until July 1, 2018, is set forth for the user's convenience.

161.400. If, at any time after the commitment of a person to a state hospital or a secure intensive community inpatient facility under ORS 161.315 to 161.351, the superintendent of the hospital or the director of the facility is of the opinion that a leave of absence from the hospital or facility would be therapeutic for the person and that such leave would pose no substantial danger to others, the superintendent or director may authorize such leave for up to 48 hours in accordance with rules adopted by the agency having jurisdiction over the person. However, the superintendent or director, before authorizing the leave of absence, shall first notify the agency for the purposes of ORS 161.326.

161.403 [1983 c.800 §14; repealed by 1993 c.77 §1]

INCHOATE CRIMES

161.405 "Attempt" described. (1) A person is guilty of an attempt to commit a crime when the person intentionally engages in conduct which constitutes a substantial step toward commission of the crime.

(2) An attempt is a:

(a) Class A felony if the offense attempted is murder or treason.

(b) Class B felony if the offense attempted is a Class A felony.

(c) Class C felony if the offense attempted is a Class B felony.

(d) Class A misdemeanor if the offense attempted is a Class C felony or an unclassified felony.

(e) Class B misdemeanor if the offense attempted is a Class A misdemeanor.

(f) Class C misdemeanor if the offense attempted is a Class B misdemeanor.

(g) Violation if the offense attempted is a Class C misdemeanor or an unclassified misdemeanor. [1971 c.743 §54]

161.425 Impossibility not a defense. In a prosecution for an attempt, it is no defense that it was impossible to commit the crime which was the object of the attempt where the conduct engaged in by the actor would be a crime if the circumstances were as the actor believed them to be. [1971 c.743 §55]

161.430 Renunciation as a defense to attempt. (1) A person is not liable under ORS 161.405 if, under circumstances manifesting a voluntary and complete renunciation of the criminal intent of the person, the person avoids the commission of the crime attempted by abandoning the criminal effort and, if mere abandonment is insufficient to accomplish this avoidance, doing everything necessary to prevent the commission of the attempted crime.

(2) The defense of renunciation is an affirmative defense. [1971 c.743 §56]

161.435 Solicitation. (1) A person commits the crime of solicitation if with the intent of causing another to engage in specific conduct constituting a crime punishable as a felony or as a Class A misdemeanor or an attempt to commit such felony or Class A misdemeanor the person commands or solicits such other person to engage in that conduct.

(2) Solicitation is a:

(a) Class A felony if the offense solicited is murder or treason.

(b) Class B felony if the offense solicited is a Class A felony.

(c) Class C felony if the offense solicited is a Class B felony.

(d) Class A misdemeanor if the offense solicited is a Class C felony.

(e) Class B misdemeanor if the offense solicited is a Class A misdemeanor. [1971 c.743 §57]

161.440 Renunciation as defense to solicitation. (1) It is a defense to the crime of solicitation that the person soliciting the crime, after soliciting another person to commit a crime, persuaded the person solicited not to commit the crime or otherwise prevented the commission of the crime, under circumstances manifesting a complete and voluntary renunciation of the criminal intent.

(2) The defense of renunciation is an affirmative defense. [1971 c.743 §58]

161.450 "Criminal conspiracy" described. (1) A person is guilty of criminal conspiracy if with the intent that conduct constituting a crime punishable as a felony or a Class A misdemeanor be performed, the person agrees with one or more persons to engage in or cause the performance of such conduct.

(2) Criminal conspiracy is a:

(a) Class A felony if an object of the conspiracy is commission of murder, treason or a Class A felony.

(b) Class B felony if an object of the conspiracy is commission of a Class B felony.

(c) Class C felony if an object of the conspiracy is commission of a Class C felony.

(d) Class A misdemeanor if an object of the conspiracy is commission of a Class A misdemeanor. [1971 c.743 §59]

161.455 Conspiratorial relationship. If a person is guilty of conspiracy, as defined in ORS 161.450, and knows that a person with whom the person conspires to commit a crime has conspired or will conspire with another person or persons to commit the same crime, the person is guilty of conspiring with such other person or persons, whether or not the person knows their identity, to commit such crime. [1971 c.743 §60]

161.460 Renunciation as defense to conspiracy. (1) It is a defense to a charge of conspiracy that the actor, after conspiring to commit a crime, thwarted commission of the crime which was the object of the conspiracy, under circumstances manifesting a complete and voluntary renunciation of the criminal purpose of the actor. Renunciation by one conspirator does not, however, affect the liability of another conspirator who does not join in the renunciation of the conspiratorial objective.

(2) The defense of renunciation is an affirmative defense. [1971 c.743 §61]

161.465 Duration of conspiracy. For the purpose of application of ORS 131.125:

(1) Conspiracy is a continuing course of conduct which terminates when the crime or crimes which are its object are completed or the agreement that they be committed is abandoned by the defendant and by those with whom the defendant conspired.

(2) Abandonment is presumed if neither the defendant nor anyone with whom the defendant conspired does any overt act in pursuance of the conspiracy during the applicable period of limitation.

(3) If an individual abandons the agreement, the conspiracy is terminated as to the individual only if and when the individual advises those with whom the individual conspired of the abandonment or the individual informs the law enforcement authorities of the existence of the conspiracy and of the participation of the individual therein. [1971 c.743 §62; 1973 c.836 §340]

161.475 Defenses to solicitation and conspiracy. (1) Except as provided in subsection (2) of this section, it is immaterial to the liability of a person who solicits or conspires with another to commit a crime that:

(a) The person or the person whom the person solicits or with whom the person conspires does not occupy a particular position or have a particular characteristic which is an element of such crime, if the person believes that one of them does; or

(b) The person whom the person solicits or with whom the person conspires is irresponsible or has an immunity to prosecution or conviction for the commission of the crime, or, in the case of conspiracy, has feigned the agreement; or

(c) The person with whom the person conspires has not been prosecuted for or convicted of the conspiracy or a crime based upon the conduct in question, or has previously been acquitted.

(2) It is a defense to a charge of solicitation or conspiracy to commit a crime that if the criminal object were achieved, the actor would not be guilty of a crime under the law defining the offense or as an accomplice under ORS 161.150 to 161.165. [1971 c.743 §63]

161.485 Multiple convictions barred in inchoate crimes. (1) It is no defense to a prosecution under ORS 161.405, 161.435 or 161.450 that the offense the defendant either attempted to commit, solicited to commit or conspired to commit was actually committed pursuant to such attempt, solicitation or conspiracy.

(2) A person shall not be convicted of more than one offense defined by ORS 161.405, 161.435 and 161.450 for conduct designed to commit or to culminate in commission of the same crime.

(3) A person shall not be convicted on the basis of the same course of conduct of both the actual commission of an offense and an attempt to commit that offense or solicitation of that offense or conspiracy to commit that offense.

(4) Nothing in this section shall be construed to bar inclusion of multiple counts charging violation of the substantive crime and ORS 161.405, 161.435 and 161.450 in a single indictment or information, provided the penal conviction is consistent with subsections (2) and (3) of this section. [1971 c.743 §64]

CLASSES OF OFFENSES

161.505 "Offense" described. An offense is conduct for which a sentence to a term of imprisonment or to a fine is provided by any law of this state or by any law or ordinance of a political subdivision of this state. An offense is either a crime, as described in ORS 161.515, or a violation, as described in ORS 153.008. [1971 c.743 §65; 1975 c.451 §173; 1981 c.626 §2; 1981 c.692 §7; 1999 c.1051 §43]

161.515 "Crime" described. (1) A crime is an offense for which a sentence of imprisonment is authorized.

(2) A crime is either a felony or a misdemeanor. [1971 c.743 §66]

161.525 "Felony" described. Except as provided in ORS 161.585, 161.705 and 161.710, a crime is a felony if it is so designated in any statute of this state or if a person convicted under a statute of this state may be sentenced to a maximum term of imprisonment of more than one year. [1971 c.743 §67; 2017 c.439 §3]

161.535 Classification of felonies. (1) Felonies are classified for the purpose of sentence into the following categories:

(a) Class A felonies;
(b) Class B felonies;
(c) Class C felonies; and
(d) Unclassified felonies.

(2) The particular classification of each felony defined in the Oregon Criminal Code, except murder under ORS 163.115 and treason under ORS 166.005, is expressly designated in the section defining the crime. An offense defined outside this code which, because of the express sentence provided is within the definition of ORS 161.525, shall be considered an unclassified felony. [1971 c.743 §68]

161.545 "Misdemeanor" described. A crime is a misdemeanor if it is so designated in any statute of this state or if a person convicted thereof may be sentenced to a maximum term of imprisonment of not more than one year. [1971 c.743 §69]

161.555 Classification of misdemeanors. (1) Misdemeanors are classified for the purpose of sentence into the following categories:

(a) Class A misdemeanors;
(b) Class B misdemeanors;
(c) Class C misdemeanors; and
(d) Unclassified misdemeanors.

(2) The particular classification of each misdemeanor defined in the Oregon Criminal Code is expressly designated in the section defining the crime. An offense defined outside this code which, because of the express sentence provided is within the definition of ORS 161.545, shall be considered an unclassified misdemeanor.

(3) An offense defined by a statute of this state, but without specification as to its classification or as to the penalty authorized upon conviction, shall be considered a Class A misdemeanor. [1971 c.743 §70]

161.565 [1971 c.743 §71; 1987 c.783 §1; 1989 c.1053 §17; 1991 c.111 §17; 1993 c.533 §4; 1997 c.852 §12; repealed by 1999 c.1051 §49]

161.566 Misdemeanor treated as violation; prosecuting attorney's election. (1) Except as provided in subsection (4) of this section, a prosecuting attorney may elect to treat any misdemeanor as a Class A violation. The election must be made by the prosecuting attorney orally at the time of the first appearance of the defendant or in writing filed on or before the time scheduled for the first appearance of the defendant. If no election is made within the time allowed, the case shall proceed as a misdemeanor.

(2) If a prosecuting attorney elects to treat a misdemeanor as a Class A violation under this section, the court shall amend the accusatory instrument to reflect the charged offense as a Class A violation and clearly denominate the offense as a Class A violation in any judgment entered in the matter. Notwithstanding ORS 153.021, the fine that a court may impose upon conviction of a violation under this section may not:

(a) Be less than the presumptive fine established by ORS 153.019 for a Class A violation; or

(b) Exceed the maximum fine established by ORS 153.018 for a Class A violation.

(3) If a prosecuting attorney elects to treat a misdemeanor as a Class A violation under this section, and the defendant fails to make any required appearance in the matter, the court may enter a default judgment against the defendant in the manner provided by ORS 153.102. Notwithstanding ORS 153.021, the fine that the court may impose under a default judgment entered pursuant to ORS 153.102 may not:

(a) Be less than the presumptive fine established by ORS 153.019 for a Class A violation; or

(b) Exceed the maximum fine established by ORS 153.018 for a Class A violation.

(4) A prosecuting attorney may not elect to treat misdemeanors created under ORS 811.540 or 813.010 as violations under the provisions of this section.

(5) The election provided for in this section may be made by a city attorney acting as prosecuting attorney in the case of municipal ordinance offenses, a county counsel acting as prosecuting attorney under a county charter in the case of county ordinance offenses, and the Attorney General acting as prosecuting attorney in those criminal actions or proceedings within the jurisdiction of the Attorney General. [1999 c.1051 §47; 2003 c.737 §89; 2011 c.597 §16; 2012 c.82 §2]

161.568 Misdemeanor treated as violation; court's election. (1) Except as provided in subsection (4) of this section, a court may elect to treat any misdemeanor as a Class A violation for the purpose of entering a default judgment under ORS 153.102 if:

(a) A complaint or information has been filed with the court for the misdemeanor;

(b) The defendant has failed to make an appearance in the proceedings required by the court or by law; and

(c) The court has given notice to the district attorney for the county and the district attorney has informed the court that the district attorney does not object to treating the misdemeanor as a Class A violation.

(2) If the court treats a misdemeanor as a Class A violation under this section, the court shall amend the accusatory instrument to reflect the charged offense as a Class A violation and clearly denominate the offense as a Class A violation in the judgment entered in the matter.

(3) Notwithstanding ORS 153.021, if the court treats a misdemeanor as a Class A violation under this section, the fine that the court may impose under a default judgment entered pursuant to ORS 153.102 may not:

(a) Be less than the presumptive fine established by ORS 153.019 for a Class A violation; or

(b) Exceed the maximum fine established by ORS 153.018 for a Class A violation.

(4) A court may not treat misdemeanors created under ORS 811.540 or 813.010 as violations under the provisions of this section. [1999 c.1051 §48; 2003 c.737 §90; 2011 c.597 §17; 2012 c.82 §3]

161.570 Felony treated as misdemeanor. (1) As used in this section, "nonperson felony" has the meaning given that term in the rules of the Oregon Criminal Justice Commission.

(2) A district attorney may elect to treat a Class C nonperson felony or a violation of ORS 475.752 (7), 475.854 (2)(b) or 475.874 (2)(b) as a Class A misdemeanor. The election must be made by the district attorney orally or in writing at the time of the first appearance of the defendant. If a district attorney elects to treat a Class C felony or a violation of ORS 475.752 (7), 475.854 (2)(b) or 475.874 (2)(b) as a Class A misdemeanor under this subsection, the court shall amend the accusatory instrument to reflect the charged offense as a Class A misdemeanor.

(3) If, at some time after the first appearance of a defendant charged with a Class C nonperson felony or a violation of ORS 475.752 (7), 475.854 (2)(b) or 475.874 (2)(b), the district attorney and the defendant agree to treat the charged offense as a Class A misdemeanor, the court may allow the offense to be treated as a Class A misdemeanor by stipulation of the parties.

(4) If a Class C felony or a violation of ORS 475.752 (7), 475.854 (2)(b) or 475.874 (2)(b) is treated as a Class A misdemeanor under this section, the court shall clearly denominate the offense as a Class A misdemeanor in any judgment entered in the matter.

(5) If no election or stipulation is made under this section, the case proceeds as a felony.

(6) Before a district attorney may make an election under subsection (2) of this section, the district attorney shall adopt written guidelines for determining when and under what circumstances the election may be made. The district attorney shall apply the guidelines uniformly.

(7) Notwithstanding ORS 161.635, the fine that a court may impose upon conviction of a misdemeanor under this section may not:

(a) Be less than the minimum fine established by ORS 137.286 for a felony; or

(b) Exceed the amount provided in ORS 161.625 for the class of felony receiving Class A misdemeanor treatment. [2003 c.645 §2; 2005 c.708 §47; 2007 c.286 §1; 2011 c.597 §18; 2013 c.591 §4; 2017 c.706 §25]

161.575 [1971 c.743 §72; repealed by 1999 c.1051 §49]

161.585 Classification of certain crimes determined by punishment. (1) When a crime punishable as a felony is also punishable by imprisonment for a maximum term of one year or by a fine, the crime shall be classed as a misdemeanor if the court imposes a punishment other than imprisonment under ORS 137.124 (1).

(2) Notwithstanding the provisions of ORS 161.525, upon conviction of a crime punishable as described in subsection (1) of this section, the crime is a felony for all purposes until one of the following events occurs, after which occurrence the crime is a misdemeanor for all purposes:

(a) Without imposing a sentence of probation, the court imposes a sentence of imprisonment other than to the legal and physical custody of the Department of Corrections.

(b) Without imposing a sentence of probation, the court imposes a fine.

(c) Upon revocation of probation, the court imposes a sentence of imprisonment other than to the legal and physical custody of the Department of Corrections.

(d) Upon revocation of probation, the court imposes a fine.

(e) The court declares the offense to be a misdemeanor, either at the time of imposing a sentence of probation, upon suspension of imposition of a part of a sentence, or on application of defendant or the parole and probation officer of the defendant thereafter.

(f) The court imposes a sentence of probation on the defendant without imposition of any other sentence upon conviction and defendant is thereafter discharged without any other sentence.

(g) Without imposing a sentence of probation and without imposing any other sentence, the court declares the offense to be a misdemeanor and discharges the defendant.

(3) The provisions of this section shall apply only to persons convicted of a felony committed prior to November 1, 1989. [1971 c.743 §73; 1987 c.320 §85; 1989 c.790 §52; 1993 c.14 §18; 2005 c.264 §15]

DISPOSITION OF OFFENDERS

161.605 Maximum terms of imprisonment for felonies. The maximum term of an indeterminate sentence of imprisonment for a felony is as follows:

(1) For a Class A felony, 20 years.

(2) For a Class B felony, 10 years.

(3) For a Class C felony, 5 years.

(4) For an unclassified felony as provided in the statute defining the crime. [1971 c.743 §74]

161.610 Enhanced penalty for use of firearm during commission of felony; pleading; minimum penalties; suspension or reduction of penalty. (1) As used in this section, "firearm" has the meaning given that term in ORS 166.210.

(2) The use or threatened use of a firearm, whether operable or inoperable, by a defendant during the commission of a felony may be pleaded in the accusatory instrument and proved at trial as an element in aggravation of the crime as provided in this section. When a crime is so pleaded, the aggravated nature of the crime may be indicated by adding the words "with a firearm" to the title of the offense. The unaggravated crime shall be considered a lesser included offense.

(3) Notwithstanding the provisions of ORS 161.605 or 137.010 (3) and except as otherwise provided in subsection (6) of this section, if a defendant is convicted of a felony having as an element the defendant's use or threatened use of a firearm during the commission of the crime, the court shall impose at least the minimum term of imprisonment as provided in subsection (4) of this section. Except as provided in ORS 144.122 and 144.126 and subsection (5) of this section, in no case shall any person punishable under this section become eligible for work release, parole, temporary leave or terminal leave until the minimum term of imprisonment is served, less a period of time equivalent to any reduction of imprisonment granted for good time served or time credits earned under ORS 421.121, nor shall the execution of the sentence imposed upon such person be suspended by the court.

(4) The minimum terms of imprisonment for felonies having as an element the defendant's use or threatened use of a firearm in the commission of the crime shall be as follows:

(a) Except as provided in subsection (5) of this section, upon the first conviction for such felony, five years, except that if the firearm is a machine gun, short-barreled rifle, short-barreled shotgun or is equipped with a firearms silencer, the term of imprisonment shall be 10 years.

(b) Upon conviction for such felony committed after punishment pursuant to paragraph (a) of this subsection or subsection (5) of this section, 10 years, except that if the firearm is a machine gun, short-barreled rifle, short-barreled shotgun or is equipped with a firearms silencer, the term of imprisonment shall be 20 years.

(c) Upon conviction for such felony committed after imprisonment pursuant to paragraph (b) of this subsection, 30 years.

(5) If it is the first time that the defendant is subject to punishment under this section, rather than impose the sentence otherwise required by subsection (4)(a) of this section, the court may:

(a) For felonies committed prior to November 1, 1989, suspend the execution of the sentence or impose a lesser term of imprisonment, when the court expressly finds mitigating circumstances justifying such lesser sentence and sets forth those circumstances in its statement on sentencing; or

(b) For felonies committed on or after November 1, 1989, impose a lesser sentence in accordance with the rules of the Oregon Criminal Justice Commission.

(6) When a defendant who is convicted of a felony having as an element the defendant's use or threatened use of a firearm during the commission of the crime is a person who was waived from juvenile court under ORS 137.707 (5)(b)(A), 419C.349, 419C.352, 419C.364 or 419C.370, the court is not required to impose a minimum term of imprisonment under this section. [1979 c.779 §2; 1985 c.552 §1; 1989 c.790 §72; 1989 c.839 §18; 1991 c.133 §3; 1993 c.692 §9; 1999 c.951 §3; 2005 c.407 §1; 2009 c.610 §5]

161.615 Maximum terms of imprisonment for misdemeanors. Sentences for misdemeanors shall be for a definite term. The court shall fix the term of imprisonment within the following maximum limitations:

(1) For a Class A misdemeanor, 364 days.

(2) For a Class B misdemeanor, 6 months.

(3) For a Class C misdemeanor, 30 days.

(4) For an unclassified misdemeanor, as provided in the statute defining the crime. [1971 c.743 §75; 2017 c.706 §22]

161.620 Sentences imposed upon waiver from juvenile court. Notwithstanding any other provision of law, a sentence imposed upon any person waived from the juvenile court under ORS 419C.349, 419C.352, 419C.364 or 419C.370 shall not include any sentence of death or life imprisonment without the possibility of release or parole nor imposition of any mandatory minimum sentence except that a mandatory minimum sentence under:

(1) ORS 163.105 (1)(c) shall be imposed; and

(2) ORS 161.610 may be imposed. [1985 c.631 §9; 1989 c.720 §3; 1993 c.33 §306; 1993 c.546 §119; 1995 c.422 §131y; 1999 c.951 §2]

Note: 161.620 was added to and made a part of ORS 161.615 to 161.685 by legislative action but was not added to any smaller series in that series. See Preface to Oregon Revised Statutes for further explanation.

161.625 Fines for felonies. (1) A sentence to pay a fine for a felony shall be a sentence to pay an amount, fixed by the court, not exceeding:

(a) $500,000 for murder or aggravated murder.

(b) $375,000 for a Class A felony.

(c) $250,000 for a Class B felony.

(d) $125,000 for a Class C felony.

(2) A sentence to pay a fine for an unclassified felony shall be a sentence to pay an amount, fixed by the court, as provided in the statute defining the crime.

(3)(a) If a person has gained money or property through the commission of a felony, then upon conviction thereof the court, in lieu of imposing the fine authorized for the crime under subsection (1) or (2) of this section, may sentence the defendant to pay an amount, fixed by the court, not exceeding double the amount of the defendant's gain from the commission of the crime.

(b) The provisions of paragraph (a) of this subsection do not apply to the felony theft of a companion animal, as defined in ORS 164.055, or a captive wild animal.

(4) As used in this section, "gain" means the amount of money or the value of property derived from the commission of the felony, less the amount of money or the value of property returned to the victim of the crime or seized by or surrendered to lawful authority before the time sentence is imposed. "Value" shall be determined by the standards established in ORS 164.115.

(5) When the court imposes a fine for a felony the court shall make a finding as to the amount of the defendant's gain from the crime. If the record does not contain sufficient evidence to support a finding the court may conduct a hearing upon the issue.

(6) Except as provided in ORS 161.655, this section does not apply to a corporation. [1971 c.743 §76; 1981 c.390 §1; 1991 c.837 §11; 1993 c.680 §36; 2003 c.615 §1; 2003 c.737 §86]

161.635 Fines for misdemeanors. (1) A sentence to pay a fine for a misdemeanor shall be a sentence to pay an amount, fixed by the court, not exceeding:

(a) $6,250 for a Class A misdemeanor.

(b) $2,500 for a Class B misdemeanor.

(c) $1,250 for a Class C misdemeanor.

(2) A sentence to pay a fine for an unclassified misdemeanor shall be a sentence to pay an amount, fixed by the court, as provided in the statute defining the crime.

(3) If a person has gained money or property through the commission of a misdemeanor, then upon conviction thereof the court, instead of imposing the fine authorized for the offense under this section, may sentence the defendant to pay an amount fixed by the court, not exceeding double the amount of the defendant's gain from the commission of the offense. In that event, ORS 161.625 (4) and (5) apply.

(4) This section does not apply to corporations. [1971 c.743 §77; 1981 c.390 §2; 1993 c.680 §30; 1995 c.545 §2; 1999 c.1051 §44; 2003 c.737 §87]

161.645 Standards for imposing fines. In determining whether to impose a fine and its amount, the court shall consider:

(1) The financial resources of the defendant and the burden that payment of a fine will impose, with due regard to the other obligations of the defendant; and

(2) The ability of the defendant to pay a fine on an installment basis or on other conditions to be fixed by the court. [1971 c.743 §78]

161.655 Fines for corporations. (1) A sentence to pay a fine when imposed on a corporation for an offense defined in the Oregon Criminal Code or for an offense defined outside this code for which no special corporate fine is specified, shall be a sentence to pay an amount, fixed by the court, not exceeding:

(a) $50,000 when the conviction is of a felony.

(b) $5,000 when the conviction is of a Class A misdemeanor or of an unclassified misdemeanor for which a term of imprisonment of more than six months is authorized.

(c) $2,500 when the conviction is of a Class B misdemeanor or of an unclassified misdemeanor for which the authorized term of imprisonment is not more than six months.

(d) $1,000 when the conviction is of a Class C misdemeanor or an unclassified misdemeanor for which the authorized term of imprisonment is not more than 30 days.

(2) A sentence to pay a fine, when imposed on a corporation for an offense defined outside the Oregon Criminal Code, if a special fine for a corporation is provided in the statute defining the offense, shall be a sentence to pay an amount, fixed by the court, as provided in the statute defining the offense.

(3) If a corporation has gained money or property through the commission of an offense, then upon conviction thereof the court, in lieu of imposing the fine authorized for the offense under subsection (1) or (2) of this section, may sentence the corporation to pay an amount, fixed by the court, not exceeding double the amount of the corporation's gain from the commission of the offense. In that event, ORS 161.625 (4) and (5) apply. [1971 c.743 §79; 1999 c.1051 §45]

161.665 Costs. (1) Except as provided in ORS 151.505, the court, only in the case of a defendant for whom it enters a judgment of conviction, may include in its sentence thereunder a money award for all costs specially incurred by the state in prosecuting the defendant. Costs include a reasonable attorney fee for counsel appointed pursuant to ORS 135.045 or 135.050 and a reasonable amount for fees and expenses incurred pursuant to preauthorization under ORS 135.055. A reasonable attorney fee is presumed to be a reasonable number of hours at the hourly rate authorized by the Public Defense Services Commission under ORS 151.216. Costs do not include expenses inherent in providing a constitutionally guaranteed jury trial or expenditures in connection with the maintenance and operation of government agencies that must be made by the public irrespective of specific violations of law.

(2) Except as provided in ORS 151.505, the court, after the conclusion of an appeal of its initial judgment of conviction, may include in its general judgment, or enter a supplemental judgment that includes, a money award that requires a convicted defendant to pay a reasonable attorney fee for counsel appointed pursuant to ORS 138.500, including counsel who is appointed under ORS 151.216 or counsel who is under contract to provide services for the proceeding under ORS 151.219, and other costs and expenses allowed by the public defense services executive director under ORS 138.500 (4). A reasonable attorney fee is presumed to be a reasonable number of hours at the hourly rate authorized by the commission under ORS 151.216.

(3) For purposes of subsections (1) and (2) of this section, compensation of counsel is determined by reference to a schedule of compensation established by the commission under ORS 151.216.

(4) The court may not sentence a defendant to pay costs under this section unless the defendant is or may be able to pay them. In determining the amount and method of payment of costs, the court shall take account of the financial resources of the defendant and the nature of the burden that payment of costs will impose.

(5) A defendant who has been sentenced to pay costs under this section and who is not in contumacious default in the payment of costs may at any time petition the court that sentenced the defendant for remission of the payment of costs or of any unpaid portion of costs. If it appears to the satisfaction of the court that payment of the amount due will impose manifest hardship on the defendant or the immediate family of the defendant, the court may enter a supplemental judgment that remits all or part of the amount due in costs, or modifies the method of payment under ORS 161.675.

(6) Except as provided in subsection (7) of this section, all moneys collected or paid under this section shall be paid into the Criminal Fine Account.

(7) The court may, in the judgment of conviction, include a money award requiring the defendant to pay the costs of extraditing the defendant to this state. Any amounts awarded to the state under this subsection must be listed separately in the money award portion of the judgment. All moneys collected or paid under this subsection shall be deposited into the Arrest and Return Account established by ORS 133.865. [1971 c.743 §80; 1981 s.s. c.3 §120; 1983 c.763 §12; 1985 c.710 §3; 1987 c.803 §26; 1989 c.1053 §11; 1991 c.460 §12; 1991 c.840 §1; 1997 c.761 §1; 2001 c.962 §§41,113; 2003 c.449 §29; 2003 c.576 §§247,248; 2003 c.615 §2; 2011 c.597 §44; 2015 c.198 §2]

161.675 Time and method of payment of fines, restitution and costs. (1) When a defendant, as a part of a sentence or as condition of probation or suspension of sentence, is required to pay a sum of money for any purpose, the court may order payment to be made immediately or within a specified period of time or in specified installments. If a defendant is sentenced to a term of imprisonment, any part of the sentence that requires the payment of a sum of money for any purpose is enforceable during the period of imprisonment if the court expressly finds that the defendant has assets to pay all or part of the amounts ordered.

(2) When a defendant whose sentence requires the payment of a sum of money for any purpose is also sentenced to probation or imposition or execution of sentence is suspended, the court may make payment of the sum of money a condition of probation or suspension of sentence.

(3) When a defendant is sentenced to probation or imposition or execution of sentence is suspended and the court requires as a part of the sentence or as a condition of the probation or suspension of sentence that the defendant pay a sum of money in installments, the court, or the court clerk or parole and probation officer if so ordered by the court, shall establish a schedule of payments to satisfy the obligation. A schedule of payments shall be reviewed by the court upon motion of the defendant at any time, so long as the obligation remains unsatisfied. [1971 c.743 §81; 1977 c.371 §4; 1985 c.46 §1; 1993 c.14 §19; 1995 c.512 §3; 2005 c.264 §16]

161.685 Effect of nonpayment of fines, restitution or costs; report to consumer reporting agency; rules. (1) When a defendant who has been sentenced or ordered to pay a fine, or to make restitution, defaults on a payment or installment ordered by the court, the court on motion of the district attorney or upon its own motion may require the defendant to show cause why the default should not be treated as contempt of court, and may issue a show cause citation or a warrant of arrest for the appearance of the defendant.

(2) If the court finds that the default constitutes contempt, the court may impose one or more of the sanctions authorized by ORS 33.105.

(3) When a fine or an order of restitution is imposed on a corporation or unincorporated association, it is the duty of the person authorized to make disbursement from the assets of the corporation or association to pay the fine or make the restitution from those assets, and if that person fails to do so, the court may hold that person in contempt.

(4) Notwithstanding ORS 33.105, the term of confinement for contempt for nonpayment of fines or failure to make restitution shall be set forth in the commitment order, and shall not exceed one day for each $25 of the fine or restitution, 30 days if the fine or order of restitution was imposed upon conviction of a violation or misdemeanor, or one year in any other case, whichever is the shorter period.

(5) If it appears to the satisfaction of the court that the default in the payment of a fine or restitution is not contempt, the court may enter an order allowing the defendant additional time for payment, reducing the amount of the payment or installments due on the payment, or revoking the fine or order of restitution in whole or in part.

(6) A default in the payment of a fine or costs or failure to make restitution or a default on an installment on a fine, costs or restitution may be collected by any means authorized by law for the enforcement of a judgment. The levy of execution or garnishment for the collection of a fine or restitution shall not discharge a defendant confined for contempt until the amount of the fine or restitution has actually been collected.

(7) The court, or the court clerk if ordered by the court, may report a default on a court-ordered payment to a consumer reporting agency.

(8) The Chief Justice of the Supreme Court shall adopt rules under ORS 1.002 establishing policies and procedures for reporting a default under subsection (7) of this section to a consumer reporting agency that may include, but are not limited to, limitations on reporting a default to a consumer reporting agency.

(9) Except as otherwise provided in this section, proceedings under this section shall be conducted:

(a) As provided in ORS 33.055, if the court seeks to impose remedial sanctions as described in ORS 33.015 to 33.155; and

(b) As provided in ORS 33.065, if the court seeks to impose punitive sanctions as described in ORS 33.015 to 33.155.

(10) Confinement under this section may be custody or incarceration, whether actual or constructive.

(11) As used in this section:

(a) "Consumer reporting agency" means any person that regularly engages for fees, dues, or on a nonprofit basis, in whole or in part, in the practice of assembling or evaluating consumer credit information or other information on consumers for the purpose of furnishing consumer reports to third parties.

(b) "Restitution" has the meaning given that term in ORS 137.103. [1971 c.743 §82; 1977 c.371 §5; 1987 c.709 §3; 1987 c.873 §28; 1991 c.724 §27a; 1995 c.79 §50; 1995 c.512 §4; 2015 c.9 §3]

AUTHORITY OF SENTENCING COURT

161.705 Reduction of certain felonies to misdemeanors. Notwithstanding ORS 161.525, the court may enter judgment of conviction for a Class A misdemeanor and make disposition accordingly when:

(1)(a) A person is convicted of any Class C felony; or

(b) A person convicted of a felony described in paragraph (a) of this subsection, of possession or delivery of marijuana or a marijuana item as defined in ORS 475B.015 constituting a Class B felony, or of a Class A felony pursuant to ORS 166.720, has successfully completed a sentence of probation; and

(2) The court, considering the nature and circumstances of the crime and the history and character of the defendant, believes that it would be unduly harsh to sentence the defendant for a felony. [1971 c.743 §83; 1977 c.745 §31; 1979 c.124 §1; 1981 c.769 §8; 2005 c.708 §48; 2009 c.610 §2; 2013 c.591 §5; 2015 c.290 §2; 2015 c.614 §125; 2017 c.21 §100]

161.710 Reduction of certain felony driving offenses after completion of sentence. Notwithstanding ORS 161.525, the court has authority, at any time after a sentence of probation has been completed, to enter judgment of conviction for a Class A misdemeanor for a person convicted of criminal driving while suspended or revoked under ORS 811.182 committed before September 1, 1999, and constituting a felony if:

(1) The suspension or revocation resulted from habitual offender status under ORS 809.640;

(2) The person successfully completed the sentence of probation; and

(3) The court finds that, considering the nature and circumstances of the crime and the history and character of the person, it would be unduly harsh for the person to continue to have a felony conviction. [2017 c.439 §2]

161.715 Standards for discharge of defendant. (1) Any court empowered to suspend imposition or execution of sentence or to sentence a defendant to probation may discharge the defendant if:

(a) The conviction is for an offense other than murder, treason or a Class A or B felony; and

(b) The court is of the opinion that no proper purpose would be served by imposing any condition upon the defendant's release.

(2) If a sentence of discharge is imposed for a felony, the court shall set forth in the record the reasons for its action.

(3) If the court imposes a sentence of discharge, the defendant shall be released with respect to the conviction for which the sentence is imposed without imprisonment, probationary supervision or conditions. The judgment entered by the court shall include a monetary obligation payable to the state in an amount equal to the minimum fine for the offense established by ORS 137.286.

(4) If a defendant pleads not guilty and is tried and found guilty, a sentence of discharge is a judgment on a conviction for all purposes, including an appeal by the defendant.

(5) If a defendant pleads guilty, a sentence of discharge is not appealable, but for all other purposes is a judgment on a conviction. [1971 c.743 §84; 1993 c.14 §20; 2003 c.576 §249; 2011 c.597 §20]

161.725 Standards for sentencing of dangerous offenders. (1) Subject to the provisions of ORS 161.737, the maximum term of an indeterminate sentence of imprisonment for a dangerous offender is 30 years, if because of the dangerousness of the defendant an extended period of confined correctional treatment or custody is required for the protection of the public and one or more of the following grounds exist:

(a) The defendant is being sentenced for a Class A felony and the defendant is suffering from a severe personality disorder indicating a propensity toward crimes that seriously endanger the life or safety of another.

(b) The defendant is being sentenced for a felony that seriously endangered the life or safety of another, the defendant has been previously convicted of a felony not related to the instant crime as a single criminal episode and the defendant is suffering from a severe personality disorder indicating a propensity toward crimes that seriously endanger the life or safety of another.

(c) The defendant is being sentenced for a felony that seriously endangered the life or safety of another, the defendant has previously engaged in unlawful conduct not related to the instant crime as a single criminal episode that seriously endangered the life or safety of another and the defendant is suffering from a severe personality disorder indicating a propensity toward crimes that seriously endanger the life or safety of another.

(2) As used in this section, "previously convicted of a felony" means:

(a) Previous conviction of a felony in a court of this state;

(b) Previous conviction in a court of the United States, other than a court-martial, of an offense which at the time of conviction of the offense was and at the time of conviction of the instant crime is punishable under the laws of the United States by death or by imprisonment in a penitentiary, prison or similar institution for a term of one year or more; or

(c) Previous conviction by a general court-martial of the United States or in a court of any other state or territory of the United States, or of the Commonwealth of Puerto Rico, of an offense which at the time of conviction of the offense was punishable by death or by imprisonment in a penitentiary, prison or similar institution for a term of one year or more and which offense also at the time of conviction of the instant crime would have been a felony if committed in this state.

(3) As used in this section, "previous conviction of a felony" does not include:

(a) An offense committed when the defendant was less than 16 years of age;

(b) A conviction rendered after the commission of the instant crime;

(c) A conviction that is the defendant's most recent conviction described in subsection (2) of this section, and the defendant was finally and unconditionally discharged from all resulting imprisonment, probation or parole more than seven years before the commission of the instant crime; or

(d) A conviction that was by court-martial of an offense denounced only by military law and triable only by court-martial.

(4) As used in this section, "conviction" means an adjudication of guilt upon a plea, verdict or finding in a criminal proceeding in a court of competent jurisdiction, but does not include an adjudication which has been expunged by pardon, reversed, set aside or otherwise rendered nugatory. [1971 c.743 §85; 1989 c.790 §75; 1993 c.334 §5; 2005 c.463 §§9,14; 2007 c.16 §4]

161.735 Procedure for determining whether defendant dangerous. (1) Upon motion of the district attorney, and if, in the opinion of the court, there is reason to believe that the defendant falls within ORS 161.725, the court shall order a presentence investigation and an examination by a psychiatrist or psychologist. The court may appoint one or more qualified psychiatrists or psychologists to examine the defendant in the local correctional facility.

(2) All costs connected with the examination shall be paid by the state.

(3) The examination performed pursuant to this section shall be completed within 30 days, subject to additional extensions not exceeding 30 days on order of the court. Each psychiatrist and psychologist appointed to examine a defendant under this section shall file with the court a written report of findings and conclusions, including an evaluation of whether the defendant is suffering from a severe personality disorder indicating a propensity toward criminal activity.

(4) No statement made by a defendant under this section or ORS 137.124 or 423.090 shall be used against the defendant in any civil proceeding or in any other criminal proceeding.

(5) Upon receipt of the examination and presentence reports the court shall set a time for a presentence hearing, unless the district attorney and the defendant waive the hearing. At the presentence hearing the district attorney and the defendant may question any psychiatrist or psychologist who examined the defendant pursuant to this section.

(6) If, after considering the evidence in the case or in the presentence hearing, the jury or, if the defendant waives the right to a jury trial, the court finds that the defendant comes within ORS 161.725, the court may sentence the defendant as a dangerous offender.

(7) In determining whether a defendant has been previously convicted of a felony for purposes of ORS 161.725, the court shall consider as prima facie evidence of the previous conviction:

(a) A copy of the judicial record of the conviction which copy is authenticated under ORS 40.510;

(b) A copy of the fingerprints of the subject of that conviction which copy is authenticated under ORS 40.510; and

(c) Testimony that the fingerprints of the subject of that conviction are those of the defendant.

(8) Subsection (7) of this section does not prohibit proof of the previous conviction by any other procedure.

(9) The facts required to be found to sentence a defendant as a dangerous offender under this section are enhancement facts, as defined in ORS 136.760, and ORS 136.765 to 136.785 apply to making determinations of those facts. [1971 c.743 §86; 1973 c.836 §341; 1981 c.892 §89a; 1983 c.740 §27; 1987 c.248 §1; 1999 c.163 §9; 2005 c.463 §§10,15; 2007 c.16 §5]

161.737 Sentence imposed on dangerous offender as departure from sentencing guidelines. (1) A sentence imposed under ORS 161.725 and 161.735 for felonies committed on or after November 1, 1989, shall constitute a departure from the sentencing guidelines created by rules of the Oregon Criminal Justice Commission. The findings made to classify the defendant as a dangerous offender under ORS 161.725 and 161.735 shall constitute substantial and compelling reasons to depart from the presumptive sentence as provided by rules of the Oregon Criminal Justice Commission.

(2) When the sentence is imposed, the sentencing judge shall indicate on the record the reasons for the departure and shall impose, in addition to the indeterminate sentence imposed under ORS 161.725, a required incarceration term that the offender must serve before release to post-prison supervision. If the presumptive sentence that would have been imposed if the court had not imposed the sentence under ORS 161.725 and 161.735 as a departure is a prison sentence, the required incarceration term shall be no less than the presumptive incarceration term and no more than twice the maximum presumptive incarceration term. If the presumptive sentence for the offense is probation, the required incarceration term shall be no less than the maximum incarceration term provided by the rule of the Oregon Criminal Justice Commission that establishes incarceration terms for dispositional departures and no more than twice that amount. However, the indeterminate sentence imposed under this section and ORS 161.725 is not subject to any guideline rule establishing limitations on the duration of departures. [1989 c.790 §77; 1993 c.334 §6]

Chapter 162 — Offenses Against the State and Public Justice

162.005 Definitions for ORS 162.005 to 162.425. As used in ORS 162.005 to 162.425, unless the context requires otherwise:

(1) "Pecuniary benefit" means gain or advantage to the beneficiary or to a third person pursuant to the desire or consent of the beneficiary, in the form of money, property, commercial interests or economic gain, but does not include a political campaign contribution reported in accordance with ORS chapter 260.

(2) "Public servant" means:

(a) A public official as defined in ORS 244.020;

(b) A person serving as an advisor, consultant or assistant at the request or direction of the state, any political subdivision thereof or of any governmental instrumentality within the state;

(c) A person nominated, elected or appointed to become a public servant, although not yet occupying the position; and

(d) Jurors. [1971 c.743 §178; 2007 c.865 §22]

162.010 [Repealed by 1971 c.743 §432]

BRIBERY

162.015 Bribe giving. (1) A person commits the crime of bribe giving if the person offers, confers or agrees to confer any pecuniary benefit upon a public servant with the intent to influence the public servant's vote, opinion, judgment, action, decision or exercise of discretion in an official capacity.

(2) Bribe giving is a Class B felony. [1971 c.743 §179]

162.020 [Repealed by 1971 c.743 §432]

162.025 Bribe receiving. (1) A public servant commits the crime of bribe receiving if the public servant:

(a) Solicits any pecuniary benefit with the intent that the vote, opinion, judgment, action, decision or exercise of discretion as a public servant will thereby be influenced; or

(b) Accepts or agrees to accept any pecuniary benefit upon an agreement or understanding that the vote, opinion, judgment, action, decision or exercise of discretion as a public servant will thereby be influenced.

(2) Bribe receiving is a Class B felony. [1971 c.743 §180]

162.030 [Amended by 1963 c.625 §3; repealed by 1971 c.743 §432]

162.035 Bribery defenses. (1) In any prosecution under ORS 162.015, it is a defense that the defendant offered, conferred or agreed to confer the pecuniary benefit as a result of the public servant's conduct constituting extortion or coercion.

(2) It is no defense to a prosecution under ORS 162.015 and 162.025 that the person sought to be influenced was not qualified to act in the desired way, whether because the person had not assumed office, lacked jurisdiction or for any other reason. [1971 c.743 §181]

162.040 [Repealed by 1971 c.743 §432]

PERJURY AND RELATED OFFENSES

162.055 Definitions for ORS 162.055 to 162.425. As used in ORS 162.055 to 162.425 and 162.465, unless the context requires otherwise:

(1) "Benefit" means gain or advantage to the beneficiary or to a third person pursuant to the desire or consent of the beneficiary.

(2) "Material" means that which could have affected the course or outcome of any proceeding or transaction. Whether a false statement is "material" in a given factual situation is a question of law.

(3) "Statement" means any representation of fact and includes a representation of opinion, belief or other state of mind where the representation clearly relates to state of mind apart from or in addition to any facts which are the subject of the representation.

(4) "Sworn statement" means any statement that attests to the truth of what is stated and that is knowingly given under any form of oath or affirmation or by declaration under penalty of perjury as described in ORCP 1 E.

(5) "Unsworn declaration" has the meaning given that term in ORS 194.805. [1971 c.743 §182; 1981 c.892 §90; 2003 c.194 §4; 2013 c.218 §18]

162.065 Perjury. (1) A person commits the crime of perjury if the person makes a false sworn statement or a false unsworn declaration in regard to a material issue, knowing it to be false.

(2) Perjury is a Class C felony. [1971 c.743 §183; 2013 c.218 §19]

162.075 False swearing. (1) A person commits the crime of false swearing if the person makes a false sworn statement or a false unsworn declaration, knowing it to be false.

(2) False swearing is a Class A misdemeanor. [1971 c.743 §184; 2013 c.218 §20]

162.085 Unsworn falsification. (1) A person commits the crime of unsworn falsification if the person knowingly makes any false written statement to a public servant in connection with an application for any benefit.

(2) Unsworn falsification is a Class B misdemeanor. [1971 c.743 §185]

162.095 Defenses to perjury and false swearing limited. It is no defense to a prosecution for perjury or false swearing that:

(1) The statement was inadmissible under the rules of evidence; or

(2) The oath or affirmation was taken or administered in an irregular manner; or

(3) The defendant mistakenly believed the false statement to be immaterial. [1971 c.743 §186]

162.105 Retraction as defense. (1) It is a defense to a prosecution for perjury or false swearing committed in an official proceeding that the defendant retracted the false statement:

(a) In a manner showing a complete and voluntary retraction of the prior false statement; and

(b) During the course of the same official proceeding in which it was made; and

(c) Before the subject matter of the official proceeding is submitted to the ultimate trier of fact.

(2) "Official proceeding," as used in this section, means a proceeding before any judicial, legislative or administrative body or officer, wherein sworn statements are received, and includes any referee, hearing examiner, commissioner, notary or other person taking sworn statements in connection with such proceedings. Statements made in separate stages of the same trial or administrative proceeding shall be considered to have been made in the course of the same proceeding. [1971 c.743 §187]

162.110 [Repealed by 1971 c.743 §432]

162.115 Corroboration of falsity required. In any prosecution for perjury or false swearing, falsity of a statement may not be established solely through contradiction by the testimony of a single witness. [1971 c.743 §188]

162.117 Public investment fraud. (1) A person commits the crime of public investment fraud if, for the purpose of influencing in any way the action of the State Treasury, the person knowingly makes any false statement or report.

(2) Public investment fraud is a Class B felony.

(3) Public investment fraud shall be classified as crime category 6 of the sentencing guidelines grid of the Oregon Criminal Justice Commission.

(4) As used in this section, "action of the State Treasury" includes any application, advance, discount, purchase, purchase agreement, repurchase agreement, commitment or loan, or any change or extension of any of them, by renewal, deferment of action or otherwise, or the acceptance, release or substitution of security therefor. [1993 c.768 §1]

Note: 162.117, 162.118, 162.119 and 162.121 were enacted into law by the Legislative Assembly but were not added to or made a part of ORS chapter 162 or any series therein by legislative action. See Preface to Oregon Revised Statutes for further explanation.

162.118 Illegal conduct by State Treasury not a defense. Illegal conduct by the State Treasury or any of its employees or agents shall not be a defense for any person charged with the crime of public investment fraud or to any person against whom any civil action is brought under ORS 30.862 and 162.117 to 162.121. [1993 c.768 §2]

Note: See note under 162.117.

162.119 Public fraud as racketeering activity. (1) Conduct constituting a violation of ORS 162.117 shall be an incident of racketeering activity for purposes of criminal actions brought under ORS 166.715 to 166.735.

(2) Conduct giving rise to the civil cause of action described in ORS 30.862 shall be an incident of racketeering activity for purposes of civil actions brought under ORS 166.715 to 166.735. [1993 c.768 §3]

Note: See note under 162.117.

162.120 [Repealed by 1971 c.743 §432]

162.121 Construction of ORS 162.117 to 162.121. The provisions of ORS 30.862 and 162.117 to 162.121 shall be liberally construed to effectuate its remedial purposes. [1993 c.768 §5]

Note: See note under 162.117.

162.130 [Repealed by 1971 c.743 §432]

ESCAPE, SUPPLYING CONTRABAND AND FAILURE TO APPEAR

162.135 Definitions for ORS 162.135 to 162.205. As used in ORS 162.135 to 162.205, unless the context requires otherwise:

(1)(a) "Contraband" means:

(A) Controlled substances as defined in ORS 475.005;

(B) Drug paraphernalia as defined in ORS 475.525;

(C) Except as otherwise provided in paragraph (b) of this subsection, currency possessed by or in the control of an inmate confined in a correctional facility; or

(D) Any article or thing which a person confined in a correctional facility, youth correction facility or state hospital is prohibited by statute, rule or order from obtaining or possessing, and whose use would endanger the safety or security of such institution or any person therein.

(b) "Contraband" does not include authorized currency possessed by an inmate in a work release facility.

(2) "Correctional facility" means any place used for the confinement of persons charged with or convicted of a crime or otherwise confined under a court order and includes but is not limited to a youth correction facility. "Correctional facility" applies to a state hospital or a secure intensive community inpatient facility only as to persons detained therein charged with or convicted of a crime, or detained therein after having been found guilty except for insanity of a crime under ORS 161.290 to 161.370.

(3) "Currency" means paper money and coins that are within the correctional institution.

(4) "Custody" means the imposition of actual or constructive restraint by a peace officer pursuant to an arrest or court order, but does not include detention in a correctional facility, youth correction facility or a state hospital.

(5) "Escape" means the unlawful departure of a person from custody or a correctional facility. "Escape" includes the unauthorized departure or absence from this state or failure to return to this state by a person who is under the jurisdiction of the Psychiatric Security Review Board under ORS 161.315 to 161.351. "Escape" does not include failure to comply with provisions of a conditional release in ORS 135.245.

(6) "Youth correction facility" means:

(a) A youth correction facility as defined in ORS 420.005; and

(b) A detention facility as defined in ORS 419A.004.

(7) "State hospital" means the Oregon State Hospital and any other hospital established by law for similar purposes.

(8) "Unauthorized departure" means the unauthorized departure of a person confined by court order in a youth correction facility or a state hospital that, because of the nature of the court order, is not a correctional facility as defined in this section, or the failure to return to custody after any form of temporary release or transitional leave from a correctional facility. [1971 c.743 §189; 1973 c.836 §342; 1983 c.740 §28; 1983 c.815 §7; 1985 c.565 §16; 1989 c.790 §53; 1991 c.809 §1; 1993 c.33 §307; 1995 c.738 §2; 1997 c.249 §47; 1999 c.504 §1; 2001 c.295 §8; 2001 c.900 §24; 2005 c.685 §10; 2007 c.14 §3; 2011 c.708 §21; 2013 c.36 §36; 2015 c.318 §8; 2017 c.442 §20]

Note: The amendments to 162.135 by section 20, chapter 442, Oregon Laws 2017, become operative July 1, 2018. See section 36, chapter 442, Oregon Laws 2017. The text that is operative until July 1, 2018, is set forth for the user's convenience.

162.135. As used in ORS 162.135 to 162.205, unless the context requires otherwise:

(1)(a) "Contraband" means:

(A) Controlled substances as defined in ORS 475.005;

(B) Drug paraphernalia as defined in ORS 475.525;

(C) Except as otherwise provided in paragraph (b) of this subsection, currency possessed by or in the control of an inmate confined in a correctional facility; or

(D) Any article or thing which a person confined in a correctional facility, youth correction facility or state hospital is prohibited by statute, rule or order from obtaining or possessing, and whose use would endanger the safety or security of such institution or any person therein.

(b) "Contraband" does not include authorized currency possessed by an inmate in a work release facility.

(2) "Correctional facility" means any place used for the confinement of persons charged with or convicted of a crime or otherwise confined under a court order and includes but is not limited to a youth correction facility. "Correctional facility" applies to a state hospital or a secure intensive community inpatient facility only as to persons detained therein charged with or convicted of a crime, or detained therein after having been found guilty except for insanity of a crime under ORS 161.290 to 161.370.

(3) "Currency" means paper money and coins that are within the correctional institution.

(4) "Custody" means the imposition of actual or constructive restraint by a peace officer pursuant to an arrest or court order, but does not include detention in a correctional facility, youth correction facility or a state hospital.

(5) "Escape" means the unlawful departure of a person from custody or a correctional facility. "Escape" includes the unauthorized departure or absence from this state or failure to return to this state by a person who is under the jurisdiction of the Psychiatric Security Review Board or under the jurisdiction of the Oregon Health Authority under ORS 161.315 to 161.351. "Escape" does not include failure to comply with provisions of a conditional release in ORS 135.245.

(6) "Youth correction facility" means:

(a) A youth correction facility as defined in ORS 420.005; and

(b) A detention facility as defined in ORS 419A.004.

(7) "State hospital" means the Oregon State Hospital and any other hospital established by law for similar purposes.

(8) "Unauthorized departure" means the unauthorized departure of a person confined by court order in a youth correction facility or a state hospital that, because of the nature of the court order, is not a correctional facility as defined in this section, or the failure to return to custody after any form of temporary release or transitional leave from a correctional facility.

162.140 [1959 c.307 §1; 1961 c.312 §1; 1963 c.499 §9; repealed by 1971 c.743 §432]

162.145 Escape in the third degree. (1) A person commits the crime of escape in the third degree if the person escapes from custody.

(2) It is a defense to a prosecution under this section that the person escaping or attempting to escape was in custody pursuant to an illegal arrest.

(3) Escape in the third degree is a Class A misdemeanor. [1971 c.743 §190]

162.150 [Repealed by 1971 c.743 §432]

162.155 Escape in the second degree. (1) A person commits the crime of escape in the second degree if:

(a) The person uses or threatens to use physical force escaping from custody; or

(b) Having been convicted or found guilty of a felony, the person escapes from custody imposed as a result thereof; or

(c) The person escapes from a correctional facility; or

(d) While under the jurisdiction of the Psychiatric Security Review Board under ORS 161.315 to 161.351, the person departs, is absent from or fails to return to this state without authorization of the board.

(2) Escape in the second degree is a Class C felony. [1971 c.743 §191; 1983 c.800 §13; 1985 c.192 §1; 2011 c.708 §22; 2017 c.442 §21]

Note: The amendments to 162.155 by section 21, chapter 442, Oregon Laws 2017, become operative July 1, 2018. See section 36, chapter 442, Oregon Laws 2017. The text that is operative until July 1, 2018, is set forth for the user's convenience.

162.155. (1) A person commits the crime of escape in the second degree if:

(a) The person uses or threatens to use physical force escaping from custody; or

(b) Having been convicted or found guilty of a felony, the person escapes from custody imposed as a result thereof; or

(c) The person escapes from a correctional facility; or

(d) While under the jurisdiction of the Psychiatric Security Review Board or under the jurisdiction of the Oregon Health Authority under ORS 161.315 to 161.351, the person departs, is absent from or fails to return to this state without authorization of the board.

(2) Escape in the second degree is a Class C felony.

162.160 [Repealed by 1971 c.743 §432]

162.165 Escape in the first degree. (1) A person commits the crime of escape in the first degree if:

(a) Aided by another person actually present, the person uses or threatens to use physical force in escaping from custody or a correctional facility; or

(b) The person uses or threatens to use a dangerous or deadly weapon escaping from custody or a correctional facility.

(2) Escape in the first degree is a Class B felony. [1971 c.743 §192]

162.175 Unauthorized departure. (1) A person commits the crime of unauthorized departure if:

(a) The person makes an unauthorized departure; or

(b) Not being an inmate therein, the person aids another in making or attempting to make an unauthorized departure.

(2) Unauthorized departure is a Class A misdemeanor. [1971 c.743 §193; 1983 c.815 §8; 1989 c.790 §54]

162.185 Supplying contraband. (1) A person commits the crime of supplying contraband if:

(a) The person knowingly introduces any contraband into a correctional facility, youth correction facility or state hospital; or

(b) Being confined in a correctional facility, youth correction facility or state hospital, the person knowingly makes, obtains or possesses any contraband.

(2) Supplying contraband is a Class C felony. [1971 c.743 §194; 1983 c.815 §9; 1997 c.249 §48]

162.193 Failure to appear; counsel for defendant cannot be witness; exception. In no prosecution under ORS 162.195 or 162.205 shall counsel representing the defendant on the underlying charge for which the defendant is alleged to have failed to appear be called to testify by the state as a witness against the defendant at any stage of the proceedings including, but not limited to, grand jury, preliminary hearing and trial. However, upon written motion by the state, and upon hearing the matter, if the court determines that no other reasonably adequate means exists to present evidence establishing the material elements of the charge, the counsel representing the defendant may be called to testify. [1989 c.759 §2]

162.195 Failure to appear in the second degree. (1) A person commits the crime of failure to appear in the second degree if the person knowingly fails to appear as required after:

(a) Having by court order been released from custody or a correctional facility under a release agreement or security release upon the condition that the person will subsequently appear personally in connection with a charge against the person of having committed a misdemeanor; or

(b) Having been released from a correctional facility subject to a forced release agreement under ORS 169.046 in connection with a charge against the person of having committed a misdemeanor.

(2) Failure to appear in the second degree is a Class A misdemeanor. [1971 c.743 §195; 1973 c.836 §343; 1993 c.533 §5; 1999 c.1051 §69; 2001 c.517 §3; 2003 c.320 §1]

162.205 Failure to appear in the first degree. (1) A person commits the crime of failure to appear in the first degree if the person knowingly fails to appear as required after:

(a) Having by court order been released from custody or a correctional facility under a release agreement or security release upon the condition that the person will subsequently appear personally in connection with a charge against the person of having committed a felony; or

(b) Having been released from a correctional facility subject to a forced release agreement under ORS 169.046 in connection with a charge against the person of having committed a felony.

(2) Failure to appear in the first degree is a Class C felony. [1971 c.743 §196; 1973 c.836 §344; 2001 c.517 §4; 2003 c.320 §2]

162.210 [Repealed by 1971 c.743 §432]

162.220 [Repealed by 1971 c.743 §432]

162.225 Definitions for ORS 162.225 to 162.375. As used in ORS 162.225 to 162.375 and 162.465, unless the context requires otherwise:

(1) "Firefighter" means any fire or forestry department employee, or authorized fire department volunteer, vested with the duty of preventing or combating fire or preventing the loss of life or property by fire.

(2) "Official proceeding" means a proceeding before any judicial, legislative or administrative body or officer, wherein sworn statements are received, and includes any referee, hearing examiner, commissioner, notary or other person taking sworn statements in connection with such proceedings.

(3) "Physical evidence" means any article, object, record, document or other evidence of physical substance.

(4) "Public record" means any book, document, paper, file, photograph, sound recording, computerized recording in machine storage, records or other materials, regardless of physical form or characteristic, made, received, filed or recorded in any government office or agency pursuant to law or in connection with the transaction of public business, whether or not confidential or restricted in use.

(5) "Testimony" means oral or written statements that may be offered by a witness in an official proceeding. [1971 c.743 §197; 1991 c.67 §34]

162.230 [Repealed by 1971 c.743 §432]

162.235 Obstructing governmental or judicial administration. (1) A person commits the crime of obstructing governmental or judicial administration if the person:

(a) Intentionally obstructs, impairs or hinders the administration of law or other governmental or judicial function by means of intimidation, force, physical or economic interference or obstacle;

(b) With intent to defraud, engages in the business of or acts in the capacity of a notary public as defined in ORS 194.215 without having received a commission as a notary public from the Secretary of State; or

(c) With intent to defraud, engages in the business of or acts in the capacity of an immigration consultant, as defined in ORS 9.280, in violation of ORS 9.160.

(2) This section shall not apply to the obstruction of unlawful governmental or judicial action or interference with the making of an arrest.

(3) Obstructing governmental or judicial administration is a Class A misdemeanor. [1971 c.743 §198; 1981 c.902 §1; 2016 c.47 §1]

162.240 [Repealed by 1971 c.743 §432]

162.245 Refusing to assist a peace officer. (1) A person commits the offense of refusing to assist a peace officer if upon command by a person known by the person to be a peace officer the person unreasonably refuses or fails to assist in effecting an authorized arrest or preventing another from committing a crime.

(2) Refusing to assist a peace officer is a Class B violation. [1971 c.743 §199; 1999 c.1051 §150]

162.247 Interfering with a peace officer or parole and probation officer. (1) A person commits the crime of interfering with a peace officer or parole and probation officer if the person, knowing that another person is a peace officer or a parole and probation officer as defined in ORS 181A.355:

(a) Intentionally acts in a manner that prevents, or attempts to prevent, a peace officer or parole and probation officer from performing the lawful duties of the officer with regards to another person; or

(b) Refuses to obey a lawful order by the peace officer or parole and probation officer.

(2) Interfering with a peace officer or parole and probation officer is a Class A misdemeanor.

(3) This section does not apply in situations in which the person is engaging in:

(a) Activity that would constitute resisting arrest under ORS 162.315; or

(b) Passive resistance. [1997 c.719 §1; 1999 c.1040 §7; 2005 c.668 §1]

Note: 162.247 was enacted into law by the Legislative Assembly but was not added to or made a part of ORS chapter 162 or any series therein by legislative action. See Preface to Oregon Revised Statutes for further explanation.

162.255 Refusing to assist in fire-fighting operations. (1) A person commits the offense of refusing to assist in fire-fighting operations if:

(a) Upon command by a person known by the person to be a firefighter the person unreasonably refuses or fails to assist in extinguishing a fire or protecting property threatened thereby; or

(b) Upon command by a person known by the person to be a firefighter or peace officer the person intentionally and unreasonably disobeys a lawful order relating to the conduct of the person in the vicinity of a fire.

(2) Subsection (1) of this section does not apply to a person working for a news organization if the person is reporting on the fire and the person does not unreasonably interfere with fire-fighting operations.

(3) Refusing to assist in fire-fighting operations is a Class B violation. [1971 c.743 §200; 1991 c.67 §35; 1999 c.1051 §151; 2005 c.626 §1]

162.257 Interfering with a firefighter or emergency medical services provider. (1) A person commits the crime of interfering with a firefighter or emergency medical services provider if the person, knowing that another person is a firefighter or emergency medical services provider, intentionally acts in a manner that prevents, or attempts to prevent, a firefighter or emergency medical services provider from performing the lawful duties of the firefighter or emergency medical services provider.

(2) Interfering with a firefighter or emergency medical services provider is a Class A misdemeanor.

(3) As used in this section, "emergency medical services provider" has the meaning given that term in ORS 682.025. [2003 c.529 §2; 2011 c.703 §26]

162.265 Bribing a witness. (1) A person commits the crime of bribing a witness if the person offers, confers or agrees to confer any pecuniary benefit upon a witness in any official proceeding, or a person the person believes may be called as a witness, with the intent that:

(a) The testimony of the person as a witness will thereby be influenced; or

(b) The person will avoid legal process summoning the person to testify; or

(c) The person will be absent from any official proceeding to which the person has been legally summoned.

(2) Bribing a witness is a Class C felony. [1971 c.743 §201]

162.275 Bribe receiving by a witness. (1) A witness in any official proceeding, or a person who believes the person may be called as a witness, commits the crime of bribe receiving by a witness if the person solicits any pecuniary benefit with the intent, or accepts or agrees to accept any pecuniary benefit upon an agreement or understanding, that:

(a) The testimony of the person as a witness will thereby be influenced; or

(b) The person will avoid legal process summoning the person to testify; or

(c) The person will be absent from any official proceeding to which the person has been legally summoned.

(2) Bribe receiving by a witness is a Class C felony. [1971 c.743 §202]

162.285 Tampering with a witness. (1) A person commits the crime of tampering with a witness if:

(a) The person knowingly induces or attempts to induce a witness or a person the person believes may be called as a witness in any official proceeding to offer false testimony or unlawfully withhold any testimony; or

(b) The person knowingly induces or attempts to induce a witness to be absent from any official proceeding to which the person has been legally summoned.

(2) Tampering with a witness is a Class C felony. [1971 c.743 §203; 1979 c.231 §1]

162.295 Tampering with physical evidence. (1) A person commits the crime of tampering with physical evidence if, with intent that it be used, introduced, rejected or unavailable in an official proceeding which is then pending or to the knowledge of such person is about to be instituted, the person:

(a) Destroys, mutilates, alters, conceals or removes physical evidence impairing its verity or availability; or

(b) Knowingly makes, produces or offers any false physical evidence; or

(c) Prevents the production of physical evidence by an act of force, intimidation or deception against any person.

(2) Tampering with physical evidence is a Class A misdemeanor. [1971 c.743 §204]

162.305 Tampering with public records. (1) A person commits the crime of tampering with public records if, without lawful authority, the person knowingly destroys, mutilates, conceals, removes, makes a false entry in or falsely alters any public record, including records relating to the Oregon State Lottery.

(2)(a) Except as provided in paragraph (b) of this subsection, tampering with public records is a Class A misdemeanor.

(b) Tampering with records relating to the Oregon State Lottery is a Class C felony. [1971 c.743 §205; 1991 c.962 §16]

162.310 [Repealed by 1971 c.743 §432]

162.315 Resisting arrest. (1) A person commits the crime of resisting arrest if the person intentionally resists a person known by the person to be a peace officer or parole and probation officer in making an arrest.

(2) As used in this section:

(a) "Arrest" has the meaning given that term in ORS 133.005 and includes, but is not limited to, the booking process.

(b) "Parole and probation officer" has the meaning given that term in ORS 181A.355.

(c) "Resists" means the use or threatened use of violence, physical force or any other means that creates a substantial risk of physical injury to any person and includes, but is not limited to, behavior clearly intended to prevent being taken into custody by overcoming the actions of the arresting officer. The behavior does not have to result in actual physical injury to an officer. Passive resistance does not constitute behavior intended to prevent being taken into custody.

(3) It is no defense to a prosecution under this section that the peace officer or parole and probation officer lacked legal authority to make the arrest or book the person, provided the officer was acting under color of official authority.

(4) Resisting arrest is a Class A misdemeanor. [1971 c.743 §206; 1989 c.877 §1; 1997 c.749 §3; 2005 c.668 §2]

162.320 [Repealed by 1971 c.743 §432]

162.322 [1961 c.649 §1; repealed by 1971 c.743 §432]

162.324 [1961 c.649 §2; repealed by 1971 c.743 §432]

162.325 Hindering prosecution. (1) A person commits the crime of hindering prosecution if, with intent to hinder the apprehension, prosecution, conviction or punishment of a person who has committed a crime punishable as a felony, or with the intent to assist a person who has committed a crime punishable as a felony in profiting or benefiting from the commission of the crime, the person:

(a) Harbors or conceals such person; or

(b) Warns such person of impending discovery or apprehension; or

(c) Provides or aids in providing such person with money, transportation, weapon, disguise or other means of avoiding discovery or apprehension; or

(d) Prevents or obstructs, by means of force, intimidation or deception, anyone from performing an act which might aid in the discovery or apprehension of such person; or

(e) Suppresses by any act of concealment, alteration or destruction physical evidence which might aid in the discovery or apprehension of such person; or

(f) Aids such person in securing or protecting the proceeds of the crime.

(2) Hindering prosecution is a Class C felony. [1971 c.743 §207]

162.326 [1961 c.649 §3; repealed by 1971 c.743 §432]

162.330 [Amended by 1961 c.649 §4; repealed by 1971 c.743 §432]

162.335 Compounding. (1) A person commits the crime of compounding if the person accepts or agrees to accept any pecuniary benefit as consideration for refraining from reporting to law enforcement authorities the commission or suspected commission of any felony or information relating to a felony.

(2) Compounding is a Class A misdemeanor. [1971 c.743 §208]

162.340 [Amended by 1955 c.660 §21; 1961 c.649 §5; repealed by 1971 c.743 §432]

162.345 Defenses for hindering or compounding limited. It is no defense to a prosecution for hindering prosecution or compounding that the principal offender is not apprehended, prosecuted, convicted or punished. [1971 c.743 §209]

162.350 [Amended by 1955 c.660 §22; repealed by 1961 c.649 §9]

162.355 Simulating legal process. (1) A person commits the crime of simulating legal process if, with the intent to harass, injure or defraud another person, the person knowingly issues or delivers to another person any document that in form and substance falsely simulates civil or criminal process.

(2) As used in this section:

(a) "Civil or criminal process" means a document or order, including, but not limited to, a summons, lien, complaint, warrant, injunction, writ, notice, pleading or subpoena, that is issued by a court or that is filed or recorded for the purpose of:

(A) Exercising jurisdiction;

(B) Representing a claim against a person or property;

(C) Directing a person to appear before a court or tribunal; or

(D) Directing a person to perform or refrain from performing a specified act.

(b) "Person" has the meaning given that term in ORS 161.015, except that in relation to a defendant, "person" means a human being, a public or private corporation, an unincorporated association or a partnership.

(3) Simulating legal process is a Class C felony. [1971 c.743 §210; 1997 c.395 §1; 2005 c.2 §1]

162.360 [Repealed by 1961 c.649 §9]

162.365 Criminal impersonation of a public servant. (1) A person commits the crime of criminal impersonation of a public servant if, with intent to obtain a benefit, to injure or defraud another or to facilitate an unlawful activity, the person does an act in the assumed character of a public servant.

(2) It is no defense to a prosecution under this section that:

(a) The office, position or title that the person pretended to hold did not in fact exist; or

(b) The unit of government that the person pretended to represent did not in fact exist.

(3)(a) Criminal impersonation of a public servant is a Class A misdemeanor.

(b) Notwithstanding paragraph (a) of this subsection, criminal impersonation of a public servant is a Class C felony if the public servant impersonated is a peace officer, judge or justice of the peace.

(4) For the purposes of this section, "public servant" includes an active member or veteran of the Armed Forces of the United States. [1971 c.743 §211; 1993 c.243 §1; 1997 c.395 §2; 2003 c.577 §12; 2007 c.510 §1; 2016 c.22 §3]

162.367 Criminal impersonation of a peace officer. (1) A person commits the crime of criminal impersonation of a peace officer if the person, with the intent to obtain a benefit or to injure or defraud another person, uses false law enforcement identification or wears a law enforcement uniform to give the impression that the person is a peace officer and does an act in that assumed character.

(2) Criminal impersonation of a peace officer is a Class C felony.

(3) As used in this section:

(a) "False law enforcement identification" means a badge or an identification card that:

(A) Identifies the possessor of the badge or card as a member of a law enforcement unit; and

(B) Was not lawfully issued to the possessor by the law enforcement unit.

(b) "Law enforcement uniform" means clothing bearing words such as "police," "sheriff," "state trooper" or "law enforcement," or clothing that is an official uniform or substantially similar to an official uniform of a law enforcement unit that would make it reasonably likely that a person would believe that the wearer is a peace officer. [1993 c.243 §2; 2005 c.259 §1]

Note: 162.367 and 162.369 were enacted into law by the Legislative Assembly but were not added to or made a part of ORS chapter 162 or any series therein by legislative action. See Preface to Oregon Revised Statutes for further explanation.

162.369 Possession of a false law enforcement identification card. (1) A person commits the crime of possession of a false law enforcement identification card if the person possesses a false law enforcement identification card.

(2) Possession of a false law enforcement identification card is a Class A misdemeanor.

(3) As used in this section, "false law enforcement identification card" means an identification card that:

(a) Identifies the possessor of the card as a member of a law enforcement unit; and

(b) Was not lawfully issued to the possessor by the law enforcement unit. [1993 c.243 §3]

Note: See note under 162.367.

162.370 [Repealed by 1961 c.649 §9]

162.375 Initiating a false report. (1) A person commits the crime of initiating a false report if the person knowingly initiates a false alarm or report that is transmitted to a fire department, law enforcement agency or other organization that deals with emergencies involving danger to life or property.

(2) Initiating a false report is a Class A misdemeanor.

(3)(a) The court shall include in the sentence of any person convicted under this section a requirement that the person repay the costs incurred in responding to and investigating the false report.

(b) If the response to the false report involved the deployment of a law enforcement special weapons and tactics (SWAT) team or a similar law enforcement group, the court shall impose, and may not suspend, a term of incarceration of at least 10 days. [1971 c.743 §212; 2013 c.490 §1; 2015 c.751 §2]

162.380 [Amended by 1953 c.531 §2; 1955 c.660 §23; repealed by 1971 c.743 §432]

162.385 Giving false information to a peace officer in connection with a citation or warrant. (1) A person commits the crime of giving false information to a peace officer in connection with a citation or warrant if the person knowingly uses or gives a false or fictitious name, address or date of birth to any peace officer when:

(a) The peace officer is issuing or serving the person a citation under authority of ORS 133.055 to 133.076 or ORS chapter 153; or

(b) There is an outstanding warrant for the person's arrest.

(2) Giving false information to a peace officer in connection with a citation or warrant is a Class A misdemeanor. [1983 c.661 §11; 1999 c.1051 §70; 2003 c.777 §1; 2007 c.771 §1; 2017 c.99 §1]

Note: 162.385 was added to and made a part of ORS chapter 133 by legislative action. It was not added to ORS chapter 162 or any series therein by legislative action. See Preface to Oregon Revised Statutes for further explanation.

162.390 [Amended by 1955 c.660 §24; repealed by 1961 c.649 §9]

162.400 [Repealed by 1971 c.743 §432]

ABUSE OF PUBLIC OFFICE

162.405 Official misconduct in the second degree. (1) A public servant commits the crime of official misconduct in the second degree if the person knowingly violates any statute relating to the office of the person.
(2) Official misconduct in the second degree is a Class C misdemeanor. [1971 c.743 §214]

162.410 [Repealed by 1961 c.649 §9]

162.415 Official misconduct in the first degree. (1) A public servant commits the crime of official misconduct in the first degree if:
(a) With intent to obtain a benefit or to harm another:
(A) The public servant knowingly fails to perform a duty imposed upon the public servant by law or one clearly inherent in the nature of office; or
(B) The public servant knowingly performs an act constituting an unauthorized exercise in official duties; or
(b) The public servant, while acting as a supervisory employee, violates ORS 162.405 and is aware of and consciously disregards the fact that the violation creates a risk of:
(A) Physical injury to a vulnerable person;
(B) The commission of a sex crime as defined in ORS 163A.005 against a vulnerable person; or
(C) The withholding from a vulnerable person of necessary and adequate food, physical care or medical attention.
(2) Official misconduct in the first degree is a Class A misdemeanor.
(3) As used in this section:
(a) "Supervisory employee" means a person having the authority, in the interest of an employer, to hire, transfer, suspend, lay off, recall, promote, discharge, assign, reward or discipline other employees.
(b) "Vulnerable person" has the meaning given that term in ORS 136.427. [1971 c.743 §215; 2017 c.519 §1]

162.420 [Repealed by 1961 c.649 §9]

162.425 Misuse of confidential information. (1) A public servant commits the crime of misuse of confidential information if in contemplation of official action by the public servant or by a governmental unit with which the public servant is associated, or in reliance on information to which the public servant has access in an official capacity and which has not been made public, the public servant acquires or aids another in acquiring a pecuniary interest in any property, transaction or enterprise which may be affected by such information or official action.
(2) Misuse of confidential information is a Class B misdemeanor. [1971 c.743 §216]

162.430 [Amended by 1961 c.649 §6; repealed by 1971 c.743 §432]

162.440 [Amended by 1961 c.649 §7; repealed by 1971 c.743 §432]

162.450 [1965 c.447 §§8,9; repealed by 1971 c.743 §432]

INTERFERENCE WITH LEGISLATIVE OPERATIONS

162.455 Interfering with legislative operations. Any person not a member of the Legislative Assembly who engages in conduct in or near the legislative chambers of either house or in or near any meeting of a joint, standing, interim or special committee of either house, wherever held, with the intention of interrupting, disrupting or otherwise interfering with the orderly conduct of business therein, or who gains or seeks to gain access to the chambers or meeting in such manner shall be guilty of a misdemeanor. [1971 c.276 §1]

162.465 Unlawful legislative lobbying. (1) A person commits the crime of unlawful legislative lobbying if, having an interest in the passage or defeat of a measure being considered by either house of the Legislative Assembly of this state, as either an agent or principal, the person knowingly attempts to influence a member of the assembly in relation to the measure without first disclosing completely to the member the true interest of the person therein, or that of the principal of the person and the person's own agency therein.

(2) Unlawful legislative lobbying is a Class B misdemeanor. [1971 c.743 §213]

162.510 [Repealed by 1971 c.743 §432]

162.520 [Repealed by 1971 c.743 §432]

162.530 [Repealed by 1971 c.743 §432]

162.540 [Repealed by 1971 c.743 §432]

162.550 [Repealed by 1971 c.743 §432]

162.560 [Repealed by 1971 c.743 §432]

162.570 [Repealed by 1971 c.743 §432]

162.580 [Repealed by 1971 c.743 §432]

162.590 [Repealed by 1971 c.743 §432]

162.600 [Repealed by 1971 c.743 §432]

162.610 [Repealed by 1971 c.743 §432]

162.620 [Repealed by 1971 c.743 §432]

162.630 [Repealed by 1971 c.743 §432]

162.640 [Repealed by 1971 c.743 §432]

162.650 [Repealed by 1971 c.743 §432]

162.655 [Repealed by 1971 c.743 §432]

162.660 [Repealed by 1971 c.743 §432]

162.670 [Repealed by 1971 c.743 §432]

162.680 [Repealed by 1971 c.743 §432]

162.690 [Repealed by 1971 c.743 §432]

162.700 [Repealed by 1971 c.743 §432]

162.710 [Repealed by 1971 c.743 §432]

162.720 [Repealed by 1971 c.743 §432]

162.730 [Repealed by 1971 c.743 §432]

162.740 [Repealed by 1971 c.743 §432]

Chapter 163 — Offenses Against Persons

HOMICIDE

163.005 Criminal homicide. (1) A person commits criminal homicide if, without justification or excuse, the person intentionally, knowingly, recklessly or with criminal negligence causes the death of another human being.

(2) "Criminal homicide" is murder, manslaughter, criminally negligent homicide or aggravated vehicular homicide.

(3) "Human being" means a person who has been born and was alive at the time of the criminal act. [1971 c.743 §87; 2007 c.867 §4]

163.010 [Amended by 1963 c.625 §4; repealed by 1971 c.743 §432]

163.020 [Amended by 1963 c.625; §5; repealed by 1971 c.743 §432]

163.030 [Repealed by 1963 c.431 §1]

163.040 [Repealed by 1971 c.743 §432]

163.050 [Repealed by 1971 c.743 §432]

163.060 [Repealed by 1969 c.684 §17]

163.070 [Repealed by 1971 c.743 §432]

163.080 [Repealed by 1971 c.743 §432]

163.090 [Amended by 1953 c.676 §2; repealed by 1957 c.396 §1 (163.091 enacted in lieu of 163.090)]

163.091 [1957 c.396 §2 (enacted in lieu of 163.090); repealed by 1971 c.743 §432]

163.095 "Aggravated murder" defined. As used in ORS 163.105 and this section, "aggravated murder" means murder as defined in ORS 163.115 which is committed under, or accompanied by, any of the following circumstances:

(1)(a) The defendant committed the murder pursuant to an agreement that the defendant receive money or other thing of value for committing the murder.

(b) The defendant solicited another to commit the murder and paid or agreed to pay the person money or other thing of value for committing the murder.

(c) The defendant committed murder after having been convicted previously in any jurisdiction of any homicide, the elements of which constitute the crime of murder as defined in ORS 163.115 or manslaughter in the first degree as defined in ORS 163.118.

(d) There was more than one murder victim in the same criminal episode as defined in ORS 131.505.

(e) The homicide occurred in the course of or as a result of intentional maiming or torture of the victim.

(f) The victim of the intentional homicide was a person under the age of 14 years.

(2)(a) The victim was one of the following and the murder was related to the performance of the victim's official duties in the justice system:

(A) A police officer as defined in ORS 181A.355;

(B) A correctional, parole and probation officer or other person charged with the duty of custody, control or supervision of convicted persons;

(C) A member of the Oregon State Police;

(D) A judicial officer as defined in ORS 1.210;

(E) A juror or witness in a criminal proceeding;

(F) An employee or officer of a court of justice;

(G) A member of the State Board of Parole and Post-Prison Supervision; or

(H) A regulatory specialist.

(b) The defendant was confined in a state, county or municipal penal or correctional facility or was otherwise in custody when the murder occurred.

(c) The defendant committed murder by means of an explosive as defined in ORS 164.055.

(d) Notwithstanding ORS 163.115 (1)(b), the defendant personally and intentionally committed the homicide under the circumstances set forth in ORS 163.115 (1)(b).

(e) The murder was committed in an effort to conceal the commission of a crime, or to conceal the identity of the perpetrator of a crime.

(f) The murder was committed after the defendant had escaped from a state, county or municipal penal or correctional facility and before the defendant had been returned to the custody of the facility. [1977 c.370 §1; 1981 c.873 §1; 1991 c.742 §13; 1991 c.837 §12; 1993 c.185 §20; 1993 c.623 §2; 1997 c.850 §1; 2005 c.264 §17; 2012 c.54 §26; 2015 c.614 §149]

163.098 Alternative proof of certain victims of aggravated murder. Notwithstanding ORS 163.095, when an element of a crime charged is that the victim of the crime is a police officer as defined in ORS 181A.355 and the crime was related to the officer's performance of official duties, the state may alternatively prove that the victim of the crime is a certified reserve officer or a reserve officer, as those terms are defined in ORS 181A.355, and the crime was related to the officer's performance of official duties. [2014 c.73 §5]

Note: 163.098 was enacted into law by the Legislative Assembly but was not added to or made a part of ORS chapter 163 or any series therein by legislative action. See Preface to Oregon Revised Statutes for further explanation.

163.100 [Amended by 1967 c.372 §12; repealed by 1971 c.743 §432]

163.103 Pleading, proof and stipulation regarding previous conviction element in prosecution for aggravated murder. (1) In a prosecution for aggravated murder under ORS 163.095 (1)(c), the state shall plead the previous conviction, and shall prove the previous conviction unless the defendant stipulates to that fact prior to trial. If the defendant so stipulates and the trial is by jury:
  (a) The court shall accept the stipulation regardless of whether or not the state agrees to it;
  (b) The defendant's stipulation to the previous conviction constitutes a judicial admission to that element of the accusatory instrument. The stipulation shall be made a part of the record of the case, but shall not be offered or received in the presence of the jury;
  (c) For the purpose of establishing the prior conviction solely as an element of the crime under ORS 163.095 (1)(c), neither the court nor the state shall reveal to the jury the previous conviction, but the previous conviction is established in the record by the defendant's stipulation; and
  (d) The court shall not submit the accusatory instrument or evidence of the previous conviction to the jury.
  (2) In a proceeding under ORS 163.095 (1)(c), the state may offer, and the court may receive and submit to the jury, evidence of the previous conviction for impeachment of the defendant or another purpose, other than establishing the conviction as an element of the offense, when the evidence of the previous conviction is otherwise admissible for that purpose. When evidence of the previous conviction has been admitted by the court, the state may comment upon, and the court may give instructions about, the evidence of the previous conviction only to the extent that the comments or instructions relate to the purpose for which the evidence was admitted.
  (3) When the defendant stipulates to the prior conviction required as an element of aggravated murder under ORS 163.095 (1)(c), if the jury finds the defendant guilty upon instruction regarding the balance of the elements of the crime, the court shall enter a judgment of guilty of aggravated murder. [1981 c.873 §3]

163.105 Sentencing options for aggravated murder. Notwithstanding the provisions of ORS chapter 144 and ORS 421.450 to 421.490:
  (1)(a) Except as otherwise provided in ORS 137.707, when a defendant is convicted of aggravated murder as defined by ORS 163.095, the defendant shall be sentenced, pursuant to ORS 163.150, to death, life imprisonment without the possibility of release or parole or life imprisonment.
  (b) A person sentenced to life imprisonment without the possibility of release or parole under this section shall not have that sentence suspended, deferred or commuted by any judicial officer, and the State Board of Parole and Post-Prison Supervision may not parole the prisoner nor reduce the period of confinement in any manner whatsoever. The Department of Corrections or any executive official may not permit the prisoner to participate in any sort of release or furlough program.
  (c) If sentenced to life imprisonment, the court shall order that the defendant shall be confined for a minimum of 30 years without possibility of parole, release to post-prison supervision, release on work release or any form of temporary leave or employment at a forest or work camp.
  (2) At any time after completion of a minimum period of confinement pursuant to subsection (1)(c) of this section, the State Board of Parole and Post-Prison Supervision, upon the petition of a prisoner so confined, shall hold a hearing to determine if the prisoner is likely to be rehabilitated within a reasonable period of time. The sole issue is whether or not the prisoner is likely to be rehabilitated within a reasonable period of time. At the hearing, the prisoner has:
  (a) The burden of proving by a preponderance of the evidence the likelihood of rehabilitation within a reasonable period of time;
  (b) The right, if the prisoner is without sufficient funds to employ an attorney, to be represented by legal counsel, appointed by the board, at board expense; and
  (c) The right to a subpoena upon a showing of the general relevance and reasonable scope of the evidence sought, provided that any subpoena issued on behalf of the prisoner must be issued by the State Board of Parole and Post-Prison Supervision pursuant to rules adopted by the board.
  (3) If, upon hearing all of the evidence, the board, upon a unanimous vote of three board members or, if the chairperson requires all voting members to participate, a unanimous vote of all voting members, finds that the prisoner is capable of rehabilitation and that the terms of the prisoner's confinement should be changed to life

imprisonment with the possibility of parole, release to post-prison supervision or work release, it shall enter an order to that effect and the order shall convert the terms of the prisoner's confinement to life imprisonment with the possibility of parole, release to post-prison supervision or work release and may set a release date. Otherwise the board shall deny the relief sought in the petition.

(4) If the board denies the relief sought in the petition, the board shall determine the date of the subsequent hearing, and the prisoner may petition for an interim hearing, in accordance with ORS 144.285.

(5) The board's final order shall be accompanied by findings of fact and conclusions of law. The findings of fact shall consist of a concise statement of the underlying facts supporting the findings as to each contested issue of fact and as to each ultimate fact required to support the board's order. [1977 c.370 §2; 1981 c.873 §4; 1985 c.3 §1; 1987 c.158 §23; 1987 c.803 §20; 1989 c.720 §1; 1991 c.126 §8; 1995 c.421 §2; 1999 c.59 §31; 1999 c.782 §5; 2007 c.717 §1; 2009 c.660 §6; 2015 c.820 §45]

163.110 [Repealed by 1971 c.743 §432]

163.115 Murder; affirmative defense to certain felony murders; sentence of life imprisonment required; minimum term. (1) Except as provided in ORS 163.118 and 163.125, criminal homicide constitutes murder:

(a) When it is committed intentionally, except that it is an affirmative defense that, at the time of the homicide, the defendant was under the influence of an extreme emotional disturbance;

(b) When it is committed by a person, acting either alone or with one or more persons, who commits or attempts to commit any of the following crimes and in the course of and in furtherance of the crime the person is committing or attempting to commit, or during the immediate flight therefrom, the person, or another participant if there be any, causes the death of a person other than one of the participants:

(A) Arson in the first degree as defined in ORS 164.325;

(B) Criminal mischief in the first degree by means of an explosive as defined in ORS 164.365;

(C) Burglary in the first degree as defined in ORS 164.225;

(D) Escape in the first degree as defined in ORS 162.165;

(E) Kidnapping in the second degree as defined in ORS 163.225;

(F) Kidnapping in the first degree as defined in ORS 163.235;

(G) Robbery in the first degree as defined in ORS 164.415;

(H) Any felony sexual offense in the first degree defined in this chapter;

(I) Compelling prostitution as defined in ORS 167.017; or

(J) Assault in the first degree, as defined in ORS 163.185, and the victim is under 14 years of age, or assault in the second degree, as defined in ORS 163.175 (1)(a) or (b), and the victim is under 14 years of age; or

(c) By abuse when a person, recklessly under circumstances manifesting extreme indifference to the value of human life, causes the death of a child under 14 years of age or a dependent person, as defined in ORS 163.205, and:

(A) The person has previously engaged in a pattern or practice of assault or torture of the victim or another child under 14 years of age or a dependent person; or

(B) The person causes the death by neglect or maltreatment.

(2) An accusatory instrument alleging murder by abuse under subsection (1)(c) of this section need not allege specific incidents of assault or torture.

(3) It is an affirmative defense to a charge of violating subsection (1)(b) of this section that the defendant:

(a) Was not the only participant in the underlying crime;

(b) Did not commit the homicidal act or in any way solicit, request, command, importune, cause or aid in the commission thereof;

(c) Was not armed with a dangerous or deadly weapon;

(d) Had no reasonable ground to believe that any other participant was armed with a dangerous or deadly weapon; and

(e) Had no reasonable ground to believe that any other participant intended to engage in conduct likely to result in death.

(4) It is an affirmative defense to a charge of violating subsection (1)(c)(B) of this section that the victim was a dependent person who was at least 18 years of age and was under care or treatment solely by spiritual means pursuant to the religious beliefs or practices of the dependent person or the guardian of the dependent person.

(5) Except as otherwise provided in ORS 163.155:

(a) A person convicted of murder, who was at least 15 years of age at the time of committing the murder, shall be punished by imprisonment for life.

(b) When a defendant is convicted of murder under this section, the court shall order that the defendant shall be confined for a minimum of 25 years without possibility of parole, release to post-prison supervision, release on work release or any form of temporary leave or employment at a forest or work camp.

(c) At any time after completion of a minimum period of confinement pursuant to paragraph (b) of this subsection, the State Board of Parole and Post-Prison Supervision, upon the petition of a prisoner so confined, shall hold a hearing to determine if the prisoner is likely to be rehabilitated within a reasonable period of time. The sole issue is whether the prisoner is likely to be rehabilitated within a reasonable period of time. At the hearing the prisoner has:

(A) The burden of proving by a preponderance of the evidence the likelihood of rehabilitation within a reasonable period of time;

(B) The right, if the prisoner is without sufficient funds to employ an attorney, to be represented by legal counsel, appointed by the board, at board expense; and

(C) The right to a subpoena upon a showing of the general relevance and reasonable scope of the evidence sought, provided that any subpoena issued on behalf of the prisoner must be issued by the State Board of Parole and Post-Prison Supervision pursuant to rules adopted by the board.

(d) If, upon hearing all of the evidence, the board, upon a unanimous vote of three board members or, if the chairperson requires all voting members to participate, a unanimous vote of all voting members, finds that the prisoner is capable of rehabilitation and that the terms of the prisoner's confinement should be changed to life imprisonment with the possibility of parole, release to post-prison supervision or work release, it shall enter an order to that effect and the order shall convert the terms of the prisoner's confinement to life imprisonment with the possibility of parole, release to post-prison supervision or work release and may set a release date. Otherwise, the board shall deny the relief sought in the petition.

(e) If the board denies the relief sought in the petition, the board shall determine the date of the subsequent hearing, and the prisoner may petition for an interim hearing, in accordance with ORS 144.285.

(f) The board's final order shall be accompanied by findings of fact and conclusions of law. The findings of fact shall consist of a concise statement of the underlying facts supporting the findings as to each contested issue of fact and as to each ultimate fact required to support the board's order.

(6) As used in this section:

(a) "Assault" means the intentional, knowing or reckless causation of physical injury to another person. "Assault" does not include the causation of physical injury in a motor vehicle accident that occurs by reason of the reckless conduct of a defendant.

(b) "Neglect or maltreatment" means a violation of ORS 163.535, 163.545 or 163.547 or a failure to provide adequate food, clothing, shelter or medical care that is likely to endanger the health or welfare of a child under 14 years of age or a dependent person. This paragraph is not intended to replace or affect the duty or standard of care required under ORS chapter 677.

(c) "Pattern or practice" means one or more previous episodes.

(d) "Torture" means the intentional infliction of intense physical pain upon an unwilling victim as a separate objective apart from any other purpose. [1971 c.743 §88; 1975 c.577 §1; 1979 c.2 §1; 1981 c.873 §5; 1985 c.763 §1; 1989 c.985 §1; 1993 c.664 §1; 1995 c.421 §3; 1995 c.657 §1; 1997 c.850 §2; 1999 c.782 §4; 2007 c.717 §2; 2009 c.660 §7; 2009 c.785 §1; 2011 c.291 §1; 2015 c.820 §46]

163.116 [1979 c.2 §3; repealed by 1981 c.873 §9]

163.117 Causing or aiding suicide as defense to charge of murder. It is a defense to a charge of murder that the defendant's conduct consisted of causing or aiding, without the use of duress or deception, another person to commit suicide. Nothing contained in this section shall constitute a defense to a prosecution for, or preclude a conviction of, manslaughter or any other crime. [1981 c.873 §8]

163.118 Manslaughter in the first degree. (1) Criminal homicide constitutes manslaughter in the first degree when:

(a) It is committed recklessly under circumstances manifesting extreme indifference to the value of human life;

(b) It is committed intentionally by a defendant under the influence of extreme emotional disturbance as provided in ORS 163.135, which constitutes a mitigating circumstance reducing the homicide that would otherwise be murder to manslaughter in the first degree and need not be proved in any prosecution;

(c) A person recklessly causes the death of a child under 14 years of age or a dependent person, as defined in ORS 163.205, and:

(A) The person has previously engaged in a pattern or practice of assault or torture of the victim or another child under 14 years of age or a dependent person; or

(B) The person causes the death by neglect or maltreatment, as defined in ORS 163.115; or

(d) It is committed recklessly or with criminal negligence by a person operating a motor vehicle while under the influence of intoxicants in violation of ORS 813.010 and:

(A) The person has at least three previous convictions for driving while under the influence of intoxicants under ORS 813.010, or its statutory counterpart in any jurisdiction, in the 10 years prior to the date of the current offense; or

(B)(i) The person has a previous conviction for any of the crimes described in subsection (2) of this section, or their statutory counterparts in any jurisdiction; and

(ii) The victim's serious physical injury in the previous conviction was caused by the person driving a motor vehicle.

(2) The previous convictions to which subsection (1)(d)(B) of this section applies are:

(a) Assault in the first degree under ORS 163.185;

(b) Assault in the second degree under ORS 163.175; or

(c) Assault in the third degree under ORS 163.165.

(3) Manslaughter in the first degree is a Class A felony.

(4) It is an affirmative defense to a charge of violating:

(a) Subsection (1)(c)(B) of this section that the victim was a dependent person who was at least 18 years of age and was under care or treatment solely by spiritual means pursuant to the religious beliefs or practices of the dependent person or the guardian of the dependent person.

(b) Subsection (1)(d)(B) of this section that the defendant was not under the influence of intoxicants at the time of the conduct that resulted in the previous conviction. [1975 c.577 §2; 1981 c.873 §6; 1997 c.850 §3; 2007 c.867 §2; 2011 c.291 §2]

163.120 [Repealed by 1971 c.743 §432]

163.125 Manslaughter in the second degree. (1) Criminal homicide constitutes manslaughter in the second degree when:

(a) It is committed recklessly;

(b) A person intentionally causes or aids another person to commit suicide; or

(c) A person, with criminal negligence, causes the death of a child under 14 years of age or a dependent person, as defined in ORS 163.205, and:

(A) The person has previously engaged in a pattern or practice of assault or torture of the victim or another child under 14 years of age or a dependent person; or

(B) The person causes the death by neglect or maltreatment, as defined in ORS 163.115.

(2) Manslaughter in the second degree is a Class B felony. [1971 c.743 §89; 1975 c.577 §3; 1997 c.850 §4; 1999 c.954 §1]

163.130 [Repealed by 1971 c.743 §432]

163.135 Extreme emotional disturbance as affirmative defense to murder; notice of expert testimony; right of state to psychiatric or psychological examination. (1) It is an affirmative defense to murder for purposes of ORS 163.115 (1)(a) that the homicide was committed under the influence of extreme emotional disturbance if the disturbance is not the result of the person's own intentional, knowing, reckless or criminally negligent act and if there is a reasonable explanation for the disturbance. The reasonableness of the explanation for the disturbance must be determined from the standpoint of an ordinary person in the actor's situation under the circumstances that the actor reasonably believed them to be. Extreme emotional disturbance does not constitute a defense to a prosecution for, or preclude a conviction of, manslaughter in the first degree or any other crime.

(2) The defendant may not introduce in the defendant's case in chief expert testimony regarding extreme emotional disturbance under this section unless the defendant gives notice of the defendant's intent to do so.

(3) The notice required must be in writing and must be filed at the time the defendant pleads not guilty. The defendant may file the notice at any time after the defendant pleads but before trial if the court determines that there was just cause for failure to file the notice at the time of the defendant's plea.

(4) If the defendant fails to file notice, the defendant may not introduce evidence for the purpose of proving extreme emotional disturbance under ORS 163.115 unless the court, in its discretion, determines that there was just cause for failure to file notice.

(5) After the defendant files notice as provided in this section, the state may have at least one psychiatrist or licensed psychologist of its selection examine the defendant in the same manner and subject to the same provisions as provided in ORS 161.315. [1971 c.743 §90; 1977 c.235 §1; 1981 c.873 §7; 2003 c.127 §1]

163.140 [Repealed by 1971 c.743 §432]

163.145 Criminally negligent homicide. (1) A person commits the crime of criminally negligent homicide when, with criminal negligence, the person causes the death of another person.

(2) Criminally negligent homicide is a Class B felony. [1971 c.743 §91; 2003 c.815 §2]

163.147 Crime category classification for manslaughter in the second degree and criminally negligent homicide. The Oregon Criminal Justice Commission shall classify manslaughter in the second degree as described in ORS 163.125 and criminally negligent homicide as described in ORS 163.145 as crime category 9 of the sentencing guidelines grid of the commission if:

(1) The manslaughter or criminally negligent homicide resulted from the operation of a motor vehicle; and

(2) The driver of the motor vehicle was driving while under the influence of intoxicants. [2003 c.815 §1]

Note: 163.147 was enacted into law by the Legislative Assembly but was not added to or made a part of ORS chapter 163 or any series therein by legislative action. See Preface to Oregon Revised Statutes for further explanation.

163.149 Aggravated vehicular homicide. (1) Criminal homicide constitutes aggravated vehicular homicide when it is committed with criminal negligence, recklessly or recklessly under circumstances manifesting extreme indifference to the value of human life by a person operating a motor vehicle while under the influence of intoxicants in violation of ORS 813.010 and:

(a) The person has a previous conviction for any of the crimes described in subsection (2) of this section, or their statutory counterparts in any jurisdiction; and

(b) The victim's death in the previous conviction was caused by the person driving a motor vehicle.

(2) The previous convictions to which subsection (1) of this section applies are:

(a) Manslaughter in the first degree under ORS 163.118;

(b) Manslaughter in the second degree under ORS 163.125; or

(c) Criminally negligent homicide under ORS 163.145.

(3) It is an affirmative defense to a prosecution under this section that the defendant was not under the influence of intoxicants at the time of the conduct that resulted in the previous conviction.

(4) Aggravated vehicular homicide is a Class A felony. [2007 c.867 §1]

Note: 163.149 was enacted into law by the Legislative Assembly but was not added to or made a part of ORS chapter 163 or any series therein by legislative action. See Preface to Oregon Revised Statutes for further explanation.

163.150 Sentencing for aggravated murder; proceedings; issues for jury. (1)(a) Upon a finding that the defendant is guilty of aggravated murder, the court, except as otherwise provided in subsection (3) of this section, shall conduct a separate sentencing proceeding to determine whether the defendant shall be sentenced to life imprisonment, as described in ORS 163.105 (1)(c), life imprisonment without the possibility of release or parole, as described in ORS 163.105 (1)(b), or death. The proceeding shall be conducted in the trial court before the trial jury as soon as practicable. If a juror for any reason is unable to perform the function of a juror, the juror shall be dismissed from the sentencing proceeding. The court shall cause to be drawn the name of one of the alternate jurors, who shall then become a member of the jury for the sentencing proceeding notwithstanding the fact that the alternate juror did not deliberate on the issue of guilt. If the defendant has pleaded guilty, the sentencing proceeding shall be conducted before a jury impaneled for that purpose. In the proceeding, evidence may be presented as to any matter that the court deems relevant to sentence including, but not limited to, victim impact evidence relating to the personal characteristics of the victim or the impact of the crime on the victim's family and any aggravating or mitigating evidence relevant to the issue in paragraph (b)(D) of this subsection; however, neither the state nor the defendant shall be allowed to introduce repetitive evidence that has previously been offered and received during the trial on the issue of guilt. The court shall instruct the jury that all evidence previously offered and received may be considered for purposes of the sentencing hearing. This paragraph shall not be construed to authorize the introduction of any evidence secured in violation of the Constitution of the United States or of the State of Oregon. The state and the defendant or the counsel of the defendant shall be permitted to present arguments for or against a sentence of death and for or against a sentence of life imprisonment with or without the possibility of release or parole.

(b) Upon the conclusion of the presentation of the evidence, the court shall submit the following issues to the jury:

(A) Whether the conduct of the defendant that caused the death of the deceased was committed deliberately and with the reasonable expectation that death of the deceased or another would result;

(B) Whether there is a probability that the defendant would commit criminal acts of violence that would constitute a continuing threat to society;

(C) If raised by the evidence, whether the conduct of the defendant in killing the deceased was unreasonable in response to the provocation, if any, by the deceased; and

(D) Whether the defendant should receive a death sentence.

(c)(A) The court shall instruct the jury to consider, in determining the issues in paragraph (b) of this subsection, any mitigating circumstances offered in evidence, including but not limited to the defendant's age, the extent and severity of the defendant's prior criminal conduct and the extent of the mental and emotional pressure under which the defendant was acting at the time the offense was committed.

(B) The court shall instruct the jury to answer the question in paragraph (b)(D) of this subsection "no" if, after considering any aggravating evidence and any mitigating evidence concerning any aspect of the defendant's character or background, or any circumstances of the offense and any victim impact evidence as described in paragraph (a) of this subsection, one or more of the jurors believe that the defendant should not receive a death sentence.

(d) The state must prove each issue submitted under paragraph (b)(A) to (C) of this subsection beyond a reasonable doubt, and the jury shall return a special verdict of "yes" or "no" on each issue considered.

(e) The court shall charge the jury that it may not answer any issue "yes," under paragraph (b) of this subsection unless it agrees unanimously.

(f) If the jury returns an affirmative finding on each issue considered under paragraph (b) of this subsection, the trial judge shall sentence the defendant to death.

(2)(a) Upon the conclusion of the presentation of the evidence, the court shall also instruct the jury that if it reaches a negative finding on any issue under subsection (1)(b) of this section, the trial court shall sentence the defendant to life imprisonment without the possibility of release or parole, as described in ORS 163.105 (1)(b), unless 10 or more members of the jury further find that there are sufficient mitigating circumstances to warrant life imprisonment, in which case the trial court shall sentence the defendant to life imprisonment as described in ORS 163.105 (1)(c).

(b) If the jury returns a negative finding on any issue under subsection (1)(b) of this section and further finds that there are sufficient mitigating circumstances to warrant life imprisonment, the trial court shall sentence the defendant to life imprisonment in the custody of the Department of Corrections as provided in ORS 163.105 (1)(c).

(3)(a) When the defendant is found guilty of aggravated murder, and ORS 137.707 (2) applies or the state advises the court on the record that the state declines to present evidence for purposes of sentencing the defendant to death, the court:

(A) Shall not conduct a sentencing proceeding as described in subsection (1) of this section, and a sentence of death shall not be ordered.

(B) Shall conduct a sentencing proceeding to determine whether the defendant shall be sentenced to life imprisonment without the possibility of release or parole as described in ORS 163.105 (1)(b) or life imprisonment as described in ORS 163.105 (1)(c). If the defendant waives all rights to a jury sentencing proceeding, the court shall conduct the sentencing proceeding as the trier of fact. The procedure for the sentencing proceeding, whether before a court or a jury, shall follow the procedure of subsection (1)(a) of this section, as modified by this subsection. In the proceeding, evidence may be presented as to any matter that the court deems relevant to sentence, including, but not limited to, victim impact evidence relating to the personal characteristics of the victim or the impact of the crime on the victim's family.

(b) Following the presentation of evidence and argument under paragraph (a) of this subsection, the court shall instruct the jury that the trial court shall sentence the defendant to life imprisonment without the possibility of release or parole as described in ORS 163.105 (1)(b), unless after considering all of the evidence submitted, 10 or more members of the jury find there are sufficient mitigating circumstances to warrant life imprisonment with the possibility of parole as described in ORS 163.105 (1)(c). If 10 or more members of the jury find there are sufficient mitigating circumstances to warrant life imprisonment with the possibility of parole, the trial court shall sentence the defendant to life imprisonment as described in ORS 163.105 (1)(c).

(c) Nothing in this subsection shall preclude the court from sentencing the defendant to life imprisonment, as described in ORS 163.105 (1)(c), or life imprisonment without the possibility of release or parole, as described in ORS 163.105 (1)(b), pursuant to a stipulation of sentence or stipulation of sentencing facts agreed to and offered by both parties if the defendant waives all rights to a jury sentencing proceeding.

(4) If any part of subsection (2) of this section is held invalid and as a result thereof a defendant who has been sentenced to life imprisonment without possibility of release or parole will instead be sentenced to life imprisonment in the custody of the Department of Corrections as provided in ORS 163.105 (2), the defendant shall be confined for a minimum of 30 years without possibility of parole, release on work release or any form of temporary leave or employment at a forest or work camp. Subsection (2) of this section shall apply only to trials commencing on or after July 19, 1989.

(5) Notwithstanding subsection (1)(a) of this section, if the trial court grants a mistrial during the sentencing proceeding, the trial court, at the election of the state, shall either:

(a) Sentence the defendant to imprisonment for life in the custody of the Department of Corrections as provided in ORS 163.105 (1)(c); or

(b) Impanel a new sentencing jury for the purpose of conducting a new sentencing proceeding to determine if the defendant should be sentenced to:

(A) Death;

(B) Imprisonment for life without the possibility of release or parole as provided in ORS 163.105 (1)(b); or

(C) Imprisonment for life in the custody of the Department of Corrections as provided in ORS 163.105 (1)(c). [1985 c.3 §3; 1987 c.320 §86; 1987 c.557 §1; 1989 c.720 §2; 1989 c.790 §135b; 1991 c.725 §2; 1991 c.885 §2; 1995 c.531 §2; 1995 c.657 §23; 1997 c.784 §1; 1999 c.1055 §1; 2001 c.306 §1; 2005 c.480 §1; 2017 c.359 §4]

163.155 Sentencing for murder of pregnant victim; proceeding; issues for jury. (1) When a defendant, who was at least 15 years of age at the time of committing the murder, is convicted of murdering a pregnant victim under ORS 163.115 (1)(a) and the defendant knew that the victim was pregnant, the defendant shall be sentenced to life imprisonment without the possibility of release or parole or to life imprisonment. The court shall conduct a sentencing proceeding to determine whether the defendant shall be sentenced to life imprisonment without the possibility of release or parole as described in subsection (4) of this section or to life imprisonment as described in subsection (5) of this section. If the defendant waives all rights to a jury sentencing proceeding, the court shall conduct the sentencing proceeding as the trier of fact. The procedure for the sentencing proceeding, whether before a court or a jury, shall follow the procedure of ORS 163.150 (1)(a), as modified by this section.

(2) Following the presentation of evidence and argument under subsection (1) of this section, the court shall instruct the jury that the trial court shall sentence the defendant to life imprisonment without the possibility of release or parole as described in subsection (4) of this section, unless after considering all of the evidence submitted, 10 or more members of the jury find there are sufficient mitigating circumstances to warrant life imprisonment with the possibility of release or parole as described in subsection (5) of this section. If 10 or more members of the jury do not find there are sufficient mitigating circumstances to warrant life imprisonment with the possibility of release or parole, the trial court shall sentence the defendant to life imprisonment without the possibility of release or parole as described in subsection (4) of this section. If 10 or more members of the jury find there are sufficient mitigating circumstances to warrant life imprisonment with the possibility of release or parole, the trial court shall sentence the defendant to life imprisonment as described in subsection (5) of this section.

(3) Nothing in this section precludes the court from sentencing the defendant to life imprisonment, as described in subsection (5) of this section, or life imprisonment without the possibility of release or parole, as described in subsection (4) of this section, pursuant to a stipulation of sentence or stipulation of sentencing facts agreed to and offered by both parties if the defendant waives all rights to a jury sentencing proceeding.

(4) A sentence of life imprisonment without the possibility of release or parole under this section may not be suspended, deferred or commuted by any judicial officer, and the State Board of Parole and Post-Prison Supervision may neither parole the prisoner nor reduce the period of confinement in any manner whatsoever. The Department of Corrections or any executive official may not permit the prisoner to participate in any sort of release or furlough program.

(5) If the defendant is sentenced to life imprisonment, the court shall order that the defendant be confined for a minimum of 30 years without possibility of parole, release to post-prison supervision, release on work release or any form of temporary leave or employment at a forest or work camp.

(6) At any time after completion of the minimum period of confinement pursuant to subsection (5) of this section, the board, upon the petition of a prisoner so confined, shall hold a hearing to determine if the prisoner is likely to be rehabilitated within a reasonable period of time. The sole issue shall be whether the prisoner is likely to be rehabilitated within a reasonable period of time. The proceeding shall be conducted in the manner prescribed for a contested case hearing under ORS chapter 183, except that:

(a) The prisoner has the burden of proving by a preponderance of the evidence the likelihood of rehabilitation within a reasonable period of time;

(b) The prisoner has the right, if the prisoner is without sufficient funds to employ an attorney, to be represented by legal counsel, appointed by the board, at board expense; and

(c) The prisoner has the right to a subpoena upon a showing of the general relevance and reasonable scope of the evidence sought, provided that any subpoena issued on behalf of the prisoner must be issued by the board pursuant to rules adopted by the board.

(7) If, upon hearing all of the evidence, the board, upon a unanimous vote of three board members or, if the chairperson requires all voting members to participate, a unanimous vote of all voting members, finds that the prisoner is capable of rehabilitation and that the terms of the prisoner's confinement should be changed to life imprisonment with the possibility of parole, release on post-prison supervision or work release, it shall enter an order to that effect and the order shall convert the terms of the prisoner's confinement to life imprisonment with the possibility of parole, release on post-prison supervision or work release and may set a release date. Otherwise the board shall deny the relief sought in the petition.

(8) Not less than two years after the denial of the relief sought in a petition under this section, the prisoner may petition again for a change in the terms of confinement. Further petitions for a change may be filed at intervals of not less than two years thereafter. [2009 c.785 §1a; 2015 c.820 §47]

Note: 163.155 was enacted into law by the Legislative Assembly but was not added to or made a part of ORS chapter 163 or any series therein by legislative action. See Preface to Oregon Revised Statutes for further explanation.

ASSAULT AND RELATED OFFENSES

163.160 Assault in the fourth degree. (1) A person commits the crime of assault in the fourth degree if the person:

(a) Intentionally, knowingly or recklessly causes physical injury to another;

(b) With criminal negligence causes physical injury to another by means of a deadly weapon; or

(c) With criminal negligence causes serious physical injury to another who is a vulnerable user of a public way, as defined in ORS 801.608, by means of a motor vehicle.

(2) Assault in the fourth degree is a Class A misdemeanor.

(3) Notwithstanding subsection (2) of this section, assault in the fourth degree under subsection (1)(a) or (b) of this section is a Class C felony if the person commits the crime of assault in the fourth degree and:

(a) The assault is committed in the immediate presence of, or is witnessed by, the person's or the victim's minor child or stepchild or a minor child residing within the household of the person or victim;

(b) The person has been previously convicted of violating this section or ORS 163.165, 163.175, 163.185, 163.187 or 163.190, or of committing an equivalent crime in another jurisdiction, and the victim in the previous conviction is the same person who is the victim of the current crime;

(c) The person has at least three previous convictions for violating this section or ORS 163.165, 163.175, 163.185, 163.187 or 163.190 or for committing an equivalent crime in another jurisdiction, in any combination; or

(d) The person commits the assault knowing that the victim is pregnant.

(4) For purposes of subsection (3) of this section, an assault is witnessed if the assault is seen or directly perceived in any other manner by the child. [1977 c.297 §5; 1997 c.694 §1; 1999 c.1073 §1; 2009 c.785 §3; 2015 c.639 §2; 2017 c.337 §1]

163.165 Assault in the third degree. (1) A person commits the crime of assault in the third degree if the person:

(a) Recklessly causes serious physical injury to another by means of a deadly or dangerous weapon;

(b) Recklessly causes serious physical injury to another under circumstances manifesting extreme indifference to the value of human life;

(c) Recklessly causes physical injury to another by means of a deadly or dangerous weapon under circumstances manifesting extreme indifference to the value of human life;

(d) Intentionally, knowingly or recklessly causes, by means other than a motor vehicle, physical injury to the operator of a public transit vehicle while the operator is in control of or operating the vehicle. As used in this paragraph, "public transit vehicle" has the meaning given that term in ORS 166.116;

(e) While being aided by another person actually present, intentionally or knowingly causes physical injury to another;

(f) While committed to a youth correction facility, intentionally or knowingly causes physical injury to another knowing the other person is a staff member while the other person is acting in the course of official duty;

(g) Intentionally, knowingly or recklessly causes physical injury to an emergency medical services provider, as defined in ORS 682.025, while the emergency medical services provider is performing official duties;

(h) Being at least 18 years of age, intentionally or knowingly causes physical injury to a child 10 years of age or younger;

(i) Intentionally, knowingly or recklessly causes, by means other than a motor vehicle, physical injury to the operator of a taxi while the operator is in control of the taxi; or

(j) Intentionally, knowingly or recklessly causes physical injury to a flagger or a highway worker while the flagger or highway worker is performing official duties.

(2)(a) Assault in the third degree is a Class C felony.

(b) Notwithstanding paragraph (a) of this subsection, assault in the third degree under subsection (1)(a) or (b) of this section is a Class B felony if:

(A) The assault resulted from the operation of a motor vehicle; and

(B) The defendant was the driver of the motor vehicle and was driving while under the influence of intoxicants.

(3) As used in this section:

(a) "Flagger" has the meaning given that term in ORS 811.230.

(b) "Highway worker" has the meaning given that term in ORS 811.230.

(c) "Staff member" means:

(A) A corrections officer as defined in ORS 181A.355, a youth correction officer, a youth correction facility staff member, a Department of Corrections or Oregon Youth Authority staff member or a person employed pursuant to a contract with the department or youth authority to work with, or in the vicinity of, inmates, youth or youth offenders; and

(B) A volunteer authorized by the department, youth authority or other entity in charge of a corrections facility to work with, or in the vicinity of, inmates, youth or youth offenders.

(d) "Youth correction facility" has the meaning given that term in ORS 162.135. [1971 c.743 §92; 1977 c.297 §3; 1991 c.475 §1; 1991 c.564 §1; 1995 c.738 §1; 1997 c.249 §49; 1999 c.1011 §1; 2001 c.104 §50; 2001 c.830 §1; 2001 c.851 §4; 2009 c.660 §39; 2009 c.783 §3; 2011 c.529 §1; 2011 c.703 §27; 2017 c.658 §1]

163.168 Crime category classification for assault in the third degree. The Oregon Criminal Justice Commission shall classify assault in the third degree that is committed under the circumstances described in ORS 163.165 (2)(b) as crime category 8 of the sentencing guidelines grid of the commission. [2009 c.660 §40]

Note: 163.168 was enacted into law by the Legislative Assembly but was not added to or made a part of ORS chapter 163 or any series therein by legislative action. See Preface to Oregon Revised Statutes for further explanation.

163.175 Assault in the second degree. (1) A person commits the crime of assault in the second degree if the person:

(a) Intentionally or knowingly causes serious physical injury to another;

(b) Intentionally or knowingly causes physical injury to another by means of a deadly or dangerous weapon; or

(c) Recklessly causes serious physical injury to another by means of a deadly or dangerous weapon under circumstances manifesting extreme indifference to the value of human life.

(2) Assault in the second degree is a Class B felony. [1971 c.743 §93; 1975 c.626 §1; 1977 c.297 §2; 2005 c.22 §110]

163.185 Assault in the first degree. (1) A person commits the crime of assault in the first degree if the person:

(a) Intentionally causes serious physical injury to another by means of a deadly or dangerous weapon;

(b) Intentionally or knowingly causes serious physical injury to a child under six years of age;

(c) Violates ORS 163.175 knowing that the victim is pregnant; or

(d) Intentionally, knowingly or recklessly causes serious physical injury to another while operating a motor vehicle under the influence of intoxicants in violation of ORS 813.010 and:

(A) The person has at least three previous convictions for driving while under the influence of intoxicants under ORS 813.010, or its statutory counterpart in any jurisdiction, in the 10 years prior to the date of the current offense; or

(B)(i) The person has a previous conviction for any of the crimes described in subsection (2) of this section, or their statutory counterparts in any jurisdiction; and

(ii) The victim's death or serious physical injury in the previous conviction was caused by the person driving a motor vehicle.

(2) The previous convictions to which subsection (1)(d)(B) of this section apply are:

(a) Manslaughter in the first degree under ORS 163.118;

(b) Manslaughter in the second degree under ORS 163.125;

(c) Criminally negligent homicide under ORS 163.145;

(d) Assault in the first degree under this section;

(e) Assault in the second degree under ORS 163.175; or

(f) Assault in the third degree under ORS 163.165.

(3) Assault in the first degree is a Class A felony.

(4) It is an affirmative defense to a prosecution under subsection (1)(d)(B) of this section that the defendant was not under the influence of intoxicants at the time of the conduct that resulted in the previous conviction. [1971 c.743 §94; 1975 c.626 §2; 1977 c.297 §1; 2005 c.513 §1; 2007 c.867 §3; 2009 c.785 §2]

163.187 Strangulation. (1) A person commits the crime of strangulation if the person knowingly impedes the normal breathing or circulation of the blood of another person by:

(a) Applying pressure on the throat or neck of the other person; or

(b) Blocking the nose or mouth of the other person.

(2) Subsection (1) of this section does not apply to legitimate medical or dental procedures or good faith practices of a religious belief.

(3) Strangulation is a Class A misdemeanor.

(4) Notwithstanding subsection (3) of this section, strangulation is a Class C felony if:

(a) The crime is committed in the immediate presence of, or is witnessed by, the person's or the victim's minor child or stepchild or a minor child residing within the household of the person or the victim;

(b) The victim is under 10 years of age;

(c) During the commission of the crime, the person used, attempted to use or threatened to use a dangerous or deadly weapon, as those terms are defined in ORS 161.015, unlawfully against another;

(d) The person has been previously convicted of violating this section or ORS 163.160, 163.165, 163.175, 163.185 or 163.190, or of committing an equivalent crime in another jurisdiction, and the victim in the previous conviction is the same person who is the victim of the current crime;

(e) The person has at least three previous convictions for violating this section or ORS 163.160, 163.165, 163.175, 163.185 or 163.190 or for committing an equivalent crime in another jurisdiction, in any combination; or

(f) The person commits the strangulation knowing that the victim is pregnant.

(5) For purposes of subsection (4)(a) of this section, a strangulation is witnessed if the strangulation is seen or directly perceived in any other manner by the child. [2003 c.577 §2, 2011 c.666 §1; 2012 c.82 §1; 2015 c.639 §1]

Note: 163.187 was added to and made a part of 163.160 to 163.208 by legislative action but was not added to any smaller series therein. See Preface to Oregon Revised Statutes for further explanation.

163.190 Menacing. (1) A person commits the crime of menacing if by word or conduct the person intentionally attempts to place another person in fear of imminent serious physical injury.

(2) Menacing is a Class A misdemeanor. [1971 c.743 §95]

163.192 Endangering a person protected by a Family Abuse Prevention Act restraining order. (1) A person commits the crime of endangering a person protected by a Family Abuse Prevention Act restraining order if the person:

(a) Has been served with the order as provided in ORS 107.718, unless service was waived under ORS 107.720 because the person appeared before the court;

(b) Intentionally engaged in conduct prohibited by the order while the order was in effect; and

(c) By engaging in the prohibited conduct, recklessly created a substantial risk of physical injury to a person protected by the order, or intentionally attempted to place a person protected by the order in fear of imminent physical injury.

(2) Endangering a person protected by a Family Abuse Prevention Act restraining order is a Class C felony. [2015 c.527 §2]

Note: 163.192 was added to and made a part of 163.160 to 163.208 by legislative action but was not added to any smaller series therein. See Preface to Oregon Revised Statutes for further explanation.

163.193 Assisting another person to commit suicide. (1) A person commits the crime of assisting another person to commit suicide if the person knowingly sells, or otherwise transfers for consideration, any substance or object, that is capable of causing death, to another person for the purpose of assisting the other person to commit suicide.

(2) This section does not apply to a person:

(a) Acting pursuant to a court order, an advance directive or power of attorney for health care pursuant to ORS 127.505 to 127.660 or a POLST, as defined in ORS 127.663;

(b) Withholding or withdrawing life-sustaining procedures or artificially administered nutrition and hydration pursuant to ORS 127.505 to 127.660; or

(c) Acting in accordance with the provisions of ORS 127.800 to 127.897.

(3) Assisting another person to commit suicide is a Class B felony. [2011 c.552 §2; 2013 c.1 §10]

Note: 163.193 was added to and made a part of 163.160 to 163.208 by legislative action but was not added to any smaller series therein. See Preface to Oregon Revised Statutes for further explanation.

163.195 Recklessly endangering another person. (1) A person commits the crime of recklessly endangering another person if the person recklessly engages in conduct which creates a substantial risk of serious physical injury to another person.

(2) Recklessly endangering another person is a Class A misdemeanor. [1971 c.743 §96]

163.196 Aggravated driving while suspended or revoked. (1) A person commits the crime of aggravated driving while suspended or revoked if the person operates a motor vehicle that causes serious physical injury to, or the death of, another person while knowingly violating ORS 811.175 or 811.182, if the suspension or revocation resulted from, or if the hardship or probationary permit violated is based upon a suspension or revocation that resulted from, a conviction for a criminal offense involving the use of a motor vehicle.

(2) Aggravated driving while suspended or revoked is a Class C felony.

(3) The Oregon Criminal Justice Commission shall classify aggravated driving while suspended or revoked as crime category 7 of the sentencing guidelines grid of the commission. [2009 c.783 §5]

Note: 163.196 was added to and made a part of ORS chapter 163 by legislative action but was not added to any smaller series therein. See Preface to Oregon Revised Statutes for further explanation.

163.197 Hazing. (1) A student organization or a member of a student organization commits the offense of hazing if, as a condition or precondition of attaining membership in the organization or of attaining any office or status in the organization, the organization or member intentionally hazes any member, potential member or person pledged to be a member of the organization.

(2)(a) A student organization that violates subsection (1) of this section commits a Class A violation.

(b) A member of a student organization who personally violates subsection (1) of this section commits a Class B violation.

(3) Consent of the person who is hazed is not a defense in a prosecution under this section.

(4) As used in this section:

(a) "Haze" means:

(A) To subject an individual to whipping, beating, striking, branding or electronic shocking, to place a harmful substance on an individual's body or to subject an individual to other similar forms of physical brutality;

(B) To subject an individual to sleep deprivation, exposure to the elements, confinement in a small space or other similar activity that subjects the individual to an unreasonable risk of harm or adversely affects the physical health or safety of the individual;

(C) To compel an individual to consume food, liquid, alcohol, cannabis, controlled substances or other substances that subject the individual to an unreasonable risk of harm or adversely affect the physical health or safety of the individual; or

(D) To induce, cause or require an individual to perform a duty or task that involves the commission of a crime or an act of hazing.

(b) "Member" includes volunteers, coaches and faculty advisers of a student organization.

(c) "Student organization" means a fraternity, sorority, athletic team or other organization that is organized or operating on a college, university or elementary or secondary school campus for the purpose of providing members an opportunity to participate in student activities of the college, university or elementary or secondary school. [1983 c.202 §2; 1999 c.1051 §152; 2009 c.493 §1; 2017 c.21 §42]

163.200 Criminal mistreatment in the second degree. (1) A person commits the crime of criminal mistreatment in the second degree if, with criminal negligence and:

(a) In violation of a legal duty to provide care for another person, the person withholds necessary and adequate food, physical care or medical attention from that person; or

(b) Having assumed the permanent or temporary care, custody or responsibility for the supervision of another person, the person withholds necessary and adequate food, physical care or medical attention from that person.

(2) Criminal mistreatment in the second degree is a Class A misdemeanor.

(3) As used in this section, "legal duty" includes but is not limited to a duty created by familial relationship, court order, contractual agreement or statutory or case law. [1973 c.627 §2; 1993 c.364 §1]

163.205 Criminal mistreatment in the first degree. (1) A person commits the crime of criminal mistreatment in the first degree if:

(a) The person, in violation of a legal duty to provide care for another person, or having assumed the permanent or temporary care, custody or responsibility for the supervision of another person, intentionally or knowingly withholds necessary and adequate food, physical care or medical attention from that other person; or

(b) The person, in violation of a legal duty to provide care for a dependent person or elderly person, or having assumed the permanent or temporary care, custody or responsibility for the supervision of a dependent person or elderly person, intentionally or knowingly:

(A) Causes physical injury or injuries to the dependent person or elderly person;

(B) Deserts the dependent person or elderly person in a place with the intent to abandon that person;

(C) Leaves the dependent person or elderly person unattended at a place for such a period of time as may be likely to endanger the health or welfare of that person;

(D) Hides the dependent person's or elderly person's money or property or takes the money or property for, or appropriates the money or property to, any use or purpose not in the due and lawful execution of the person's responsibility;

(E) Takes charge of a dependent or elderly person for the purpose of fraud;

(F) Leaves the dependent person or elderly person, or causes the dependent person or elderly person to enter or remain, in or upon premises:

(i) Where a cannabinoid extract as defined in ORS 475B.015 is being processed; and

(ii) That have not been licensed under ORS 475B.090; or

(G) Leaves the dependent person or elderly person, or causes the dependent person or elderly person to enter or remain, in or upon premises where a chemical reaction involving one or more precursor substances:

(i) Is occurring as part of unlawfully manufacturing a controlled substance or grinding, soaking or otherwise breaking down a precursor substance for the unlawful manufacture of a controlled substance; or

(ii) Has occurred as part of unlawfully manufacturing a controlled substance or grinding, soaking or otherwise breaking down a precursor substance for the unlawful manufacture of a controlled substance and the premises have not been certified as fit for use under ORS 453.885.

(2) As used in this section:

(a) "Controlled substance" has the meaning given that term in ORS 475.005.

(b) "Dependent person" means a person who because of either age or a physical or mental disability is dependent upon another to provide for the person's physical needs.

(c) "Elderly person" means a person 65 years of age or older.

(d) "Legal duty" includes but is not limited to a duty created by familial relationship, court order, contractual agreement or statutory or case law.

(e) "Precursor substance" has the meaning given that term in ORS 475.940.

(3) Criminal mistreatment in the first degree is a Class C felony. [1973 c.627 §3; 1981 c.486 §1; 1993 c.364 §2; 2005 c.708 §1; 2017 c.21 §43]

163.206 Exceptions to criminal mistreatment. ORS 163.200 and 163.205 do not apply:

(1) To a person acting pursuant to a court order, an advance directive or a power of attorney for health care pursuant to ORS 127.505 to 127.660 or a POLST, as defined in ORS 127.663;

(2) To a person withholding or withdrawing life-sustaining procedures or artificially administered nutrition and hydration pursuant to ORS 127.505 to 127.660;

(3) When a competent person refuses food, physical care or medical care;

(4) To a person who provides an elderly person or a dependent person who is at least 18 years of age with spiritual treatment through prayer from a duly accredited practitioner of spiritual treatment as provided in ORS 124.095, in lieu of medical treatment, in accordance with the tenets and practices of a recognized church or religious denomination of which the elderly or dependent person is a member or an adherent; or

(5) To a duly accredited practitioner of spiritual treatment as provided in ORS 124.095. [1993 c.364 §3; 1995 c.79 §51; 1999 c.954 §5; 2009 c.595 §1190; 2011 c.291 §4]

Note: 163.206 was enacted into law by the Legislative Assembly but was not added to or made a part of ORS chapter 163 or any series therein by legislative action. See Preface to Oregon Revised Statutes for further explanation.

163.207 Female genital mutilation. (1) A person commits the crime of female genital mutilation if the person:

(a) Knowingly circumcises, excises or infibulates the whole or any part of the labia majora, labia minora or clitoris of a child; or

(b) Is the parent, guardian or other person legally responsible for the care or custody of a child and knowingly allows the circumcision, excision or infibulation of the whole or any part of the child's labia majora, labia minora or clitoris.

(2) Female genital mutilation is a Class B felony.

(3)(a) A person who circumcises, excises or infibulates the whole or any part of a child's labia majora, labia minora or clitoris does not violate subsection (1) of this section if:

(A) The person is a physician, licensed to practice in this state; and

(B) The surgery is medically necessary for the physical well-being of the child.

(b) In determining medical necessity for purposes of paragraph (a)(B) of this subsection, a person may not consider the effect on the child of the child's belief that the surgery is required as a matter of custom or ritual. [1999 c.737 §1]

Note: 163.207 was enacted into law by the Legislative Assembly but was not added to or made a part of ORS chapter 163 or any series therein by legislative action. See Preface to Oregon Revised Statutes for further explanation.

163.208 Assaulting a public safety officer. (1) A person commits the crime of assaulting a public safety officer if the person intentionally or knowingly causes physical injury to the other person, knowing the other person to be a peace officer, corrections officer, youth correction officer, parole and probation officer, animal control officer, firefighter or staff member, and while the other person is acting in the course of official duty.

(2) Assaulting a public safety officer is a Class C felony.

(3)(a) Except as otherwise provided in paragraph (b) of this subsection, a person convicted under this section shall be sentenced to not less than seven days of imprisonment and shall not be granted bench parole or suspension of sentence nor released on a sentence of probation before serving at least seven days of the sentence of confinement.

(b) A person convicted under this section shall be sentenced to not less than 14 days of imprisonment and shall not be granted bench parole or suspension of sentence nor released on a sentence of probation before serving at least 14 days of the sentence of confinement if the victim is a peace officer.

(4) As used in this section:

(a) "Animal control officer" has the meaning given that term in ORS 609.500; and

(b) "Staff member" means:

(A) A corrections officer as defined in ORS 181A.355, a youth correction officer, a Department of Corrections or Oregon Youth Authority staff member or a person employed pursuant to a contract with the department or youth authority to work with, or in the vicinity of, inmates or youth offenders; and

(B) A volunteer authorized by the department, youth authority or other entity in charge of a corrections facility to work with, or in the vicinity of, inmates or youth offenders. [1981 c.783 §2; 1993 c.14 §21; 1993 c.358 §1; 1995 c.651 §4; 1999 c.1040 §14; 2001 c.104 §51; 2001 c.828 §1; 2003 c.327 §1]

163.210 [Repealed by 1971 c.743 §432]

163.211 Definitions for ORS 163.211 to 163.213. As used in ORS 163.211 to 163.213:

(1) "Corrections officer" and "parole and probation officer" have the meanings given those terms in ORS 181A.355.

(2) "Mace, tear gas, pepper mace or any similar deleterious agent" means a sternutator, lacrimator or any substance composed of a mixture of a sternutator or lacrimator including, but not limited to, chloroacetophenone, alpha-chloroacetophenone, phenylchloromethylketone, orthochlorobenzalmalononitrile, oleoresin capsicum or a

chemically similar sternutator or lacrimator by whatever name known, or phosgene or other gas or substance capable of generating offensive, noxious or suffocating fumes, gases or vapor or capable of immobilizing a person.

(3) "Tear gas weapon" includes:

(a) Any shell, cartridge or bomb capable of being discharged or exploded, when the discharge or explosion will cause or permit the release or emission of tear gas or oleoresin capsicum.

(b) Any revolver, pistol, fountain pen gun, billy or other form of device, portable or fixed, intended for the projection or release of tear gas or oleoresin capsicum. [1995 c.651 §1]

Note: 163.211 to 163.213 were enacted into law by the Legislative Assembly but were not added to or made a part of ORS chapter 163 or any series therein by legislative action. See Preface to Oregon Revised Statutes for further explanation.

163.212 Unlawful use of an electrical stun gun, tear gas or mace in the second degree. (1) A person commits the crime of unlawful use of an electrical stun gun, tear gas or mace in the second degree if the person recklessly discharges an electrical stun gun, tear gas weapon, mace, tear gas, pepper mace or any similar deleterious agent against another person.

(2) Unlawful use of an electrical stun gun, tear gas or mace in the second degree is a Class A misdemeanor. [1995 c.651 §2]

Note: See note under 163.211.

163.213 Unlawful use of an electrical stun gun, tear gas or mace in the first degree. (1) A person commits the crime of unlawful use of an electrical stun gun, tear gas or mace in the first degree if the person knowingly discharges or causes to be discharged any electrical stun gun, tear gas weapon, mace, tear gas, pepper mace or any similar deleterious agent against another person, knowing the other person to be a peace officer, corrections officer, parole and probation officer, firefighter or emergency medical services provider and while the other person is acting in the course of official duty.

(2) Unlawful use of an electrical stun gun, tear gas or mace in the first degree is a Class C felony. [1995 c.651 §3; 2011 c.703 §50]

Note: See note under 163.211.

KIDNAPPING AND RELATED OFFENSES

163.215 Definitions for ORS 163.215 to 163.257. As used in ORS 163.215 to 163.257, unless the context requires otherwise:

(1) "Without consent" means that the taking or confinement is accomplished by force, threat or deception, or, in the case of a person under 16 years of age or who is otherwise incapable of giving consent, that the taking or confinement is accomplished without the consent of the lawful custodian of the person.

(2) "Lawful custodian" means a parent, guardian or other person responsible by authority of law for the care, custody or control of another.

(3) "Relative" means a parent, ancestor, brother, sister, uncle or aunt. [1971 c.743 §97]

163.220 [Repealed by 1971 c.743 §432]

163.225 Kidnapping in the second degree. (1) A person commits the crime of kidnapping in the second degree if, with intent to interfere substantially with another's personal liberty, and without consent or legal authority, the person:

(a) Takes the person from one place to another; or

(b) Secretly confines the person in a place where the person is not likely to be found.

(2) It is a defense to a prosecution under subsection (1) of this section if:

(a) The person taken or confined is under 16 years of age;

(b) The defendant is a relative of that person; and

(c) The sole purpose of the person is to assume control of that person.

(3) Kidnapping in the second degree is a Class B felony. [1971 c.743 §98; 2005 c.22 §111]

163.230 [Repealed by 1971 c.743 §432]

163.235 Kidnapping in the first degree. (1) A person commits the crime of kidnapping in the first degree if the person violates ORS 163.225 with any of the following purposes:

(a) To compel any person to pay or deliver money or property as ransom;

(b) To hold the victim as a shield or hostage;

(c) To cause physical injury to the victim;

(d) To terrorize the victim or another person; or

(e) To further the commission or attempted commission of any of the following crimes against the victim:

(A) Rape in the first degree, as defined in ORS 163.375 (1)(b);

(B) Sodomy in the first degree, as defined in ORS 163.405 (1)(b); or

(C) Unlawful sexual penetration in the first degree, as defined in ORS 163.411 (1)(b).

(2) Kidnapping in the first degree is a Class A felony. [1971 c.743 §99; 2005 c.22 §112; 2009 c.660 §43]

163.240 [Repealed by 1971 c.743 §432]

163.245 Custodial interference in the second degree. (1) A person commits the crime of custodial interference in the second degree if, knowing or having reason to know that the person has no legal right to do so, the person takes, entices or keeps another person from the other person's lawful custodian or in violation of a valid joint custody order with intent to hold the other person permanently or for a protracted period.

(2) Expenses incurred by a lawful custodial parent or a parent enforcing a valid joint custody order in locating and regaining physical custody of the person taken, enticed or kept in violation of this section are "economic damages" for purposes of restitution under ORS 137.103 to 137.109.

(3) Custodial interference in the second degree is a Class C felony. [1971 c.743 §100; 1981 c.774 §1; 1987 c.795 §7; 2005 c.564 §6]

163.250 [Repealed by 1971 c.743 §432]

163.255 [1955 c.530 §1; repealed by 1971 c.743 §432]

163.257 Custodial interference in the first degree. (1) A person commits the crime of custodial interference in the first degree if the person violates ORS 163.245 and:

(a) Causes the person taken, enticed or kept from the lawful custodian or in violation of a valid joint custody order to be removed from the state; or

(b) Exposes that person to a substantial risk of illness or physical injury.

(2) Expenses incurred by a lawful custodial parent or a parent enforcing a valid joint custody order in locating and regaining physical custody of the person taken, enticed or kept in violation of this section are "economic damages" for purposes of restitution under ORS 137.103 to 137.109.

(3) Custodial interference in the first degree is a Class B felony. [1971 c.743 §101; 1981 c.774 §2; 1987 c.795 §8; 2005 c.564 §7]

163.260 [Amended by 1955 c.366 §1; repealed by 1971 c.743 §432]

163.261 Definitions for ORS 163.263 and 163.264. As used in ORS 163.263 and 163.264, "services" means activities performed by one person under the supervision or for the benefit of another person. [2007 c.811 §1]

Note: 163.261 to 163.269 were enacted into law by the Legislative Assembly but were not added to or made a part of ORS chapter 163 or any series therein by legislative action. See Preface to Oregon Revised Statutes for further explanation.

163.263 Subjecting another person to involuntary servitude in the second degree. (1) A person commits the crime of subjecting another person to involuntary servitude in the second degree if the person knowingly and without lawful authority forces or attempts to force the other person to engage in services by:

(a) Abusing or threatening to abuse the law or legal process;

(b) Destroying, concealing, removing, confiscating or possessing an actual or purported passport or immigration document or another actual or purported government identification document of a person;

(c) Threatening to report a person to a government agency for the purpose of arrest or deportation;

(d) Threatening to collect an unlawful debt; or

(e) Instilling in the other person a fear that the actor will withhold from the other person the necessities of life, including but not limited to lodging, food and clothing.

(2) Subjecting another person to involuntary servitude in the second degree is a Class C felony. [2007 c.811 §3]

Note: See note under 163.261.

163.264 Subjecting another person to involuntary servitude in the first degree. (1) A person commits the crime of subjecting another person to involuntary servitude in the first degree if the person knowingly and without lawful authority forces or attempts to force the other person to engage in services by:

(a) Causing or threatening to cause the death of or serious physical injury to a person; or

(b) Physically restraining or threatening to physically restrain a person.

(2) Subjecting another person to involuntary servitude in the first degree is a Class B felony. [2007 c.811 §2]

Note: See note under 163.261.

163.266 Trafficking in persons. (1) A person commits the crime of trafficking in persons if the person knowingly recruits, entices, harbors, transports, provides or obtains by any means, or attempts to recruit, entice, harbor, transport, provide or obtain by any means, another person and:

(a) The person knows that the other person will be subjected to involuntary servitude as described in ORS 163.263 or 163.264;

(b) The person knows or recklessly disregards the fact that force, fraud or coercion will be used to cause the other person to engage in a commercial sex act; or

(c) The person knows or recklessly disregards the fact that the other person is under 18 years of age and will be used in a commercial sex act.

(2) A person commits the crime of trafficking in persons if the person knowingly benefits financially or receives something of value from participation in a venture that involves an act prohibited by subsection (1) of this section or ORS 163.263 or 163.264.

(3) As used in this section, "commercial sex act" means sexual conduct or sexual contact, as those terms are defined in ORS 167.002, performed in return for a fee or anything of value.

(4) Violation of subsection (1)(a) or (2) of this section is a Class B felony.

(5) Violation of subsection (1)(b) or (c) of this section is a Class A felony. [2007 c.811 §4; 2013 c.720 §1; 2017 c.395 §1]

Note: See note under 163.261.

163.269 Victim assertion of defense of duress. A person who is the victim of a crime described in ORS 163.263, 163.264 or 163.266 may assert the defense of duress, as described in ORS 161.270, if the person is prosecuted for conduct that constitutes services under ORS 163.261, that the person was caused to provide. [2007 c.811 §10]

Note: See note under 163.261.

163.270 [Amended by 1955 c.371 §1; 1957 c.640 §1; repealed by 1971 c.743 §432]

COERCION

163.275 Coercion. (1) A person commits the crime of coercion when the person compels or induces another person to engage in conduct from which the other person has a legal right to abstain, or to abstain from engaging in conduct in which the other person has a legal right to engage, by means of instilling in the other person a fear that, if the other person refrains from the conduct compelled or induced or engages in conduct contrary to the compulsion or inducement, the actor or another will:

(a) Unlawfully cause physical injury to some person;

(b) Unlawfully cause physical injury to some animal;

(c) Unlawfully cause damage to property;

(d) Engage in conduct constituting a crime;

(e) Falsely accuse some person of a crime or cause criminal charges to be instituted against the person;

(f) Cause or continue a strike, boycott or other collective action injurious to some person's business, except that such a threat is not deemed coercive when the act or omission compelled is for the benefit of the group in whose interest the actor purports to act;

(g) Testify falsely or provide false information or withhold testimony or information with respect to another's legal claim or defense; or

(h) Unlawfully use or abuse the person's position as a public servant by performing some act within or related to official duties, or by failing or refusing to perform an official duty, in such manner as to affect some person adversely.

(2) Coercion is a Class C felony. [1971 c.743 §102; 1983 c.546 §4; 1985 c.338 §1; 2007 c.71 §45; 2015 c.751 §1]

163.280 [Amended by 1957 c.640 §2; repealed by 1971 c.743 §432]

163.285 Defense to coercion. In any prosecution for coercion committed by instilling in the victim a fear that the victim or another person would be charged with a crime, it is a defense that the defendant reasonably believed the threatened charge to be true and that the sole purpose of the defendant was to compel or induce the victim to take reasonable action to make good the wrong which was the subject of the threatened charge. [1971 c.743 §103]

163.290 [Repealed by 1971 c.743 §432]

163.300 [Repealed by 1971 c.743 §432]

SEXUAL OFFENSES

163.305 Definitions. As used in chapter 743, Oregon Laws 1971, unless the context requires otherwise:
(1) "Forcible compulsion" means to compel by:
(a) Physical force; or
(b) A threat, express or implied, that places a person in fear of immediate or future death or physical injury to self or another person, or in fear that the person or another person will immediately or in the future be kidnapped.
(2) "Mentally defective" means that a person suffers from a qualifying mental disorder that renders the person incapable of appraising the nature of the conduct of the person.
(3) "Mentally incapacitated" means that a person is rendered incapable of appraising or controlling the conduct of the person at the time of the alleged offense.
(4) "Oral or anal sexual intercourse" means sexual conduct between persons consisting of contact between the sex organs of one person and the mouth or anus of another.
(5) "Physically helpless" means that a person is unconscious or for any other reason is physically unable to communicate unwillingness to an act.
(6) "Sexual contact" means any touching of the sexual or other intimate parts of a person or causing such person to touch the sexual or other intimate parts of the actor for the purpose of arousing or gratifying the sexual desire of either party.
(7) "Sexual intercourse" has its ordinary meaning and occurs upon any penetration, however slight; emission is not required. [1971 c.743 §104; 1975 c.461 §1; 1977 c.844 §1; 1979 c.744 §7; 1983 c.500 §1; 1999 c.949 §1; 2009 c.770 §1; 2017 c.318 §2; 2017 c.634 §17]

Note: Legislative Counsel has substituted "chapter 743, Oregon Laws 1971," for the words "this Act" in section 104, chapter 743, Oregon Laws 1971, compiled as 163.305. Specific ORS references have not been substituted, pursuant to 173.160. These sections may be determined by referring to the 1971 Comparative Section Table located in Volume 20 of ORS.

163.310 [Renumbered 166.180]

163.315 Incapacity to consent; effect of lack of resistance. (1) A person is considered incapable of consenting to a sexual act if the person is:
(a) Under 18 years of age;
(b) Mentally defective;
(c) Mentally incapacitated; or
(d) Physically helpless.
(2) A lack of verbal or physical resistance does not, by itself, constitute consent but may be considered by the trier of fact along with all other relevant evidence. [1971 c.743 §105; 1999 c.949 §2; 2001 c.104 §52]

163.320 [Renumbered 166.190]

163.325 Ignorance or mistake as a defense. (1) In any prosecution under ORS 163.355 to 163.445 in which the criminality of conduct depends on a child's being under the age of 16, it is no defense that the defendant did not know the child's age or that the defendant reasonably believed the child to be older than the age of 16.
(2) When criminality depends on the child's being under a specified age other than 16, it is an affirmative defense for the defendant to prove that the defendant reasonably believed the child to be above the specified age at the time of the alleged offense.
(3) In any prosecution under ORS 163.355 to 163.445 in which the victim's lack of consent is based solely upon the incapacity of the victim to consent because the victim is mentally defective, mentally incapacitated or physically helpless, it is an affirmative defense for the defendant to prove that at the time of the alleged offense the defendant did not know of the facts or conditions responsible for the victim's incapacity to consent. [1971 c.743 §106]

163.330 [Repealed by 1971 c.743 §432]

163.335 [1971 c.743 §107; repealed by 1977 c.844 §2]

163.340 [Repealed by 1971 c.743 §432]

163.345 Age as a defense in certain cases. (1) In any prosecution under ORS 163.355, 163.365, 163.385, 163.395, 163.415, 163.425, 163.427 or 163.435 in which the victim's lack of consent was due solely to incapacity to consent by reason of being less than a specified age, it is a defense that the actor was less than three years older than the victim at the time of the alleged offense.

(2) In any prosecution under ORS 163.408, when the object used to commit the unlawful sexual penetration was the hand or any part thereof of the actor and in which the victim's lack of consent was due solely to incapacity to consent by reason of being less than a specified age, it is a defense that the actor was less than three years older than the victim at the time of the alleged offense.

(3) In any prosecution under ORS 163.445 in which the victim's lack of consent was due solely to incapacity to consent by reason of being less than a specified age, it is a defense that the actor was less than three years older than the victim at the time of the alleged offense if the victim was at least 15 years of age at the time of the alleged offense. [1971 c.743 §108; 1991 c.386 §3; 1991 c.830 §4; 1999 c.626 §24; amendments by 1999 c.626 §45 repealed by 2001 c.884 §1]

163.355 Rape in the third degree. (1) A person commits the crime of rape in the third degree if the person has sexual intercourse with another person under 16 years of age.

(2) Rape in the third degree is a Class C felony. [1971 c.743 §109; 1991 c.628 §1]

163.365 Rape in the second degree. (1) A person who has sexual intercourse with another person commits the crime of rape in the second degree if the other person is under 14 years of age.

(2) Rape in the second degree is a Class B felony. [1971 c.743 §110; 1989 c.359 §1; 1991 c.628 §2]

163.375 Rape in the first degree. (1) A person who has sexual intercourse with another person commits the crime of rape in the first degree if:

(a) The victim is subjected to forcible compulsion by the person;

(b) The victim is under 12 years of age;

(c) The victim is under 16 years of age and is the person's sibling, of the whole or half blood, the person's child or the person's spouse's child; or

(d) The victim is incapable of consent by reason of mental defect, mental incapacitation or physical helplessness.

(2) Rape in the first degree is a Class A felony. [1971 c.743 §111; 1989 c.359 §2; 1991 c.628 §3]

163.385 Sodomy in the third degree. (1) A person commits the crime of sodomy in the third degree if the person engages in oral or anal sexual intercourse with another person under 16 years of age or causes that person to engage in oral or anal sexual intercourse.

(2) Sodomy in the third degree is a Class C felony. [1971 c.743 §112; 2017 c.318 §3]

163.395 Sodomy in the second degree. (1) A person who engages in oral or anal sexual intercourse with another person or causes another to engage in oral or anal sexual intercourse commits the crime of sodomy in the second degree if the victim is under 14 years of age.

(2) Sodomy in the second degree is a Class B felony. [1971 c.743 §113; 1989 c.359 §3; 2017 c.318 §4]

163.405 Sodomy in the first degree. (1) A person who engages in oral or anal sexual intercourse with another person or causes another to engage in oral or anal sexual intercourse commits the crime of sodomy in the first degree if:

(a) The victim is subjected to forcible compulsion by the actor;

(b) The victim is under 12 years of age;

(c) The victim is under 16 years of age and is the actor's brother or sister, of the whole or half blood, the son or daughter of the actor or the son or daughter of the actor's spouse; or

(d) The victim is incapable of consent by reason of mental defect, mental incapacitation or physical helplessness.

(2) Sodomy in the first degree is a Class A felony. [1971 c.743 §114; 1989 c.359 §4; 2017 c.318 §5]

163.408 Unlawful sexual penetration in the second degree. (1) Except as permitted under ORS 163.412, a person commits the crime of unlawful sexual penetration in the second degree if the person penetrates the vagina, anus or penis of another with any object other than the penis or mouth of the actor and the victim is under 14 years of age.

(2) Unlawful sexual penetration in the second degree is a Class B felony. [1981 c.549 §2; 1989 c.359 §5; 1991 c.386 §1]

163.410 [Repealed by 1971 c.743 §432]

163.411 Unlawful sexual penetration in the first degree. (1) Except as permitted under ORS 163.412, a person commits the crime of unlawful sexual penetration in the first degree if the person penetrates the vagina, anus or penis of another with any object other than the penis or mouth of the actor and:
(a) The victim is subjected to forcible compulsion;
(b) The victim is under 12 years of age; or
(c) The victim is incapable of consent by reason of mental defect, mental incapacitation or physical helplessness.
(2) Unlawful sexual penetration in the first degree is a Class A felony. [1981 c.549 §3; 1989 c.359 §6; 1991 c.386 §2]

163.412 Exceptions to unlawful sexual penetration prohibition. Nothing in ORS 163.408, 163.411 or 163.452 prohibits a penetration described in those sections when:
(1) The penetration is part of a medically recognized treatment or diagnostic procedure; or
(2) The penetration is accomplished by a peace officer or a corrections officer acting in official capacity, or by medical personnel at the request of such an officer, in order to search for weapons, contraband or evidence of crime. [1981 c.549 §4; 2005 c.488 §5]

163.413 Purchasing sex with a minor. (1) A person commits the crime of purchasing sex with a minor if the person pays, or offers or agrees to pay, a fee to engage in sexual intercourse or sexual contact with a minor, a police officer posing as a minor or an agent of a police officer posing as a minor.
(2)(a) If the person does not have a prior conviction under this section at the time of the offense, purchasing sex with a minor is a Class C felony and the person may use a defense described in ORS 163.325 only if the minor or, in the case of a police officer or agent of a police officer posing as a minor, the age of the purported minor as reported to the defendant was at least 16 years of age.
(b) If the person has one or more prior convictions under this section at the time of the offense, purchasing sex with a minor is a Class B felony, the state need not prove that the person knew the minor or, in the case of a police officer or agent of a police officer posing as a minor, the purported minor was under 18 years of age and the person may not use a defense described in ORS 163.325.
(3)(a) When a person is convicted under this section, in addition to any other sentence that may be imposed, the court shall impose and may not suspend the sentence described in paragraph (b) of this subsection.
(b) The mandatory minimum sentences that apply to paragraph (a) of this subsection are as follows:
(A) For a person's first conviction, a fine in the amount of $10,000, a term of incarceration of at least 30 days and completion of a john school program.
(B) For a person's second or subsequent conviction, a fine in the amount of $20,000 and the court shall designate the offense as a sex crime under ORS 163A.005.
(c) Notwithstanding paragraphs (a) and (b) of this subsection, if the court determines that the person is unable to pay the full amount of the mandatory minimum fine, the court shall impose and may not suspend a fine in an amount the court determines the person is able to pay.
(d) For a person's first conviction under this section, the court may designate the offense as a sex crime under ORS 163A.005 if the court finds that the circumstances of the offense and the age of the minor or, in the case of a police officer or agent of a police officer posing as a minor, the purported minor as reported to the defendant require the defendant to register and report as a sex offender for the safety of the community.
(4) As used in this section:
(a) "John school" means any course, class or program intended to educate and prevent recidivism of persons who have been arrested for, charged with or convicted of commercial sexual solicitation or purchasing sex with a minor or attempting to engage in commercial sexual solicitation or purchase sex with a minor.
(b) "Minor" means a person under 18 years of age.
(c) "Police officer" has the meaning given that term in ORS 181A.355. [2013 c.720 §4; 2015 c.98 §6; 2015 c.101 §2]

163.415 Sexual abuse in the third degree. (1) A person commits the crime of sexual abuse in the third degree if:
(a) The person subjects another person to sexual contact and:
(A) The victim does not consent to the sexual contact; or
(B) The victim is incapable of consent by reason of being under 18 years of age; or
(b) For the purpose of arousing or gratifying the sexual desire of the person or another person, the person intentionally propels any dangerous substance at a victim without the consent of the victim.
(2) Sexual abuse in the third degree is a Class A misdemeanor.

(3) As used in this section, "dangerous substance" means blood, urine, semen or feces. [1971 c.743 §115; 1979 c.489 §1; 1991 c.830 §1; 1995 c.657 §11; 1995 c.671 §9; 2009 c.616 §1]

163.420 [Repealed by 1971 c.743 §432]

163.425 Sexual abuse in the second degree. (1) A person commits the crime of sexual abuse in the second degree when:

(a) The person subjects another person to sexual intercourse, oral or anal sexual intercourse or, except as provided in ORS 163.412, penetration of the vagina, anus or penis with any object other than the penis or mouth of the actor and the victim does not consent thereto; or

(b)(A) The person violates ORS 163.415 (1)(a)(B);

(B) The person is 21 years of age or older; and

(C) At any time before the commission of the offense, the person was the victim's coach as defined in ORS 163.426.

(2) Sexual abuse in the second degree is a Class C felony. [1971 c.743 §116; 1983 c.564 §1; 1991 c.386 §14; 1991 c.830 §2; 2009 c.876 §2; 2017 c.318 §6]

163.426 Crime category classification for sexual abuse in the second degree. (1) As used in this section, "coach" means a person who instructs or trains an individual or members of a team in a sport.

(2) The Oregon Criminal Justice Commission shall classify sexual abuse in the second degree as described in ORS 163.425 (1)(a) as a crime category 8 of the sentencing guidelines grid of the commission if:

(a) The victim is incapable of consent by reason of being under 18 years of age;

(b) The offender is 21 years of age or older; and

(c) At any time before the commission of the offense, the offender was the victim's coach. [2009 c.876 §1]

Note: 163.426 was enacted into law by the Legislative Assembly but was not added to or made a part of ORS chapter 163 or any series therein by legislative action. See Preface to Oregon Revised Statutes for further explanation.

163.427 Sexual abuse in the first degree. (1) A person commits the crime of sexual abuse in the first degree when that person:

(a) Subjects another person to sexual contact and:

(A) The victim is less than 14 years of age;

(B) The victim is subjected to forcible compulsion by the actor; or

(C) The victim is incapable of consent by reason of being mentally defective, mentally incapacitated or physically helpless; or

(b) Intentionally causes a person under 18 years of age to touch or contact the mouth, anus or sex organs of an animal for the purpose of arousing or gratifying the sexual desire of a person.

(2) Sexual abuse in the first degree is a Class B felony. [1991 c.830 §3; 1995 c.657 §12; 1995 c.671 §10]

Note: 163.427 was enacted into law by the Legislative Assembly but was not added to or made a part of ORS chapter 163 or any series therein by legislative action. See Preface to Oregon Revised Statutes for further explanation.

163.430 [Amended by 1967 c.359 §683; repealed by 1971 c.743 §432]

163.431 Definitions for ORS 163.431 to 163.434. As used in ORS 163.431 to 163.434:

(1) "Child" means a person who the defendant reasonably believes to be under 16 years of age.

(2) "Online communication" means communication that occurs via telephone text messaging, electronic mail, personal or instant messaging, chat rooms, bulletin boards or any other transmission of information by wire, radio, optical cable, cellular system, electromagnetic system or other similar means.

(3) "Sexual contact" has the meaning given that term in ORS 163.305.

(4) "Sexually explicit conduct" has the meaning given that term in ORS 163.665.

(5) "Solicit" means to invite, request, seduce, lure, entice, persuade, prevail upon, coax, coerce or attempt to do so. [2007 c.876 §1; 2009 c.517 §1]

Note: 163.431 to 163.434 were added to and made a part of ORS chapter 163 by legislative action but were not added to any smaller series therein. See Preface to Oregon Revised Statutes for further explanation.

163.432 Online sexual corruption of a child in the second degree. (1) A person commits the crime of online sexual corruption of a child in the second degree if the person is 18 years of age or older and:

(a) For the purpose of arousing or gratifying the sexual desire of the person or another person, knowingly uses an online communication to solicit a child to engage in sexual contact or sexually explicit conduct; and

(b) Offers or agrees to physically meet with the child.

(2) Online sexual corruption of a child in the second degree is a Class C felony. [2007 c.876 §2]

Note: See note under 163.431.

163.433 Online sexual corruption of a child in the first degree. (1) A person commits the crime of online sexual corruption of a child in the first degree if the person violates ORS 163.432 and intentionally takes a substantial step toward physically meeting with or encountering the child.

(2) Online sexual corruption of a child in the first degree is a Class B felony. [2007 c.876 §3]

Note: See note under 163.431.

163.434 Provisions applicable to online sexual corruption of a child. (1) It is an affirmative defense to a prosecution for online sexual corruption of a child in the first or second degree that the person was not more than three years older than the person reasonably believed the child to be.

(2) It is not a defense to a prosecution for online sexual corruption of a child in the first or second degree that the person was in fact communicating with a law enforcement officer, as defined in ORS 163.730, or a person working under the direction of a law enforcement officer, who is 16 years of age or older.

(3) Online sexual corruption of a child in the first or second degree is committed in either the county in which the communication originated or the county in which the communication was received. [2007 c.876 §4]

Note: See note under 163.431.

163.435 Contributing to the sexual delinquency of a minor. (1) A person 18 years of age or older commits the crime of contributing to the sexual delinquency of a minor if:

(a) Being a male, he engages in sexual intercourse with a female under 18 years of age; or

(b) Being a female, she engages in sexual intercourse with a male under 18 years of age; or

(c) The person engages in oral or anal sexual intercourse with another person under 18 years of age or causes that person to engage in oral or anal sexual intercourse.

(2) Contributing to the sexual delinquency of a minor is a Class A misdemeanor. [1971 c.743 §117; 2017 c.318 §7]

163.440 [Repealed by 1971 c.743 §432]

163.445 Sexual misconduct. (1) A person commits the crime of sexual misconduct if the person engages in sexual intercourse or oral or anal sexual intercourse with an unmarried person under 18 years of age.

(2) Sexual misconduct is a Class C misdemeanor. [1971 c.743 §118; 2017 c.318 §8]

163.448 Definitions for ORS 163.452 and 163.454. As used in ORS 163.452 and 163.454, "correctional facility" has the meaning given that term in ORS 162.135. [2005 c.488 §2]

163.450 [Repealed by 1971 c.743 §432]

163.452 Custodial sexual misconduct in the first degree. (1) A person commits the crime of custodial sexual misconduct in the first degree if the person:

(a) Engages in sexual intercourse or oral or anal sexual intercourse with another person or penetrates the vagina, anus or penis of another person with any object other than the penis or mouth of the actor knowing that the other person is:

(A) In the custody of a law enforcement agency following arrest;

(B) Confined or detained in a correctional facility;

(C) Participating in an inmate or offender work crew or work release program; or

(D) On probation, parole, post-prison supervision or other form of conditional or supervised release; and

(b) Is employed by or under contract with the state or local agency that:

(A) Employs the officer who arrested the other person;

(B) Operates the correctional facility in which the other person is confined or detained;

(C) Is responsible for supervising the other person in a work crew or work release program or on probation, parole, post-prison supervision or other form of conditional or supervised release; or

(D) Engages the other person in work or on-the-job training pursuant to ORS 421.354 (1).

(2) Consent of the other person to sexual intercourse, oral or anal sexual intercourse or the sexual penetration is not a defense to a prosecution under this section.

(3) Lack of supervisory authority over the other person is an affirmative defense to a prosecution under this section when the other person is on probation, parole, post-prison supervision or other form of conditional or supervised release.

(4) Custodial sexual misconduct in the first degree is a Class C felony. [2005 c.488 §3; 2017 c.318 §9]

163.454 Custodial sexual misconduct in the second degree. (1) A person commits the crime of custodial sexual misconduct in the second degree if the person:

(a) Engages in sexual contact with another person knowing that the other person is:

(A) In the custody of a law enforcement agency following arrest;

(B) Confined or detained in a correctional facility;

(C) Participating in an inmate or offender work crew or work release program; or

(D) On probation, parole, post-prison supervision or other form of conditional or supervised release; and

(b) Is employed by or under contract with the state or local agency that:

(A) Employs the officer who arrested the other person;

(B) Operates the correctional facility in which the other person is confined or detained;

(C) Is responsible for supervising the other person in a work crew or work release program or on probation, parole, post-prison supervision or other form of conditional or supervised release; or

(D) Engages the other person in work or on-the-job training pursuant to ORS 421.354 (1).

(2) Consent of the other person to sexual contact is not a defense to a prosecution under this section.

(3) Lack of supervisory authority over the other person is an affirmative defense to a prosecution under this section when the other person is on probation, parole, post-prison supervision or other form of conditional or supervised release.

(4) Custodial sexual misconduct in the second degree is a Class A misdemeanor. [2005 c.488 §4]

163.455 [1971 c.743 §119; repealed by 1983 c.546 §1]

163.460 [Repealed by 1971 c.743 §432]

163.465 Public indecency. (1) A person commits the crime of public indecency if while in, or in view of, a public place the person performs:

(a) An act of sexual intercourse;

(b) An act of oral or anal sexual intercourse; or

(c) An act of exposing the genitals of the person with the intent of arousing the sexual desire of the person or another person.

(2)(a) Public indecency is a Class A misdemeanor.

(b) Notwithstanding paragraph (a) of this subsection, public indecency is a Class C felony if the person has a prior conviction for public indecency or a crime described in ORS 163.355 to 163.445 or for a crime in another jurisdiction that, if committed in this state, would constitute public indecency or a crime described in ORS 163.355 to 163.445. [1971 c.743 §120; 1999 c.962 §1; 2005 c.434 §1; 2017 c.318 §10]

163.466 Classification of felony public indecency. The Oregon Criminal Justice Commission shall classify felony public indecency as a person felony and crime category 6 of the sentencing guidelines grid of the commission. [1999 c.962 §3]

Note: 163.466 was enacted into law by the Legislative Assembly but was not added to or made a part of ORS chapter 163 or any series therein by legislative action. See Preface to Oregon Revised Statutes for further explanation.

163.467 Private indecency. (1) A person commits the crime of private indecency if the person exposes the genitals of the person with the intent of arousing the sexual desire of the person or another person and:

(a) The person is in a place where another person has a reasonable expectation of privacy;

(b) The person is in view of the other person;

(c) The exposure reasonably would be expected to alarm or annoy the other person; and

(d) The person knows that the other person did not consent to the exposure.

(2) Private indecency is a Class A misdemeanor.

(3) Subsection (1) of this section does not apply to a person who commits the act described in subsection (1) of this section if the person cohabits with and is involved in a sexually intimate relationship with the other person.

(4) For purposes of this section, "place where another person has a reasonable expectation of privacy" includes, but is not limited to, residences, yards of residences, working areas and offices. [1999 c.869 §2]

163.470 [Repealed by 1971 c.743 §432]

163.472 Unlawful dissemination of an intimate image. (1) A person commits the crime of unlawful dissemination of an intimate image if:

(a) The person, with the intent to harass, humiliate or injure another person, knowingly causes to be disclosed through an Internet website an identifiable image of the other person whose intimate parts are visible or who is engaged in sexual conduct;

(b) The person knows or reasonably should have known that the other person does not consent to the disclosure;

(c) The other person is harassed, humiliated or injured by the disclosure; and

(d) A reasonable person would be harassed, humiliated or injured by the disclosure.

(2)(a) Except as provided in paragraph (b) of this subsection, unlawful dissemination of an intimate image is a Class A misdemeanor.

(b) Unlawful dissemination of an intimate image is a Class C felony if the person has a prior conviction under this section at the time of the offense.

(3) As used in this section:

(a) "Disclose" includes, but is not limited to, transfer, publish, distribute, exhibit, advertise and offer.

(b) "Image" includes, but is not limited to, a photograph, film, videotape, recording, digital picture and other visual reproduction, regardless of the manner in which the image is stored.

(c) "Information content provider" has the meaning given that term in 47 U.S.C. 230(f).

(d) "Interactive computer service" has the meaning given that term in 47 U.S.C. 230(f).

(e) "Intimate parts" means uncovered human genitals, pubic areas or female nipples.

(f) "Sexual conduct" means sexual intercourse or oral or anal sexual intercourse, as those terms are defined in ORS 163.305, or masturbation.

(4) This section does not apply to:

(a) Activity by law enforcement agencies investigating and prosecuting criminal offenses;

(b) Legitimate medical, scientific or educational activities;

(c) Legal proceedings, when disclosure is consistent with common practice in civil proceedings or necessary for the proper functioning of the criminal justice system;

(d) The reporting of unlawful conduct to a law enforcement agency;

(e) Disclosures that serve a lawful public interest;

(f) Disclosures of images:

(A) Depicting the other person voluntarily displaying, in a public area, the other person's intimate parts or engaging in sexual conduct; or

(B) Originally created for a commercial purpose with the consent of the other person; or

(g) The provider of an interactive computer service for an image of intimate parts provided by an information content provider. [2015 c.379 §1; 2017 c.318 §11]

Note: 163.472 was enacted into law by the Legislative Assembly but was not added to or made a part of ORS chapter 163 or any series therein by legislative action. See Preface to Oregon Revised Statutes for further explanation.

163.475 [1975 c.176 §2; 1977 c.822 §1; repealed by 1981 c.892 §98]

163.476 Unlawfully being in a location where children regularly congregate. (1) A person commits the crime of unlawfully being in a location where children regularly congregate if the person:

(a)(A) Has been designated a sexually violent dangerous offender under ORS 137.765;

(B) Has been classified as a level three sex offender under ORS 163A.100 (3), is an unclassified adult sex offender designated as predatory prior to January 1, 2014, or is a person whom the State Board of Parole and Post-Prison Supervision or the Psychiatric Security Review Board has classified as a level three sex offender under section 7 (2)(b), chapter 708, Oregon Laws 2013, and does not have written approval from the State Board of Parole and Post-Prison Supervision or the person's supervisory authority or supervising officer to be in or upon the specific premises;

(C) Has been sentenced as a dangerous offender under ORS 161.725 upon conviction of a sex crime; or

(D) Has been given a similar designation or been sentenced under a similar law of another jurisdiction; and

(b) Knowingly enters or remains in or upon premises where persons under 18 years of age regularly congregate.

(2) As used in this section:

(a) "Premises where persons under 18 years of age regularly congregate" means schools, child care centers, playgrounds, other places intended for use primarily by persons under 18 years of age and places where persons under 18 years of age gather for regularly scheduled educational and recreational programs.

(b) "Sex crime" has the meaning given that term in ORS 163A.005.

(3) Unlawfully being in a location where children regularly congregate is a Class A misdemeanor. [2005 c.811 §1; 2013 c.708 §12; 2015 c.820 §17; 2017 c.442 §34]

Note 1: The amendments to 163.476 by section 34, chapter 442, Oregon Laws 2017, become operative July 1, 2018. See section 36, chapter 442, Oregon Laws 2017. The text that is operative until July 1, 2018, is set forth for the user's convenience.

163.476. (1) A person commits the crime of unlawfully being in a location where children regularly congregate if the person:

(a)(A) Has been designated a sexually violent dangerous offender under ORS 137.765;

(B) Has been classified as a level three sex offender under ORS 163A.100 (3), is an unclassified adult sex offender designated as predatory prior to January 1, 2014, or is a person whom the State Board of Parole and Post-Prison Supervision, the Psychiatric Security Review Board or the Oregon Health Authority has classified as a level three sex offender under section 7 (2)(b), chapter 708, Oregon Laws 2013, and does not have written approval from the State Board of Parole and Post-Prison Supervision or the person's supervisory authority or supervising officer to be in or upon the specific premises;

(C) Has been sentenced as a dangerous offender under ORS 161.725 upon conviction of a sex crime; or

(D) Has been given a similar designation or been sentenced under a similar law of another jurisdiction; and

(b) Knowingly enters or remains in or upon premises where persons under 18 years of age regularly congregate.

(2) As used in this section:

(a) "Premises where persons under 18 years of age regularly congregate" means schools, child care centers, playgrounds, other places intended for use primarily by persons under 18 years of age and places where persons under 18 years of age gather for regularly scheduled educational and recreational programs.

(b) "Sex crime" has the meaning given that term in ORS 163A.005.

(3) Unlawfully being in a location where children regularly congregate is a Class A misdemeanor.

Note 2: The amendments to 163.476 by section 24, chapter 820, Oregon Laws 2015, become operative January 1, 2019. See section 26, chapter 820, Oregon Laws 2015. The text that is operative on and after January 1, 2019, is set forth for the user's convenience.

163.476. (1) A person commits the crime of unlawfully being in a location where children regularly congregate if the person:

(a)(A) Has been designated a sexually violent dangerous offender under ORS 137.765;

(B) Has been classified as a level three sex offender under ORS 163A.100 (3), and does not have written approval from the State Board of Parole and Post-Prison Supervision or the person's supervisory authority or supervising officer to be in or upon the specific premises;

(C) Has been sentenced as a dangerous offender under ORS 161.725 upon conviction of a sex crime; or

(D) Has been given a similar designation or been sentenced under a similar law of another jurisdiction; and

(b) Knowingly enters or remains in or upon premises where persons under 18 years of age regularly congregate.

(2) As used in this section:

(a) "Premises where persons under 18 years of age regularly congregate" means schools, child care centers, playgrounds, other places intended for use primarily by persons under 18 years of age and places where persons under 18 years of age gather for regularly scheduled educational and recreational programs.

(b) "Sex crime" has the meaning given that term in ORS 163A.005.

(3) Unlawfully being in a location where children regularly congregate is a Class A misdemeanor.

Note 3: 163.476 and 163.479 were enacted into law by the Legislative Assembly but were not added to or made a part of ORS chapter 163 or any series therein by legislative action. See Preface to Oregon Revised Statutes for further explanation.

163.477 [1979 c.706 §3; repealed by 1985 c.557 §10]

163.479 Unlawful contact with a child. (1) A person commits the crime of unlawful contact with a child if the person:

(a)(A) Has been designated a sexually violent dangerous offender under ORS 137.765;

(B) Has been classified as a level three sex offender under ORS 163A.100 (3);

(C) Is an unclassified adult sex offender designated as predatory prior to January 1, 2014, or a person whom the State Board of Parole and Post-Prison Supervision or the Psychiatric Security Review Board has classified as a level three sex offender under section 7 (2)(b), chapter 708, Oregon Laws 2013;

(D) Has been sentenced as a dangerous offender under ORS 161.725 upon conviction of a sex crime; or

(E) Has been given a similar designation or been sentenced under a similar law of another jurisdiction; and

(b) Knowingly contacts a child with the intent to commit a crime or for the purpose of arousing or satisfying the sexual desires of the person or another person.

(2) As used in this section:

(a) "Child" means a person under 18 years of age.

(b) "Contact" means to communicate in any manner.

(c) "Sex crime" has the meaning given that term in ORS 163A.005.

(3) Unlawful contact with a child is a Class C felony. [2005 c.811 §2; 2013 c.708 §13; 2015 c.820 §18; 2017 c.442 §35]

Note 1: The amendments to 163.479 by section 35, chapter 442, Oregon Laws 2017, become operative July 1, 2018. See section 36, chapter 442, Oregon Laws 2017. The text that is operative until July 1, 2018, is set forth for the user's convenience.

163.479. (1) A person commits the crime of unlawful contact with a child if the person:

(a)(A) Has been designated a sexually violent dangerous offender under ORS 137.765;

(B) Has been classified as a level three sex offender under ORS 163A.100 (3);

(C) Is an unclassified adult sex offender designated as predatory prior to January 1, 2014, or a person whom the State Board of Parole and Post-Prison Supervision, the Psychiatric Security Review Board or the Oregon Health Authority has classified as a level three sex offender under section 7 (2)(b), chapter 708, Oregon Laws 2013;

(D) Has been sentenced as a dangerous offender under ORS 161.725 upon conviction of a sex crime; or

(E) Has been given a similar designation or been sentenced under a similar law of another jurisdiction; and

(b) Knowingly contacts a child with the intent to commit a crime or for the purpose of arousing or satisfying the sexual desires of the person or another person.

(2) As used in this section:

(a) "Child" means a person under 18 years of age.

(b) "Contact" means to communicate in any manner.

(c) "Sex crime" has the meaning given that term in ORS 163A.005.

(3) Unlawful contact with a child is a Class C felony.

Note 2: The amendments to 163.479 by section 25, chapter 820, Oregon Laws 2015, become operative January 1, 2019. See section 26, chapter 820, Oregon Laws 2015. The text that is operative on and after January 1, 2019, is set forth for the user's convenience.

163.479. (1) A person commits the crime of unlawful contact with a child if the person:

(a)(A) Has been designated a sexually violent dangerous offender under ORS 137.765;

(B) Has been classified as a level three sex offender under ORS 163A.100 (3);

(C) Has been sentenced as a dangerous offender under ORS 161.725 upon conviction of a sex crime; or

(D) Has been given a similar designation or been sentenced under a similar law of another jurisdiction; and

(b) Knowingly contacts a child with the intent to commit a crime or for the purpose of arousing or satisfying the sexual desires of the person or another person.

(2) As used in this section:

(a) "Child" means a person under 18 years of age.

(b) "Contact" means to communicate in any manner.

(c) "Sex crime" has the meaning given that term in ORS 163A.005.

(3) Unlawful contact with a child is a Class C felony.

Note 3: See note 3 under 163.476.

163.480 [Amended by 1963 c.406 §1; repealed by 1971 c.743 §432]

163.483 [1979 c.706 §2; 1983 c.740 §30; repealed by 1985 c.557 §10]

163.485 [1979 c.706 §4; repealed by 1985 c.557 §10]

163.490 [Repealed by 1971 c.743 §432]

163.495 [1979 c.706 §5; 1987 c.158 §25; 1987 c.864 §14; renumbered 163.676 in 1987]

163.500 [Repealed by 1971 c.743 §432]

OFFENSES AGAINST FAMILY

163.505 Definitions for certain provisions of ORS 163.505 to 163.575. As used in ORS 163.505 to 163.575, unless the context requires otherwise:

(1) "Controlled substance" has the meaning given that term in ORS 475.005.

(2) "Descendant" includes persons related by descending lineal consanguinity, stepchildren and lawfully adopted children.

(3) "Precursor substance" has the meaning given that term in ORS 475.940.

(4) "Support" includes, but is not limited to, necessary and proper shelter, food, clothing, medical attention and education. [1971 c.743 §170; 2005 c.708 §3]

163.515 Bigamy. (1) A person commits the crime of bigamy if the person knowingly marries or purports to marry another person at a time when either is lawfully married.

(2) Bigamy is a Class C felony. [1971 c.743 §171]

163.525 Incest. (1) A person commits the crime of incest if the person marries or engages in sexual intercourse or oral or anal sexual intercourse with a person whom the person knows to be related to the person, either legitimately or illegitimately, as an ancestor, descendant or brother or sister of either the whole or half blood.

(2) Incest is a Class C felony. [1971 c.743 §172; 2017 c.318 §12]

163.535 Abandonment of a child. (1) A person commits the crime of abandonment of a child if, being a parent, lawful guardian or other person lawfully charged with the care or custody of a child under 15 years of age, the person deserts the child in any place with intent to abandon it.

(2) Abandonment of a child is a Class C felony.

(3) It is an affirmative defense to a charge of violating subsection (1) of this section that the child was left in accordance with ORS 418.017. [1971 c.743 §173; 2001 c.597 §2]

163.537 Buying or selling a person under 18 years of age. (1) A person commits the crime of buying or selling a person under 18 years of age if the person buys, sells, barters, trades or offers to buy or sell the legal or physical custody of a person under 18 years of age.

(2) Subsection (1) of this section does not:

(a) Prohibit a person in the process of adopting a child from paying the fees, costs and expenses related to the adoption as allowed in ORS 109.311.

(b) Prohibit a negotiated satisfaction of child support arrearages or other settlement in favor of a parent of a child in exchange for consent of the parent to the adoption of the child by the current spouse of the child's other parent.

(c) Apply to fees for services charged by the Department of Human Services or adoption agencies licensed under ORS 412.001 to 412.161 and 412.991 and ORS chapter 418.

(d) Apply to fees for services in an adoption pursuant to a surrogacy agreement.

(e) Prohibit discussion or settlement of disputed issues between parties in a domestic relations proceeding.

(3) Buying or selling a person under 18 years of age is a Class B felony. [1997 c.561 §2]

163.545 Child neglect in the second degree. (1) A person having custody or control of a child under 10 years of age commits the crime of child neglect in the second degree if, with criminal negligence, the person leaves the child unattended in or at any place for such period of time as may be likely to endanger the health or welfare of such child.

(2) Child neglect in the second degree is a Class A misdemeanor. [1971 c.743 §174; 1991 c.832 §2]

163.547 Child neglect in the first degree. (1)(a) A person having custody or control of a child under 16 years of age commits the crime of child neglect in the first degree if the person knowingly leaves the child, or allows the child to stay:

(A) In a vehicle where controlled substances or cannabinoid extracts as defined in ORS 475B.015 are being criminally delivered or manufactured;

(B) In or upon premises, or in the immediate proximity of premises, where a cannabinoid extract as defined in ORS 475B.015 is being processed, if the premises have not been licensed under ORS 475B.090;

(C) In or upon premises and in the immediate proximity where controlled substances are criminally delivered or manufactured for consideration or profit or where a chemical reaction involving one or more precursor substances:

(i) Is occurring as part of unlawfully manufacturing a controlled substance or grinding, soaking or otherwise breaking down a precursor substance for the unlawful manufacture of a controlled substance; or

(ii) Has occurred as part of unlawfully manufacturing a controlled substance or grinding, soaking or otherwise breaking down a precursor substance for the unlawful manufacture of a controlled substance and the premises have not been certified as fit for use under ORS 453.885; or

(D) In or upon premises that have been determined to be not fit for use under ORS 453.855 to 453.912.

(b) As used in this subsection, "vehicle" and "premises" do not include public places, as defined in ORS 161.015.

(2) Child neglect in the first degree is a Class B felony.

(3) Subsection (1) of this section does not apply if the controlled substance is marijuana and is delivered for no consideration.

(4) The Oregon Criminal Justice Commission shall classify child neglect in the first degree as crime category 6 of the sentencing guidelines grid of the commission if the controlled substance being delivered or manufactured is methamphetamine. [1991 c.832 §1; 2001 c.387 §1; 2001 c.870 §11; 2005 c.708 §2; 2017 c.21 §44]

Note: 163.547 was enacted into law by the Legislative Assembly but was not added to or made a part of ORS chapter 163 or any series therein by legislative action. See Preface to Oregon Revised Statutes for further explanation.

163.555 Criminal nonsupport. (1) A person commits the crime of criminal nonsupport if, being the parent, lawful guardian or other person lawfully charged with the support of a child under 18 years of age, born in or out of wedlock, the person knowingly fails to provide support for such child.

(2) It is no defense to a prosecution under this section that either parent has contracted a subsequent marriage, that issue has been born of a subsequent marriage, that the defendant is the parent of issue born of a prior marriage or that the child is being supported by another person or agency.

(3) It is an affirmative defense to a prosecution under this section that the defendant has a lawful excuse for failing to provide child support.

(4) If the defendant intends to rely on the affirmative defense created in subsection (3) of this section, the defendant must give the district attorney written notice of the intent to do so at least 30 days prior to trial. The notice must describe the nature of the lawful excuse upon which the defendant proposes to rely. If the defendant fails to file notice as required by this subsection, the defendant may not introduce evidence of a lawful excuse unless the court finds there was just cause for the defendant's failure to file the notice within the required time.

(5) Criminal nonsupport is a Class C felony. [1971 c.743 §175; 1993 c.33 §308; 1999 c.954 §3; 2005 c.502 §1]

163.565 Evidence of parentage; confidentiality between spouses not applicable; spouses competent and compellable witnesses. (1) Proof that a child was born during the time a person lived and cohabited with the child's mother, or held the child's mother out as that person's spouse in a marriage, is prima facie evidence that the person is the parent of the child. This subsection does not exclude any other legal evidence tending to establish the parental relationship.

(2) No provision of law prohibiting the disclosure of confidential communications between spouses in a marriage apply to prosecutions for criminal nonsupport. A spouse is a competent and compellable witness for or against either party. [1971 c.743 §176; 2015 c.629 §30; 2017 c.651 §36]

163.575 Endangering the welfare of a minor. (1) A person commits the offense of endangering the welfare of a minor if the person knowingly:

(a) Induces, causes or permits an unmarried person under 18 years of age to witness an act of sexual conduct or sadomasochistic abuse as defined in ORS 167.060;

(b) Permits a person under 18 years of age to enter or remain in a place where unlawful activity involving controlled substances or cannabis is maintained or conducted;

(c) Induces, causes or permits a person under 18 years of age to participate in gambling as defined in ORS 167.117; or

(d) Sells to a person under 18 years of age any device in which cannabis, cocaine or any controlled substance, as defined in ORS 475.005, is burned and the principal design and use of which is directly or indirectly to deliver cannabis smoke, cocaine smoke or smoke from any controlled substance into the human body, including but not limited to:

(A) Pipes, water pipes, hookahs, wooden pipes, carburetor pipes, electric pipes, air driven pipes, corncob pipes, meerschaum pipes and ceramic pipes, with or without screens, permanent screens, hashish heads or punctured metal bowls;

(B) Carburetion tubes and devices, including carburetion masks;

(C) Bongs;

(D) Chillums;

(E) Ice pipes or chillers;

(F) Rolling papers and rolling machines; and

(G) Cocaine free basing kits.

(2) Endangering the welfare of a minor is a Class A misdemeanor. [1971 c.743 §177; 1973 c.827 §20; 1979 c.744 §8; 1981 c.838 §1; 1983 c.740 §31; 1991 c.970 §5; 1995 c.79 §52; 1999 c.1051 §153; 2011 c.597 §79; 2014 c.20 §1; 2015 c.158 §5; 2017 c.21 §45; 2017 c.701 §18]

163.577 Failing to supervise a child. (1) A person commits the offense of failing to supervise a child if the person is the parent, lawful guardian or other person lawfully charged with the care or custody of a child under 15 years of age and the child:

(a) Commits an act that brings the child within the jurisdiction of the juvenile court under ORS 419C.005;

(b) Violates a curfew law of a county or any other political subdivision; or

(c) Fails to attend school as required under ORS 339.010.

(2) Nothing in this section applies to a child-caring agency as defined in ORS 418.205 or to foster parents.

(3) In a prosecution of a person for failing to supervise a child under subsection (1)(a) of this section, it is an affirmative defense that the person:

(a) Is the victim of the act that brings the child within the jurisdiction of the juvenile court; or

(b) Reported the act to the appropriate authorities.

(4) In a prosecution of a person for failing to supervise a child under subsection (1) of this section, it is an affirmative defense that the person took reasonable steps to control the conduct of the child at the time the person is alleged to have failed to supervise the child.

(5)(a) Except as provided in subsection (6) or (7) of this section, in a prosecution of a person for failing to supervise a child under subsection (1)(a) of this section, the court shall order the person to pay restitution under ORS 137.103 to 137.109 to a victim for economic damages arising from the act of the child that brings the child within the jurisdiction of the juvenile court.

(b) The amount of restitution ordered under this subsection may not exceed $2,500.

(6) If a person pleads guilty or is found guilty of failing to supervise a child under this section and if the person has not previously been convicted of failing to supervise a child, the court:

(a) Shall warn the person of the penalty for future convictions of failing to supervise a child and shall suspend imposition of sentence.

(b) May not order the person to pay restitution under this section.

(7)(a) If a person pleads guilty or is found guilty of failing to supervise a child under this section and if the person has only one prior conviction for failing to supervise a child, the court, with the consent of the person, may suspend imposition of sentence and order the person to complete a parent effectiveness program approved by the court. Upon the person's completion of the parent effectiveness program to the satisfaction of the court, the court may discharge the person. If the person fails to complete the parent effectiveness program to the satisfaction of the court, the court may impose a sentence authorized by this section.

(b) There may be only one suspension of sentence under this subsection with respect to a person.

(8) The juvenile court has jurisdiction over a first offense of failing to supervise a child under this section.

(9) Failing to supervise a child is a Class A violation. [1995 c.593 §1; 1999 c.1051 §154; 2003 c.670 §5; 2005 c.564 §8]

Note: 163.577 was enacted into law by the Legislative Assembly but was not added to or made a part of ORS chapter 163 or any series therein by legislative action. See Preface to Oregon Revised Statutes for further explanation.

163.580 Display of sign concerning sale of smoking devices. (1) A person who sells any of the smoking devices listed in ORS 163.575 (1)(d) shall display a sign clearly stating that the sale of such devices to persons under 18 years of age is prohibited by law.

(2) A person who violates this section commits a Class B violation. [1981 c.838 §2; 1999 c.1051 §155; 2015 c.158 §32; 2017 c.701 §19]

Note: 163.580 was enacted into law by the Legislative Assembly but was not added to or made a part of ORS chapter 163 or any series therein by legislative action. See Preface to Oregon Revised Statutes for further explanation.

163.605 [1971 c.743 §287; repealed by 1985 c.366 §1]

163.610 [Repealed by 1971 c.743 §432]

163.620 [Repealed by 1971 c.743 §432]

163.630 [Repealed by 1971 c.743 §432]

163.635 [1955 c.308 §1; repealed by 1971 c.743 §432]

163.640 [Repealed by 1971 c.743 §432]

163.650 [Repealed by 1971 c.743 §432]

163.660 [Repealed by 1971 c.743 §432]

VISUAL RECORDING OF SEXUAL CONDUCT OF CHILDREN

163.665 Definitions. As used in ORS 163.665 to 163.693:

(1) "Child" means a person who is less than 18 years of age, and any reference to a child in relation to a visual recording of the child is a reference to a person who was less than 18 years of age at the time the original image in

the visual recording was created and not the age of the person at the time of an alleged offense relating to the subsequent reproduction, use or possession of the visual recording.

(2) "Child abuse" means conduct that constitutes, or would constitute if committed in this state, a crime in which the victim is a child.

(3) "Sexually explicit conduct" means actual or simulated:

(a) Sexual intercourse or deviant sexual intercourse;

(b) Genital-genital, oral-genital, anal-genital or oral-anal contact, whether between persons of the same or opposite sex or between humans and animals;

(c) Penetration of the vagina or rectum by any object other than as part of a medical diagnosis or treatment or as part of a personal hygiene practice;

(d) Masturbation;

(e) Sadistic or masochistic abuse; or

(f) Lewd exhibition of sexual or other intimate parts.

(4) "Visual depiction" includes, but is not limited to, visual recordings, pictures and computer-generated images and pictures, whether made or produced by electronic, mechanical or other means.

(5) "Visual recording" includes, but is not limited to, photographs, films, videotapes and computer and other digital pictures, regardless of the manner in which the recording is stored. [1985 c.557 §2; 1987 c.864 §1; 1991 c.664 §4; 1995 c.768 §4; 1997 c.719 §5; 2011 c.515 §1]

163.670 Using child in display of sexually explicit conduct. (1) A person commits the crime of using a child in a display of sexually explicit conduct if the person employs, authorizes, permits, compels or induces a child to participate or engage in sexually explicit conduct for any person to observe or to record in a visual recording.

(2) Using a child in a display of sexually explicit conduct is a Class A felony. [1985 c.557 §3; 1987 c.864 §3; 1991 c.664 §5; 2011 c.515 §2]

163.672 [1991 c.664 §2; repealed by 1995 c.768 §16]

163.673 [1987 c.864 §4; 1991 c.664 §6; repealed by 1995 c.768 §16]

163.675 [1985 c.557 §4; repealed by 1987 c.864 §15]

163.676 Exemption from prosecution under ORS 163.684. (1) No employee is liable to prosecution under ORS 163.684 or under any city or home rule county ordinance for exhibiting or possessing with intent to exhibit any obscene matter or performance provided the employee is acting within the scope of regular employment at a showing open to the public.

(2) As used in this section, "employee" means any person regularly employed by the owner or operator of a motion picture theater if the person has no financial interest other than salary or wages in the ownership or operation of the motion picture theater, no financial interest in or control over the selection of the motion pictures shown in the theater, and is working within the motion picture theater where the person is regularly employed, but does not include a manager of the motion picture theater. [Formerly 163.495; 1995 c.768 §5]

163.677 [1987 c.864 §5; 1991 c.664 §7; repealed by 1995 c.768 §16]

163.680 [1985 c.557 §5; 1987 c.158 §26; 1987 c.864 §9; 1991 c.664 §8; repealed by 1995 c.768 §16]

163.682 Exceptions to ORS 163.665 to 163.693. The provisions of ORS 163.665 to 163.693 do not apply to:

(1) Any legitimate medical procedure performed by or under the direction of a person licensed to provide medical services for the purpose of medical diagnosis or treatment, including the recording of medical procedures;

(2) Any activity undertaken in the course of bona fide law enforcement activity or necessary to the proper functioning of the criminal justice system, except that this exception shall not apply to any activity prohibited by ORS 163.670;

(3) Any bona fide educational activity, including studies and lectures, in the fields of medicine, psychotherapy, sociology or criminology, except that this exception shall not apply to any activity prohibited by ORS 163.670;

(4) Obtaining, viewing or possessing a visual recording as part of a bona fide treatment program for sexual offenders; or

(5) A public library, as defined in ORS 357.400, or a library exempt from taxation under ORS 307.090 or 307.130, except that these exceptions do not apply to any activity prohibited by ORS 163.670. [1991 c.664 §3; 2011 c.515 §9]

163.683 [1987 c.864 §11; repealed by 1991 c.664 §12]

163.684 Encouraging child sexual abuse in the first degree. (1) A person commits the crime of encouraging child sexual abuse in the first degree if the person:

(a)(A) Knowingly develops, duplicates, publishes, prints, disseminates, exchanges, displays, finances, attempts to finance or sells a visual recording of sexually explicit conduct involving a child or knowingly possesses, accesses or views such a visual recording with the intent to develop, duplicate, publish, print, disseminate, exchange, display or sell it; or

(B) Knowingly brings into this state, or causes to be brought or sent into this state, for sale or distribution, a visual recording of sexually explicit conduct involving a child; and

(b) Knows or is aware of and consciously disregards the fact that creation of the visual recording of sexually explicit conduct involved child abuse.

(2) Encouraging child sexual abuse in the first degree is a Class B felony. [1995 c.768 §2; 2011 c.515 §3]

163.685 [1985 c.557 §6; 1987 c.864 §12; repealed by 1991 c.664 §12]

163.686 Encouraging child sexual abuse in the second degree. (1) A person commits the crime of encouraging child sexual abuse in the second degree if the person:

(a)(A)(i) Knowingly possesses or controls, or knowingly accesses with the intent to view, a visual recording of sexually explicit conduct involving a child for the purpose of arousing or satisfying the sexual desires of the person or another person; or

(ii) Knowingly pays, exchanges or gives anything of value to obtain or view a visual recording of sexually explicit conduct involving a child for the purpose of arousing or satisfying the sexual desires of the person or another person; and

(B) Knows or is aware of and consciously disregards the fact that creation of the visual recording of sexually explicit conduct involved child abuse; or

(b)(A) Knowingly pays, exchanges or gives anything of value to observe sexually explicit conduct by a child or knowingly observes, for the purpose of arousing or gratifying the sexual desire of the person, sexually explicit conduct by a child; and

(B) Knows or is aware of and consciously disregards the fact that the conduct constitutes child abuse.

(2) Encouraging child sexual abuse in the second degree is a Class C felony. [1995 c.768 §3; 2011 c.515 §4]

163.687 Encouraging child sexual abuse in the third degree. (1) A person commits the crime of encouraging child sexual abuse in the third degree if the person:

(a)(A)(i) Knowingly possesses or controls, or knowingly accesses with the intent to view, a visual recording of sexually explicit conduct involving a child for the purpose of arousing or satisfying the sexual desires of the person or another person; or

(ii) Knowingly pays, exchanges or gives anything of value to obtain or view a visual recording of sexually explicit conduct involving a child for the purpose of arousing or satisfying the sexual desires of the person or another person; and

(B) Knows or fails to be aware of a substantial and unjustifiable risk that the creation of the visual recording of sexually explicit conduct involved child abuse; or

(b)(A) Knowingly pays, exchanges or gives anything of value to observe sexually explicit conduct by a child or knowingly observes, for the purpose of arousing or gratifying the sexual desire of the person, sexually explicit conduct by a child; and

(B) Knows or fails to be aware of a substantial and unjustifiable risk that the conduct constitutes child abuse.

(2) Encouraging child sexual abuse in the third degree is a Class A misdemeanor. [1995 c.768 §3a; 2011 c.515 §5]

163.688 Possession of materials depicting sexually explicit conduct of a child in the first degree. (1) A person commits the crime of possession of materials depicting sexually explicit conduct of a child in the first degree if the person:

(a) Knowingly possesses, accesses or views a visual depiction of sexually explicit conduct involving a child or a visual depiction of sexually explicit conduct that appears to involve a child; and

(b) Uses the visual depiction to induce a child to participate or engage in sexually explicit conduct.

(2) Possession of materials depicting sexually explicit conduct of a child in the first degree is a Class B felony. [1997 c.719 §3; 2011 c.515 §6]

163.689 Possession of materials depicting sexually explicit conduct of a child in the second degree. (1) A person commits the crime of possession of materials depicting sexually explicit conduct of a child in the second degree if the person:

(a) Knowingly possesses, accesses or views a visual depiction of sexually explicit conduct involving a child or a visual depiction of sexually explicit conduct that appears to involve a child; and

(b) Intends to use the visual depiction to induce a child to participate or engage in sexually explicit conduct.

(2) Possession of materials depicting sexually explicit conduct of a child in the second degree is a Class C felony. [1997 c.719 §4; 2011 c.515 §7]

163.690 Lack of knowledge of age of child as affirmative defense. It is an affirmative defense to any prosecution under ORS 163.684, 163.686, 163.687 or 163.693 that the defendant, at the time of engaging in the conduct prohibited therein, did not know and did not have reason to know that the relevant sexually explicit conduct involved a child. [1985 c.557 §7; 1987 c.864 §13; 1991 c.664 §9; 1995 c.768 §7]

163.693 Failure to report child pornography. (1) As used in this section:
(a) "Computer technician" means a person who repairs, installs or otherwise services a computer, computer network or computer system for compensation.
(b) "Processor of photographic images" means a person who develops, processes, reproduces, transfers, edits or enhances photographic film into negatives, slides, prints, movies, digital images or video.
(2) A processor of photographic images or a computer technician who reasonably believes the processor or technician has observed a visual recording of a child involved in sexually explicit conduct shall report the name and address, if known, of the person requesting the processing or of the owner or person in possession of the computer, computer network or computer system to:
(a) The CyberTipline at the National Center for Missing and Exploited Children;
(b) The local office of the Department of Human Services; or
(c) A law enforcement agency within the county where the processor or technician making the report is located at the time the visual recording is observed.
(3) Nothing in this section requires a processor of photographic images or a computer technician to monitor any user, subscriber or customer or to search for prohibited materials or media.
(4) Any person, their employer or a third party complying with this section in good faith shall be immune from civil or criminal liability in connection with making the report, except for willful or wanton misconduct.
(5) A person commits the crime of failure to report child pornography if the person violates the provisions of this section.
(6) Failure to report child pornography is a Class A misdemeanor. [1987 c.864 §7; 1991 c.664 §10; 2011 c.515 §§8,11a]

163.695 [1987 c.864 §8; 1991 c.664 §11; 1995 c.768 §7; repealed by 2001 c.666 §56]

163.696 [2001 c.666 §49; repealed by 2005 c.830 §48]

INVASION OF PRIVACY

163.700 Invasion of personal privacy in the second degree. (1) Except as provided in ORS 163.702, a person commits the crime of invasion of personal privacy in the second degree if:
(a)(A) For the purpose of arousing or gratifying the sexual desire of the person, the person is in a location to observe another person in a state of nudity without the consent of the other person; and
(B) The other person is in a place and circumstances where the person has a reasonable expectation of personal privacy; or
(b)(A) The person knowingly makes or records a photograph, motion picture, videotape or other visual recording of another person's intimate area without the consent of the other person; and
(B) The person being recorded has a reasonable expectation of privacy concerning the intimate area.
(2) As used in this section and ORS 163.701:
(a) "Intimate area" means nudity, or undergarments that are being worn by a person and are covered by clothing.
(b) "Makes or records a photograph, motion picture, videotape or other visual recording" includes, but is not limited to:
(A) Making or recording or employing, authorizing, permitting, compelling or inducing another person to make or record a photograph, motion picture, videotape or other visual recording.
(B) Making or recording a photograph, motion picture, videotape or other visual recording through the use of an unmanned aircraft system as defined in ORS 837.300, even if the unmanned aircraft system is operated for commercial purposes in compliance with authorization granted by the Federal Aviation Administration.
(c) "Nudity" means any part of the uncovered or less than opaquely covered:
(A) Genitals;
(B) Pubic area; or
(C) Female breast below a point immediately above the top of the areola.
(d) "Places and circumstances where the person has a reasonable expectation of personal privacy" includes, but is not limited to, a bathroom, dressing room, locker room that includes an enclosed area for dressing or showering, tanning booth and any area where a person undresses in an enclosed space that is not open to public view.

(e) "Public view" means that an area can be readily seen and that a person within the area can be distinguished by normal unaided vision when viewed from a public place as defined in ORS 161.015.

(f) "Reasonable expectation of privacy concerning the intimate area" means that the person intended to protect the intimate area from being seen and has not exposed the intimate area to public view.

(3) Invasion of personal privacy in the second degree is a Class A misdemeanor. [1997 c.697 §1; 2001 c.330 §1; 2009 c.877 §1; 2013 c.1 §11; 2015 c.321 §§1,4; 2016 c.72 §11]

Note: 163.700, 163.701 and 163.702 were enacted into law by the Legislative Assembly but were not added to or made a part of ORS chapter 163 or any series therein by legislative action. See Preface to Oregon Revised Statutes for further explanation.

163.701 Invasion of personal privacy in the first degree. (1) Except as provided in ORS 163.702, a person commits the crime of invasion of personal privacy in the first degree if:

(a)(A) The person knowingly makes or records a photograph, motion picture, videotape or other visual recording of another person in a state of nudity without the consent of the other person; and

(B) At the time the visual recording is made or recorded the person being recorded is in a place and circumstances where the person has a reasonable expectation of personal privacy; or

(b) The person violates ORS 163.700 and, at the time of the offense, has a prior conviction for:

(A) Invasion of personal privacy in any degree, public indecency, private indecency or a sex crime as defined in ORS 163A.005; or

(B) The statutory counterpart of an offense described in subparagraph (A) of this paragraph in another jurisdiction.

(2)(a) Invasion of personal privacy in the first degree is a Class C felony.

(b) The Oregon Criminal Justice Commission shall classify invasion of personal privacy in the first degree as crime category 6 of the sentencing guidelines grid of the commission.

(3) The court may designate invasion of personal privacy in the first degree as a sex crime under ORS 163A.005 if the court finds that the circumstances of the offense require the defendant to register and report as a sex offender for the safety of the community. [2015 c.645 §2]

Note: See note under 163.700.

163.702 Exceptions to ORS 163.700 and 163.701. (1) The provisions of ORS 163.700 and 163.701 do not apply to:

(a) Any legitimate medical procedure performed by or under the direction of a person licensed to provide medical service for the purpose of medical diagnosis, treatment, education or research, including, but not limited to, the recording of medical procedures; and

(b) Any activity undertaken in the course of bona fide law enforcement or corrections activity or necessary to the proper functioning of the criminal justice system, including but not limited to the operation and management of jails, prisons and other youth and adult corrections facilities.

(2) The provisions of ORS 163.701 (1)(a) do not apply to a visual recording of a person under 12 years of age if:

(a) The person who makes or records the visual recording is the father, mother, sibling, grandparent, aunt, uncle or first cousin, by blood, adoption or marriage, of the person under 12 years of age; and

(b) The visual recording is made or recorded for a purpose other than arousing or gratifying the sexual desire of the person or another person. [1997 c.697 §2; 2009 c.877 §2; 2015 c.645 §7]

Note: See note under 163.700.

MISCELLANEOUS

163.705 Polygraph examination of victims in certain criminal cases prohibited. No district attorney or other law enforcement officer or investigator involved in the investigation or prosecution of crimes, or any employee thereof, shall require any complaining witness in a case involving the use of force, violence, duress, menace or threat of physical injury in the commission of any sex crime under ORS 163.305 to 163.575, to submit to a polygraph examination as a prerequisite to filing an accusatory pleading. [1981 c.877 §1]

163.707 Forfeiture of motor vehicle used in drive-by shooting. (1) A motor vehicle used by the owner in a drive-by shooting is subject to civil in rem forfeiture.

(2) Seizure and forfeiture proceedings under this section shall be conducted in accordance with ORS chapter 131A.

(3) As used in this section, "drive-by shooting" means discharge of a firearm from a motor vehicle while committing or attempting to commit:

(a) Aggravated murder under ORS 163.095;

(b) Murder under ORS 163.115;

(c) Manslaughter in any degree under ORS 163.118 or 163.125;

(d) Assault in any degree under ORS 163.160, 163.165, 163.175 or 163.185;

(e) Menacing under ORS 163.190;

(f) Recklessly endangering another person under ORS 163.195;

(g) Assaulting a public safety officer under ORS 163.208; or

(h) Intimidation in any degree under ORS 166.155 or 166.165. [1999 c.870 §1; 2009 c.78 §57]

Note: 163.707 was enacted into law by the Legislative Assembly but was not added to or made a part of ORS chapter 163 or any series therein by legislative action. See Preface to Oregon Revised Statutes for further explanation.

163.709 Unlawful directing of light from a laser pointer. (1) A person commits the offense of unlawful directing of light from a laser pointer if the person knowingly directs light from a laser pointer at another person without the consent of the other person and the other person is:

(a) A peace officer as defined in ORS 161.015 who is acting in the course of official duty; or

(b) A uniformed private security professional as defined in ORS 181A.840 who is on duty.

(2) The offense described in this section, unlawful directing of light from a laser pointer, is a Class A misdemeanor.

(3) As used in this section, "laser pointer" means a device that emits light amplified by the stimulated emission of radiation that is visible to the human eye. [1999 c.757 §1; 2005 c.447 §9]

Note: 163.709 was enacted into law by the Legislative Assembly but was not added to or made a part of ORS chapter 163 or any series therein by legislative action. See Preface to Oregon Revised Statutes for further explanation.

163.715 Unlawful use of a global positioning system device. (1) A person commits the crime of unlawful use of a global positioning system device if the person knowingly affixes a global positioning system device to a motor vehicle without consent of the owner of the motor vehicle.

(2)(a) Except as provided in paragraph (b) of this subsection, unlawful use of a global positioning system device is a Class A misdemeanor.

(b) Unlawful use of a global positioning system device is a Class C felony if, at the time of the offense, the person:

(A) Has been previously convicted of stalking under ORS 163.732, violating a court's stalking order under ORS 163.750 or committing an equivalent crime in another jurisdiction; or

(B) Is the subject of a citation issued under ORS 163.735, an order issued under ORS 30.866, 107.700 to 107.735 or 163.738 or another court order prohibiting the person from contacting another person.

(3) This section does not apply to:

(a) A police officer who affixes a global positioning system device to a motor vehicle pursuant to a warrant or court order; or

(b) A person who affixes a global positioning system device to a motor vehicle operated by a motor carrier.

(4) As used in this section:

(a) "Global positioning system device" means an electronic device that permits the tracking of a person or object by means of global positioning system coordinates.

(b) "Motor carrier" has the meaning given that term in ORS 825.005.

(c) "Police officer" has the meaning given that term in ORS 133.525. [2017 c.649 §1]

Note: 163.715 was enacted into law by the Legislative Assembly but was not added to or made a part of ORS chapter 163 or any series therein by legislative action. See Preface to Oregon Revised Statutes for further explanation.

STALKING

163.730 Definitions for ORS 30.866 and 163.730 to 163.750. As used in ORS 30.866 and 163.730 to 163.750, unless the context requires otherwise:

(1) "Alarm" means to cause apprehension or fear resulting from the perception of danger.

(2) "Coerce" means to restrain, compel or dominate by force or threat.

(3) "Contact" includes but is not limited to:

(a) Coming into the visual or physical presence of the other person;

(b) Following the other person;

(c) Waiting outside the home, property, place of work or school of the other person or of a member of that person's family or household;

(d) Sending or making written or electronic communications in any form to the other person;

(e) Speaking with the other person by any means;

(f) Communicating with the other person through a third person;

(g) Committing a crime against the other person;

(h) Communicating with a third person who has some relationship to the other person with the intent of affecting the third person's relationship with the other person;

(i) Communicating with business entities with the intent of affecting some right or interest of the other person;

(j) Damaging the other person's home, property, place of work or school;

(k) Delivering directly or through a third person any object to the home, property, place of work or school of the other person; or

(L) Service of process or other legal documents unless the other person is served as provided in ORCP 7 or 9.

(4) "Household member" means any person residing in the same residence as the victim.

(5) "Immediate family" means father, mother, child, sibling, spouse, grandparent, stepparent and stepchild.

(6) "Law enforcement officer" means:

(a) A person employed in this state as a police officer by:

(A) A county sheriff, constable or marshal;

(B) A police department established by a university under ORS 352.121 or 353.125; or

(C) A municipal or state police agency; or

(b) An authorized tribal police officer as defined in ORS 181A.680.

(7) "Repeated" means two or more times.

(8) "School" means a public or private institution of learning or a child care facility. [1993 c.626 §1; 1995 c.278 §27; 1995 c.353 §1; 2001 c.870 §1; 2007 c.71 §46; 2009 c.359 §2; 2011 c.644 §§24,66,73; 2013 c.180 §§25,26; 2015 c.174 §12]

Note: 163.730 to 163.753 were enacted into law by the Legislative Assembly but were not added to or made a part of ORS chapter 163 or any series therein by legislative action. See Preface to Oregon Revised Statutes for further explanation.

163.732 Stalking. (1) A person commits the crime of stalking if:

(a) The person knowingly alarms or coerces another person or a member of that person's immediate family or household by engaging in repeated and unwanted contact with the other person;

(b) It is objectively reasonable for a person in the victim's situation to have been alarmed or coerced by the contact; and

(c) The repeated and unwanted contact causes the victim reasonable apprehension regarding the personal safety of the victim or a member of the victim's immediate family or household.

(2)(a) Stalking is a Class A misdemeanor.

(b) Notwithstanding paragraph (a) of this subsection, stalking is a Class C felony if the person has a prior conviction for:

(A) Stalking; or

(B) Violating a court's stalking protective order.

(c) When stalking is a Class C felony pursuant to paragraph (b) of this subsection, stalking shall be classified as a person felony and as crime category 8 of the sentencing guidelines grid of the Oregon Criminal Justice Commission. [1993 c.626 §2; 1995 c.353 §2]

Note: See note under 163.730.

163.735 Citation; form. (1) Upon a complaint initiated as provided in ORS 163.744, a law enforcement officer shall issue a citation ordering the person to appear in court within three judicial days and show cause why the court should not enter a court's stalking protective order when the officer has probable cause to believe that:

(a) The person intentionally, knowingly or recklessly engages in repeated and unwanted contact with the other person or a member of that person's immediate family or household thereby alarming or coercing the other person;

(b) It is objectively reasonable for a person in the victim's situation to have been alarmed or coerced by the contact; and

(c) The repeated and unwanted contact causes the victim reasonable apprehension regarding the personal safety of the victim or a member of the victim's immediate family or household.

(2) The Department of State Police shall develop and distribute a form for the citation. The form shall be uniform throughout the state and shall contain substantially the following in addition to any other material added by the department:

OFFICER:_____
AGENCY:_____
PETITIONER:_____
PERSON TO BE PROTECTED IF OTHER THAN PETITIONER:_____
RESPONDENT:_____

On behalf of petitioner, I affirm that I am a law enforcement officer in the State of Oregon.

You, the respondent, must appear at _____ (name and location of court at which respondent is to appear) on _____ (date and time respondent is to appear in court). At this hearing, you must be prepared to establish why the court should not enter a court's stalking protective order which shall be for an unlimited duration unless limited by law or court order. If you fail to appear at this hearing, the court shall immediately issue a warrant for your arrest and shall enter a court's stalking protective order.

If the court issues a stalking protective order at this hearing, and while the protective order is in effect, federal law may prohibit you from:

Traveling across state lines or tribal land lines with the intent to violate this order and then violating this order.

Causing the person protected by the order, if the person is your spouse or intimate partner, to cross state lines or tribal land lines for your purpose of violating the order.

Possessing, receiving, shipping or transporting any firearm or firearm ammunition.

Whether or not a stalking protective order is in effect, federal law may prohibit you from:

Traveling across state lines or tribal land lines with the intent to injure or harass another person and during, or because of, that travel placing that person in reasonable fear of death or serious bodily injury to that person or to a member of that person's immediate family.

Traveling across state lines or tribal land lines with the intent to injure your spouse or intimate partner and then intentionally committing a crime of violence causing bodily injury to that person.

Causing your spouse or intimate partner to travel across state lines or tribal land lines if your intent is to cause bodily injury to that person or if the travel results in your causing bodily injury to that person.

It has been alleged that you have alarmed or coerced the petitioner, or person to be protected if other than the petitioner. If you engage in contact that alarms or coerces the petitioner, or person to be protected if other than the petitioner, in violation of ORS 163.732, you may be arrested for the crime of stalking.

Date: _____ Time: _____

Signed: _____
　　(Respondent)
Signed: _____
　　(Law enforcement officer).

_____ [1993 c.626 §3; 1995 c.353 §3; 1999 c.1052 §10]

Note: See note under 163.730.

163.738 Effect of citation; contents; hearing; court's order; use of statements made at hearing. (1)(a) A citation shall notify the respondent of a circuit court hearing where the respondent shall appear at the place and time set forth in the citation. The citation shall contain:

(A) The name of the court at which the respondent is to appear;

(B) The name of the respondent;

(C) A copy of the stalking complaint;

(D) The date, time and place at which the citation was issued;

(E) The name of the law enforcement officer who issued the citation;

(F) The time, date and place at which the respondent is to appear in court;

(G) Notice to the respondent that failure to appear at the time, date and place set forth in the citation shall result in the respondent's arrest and entry of a court's stalking protective order; and

(H) Notice to the respondent of potential liability under federal law for the possession or purchase of firearms or firearm ammunition and for other acts prohibited by 18 U.S.C. 2261 to 2262.

(b) The officer shall notify the petitioner in writing of the place and time set for the hearing.

(2)(a) The hearing shall be held as indicated in the citation. At the hearing, the petitioner may appear in person or by telephonic appearance. The respondent shall be given the opportunity to show cause why a court's stalking protective order should not be entered. The hearing may be continued for up to 30 days. The court may enter:

(A) A temporary stalking protective order pending further proceedings; or

(B) A court's stalking protective order if the court finds by a preponderance of the evidence that:

(i) The person intentionally, knowingly or recklessly engages in repeated and unwanted contact with the other person or a member of that person's immediate family or household thereby alarming or coercing the other person;

(ii) It is objectively reasonable for a person in the victim's situation to have been alarmed or coerced by the contact; and

(iii) The repeated and unwanted contact causes the victim reasonable apprehension regarding the personal safety of the victim or a member of the victim's immediate family or household.

(b) In the order, the court shall specify the conduct from which the respondent is to refrain, which may include all contact listed in ORS 163.730 and any attempt to make contact listed in ORS 163.730. The order is of unlimited duration unless limited by law. If the respondent was provided notice and an opportunity to be heard, the court shall also include in the order, when appropriate, terms and findings sufficient under 18 U.S.C. 922 (d)(8) and (g)(8) to affect the respondent's ability to possess firearms and ammunition or engage in activities involving firearms.

(3) The circuit court may enter an order under this section against a minor respondent without appointment of a guardian ad litem.

(4) If the respondent fails to appear at the time, date and place specified in the citation, the circuit court shall issue a warrant of arrest as provided in ORS 133.110 in order to ensure the appearance of the respondent at court and shall enter a court's stalking protective order.

(5) The circuit court may also order the respondent to undergo mental health evaluation and, if indicated by the evaluation, treatment. If the respondent is without sufficient resources to obtain the evaluation or treatment, or both, the court shall refer the respondent to the mental health agency designated by the community mental health director for evaluation or treatment, or both.

(6) If the circuit court, the mental health evaluator or any other persons have probable cause to believe that the respondent is dangerous to self or others or is unable to provide for basic personal needs, the court shall initiate commitment procedures as provided in ORS 426.070 or 426.180.

(7) A law enforcement officer shall report the results of any investigation arising from a complaint under ORS 163.744 to the district attorney within three days after presentation of the complaint.

(8) Except for purposes of impeachment, a statement made by the respondent at a hearing under this section may not be used as evidence in a prosecution for stalking as defined in ORS 163.732 or for violating a court's stalking protective order as defined in ORS 163.750. [1993 c.626 §4; 1995 c.353 §4; 1997 c.863 §6; 1999 c.1052 §2; 2003 c.292 §2]

Note: See note under 163.730.

163.741 Service of stalking protective order; entry of order into law enforcement data systems. (1) Service of a stalking protective order shall be made by personal delivery of a copy of the order to the respondent. The respondent need not be served if an order of the court indicates that the respondent appeared in person before the court.

(2) Whenever a stalking protective order, as authorized by ORS 163.735 or 163.738, is served on a respondent, the person serving the order shall immediately deliver to the county sheriff a true copy of proof of service, on which it is stated that personal service of the order was made on the respondent, and a copy of the order. Proof of service may be made by affidavit or by declaration under penalty of perjury in the form required by ORCP 1 E. If service of the order is not required under subsection (1) of this section, a copy of the order must be delivered to the sheriff by the court. Upon receipt of a copy of the order and notice of completion of any required service by a member of a law enforcement agency, the county sheriff shall immediately enter the order into the Law Enforcement Data System maintained by the Department of State Police and into the databases of the National Crime Information Center of the United States Department of Justice. If the order was served on the respondent by a person other than a member of a law enforcement agency, the county sheriff shall enter the order into the Law Enforcement Data System and databases of the National Crime Information Center upon receipt of a true copy of proof of service. The sheriff shall provide the complainant with a true copy of any required proof of service. Entry into the Law Enforcement Data System constitutes notice to all law enforcement agencies of the existence of the order. Law enforcement agencies shall establish procedures adequate to ensure that an officer at the scene of an alleged violation of the order may be informed of the existence and terms of the order. The order is fully enforceable in any county in this state.

(3) When a stalking protective order has been entered into the Law Enforcement Data System and the databases of the National Crime Information Center of the United States Department of Justice under subsection (1) of this section, a county sheriff shall cooperate with a request from a law enforcement agency from any other jurisdiction to verify the existence of the stalking protective order or to transmit a copy of the order to the requesting jurisdiction.

(4) When a stalking protective order is terminated by order of the court, the clerk of the court shall immediately deliver a copy of the termination order to the county sheriff with whom the original order was filed. Upon receipt of the termination order, the county sheriff shall promptly remove the original order from the Law Enforcement Data System and the databases of the National Crime Information Center of the United States Department of Justice. [1993 c.626 §5; 1999 c.1052 §3; 2007 c.255 §11; 2009 c.364 §3; 2011 c.269 §6; 2015 c.121 §25]

Note: See note under 163.730.

163.744 Initiation of action seeking citation; complaint form. (1) A person may initiate an action seeking a citation under ORS 163.735 by presenting a complaint to a law enforcement officer or to any law enforcement agency. The complaint shall be a statement setting forth with particularity the conduct that is the basis for the complaint. The petitioner must affirm the truth of the facts in the complaint.

(2) The Department of State Police shall develop and distribute the form of the complaint. The form shall include the standards for reviewing the complaint and for action. The form shall be uniform throughout the state and shall include substantially the following material:

STALKING COMPLAINT

Name of petitioner (person presenting complaint): _____
Name of person being stalked if other than the petitioner: _____

_____
Name of respondent (alleged stalker):

_____
Description of respondent:
_____
_____
_____

Length of period of conduct:
_____

Description of relationship (if any) between petitioner or person being stalked, if other than the petitioner, and respondent:
_____
_____

Description of contact:
_____
_____
_____
_____
_____

Subscribed to and affirmed by:
_____

(signature of petitioner)
(printed name of petitioner) _____
    Dated: _____

---

(3) A parent may present a complaint to protect a minor child. A guardian may present a complaint to protect a dependent person.

(4) By signing the complaint, a person is making a sworn statement for purposes of ORS 162.055 to 162.425. [1993 c.626 §6; 1995 c.353 §5]

Note: See note under 163.730.

163.747 [1993 c.626 §7; repealed by 1995 c.353 §10]

163.750 Violating a court's stalking protective order. (1) A person commits the crime of violating a court's stalking protective order when:

(a) The person has been served with a court's stalking protective order as provided in ORS 30.866 or 163.738 or if further service was waived under ORS 163.741 because the person appeared before the court;

(b) The person, subsequent to the service of the order, has engaged intentionally, knowingly or recklessly in conduct prohibited by the order; and

(c) If the conduct is prohibited contact as defined in ORS 163.730 (3)(d), (e), (f), (h) or (i), the subsequent conduct has created reasonable apprehension regarding the personal safety of a person protected by the order.

(2)(a) Violating a court's stalking protective order is a Class A misdemeanor.

(b) Notwithstanding paragraph (a) of this subsection, violating a court's stalking protective order is a Class C felony if the person has a prior conviction for:

(A) Stalking; or

(B) Violating a court's stalking protective order.

(c) When violating a court's stalking protective order is a Class C felony pursuant to paragraph (b) of this subsection, violating a court's stalking protective order shall be classified as a person felony and as crime category 8 of the sentencing guidelines grid of the Oregon Criminal Justice Commission. [1993 c.626 §8; 1995 c.353 §7]

Note: See note under 163.730.

163.753 Immunity of officer acting in good faith. A law enforcement officer acting in good faith shall not be liable in any civil action for issuing or not issuing a citation under ORS 163.735. [1993 c.626 §11; 1995 c.353 §9]

Note: See note under 163.730.

163.755 Conduct for which stalking protective order may not be issued. (1) Nothing in ORS 30.866 or 163.730 to 163.750 shall be construed to permit the issuance of a court's stalking protective order under ORS 30.866 or 163.738, the issuance of a citation under ORS 163.735, a criminal prosecution under ORS 163.732 or a civil action under ORS 30.866:
(a) For conduct that is authorized or protected by the labor laws of this state or of the United States.
(b) By or on behalf of a person who is in the legal or physical custody of a law enforcement unit or is in custody under ORS chapter 419C.
(c) By or on behalf of a person not described in paragraph (b) of this subsection to or against another person who:
(A) Is a parole and probation officer or an officer, employee or agent of a law enforcement unit, a county juvenile department or the Oregon Youth Authority; and
(B) Is acting within the scope of the other person's official duties.
(2) As used in this section, "law enforcement unit" and "parole and probation officer" have the meanings given those terms in ORS 181A.355. [1995 c.353 §8; 2003 c.292 §1]

Note: 163.755 was enacted into law by the Legislative Assembly but was not added to or made a part of ORS chapter 163 or any series therein by legislative action. See Preface to Oregon Revised Statutes for further explanation.

SEXUAL ABUSE RESTRAINING ORDERS

163.760 Definitions for ORS 163.760 to 163.777. As used in ORS 163.760 to 163.777:
(1) "Declaration under penalty of perjury," "family or household members," "interfere," "intimidate," "menace" and "molest" have the meanings given those terms in ORS 107.705.
(2) "Sexual abuse" means sexual contact with:
(a) A person who does not consent to the sexual contact; or
(b) A person who is considered incapable of consenting to a sexual act under ORS 163.315, unless the sexual contact would be lawful under ORS 163.325 or 163.345.
(3) "Sexual contact" has the meaning given that term in ORS 163.305. [2013 c.687 §1; 2015 c.121 §21]

Note: 163.760 to 163.777 were enacted into law by the Legislative Assembly but were not added to or made a part of ORS chapter 163 or any series therein by legislative action. See Preface to Oregon Revised Statutes for further explanation.

163.763 Petition to circuit court for relief; burden of proof. (1) A person who has been subjected to sexual abuse and who reasonably fears for the person's physical safety may petition the circuit court for a restraining order if:
(a) The person and the respondent are not family or household members;
(b) The respondent is at least 18 years of age; and
(c) The respondent is not prohibited from contacting the person pursuant to a foreign restraining order as defined in ORS 24.190, an order issued under ORS 30.866, 124.015, 124.020, 163.738 or 419B.845 or an order entered in a criminal action.
(2)(a) A petition seeking relief under ORS 163.760 to 163.777 must be filed in the circuit court for the county in which the petitioner or the respondent resides. The petition may be filed, without the appointment of a guardian ad litem, by a person who is at least 12 years of age or by a parent or lawful guardian of a person who is under 18 years of age.
(b) The petition must allege that:
(A) The petitioner reasonably fears for the petitioner's physical safety with respect to the respondent; and
(B) The respondent subjected the petitioner to sexual abuse within the 180 days preceding the filing of the petition.
(c) The petition must include allegations made under oath or affirmation or a declaration under penalty of perjury.
(d) The petitioner has the burden of proving a claim under ORS 163.760 to 163.777 by a preponderance of the evidence.
(3) The following periods of time may not be counted for the purpose of computing the 180-day period described in this section and ORS 163.765:
(a) Any time during which the respondent is incarcerated.
(b) Any time during which the respondent has a principal residence more than 100 miles from the principal residence of the petitioner.

(c) Any time during which the respondent is subject to an order described in subsection (1)(c) of this section. [2013 c.687 §2; 2015 c.121 §22]

Note: See note under 163.760.

163.765 Restraining order; service of order; request for hearing. (1) When a petition is filed in accordance with ORS 163.763, the circuit court shall hold an ex parte hearing in person or by telephone on the day the petition is filed or on the following judicial day. Upon a finding that it is objectively reasonable for a person in the petitioner's situation to fear for the person's physical safety if an order granting relief under ORS 163.760 to 163.777 is not entered and that the respondent has subjected the petitioner to sexual abuse within the 180 days preceding the filing of the petition, the circuit court:

(a) Shall enter an order restraining the respondent from contacting the petitioner and from intimidating, molesting, interfering with or menacing the petitioner, or attempting to intimidate, molest, interfere with or menace the petitioner.

(b) If the petitioner requests, may order:

(A) That the respondent be restrained from contacting the petitioner's children or family or household members;

(B) That the respondent be restrained from entering, or attempting to enter, a reasonable area surrounding the petitioner's residence;

(C) That the respondent be restrained from intimidating, molesting, interfering with or menacing any children or family or household members of the petitioner, or attempting to intimidate, molest, interfere with or menace any children or family or household members of the petitioner;

(D) That the respondent be restrained from entering, or attempting to enter, any premises and a reasonable area surrounding the premises when necessary to prevent the respondent from intimidating, molesting, interfering with or menacing the petitioner or the petitioner's children or family or household members; and

(E) Other relief necessary to provide for the safety and welfare of the petitioner or the petitioner's children or family or household members.

(2) If the respondent is restrained from entering or attempting to enter an area surrounding the petitioner's residence or any other premises, the restraining order must specifically describe the area or premises.

(3) When the circuit court enters a restraining order under this section, the court shall set a security amount for the violation of the order.

(4) If the circuit court enters a restraining order under subsection (1) of this section:

(a) The clerk of the court shall provide, without charge, the number of certified true copies of the petition and the restraining order necessary to provide the petitioner with one copy and to effect service and shall have a true copy of the petition and the restraining order delivered to the county sheriff for service upon the respondent, unless the circuit court finds that further service is unnecessary because the respondent appeared in person before the court. In addition and upon request by the petitioner, the clerk of the court shall provide the petitioner, without charge, two exemplified copies of the petition and the restraining order.

(b) The county sheriff shall serve the respondent personally unless the petitioner elects to have the respondent served personally by another party. Proof of service shall be made in accordance with ORS 163.773. When the restraining order does not contain the respondent's date of birth and service is effected by the sheriff, the sheriff shall verify the respondent's date of birth with the respondent and shall record that date on the restraining order or proof of service entered into the Law Enforcement Data System under ORS 163.773.

(5) If the county sheriff:

(a) Determines that the restraining order and petition are incomplete, the sheriff shall return the restraining order and petition to the clerk of the court. The clerk of the court shall notify the petitioner, at the address provided by the petitioner, of the error or omission.

(b) Cannot complete service within 10 days after accepting the restraining order and petition, the sheriff shall notify the petitioner, at the address provided by the petitioner, that the documents have not been served. If the petitioner does not respond within 10 days, the sheriff shall hold the restraining order and petition for future service and file a return to the clerk of the court showing that service was not completed.

(6)(a) Within 30 days after a restraining order is served under this section, the respondent may request a circuit court hearing upon any relief granted.

(b) If the respondent requests a hearing under paragraph (a) of this subsection, the clerk of the court shall notify the petitioner of the date and time of the hearing and shall supply the petitioner with a copy of the respondent's request for a hearing. The petitioner shall give the clerk of the court information sufficient to allow such notification.

(7) If the respondent fails to request a hearing within 30 days after a restraining order is served, the restraining order is confirmed by operation of law.

(8) A restraining order entered under this section is effective for a period of one year, unless the restraining order is renewed, modified or terminated in accordance with ORS 163.760 to 163.777. [2013 c.687 §3]

Note: See note under 163.760.

163.767 Hearing; order; certificate of compliance; consent agreement. (1) If the respondent requests a hearing under ORS 163.765 (6), the circuit court shall hold the hearing within 21 days after the request. At the hearing, the circuit court may terminate or modify the restraining order issued under ORS 163.765.

(2)(a) If service of a notice of hearing is inadequate to provide a party with sufficient notice of the hearing, the circuit court may extend the date of the hearing for up to five days so that the party may seek representation.

(b) If one party is represented by an attorney at the hearing, the circuit court may extend the date of the hearing for up to five days at the other party's request so that the other party may seek representation.

(3) If the circuit court continues the restraining order issued under ORS 163.765, with or without modification, at a hearing about which the respondent received actual notice and the opportunity to be heard, the court shall include in the restraining order a certificate in substantially the following form in a separate section immediately above the signature of the judge:

CERTIFICATE OF COMPLIANCE
WITH THE VIOLENCE
AGAINST WOMEN ACT OF 1994

This protective order meets all full faith and credit requirements of the Violence Against Women Act of 1994, 18 U.S.C. 2265. This court has jurisdiction over the parties and the subject matter. The respondent was afforded notice and timely opportunity to be heard as provided by the law of this jurisdiction. This protective order is valid and entitled to enforcement in this and all other jurisdictions.

---

(4) The circuit court may approve a consent agreement if the court determines that the agreement provides sufficient protections to the petitioner. The circuit court may not approve a term in a consent agreement that provides for restraint of a party to the agreement unless the other party petitioned for and was granted a restraining order issued under ORS 163.765.

(5) A restraining order entered under this section, or a consent agreement entered into under this section, shall continue for a period of one year from the date of the restraining order issued under ORS 163.765, unless the restraining order is renewed, modified or terminated in accordance with ORS 163.775. [2013 c.687 §4]

Note: See note under 163.760.

163.770 Appearance by telephone or electronic communication device. (1) A party may file a motion under ORS 45.400 requesting that the circuit court allow the appearance of the party or a witness by telephone or by other two-way electronic communication device in a proceeding under ORS 163.760 to 163.777.

(2) In determining whether to allow written notice less than 30 days before the proceeding under ORS 45.400 (2), the circuit court shall consider the expedited nature of a proceeding under ORS 163.760 to 163.777.

(3) In addition to the factors listed in ORS 45.400 (3)(b) that would support a finding of good cause, the circuit court shall consider whether the safety or welfare of the party or witness would be threatened if testimony were required to be provided in person at a proceeding under ORS 163.760 to 163.777.

(4) A motion or good cause determination is not required for ex parte hearings held by telephone under ORS 163.765. [2013 c.687 §5; 2017 c.240 §4]

Note: See note under 163.760.

163.773 Enforcement of restraining order; service by sheriff; termination order; contempt proceeding. (1)(a) When a restraining order is issued in accordance with ORS 163.760 to 163.777 and the person to be restrained has actual notice of the restraining order, the clerk of the court or any other person serving the petition and the restraining order shall immediately deliver to a county sheriff copies of the petition and the restraining order and a true copy of proof of service on which it is stated that the petition and the restraining order were served personally on the respondent. Proof of service may be made by affidavit or by declaration under penalty of perjury. If a restraining order entered by the circuit court recites that the respondent appeared in person before the court, the necessity for service of the restraining order and proof of service is waived.

(b) Upon receipt of a copy of the restraining order and notice of completion of any required service by a member of a law enforcement agency, the county sheriff shall immediately enter the restraining order into the Law Enforcement Data System maintained by the Department of State Police and the databases of the National Crime Information Center of the United States Department of Justice. If the petition and the restraining order were served on the respondent by a person other than a member of a law enforcement agency, the county sheriff shall enter the restraining order into the Law Enforcement Data System and the databases of the National Crime Information Center upon receipt of a true copy of proof of service. The sheriff shall provide the petitioner with a true copy of any required proof of service.

(c) Entry into the Law Enforcement Data System constitutes notice to all law enforcement agencies of the existence of the restraining order. Law enforcement agencies shall establish procedures adequate to ensure that an officer at the scene of an alleged violation of the restraining order may be informed of the existence and terms of the restraining order. The restraining order is fully enforceable in any county or tribal land in this state.

(d) When a restraining order has been entered into the Law Enforcement Data System and the databases of the National Crime Information Center of the United States Department of Justice under this subsection, a county sheriff shall cooperate with a request from a law enforcement agency from any other jurisdiction to verify the existence of the restraining order or to transmit a copy of the restraining order to the requesting jurisdiction.

(2) A sheriff may serve a restraining order issued under ORS 163.760 to 163.777 in the county in which the sheriff was elected and in any county that is adjacent to the county in which the sheriff was elected.

(3)(a) A sheriff may serve and enter into the Law Enforcement Data System a copy of a restraining order issued under ORS 163.760 to 163.777 that was transmitted to the sheriff by a circuit court or law enforcement agency through an electronic communication device. Before transmitting a copy of a restraining order to a sheriff under this subsection through an electronic communication device, the person transmitting the copy must receive confirmation from the sheriff's office that an electronic communication device is available and operating.

(b) For purposes of this subsection, "electronic communication device" means a device by which any kind of electronic communication can be made, including but not limited to communication by telephonic facsimile and electronic mail.

(4) When a circuit court enters an order terminating a restraining order issued under ORS 163.760 to 163.777 before the expiration date, the clerk of the court shall immediately deliver a copy of the termination order to the county sheriff with whom the original restraining order was filed. Upon receipt of the termination order, the county sheriff shall promptly remove the original restraining order from the Law Enforcement Data System and the databases of the National Crime Information Center of the United States Department of Justice.

(5)(a) A contempt proceeding for an alleged violation of a restraining order issued under ORS 163.760 to 163.777 must be conducted by the circuit court that issued the restraining order or by the circuit court for the county in which the alleged violation of the restraining order occurs. If contempt proceedings are initiated in the circuit court for the county in which the alleged violation of the restraining order occurs, the person initiating the contempt proceedings shall file with the court a copy of the restraining order that is certified by the clerk of the court that originally issued the restraining order. Upon filing of the certified copy of the restraining order, the circuit court shall enforce the restraining order as though that court had originally issued the restraining order.

(b) Pending a contempt hearing for an alleged violation of a restraining order issued under ORS 163.760 to 163.777, a person arrested and taken into custody pursuant to ORS 133.310 may be released as provided in ORS 135.230 to 135.290.

(c) Service of process or other legal documents upon the petitioner is not a violation of a restraining order entered under ORS 163.760 to 163.777 if the petitioner is served as provided in ORCP 7 or 9. [2013 c.687 §6; 2015 c.121 §23]

Note: See note under 163.760.

163.775 Renewal and modification of restraining order. (1)(a) A circuit court may renew a restraining order entered under ORS 163.760 to 163.777 upon a finding that it is objectively reasonable for a person in the petitioner's situation to fear for the person's physical safety if the restraining order is not renewed. A finding that the respondent has subjected the petitioner to additional sexual abuse is not required.

(b) A circuit court may renew a restraining order on the basis of an ex parte petition alleging facts supporting the required finding. The petition must include allegations made under oath or affirmation or a declaration under penalty of perjury. If the renewal order is granted, the provisions of ORS 163.765 (4) to (8) and 163.767 (3) apply, except that the court may hear no issue other than the basis for renewal, unless requested in the hearing request form and thereafter agreed to by the petitioner. The circuit court shall hold a hearing required under this paragraph within 21 days after the respondent's request.

(2) At any time after the time period set forth in ORS 163.765 (6):

(a) A party may request that the circuit court modify terms in the restraining order for good cause shown.

(b) A petitioner may request that the circuit court remove terms in the restraining order or make terms in the order less restrictive. Application to the circuit court under this paragraph may be by ex parte motion.

(3) The clerk of the court shall provide without charge the number of certified true copies of the request for modification of the restraining order and notice of hearing necessary to effect service and, at the election of the party requesting the modification, shall have a true copy of the request and notice delivered to the county sheriff for service upon the other party.

(4) The county sheriff shall serve the other party with a request for modification of a restraining order under subsection (2)(a) of this section by personal service, unless the party requesting the modification elects to have the other party personally served by a private party or unless otherwise ordered by the circuit court.

(5) The provisions of ORS 163.767 (3) apply to a modification of a restraining order under this section.

(6) The clerk of the court shall deliver a copy of an order of modification entered under this section to the county sheriff for service and entry into the Law Enforcement Data System as provided in ORS 163.773.

(7)(a) The county sheriff shall serve a copy of an order of modification:

(A) Entered under subsection (2)(a) of this section by personal service on the nonrequesting party.

(B) Entered under subsection (2)(b) of this section by mailing a copy of the order of modification to the respondent by first class mail.

(b) If the order of modification recites that the respondent appeared in person before the circuit court, the necessity for service of the order and proof of service is waived.

(8) A restraining order entered under ORS 163.760 to 163.777 may not be terminated on motion of the petitioner, unless the motion is notarized. [2013 c.687 §7; 2015 c.121 §24]

Note: See note under 163.760.

163.777 Fees or undertaking may not be required; forms and brochures. (1)(a) A filing fee, service fee or hearing fee may not be charged for proceedings seeking only the relief provided under ORS 163.760 to 163.777.

(b) An undertaking may not be required in any proceeding under ORS 163.760 to 163.777.

(2) A proceeding under ORS 163.760 to 163.777 is in addition to any other available civil or criminal remedies.

(3)(a) After obtaining the approval of the Chief Justice of the Supreme Court, the Attorney General's Sexual Assault Task Force shall produce:

(A) The forms for petitions and restraining orders, hearing requests and any related forms for use under ORS 163.760 to 163.777; and

(B) An instructional brochure explaining the rights set forth in ORS 163.760 to 163.777.

(b) After obtaining the approval of the Chief Justice of the Supreme Court of the forms and instructional brochures produced pursuant to this subsection, the Attorney General's Sexual Assault Task Force shall provide the forms and copies of the instructional brochure to the clerks of the circuit court who shall make the forms and brochures available to the public. [2013 c.687 §8]

Note: The amendments to 163.777 by section 10, chapter 687, Oregon Laws 2013, become operative July 1, 2021. See section 9, chapter 687, Oregon Laws 2013. The text that is operative on and after July 1, 2021, is set forth for the user's convenience.

163.777. (1)(a) A filing fee, service fee or hearing fee may not be charged for proceedings seeking only the relief provided under ORS 163.760 to 163.777.

(b) An undertaking may not be required in any proceeding under ORS 163.760 to 163.777.

(2) A proceeding under ORS 163.760 to 163.777 is in addition to any other available civil or criminal remedies.

(3)(a) The State Court Administrator shall produce:

(A) The forms for petitions and restraining orders, hearing requests and any related forms for use under ORS 163.760 to 163.777; and

(B) An instructional brochure explaining the rights set forth in ORS 163.760 to 163.777.

(b) The State Court Administrator shall provide the forms and copies of the instructional brochure to the clerks of the circuit court who shall make the forms and brochures available to the public.

Note: See note under 163.760.

Chapter 163A — Sex Offender Reporting and Classification

REPORTING

163A.005 Definitions for ORS 163A.005 to 163A.235. As used in ORS 163A.005 to 163A.235:

(1) "Another United States court" means a federal court, a military court, the tribal court of a federally recognized Indian tribe or a court of:

(a) A state other than Oregon;

(b) The District of Columbia;

(c) The Commonwealth of Puerto Rico;

(d) Guam;

(e) American Samoa;

(f) The Commonwealth of the Northern Mariana Islands; or

(g) The United States Virgin Islands.

(2) "Attends" means is enrolled on a full-time or part-time basis.

(3)(a) "Correctional facility" means any place used for the confinement of persons:

(A) Charged with or convicted of a crime or otherwise confined under a court order.

(B) Found to be within the jurisdiction of the juvenile court for having committed an act that if committed by an adult would constitute a crime.

(b) "Correctional facility" applies to a state hospital or a secure intensive community inpatient facility only as to persons detained therein charged with or convicted of a crime, or detained therein after being found guilty except for insanity under ORS 161.290 to 161.370 or responsible except for insanity under ORS 419C.411.

(4) "Institution of higher education" means a public or private educational institution that provides a program of post-secondary education.

(5) "Sex crime" means:

(a) Rape in any degree;

(b) Sodomy in any degree;

(c) Unlawful sexual penetration in any degree;

(d) Sexual abuse in any degree;

(e) Incest with a child victim;

(f) Using a child in a display of sexually explicit conduct;

(g) Encouraging child sexual abuse in any degree;

(h) Transporting child pornography into the state;

(i) Paying for viewing a child's sexually explicit conduct;

(j) Compelling prostitution;

(k) Promoting prostitution;

(L) Kidnapping in the first degree if the victim was under 18 years of age;

(m) Contributing to the sexual delinquency of a minor;

(n) Sexual misconduct if the offender is at least 18 years of age;

(o) Possession of materials depicting sexually explicit conduct of a child in the first degree;

(p) Kidnapping in the second degree if the victim was under 18 years of age, except by a parent or by a person found to be within the jurisdiction of the juvenile court;

(q) Online sexual corruption of a child in any degree if the offender reasonably believed the child to be more than five years younger than the offender;

(r) Luring a minor, if:

(A) The offender reasonably believed the minor or, in the case of a police officer or agent of a police officer posing as a minor, the purported minor to be more than five years younger than the offender or under 16 years of age; and

(B) The court designates in the judgment that the offense is a sex crime;

(s) Sexual assault of an animal;

(t) Public indecency or private indecency, if the person has a prior conviction for a crime listed in this subsection;

(u) Trafficking in persons as described in ORS 163.266 (1)(b) or (c);

(v) Purchasing sex with a minor if the court designates the offense as a sex crime pursuant to ORS 163.413 (3)(d), or the offense is the defendant's second or subsequent conviction under ORS 163.413 (3)(b)(B);

(w) Invasion of personal privacy in the first degree, if the court designates the offense as a sex crime pursuant to ORS 163.701 (3);

(x) Any attempt to commit any of the crimes listed in paragraphs (a) to (w) of this subsection;

(y) Burglary, when committed with intent to commit any of the offenses listed in paragraphs (a) to (w) of this subsection; or

(z) Criminal conspiracy if the offender agrees with one or more persons to engage in or cause the performance of an offense listed in paragraphs (a) to (w) of this subsection.

(6) "Sex offender" means a person who:

(a) Has been convicted of a sex crime;

(b) Has been found guilty except for insanity of a sex crime;

(c) Has been convicted in another United States court of a crime:

(A) That would constitute a sex crime if committed in this state; or

(B) For which the person would have to register as a sex offender in that court's jurisdiction, or as required under federal law, regardless of whether the crime would constitute a sex crime in this state; or

(d) Is described in ORS 163A.025 (1).

(7) "Works" or "carries on a vocation" means full-time or part-time employment for more than 14 days within one calendar year whether financially compensated, volunteered or for the purpose of governmental or educational benefit. [Formerly 181.805]

163A.010 Reporting by sex offender discharged, paroled or released from correctional facility or another United States jurisdiction. (1) The agency to which a person reports under subsection (3) of this section shall complete a sex offender registration form concerning the person when the person reports under subsection (3) of this section.

(2) Subsection (3) of this section applies to a person who:

(a) Is discharged, paroled or released on any form of supervised or conditional release from a jail, prison or other correctional facility or detention facility in this state at which the person was confined as a result of:

(A) Conviction of a sex crime or a crime for which the person would have to register as a sex offender under federal law; or

(B) Having been found guilty except for insanity of a sex crime;

(b) Is paroled to this state under ORS 144.610 after being convicted in another United States court of a crime:

(A) That would constitute a sex crime if committed in this state; or

94

(B) For which the person would have to register as a sex offender in that court's jurisdiction, or as required under federal law, regardless of whether the crime would constitute a sex crime in this state; or

(c) Is discharged by the court under ORS 161.329 after having been found guilty except for insanity of a sex crime.

(3)(a) A person described in subsection (2) of this section shall report, in person, to the Department of State Police, a city police department or a county sheriff's office, in the county to which the person was discharged, paroled or released or in which the person was otherwise placed:

(A) Within 10 days following discharge, release on parole, post-prison supervision or other supervised or conditional release;

(B) Within 10 days of a change of residence;

(C) Once each year within 10 days of the person's birth date, regardless of whether the person changed residence;

(D) Within 10 days of the first day the person works at, carries on a vocation at or attends an institution of higher education; and

(E) Within 10 days of a change in work, vocation or attendance status at an institution of higher education.

(b) If a person required to report under this subsection has complied with the initial reporting requirement under paragraph (a)(A) of this subsection, the person shall subsequently report, in person, in the circumstances specified in paragraph (a) of this subsection, as applicable, to the Department of State Police, a city police department or a county sheriff's office, in the county of the person's last reported residence.

(c) Notwithstanding paragraphs (a) and (b) of this subsection, during the period of supervision or custody authorized by law, the Oregon Youth Authority may authorize a youth offender committed to its supervision and custody by order of the juvenile court or a person placed in its physical custody under ORS 137.124 or any other provision of law to report to the authority regardless of the youth offender's or the person's last reported residence.

(d) In the event that a person reports to the authority under this subsection, the authority shall register the person.

(e) The obligation to report under this subsection terminates if the conviction or adjudication that gave rise to the obligation is reversed or vacated or if the registrant is pardoned.

(4) As part of the registration and reporting requirements of this section:

(a) The person required to report shall:

(A) Provide the information necessary to complete the sex offender registration form and sign the form as required; and

(B) Submit to the requirements described in paragraph (b) of this subsection.

(b) The Department of State Police, Oregon Youth Authority, city police department or county sheriff's office:

(A) Shall photograph the person when the person initially reports under this section and each time the person reports annually under this section;

(B) May photograph the person or any identifying scars, marks or tattoos located on the person when the person reports under any of the circumstances described in this section; and

(C) Shall fingerprint the person if the person's fingerprints are not included in the record file of the Department of State Police. [Formerly 181.806; 2016 c.95 §4]

163A.015 Reporting by sex offender discharged, released or placed on probation by court or another United States jurisdiction. (1) The agency to which a person reports under subsection (4) of this section shall complete a sex offender registration form concerning the person when the person reports under subsection (4) of this section.

(2) Subsection (4) of this section applies to a person who is discharged, released or placed on probation:

(a) By the court after being convicted in this state of a sex crime;

(b) By a federal court after being convicted of a crime for which the person would have to register as a sex offender under federal law, regardless of whether the crime would constitute a sex crime in this state; or

(c) To or in this state under ORS 144.610 after being convicted in another United States court of a crime:

(A) That would constitute a sex crime if committed in this state; or

(B) For which the person would have to register as a sex offender in that court's jurisdiction, regardless of whether the crime would constitute a sex crime in this state.

(3) The court shall ensure that the person completes a form that documents the person's obligation to report under ORS 163A.010 or this section. No later than three working days after the person completes the form required by this subsection, the court shall ensure that the form is sent to the Department of State Police.

(4)(a) A person described in subsection (2) of this section shall report, in person, to the Department of State Police, a city police department or a county sheriff's office, in the county to which the person was discharged or released or in which the person was placed on probation:

(A) Within 10 days following discharge, release or placement on probation;

(B) Within 10 days of a change of residence;

(C) Once each year within 10 days of the person's birth date, regardless of whether the person changed residence;

(D) Within 10 days of the first day the person works at, carries on a vocation at or attends an institution of higher education; and

(E) Within 10 days of a change in work, vocation or attendance status at an institution of higher education.

(b) If a person required to report under this subsection has complied with the initial reporting requirement under paragraph (a)(A) of this subsection, the person shall subsequently report, in person, in the circumstances specified in paragraph (a) of this subsection, as applicable, to the Department of State Police, a city police department or a county sheriff's office, in the county of the person's last reported residence.

(c) The obligation to report under this subsection terminates if the conviction or adjudication that gave rise to the obligation is reversed or vacated or if the registrant is pardoned.

(5) As part of the registration and reporting requirements of this section:

(a) The person required to report shall:

(A) Provide the information necessary to complete the sex offender registration form and sign the form as required; and

(B) Submit to the requirements described in paragraph (b) of this subsection.

(b) The Department of State Police, the city police department or the county sheriff's office:

(A) Shall photograph the person when the person initially reports under this section and each time the person reports annually under this section;

(B) May photograph the person or any identifying scars, marks or tattoos located on the person when the person reports under any of the circumstances described in this section; and

(C) Shall fingerprint the person if the person's fingerprints are not included in the record file of the Department of State Police. [Formerly 181.807]

163A.020 Reporting by sex offender upon moving into state; reporting by certain nonresidents and certain residents. (1)(a) When a person described in subsection (6) of this section moves into this state and is not otherwise required by ORS 163A.010, 163A.015 or 163A.025 to report, the person shall report, in person, to the Department of State Police, a city police department or a county sheriff's office, in the county of the person's residence:

(A) No later than 10 days after moving into this state;

(B) Within 10 days of a change of residence;

(C) Once each year within 10 days of the person's birth date, regardless of whether the person changed residence;

(D) Within 10 days of the first day the person works at, carries on a vocation at or attends an institution of higher education; and

(E) Within 10 days of a change in work, vocation or attendance status at an institution of higher education.

(b) If a person required to report under this subsection has complied with the initial reporting requirement under paragraph (a)(A) of this subsection, the person shall subsequently report, in person, in the circumstances specified in paragraph (a) of this subsection, as applicable, to the Department of State Police, a city police department or a county sheriff's office, in the county of the person's last reported residence.

(2)(a) When a person described in ORS 163A.010 (2) or 163A.015 (2) or subsection (6) of this section attends school or works in this state, resides in another state and is not otherwise required by ORS 163A.010, 163A.015 or 163A.025 to report, the person shall report, in person, to the Department of State Police, a city police department or a county sheriff's office, in the county in which the school or place of work is located, no later than 10 days after:

(A) The first day of school attendance or the 14th day of employment in this state; and

(B) A change in school enrollment or employment.

(b) As used in this subsection, "attends school" means enrollment in any type of school on a full-time or part-time basis.

(3)(a) When a person described in subsection (6) of this section resides in this state at the time of the conviction or adjudication giving rise to the obligation to report, continues to reside in this state following the conviction or adjudication and is not otherwise required by ORS 163A.010, 163A.015 or 163A.025 to report, the person shall report, in person, to the Department of State Police, a city police department or a county sheriff's office, in the county of the person's residence:

(A) Within 10 days following:

(i) Discharge, release on parole or release on any form of supervised or conditional release, from a jail, prison or other correctional facility or detention facility; or

(ii) Discharge, release or placement on probation, by another United States court;

(B) Within 10 days of a change of residence;

(C) Once each year within 10 days of the person's birth date, regardless of whether the person has changed residence;

(D) Within 10 days of the first day the person works at, carries on a vocation at or attends an institution of higher education; and

(E) Within 10 days of a change in work, vocation or attendance status at an institution of higher education.

(b) If a person required to report under this subsection has complied with the applicable initial reporting requirement under paragraph (a)(A) of this subsection, the person shall subsequently report, in person, in the circumstances specified in paragraph (a) of this subsection, as applicable, to the Department of State Police, a city police department or a county sheriff's office, in the county of the person's last reported residence.

(4) When a person reports under this section, the agency to which the person reports shall complete a sex offender registration form concerning the person.

(5) The obligation to report under this section terminates if the conviction or adjudication that gave rise to the obligation is reversed or vacated or if the registrant is pardoned.

(6) Subsections (1) to (5) of this section apply to a person convicted in another United States court of a crime:

(a) That would constitute a sex crime if committed in this state; or

(b) For which the person would have to register as a sex offender in that court's jurisdiction, or as required under federal law, regardless of whether the crime would constitute a sex crime in this state.

(7) As part of the registration and reporting requirements of this section:

(a) The person required to report shall:

(A) Provide the information necessary to complete the sex offender registration form and sign the form as required; and

(B) Submit to the requirements described in paragraph (b) of this subsection.

(b) The Department of State Police, the city police department or the county sheriff's office:

(A) Shall photograph the person when the person initially reports under this section, each time the person reports annually under subsection (1)(a)(C) or (3)(a)(C) of this section and each time the person reports under subsection (2)(a)(B) of this section;

(B) May photograph the person or any identifying scars, marks or tattoos located on the person when the person reports under any of the circumstances described in this section; and

(C) Shall fingerprint the person if the person's fingerprints are not included in the record file of the Department of State Police. [Formerly 181.808]

163A.025 Reporting by sex offender adjudicated in juvenile court. (1) A person found to be within the jurisdiction of the juvenile court under ORS 419C.005, or found by the juvenile court to be responsible except for insanity under ORS 419C.411, for having committed an act that, if committed by an adult, would constitute a felony sex crime shall report as a sex offender as described in subsections (2) to (4) of this section, unless the juvenile court enters an order under ORS 163A.130 or 163A.135 relieving the person of the obligation to report, if:

(a) The person has been ordered under ORS 163A.030 to report as a sex offender;

(b) The person was adjudicated, and the jurisdiction of the juvenile court or the Psychiatric Security Review Board over the person ended, prior to August 12, 2015;

(c) The person was adjudicated prior to August 12, 2015, and the jurisdiction of the juvenile court or the Psychiatric Security Review Board over the person ended after August 12, 2015, and before April 4, 2016; or

(d) The person has been found in a juvenile adjudication in another United States court to have committed an act while the person was under 18 years of age that would constitute a felony sex crime if committed in this state by an adult.

(2) A person described in subsection (1)(a) or (d) of this section, or a person described in subsection (1)(c) of this section who did not make an initial report prior to April 4, 2016, who resides in this state shall make an initial report, in person, to the Department of State Police, a city police department or a county sheriff's office as follows:

(a) The person shall report no later than 10 days after the date of the court order requiring the person to report under ORS 163A.030;

(b) If the person is adjudicated for the act giving rise to the obligation to report in another United States court and the person is found to have committed an act that if committed by an adult in this state would constitute:

(A) A Class A or Class B felony sex crime:

(i) If the person is not a resident of this state at the time of the adjudication, the person shall make the initial report to the Department of State Police, a city police department or a county sheriff's office, in the county of the person's residence, no later than 10 days after the date the person moves into this state; or

(ii) If the person is a resident of this state at the time of the adjudication, the person shall make the initial report to the Department of State Police, a city police department or a county sheriff's office, in the county of the person's residence, no later than 10 days after the date the person is discharged, released or placed on probation or any other form of supervised or conditional release by the other United States court or, if the person is confined in a correctional facility by the other United States court, no later than 10 days after the date the person is discharged or otherwise released from the facility.

(B) A Class C felony sex crime:

(i) If the person is not a resident of this state at the time of the adjudication, the person shall make the initial report to the Department of State Police, a city police department or a county sheriff's office, in the county of the person's residence, no later than six months after the date the person moves into this state; or

(ii) If the person is a resident of this state at the time of the adjudication, the person shall make the initial report to the Department of State Police, a city police department or a county sheriff's office, in the county of the person's residence, no later than 10 days after the date the person is discharged, released or placed on probation or any other form of supervised or conditional release by the other United States court or, if the person is confined in a correctional facility by the other United States court, no later than 10 days after the date the person is discharged or otherwise released from the facility; or

(c) For persons described in subsection (1)(c) of this section who did not make an initial report prior to April 4, 2016, the person shall report no later than 120 days after April 4, 2016.

(3) After making the initial report described in subsection (2) of this section or, for a person described in subsection (1)(c) of this section who made an initial report prior to April 4, 2016, or a person described in subsection (1)(b) of this section, beginning after April 4, 2016, the person shall report, in person, to the Department of State Police, a city police department or a county sheriff's office, in the county of the person's last reported residence:

(a) Within 10 days of a change of residence;

(b) Once each year within 10 days of the person's birth date, regardless of whether the person changed residence;

(c) Within 10 days of the first day the person works at, carries on a vocation at or attends an institution of higher education; and

(d) Within 10 days of a change in work, vocation or attendance status at an institution of higher education.

(4) When a person described in subsection (1) of this section attends school or works in this state, resides in another state and is not otherwise required to report as a sex offender under this section or ORS 163A.010, 163A.015 or 163A.020, the person shall report, in person, to the Department of State Police, a city police department or a county sheriff's office, in the county in which the person attends school or works, no later than 10 days after:

(a) The first day of school attendance or the 14th day of employment in this state; and

(b) A change in school enrollment or employment.

(5) The agency to which a person reports under this section shall complete a sex offender registration form concerning the person when the person reports under this section.

(6) As part of the registration and reporting requirements of this section:

(a) The person required to report shall:

(A) Provide the information necessary to complete the sex offender registration form and sign the form as required; and

(B) Submit to the requirements described in paragraph (b) of this subsection.

(b) The Department of State Police, Oregon Youth Authority, county juvenile department, city police department or county sheriff's office:

(A) Shall photograph the person when the person initially reports under this section and each time the person reports annually under this section;

(B) May photograph the person or any identifying scars, marks or tattoos located on the person when the person reports under any of the circumstances described in this section; and

(C) Shall fingerprint the person if the person's fingerprints are not included in the record file of the Department of State Police.

(7) The obligation to report under this section is terminated if the adjudication that gave rise to the obligation is reversed or vacated.

(8) Notwithstanding subsections (2) and (3) of this section:

(a) The Oregon Youth Authority may authorize a youth offender committed to its custody and supervision by order of the juvenile court, or a person placed in its physical custody under ORS 137.124 or any other provision of law, to report to the authority regardless of the youth offender's or the person's last reported residence.

(b) A county juvenile department may authorize a youth offender or young person, as those terms are defined in ORS 419A.004, to report to the department, regardless of the county of the youth offender's or the young person's last reported residence.

(c) In the event that a person reports to the authority or the department under this subsection, the authority or the department shall register the person. [Formerly 181.809; 2016 c.95 §1]

163A.030 Hearing on issue of reporting by sex offender adjudicated in juvenile court; right to counsel. (1)(a) Except as provided in subsection (6) of this section, the juvenile court shall hold a hearing on the issue of reporting as a sex offender by a person who has been found to be within the jurisdiction of the juvenile court under ORS 419C.005, or found by the juvenile court to be responsible except for insanity under ORS 419C.411, for having committed an act that if committed by an adult would constitute a felony sex crime if:

(A) The person was adjudicated on or after August 12, 2015; or

(B) The person was adjudicated before August 12, 2015, and was still under the jurisdiction of the juvenile court or the Psychiatric Security Review Board on April 4, 2016.

(b) Unless the court continues the hearing described in this section for good cause, the hearing must be held:

(A) During the six-month period before the termination of juvenile court jurisdiction over the person; or

(B) During the six-month period after the court receives the notice described in subsection (2) of this section from the Psychiatric Security Review Board, if the person was placed under the jurisdiction of the board.

(c) The court shall notify the person of the person's right to a hearing under this section upon finding the person within the jurisdiction of the juvenile court under ORS 419C.005.

(2)(a) The county or state agency responsible for supervising the person shall notify the person and the juvenile court when the agency determines that termination of jurisdiction is likely to occur within six months.

(b) If the Psychiatric Security Review Board discharges a person prior to the end of the board's jurisdiction over the person, the board shall notify the juvenile court within three business days after the discharge date.

(3) Upon receipt of the notice described in subsection (2) of this section, the court shall:

(a) Appoint an attorney for the person as described in subsection (4) of this section;

(b) Set an initial hearing date; and

(c) Notify the parties and the juvenile department or the Psychiatric Security Review Board, if the department or board is supervising or has jurisdiction over the person, of the hearing at least 60 days before the hearing date.

(4)(a) A person who is the subject of a hearing under this section has the right to be represented by a suitable attorney possessing skills and experience commensurate with the nature and complexity of the case, to consult with the attorney prior to the hearing and, if financially eligible, to have a suitable attorney appointed at state expense.

(b) In order to comply with the right to counsel under paragraph (a) of this subsection, the court may:

(A) Continue the appointment of the attorney appointed under ORS 419C.200 at the time of disposition;

(B) Set a date prior to the hearing under this section in order to reappoint the attorney appointed under ORS 419C.200; or

(C) Appoint or reappoint an attorney at any time in response to a request by the person who is the subject of a hearing under this section.

(5)(a) The district attorney shall notify the victim prior to the hearing of the right to appear and the right to be heard under ORS 419C.273.

(b) If the person is under the jurisdiction of the Psychiatric Security Review Board, the board shall notify the following of the hearing:

(A) The mental health agency providing services to the person, if any;

(B) The person's board defense attorney; and

(C) The assistant attorney general representing the state at board hearings.

(6)(a) A person may waive the right to the hearing described in this section after consultation with the person's attorney. If the court finds that the person has knowingly waived the right to a hearing, the court shall enter an order requiring the person to report as a sex offender under ORS 163A.025.

(b) If a person fails to appear at a hearing described in this section, the court may enter an order requiring the person to report as a sex offender under ORS 163A.025.

(7) At the hearing described in subsection (1) of this section:

(a) The district attorney, the victim, the person and the juvenile department or a representative of the Oregon Youth Authority shall have an opportunity to be heard.

(b) The person who is the subject of the hearing has the burden of proving by clear and convincing evidence that the person is rehabilitated and does not pose a threat to the safety of the public. If the court finds that the person has not met the burden of proof, the court shall enter an order requiring the person to report as a sex offender under ORS 163A.025.

(8) In determining whether the person has met the burden of proof, the juvenile court may consider but need not be limited to considering:

(a) The extent and impact of any physical or emotional injury to the victim;

(b) The nature of the act that subjected the person to the duty of reporting as a sex offender;

(c) Whether the person used or threatened to use force in committing the act;

(d) Whether the act was premeditated;

(e) Whether the person took advantage of a position of authority or trust in committing the act;

(f) The age of any victim at the time of the act, the age difference between any victim and the person and the number of victims;

(g) The vulnerability of the victim;

(h) Other acts committed by the person that would be crimes if committed by an adult and criminal activities engaged in by the person before and after the adjudication;

(i) Statements, documents and recommendations by or on behalf of the victim or the parents of the victim;

(j) The person's willingness to accept personal responsibility for the act and personal accountability for the consequences of the act;

(k) The person's ability and efforts to pay the victim's expenses for counseling and other trauma-related expenses or other efforts to mitigate the effects of the act;

(L) Whether the person has participated in and satisfactorily completed a sex offender treatment program or any other intervention, and if so the juvenile court may also consider:

(A) The availability, duration and extent of the treatment activities;

(B) Reports and recommendations from the providers of the treatment;

(C) The person's compliance with court, board or supervision requirements regarding treatment; and

(D) The quality and thoroughness of the treatment program;

(m) The person's academic and employment history;

(n) The person's use of drugs or alcohol before and after the adjudication;

(o) The person's history of public or private indecency;

(p) The person's compliance with and success in completing the terms of supervision;

(q) The results of psychological examinations of the person;

(r) The protection afforded the public by records of sex offender registration; and

(s) Any other relevant factors.

(9) In a hearing under this section, the juvenile court may receive testimony, reports and other evidence, without regard to whether the evidence is admissible under ORS 40.010 to 40.210 and 40.310 to 40.585, if the evidence is relevant evidence related to the determination and findings required under this section. As used in this subsection, "relevant evidence" has the meaning given that term in ORS 40.150.

(10)(a) In a hearing under this section, the Oregon Youth Authority or the juvenile department, if either agency is supervising the person, or the Psychiatric Security Review Board, if the board has jurisdiction over the person, shall file with the juvenile court the following records and materials in the possession of the agency or board at least 45 days prior to the hearing unless good cause is shown:

(A) Evaluations and treatment records concerning the person conducted by a clinician or program operating under the standards of practice for the evaluation and treatment of juvenile sex offenders adopted by the Sex Offender Treatment Board under ORS 675.400, and recommendations contained therein regarding the need for the person to register in order to protect the public from future sex crimes;

(B) All examination preparation material and examination records from polygraph examinations conducted by or for the treatment provider, juvenile department or Oregon Youth Authority; and

(C) The Psychiatric Security Review Board exhibit file.

(b) Any records and materials filed with the court under this subsection shall be made available to the parties in accordance with ORS 419A.255.

(11) When the juvenile court enters an order described in subsection (7)(b) of this section, the court shall ensure that the person completes a form that documents the person's obligation to report under ORS 163A.025. No later than three business days after the person completes the form required by this subsection, the court shall ensure that the form is sent to the Department of State Police.

(12) Notwithstanding ORS 419C.005 (4)(c), (d) and (e), the juvenile court retains jurisdiction over a person for purposes of this section.

(13) As used in this section, "parties" means the person, the state as represented by the district attorney or the juvenile department, and the Oregon Youth Authority or other child care agency, if the person is temporarily committed to the authority or agency. [2015 c.820 §31; 2016 c.95 §2]

Note: Sections 3 and 10, chapter 95, Oregon Laws 2016, provide:

Sec. 3. (1) A person found to be within the jurisdiction of the juvenile court under ORS 419C.005, or found by the juvenile court to be responsible except for insanity under ORS 419C.411, for having committed an act that, if committed by an adult, would constitute a felony sex crime, who was adjudicated before August 12, 2015, and was still under the jurisdiction of the juvenile court on August 12, 2015, and who ceased to be under the jurisdiction of the juvenile court before the effective date of this 2016 Act [April 4, 2016], is entitled to a hearing on the issue of reporting as a sex offender as described in this section.

(2)(a) A county or state agency that was responsible for supervising or that had jurisdiction over a person described in subsection (1) of this section while the person was under juvenile court or Psychiatric Security Review Board jurisdiction shall, within 90 days of the effective date of this 2016 Act:

(A) Send written notice of the right to a hearing to the last-known address of the person and to the person's most recent attorney of record, if available. The notice shall inform the person that, in order to have a hearing, the person must file a written request for the hearing with the juvenile court. The notice must also inform the person that the person shall report as required under ORS 163A.025 beginning 120 days after the effective date of this 2016 Act.

(B) Send written notice to the juvenile court identifying the person.

(b) Upon receiving the notice described in paragraph (a) of this subsection, the court shall appoint an attorney for the person for the limited purpose of assisting the person to decide whether to file, and to file, a request for a hearing under this section.

(3) Upon receiving a written request from a person for a hearing under this section, and after confirming the person's eligibility for the hearing, the court shall:

(a) Appoint an attorney for the person in accordance with ORS 163A.030 (4);

(b) Set an initial hearing date within six months after receiving the request; and

(c) Notify the parties and the juvenile department or the Psychiatric Security Review Board, if the department or board supervised or had jurisdiction over the person, of the hearing date.

(4)(a) The district attorney shall notify the victim prior to a hearing under this section of the right to appear and the right to be heard under ORS 419C.273.

(b) If the person was under the jurisdiction of the Psychiatric Security Review Board, the board shall notify the following of the hearing:

(A) The mental health agency providing services to the person, if any;

(B) The person's board defense attorney; and

(C) The assistant attorney general representing the state at board hearings.

(5) A person may waive the right to the hearing described in this section after consultation with the person's attorney. If the court finds that the person has knowingly waived the right to a hearing, the court shall enter an order requiring the person to report as a sex offender as required under ORS 163A.025 and shall send a certified copy of the order to the Department of State Police.

(6) At the hearing described in subsection (1) of this section:

(a) The district attorney, the victim, the person and the juvenile department or a representative of the Oregon Youth Authority shall have an opportunity to be heard.

(b) The person who is the subject of the hearing has the burden of proving by clear and convincing evidence that the person is rehabilitated and does not pose a threat to the safety of the public. If the court finds that the person has not met the burden of proof, the court shall enter an order requiring the person to report as a sex offender as required under ORS 163A.025.

(7) In determining whether the person has met the burden of proof, the juvenile court may consider but need not be limited to considering:

(a) The extent and impact of any physical or emotional injury to the victim;

(b) The nature of the act that subjected the person to the duty of reporting as a sex offender;

(c) Whether the person used or threatened to use force in committing the act;

(d) Whether the act was premeditated;

(e) Whether the person took advantage of a position of authority or trust in committing the act;

(f) The age of any victim at the time of the act, the age difference between any victim and the person, and the number of victims;

(g) The vulnerability of the victim;

(h) Other acts committed by the person that would be crimes if committed by an adult and criminal activities engaged in by the person before and after the adjudication;

(i) Statements, documents and recommendations by or on behalf of the victim or the parents of the victim;

(j) The person's willingness to accept personal responsibility for the act and personal accountability for the consequences of the act;

(k) The person's ability and efforts to pay the victim's expenses for counseling and other trauma-related expenses or other efforts to mitigate the effects of the act;

(L) Whether the person has participated in and satisfactorily completed a sex offender treatment program or any other intervention and, if so, the juvenile court may also consider:

(A) The availability, duration and extent of the treatment activities;

(B) Reports and recommendations from the providers of the treatment;

(C) The person's compliance with court, board or supervision requirements regarding treatment; and

(D) The quality and thoroughness of the treatment program;

(m) The person's academic and employment history;

(n) The person's use of drugs or alcohol before and after the adjudication;

(o) The person's history of public or private indecency;

(p) The person's compliance with and success in completing the terms of supervision;

(q) The results of psychological examinations of the person;

(r) The protection afforded the public by records of sex offender registration; and

(s) Any other relevant factors.

(8) In a hearing under this section, the juvenile court may receive testimony, reports and other evidence, without regard to whether the evidence is admissible under ORS 40.010 to 40.210 and 40.310 to 40.585, if the evidence is relevant evidence, as defined in ORS 40.150, related to the determination and findings required under this section.

(9)(a) In a hearing under this section, the Oregon Youth Authority or the juvenile department, if either agency supervised the person, or the Psychiatric Security Review Board, if the board had jurisdiction over the person, shall file with the juvenile court the following records and materials in the possession of the agency or board at least 45 days prior to the hearing unless good cause is shown:

(A) Evaluations and treatment records concerning the person conducted or maintained by a clinician or program operating under the standards of practice for the evaluation and treatment of juvenile sex offenders adopted by the Sex Offender Treatment Board under ORS 675.400, and recommendations contained in the evaluations and treatment records regarding the need for the person to register in order to protect the public from future sex crimes;

(B) All examination preparation material and examination records from polygraph examinations conducted by or for the treatment provider, juvenile department or Oregon Youth Authority; and

(C) The Psychiatric Security Review Board exhibit file.

(b) Any records and materials filed with the court under this subsection shall be made available to the parties in accordance with ORS 419A.255.

(10) When the juvenile court enters an order described in subsection (5) or (6)(b) of this section, the court shall ensure that the person completes a form that documents the person's obligation to report under ORS 163A.025. No later than three business days after the person completes the form required by this subsection, the court shall ensure that the form is sent to the Department of State Police.

(11) Notwithstanding ORS 419C.005 (4)(c), (d) and (e), the juvenile court retains jurisdiction over a person for purposes of this section.

(12) If the court finds that the person has met the burden of proof as described in subsection (6)(b) of this section, the court shall enter an order that the person is not required to report as a sex offender and shall send a certified copy of the order to the Department of State Police.

(13) If the court has not received a written request for a hearing prior to July 1, 2018, the person may not request a hearing under this section.

(14) As used in this section, "parties" means the person, the state as represented by the district attorney or the juvenile department, and the Oregon Youth Authority or other child care agency, if the person was committed to the authority or agency. [2016 c.95 §3]

Sec. 10. Section 3 of this 2016 Act is repealed on July 1, 2018. [2016 c.95 §10]

163A.035 Registration forms; Department of State Police to provide; distribution of information; rules; fee. (1) Agencies registering offenders under ORS 163A.010, 163A.015, 163A.020 and 163A.025 shall use forms and procedures adopted by the Department of State Police by administrative rule. The department shall include places on the form to list all the names used by the offender and the address of the offender. No later than three working days after registration, the agency or official completing the form shall forward the registration information to the department in the manner prescribed by the department.

(2) The department shall enter into the Law Enforcement Data System the sex offender information obtained from the sex offender registration forms. If a conviction or adjudication that gave rise to the registration obligation is reversed or vacated or if the registrant is pardoned, the department shall remove from the Law Enforcement Data System the sex offender information obtained from the form.

(3) The Law Enforcement Data System may send sex offender information to the National Crime Information Center as part of the national sex offender registry in accordance with appropriate state and federal procedures.

(4) If the person is no longer under supervision, the department shall verify the residence address of a person determined to be a sexually violent dangerous offender as defined in ORS 137.765 every 90 days by mailing a verification form to the person at the person's last reported residence address. No later than 10 days after receiving the form, the person shall sign and return the form to the department.

(5) The department shall assess a person who is required to report under ORS 163A.010, 163A.015, 163A.020 or 163A.025 and who is not under supervision a fee of $70 each year. Moneys received by the department under this subsection are continuously appropriated to the department for the purpose of carrying out the department's duties under ORS 163A.005 to 163A.235. [Formerly 181.810]

163A.040 Failure to report as sex offender; defense. (1) A person who is required to report as a sex offender in accordance with the applicable provisions of ORS 163A.010, 163A.015, 163A.020 or 163A.025 and who has knowledge of the reporting requirement commits the crime of failure to report as a sex offender if the person:

(a) Fails to make the initial report to an agency;

(b) Fails to report when the person works at, carries on a vocation at or attends an institution of higher education;

(c) Fails to report following a change of school enrollment or employment status, including enrollment, employment or vocation status at an institution of higher education;

(d) Fails to report following a change of residence;

(e) Fails to make an annual report;

(f) Fails to provide complete and accurate information;

(g) Fails to sign the sex offender registration form as required;

(h) Fails or refuses to participate in a sex offender risk assessment as directed by the State Board of Parole and Post-Prison Supervision, Psychiatric Security Review Board, Oregon Health Authority or supervisory authority; or

(i) Fails to submit to fingerprinting or to having a photograph taken of the person's face, identifying scars, marks or tattoos.

(2)(a) It is an affirmative defense to a charge of failure to report under subsection (1)(d) of this section by a person required to report under ORS 163A.010 (3)(a)(B), 163A.015 (4)(a)(B) or 163A.025 (3)(a) that the person reported, in person, within 10 days of a change of residence to the Department of State Police, a city police department or a county sheriff's office, in the county of the person's new residence, if the person otherwise complied with all reporting requirements.

(b) It is an affirmative defense to a charge of failure to report under subsection (1)(a) of this section by a person required to report under ORS 163A.025 (2)(b)(A)(i) that the person reported, in person, to the Department of State Police in Marion County, Oregon, within 10 days of moving into this state.

(c) It is an affirmative defense to a charge of failure to report under subsection (1)(a) of this section by a person required to report under ORS 163A.025 (2)(b)(B)(i) that the person reported, in person, to the Department of State Police in Marion County, Oregon, within six months of moving into this state.

(d) It is an affirmative defense to a charge of failure to report under subsection (1) of this section by a person required to report under ORS 163A.025 (2)(b)(A)(ii) or (B)(ii) that the person reported, in person, to the Department of State Police in Marion County, Oregon, if the person otherwise complied with all reporting requirements.

(e) It is an affirmative defense to a charge of failure to report under subsection (1) of this section by a person required to report under ORS 163A.025 (3) that the person reported, in person, to the Department of State Police, a city police department or a county sheriff's office, in the county of the person's residence, if the person otherwise complied with all reporting requirements.

(f) It is an affirmative defense to a charge of failure to report under subsection (1) of this section by a person required to report under ORS 163A.010 (3) that the person reported to the Oregon Youth Authority if the person establishes that the authority registered the person under ORS 163A.010 (3)(c).

(g) It is an affirmative defense to a charge of failure to report under subsection (1) of this section by a person required to report under ORS 163A.025 (2) or (3) that the person reported to the Oregon Youth Authority or a county juvenile department if the person establishes that the authority or department registered the person under ORS 163A.025 (8).

(3)(a) Except as otherwise provided in paragraph (b) of this subsection, failure to report as a sex offender is a Class A misdemeanor.

(b) Failure to report as a sex offender is a Class C felony if the person violates:

(A) Subsection (1)(a) of this section; or

(B) Subsection (1)(b), (c), (d) or (g) of this section and the crime for which the person is required to report is a felony.

(4) A person who fails to sign and return an address verification form as required by ORS 163A.035 (4) commits a violation. [Formerly 181.812; 2016 c.95 §4a; 2017 c.418 §1]

Note: The amendments to 163A.040 by section 2, chapter 418, Oregon Laws 2017, become operative January 1, 2022. See section 3, chapter 418, Oregon Laws 2017. The text that is operative on and after January 1, 2022, is set forth for the user's convenience.

163A.040. (1) A person who is required to report as a sex offender in accordance with the applicable provisions of ORS 163A.010, 163A.015, 163A.020 or 163A.025 and who has knowledge of the reporting requirement commits the crime of failure to report as a sex offender if the person:

(a) Fails to make the initial report to an agency;

(b) Fails to report when the person works at, carries on a vocation at or attends an institution of higher education;

(c) Fails to report following a change of school enrollment or employment status, including enrollment, employment or vocation status at an institution of higher education;

(d) Moves to a new residence and fails to report the move and the person's new address;

(e) Fails to make an annual report;

(f) Fails to provide complete and accurate information;

(g) Fails to sign the sex offender registration form as required;

(h) Fails or refuses to participate in a sex offender risk assessment as directed by the State Board of Parole and Post-Prison Supervision, Psychiatric Security Review Board, Oregon Health Authority or supervisory authority; or

(i) Fails to submit to fingerprinting or to having a photograph taken of the person's face, identifying scars, marks or tattoos.

(2)(a) It is an affirmative defense to a charge of failure to report under subsection (1)(d) of this section by a person required to report under ORS 163A.010 (3)(a)(B), 163A.015 (4)(a)(B) or 163A.025 (3)(a) that the person reported, in person, within 10 days of a change of residence to the Department of State Police, a city police department or a county sheriff's office, in the county of the person's new residence, if the person otherwise complied with all reporting requirements.

(b) It is an affirmative defense to a charge of failure to report under subsection (1)(a) of this section by a person required to report under ORS 163A.025 (2)(b)(A)(i) that the person reported, in person, to the Department of State Police in Marion County, Oregon, within 10 days of moving into this state.

(c) It is an affirmative defense to a charge of failure to report under subsection (1)(a) of this section by a person required to report under ORS 163A.025 (2)(b)(B)(i) that the person reported, in person, to the Department of State Police in Marion County, Oregon, within six months of moving into this state.

(d) It is an affirmative defense to a charge of failure to report under subsection (1) of this section by a person required to report under ORS 163A.025 (2)(b)(A)(ii) or (B)(ii) that the person reported, in person, to the Department of State Police in Marion County, Oregon, if the person otherwise complied with all reporting requirements.

(e) It is an affirmative defense to a charge of failure to report under subsection (1) of this section by a person required to report under ORS 163A.025 (3) that the person reported, in person, to the Department of State Police, a city police department or a county sheriff's office, in the county of the person's residence, if the person otherwise complied with all reporting requirements.

(f) It is an affirmative defense to a charge of failure to report under subsection (1) of this section by a person required to report under ORS 163A.010 (3) that the person reported to the Oregon Youth Authority if the person establishes that the authority registered the person under ORS 163A.010 (3)(c).

(g) It is an affirmative defense to a charge of failure to report under subsection (1) of this section by a person required to report under ORS 163A.025 (2) or (3) that the person reported to the Oregon Youth Authority or a county juvenile department if the person establishes that the authority or department registered the person under ORS 163A.025 (8).

(3)(a) Except as otherwise provided in paragraph (b) of this subsection, failure to report as a sex offender is a Class A misdemeanor.

(b) Failure to report as a sex offender is a Class C felony if the person violates:

(A) Subsection (1)(a) of this section; or

(B) Subsection (1)(b), (c), (d) or (g) of this section and the crime for which the person is required to report is a felony.

(4) A person who fails to sign and return an address verification form as required by ORS 163A.035 (4) commits a violation.

163A.045 Purpose of sex offender reporting obligation; rules. (1) The purpose of ORS 163A.005 to 163A.235 is to assist law enforcement agencies in preventing future sex offenses.

(2) The Department of State Police may adopt rules to carry out the responsibilities of the department under ORS 163A.005 to 163A.235. [Formerly 181.814]

163A.050 Notice of reporting obligation to be given by court; procedure at intake. (1) When the court imposes sentence upon a person convicted of a sex crime or finds a person guilty except for insanity of a sex crime, the court shall notify the person of the obligation to report as a sex offender under ORS 163A.010 and 163A.015.

(2) At the initial intake for incarceration or release on any type of supervised release, the sex offender shall complete a form that documents the offender's obligation to report under ORS 163A.010 or 163A.015 and the effect described in ORS 163A.115 of failing to submit to a sex offender risk assessment. The Department of State Police shall develop and provide the form. No later than three working days after the sex offender completes the form, the person responsible for the intake process shall send the form to the Department of State Police. [Formerly 181.815; 2017 c.233 §1]

163A.055 Notice required when offender moves to another state. When the Department of State Police learns that a person required to report under ORS 163A.010, 163A.015, 163A.020 or 163A.025 is moving to another state, the department shall notify the appropriate criminal justice agency of that state of that fact. The department is not responsible for registering and tracking a person once the person has moved from this state. [Formerly 181.816]

163A.060 Offender profiling. (1) For those sex offenders classified as a level three sex offender under ORS 163A.100 (3), or designated as a predatory sex offender prior to January 1, 2014, the supervising agency or the agency making the classification or designation shall provide the Department of State Police, by electronic or other means, at the termination of supervision, with the following information for the purpose of offender profiling:

(a) Presentence investigations;

(b) Violation reports;

(c) Parole and probation orders;

(d) Conditions of parole and probation and other corrections records;

(e) Sex offender risk assessments; and

(f) Any other information that the supervising agency or the agency making the classification or designation determines is appropriate disclosure of which is not otherwise prohibited by law.

(2) The Oregon Youth Authority and county juvenile departments shall provide access to information in their files to the Oregon State Police for the purpose of offender profiling.

(3)(a) Except as otherwise provided by law, the Oregon State Police may not disclose information received under subsection (1) or (2) of this section.

(b) The Department of State Police may release information on the methodology of offenses and behavior profiles derived from information received under subsection (1) or (2) of this section to local law enforcement agencies. [Formerly 181.817]

163A.065 Immunity. A public agency and its employees are immune from liability, both civil and criminal, for the good faith performance of the agency's or employee's duties under ORS 163A.005 to 163A.235. [Formerly 181.818]

CLASSIFICATION

163A.100 Risk assessment methodology; rules. The State Board of Parole and Post-Prison Supervision shall, in consultation with community corrections agencies, adopt by rule a sex offender risk assessment methodology for use in classifying sex offenders. Application of the risk assessment methodology to a sex offender must result in placing the sex offender in one of the following levels:

(1) A level one sex offender who presents the lowest risk of reoffending and requires a limited range of notification.

(2) A level two sex offender who presents a moderate risk of reoffending and requires a moderate range of notification.

(3) A level three sex offender who presents the highest risk of reoffending and requires the widest range of notification. [Formerly 181.800]

163A.105 When risk assessments performed; classification into risk level; review; rules. (1) When a person convicted of a crime described in ORS 163.355 to 163.427 is sentenced to a term of imprisonment in a Department of Corrections institution for that crime, the State Board of Parole and Post-Prison Supervision shall assess the person utilizing the risk assessment methodology described in ORS 163A.100. The board shall apply the results of the assessment to place the person in one of the levels described in ORS 163A.100 before the person is released from custody.

(2) When a person convicted of a sex crime is sentenced to a term of incarceration in a jail, or is discharged, released or placed on probation by the court, the supervisory authority as defined in ORS 144.087 shall assess the person utilizing the risk assessment methodology described in ORS 163A.100 and apply the results of the assessment to place the person in one of the levels described in ORS 163A.100 no later than 90 days after the person is released from jail or discharged, released or placed on probation by the court.

(3)(a) When a person is found guilty except for insanity of a sex crime, the Psychiatric Security Review Board shall assess the person utilizing the risk assessment methodology described in ORS 163A.100 and apply the results of the assessment to place the person in one of the levels described in ORS 163A.100 no later than 90 days after the person is:

(A) Placed on conditional release by the Psychiatric Security Review Board;

(B) Discharged from the jurisdiction of the Psychiatric Security Review Board;

(C) Placed on conditional release by the court pursuant to ORS 161.327; or

(D) Discharged by the court pursuant to ORS 161.329.

(b) If the State Board of Parole and Post-Prison Supervision previously completed a risk assessment and assigned a classification level described in ORS 163A.100 for a person described in paragraph (a) of this subsection, the Psychiatric Security Review Board need not complete a reassessment for an initial classification.

(c) The court shall notify the Psychiatric Security Review Board when the court conditionally releases or discharges a person described in paragraph (a) of this subsection.

(d) The Psychiatric Security Review Board shall notify the State Board of Parole and Post-Prison Supervision no later than seven days after the Psychiatric Security Review Board conditionally releases or discharges a person who has a prior sex crime conviction that obligates the person to report as a sex offender, unless the person has also been found guilty except for insanity of a sex crime that obligates the person to report as a sex offender.

(4)(a) Within 90 days after receiving notice of a person's obligation to report in this state from the Department of State Police, the State Board of Parole and Post-Prison Supervision shall assess the person utilizing the risk assessment methodology described in ORS 163A.100 and apply the results of the assessment to place the person in one of the levels described in ORS 163A.100 if the person has been convicted in another United States court of a crime:

(A) That would constitute a sex crime if committed in this state; or

(B) For which the person would have to register as a sex offender in that court's jurisdiction, or as required under federal law, regardless of whether the crime would constitute a sex crime in this state.

(b) If a person has been convicted of a sex crime and was sentenced to a term of imprisonment in a Department of Corrections institution for that sex crime, but was not subjected to a risk assessment utilizing the risk assessment methodology described in ORS 163A.100 before release under subsection (1) of this section, within 90 days after the person's release the State Board of Parole and Post-Prison Supervision shall assess the person utilizing the risk assessment methodology described in ORS 163A.100 and apply the results of the assessment to place the person in one of the levels described in ORS 163A.100.

(5) When the State Board of Parole and Post-Prison Supervision, the Psychiatric Security Review Board or a supervisory authority applies the results of a risk assessment to place a person in one of the levels described in ORS 163A.100, the agency shall notify the Department of State Police of the results of the risk assessment within three business days after the agency's classification. Upon receipt, the Department of State Police shall enter the results of the risk assessment into the Law Enforcement Data System.

(6) The State Board of Parole and Post-Prison Supervision, the Psychiatric Security Review Board or a supervisory authority may reassess or reclassify a person placed in one of the levels described in ORS 163A.100 under this section if the classifying board or authority determines that a factual mistake caused an erroneous assessment or classification.

(7)(a) A person classified under this section as a level two or level three sex offender as described in ORS 163A.100 may petition the classifying board or authority for review. The petition may be filed no later than 60 days after the person receives notice of the classification.

(b) Upon receipt of a petition described in this subsection, the classifying board or authority shall afford the person an opportunity to be heard as to all factual questions related to the classification.

(c) After providing the person with notice and an opportunity to be heard in accordance with this subsection, the board or authority shall classify the person in accordance with the classifications described in ORS 163A.100, based on all of the information available to the classifying board or authority.

(8)(a) If the State Board of Parole and Post-Prison Supervision, the Psychiatric Security Review Board or a supervisory authority does not classify a person under ORS 163A.100 because the person has failed or refused to participate in a sex offender risk assessment as directed by the board or authority, the classifying board or authority shall classify the person as a level three sex offender under ORS 163A.100 (3).

(b) If person classified as a level three sex offender under this subsection notifies the classifying board or authority of the willingness to participate in a sex offender risk assessment, the classifying board or authority shall perform the assessment and classify the person in one of the levels described in ORS 163A.100.

(9) The State Board of Parole and Post-Prison Supervision and the Psychiatric Security Review Board may adopt rules to carry out the provisions of this section. [Formerly 181.801; 2017 c.442 §30; 2017 c.488 §2]

Note: The amendments to 163A.105 by section 30, chapter 442, Oregon Laws 2017, become operative July 1, 2018. See section 36, chapter 442, Oregon Laws 2017. The text that is operative until July 1, 2018, including amendments by section 2, chapter 488, Oregon Laws 2017, is set forth for the user's convenience.

163A.105. (1) When a person convicted of a crime described in ORS 163.355 to 163.427 is sentenced to a term of imprisonment in a Department of Corrections institution for that crime, the State Board of Parole and Post-Prison Supervision shall assess the person utilizing the risk assessment methodology described in ORS 163A.100. The board shall apply the results of the assessment to place the person in one of the levels described in ORS 163A.100 before the person is released from custody.

(2) When a person convicted of a sex crime is sentenced to a term of incarceration in a jail, or is discharged, released or placed on probation by the court, the supervisory authority as defined in ORS 144.087 shall assess the person utilizing the risk assessment methodology described in ORS 163A.100 and apply the results of the assessment to place the person in one of the levels described in ORS 163A.100 no later than 90 days after the person is released from jail or discharged, released or placed on probation by the court.

(3)(a) When a person is found guilty except for insanity of a sex crime, the Psychiatric Security Review Board shall assess the person utilizing the risk assessment methodology described in ORS 163A.100 and apply the results of the assessment to place the person in one of the levels described in ORS 163A.100 no later than 90 days after the person is:

(A) Placed on conditional release by the Psychiatric Security Review Board or the Oregon Health Authority;

(B) Discharged from the jurisdiction of the Psychiatric Security Review Board or the Oregon Health Authority;

(C) Placed on conditional release by the court pursuant to ORS 161.327; or

(D) Discharged by the court pursuant to ORS 161.329.

(b) If the State Board of Parole and Post-Prison Supervision previously completed a risk assessment and assigned a classification level described in ORS 163A.100 for a person described in paragraph (a) of this subsection, the Psychiatric Security Review Board need not complete a reassessment for an initial classification.

(c) The court shall notify the Psychiatric Security Review Board when the court conditionally releases or discharges a person described in paragraph (a) of this subsection.

(d) The Psychiatric Security Review Board or the Oregon Health Authority shall notify the State Board of Parole and Post-Prison Supervision no later than seven days after the Psychiatric Security Review Board or the authority conditionally releases or discharges a person who has a prior sex crime conviction that obligates the person to report as a sex offender, unless the person has also been found guilty except for insanity of a sex crime that obligates the person to report as a sex offender.

(4)(a) Within 90 days after receiving notice of a person's obligation to report in this state from the Department of State Police, the State Board of Parole and Post-Prison Supervision shall assess the person utilizing the risk assessment methodology described in ORS 163A.100 and apply the results of the assessment to place the person in one of the levels described in ORS 163A.100 if the person has been convicted in another United States court of a crime:

(A) That would constitute a sex crime if committed in this state; or

(B) For which the person would have to register as a sex offender in that court's jurisdiction, or as required under federal law, regardless of whether the crime would constitute a sex crime in this state.

(b) If a person has been convicted of a sex crime and was sentenced to a term of imprisonment in a Department of Corrections institution for that sex crime, but was not subjected to a risk assessment utilizing the risk assessment methodology described in ORS 163A.100 before release under subsection (1) of this section, within 90 days after the person's release the State Board of Parole and Post-Prison Supervision shall assess the person utilizing the risk assessment methodology described in ORS 163A.100 and apply the results of the assessment to place the person in one of the levels described in ORS 163A.100.

(5) When the State Board of Parole and Post-Prison Supervision, the Psychiatric Security Review Board or a supervisory authority applies the results of a risk assessment to place a person in one of the levels described in ORS 163A.100, the agency shall notify the Department of State Police of the results of the risk assessment within three business days after the agency's classification. Upon receipt, the Department of State Police shall enter the results of the risk assessment into the Law Enforcement Data System.

(6) The State Board of Parole and Post-Prison Supervision, the Psychiatric Security Review Board or a supervisory authority may reassess or reclassify a person placed in one of the levels described in ORS 163A.100

under this section if the classifying board or authority determines that a factual mistake caused an erroneous assessment or classification.

(7)(a) A person classified under this section as a level two or level three sex offender as described in ORS 163A.100 may petition the classifying board or authority for review. The petition may be filed no later than 60 days after the person receives notice of the classification.

(b) Upon receipt of a petition described in this subsection, the classifying board or authority shall afford the person an opportunity to be heard as to all factual questions related to the classification.

(c) After providing the person with notice and an opportunity to be heard in accordance with this subsection, the board or authority shall classify the person in accordance with the classifications described in ORS 163A.100, based on all of the information available to the classifying board or authority.

(8)(a) If the State Board of Parole and Post-Prison Supervision, the Psychiatric Security Review Board or a supervisory authority does not classify a person under ORS 163A.100 because the person has failed or refused to participate in a sex offender risk assessment as directed by the board or authority, the classifying board or authority shall classify the person as a level three sex offender under ORS 163A.100 (3).

(b) If person classified as a level three sex offender under this subsection notifies the classifying board or authority of the willingness to participate in a sex offender risk assessment, the classifying board or authority shall perform the assessment and classify the person in one of the levels described in ORS 163A.100.

(9) The State Board of Parole and Post-Prison Supervision and the Psychiatric Security Review Board may adopt rules to carry out the provisions of this section.

163A.110 Applicability of ORS 163A.105. (1) ORS 163A.105 applies to persons for whom the event triggering the obligation to make an initial report under ORS 163A.010 (3)(a)(A), 163A.015 (4)(a)(A) or 163A.020 (1)(a)(A), (2)(a)(A) or (3)(a)(A) occurs on or after January 1, 2014.

(2) As used in this section, "event triggering the obligation to make an initial report" means:

(a) If the initial report is described in ORS 163A.010 (3)(a)(A):

(A) Discharge, parole or release on any form of supervised or conditional release from a jail, prison or other correctional facility in this state;

(B) Parole to this state under ORS 144.610 after being convicted in another United States court of a crime that would constitute a sex crime if committed in this state; or

(C) Discharge by the court under ORS 161.329.

(b) If the initial report is described in ORS 163A.015 (4)(a)(A), discharge, release or placement on probation:

(A) By the court; or

(B) To or in this state under ORS 144.610 after being convicted in another United States court of a crime that would constitute a sex crime if committed in this state.

(c) If the initial report is described in ORS 163A.020 (1)(a)(A), moving into this state.

(d) If the initial report is described in ORS 163A.020 (2)(a)(A), the first day of school attendance or the 14th day of employment in this state.

(e) If the initial report is described in ORS 163A.020 (3)(a)(A):

(A) Discharge, release on parole or release on any form of supervised or conditional release, from a jail, prison or other correctional facility or detention facility; or

(B) Discharge, release or placement on probation, by another United States court. [Formerly 181.802; 2017 c.488 §5]

Note: Section 7, chapter 708, Oregon Laws 2013, provides:

Sec. 7. Existing registrants. (1) As used in this section and ORS 163A.200 to 163A.210:

(a) "Event triggering the obligation to make an initial report" has the meaning given that term in ORS 163A.110.

(b) "Existing registrant" means a person for whom the event triggering the obligation to make an initial report under ORS 163A.010 (3)(a)(A), 163A.015 (4)(a)(A) or 163A.020 (1)(a)(A), (2)(a)(A) or (3)(a)(A) occurs before January 1, 2014.

(2)(a) No later than December 1, 2022, the State Board of Parole and Post-Prison Supervision shall classify existing registrants in one of the levels described in ORS 163A.100. No later than February 1, 2023, the Department of State Police shall enter the results of the classifications described in this section into the Law Enforcement Data System.

(b) The board shall classify an existing registrant as a level three sex offender under ORS 163A.100 (3), if:

(A) The person was previously designated a predatory sex offender and the designation was made after the person was afforded notice and an opportunity to be heard as to all factual questions at a meaningful time and in a meaningful manner; or

(B) The person is a sexually violent dangerous offender under ORS 137.765.

(c) The Psychiatric Security Review Board may complete the risk assessment of an existing registrant who is under the jurisdiction of the Psychiatric Security Review Board, regardless of whether the person has been found guilty except for insanity of a sex crime or was previously convicted of a sex crime, if the State Board of Parole and Post-Prison Supervision and the Psychiatric Security Review Board mutually agree that the Psychiatric Security

Review Board has adequate resources to perform the assessment and that the performance of the assessment by the Psychiatric Security Review Board would assist in classifying the existing registrant in a more timely manner.

(3) As soon as practicable following the classification of an existing registrant under this section, the classifying board shall notify the person of the classification by mail.

(4)(a) An existing registrant who seeks review of a classification made under this section as a level two or level three sex offender as described in ORS 163A.100 may petition the classifying board for review. The petition may be filed no later than 60 days after the board provides the notice described in subsection (3) of this section.

(b) Upon receipt of a petition described in this subsection, the classifying board shall afford the person an opportunity to be heard as to all factual questions related to the classification.

(c) After providing the person with notice and an opportunity to be heard in accordance with this subsection, the board shall classify the person in accordance with the classifications described in ORS 163A.100, based on all of the information available to the classifying board.

(5) The boards shall adopt rules to carry out the provisions of this section.

(6) An existing registrant may not petition for reclassification or relief from the obligation to report as a sex offender as provided in ORS 163A.125 until either all existing registrants have been classified in one of the levels described in ORS 163A.100 or December 1, 2018, whichever occurs first.

(7) Notwithstanding ORS 163A.225 or any other provision of law, the Department of State Police may until December 1, 2018, continue to use the Internet to make information available to the public concerning any adult sex offender designated as predatory as authorized by the law in effect on December 31, 2013.

(8)(a) If the State Board of Parole and Post-Prison Supervision or the Psychiatric Security Review Board does not classify an existing registrant under ORS 163A.100 because the person has failed or refused to participate in a sex offender risk assessment as directed by the State Board of Parole and Post-Prison Supervision or the Psychiatric Security Review Board, the appropriate board shall classify the person as a level three sex offender under ORS 163A.100 (3).

(b) If an existing registrant classified as a level three sex offender under this subsection notifies the State Board of Parole and Post-Prison Supervision or the Psychiatric Security Review Board of the willingness to participate in a sex offender risk assessment, the appropriate board shall perform the assessment and classify the existing registrant in one of the levels described in ORS 163A.100.

(9) The State Board of Parole and Post-Prison Supervision or the Psychiatric Security Review Board may reassess or reclassify an existing registrant placed in one of the levels described in ORS 163A.100 under this section if the classifying board determines that a factual mistake caused an erroneous assessment or classification. [2013 c.708 §7; 2015 c.820 §27; 2017 c.442 §31; 2017 c.488 §1]

Note: The amendments to section 7, chapter 708, Oregon Laws 2013, by section 31, chapter 442, Oregon Laws 2017, become operative July 1, 2018. See section 36, chapter 442, Oregon Laws 2017. The text that is operative until July 1, 2018, including amendments by section 27, chapter 820, Oregon Laws 2015, and section 1, chapter 488, Oregon Laws 2017, is set forth for the user's convenience.

Sec. 7. (1) As used in this section and ORS 163A.200 to 163A.210:

(a) "Event triggering the obligation to make an initial report" has the meaning given that term in ORS 163A.110.

(b) "Existing registrant" means a person for whom the event triggering the obligation to make an initial report under ORS 163A.010 (3)(a)(A), 163A.015 (4)(a)(A) or 163A.020 (1)(a)(A), (2)(a)(A) or (3)(a)(A) occurs before January 1, 2014.

(2)(a) No later than December 1, 2022, the State Board of Parole and Post-Prison Supervision shall classify existing registrants in one of the levels described in ORS 163A.100. No later than February 1, 2023, the Department of State Police shall enter the results of the classifications described in this section into the Law Enforcement Data System.

(b) The board shall classify an existing registrant as a level three sex offender under ORS 163A.100 (3), if:

(A) The person was previously designated a predatory sex offender and the designation was made after the person was afforded notice and an opportunity to be heard as to all factual questions at a meaningful time and in a meaningful manner; or

(B) The person is a sexually violent dangerous offender under ORS 137.765.

(c) The Psychiatric Security Review Board may complete the risk assessment of an existing registrant who is under the jurisdiction of the Psychiatric Security Review Board or the Oregon Health Authority, regardless of whether the person has been found guilty except for insanity of a sex crime or was previously convicted of a sex crime, if the State Board of Parole and Post-Prison Supervision and the Psychiatric Security Review Board mutually agree that the Psychiatric Security Review Board has adequate resources to perform the assessment and that the performance of the assessment by the Psychiatric Security Review Board would assist in classifying the existing registrant in a more timely manner.

(3) As soon as practicable following the classification of an existing registrant under this section, the classifying board shall notify the person of the classification by mail.

(4)(a) An existing registrant who seeks review of a classification made under this section as a level two or level three sex offender as described in ORS 163A.100 may petition the classifying board for review. The petition may be filed no later than 60 days after the board provides the notice described in subsection (3) of this section.

(b) Upon receipt of a petition described in this subsection, the classifying board shall afford the person an opportunity to be heard as to all factual questions related to the classification.

(c) After providing the person with notice and an opportunity to be heard in accordance with this subsection, the board shall classify the person in accordance with the classifications described in ORS 163A.100, based on all of the information available to the classifying board.

(5) The boards shall adopt rules to carry out the provisions of this section.

(6) An existing registrant may not petition for reclassification or relief from the obligation to report as a sex offender as provided in ORS 163A.125 until either all existing registrants have been classified in one of the levels described in ORS 163A.100 or December 1, 2018, whichever occurs first.

(7) Notwithstanding ORS 163A.225 or any other provision of law, the Department of State Police may until December 1, 2018, continue to use the Internet to make information available to the public concerning any adult sex offender designated as predatory as authorized by the law in effect on December 31, 2013.

(8)(a) If the State Board of Parole and Post-Prison Supervision or the Psychiatric Security Review Board does not classify an existing registrant under ORS 163A.100 because the person has failed or refused to participate in a sex offender risk assessment as directed by the State Board of Parole and Post-Prison Supervision or the Psychiatric Security Review Board, the appropriate board shall classify the person as a level three sex offender under ORS 163A.100 (3).

(b) If an existing registrant classified as a level three sex offender under this subsection notifies the State Board of Parole and Post-Prison Supervision or the Psychiatric Security Review Board of the willingness to participate in a sex offender risk assessment, the appropriate board shall perform the assessment and classify the existing registrant in one of the levels described in ORS 163A.100.

(9) The State Board of Parole and Post-Prison Supervision or the Psychiatric Security Review Board may reassess or reclassify an existing registrant placed in one of the levels described in ORS 163A.100 under this section if the classifying board determines that a factual mistake caused an erroneous assessment or classification.

163A.115 When certain classification required; persons ineligible for relief from reporting obligation. Notwithstanding any other provision of law:

(1) A person who is a sexually violent dangerous offender under ORS 137.765:

(a) Must be classified as a level three sex offender under ORS 163A.100 (3); and

(b) Is not eligible for relief from the obligation to report as a sex offender or reclassification as a level two sex offender under ORS 163A.100 (2), pursuant to a petition filed under ORS 163A.125.

(2) A person who has been convicted or found guilty except for insanity of one of the following offenses is not eligible for relief from the obligation to report as a sex offender pursuant to a petition filed under ORS 163A.125 (1):

(a) Rape in the first degree;

(b) Sodomy in the first degree;

(c) Unlawful sexual penetration in the first degree;

(d) Kidnapping in the first degree as described in ORS 163.235 (1)(e) or when the victim is under 18 years of age; or

(e) Burglary in the first degree when committed with the intent to commit any of the offenses listed in ORS 163A.005 (5)(a) to (w).

(3) A person classified as a level three sex offender under section 7 (2)(b), chapter 708, Oregon Laws 2013, is not eligible for relief from the obligation to report as a sex offender pursuant to a petition filed under ORS 163A.125 (1). [Formerly 181.803]

Note: Section 35, chapter 708, Oregon Laws 2013, provides:

Sec. 35. (1) Sections 4 to 6 of this 2013 Act [163A.115, 163A.125 and 163A.215] apply to persons for whom the event triggering the obligation to make an initial report, as defined in section 3 of this 2013 Act [163A.110], occurs on or after January 1, 2014.

(2) Notwithstanding section 7 or 38 of this 2013 Act or any other provision of law, notification to the public for persons for whom the event triggering the obligation to make an initial report, as defined in section 3 of this 2013 Act, occurs before January 1, 2014, shall continue to be governed by the law in effect on December 31, 2013. [2013 c.708 §35]

Note: The amendments to section 35, chapter 708, Oregon Laws 2013, by section 36, chapter 708, Oregon Laws 2013, become operative January 1, 2023. See section 37, chapter 708, Oregon Laws 2013, as amended by section 29, chapter 820, Oregon Laws 2015, and section 4, chapter 488, Oregon Laws 2017. The text that is operative on and after January 1, 2023, is set forth for the user's convenience.

Sec. 35. Sections 4 to 6 of this 2013 Act [163A.115, 163A.125 and 163A.215] apply to persons for whom the event triggering the obligation to make an initial report, as defined in section 3 of this 2013 Act [163A.110], occurs before, on or after January 1, 2014.

RECLASSIFICATION AND RELIEF FROM REPORTING

163A.120 Relief from reporting obligation. (1)(a) No sooner than 10 years after termination of supervision on probation, conditional release, parole or post-prison supervision, a person required to report under ORS 163A.010, 163A.015 or 163A.020 may file a petition in circuit court for an order relieving the person of the duty to report. The person must pay the filing fee established under ORS 21.135. A petition may be filed under this section only if:

(A) The person has only one conviction for a sex crime;

(B) The sex crime was a misdemeanor or Class C felony or, if committed in another state, would have been a misdemeanor or Class C felony if committed in this state; and

(C) The person has not been determined to be a predatory sex offender prior to January 1, 2014.

(b)(A) Except as otherwise provided in this paragraph, the petition must be filed in the circuit court of the county in which the person was convicted of the sex crime.

(B) If the person was convicted of the sex crime in another state, the petition must be filed in the circuit court of the county in which the person resides.

(c) The district attorney of the county in which the petition is filed shall be named and served as the respondent in the petition.

(2) The court shall hold a hearing on the petition. In determining whether to grant the relief requested, the court shall consider:

(a) The nature of the offense that required reporting;

(b) The age and number of victims;

(c) The degree of violence involved in the offense;

(d) Other criminal and relevant noncriminal behavior of the petitioner both before and after the conviction that required reporting;

(e) The period of time during which the petitioner has not reoffended;

(f) Whether the petitioner has successfully completed a court-approved sex offender treatment program; and

(g) Any other relevant factors.

(3) If the court is satisfied by clear and convincing evidence that the petitioner is rehabilitated and that the petitioner does not pose a threat to the safety of the public, the court shall enter an order relieving the petitioner of the duty to report. When the court enters an order under this subsection, the petitioner shall send a certified copy of the court order to the Department of State Police. [Formerly 181.820]

Note: 163A.120 (formerly 181.820) is repealed January 1, 2023. See section 34, chapter 708, Oregon Laws 2013, as amended by section 28, chapter 820, Oregon Laws 2015, and section 3, chapter 488, Oregon Laws 2017.

163A.125 Relief from reporting obligation for sex offenders classified under ORS 163A.100; reclassification; procedure. (1)(a) A person who is required to report as a sex offender under ORS 163A.010, 163A.015 or 163A.020 due to a conviction for a sex crime and is classified as a level one sex offender under ORS 163A.100 (1) may petition the State Board of Parole and Post-Prison Supervision to relieve the person from the obligation to report as a sex offender under ORS 163A.010, 163A.015 or 163A.020.

(b) A person who is required to report as a sex offender under ORS 163A.010, 163A.015 or 163A.020 due to being found guilty except for insanity under ORS 161.295 for a sex crime, and is classified as a level one sex offender under ORS 163A.100 (1), may petition the Psychiatric Security Review Board to relieve the person from the obligation to report as a sex offender under ORS 163A.010, 163A.015 or 163A.020.

(c)(A) Except as otherwise provided in subparagraph (B) of this paragraph, a person described in paragraph (a) or (b) of this subsection may file the petition no sooner than five years after the date supervision for the sex crime is terminated or, if the person was not subject to supervision for the sex crime, five years after the date the person was discharged from the jurisdiction of the court, Psychiatric Security Review Board or Oregon Health Authority.

(B) A person who was reclassified under subsection (2) of this section from a level two sex offender under ORS 163A.100 (2) to a level one sex offender under ORS 163A.100 (1) may file the petition no sooner than five years after the date of reclassification.

(d) Notwithstanding paragraph (c) of this subsection, if a person is required to report because of a conviction or finding of guilty except for insanity from another United States court as that term is defined in ORS 163A.005, the person may not petition for relief from reporting as a sex offender in Oregon unless the laws of the jurisdiction where the person was convicted or found guilty except for insanity would permit a petition for relief from reporting as a sex offender.

(2)(a) A person who is required to report as a sex offender under ORS 163A.010, 163A.015 or 163A.020 due to a conviction for a sex crime and is classified as a level three sex offender under ORS 163A.100 (3) may petition the

State Board of Parole and Post-Prison Supervision to reclassify the person as a level two sex offender under ORS 163A.100 (2).

(b) A person who is required to report as a sex offender under ORS 163A.010, 163A.015 or 163A.020 due to being found guilty except for insanity under ORS 161.295 for a sex crime, and is classified as a level three sex offender under ORS 163A.100 (3), may petition the Psychiatric Security Review Board to reclassify the person as a level two sex offender under ORS 163A.100 (2).

(c) A person who is required to report as a sex offender under ORS 163A.010, 163A.015 or 163A.020 due to a conviction for a sex crime and is classified as a level two sex offender under ORS 163A.100 (2) may petition the State Board of Parole and Post-Prison Supervision to reclassify the person as a level one sex offender under ORS 163A.100 (1).

(d) A person who is required to report as a sex offender under ORS 163A.010, 163A.015 or 163A.020 due to being found guilty except for insanity under ORS 161.295 for a sex crime, and is classified as a level two sex offender under ORS 163A.100 (2), may petition the Psychiatric Security Review Board to reclassify the person as a level one sex offender under ORS 163A.100 (1).

(e) The petition described in this subsection may be filed no sooner than 10 years after the date supervision for the sex crime is terminated or, if the person was not subject to supervision for the sex crime, 10 years after the date the person was discharged from the jurisdiction of the court, Psychiatric Security Review Board or Oregon Health Authority.

(3)(a) The State Board of Parole and Post-Prison Supervision or the Psychiatric Security Review Board shall deny a petition filed under this section if, at any time after the person is convicted or found guilty except for insanity of a sex crime, the person is convicted of or found guilty except for insanity of a person felony or a person Class A misdemeanor, as those terms are defined in the rules of the Oregon Criminal Justice Commission.

(b) The appropriate board shall deny a petition filed under subsection (2)(c) or (d) of this section if the board has previously reclassified the person as a level two sex offender under ORS 163A.100 (2) as the result of a petition filed under subsection (2)(a) or (b) of this section.

(4)(a) Except as otherwise provided in subsection (3) of this section, if a person files a petition under subsection (1) of this section, the State Board of Parole and Post-Prison Supervision or the Psychiatric Security Review Board shall hold a hearing. At the hearing, the board shall enter an order relieving the person of the obligation to report as a sex offender under ORS 163A.010, 163A.015 or 163A.020 if the board determines, by clear and convincing evidence, that the person:

(A) Is statistically unlikely to reoffend; and

(B) Does not pose a threat to the safety of the public.

(b)(A) Except as otherwise provided in subsection (3) of this section, if a person files a petition under subsection (2)(a) or (b) of this section, the State Board of Parole and Post-Prison Supervision or the Psychiatric Security Review Board shall hold a hearing. At the hearing, the board shall enter an order reclassifying the person as a level two sex offender under ORS 163A.100 (2) if, after completion of a new risk assessment utilizing the risk assessment methodology described in ORS 163A.100, the person is classified as presenting a low or moderate risk of reoffending and the board determines that a lower level of notification is sufficient to protect public safety.

(B) Except as otherwise provided in subsection (3) of this section, if a person files a petition under subsection (2)(c) or (d) of this section, the State Board of Parole and Post-Prison Supervision or the Psychiatric Security Review Board shall hold a hearing. At the hearing, the board shall enter an order reclassifying the person as a level one sex offender under ORS 163A.100 (1) if, after completion of a new risk assessment utilizing the risk assessment methodology described in ORS 163A.100, the person is classified as presenting a low risk of reoffending and the board determines that a lower level of notification is sufficient to protect public safety.

(5) In making the determinations described in subsection (4) of this section, the State Board of Parole and Post-Prison Supervision or the Psychiatric Security Review Board shall consider:

(a) The nature of and degree of violence involved in the offense that requires reporting;

(b) The age and number of victims of the offense that requires reporting;

(c) The age of the person at the time of the offense that requires reporting;

(d) The length of time since the offense that requires reporting and the time period during which the person has not reoffended;

(e) The person's performance on supervision for the offense that requires reporting;

(f) Whether the person has participated in or successfully completed a court-approved sex offender treatment program or any other rehabilitative programs;

(g) The person's stability in employment and housing;

(h) The person's community and personal support system;

(i) Other criminal and relevant noncriminal behavior of the person both before and after the offense that requires reporting; and

(j) Any other relevant factors.

(6)(a) The Attorney General may represent the state at a hearing conducted under this section unless the district attorney of the county in which the person was convicted or, if the conviction for which the person is required to report as a sex offender was entered in another United States court, the district attorney of the county in which the person resides, elects to represent the state.

(b) If a district attorney elects to represent the state, the district attorney shall give timely written notice of the election to the Attorney General, the State Board of Parole and Post-Prison Supervision or the Psychiatric Security Review Board and the person who is the subject of the hearing.

(c) If the district attorney declines to represent the state, the district attorney shall cooperate with the Attorney General in securing the material necessary to represent the state.

(7)(a) When the State Board of Parole and Post-Prison Supervision or the Psychiatric Security Review Board enters an order under this section relieving a person of the obligation to report as a sex offender under ORS 163A.010, 163A.015 or 163A.020 or enters an order reclassifying a person as a level two sex offender under ORS 163A.100 (2) or as a level one sex offender under ORS 163A.100 (1), the board shall forward a copy of the order to the Department of State Police.

(b) Upon receipt of an order relieving a person of the obligation to report, the department shall remove from the Law Enforcement Data System the sex offender information obtained from the sex offender registration form submitted under ORS 163A.010, 163A.015 or 163A.020.

(c) Upon receipt of an order reclassifying a person as a level two sex offender under ORS 163A.100 (2) or as a level one sex offender under ORS 163A.100 (1), the department shall update the Law Enforcement Data System to reflect the reclassification.

(8) The State Board of Parole and Post-Prison Supervision and the Psychiatric Security Review Board shall adopt rules to carry out the provisions of this section. The rules may include a filing fee in an amount determined by the appropriate board. All fees paid under this subsection shall be deposited into the General Fund and credited to the account of the appropriate board.

(9) As used in this section, "supervision" means probation, parole, post-prison supervision or any other form of supervised or conditional release. [Formerly 181.821]

Note: See notes under 163A.115.

163A.130 Relief from reporting obligation for juvenile offenders adjudicated in Oregon. (1) A person required to report as a sex offender under ORS 163A.025 (1)(a), (b) or (c), or required to report as a sex offender under the laws of another state as a result of an adjudication in an Oregon juvenile court, may file a petition for an order relieving the person of the obligation to report. The person must pay the filing fee established under ORS 21.135. If the person resides:

(a) In this state and is required to report under ORS 163A.025 (2) or (3), the petition must be filed in the juvenile court in which the person was adjudicated for the act that requires reporting.

(b) In another state and is required to report under ORS 163A.025 (4), the petition must be filed in the juvenile court in the county in which the person attends school or works.

(c) In another state and is required to report under the laws of the other state, the petition must be filed in the juvenile court in which the person was adjudicated for the act that requires reporting.

(2) If the act giving rise to the obligation to report would constitute:

(a) A Class A or Class B felony sex crime if committed by an adult, the petition may be filed no sooner than two years after the termination of juvenile court jurisdiction over the person or, if the person is placed under the jurisdiction of the Psychiatric Security Review Board, no sooner than two years after the person is discharged from the jurisdiction of the board.

(b) A Class C felony sex crime if committed by an adult, the petition may be filed no sooner than 30 days before the termination of juvenile court jurisdiction over the person or, if the person is placed under the jurisdiction of the Psychiatric Security Review Board, no sooner than 30 days before the person is discharged from the jurisdiction of the board.

(3)(a) The juvenile court in which a petition under this section is filed may transfer the matter to the juvenile court of the county that last supervised the person if the court determines that the convenience of the parties, the victim and witnesses require the transfer.

(b) The juvenile court has exclusive original jurisdiction in any proceeding under this section.

(c) The person, the district attorney and the juvenile department are parties to a hearing on a petition filed under this section.

(4) The person filing the petition has the burden of proving by clear and convincing evidence that the person is rehabilitated and does not pose a threat to the safety of the public. In determining whether the person has met the burden of proof, the juvenile court may consider but need not be limited to considering:

(a) The extent and impact of any physical or emotional injury to the victim;

(b) The nature of the act that subjected the person to the obligation of reporting as a sex offender;

(c) Whether the person used or threatened to use force in committing the act;

(d) Whether the act was premeditated;

(e) Whether the person took advantage of a position of authority or trust in committing the act;

(f) The age of any victim at the time of the act, the age difference between any victim and the person and the number of victims;

(g) The vulnerability of the victim;

(h) Other acts committed by the person that would be crimes if committed by an adult and criminal activities engaged in by the person before and after the adjudication;

(i) Statements, documents and recommendations by or on behalf of the victim or the parents of the victim;

(j) The person's willingness to accept personal responsibility for the act and personal accountability for the consequences of the act;

(k) The person's ability and efforts to pay the victim's expenses for counseling and other trauma-related expenses or other efforts to mitigate the effects of the act;

(L) Whether the person has participated in and satisfactorily completed a sex offender treatment program or any other intervention, and if so the juvenile court may also consider:

(A) The availability, duration and extent of the treatment activities;

(B) Reports and recommendations from the providers of the treatment;

(C) The person's compliance with court, board or supervision requirements regarding treatment; and

(D) The quality and thoroughness of the treatment program;

(m) The person's academic and employment history;

(n) The person's use of drugs or alcohol before and after the adjudication;

(o) The person's history of public or private indecency;

(p) The person's compliance with and success in completing the terms of supervision;

(q) The results of psychological examinations of the person;

(r) The protection afforded the public by the continued existence of the records; and

(s) Any other relevant factors.

(5) In a hearing under this section, the juvenile court may receive testimony, reports and other evidence without regard to whether the evidence is admissible under ORS 40.010 to 40.210 and 40.310 to 40.585 if the evidence is relevant to the determination and findings required under this section. As used in this subsection, "relevant evidence" has the meaning given that term in ORS 40.150.

(6) When a petition is filed under this section, the state has the right to have a psychosexual evaluation of the person conducted. The state shall file notice with the juvenile court of its intention to have the person evaluated. If the person objects to the evaluator chosen by the state, the juvenile court for good cause shown may direct the state to select a different evaluator.

(7) As soon as practicable after a petition has been filed under this section, the district attorney or juvenile department shall make a reasonable effort to notify the victim of the crime that the person has filed a petition seeking relief under this section and, if the victim has requested, to inform the victim of the date, time and place of a hearing on the petition in advance of the hearing.

(8)(a) When a petition filed under this section is filed:

(A) While the person is under the jurisdiction of the juvenile court or the Psychiatric Security Review Board or less than three years after the date the jurisdiction is terminated, the court shall hold a hearing no sooner than 60 days and no later than 120 days after the date of filing.

(B) Three years or more after the date the juvenile court or board jurisdiction is terminated, the court shall hold a hearing no sooner than 90 days and no later than 150 days after the date of filing.

(b) Notwithstanding paragraph (a) of this subsection, upon a showing of good cause, the court may extend the period of time in which a hearing on the petition must be held.

(9)(a) When the person proves by clear and convincing evidence that the person is rehabilitated and does not pose a threat to the safety of the public, the court shall grant the petition.

(b) Notwithstanding paragraph (a) of this subsection, the court may not grant a petition filed under this section before the date the juvenile court or board jurisdiction over the person is terminated.

(10) When a juvenile court enters an order relieving a person of the requirement to report under ORS 163A.025, the person shall send a certified copy of the juvenile court order to the Department of State Police.

(11) If a person commits an act that could be charged as a sex crime listed in ORS 137.707 and the person is 15, 16 or 17 years of age at the time the act is committed, the state and the person may stipulate that the person may not petition for relief under this section as part of an agreement that the person be subject to the jurisdiction of the juvenile court rather than being prosecuted as an adult under ORS 137.707.

(12) When a petition is filed under subsection (2)(b) of this section before the termination of juvenile court or board jurisdiction, if the person, or the parent or guardian of the person if the person is less than 18 years of age, requests counsel and is without sufficient financial means to employ suitable counsel to represent the person, for purposes of the petition described in this section, the court shall appoint suitable counsel to represent the person. Appointment of counsel under this subsection is subject to ORS 419C.200, 419C.203, 419C.206 and 419C.209. [Formerly 181.823; 2016 c.95 §5]

163A.135 Relief from reporting obligation for juvenile offenders adjudicated in another United States jurisdiction. (1) Except as provided in subsection (7) of this section, a person required to report under ORS

163A.025 (1)(d) may file a petition in the juvenile court for an order relieving the person of the duty to report. The person must pay the filing fee established under ORS 21.135. If the person resides:

(a) In this state and is required to report under ORS 163A.025 (2) or (3), the petition must be filed in the juvenile court of the county in which the person resides.

(b) In another state and is required to report under ORS 163A.025 (4), the petition must be filed in the juvenile court of the county in which the person attends school or works.

(2) If the act giving rise to the obligation to report would constitute:

(a) A Class A or Class B felony sex crime if committed in this state by an adult, the petition may be filed no sooner than two years after the termination of the other United States court's jurisdiction over the person.

(b) A Class C felony sex crime if committed in this state by an adult, the petition may be filed no sooner than 30 days before the termination of the other United States court's jurisdiction over the person.

(3) The person filing the petition must submit with the petition all releases and waivers necessary to allow the district attorney for the county in which the petition is filed to obtain the following documents from the jurisdiction in which the person was adjudicated for the act for which reporting is required:

(a) The juvenile court petition;

(b) The dispositional report to the court;

(c) The order of adjudication or jurisdiction;

(d) Any other relevant court documents;

(e) The police report relating to the act for which reporting is required;

(f) The order terminating jurisdiction for the act for which reporting is required; and

(g) The evaluation and treatment records or reports of the person that are related to the act for which reporting is required.

(4) A person filing a petition under this section has the burden of proving by clear and convincing evidence that the person is rehabilitated and does not pose a threat to the safety of the public.

(5) Unless the court finds good cause for a continuance, the court shall hold a hearing on the petition no sooner than 90 days and no later than 150 days after the date the petition is filed.

(6) If a person who files a petition under this section is required to report as a sex offender for having committed an act that if committed in this state could have subjected the person to prosecution as an adult under ORS 137.707, the court may not grant the petition notwithstanding the fact that the person has met the burden of proof established in subsection (4) of this section unless the court determines that to do so is in the interest of public safety.

(7) This section does not apply to a person who is required to register as a sex offender for life in the jurisdiction in which the offense occurred.

(8) In a hearing under this section, the court may receive testimony, reports and other evidence without regard to whether the evidence is admissible under ORS 40.010 to 40.210 and 40.310 to 40.585 if the evidence is relevant to the determination and findings required under this section. As used in this subsection, "relevant evidence" has the meaning given that term in ORS 40.150.

(9) If the court is satisfied by clear and convincing evidence that the person is rehabilitated and that the person does not pose a threat to the safety of the public, the court shall enter an order relieving the person of the duty to report. When the court enters an order under this subsection, the person shall send a certified copy of the court order to the Department of State Police. [Formerly 181.826; 2016 c.95 §6]

163A.140 Relief from reporting obligation; circumstances; order. A person otherwise required to report under ORS 163A.010, 163A.015, 163A.020 or 163A.025 is not required to report, and if currently reporting is no longer required to report, if:

(1)(a) The person has been convicted of:

(A) Rape in the third degree as defined in ORS 163.355;

(B) Sodomy in the third degree as defined in ORS 163.385;

(C) Sexual abuse in the third degree as defined in ORS 163.415;

(D) Contributing to the sexual delinquency of a minor as defined in ORS 163.435;

(E) Sexual misconduct as defined in ORS 163.445; or

(F) An attempt to commit an offense listed in subparagraphs (A) to (E) of this paragraph;

(b) The person has been found guilty except for insanity of an offense listed in paragraph (a) of this subsection;

(c) The person has been found to be within the jurisdiction of the juvenile court for having committed an act that if committed by an adult would constitute an offense listed in paragraph (a)(A) or (B) of this subsection; or

(d) The person is paroled to this state under ORS 144.610 after being convicted in another United States court of a crime that would constitute an offense listed in paragraph (a) of this subsection;

(2)(a) The person is less than five years older than the victim;

(b) The victim's lack of consent was due solely to incapacity to consent by reason of being less than a specified age;

(c) The victim was at least 14 years of age at the time of the offense or act;

(d) Except for the convictions or findings described in subsection (1) of this section, the person has not been convicted of, found guilty except for insanity of, or found to be within the jurisdiction of the juvenile court based on, a

114

sex crime or an offense, in another United States court, for conduct that if committed in this state would constitute a sex crime; and

(e) Each conviction or finding described in subsection (1) of this section involved the same victim; and

(3) The court enters an order relieving the person of the requirement to report under ORS 163A.145 or 163A.150. [Formerly 181.830]

163A.145 Procedure for relief under ORS 163A.140; upon conviction or adjudication. (1) When a person is convicted of an offense or adjudicated for an act described in ORS 163A.140 (1), the court shall determine whether the person is required to report under ORS 163A.010 or 163A.015.

(2) The court shall enter an order relieving the person of the requirement to report, unless:

(a) The court finds by a preponderance of the evidence that the person does not meet the eligibility requirements described in ORS 163A.140; or

(b) The district attorney and the person stipulate that the person is required to report.

(3) The state has the burden of proving that the person does not meet the eligibility requirements described in ORS 163A.140.

(4) If the court relieves the person from the requirement to report, the person shall send a certified copy of the court order to the Department of State Police. [Formerly 181.832]

163A.150 Procedure for relief under ORS 163A.140; after conviction or adjudication; testimony of victim. (1) A person who meets the criteria described in ORS 163A.140 and seeks relief from the requirement to report under ORS 163A.010, 163A.015 or 163A.020 shall:

(a) If the person was convicted in this state of the offense or adjudicated in this state for the act giving rise to the obligation to report, file a motion for relief from the requirement to report and an affidavit of eligibility with the circuit court of the county in which the person was convicted or adjudicated and serve a copy of the motion and affidavit on the district attorney for that county.

(b) If the person was convicted in another United States court of the offense or adjudicated in another United States court for the act giving rise to the obligation to report, file a petition for relief from the requirement to report and an affidavit of eligibility with the circuit court of the county in which the person resides and serve a copy of the petition and affidavit on the district attorney for that county.

(2) A person filing a motion or petition under subsection (1) of this section must pay the filing fee established under ORS 21.135. The court shall schedule a hearing more than 90 days from the date of the filing. The court shall notify the person and the district attorney of the date of the hearing.

(3)(a) Upon receipt of the affidavit described in subsection (1) of this section, the district attorney shall determine whether the district attorney contests the request for relief.

(b) If the district attorney does not contest the request for relief, the district attorney shall submit an order to the court relieving the person of the reporting requirements described in ORS 163A.010, 163A.015 or 163A.020. The court shall enter the order.

(c) If the district attorney contests the request for relief, the district attorney shall notify the person of that determination within 90 days after receipt of the affidavit.

(4) At the hearing, the person has the burden of proving that the person meets the eligibility requirements described in ORS 163A.140.

(5)(a) At the hearing, the victim of the offense or act giving rise to the obligation to report:

(A) May testify voluntarily upon request.

(B) May be compelled by the person to testify only if the court issues an order allowing a subpoena upon the motion of the person.

(b) A copy of the motion for a subpoena under this subsection must be served on the district attorney.

(c) The court may not issue an order allowing a subpoena under this subsection unless the person can demonstrate good cause by showing that the victim's testimony is material and favorable to the person's request for relief.

(d) If the court grants an order allowing a subpoena under this subsection, the court may allow the victim to appear by telephone or other communication device approved by the court.

(6)(a) If the court finds, by a preponderance of the evidence, that the person meets the eligibility requirements described in ORS 163A.140, the court shall enter an order granting the request for relief from the requirement to report.

(b) If the court does not make the finding described in paragraph (a) of this subsection, the court shall enter an order denying the request for relief.

(7)(a) If the court relieves the person from the requirement to report, the person shall send a certified copy of the court order to the Department of State Police.

(b) Upon receipt of the order, the Department of State Police shall remove from the Law Enforcement Data System the sex offender information obtained from the sex offender registration form submitted under ORS 163A.010, 163A.015 or 163A.020.

(8) The order entered under subsection (6) of this section is not subject to appeal.

(9) The Oregon Evidence Code and the Oregon Rules of Civil Procedure do not apply to the hearing described in subsection (2) of this section. [Formerly 181.833]

PROVISION OF RECORDS BY AGENCIES

163A.200 Provision of records by Psychiatric Security Review Board and Oregon Health Authority. (1) Notwithstanding ORS 179.505, the Psychiatric Security Review Board and the Oregon Health Authority shall provide to the State Board of Parole and Post-Prison Supervision any records that would assist the State Board of Parole and Post-Prison Supervision in:

(a) Performing an initial classification of a person into one of the three levels described in ORS 163A.100, as required by ORS 163A.105;

(b) Deciding whether to reclassify a person as a level one or a level two sex offender or relieve the person from the obligation to report as a sex offender, as described in ORS 163A.125; or

(c) Conducting a risk assessment of a person who is an existing registrant to classify the person into one of the three levels described in ORS 163A.100, as required by section 7, chapter 708, Oregon Laws 2013.

(2) The State Board of Parole and Post-Prison Supervision may not release any records obtained pursuant to this section to any other agency or person unless authorized by law to do so. [2015 c.820 §19]

Note: 163A.200 to 163A.210 were enacted into law by the Legislative Assembly but were not added to or made a part of ORS chapter 163A or any series therein by legislative action. See Preface to Oregon Revised Statutes for further explanation.

163A.205 Provision of records by Oregon Health Authority. (1) Notwithstanding ORS 179.505, the Oregon Health Authority shall provide to the Psychiatric Security Review Board any records that would assist the board in:

(a) Performing an initial classification of a person into one of the three levels described in ORS 163A.100, as required by ORS 163A.105;

(b) Deciding whether to reclassify a person as a level one or a level two sex offender or relieve the person from the obligation to report as a sex offender, as described in ORS 163A.125; or

(c) Conducting a risk assessment of a person who is an existing registrant to classify the person into one of the three levels described in ORS 163A.100, as required by section 7, chapter 708, Oregon Laws 2013.

(2) The board may not release any records obtained pursuant to this section to any other agency or person unless authorized by law to do so. [2015 c.820 §20]

Note: See note under 163A.200.

163A.210 Provision of records by Oregon Youth Authority and juvenile department. Notwithstanding ORS 419A.257 or any other provision of law, the Oregon Youth Authority and the juvenile department may disclose and provide copies of reports and other materials relating to a child, ward, youth or youth offender's history and prognosis to the Psychiatric Security Review Board or the State Board of Parole and Post-Prison Supervision in order for the boards to determine whether to reclassify the person as a level one or a level two sex offender or relieve the person from the obligation to report as a sex offender, as described in ORS 163A.125, or whether to classify a person who is an existing registrant into one of the three levels described in ORS 163A.100, as required by section 7, chapter 708, Oregon Laws 2013. [2015 c.820 §21; 2017 c.442 §32; 2017 c.488 §6]

Note: See note under 163A.200.

RELEASE OF INFORMATION

163A.215 Release of sex offender information according to classification. (1)(a) A notifying agency or a supervising agency shall release, upon request, any information that may be necessary to protect the public concerning sex offenders who reside in a specific area or concerning a specific sex offender.

(b) A notifying agency or a supervising agency may release sex offender information to a law enforcement agency if the notifying agency or supervising agency determines that the release of information is in the public interest.

(c) In addition to the release of information described in this subsection and ORS 137.540, 144.260 and 441.373, a notifying agency or a supervising agency may release sex offender information to the public in accordance with subsections (2) to (4) of this section.

(2) If the sex offender is classified as a level three sex offender under ORS 163A.100 (3):

(a) The Department of State Police shall release sex offender information on a website maintained by the department; and

(b) The supervising agency or a notifying agency may release sex offender information to:

(A) A person that resides with the sex offender;

(B) A person with whom the sex offender has a significant relationship;

(C) Residential neighbors and churches, community parks, schools and child care centers, convenience stores, businesses and other places that children or other potential victims may frequent;

(D) A long term care facility, as defined in ORS 442.015, or a residential care facility, as defined in ORS 443.400, if the agency knows that the sex offender is seeking admission to the facility; and

(E) Local or regional media sources.

(3) Notwithstanding subsection (2)(a) of this section, the Department of State Police may not use the Internet to make available to the public information concerning a sex offender classified as a level three sex offender under ORS 163A.100 (3) while the person is under the supervision of the Psychiatric Security Review Board, unless the department is authorized to do so by a request of the supervising agency.

(4) If the sex offender is classified as a level two sex offender under ORS 163A.100 (2), the supervising agency or a notifying agency may release sex offender information to the persons or entities described in subsection (2)(b)(A) to (D) of this section.

(5) If the sex offender is classified as a level one sex offender under ORS 163A.100 (1), the supervising agency or a notifying agency may release sex offender information to a person described in subsection (2)(b)(A) of this section.

(6) As used in this section:

(a) "Notifying agency" means the Department of State Police, a city police department, a county sheriff's office or a police department established by a university under ORS 352.121.

(b) "Sex offender information" means information that the Department of State Police determines by rule is appropriate for release to the public.

(c) "Supervising agency" means a governmental entity responsible for supervising a person required to report as a sex offender under ORS 163A.010 or 163A.015. [Formerly 181.835; 2017 c.442 §33]

Note: The amendments to 163A.215 by section 33, chapter 442, Oregon Laws 2017, become operative July 1, 2018. See section 36, chapter 442, Oregon Laws 2017. The text that is operative until July 1, 2018, is set forth for the user's convenience.

163A.215. (1)(a) A notifying agency or a supervising agency shall release, upon request, any information that may be necessary to protect the public concerning sex offenders who reside in a specific area or concerning a specific sex offender.

(b) A notifying agency or a supervising agency may release sex offender information to a law enforcement agency if the notifying agency or supervising agency determines that the release of information is in the public interest.

(c) In addition to the release of information described in this subsection and ORS 137.540, 144.260 and 441.373, a notifying agency or a supervising agency may release sex offender information to the public in accordance with subsections (2) to (4) of this section.

(2) If the sex offender is classified as a level three sex offender under ORS 163A.100 (3):

(a) The Department of State Police shall release sex offender information on a website maintained by the department; and

(b) The supervising agency or a notifying agency may release sex offender information to:

(A) A person that resides with the sex offender;

(B) A person with whom the sex offender has a significant relationship;

(C) Residential neighbors and churches, community parks, schools and child care centers, convenience stores, businesses and other places that children or other potential victims may frequent;

(D) A long term care facility, as defined in ORS 442.015, or a residential care facility, as defined in ORS 443.400, if the agency knows that the sex offender is seeking admission to the facility; and

(E) Local or regional media sources.

(3) Notwithstanding subsection (2)(a) of this section, the Department of State Police may not use the Internet to make available to the public information concerning a sex offender classified as a level three sex offender under ORS 163A.100 (3) while the person is under the supervision of the Psychiatric Security Review Board or the Oregon Health Authority, unless the department is authorized to do so by a request of the supervising agency.

(4) If the sex offender is classified as a level two sex offender under ORS 163A.100 (2), the supervising agency or a notifying agency may release sex offender information to the persons or entities described in subsection (2)(b)(A) to (D) of this section.

(5) If the sex offender is classified as a level one sex offender under ORS 163A.100 (1), the supervising agency or a notifying agency may release sex offender information to a person described in subsection (2)(b)(A) of this section.

(6) As used in this section:

(a) "Notifying agency" means the Department of State Police, a city police department, a county sheriff's office or a police department established by a university under ORS 352.121.

(b) "Sex offender information" means information that the Department of State Police determines by rule is appropriate for release to the public.

(c) "Supervising agency" means a governmental entity responsible for supervising a person required to report as a sex offender under ORS 163A.010 or 163A.015.

Note: See notes under 163A.115.

163A.220 Internet website. The Department of State Police shall consider:
(1) Contracting with a private vendor to build and maintain the website required by ORS 163A.215 (2)(a).
(2) Adding links on the website required by ORS 163A.215 (2)(a) that connect to other sex offender websites run by Oregon counties and by the federal government. [Formerly 181.836]

163A.225 Release of information concerning sex offender adjudicated in juvenile court. (1)(a) Except as otherwise provided in this section, when a sex offender is under the supervision of the Oregon Youth Authority or a county juvenile department for the first time as a result of committing an act that if committed by an adult would constitute a sex crime, the Department of State Police, city police department or county sheriff's office shall release, upon request, only:
(A) The sex offender's name and year of birth;
(B) The name and zip code of the city where the sex offender resides;
(C) The name and telephone number of a contact person at the agency that is supervising the sex offender; and
(D) The name of institutions of higher education that the sex offender attends or at which the sex offender works or carries on a vocation.
(b) Notwithstanding paragraph (a) of this section, the Oregon Youth Authority or a county juvenile department shall release, upon request, any information that may be necessary to protect the public concerning a sex offender under the supervision of the authority or department.
(2) Except as otherwise limited by subsection (1)(a) of this section regarding persons who are under supervision for the first time as sex offenders, the Department of State Police, a city police department or a county sheriff's office shall release, upon request, any information that may be necessary to protect the public concerning sex offenders required to report under ORS 163A.025 who reside in a specific area or concerning a specific sex offender required to report under ORS 163A.025. However, the entity releasing the information may not release the identity of a victim of a sex crime.
(3)(a) The Department of State Police may make the information described in subsections (1) and (2) of this section available to the public, without the need for a request, by electronic or other means. The Department of State Police shall make information about a person who is under supervision for the first time as a result of committing an act that if committed by an adult would constitute a sex crime accessible only by the use of the sex offender's name. For all other sex offenders required to report under ORS 163A.025, the Department of State Police may make the information accessible in any manner the department chooses.
(b) Notwithstanding paragraph (a) of this subsection, the Department of State Police may not use the Internet to make information available to the public. [Formerly 181.837]

163A.230 Victim access to sex offender information; toll-free telephone number. (1)(a) When information about a person is first entered into the Law Enforcement Data System under ORS 163A.035, the person will be assigned a registry identification number.
(b) A victim shall be issued a victim identification number and shall be given the registry identification number of the person who committed the crime against the victim:
(A) At any time, upon request by the victim; and
(B) Upon verification of the identification of the victim.
(2) The Department of State Police shall establish a toll-free telephone number to provide victims with updates on the prison status, release information, parole status and any other information authorized for release under ORS 163A.005 to 163A.235 regarding the person who committed the crime against the victim. The telephone line shall be operational within the state during normal working hours.
(3) Access of the victim to the telephone line shall be revoked if the victim makes public, or otherwise misuses, information received.
(4) When a victim receives notification under ORS 144.750 of upcoming parole release hearings, or at any other time that the victim is notified concerning the offender, the victim shall be provided a notice of rights under this section and information about the toll-free telephone number. [Formerly 181.843]

163A.235 Agreements to resolve concerns about community notification. Upon the request of the Department of State Police, a city police department, a county sheriff's office or a supervising agency, a supervising agency or an agency having responsibility for community notification shall enter into agreements to resolve concerns regarding community notification. As used in this section:
(1) "Community notification" means the disclosure of information to the public as provided in ORS 163A.005 to 163A.235.
(2) "Supervising agency" means a governmental entity responsible for supervising a person required to report under ORS 163A.010, 163A.015 or 163A.025. [Formerly 181.845]

118

ORS sections in this chapter were amended or repealed by the Legislative Assembly during its 2018 regular session. See the table of ORS sections amended or repealed during the 2018 regular session: 2018 A&R Tables

New sections of law were enacted by the Legislative Assembly during its 2018 regular session and pertain to or are likely to be compiled in this ORS chapter. See sections in the following 2018 Oregon Laws chapters: 2018 Session Laws 0076

DEFINITIONS

164.005 Definitions. As used in chapter 743, Oregon Laws 1971, unless the context requires otherwise:

(1) "Appropriate property of another to oneself or a third person" or "appropriate" means to:

(a) Exercise control over property of another, or to aid a third person to exercise control over property of another, permanently or for so extended a period or under such circumstances as to acquire the major portion of the economic value or benefit of such property; or

(b) Dispose of the property of another for the benefit of oneself or a third person.

(2) "Deprive another of property" or "deprive" means to:

(a) Withhold property of another or cause property of another to be withheld from that person permanently or for so extended a period or under such circumstances that the major portion of its economic value or benefit is lost to that person; or

(b) Dispose of the property in such manner or under such circumstances as to render it unlikely that an owner will recover such property.

(3) "Obtain" includes, but is not limited to, the bringing about of a transfer or purported transfer of property or of a legal interest therein, whether to the obtainer or another.

(4) "Owner of property taken, obtained or withheld" or "owner" means any person who has a right to possession thereof superior to that of the taker, obtainer or withholder.

(5) "Property" means any article, substance or thing of value, including, but not limited to, money, tangible and intangible personal property, real property, choses-in-action, evidence of debt or of contract. [1971 c.743 §121]

Note: Legislative Counsel has substituted "chapter 743, Oregon Laws 1971," for the words "this Act" in sections 121 and 131, chapter 743, Oregon Laws 1971, compiled as 164.005 and 164.115. Specific ORS references have not been substituted, pursuant to 173.160. These sections may be determined by referring to the 1971 Comparative Section Table located in Volume 20 of ORS.

164.010 [Amended by 1959 c.236 §1; repealed by 1971 c.743 §432]

THEFT AND RELATED OFFENSES

164.015 "Theft" described. A person commits theft when, with intent to deprive another of property or to appropriate property to the person or to a third person, the person:

(1) Takes, appropriates, obtains or withholds such property from an owner thereof;

(2) Commits theft of property lost, mislaid or delivered by mistake as provided in ORS 164.065;

(3) Commits extortion as provided in ORS 164.075 by compelling or inducing another person to deliver property;

(4) Commits theft by deception as provided in ORS 164.085; or

(5) Commits theft by receiving as provided in ORS 164.095. [1971 c.743 §123; 2007 c.71 §47; 2016 c.47 §7]

164.020 [Amended by 1959 c.236 §2; repealed by 1971 c.743 §432]

164.025 Consolidation of theft offenses; pleading and proof. (1) Except for the crime of extortion, conduct denominated theft under ORS 164.015 constitutes a single offense.

(2) If it is an element of the crime charged that property was taken by extortion, an accusation of theft must so specify. In all other cases an accusation of theft is sufficient if it alleges that the defendant committed theft of property of the nature or value required for the commission of the crime charged without designating the particular way or manner in which the theft was committed.

(3) Proof that the defendant engaged in conduct constituting theft as defined in ORS 164.015 is sufficient to support any indictment, information or complaint for theft other than one charging extortion. An accusation of extortion must be supported by proof establishing extortion. [1971 c.743 §122; 2016 c.47 §8]

164.030 [Amended by 1955 c.37 §1; 1959 c.236 §3; repealed by 1971 c.743 §432]

164.035 Defenses. (1) In a prosecution for theft it is a defense that the defendant acted under an honest claim of right, in that:

(a) The defendant was unaware that the property was that of another; or

(b) The defendant reasonably believed that the defendant was entitled to the property involved or had a right to acquire or dispose of it as the defendant did.

(2) In a prosecution for extortion committed by instilling in the victim a fear that the victim or another person would be charged with a crime, it is a defense that the defendant reasonably believed the threatened charge to be true and that the sole purpose of the defendant was to compel or induce the victim to take reasonable action to make good the wrong which was the subject of the threatened charge.

(3) In a prosecution for theft by receiving, it is a defense that the defendant received, retained, concealed or disposed of the property with the intent of restoring it to the owner.

(4) It is a defense that the property involved was that of the defendant's spouse, unless the parties were not living together as spouses in a marriage and were living in separate abodes at the time of the alleged theft. [1971 c.743 §132; 2001 c.104 §53; 2015 c.629 §31; 2016 c.47 §9]

164.040 [Amended by 1959 c.236 §4; repealed by 1971 c.743 §432]

164.043 Theft in the third degree. (1) A person commits the crime of theft in the third degree if:

(a) By means other than extortion, the person commits theft as defined in ORS 164.015; and

(b) The total value of the property in a single or an aggregate transaction is less than $100.

(2) Theft in the third degree is a Class C misdemeanor. [1987 c.907 §2; 2009 c.11 §11; 2009 c.16 §1]

164.045 Theft in the second degree. (1) A person commits the crime of theft in the second degree if:

(a) By means other than extortion, the person commits theft as defined in ORS 164.015; and

(b) The total value of the property in a single or aggregate transaction is $100 or more and less than $1,000.

(2) Theft in the second degree is a Class A misdemeanor. [1971 c.743 §124; 1987 c.907 §3; 1993 c.680 §19; 2009 c.11 §12; 2009 c.16 §2]

164.050 [Repealed by 1965 c.253 §153]

164.055 Theft in the first degree. (1) A person commits the crime of theft in the first degree if, by means other than extortion, the person commits theft as defined in ORS 164.015 and:

(a) The total value of the property in a single or aggregate transaction is $1,000 or more;

(b) The theft is committed during a riot, fire, explosion, catastrophe or other emergency in an area affected by the riot, fire, explosion, catastrophe or other emergency;

(c) The theft is theft by receiving committed by buying, selling, borrowing or lending on the security of the property;

(d) The subject of the theft is a firearm or explosive;

(e) The subject of the theft is a livestock animal, a companion animal or a wild animal removed from habitat or born of a wild animal removed from habitat, pursuant to ORS 497.308 (2)(c); or

(f) The subject of the theft is a precursor substance.

(2) As used in this section:

(a) "Companion animal" means a dog or cat possessed by a person, business or other entity for purposes of companionship, security, hunting, herding or providing assistance in relation to a physical disability.

(b) "Explosive" means a chemical compound, mixture or device that is commonly used or intended for the purpose of producing a chemical reaction resulting in a substantially instantaneous release of gas and heat, including but not limited to dynamite, blasting powder, nitroglycerin, blasting caps and nitrojelly, but excluding fireworks as defined in ORS 480.111, black powder, smokeless powder, small arms ammunition and small arms ammunition primers.

(c) "Firearm" has the meaning given that term in ORS 166.210.

(d) "Livestock animal" means a ratite, psittacine, horse, gelding, mare, filly, stallion, colt, mule, ass, jenny, bull, steer, cow, calf, goat, sheep, lamb, llama, pig or hog.

(e) "Precursor substance" has the meaning given that term in ORS 475.940.

(3) Theft in the first degree is a Class C felony. [1971 c.743 §125; 1973 c.405 §1; 1983 c.740 §32; 1987 c.907 §4; 1991 c.837 §9; 1993 c.252 §5; 1993 c.680 §20; 2005 c.706 §10; 2009 c.16 §3; 2009 c.610 §6; 2013 c.24 §11]

164.057 Aggravated theft in the first degree. (1) A person commits the crime of aggravated theft in the first degree, if:

(a) The person violates ORS 164.055 with respect to property, other than a motor vehicle used primarily for personal rather than commercial transportation; and

(b) The value of the property in a single or aggregate transaction is $10,000 or more.

(2) Aggravated theft in the first degree is a Class B felony. [1987 c.907 §5]

164.060 [Repealed by 1965 c.253 §153]

164.061 Sentence for aggravated theft in the first degree when victim 65 years of age or older. When a person is convicted of aggravated theft in the first degree under ORS 164.057, the court shall sentence the person to a term of incarceration ranging from 16 months to 45 months, depending on the person's criminal history, if:

(1) The victim of the theft was 65 years of age or older at the time of the commission of the offense; and

(2) The value of the property stolen from the victim described in subsection (1) of this section, in a single or aggregate transaction, is $10,000 or more. [2008 c.14 §4]

Note: 164.061 was enacted into law but was not added to or made a part of ORS chapter 164 or any series therein by law. See Preface to Oregon Revised Statutes for further explanation.

164.063 Disproportionate impact; rules. (1) As used in this section, "disproportionate impact" means that, in a case of theft in the first degree under ORS 164.055 or aggravated theft in the first degree under ORS 164.057:

(a) The offender caused damage to property during the commission of the theft and the cost to restore the damaged property to the condition the property was in immediately before the theft is more than three times the value of the property that was the subject of the theft; or

(b) The theft of the property creates a hazard to public health or safety or the environment.

(2) The Oregon Criminal Justice Commission shall adopt rules that establish disproportionate impact as an aggravating factor that a court may consider as a substantial and compelling reason to impose an upward departure from a presumptive sentence under the rules of the commission. [2009 c.811 §7]

Note: 164.063 was enacted into law by the Legislative Assembly but was not added to or made a part of ORS chapter 164 or any series therein by legislative action. See Preface to Oregon Revised Statutes for further explanation.

164.065 Theft of lost, mislaid property. A person who comes into control of property of another that the person knows or has good reason to know to have been lost, mislaid or delivered under a mistake as to the nature or amount of the property or the identity of the recipient, commits theft if, with intent to deprive the owner thereof, the person fails to take reasonable measures to restore the property to the owner. [1971 c.743 §126]

164.070 [Amended by 1965 c.253 §131; repealed by 1971 c.743 §432]

164.075 Extortion. (1) A person commits the crime of extortion when the person compels or induces another person to either deliver property or services to the person or to a third person, or refrain from reporting unlawful conduct to a law enforcement agency, by instilling in the other person a fear that, if the property or services are not so delivered or if the unlawful conduct is reported, the actor or a third person will in the future:

(a) Unlawfully cause physical injury to some person;

(b) Unlawfully cause damage to property;

(c) Engage in other conduct constituting a crime;

(d) Accuse some person of a crime or cause criminal charges to be instituted against the person;

(e) Report the immigration status, or suspected immigration status, of the other person, or some other person known to the other person, to a law enforcement agency;

(f) Cause or continue a strike, boycott or other collective action injurious to some person's business, except that such conduct is not considered extortion when the property is demanded or received for the benefit of the group in whose interest the actor purports to act;

(g) Testify falsely or provide false information or withhold testimony or information with respect to another's legal claim or defense; or

(h) Unlawfully use or abuse the position as a public servant by performing some act within or related to official duties, or by failing or refusing to perform an official duty, in such manner as to affect some person adversely.

(2) Extortion is a Class B felony. [1971 c.743 §127; 1987 c.158 §27; 2007 c.71 §48; 2016 c.47 §2]

164.080 [Repealed by 1971 c.743 §432]

164.085 Theft by deception. (1) A person, who obtains property of another thereby, commits theft by deception when, with intent to defraud, the person:

(a) Creates or confirms another's false impression of law, value, intention or other state of mind that the actor does not believe to be true;

(b) Fails to correct a false impression that the person previously created or confirmed;

(c) Prevents another from acquiring information pertinent to the disposition of the property involved;

(d) Sells or otherwise transfers or encumbers property, failing to disclose a lien, adverse claim or other legal impediment to the enjoyment of the property, whether such impediment is or is not valid, or is or is not a matter of official record; or

(e) Promises performance that the person does not intend to perform or knows will not be performed.

(2) "Deception" does not include falsity as to matters having no pecuniary significance, or representations unlikely to deceive ordinary persons in the group addressed. For purposes of this subsection, the theft of a companion animal, as defined in ORS 164.055, or a captive wild animal is a matter having pecuniary significance.

(3) In a prosecution for theft by deception, the defendant's intention or belief that a promise would not be performed may not be established by or inferred from the fact alone that such promise was not performed.

(4) In a prosecution for theft by deception committed by means of a bad check, it is prima facie evidence of knowledge that the check or order would not be honored if:

(a) The drawer has no account with the drawee at the time the check or order is drawn or uttered; or

(b) Payment is refused by the drawee for lack of funds, upon presentation within 30 days after the date of utterance, and the drawer fails to make good within 10 days after receiving notice of refusal. [1971 c.743 §128; 1991 c.837 §10; 2007 c.71 §49]

164.090 [Repealed by 1971 c.743 §432]

164.095 Theft by receiving. (1) A person commits theft by receiving if the person receives, retains, conceals or disposes of property of another knowing or having good reason to know that the property was the subject of theft.

(2) It is a defense to a charge of violating subsection (1) of this section if:

(a) The person is a scrap metal business as defined in ORS 165.116 or an agent or employee of a scrap metal business;

(b) The person receives or retains metal property as defined in ORS 165.116; and

(c) The person makes a report in accordance with ORS 165.118 (3)(a).

(3) "Receiving" means acquiring possession, control or title, or lending on the security of the property. [1971 c.743 §129; 2009 c.811 §9]

164.098 Organized retail theft. (1) A person commits the crime of organized retail theft if, acting in concert with another person:

(a) The person violates ORS 164.015 or aids or abets the other person to violate ORS 164.015;

(b) The subject of the theft is merchandise and the merchandise is taken from a mercantile establishment; and

(c) The aggregate value of the merchandise taken within any 90-day period exceeds $5,000.

(2) As used in this section:

(a) "Merchandise" has the meaning given that term in ORS 30.870.

(b) "Mercantile establishment" has the meaning given that term in ORS 30.870.

(3) Organized retail theft is a Class B felony. [2007 c.498 §2]

Note: 164.098 was added to and made a part of ORS chapter 164 by legislative action but was not added to any smaller series therein. See Preface to Oregon Revised Statutes for further explanation.

164.100 [Repealed by 1971 c.743 §432]

164.105 Right of possession. Right of possession of property is as follows:

(1) A person who has obtained possession of property by theft or other illegal means shall be deemed to have a right of possession superior to that of another person who takes, obtains or withholds the property from that person by means of theft.

(2) A joint or common owner of property shall not be deemed to have a right of possession of the property superior to that of any other joint or common owner of the property.

(3) In the absence of a specific agreement to the contrary, a person in lawful possession of property shall be deemed to have a right of possession superior to that of a person having only a security interest in the property, even if legal title to the property lies with the holder of the security interest pursuant to a conditional sale contract or other security agreement. [1971 c.743 §130; 1987 c.158 §28]

164.110 [Repealed by 1971 c.743 §432]

164.115 Value of property. For the purposes of chapter 743, Oregon Laws 1971, the value of property shall be ascertained as follows:

(1) Except as otherwise specified in this section, value means the market value of the property at the time and place of the crime, or if such cannot reasonably be ascertained, the cost of replacement of the property within a reasonable time after the crime.

(2) Whether or not they have been issued or delivered, certain written instruments, not including those having a readily ascertainable market value, shall be evaluated as follows:

(a) The value of an instrument constituting an evidence of debt, including, but not limited to, a check, draft or promissory note, shall be considered the amount due or collectible thereon or thereby.

(b) The value of any other instrument which creates, releases, discharges or otherwise affects any valuable legal right, privilege or obligation shall be considered the greatest amount of economic loss which the owner might reasonably suffer because of the loss of the instrument.

(3) The value of a gambling chip, token, imitation currency or similar device is its face value.

(4) The value of the wildlife listed in ORS 496.705 is the amount of damages as specified in ORS 496.705.

(5) When the value of property cannot reasonably be ascertained, it shall be presumed to be an amount less than $50 in a case of theft, and less than $500 in any other case.

(6) The value of single theft transactions may be added together if the thefts were committed:

(a) Against multiple victims by similar means within a 30-day period; or

(b) Against the same victim, or two or more persons who are joint owners, within a 180-day period. [1971 c.743 §131; 1987 c.907 §6; 1993 c.680 §22; 1997 c.867 §18; 2011 c.363 §2]

Note: See note under 164.005.

164.125 Theft of services. (1) A person commits the crime of theft of services if:

(a) With intent to avoid payment therefor, the person obtains services that are available only for compensation, by force, threat, deception or other means to avoid payment for the services; or

(b) Having control over the disposition of labor or of business, commercial or industrial equipment or facilities of another, the person uses or diverts to the use of the person or a third person such labor, equipment or facilities with intent to derive for the person or the third person a commercial benefit to which the person or the third person is not entitled.

(2) As used in this section, "services" includes, but is not limited to, labor, professional services, toll facilities, transportation, communications service, entertainment, the supplying of food, lodging or other accommodations in hotels, restaurants or elsewhere, the supplying of equipment for use, and the supplying of commodities of a public utility nature such as gas, electricity, steam and water. "Communication service" includes, but is not limited to, use of telephone, computer and cable television systems.

(3) Absconding without payment or offer to pay for hotel, restaurant or other services for which compensation is customarily paid immediately upon the receiving of them is prima facie evidence that the services were obtained with intent to avoid payment therefor. Obtaining the use of any communication system the use of which is available only for compensation, including but not limited to telephone, computer and cable television systems, or obtaining the use of any services of a public utility nature, without payment or offer to pay for such use is prima facie evidence that the obtaining of the use of such system or the use of such services was gained with intent to avoid payment therefor.

(4) The value of single theft transactions may be added together if the thefts were committed:

(a) Against multiple victims by a similar means within a 30-day period; or

(b) Against the same victim, or two or more persons who are joint owners, within a 180-day period.

(5) Theft of services is:

(a) A Class C misdemeanor if the aggregate total value of services that are the subject of the theft is less than $100;

(b) A Class A misdemeanor if the aggregate total value of services that are the subject of the theft is $100 or more and less than $1,000;

(c) A Class C felony if the aggregate total value of services that are the subject of the theft is $1,000 or more; and

(d) A Class B felony if the aggregate total value of services that are the subject of the theft is $10,000 or more. [1971 c.743 §133; 1973 c.133 §1; 1985 c.537 §1; 1987 c.907 §8; 1993 c.680 §21; 2009 c.16 §4]

164.130 Application of ORS 164.125 to telephone or telegraph services; jurisdiction. (1) ORS 164.125 shall apply when the telephone or telegraph communication involved either originates or terminates, or both originates and terminates, in this state, or when the charges for service would have been billable, in normal course, by a person providing telephone or telegraph service in this state, but for the fact that the charge for service was avoided, or attempted to be avoided by one or more of the means set forth in ORS 164.125.

(2) Jurisdiction of an offense under ORS 164.125 is in the jurisdictional territory where the telephone or telegraph communication involved in the offense originates or where it terminates, or the jurisdictional territory to which the bill for the service is sent or would have been sent but for the fact that the service was obtained or attempted to be obtained by one or more of the means set forth in ORS 164.125. [1973 c.133 §3]

164.132 Unlawful distribution of cable television equipment. (1) A person commits the crime of unlawful distribution of cable television equipment if the person knowingly manufactures, imports into this state, distributes, sells, offers for sale, rental or use, possesses for sale, rental or use, or advertises for sale, rental or use, any device designed to make available the unauthorized reception of cable television signals.

123

(2) Unlawful distribution of cable television equipment is a Class B misdemeanor. [1985 c.537 §3]

164.135 Unauthorized use of a vehicle. (1) A person commits the crime of unauthorized use of a vehicle when:

(a) The person takes, operates, exercises control over, rides in or otherwise uses another's vehicle, boat or aircraft without consent of the owner;

(b) Having custody of a vehicle, boat or aircraft pursuant to an agreement between the person or another and the owner thereof whereby the person or another is to perform for compensation a specific service for the owner involving the maintenance, repair or use of such vehicle, boat or aircraft, the person intentionally uses or operates it, without consent of the owner, for the person's own purpose in a manner constituting a gross deviation from the agreed purpose; or

(c) Having custody of a vehicle, boat or aircraft pursuant to an agreement with the owner thereof whereby such vehicle, boat or aircraft is to be returned to the owner at a specified time, the person knowingly retains or withholds possession thereof without consent of the owner for so lengthy a period beyond the specified time as to render such retention or possession a gross deviation from the agreement.

(2) Unauthorized use of a vehicle, boat or aircraft is a Class C felony.

(3) Subsection (1)(a) of this section does not apply to a person who rides in or otherwise uses a public transit vehicle, as defined in ORS 166.116, if the vehicle is being operated by an authorized operator within the scope of the operator's employment. [1971 c.743 §134; 2001 c.851 §1; 2007 c.71 §50]

164.138 Criminal possession of a rented or leased motor vehicle. (1) A person commits the offense of criminal possession of a rented or leased motor vehicle if:

(a) After renting a motor vehicle from a commercial renter of motor vehicles under a written agreement that provides for the return of the motor vehicle to a particular place at a particular time, the person fails to return the motor vehicle as specified, is thereafter served in accordance with subsection (2) of this section with a written demand to return the motor vehicle and knowingly fails to return the motor vehicle within three calendar days from the date of the receipt or refusal of the demand; or

(b) After leasing a motor vehicle from a commercial lessor of motor vehicles under a written agreement that provides for periodic lease payments, the person fails to pay the lessor a periodic payment when due for a period of 45 days, is thereafter served with a written demand to return the motor vehicle in accordance with subsection (2) of this section and knowingly fails to return the motor vehicle within three calendar days from the date of the receipt or refusal of the demand.

(2)(a) Service of written demand under this section shall be accomplished by delivery through any commercial overnight service that can supply a delivery receipt. The demand shall be sent to the person who obtained the motor vehicle by rental or lease at the address stated in the rental or lease agreement and any other address of the person provided by the person to the renter or lessor. The person is responsible for providing correct current address information to the renter or lessor until the motor vehicle is returned.

(b) The person shall be considered to have refused the written demand if the commercial delivery service determines that the demand is not deliverable to the person at the address or addresses provided by the person.

(3) A bona fide contract dispute with the lessor or renter shall be an affirmative defense to a charge of criminal possession of a rented or leased motor vehicle.

(4) Criminal possession of a rented or leased motor vehicle is a Class C felony. [2007 c.684 §1]

Note: 164.138 was enacted into law by the Legislative Assembly but was not added to or made a part of ORS chapter 164 or any series therein by legislative action. See Preface to Oregon Revised Statutes for further explanation.

164.140 Criminal possession of rented or leased personal property. (1) A person is guilty of criminal possession of rented or leased personal property if:

(a) After renting an item of personal property from a commercial renter of personal property under a written agreement which provides for the return of the item to a particular place at a particular time, the person fails to return the item as specified, is thereafter served by mail with a written demand to return the item, and knowingly fails to return the item within 10 business days from the date of mailing of the demand; or

(b) After leasing an item of personal property from a commercial lessor of personal property under a written agreement which provides for periodic lease payments, the person fails to pay the lessor a periodic payment when due for a period of 45 days, is thereafter served by mail with a written demand to return the item, and knowingly fails to return the item within 10 business days from the date of mailing of the demand.

(2) Service of written demand under this section shall be accomplished by certified mail sent to the person who obtained the item of personal property by rental or lease, sent to the address stated in the rental or lease agreement and any other address of the person provided by the person to the renter or lessor. The person is responsible for providing correct current address information to the renter or lessor until the item of personal property is returned.

(3) A bona fide contract dispute with the lessor or renter shall be an affirmative defense to a charge of criminal possession of rented or leased personal property.

(4) For purposes of this section, the value of property shall be ascertained as provided in ORS 164.115. Criminal possession of rented or leased personal property is:

(a) A Class A misdemeanor if the aggregate total value of the personal property not returned is under $500.

(b) A Class C felony if the aggregate total value of the personal property not returned is $500 or more. [1979 c.476 §3; 1987 c.907 §9]

MAIL-RELATED OFFENSES

164.160 Definitions. As used in this section and ORS 164.162:

(1) "Authorized depository" means a mailbox, post office box or rural box used by postal customers to deposit outgoing mail or used by the Postal Service to deliver incoming mail.

(2) "Mail" means any letter, card, parcel or other material that:

(a) Is sent or delivered by means of the Postal Service;

(b) Has postage affixed by the postal customer or Postal Service or has been accepted for delivery by the Postal Service; and

(c) Is placed in any authorized depository or mail receptacle or given to any Postal Service employee for delivery.

(3) "Mail receptacle" means any location used by the Postal Service or postal customers to place outgoing mail or receive incoming mail.

(4) "Postage" means a Postal Service stamp, permit imprint, meter strip or other authorized indication of prepayment for service provided or authorized by the Postal Service for collection and delivery of mail.

(5) "Postal Service" means the United States Postal Service. [1999 c.920 §1]

Note: 164.160, 164.162 and 164.164 were enacted into law by the Legislative Assembly but were not added to or made a part of ORS chapter 164 or any series therein by legislative action. See Preface to Oregon Revised Statutes for further explanation.

164.162 Mail theft or receipt of stolen mail. (1) A person commits the crime of mail theft or receipt of stolen mail if the person intentionally:

(a) Takes or, by fraud or deception, obtains mail from a post office, postal station, mail receptacle, authorized depository or mail carrier;

(b) Takes from mail any article contained therein;

(c) Secretes, embezzles or destroys mail or any article contained therein;

(d) Takes or, by fraud or deception, obtains mail that has been delivered to or left for collection on or adjacent to a mail receptacle or authorized depository; or

(e) Buys, receives, conceals or possesses mail or any article contained therein knowing that the mail or article has been unlawfully taken or obtained.

(2) Mail theft or receipt of stolen mail is a Class C felony. [1999 c.920 §2; 2008 c.14 §10; 2009 c.660 §§9,14]

Note: See note under 164.160.

164.164 Defense in prosecution under ORS 164.162; applicability of ORS 164.162. (1) In a prosecution under ORS 164.162, it is a defense that the defendant acted under an honest claim of right in that:

(a) The defendant was unaware that the property was that of another person;

(b) The defendant reasonably believed that the defendant was entitled to the property involved or had a right to acquire or dispose of it as the defendant did; or

(c) The property involved was that of the defendant's spouse, unless the parties were not living together as spouses in a marriage and were living in separate abodes at the time of the alleged offense.

(2)(a) ORS 164.162 does not apply to employees charged with the operation of facilities listed in paragraph (b) of this subsection when the employees are carrying out their official duties to protect the safety and security of the facilities.

(b) The facilities to which paragraph (a) of this subsection applies are juvenile detention facilities and local correctional facilities as defined in ORS 169.005, detention facilities as defined in ORS 419A.004, youth correction facilities as defined in ORS 420.005 and Department of Corrections institutions as defined in ORS 421.005. [1999 c.920 §3; 2015 c.629 §32]

Note: See note under 164.160.

MONEY LAUNDERING

164.170 Laundering a monetary instrument. (1) A person commits the crime of laundering a monetary instrument if the person:

(a) Knowing that the property involved in a financial transaction represents the proceeds of some form, though not necessarily which form, of unlawful activity, conducts or attempts to conduct a financial transaction that involves the proceeds of unlawful activity:

(A) With the intent to promote the carrying on of unlawful activity; or

(B) Knowing that the transaction is designed in whole or in part to:

(i) Conceal or disguise the nature, location, source, ownership or control of the proceeds of unlawful activity; or

(ii) Avoid a transaction reporting requirement under federal law;

(b) Transports, transmits or transfers or attempts to transport, transmit or transfer a monetary instrument or funds:

(A) With the intent to promote the carrying on of unlawful activity; or

(B) Knowing that the monetary instrument or funds involved in the transportation, transmission or transfer represent the proceeds of some form, though not necessarily which form, of unlawful activity and knowing that the transportation, transmission or transfer is designed, in whole or in part, to:

(i) Conceal or disguise the nature, location, source, ownership or control of the proceeds of unlawful activity; or

(ii) Avoid a transaction reporting requirement under federal law; or

(c) Intentionally conducts or attempts to conduct a financial transaction involving property represented to be the proceeds of unlawful activity or property used to conduct or facilitate unlawful activity to:

(A) Promote the carrying on of unlawful activity;

(B) Conceal or disguise the nature, location, source, ownership or control of property believed to be the proceeds of unlawful activity; or

(C) Avoid a transaction reporting requirement under federal law.

(2)(a) Laundering a monetary instrument is a Class B felony.

(b) In addition to any other sentence of imprisonment or fine that a court may impose and notwithstanding ORS 161.625, a court may include in the sentence of a person convicted under this section a fine in an amount equal to the value of the property, funds or monetary instruments involved in the unlawful transaction.

(3) For purposes of subsection (1)(b)(B) of this section, the state may establish the defendant's knowledge through evidence that a peace officer, federal officer or another person acting at the direction of or with the approval of a peace officer or federal officer represented the matter specified in subsection (1)(b)(B) of this section as true and the defendant's subsequent statements or actions indicate that the defendant believed the representations to be true.

(4) For purposes of subsection (1)(c) of this section, "represented" includes, but is not limited to, any representation made by a peace officer, federal officer or another person acting at the direction of or with the approval of a peace officer or federal officer.

(5) As used in this section:

(a) "Conducts" includes initiating, concluding or participating in the initiation or conclusion of a transaction.

(b) "Federal officer" has the meaning given that term in ORS 133.005.

(c) "Financial institution" has the meaning given that term in ORS 706.008.

(d) "Financial transaction" means a transaction involving:

(A) The movement of funds by wire or other means;

(B) One or more monetary instruments;

(C) The transfer of title to any real property, vehicle, vessel or aircraft; or

(D) The use of a financial institution.

(e) "Monetary instrument" means:

(A) Coin or currency of the United States or of any other country, traveler's checks, personal checks, bank checks, cashier's checks, money orders, foreign bank drafts of any foreign country or gold, silver or platinum bullion or coins; or

(B) Investment securities or negotiable instruments, in bearer form or otherwise in such form that title passes upon delivery.

(f) "Peace officer" has the meaning given that term in ORS 133.005.

(g) "Transaction" includes a purchase, sale, loan, pledge, gift, transfer, delivery or other disposition and, with respect to a financial institution, includes a deposit, withdrawal, transfer between accounts, exchange of currency, loan, extension of credit, purchase or sale of any stock, bond, certificate of deposit or other monetary instrument, use of a safe deposit box or any other payment, transfer or delivery by, through or to a financial institution by whatever means.

(h) "Unlawful activity" means any act constituting a felony under state, federal or foreign law. [1999 c.878 §1]

Note: 164.170, 164.172 and 164.174 were enacted into law by the Legislative Assembly but were not added to or made a part of ORS chapter 164 or any series therein by legislative action. See Preface to Oregon Revised Statutes for further explanation.

164.172 Engaging in a financial transaction in property derived from unlawful activity. (1) A person commits the crime of engaging in a financial transaction in property derived from unlawful activity if the person knowingly engages in or attempts to engage in a financial transaction in property that:

(a) Constitutes, or is derived from, the proceeds of unlawful activity;

(b) Is of a value greater than $10,000; and

(c) The person knows is derived from or represents the proceeds of some form, though not necessarily which form, of unlawful activity.

(2)(a) Engaging in a financial transaction in property derived from unlawful activity is a Class C felony.

(b) In addition to any other sentence of imprisonment or fine that a court may impose and notwithstanding ORS 161.625, a court may include in the sentence of a person convicted under this section a fine in an amount equal to the value of the property involved in the unlawful transaction.

(3) As used in this section:

(a) "Financial transaction" has the meaning given that term in ORS 164.170. "Financial transaction" does not include any transaction necessary to preserve a person's right to representation as guaranteed by section 11, Article I of the Oregon Constitution, and the Sixth Amendment to the United States Constitution.

(b) "Unlawful activity" has the meaning given that term in ORS 164.170. [1999 c.878 §2]

Note: See note under 164.170.

164.174 Exceptions. Nothing in ORS 164.170 or 164.172 or the amendments to ORS 166.715 by section 4, chapter 878, Oregon Laws 1999, is intended to allow the prosecution of a corporation, business, partnership, limited liability company, limited liability partnership or any similar entity, or an employee or agent of such an entity, that makes a good faith effort to comply with federal and state laws governing the entity. [1999 c.878 §3]

Note: See note under 164.170.

BURGLARY AND CRIMINAL TRESPASS

164.205 Definitions for ORS 164.205 to 164.270. As used in ORS 164.205 to 164.270, except as the context requires otherwise:

(1) "Building," in addition to its ordinary meaning, includes any booth, vehicle, boat, aircraft or other structure adapted for overnight accommodation of persons or for carrying on business therein. Where a building consists of separate units, including, but not limited to, separate apartments, offices or rented rooms, each unit is, in addition to being a part of such building, a separate building.

(2) "Dwelling" means a building which regularly or intermittently is occupied by a person lodging therein at night, whether or not a person is actually present.

(3) "Enter or remain unlawfully" means:

(a) To enter or remain in or upon premises when the premises, at the time of such entry or remaining, are not open to the public and when the entrant is not otherwise licensed or privileged to do so;

(b) To fail to leave premises that are open to the public after being lawfully directed to do so by the person in charge;

(c) To enter premises that are open to the public after being lawfully directed not to enter the premises; or

(d) To enter or remain in a motor vehicle when the entrant is not authorized to do so.

(4) "Open to the public" means premises which by their physical nature, function, custom, usage, notice or lack thereof or other circumstances at the time would cause a reasonable person to believe that no permission to enter or remain is required.

(5) "Person in charge" means a person, a representative or employee of the person who has lawful control of premises by ownership, tenancy, official position or other legal relationship. "Person in charge" includes, but is not limited to the person, or holder of a position, designated as the person or position-holder in charge by the Governor, board, commission or governing body of any political subdivision of this state.

(6) "Premises" includes any building and any real property, whether privately or publicly owned. [1971 c.743 §135; 1983 c.740 §33; 1999 c.1040 §10; 2003 c.444 §1; 2015 c.10 §1]

164.210 [Repealed by 1971 c.743 §432]

164.215 Burglary in the second degree. (1) Except as otherwise provided in ORS 164.255, a person commits the crime of burglary in the second degree if the person enters or remains unlawfully in a building with intent to commit a crime therein.

(2) Burglary in the second degree is a Class C felony. [1971 c.743 §136; 1993 c.680 §24]

164.220 [Repealed by 1971 c.743 §432]

164.225 Burglary in the first degree. (1) A person commits the crime of burglary in the first degree if the person violates ORS 164.215 and the building is a dwelling, or if in effecting entry or while in a building or in immediate flight therefrom the person:

(a) Is armed with a burglary tool or theft device as defined in ORS 164.235 or a deadly weapon;

(b) Causes or attempts to cause physical injury to any person; or

(c) Uses or threatens to use a dangerous weapon.

(2) Burglary in the first degree is a Class A felony. [1971 c.743 §137; 2003 c.577 §10]

164.230 [Repealed by 1971 c.743 §432]

164.235 Possession of a burglary tool or theft device. (1) A person commits the crime of possession of a burglary tool or theft device if the person possesses a burglary tool or theft device and the person:

(a) Intends to use the tool or device to commit or facilitate a forcible entry into premises or a theft by a physical taking; or

(b) Knows that another person intends to use the tool or device to commit or facilitate a forcible entry into premises or a theft by a physical taking.

(2) For purposes of this section, "burglary tool or theft device" means an acetylene torch, electric arc, burning bar, thermal lance, oxygen lance or other similar device capable of burning through steel, concrete or other solid material, or nitroglycerine, dynamite, gunpowder or any other explosive, tool, instrument or other article adapted or designed for committing or facilitating a forcible entry into premises or theft by a physical taking.

(3) Possession of a burglary tool or theft device is a Class A misdemeanor. [1971 c.743 §138; 1999 c.1040 §13; 2003 c.577 §9]

164.240 [Amended by 1959 c.99 §1; repealed by 1971 c.743 §432]

164.243 Criminal trespass in the second degree by a guest. A guest commits the crime of criminal trespass in the second degree if that guest intentionally remains unlawfully in a transient lodging after the departure date of the guest's reservation without the approval of the hotelkeeper. "Guest" means a person who is registered at a hotel and is assigned to transient lodging, and includes any individual accompanying the person. [1979 c.856 §2]

164.245 Criminal trespass in the second degree. (1) A person commits the crime of criminal trespass in the second degree if the person enters or remains unlawfully in a motor vehicle or in or upon premises.

(2) Criminal trespass in the second degree is a Class C misdemeanor. [1971 c.743 §139; 1999 c.1040 §9]

164.250 [Repealed by 1971 c.743 §432]

164.255 Criminal trespass in the first degree. (1) A person commits the crime of criminal trespass in the first degree if the person:

(a) Enters or remains unlawfully in a dwelling;

(b) Having been denied future entry to a building pursuant to a merchant's notice of trespass, reenters the building during hours when the building is open to the public with the intent to commit theft therein;

(c) Enters or remains unlawfully upon railroad yards, tracks, bridges or rights of way; or

(d) Enters or remains unlawfully in or upon premises that have been determined to be not fit for use under ORS 453.855 to 453.912.

(2) Subsection (1)(d) of this section does not apply to the owner of record of the premises if:

(a) The owner notifies the law enforcement agency having jurisdiction over the premises that the owner intends to enter the premises;

(b) The owner enters or remains on the premises for the purpose of inspecting or decontaminating the premises or lawfully removing items from the premises; and

(c) The owner has not been arrested for, charged with or convicted of a criminal offense that contributed to the determination that the premises are not fit for use.

(3) Criminal trespass in the first degree is a Class A misdemeanor. [1971 c.743 §140; 1993 c.680 §23; 1999 c.837 §1; 2001 c.386 §1; 2003 c.527 §1]

164.260 [Repealed by 1971 c.743 §432]

164.265 Criminal trespass while in possession of a firearm. (1) A person commits the crime of criminal trespass while in possession of a firearm who, while in possession of a firearm, enters or remains unlawfully in or upon premises.

(2) Criminal trespass while in possession of a firearm is a Class A misdemeanor. [1979 c.603 §2]

164.270 Closure of premises to motor-propelled vehicles. (1) For purposes of ORS 164.245, a landowner or an agent of the landowner may close the privately owned premises of the landowner to motor-propelled vehicles by posting signs on or near the boundaries of the closed premises at the normal points of entry as follows:

(a) Signs must be no smaller than eight inches in height and 11 inches in width;

(b) Signs must contain the words "Closed to Motor-propelled Vehicles" or words to that effect in letters no less than one inch in height;

(c) Signs must display the name, business address and phone number, if any, of the landowner or agent of the landowner; and

(d) Signs must be posted at normal points of entry and be no further apart than 350 yards.

(2) A person violates ORS 164.245 if the person operates or rides upon or within a motor-propelled vehicle upon privately owned premises when the premises are posted as provided in this section and the person does not have written authorization to operate a motor-propelled vehicle upon the premises.

(3) Nothing contained in this section prevents emergency or law enforcement vehicles from entering upon land closed to motor-propelled vehicles. [1981 c.394 §2]

164.272 Unlawful entry into a motor vehicle. (1) A person commits the crime of unlawful entry into a motor vehicle if the person enters a motor vehicle, or any part of a motor vehicle, with the intent to commit a crime.

(2) Unlawful entry into a motor vehicle is a Class A misdemeanor.

(3) As used in this section, "enters" includes, but is not limited to, inserting:

(a) Any part of the body; or

(b) Any object connected with the body. [1995 c.782 §1]

Note: 164.272 was enacted into law by the Legislative Assembly but was not added to or made a part of ORS chapter 164 or any series therein by legislative action. See Preface to Oregon Revised Statutes for further explanation.

164.274 Definitions for ORS 164.276 and 164.278. As used in ORS 164.276 and 164.278:

(1) "Coach" means a person who instructs or trains members of a team or directs the strategy of a team participating in a sports event.

(2) "Inappropriate behavior" means:

(a) Engaging in fighting or in violent, tumultuous or threatening behavior;

(b) Violating the rules of conduct governing coaches, team players and spectators at a sports event;

(c) Publicly insulting another person by abusive words or gestures in a manner intended to provoke a violent response; or

(d) Intentionally subjecting another person to offensive physical contact.

(3) "Premises" has the meaning given that term in ORS 164.205.

(4) "Spectator" means any person, other than a team player or coach, who attends a sports event.

(5) "Sports official" has the meaning given that term in ORS 30.882. [2003 c.629 §1]

Note: 164.274 to 164.278 were enacted into law by the Legislative Assembly but were not added to or made a part of ORS chapter 164 or any series therein by legislative action. See Preface to Oregon Revised Statutes for further explanation.

164.276 Authority of sports official to expel persons from sports event. A sports official may order a coach, team player or spectator to leave the premises at which a sports event is taking place and at which the sports official is officiating if the coach, team player or spectator is engaging in inappropriate behavior. [2003 c.629 §2]

Note: See note under 164.274.

164.278 Criminal trespass at a sports event. (1) A person commits the crime of criminal trespass at a sports event if the person:

(a) Is a coach, team player or spectator at a sports event;

(b) Engages in inappropriate behavior;

(c) Has been ordered by a sports official to leave the premises at which the sports event is taking place; and

(d) Fails to leave the premises or returns to the premises during the period of time when reentry has been prohibited.

(2) Criminal trespass at a sports event is a Class C misdemeanor. [2003 c.629 §3]

Note: See note under 164.274.

ARSON, CRIMINAL MISCHIEF AND RELATED OFFENSES

164.305 Definitions for ORS 164.305 to 164.377. As used in ORS 164.305 to 164.377, except as the context requires otherwise:

(1) "Protected property" means any structure, place or thing customarily occupied by people, including "public buildings" as defined by ORS 479.168 and "forestland," as defined by ORS 477.001.

(2) "Property of another" means property in which anyone other than the actor has a legal or equitable interest that the actor has no right to defeat or impair, even though the actor may also have such an interest in the property. [1971 c.743 §141; 1977 c.640 §1; 1989 c.584 §1; 2003 c.543 §1]

164.310 [Amended by 1957 c.653 §1; 1959 c.302 §2; repealed by 1971 c.743 §432]

164.315 Arson in the second degree. (1) A person commits the crime of arson in the second degree if:
(a) By starting a fire or causing an explosion, the person intentionally damages:
(A) Any building of another that is not protected property; or
(B) Any property of another and the damages to the property exceed $750; or
(b) By knowingly engaging in the manufacture of methamphetamine, the person causes fire or causes an explosion that damages property described in paragraph (a) of this subsection.
(2) Arson in the second degree is a Class C felony. [1971 c.743 §143; 2001 c.432 §1; 2005 c.706 §3]

164.320 [Amended by 1959 c.77 §1; repealed by 1971 c.743 §432]

164.325 Arson in the first degree. (1) A person commits the crime of arson in the first degree if:
(a) By starting a fire or causing an explosion, the person intentionally damages:
(A) Protected property of another;
(B) Any property, whether the property of the person or the property of another person, and such act recklessly places another person in danger of physical injury or protected property of another in danger of damage; or
(C) Any property, whether the property of the person or the property of another person, and recklessly causes serious physical injury to a firefighter or peace officer acting in the line of duty relating to the fire; or
(b) By knowingly engaging in the manufacture of methamphetamine, the person causes fire or causes an explosion that damages property described in paragraph (a) of this subsection.
(2) Arson in the first degree is a Class A felony. [1971 c.743 §144; 1991 c.946 §1; 2005 c.706 §4]

164.330 [Repealed by 1971 c.743 §432]

164.335 Reckless burning. (1) A person commits the crime of reckless burning if the person recklessly damages property of another by fire or explosion.
(2) Reckless burning is a Class A misdemeanor. [1971 c.743 §142]

164.338 Arson incident to the manufacture of a controlled substance in the second degree. (1) A person commits the crime of arson incident to the manufacture of a controlled substance in the second degree if, by knowingly engaging in the manufacture of a controlled substance, the person causes a fire or causes an explosion that damages:
(a) Any building of another that is not protected property; or
(b) Any property of another and the damages to the property exceed $750.
(2) Arson incident to the manufacture of a controlled substance in the second degree is a Class C felony.
(3) As used in this section and ORS 164.342, "controlled substance" and "manufacture" have the meanings given those terms in ORS 475.005. [2017 c.248 §2]

164.340 [Repealed by 1971 c.743 §432]

164.342 Arson incident to the manufacture of a controlled substance in the first degree. (1) A person commits the crime of arson incident to the manufacture of a controlled substance in the first degree if, by knowingly engaging in the manufacture of a controlled substance, the person causes a fire or causes an explosion that damages:
(a) The protected property of another;
(b) Any property, whether the property of the person or the property of another person, if the fire or explosion recklessly places another person in danger of physical injury or protected property of another in danger of damage; or
(c) Any property, whether the property of the person or the property of another person, if the fire or explosion recklessly causes serious physical injury to a firefighter or peace officer acting in the line of duty relating to the fire or explosion.
(2) Arson incident to the manufacture of a controlled substance in the first degree is a Class A felony. [2017 c.248 §3]

164.345 Criminal mischief in the third degree. (1) A person commits the crime of criminal mischief in the third degree if, with intent to cause substantial inconvenience to the owner or to another person, and having no right to do so nor reasonable ground to believe that the person has such right, the person tampers or interferes with property of another.

(2) Criminal mischief in the third degree is a Class C misdemeanor. [1971 c.743 §145]

164.350 [Repealed by 1971 c.743 §432]

164.354 Criminal mischief in the second degree. (1) A person commits the crime of criminal mischief in the second degree if:

(a) The person violates ORS 164.345, and as a result thereof, damages property in an amount exceeding $500; or

(b) Having no right to do so nor reasonable ground to believe that the person has such right, the person intentionally damages property of another, or, the person recklessly damages property of another in an amount exceeding $500.

(2) Criminal mischief in the second degree is a Class A misdemeanor. [1971 c.743 §146; 2009 c.16 §5]

164.355 [1967 c.378 §§1,2,3,4; 1969 c.287 §1; repealed by 1971 c.743 §432]

164.360 [Repealed by 1971 c.743 §432]

164.362 [1957 c.714 §§1,6(1); repealed by 1971 c.743 §432]

164.364 [1957 c.714 §§4,5; repealed by 1971 c.743 §432]

164.365 Criminal mischief in the first degree. (1) A person commits the crime of criminal mischief in the first degree who, with intent to damage property, and having no right to do so nor reasonable ground to believe that the person has such right:

(a) Damages or destroys property of another:

(A) In an amount exceeding $1,000;

(B) By means of an explosive;

(C) By starting a fire in an institution while the person is committed to and confined in the institution;

(D) Which is a livestock animal as defined in ORS 164.055;

(E) Which is the property of a public utility, telecommunications carrier, railroad, public transportation facility or medical facility used in direct service to the public; or

(F) By intentionally interfering with, obstructing or adulterating in any manner the service of a public utility, telecommunications carrier, railroad, public transportation facility or medical facility; or

(b) Intentionally uses, manipulates, arranges or rearranges the property of a public utility, telecommunications carrier, railroad, public transportation facility or medical facility used in direct service to the public so as to interfere with its efficiency.

(2) As used in subsection (1) of this section:

(a) "Institution" includes state and local correctional facilities, mental health facilities, juvenile detention facilities and state training schools.

(b) "Medical facility" means a health care facility as defined in ORS 442.015, a licensed physician's office or anywhere a licensed medical practitioner provides health care services.

(c) "Public utility" has the meaning provided for that term in ORS 757.005 and includes any cooperative, people's utility district or other municipal corporation providing an electric, gas, water or other utility service.

(d) "Railroad" has the meaning provided for that term in ORS 824.020.

(e) "Public transportation facility" means any property, structure or equipment used for or in connection with the transportation of persons for hire by rail, air or bus, including any railroad cars, buses or airplanes used to carry out such transportation.

(f) "Telecommunications carrier" has the meaning given that term in ORS 133.721.

(3) Criminal mischief in the first degree is a Class C felony. [1971 c.743 §147; 1973 c.133 §6; 1975 c.344 §1; 1979 c.805 §1; 1983 c.740 §33a; 1987 c.447 §104; 1987 c.907 §10; 1989 c.584 §2; 1991 c.837 §13; 1991 c.946 §2; 1993 c.94 §1; 1993 c.332 §3; 1999 c.1040 §11; 1999 c.1093 §2; 2003 c.543 §4; 2009 c.16 §6]

164.366 [1957 c.714 §§2,6(2); repealed by 1971 c.743 §432]

164.367 Determining value of damage; aggregation. For purposes of ORS 164.345, 164.354 and 164.365, the value of damage done during single incidents of criminal mischief may be added together if the incidents of criminal mischief were committed:

(1) Against multiple victims in the same course of conduct; or

(2) Against the same victim, or two or more persons who are joint owners, within a 30-day period. [1999 c.1040 §12]

Note: 164.367 was enacted into law by the Legislative Assembly but was not added to or made a part of ORS chapter 164 or any series therein by legislative action. See Preface to Oregon Revised Statutes for further explanation.

164.368 [1957 c.714 §3; repealed by 1971 c.743 §432]

164.369 [1989 c.584 §4; 2003 c.543 §5; renumbered 167.337 in 2003]

164.370 [Repealed by 1971 c.743 §432]

164.373 Tampering with cable television equipment. (1) A person commits the crime of tampering with cable television equipment if the person:

(a) Knowingly tampers or otherwise interferes with or connects to by any means, whether mechanical, electrical, acoustical or other means, any cable, wire or other device used for the distribution of cable television service, without authority of the provider of such service; or

(b) Knowingly permits another person to tamper or otherwise interfere with, or connect to by any means, whether mechanical, electrical, acoustical or other means, any cable, wire or other device used for the distribution of cable television service, such tampering, interfering or connecting being upon premises under the control of such first person or intended for the benefit of such first person, without authority of the provider of such service.

(2) Tampering with cable television equipment is a Class B misdemeanor. [1985 c.537 §5]

164.377 Computer crime. (1) As used in this section:

(a) To "access" means to instruct, communicate with, store data in, retrieve data from or otherwise make use of any resources of a computer, computer system or computer network.

(b) "Computer" means, but is not limited to, an electronic, magnetic, optical electrochemical or other high-speed data processing device that performs logical, arithmetic or memory functions by the manipulations of electronic, magnetic or optical signals or impulses, and includes the components of a computer and all input, output, processing, storage, software or communication facilities that are connected or related to such a device in a system or network.

(c) "Computer network" means, but is not limited to, the interconnection of communication lines, including microwave or other means of electronic communication, with a computer through remote terminals or a complex consisting of two or more interconnected computers.

(d) "Computer program" means, but is not limited to, a series of instructions or statements, in a form acceptable to a computer, which permits the functioning of a computer system in a manner designed to provide appropriate products from or usage of such computer system.

(e) "Computer software" means, but is not limited to, computer programs, procedures and associated documentation concerned with the operation of a computer system.

(f) "Computer system" means, but is not limited to, a set of related, connected or unconnected, computer equipment, devices and software. "Computer system" also includes any computer, device or software owned or operated by the Oregon State Lottery or rented, owned or operated by another person or entity under contract to or at the direction of the Oregon State Lottery.

(g) "Data" means a representation of information, knowledge, facts, concepts, computer software, computer programs or instructions. "Data" may be in any form, in storage media, or as stored in the memory of the computer, or in transit, or presented on a display device. "Data" includes, but is not limited to, computer or human readable forms of numbers, text, stored voice, graphics and images.

(h) "Intimate image" means a photograph, film, video, recording, digital picture or other visual reproduction of a person whose intimate parts are visible or who is engaged in sexual conduct.

(i) "Intimate parts" means uncovered human genitals, pubic areas or female nipples.

(j) "Property" includes, but is not limited to, financial instruments, information, including electronically produced data, and computer software and programs in either computer or human readable form, intellectual property and any other tangible or intangible item of value.

(k) "Proprietary information" includes any scientific, technical or commercial information including any design, process, procedure, list of customers, list of suppliers, customers' records or business code or improvement thereof that is known only to limited individuals within an organization and is used in a business that the organization conducts. The information must have actual or potential commercial value and give the user of the information an opportunity to obtain a business advantage over competitors who do not know or use the information.

(L) "Services" includes, but is not limited to, computer time, data processing and storage functions.

(m) "Sexual conduct" means sexual intercourse or oral or anal sexual intercourse, as those terms are defined in ORS 163.305, or masturbation.

(2) Any person commits computer crime who knowingly accesses, attempts to access or uses, or attempts to use, any computer, computer system, computer network or any part thereof for the purpose of:

(a) Devising or executing any scheme or artifice to defraud;

(b) Obtaining money, property or services by means of false or fraudulent pretenses, representations or promises; or

(c) Committing theft, including, but not limited to, theft of proprietary information or theft of an intimate image.

(3) Any person who knowingly and without authorization alters, damages or destroys any computer, computer system, computer network, or any computer software, program, documentation or data contained in such computer, computer system or computer network, commits computer crime.

(4) Any person who knowingly and without authorization uses, accesses or attempts to access any computer, computer system, computer network, or any computer software, program, documentation or data contained in such computer, computer system or computer network, commits computer crime.

(5)(a) A violation of the provisions of subsection (2) or (3) of this section shall be a Class C felony. Except as provided in paragraph (b) of this subsection, a violation of the provisions of subsection (4) of this section shall be a Class A misdemeanor.

(b) Any violation of this section relating to a computer, computer network, computer program, computer software, computer system or data owned or operated by the Oregon State Lottery or rented, owned or operated by another person or entity under contract to or at the direction of the Oregon State Lottery Commission shall be a Class C felony. [1985 c.537 §8; 1989 c.737 §1; 1991 c.962 §17; 2001 c.870 §18; 2015 c.350 §1; 2017 c.318 §13]

164.380 [Repealed by 1971 c.743 §432]

GRAFFITI-RELATED OFFENSES

164.381 Definitions. As used in ORS 137.131, 164.381 to 164.386 and 419C.461:

(1) "Graffiti" means any inscriptions, words, figures or designs that are marked, etched, scratched, drawn, painted, pasted or otherwise affixed to the surface of property.

(2) "Graffiti implement" means paint, ink, chalk, dye or other substance or any instrument or article designed or adapted for spraying, marking, etching, scratching or carving surfaces. [1995 c.615 §1]

Note: 164.381 to 164.388 were enacted into law by the Legislative Assembly but were not added to or made a part of ORS chapter 164 or any series therein by legislative action. See Preface to Oregon Revised Statutes for further explanation.

164.383 Unlawfully applying graffiti. (1) A person commits the offense of unlawfully applying graffiti if the person, having no right to do so nor reasonable ground to believe that the person has such right, intentionally damages property of another by applying graffiti to the property.

(2) Unlawfully applying graffiti is a Class A violation. Upon a conviction for unlawfully applying graffiti, a court, in addition to any fine it imposes and pursuant to ORS 137.128 but notwithstanding ORS 137.129, may order the defendant to perform up to 100 hours of community service. The community service must include removing graffiti, either those that the defendant created or those created by another, or both.

(3) If the court orders community service, the community service must be completed within six months after entry of the order unless the person shows good cause why community service cannot be completed within the six-month time period. [1995 c.615 §2; 1999 c.1051 §156]

Note: See note under 164.381.

164.385 [1967 c.243 §1; repealed by 1971 c.743 §432]

164.386 Unlawfully possessing a graffiti implement. (1) A person commits the offense of unlawfully possessing a graffiti implement if the person possesses a graffiti implement with the intent of using the graffiti implement in violation of ORS 164.383.

(2) Unlawfully possessing a graffiti implement is a Class C violation. Upon a conviction for unlawfully possessing a graffiti implement, a court, in addition to any fine it imposes and pursuant to ORS 137.128 but notwithstanding ORS 137.129, may order the defendant to perform up to 50 hours of community service. The community service must include removing graffiti, either those that the defendant created or those created by another, or both.

(3) If the court orders community service, the community service must be completed within six months after entry of the order unless the person shows good cause why community service cannot be completed within the six-month time period. [1995 c.615 §3; 1999 c.1051 §157]

Note: See note under 164.381.

164.388 Preemption. The provisions of ORS 137.131, 164.381 to 164.386 and 419C.461 are not intended to preempt any local regulation of graffiti or graffiti-related activities or any prosecution under ORS 164.345, 164.354 or 164.365. [1995 c.615 §7; 1999 c.1040 §6]

Note: See note under 164.381.

164.390 [1959 c.626 §§1,4; repealed by 1971 c.743 §432]

164.392 [1959 c.626 §§2,3; repealed by 1971 c.743 §432]

ROBBERY

164.395 Robbery in the third degree. (1) A person commits the crime of robbery in the third degree if in the course of committing or attempting to commit theft or unauthorized use of a vehicle as defined in ORS 164.135 the person uses or threatens the immediate use of physical force upon another person with the intent of:
　(a) Preventing or overcoming resistance to the taking of the property or to retention thereof immediately after the taking; or
　(b) Compelling the owner of such property or another person to deliver the property or to engage in other conduct which might aid in the commission of the theft or unauthorized use of a vehicle.
　(2) Robbery in the third degree is a Class C felony. [1971 c.743 §148; 2003 c.357 §1]

164.405 Robbery in the second degree. (1) A person commits the crime of robbery in the second degree if the person violates ORS 164.395 and the person:
　(a) Represents by word or conduct that the person is armed with what purports to be a dangerous or deadly weapon; or
　(b) Is aided by another person actually present.
　(2) Robbery in the second degree is a Class B felony. [1971 c.743 §149]

164.410 [Repealed by 1971 c.743 §432]

164.415 Robbery in the first degree. (1) A person commits the crime of robbery in the first degree if the person violates ORS 164.395 and the person:
　(a) Is armed with a deadly weapon;
　(b) Uses or attempts to use a dangerous weapon; or
　(c) Causes or attempts to cause serious physical injury to any person.
　(2) Robbery in the first degree is a Class A felony. [1971 c.743 §150; 2007 c.71 §51]

164.420 [Repealed by 1971 c.743 §432]

164.430 [Repealed by 1971 c.743 §432]

164.440 [Amended by 1969 c.511 §1; repealed by 1971 c.404 §8 and by 1971 c.743 §432]

164.450 [Repealed by 1971 c.743 §432]

164.452 [1965 c.100 §300; repealed by 1971 c.743 §432]

164.455 [1953 c.535 §1; 1959 c.687 §2; 1965 c.453 §1; repealed by 1971 c.743 §432]

164.460 [Amended by 1957 c.470 §1; 1959 c.530 §2; 1969 c.501 §3; repealed by 1971 c.743 §432]

164.462 [1963 c.552 §§1,2; 1965 c.450 §1; repealed by 1971 c.743 §432]

164.465 [1953 c.430 §1; 1959 c.687 §3; repealed by 1971 c.743 §432]

164.470 [Amended by 1969 c.594 §1; repealed by 1971 c.743 §432]

164.480 [Repealed by 1971 c.743 §432]

164.485 [1969 c.652 §1; repealed by 1971 c.743 §432]

164.490 [1969 c.652 §2; repealed by 1971 c.743 §432]

164.500 [1969 c.652 §§3,4,6; repealed by 1971 c.743 §432]

164.505 [1969 c.652 §5; repealed by 1971 c.743 §432]

164.510 [Repealed by 1971 c.743 §432]

164.520 [Repealed by 1971 c.743 §432]

164.530 [Repealed by 1971 c.743 §432]

164.540 [Repealed by 1971 c.743 §432]

164.550 [Repealed by 1971 c.743 §432]

164.555 [1963 c.552 §3; repealed by 1971 c.743 §432]

164.560 [Repealed by 1971 c.743 §432]

164.570 [Repealed by 1971 c.743 §432]

164.580 [Amended by 1959 c.580 §103; repealed by 1971 c.743 §432]

164.590 [Repealed by 1971 c.743 §432]

164.610 [Repealed by 1971 c.743 §432]

164.620 [Repealed by 1971 c.743 §432]

164.630 [Repealed by 1971 c.743 §432]

164.635 [1961 c.310 §2; 1967 c.332 §1; repealed by 1971 c.743 §432]

164.640 [Repealed by 1971 c.743 §432]

164.650 [Repealed by 1971 c.743 §432]

164.660 [Amended by 1967 c.390 §1; repealed by 1971 c.743 §432]

164.670 [Amended by 1965 c.552 §1; repealed by 1971 c.743 §432]

164.680 [Repealed by 1971 c.743 §432]

164.690 [Repealed by 1971 c.743 §432]

164.700 [1965 c.594 §1; repealed by 1971 c.743 §432]

164.710 [Amended by 1969 c.517 §1; repealed by 1971 c.743 §432]

164.720 [Repealed by 1971 c.743 §432]

164.730 [Amended by 1967 c.351 §1; repealed by 1971 c.743 §432]

164.740 [Repealed by 1971 c.743 §432]

164.750 [1969 c.584 §1; repealed by 1971 c.743 §432]

164.760 [1969 c.584 §§2,3; repealed by 1971 c.743 §432]

164.770 [1969 c.584 §4; repealed by 1971 c.743 §432]

LITTERING

164.775 Deposit of trash within 100 yards of waters or in waters; license suspensions; civil penalties; credit for work in lieu of fine. (1) It is unlawful for any person to discard any glass, cans or other trash, rubbish, debris or litter on land within 100 yards of any of the waters of the state, as defined in ORS 468B.005, other than in receptacles provided for the purpose of holding such trash, rubbish, debris or litter.

(2) It is unlawful for any person to discard any glass, cans or other similar refuse in any waters of the state, as defined in ORS 468B.005.

(3) In addition to or in lieu of the penalties provided for violation of any provision of this section, the court in which any individual is convicted of a violation of this section may order suspension of certain permits or licenses for a period not to exceed 90 days if the court finds that the violation occurred during or in connection with the exercise of the privilege granted by the permit or license. The permits and licenses to which this section applies are motor vehicle operator's permits or licenses, hunting licenses, fishing licenses or boat registrations.

(4)(a) Any person sentenced under subsection (6) of this section to pay a fine for violation of this section shall be permitted, in default of the payment of the fine, to work at clearing rubbish, trash and debris from the lands and waters described by subsections (1) and (2) of this section. Credit in compensation for such work shall be allowed at the rate of $25 for each day of work.

(b) In any case, upon conviction, if punishment by imprisonment is imposed upon the defendant, the form of the sentence shall include that the defendant shall be punished by confinement at labor clearing rubbish, trash and debris from the lands and waters described by subsections (1) and (2) of this section, for not less than one day nor more than five days.

(5) A citation conforming to the requirements of ORS 133.066 shall be used for all violations of subsection (1) or (2) of this section in the state.

(6) Violation of this section is a Class B misdemeanor.

(7) In addition to and not in lieu of the criminal penalty authorized by subsection (6) of this section, the civil penalty authorized by ORS 468.140 may be imposed for violation of this section.

(8) Nothing in this section or ORS 164.785 prohibits the operation of a disposal site, as defined in ORS 459.005, for which a permit is required by the Department of Environmental Quality, for which such a permit has been issued and which is being operated and maintained in accordance with the terms and conditions of such permit. [Formerly 449.107; 1999 c.1051 §132]

164.780 [1969 c.584 §5; repealed by 1971 c.743 §432]

164.785 Placing offensive substances in waters, on highways or other property. (1)(a) It is unlawful for any person, including a person in the possession or control of any land, to discard any dead animal carcass or part thereof, excrement, putrid, nauseous, noisome, decaying, deleterious or offensive substance into or in any other manner befoul, pollute or impair the quality of any spring, river, brook, creek, branch, well, irrigation drainage ditch, irrigation ditch, cistern or pond of water.

(b)(A) In a prosecution under this subsection, it is a defense that:

(i) The dead animal carcass that is discarded is a fish carcass;

(ii) The person returned the fish carcass to the water from which the person caught the fish; and

(iii) The person retained proof of compliance with any provisions regarding angling prescribed by the State Fish and Wildlife Commission pursuant to ORS 496.162.

(B) As used in this paragraph, "fish carcass" means entrails, gills, head, skin, fins and backbone.

(2) It is unlawful for any person to place or cause to be placed any polluting substance listed in subsection (1) of this section into any road, street, alley, lane, railroad right of way, lot, field, meadow or common. It is unlawful for an owner thereof to knowingly permit any polluting substances to remain in any of the places described in this subsection to the injury of the health or to the annoyance of any citizen of this state. Every 24 hours after conviction for violation of this subsection during which the violator permits the polluting substances to remain is an additional offense against this subsection.

(3) Nothing in this section shall apply to the storage or spreading of manure or like substance for agricultural, silvicultural or horticultural purposes, except that no sewage sludge, septic tank or cesspool pumpings shall be used for these purposes unless treated and applied in a manner approved by the Department of Environmental Quality.

(4) Violation of this section is a Class A misdemeanor.

(5) The Department of Environmental Quality may impose the civil penalty authorized by ORS 468.140 for violation of this section. [Formerly 449.105; 1983 c.257 §1; 1987 c.325 §1; 2013 c.132 §1]

164.805 Offensive littering. (1) A person commits the crime of offensive littering if the person creates an objectionable stench or degrades the beauty or appearance of property or detracts from the natural cleanliness or safety of property by intentionally:

(a) Discarding or depositing any rubbish, trash, garbage, debris or other refuse upon the land of another without permission of the owner, or upon any public way or in or upon any public transportation facility;

(b) Draining, or causing or permitting to be drained, sewage or the drainage from a cesspool, septic tank, recreational or camping vehicle waste holding tank or other contaminated source, upon the land of another without permission of the owner, or upon any public way; or

(c) Permitting any rubbish, trash, garbage, debris or other refuse to be thrown from a vehicle that the person is operating. This subsection does not apply to a person operating a vehicle transporting passengers for hire subject to regulation by the Department of Transportation or a person operating a school bus described under ORS 801.460.

(2) As used in this section:

(a) "Public transportation facility" has the meaning given that term in ORS 164.365.

(b) "Public way" includes, but is not limited to, roads, streets, alleys, lanes, trails, beaches, parks and all recreational facilities operated by the state, a county or a local municipality for use by the general public.

(3) Offensive littering is a Class C misdemeanor. [1971 c.743 §283; 1975 c.344 §2; 1983 c.338 §897; 1985 c.420 §20; 2007 c.71 §52; 2015 c.138 §2]

164.810 [Repealed by 1971 c.743 §432]

UNLAWFUL TRANSPORT

164.813 Unlawful cutting and transport of special forest products. (1) As used in this section:

(a) "Harvest" means to separate by cutting, digging, prying, picking, peeling, breaking, pulling, splitting or otherwise removing a special forest product from:

(A) Its physical connection or point of contact with the ground or vegetation upon which it was growing; or

(B) The place or position where it lay.

(b) "Special forest products" means:

(A) Plants, plant parts, fruit, fungi, parts of fungi, rocks or minerals that are identified in State Board of Forestry rules as special forest products;

(B) Firewood;

(C) Trees or parts of trees of a species identified in board rules as a forest tree species not normally used in commercial forest harvests; and

(D) Other items identified by the board by rule as special forest products.

(c) "Special forest products" does not mean mill ends, driftwood and artificially fabricated fireplace logs.

(d) "Transportation" means the physical conveyance of special forest products away from a harvest or collection site and includes, but is not limited to, transportation in or on:

(A) A motor vehicle or trailer, both as defined for purposes of the Oregon Vehicle Code;

(B) A boat, barge, raft or other water vessel; or

(C) An airplane, helicopter, balloon or other aircraft.

(2) Subject to subsection (6) of this section, it is unlawful for any person other than the landowner to cut or split wood into special forest products or to harvest or remove special forest products from a place unless the person has in possession a written permit to do so from the owner of the land from which the wood is cut or the special forest products taken. The written permit required under this subsection must set forth:

(a) The date of the permit;

(b) The name, address, telephone number and signature of the person granting the permit;

(c) The name, address and telephone number of the person to whom the permit is granted;

(d) The amount and kind of wood, by species, to be cut or split or the amount and kind of special forest products to be taken;

(e) A description of the premises from which the wood is to be cut or the special forest products taken. The description may be by legal description, tax account number or other description clearly identifying the premises; and

(f) The date of expiration of the permit.

(3) Subject to subsection (6) of this section, it is unlawful for a person to transport special forest products without possessing a permit as described in subsection (2) of this section or a document of sale showing title to the special forest products. A document of sale must be signed by the landowner, seller or donor, and must set forth:

(a) The date of the document;

(b) The name, address and telephone number of the seller or donor of the special forest products;

(c) The name, address and telephone number of the purchaser or donee;

(d) The amount and kind of special forest products sold, by species; and

(e) A description of the premises from which the special forest products were taken. The description may be by legal description, tax account number or other description clearly identifying the premises, or by street address in the event of purchase from a woodlot or fuel dealer or dealer in other special forest products.

(4) Except as provided in subsection (7) of this section, any person who engages in the purchase or other acquisition of special forest products for resale, other than special forest products acquired from property owned by that person, shall keep records of such purchases or acquisitions for a period of one year from the date of purchase or acquisition. The records shall be made available to any peace officer upon request and shall reveal:

(a) The date of purchase or acquisition;

(b) The name, address, telephone number and signature of the person from whom the special forest products were obtained and the date they were obtained;

(c) The license number of any vehicle used to deliver the special forest products to the dealer for resale;

(d) The quantity of special forest products purchased or acquired; and

(e) The name and address of the landowner from whose land the special forest product was harvested.

(5) Any permit for the removal of special forest products from public lands issued or required by the United States Forest Service or the Bureau of Land Management is:

(a) Sufficient for the purposes of subsections (2) and (3) of this section, regardless of whether the permit conforms to the specific requirements as to content set forth in subsections (2) and (3) of this section; and

(b) Valid only for the purposes and public lands locations identified in the permit.

(6) Subsections (2) and (3) of this section do not apply to the following activities conducted on public lands:

(a) The cutting or transportation of wild edible fungi occupying a volume at harvest of one gallon or less;

(b) The cutting or transportation of special forest products, described in subsection (1)(b)(B) and (C) of this section, having a total volume of less than 27 cubic feet;

(c) The cutting or transportation of special forest products, other than those specified in paragraphs (a) and (b) of this subsection, having a total volume of less than 12 cubic feet;

(d) The cutting or transportation of coniferous trees that are subject to the provisions of ORS 164.825;

(e) The cutting or transportation of special forest products by the owner of the land from which they were taken or by the owner's agent; or

(f) The transportation of special forest products by a common carrier or contract carrier.

(7) Subsection (4) of this section does not apply to a person who purchases cedar products that are special forest products and who complies with the record keeping requirements of ORS 165.109.

(8) Violation of any provision of subsections (2) to (4) of this section is a Class B misdemeanor. [1981 c.645 §2; 1989 c.368 §1; 1993 c.167 §1; 1995 c.75 §1; 2013 c.276 §§1,2]

164.814 State Forester required to develop forms for special forest products. The State Forester shall develop a typical form for the permit and document of sale required by ORS 164.813 and for the records required by ORS 164.813 (4). The State Forester shall make copies of the forms available. Use of the forms is not required. [1995 c.75 §2; 2013 c.276 §3]

Note: 164.814 was enacted into law by the Legislative Assembly but was not added to or made a part of ORS chapter 164 or any series therein by legislative action. See Preface to Oregon Revised Statutes for further explanation.

164.815 Unlawfully transporting hay. (1) A person commits the crime of unlawfully transporting hay if the person knowingly transports more than 20 bales of hay on a public highway without having in possession a transportation certificate signed by the producer or the agent of the producer showing:

(a) The amount of hay in possession and the date of acquisition of it;

(b) The price paid or agreed to be paid for the hay or other terms of the transportation or sale contract;

(c) The location where the hay was loaded and its destination;

(d) The total number of bales or other units and the method of bailing or packaging; and

(e) The type of hay.

(2) Subsection (1) of this section does not apply to transportation of hay:

(a) By the producer thereof or the agent of the producer who has in possession written evidence of authority to transport the hay for the producer; or

(b) By a person or the agent of the person under contract to transport the hay for the producer.

(3) As used in this section:

(a) "Hay" means grasses, legumes or other forage plants grown in Oregon and intended for use as a feed.

(b) "Producer" means a person who raises and harvests hay on land the person owns or leases and who is delivering that hay from the field to a place of storage or sale or to a feedlot for livestock.

(4) Unlawfully transporting hay is a Class C misdemeanor. [1971 c.743 §288a; 1973 c.445 §1]

164.820 [Amended by 1971 c.647 §1; repealed by 1971 c.743 §432]

164.825 Cutting and transport of coniferous trees without permit or bill of sale. (1) It is unlawful for any person to cut more than five coniferous trees unless the person has in possession written permission to do so from the owner of the land from which the trees are cut. The written permit required under this subsection must set forth:

(a) The date of the permit;

(b) The name, address, telephone number and signature of the person granting the permit;

(c) The name, address and telephone number of the person to whom the permit is granted;

(d) The number of trees, by species, to be cut;

(e) A description of the premises from which the trees are to be cut. The description may be by legal description or tax account number; and

(f) The date of expiration of the permit.

(2) It is unlawful for any person to transport over the highways of this state more than five coniferous trees without possessing a cutting permit as described in subsection (1) of this section or a document of title showing title thereto. A document of sale must be signed by the landowner, seller or donor, and shall set forth:

(a) The date of the document;

(b) The name, address and telephone number of the seller or donor of the trees;

(c) The name, address and telephone number of the purchaser or donee of the trees;

(d) The number of trees, by species, sold or transferred by the permit or document of sale; and

(e) A description of the premises from which the trees were taken. The description may be by legal description, tax account number or other description clearly identifying the premises.

(3) The provisions of subsections (1) and (2) of this section do not apply to:

(a) The transportation of trees in the course of transplantation, with their roots intact.

(b) The cutting or transportation of coniferous trees by the owner of the land from which they were taken or by the owner's agent.

(c) The transportation of coniferous trees by a common carrier or contract carrier.

(4) Violation of the provisions of subsection (1) or (2) of this section is a Class B misdemeanor. [1971 c.743 §295; 1981 c.645 §6]

164.828 Ownership as affirmative defense under ORS 164.813 and 164.825. It is an affirmative defense to any charge under ORS 164.813 or 164.825 that the defendant is in fact the owner of the trees or special forest products cut or transported. [1981 c.645 §7; 1993 c.167 §2]

Note: 164.828 was enacted into law by the Legislative Assembly but was not added to or made a part of ORS chapter 164 or any series therein by legislative action. See Preface to Oregon Revised Statutes for further explanation.

164.830 [Repealed by 1971 c.743 §432]

164.835 Investigation to prevent violations of ORS 164.813 and 164.825. (1) All peace officers shall note and investigate the cutting and transportation of coniferous trees and special forest products as defined in ORS 164.813 for the purpose of preventing violations of ORS 164.813 and 164.825.

(2) Justice courts and circuit courts have concurrent jurisdiction of violations of ORS 164.813 and 164.825. [1971 c.743 §296; 1981 c.645 §3; 1993 c.167 §3]

164.840 [Repealed by 1971 c.743 §432]

164.845 Arrest, summons for cutting or transport of trees or special forest products; effect of failure to appear. (1) Whenever any peace officer has reasonable cause to believe that a person is cutting or transporting trees or special forest products in violation of ORS 164.813 (2) or (3) or 164.825, the peace officer may arrest the person without a warrant and take the person before any court having jurisdiction of the offense. The court shall proceed without delay to hear, try and determine the matter and enter judgment according to the allegations and proofs.

(2) The peace officer making the arrest, if not immediately taking the person arrested into custody, may issue a summons to the person. The summons shall direct the person to appear at the court named in the summons to answer a complaint to be filed therewith. The violation shall be noted on the summons, which shall be dated and signed by the peace officer.

(3) Any person to whom a summons is issued under this section who fails to appear at the time and place specified therein commits a Class B misdemeanor. [1971 c.743 §297; 1981 c.645 §4; 1993 c.167 §4; 2013 c.276 §4]

164.850 [Repealed by 1971 c.743 §432]

164.855 Seizure of trees or special forest products cut or transported in violation of ORS 164.813 or 164.825. (1) Whenever any peace officer has reasonable cause for believing that a person is cutting or transporting trees or special forest products in violation of ORS 164.813 (2) or (3) or 164.825, the peace officer may, at the time of making the arrest or issuing the summons, under ORS 164.845, seize and take possession of the trees or special forest products. The peace officer shall hold the trees or special forest products subject to the order of the court before which the arrested person is ordered to appear. If the owner of the trees or special forest products appears before the court within 48 hours after the seizure thereof and presents satisfactory evidence of ownership, the court shall order the peace officer to deliver the trees or special forest products to the owner. If the owner does not appear within the 48-hour period and prove ownership of the trees or special forest products, the court may direct the peace officer to sell the trees or special forest products in any manner and for any price that appears to the court to be warranted. If the trees or special forest products have no value, the court may direct the officer to destroy them in any manner practicable. The proceeds of the sale, less the reasonable expenses thereof, shall be paid to the treasurer of the county in which the trees or special forest products are sold. At any time within one year after the seizure of the trees or special forest products the owner thereof may appear before the court, and, upon presentation of satisfactory evidence of ownership, the court shall direct the treasurer of the county to pay the proceeds to the owner. If the owner does not appear within one year from the seizure of the trees or special forest products and prove a right to the proceeds, the proceeds shall thereafter belong to the county, and may be disposed of as the county court may direct.

(2) The return of the trees or special forest products or the payment of the proceeds shall not preclude the court from imposing any fine or penalty for any violation of ORS 164.825 to 164.855. [1971 c.743 §298; 1981 c.645 §5; 1993 c.167 §5; 2013 c.276 §5]

164.857 Unlawfully transporting metal property. (1) A person commits the offense of unlawfully transporting metal property if the person transports metal property on a public highway or on premises open to the public with the intent to deliver the metal property to a scrap metal business and the person does not have a metal transportation certificate in the person's possession.

(2) A seller or transferor of metal property that has reason to believe that a buyer or transferee intends to obtain the metal property for delivery to a scrap metal business shall provide the buyer or transferee with a metal transportation certificate.

(3) A metal transportation certificate must include:

(a) The date the metal property was acquired and the amount and type of metal property that the person is transporting;

(b) The location where the metal property was loaded and the destination of the metal property;

(c) The name, address and telephone number of the seller or the transferor;

(d) The signature of the seller or transferor or the authorized agent of the seller or transferor; and

(e) The name, address and telephone number of the person transporting the metal property.

(4) The Department of State Police shall create a form that may serve as a metal transportation certificate and shall make the form available on the department's website.

(5) It is a defense to a charge of unlawfully transporting metal property that the person transporting the metal property is the owner of the property or an agent or employee of the owner of the property.

(6) Unlawfully transporting metal property is a Class C misdemeanor.

(7) As used in this section:

(a) "Agent or employee of the owner of the property" includes a motor carrier as defined in ORS 825.005 that is operating in accordance with the provisions of ORS chapter 825.

(b) "Metal property" and "scrap metal business" have the meanings given those terms in ORS 165.116. [2009 c.811 §3; 2010 c.56 §4]

Note: 164.857 was enacted into law by the Legislative Assembly but was not added to or made a part of ORS chapter 164 or any series therein by legislative action. See Preface to Oregon Revised Statutes for further explanation.

164.860 [Repealed by 1971 c.743 §432]

164.863 Unlawful transport of meat animal carcasses. (1) Except as provided in subsection (2) of this section, it shall be unlawful for any person to transport the carcass or a primal cut thereof of any meat animal on a public highway without having in possession a transportation certificate signed by the owner or the agent of the owner showing:

(a) The location where the carcass or primal cut was loaded and its destination;

(b) The quantity in possession and the date of acquisition of it; and

(c) Transportation or bill of sale.

(2) Subsection (1) of this section does not apply to the carcass or meat of a meat animal:

(a) That is transported by common carrier;

(b) That is marked, tagged or otherwise identified as required by ORS chapter 619;

(c) That is marked, tagged or identified as required by ORS 603.045 (2), or that is the subject of the certificate and tags described in ORS 603.045 (4); or

(d) That is marked, tagged or otherwise identified as having been previously inspected under the Federal Meat Inspection Act.

(3) As used in this section:

(a) "Common carrier" means:

(A) Any person who transports for hire or who purports to be to the public as willing to transport for hire, compensation or consideration by motor vehicle, persons or property, or both, for those who may choose to employ the person; or

(B) Any person who leases, rents or otherwise provides a motor vehicle for the use of others and who in connection therewith in the regular course of business provides, procures or arranges for, directly, indirectly or by course of dealing, a driver or operator therefor.

(b) "Federal Meat Inspection Act" means the Act so entitled approved March 4, 1907, (34 Stat. 1260), as amended by the Wholesome Meat Act (81 Stat. 584).

(c) "Meat animal" means any live cattle, equines, sheep, goats or swine.

(d) "Meat" or "meat product" means any edible muscle, except any muscle found in the lips, snout or ears of meat animals, which is skeletal or found in the tongue, diaphragm, heart or esophagus, with or without any accompanying and overlying fat, and any portion of bone, skin, sinew, nerve or blood vessels normally accompanying the muscle tissue and not separated from it in the process of dressing or as otherwise prescribed by the Department of Agriculture.

(4) Unlawfully transporting the carcass or primal cut of a meat animal is a Class C misdemeanor.

(5) For the purpose of this section "primal cut" of cattle and equines means round, loin, flank, rib, chuck, brisket, plate or shank; of pork means ham, loin, side, spareribs, shoulder or jowl; of sheep and goats means rib or rack, loin, leg or shoulder. [1975 c.201 §2]

MISCELLANEOUS

164.864 Definitions for ORS 164.864 to 164.882. As used in ORS 164.865, 164.866, 164.868, 164.869, 164.872, 164.873, 164.875 and 164.882 and this section, unless the context requires otherwise:

(1) "Audiovisual recording function" means the capability of a device to record or transmit a motion picture or any part of a motion picture by means of any technology now known or later developed.

(2) "Commercial enterprise" means a business operating in intrastate or interstate commerce for profit. "Commercial enterprise" does not include:

(a) Activities by schools, libraries or religious organizations;

(b) Activities incidental to a bona fide scholastic or critical endeavor;

(c) Activities incidental to the marketing or sale of recording devices; and

(d) Activities involving the recording of school or religious events or activities.

(3) "Fixed" means embodied in a recording or other tangible medium of expression, by or under the authority of the author, so that the matter embodied is sufficiently permanent or stable to permit it to be perceived, reproduced or otherwise communicated for a period of more than transitory duration.

(4) "Live performance" means a recitation, rendering or playing of musical instruments or vocal arrangements in an audible sequence in a public performance.

(5) "Manufacturer" means the entity authorizing the duplication of a specific recording, but shall not include the manufacturer of the cartridge or casing itself.

(6) "Master recording" means the master disk, master tape, master film or other device used for reproducing recorded sound from which a sound recording is directly or indirectly derived.

(7) "Motion picture" includes any motion picture, regardless of length or content, that is exhibited in a motion picture theater, exhibited on television to paying customers or under the sponsorship of a paying advertiser or produced and exhibited for scientific research or educational purposes. "Motion picture" does not include amateur films that are shown free or at cost to friends, neighbors or civic groups.

(8) "Motion picture theater" means a movie theater, screening room or other venue that is being utilized primarily for the exhibition of a motion picture.

(9) "Owner" means a person who owns the sounds fixed in a master phonograph record, master disk, master tape, master film or other recording on which sound is or can be recorded and from which the transferred recorded sounds are directly or indirectly derived.

(10) "Recording" means a tangible medium on which information, sounds or images, or any combination thereof, are recorded or otherwise stored. Medium includes, but is not limited to, an original phonograph record, disk, tape, audio or video cassette, wire, film or other medium now existing or developed later on which sounds, images or both are or can be recorded or otherwise stored or a copy or reproduction that duplicates in whole or in part the original.

(11) "Sound recording" means any reproduction of a master recording.

(12) "Videotape" means a reel of tape upon which a motion picture is electronically or magnetically imprinted by means of an electronic video recorder and which may be used in video playback equipment to project or display the motion picture on a television screen. [1993 c.95 §1; 2001 c.666 §§30,42; 2005 c.459 §§3,4; 2005 c.830 §22]

Note: 164.864, 164.866, 164.867, 164.868, 164.869, 164.872 and 164.873 were enacted into law by the Legislative Assembly but were not added to or made a part of ORS chapter 164 or any series therein by legislative action. See Preface to Oregon Revised Statutes for further explanation.

164.865 Unlawful sound recording. (1) A person commits the crime of unlawful sound recording if the person:

(a) Reproduces for sale any sound recording without the written consent of the owner of the master recording; or

(b) Knowingly sells, offers for sale or advertises for sale any sound recording that has been reproduced without the written consent of the owner of the master recording.

(2) Unlawful sound recording is a Class B misdemeanor. [1973 c.747 §1; 1993 c.95 §3]

164.866 Civil action for injuries caused by criminal acts. Nothing in ORS 164.864, 164.865, 164.868, 164.869, 164.872, 164.873 or 164.875 or this section limits or impairs the right of a person injured by the criminal acts of a defendant to sue and recover damages from the defendant in a civil action. [1993 c.95 §11; 2001 c.666 §§31,43; 2005 c.830 §23]

Note: See note under 164.864.

164.867 Applicability of ORS 164.868, 164.869 and 164.872. The provisions of ORS 164.868, 164.869 and 164.872 apply only to persons operating commercial enterprises. [1993 c.95 §2]

Note: See note under 164.864.

164.868 Unlawful labeling of a sound recording. (1) A person commits unlawful labeling of a sound recording if the person:

(a) Fails to disclose the origin of a sound recording when the person knowingly advertises or offers for sale or resale, sells, resells, rents, leases, or lends or possesses for any of these purposes, any sound recording that does not contain the true name and address of the manufacturer in a prominent place on the cover, jacket or label of the sound recording; and

(b) Possesses five or more duplicate copies or 20 or more individual copies of recordings produced without consent of the owner or performer and the recordings are intended for sale or distribution in violation of this section.

(2) Unlawful labeling of a sound recording is a Class C felony. [1993 c.95 §7]

Note: See note under 164.864.

164.869 Unlawful recording of a live performance. (1) A person commits unlawful recording of a live performance if the person:

(a)(A) Advertises or offers for sale, sells, rents, transports, or causes the sale, resale, rental or transportation of, or possesses for one or more of these purposes, a recording containing sounds of a live performance with the knowledge that the live performance has been recorded or fixed without the consent of the owner; or

(B) With the intent to sell, records or fixes, or causes to be recorded or fixed on a recording, a live performance with the knowledge that the live performance has been recorded or fixed without the consent of the owner; and

(b) Possesses five or more duplicate copies or 20 or more individual copies of recordings produced without consent of the owner or performer and the recordings are intended for sale or distribution in violation of this section.

(2) Unlawful recording of a live performance is a Class C felony.

(3) For purposes of subsections (1) and (2) of this section, in the absence of a written agreement or law to the contrary, the performer of a live performance is presumed to own the rights to record or fix the performance.

(4) A person who is authorized to maintain custody and control over business records that reflect whether or not the owner of the live performance consented to having the live performance recorded or fixed is a proper witness in a proceeding regarding the issue of consent. [1993 c.95 §§5,6]

Note: See note under 164.864.

164.870 [Repealed by 1957 c.269 §1; (164.871 enacted in lieu of 164.870)]

164.871 [1957 c.269 §2 (enacted in lieu of 164.870); repealed by 1971 c.743 §432]

164.872 Unlawful labeling of a videotape recording. (1) A person commits unlawful labeling of a videotape recording if the person:

(a) Fails to disclose the origin of a recording when the person knowingly advertises or offers for sale or resale, or sells, resells, rents, leases or lends, or possesses for any of these purposes, any videotape recording that does not contain the true name and address of the manufacturer in a prominent place on the cover, jacket or label of the videotape recording; and

(b) Possesses five or more duplicate copies or 20 or more individual copies of videotape recordings produced without consent of the owner or performer and the videotape recordings are intended for sale or distribution in violation of this section.

(2) Unlawful labeling of a videotape recording is a Class C felony. [1993 c.95 §8]

Note: See note under 164.864.

164.873 Exemptions from ORS 164.865, 164.868, 164.869, 164.872 and 164.875. (1) The provisions of ORS 164.872 and 164.875 do not apply to:

(a) The production of a videotape of a motion picture that is defined as a public record under ORS 192.005 (5), in accordance with ORS 192.005 to 192.170 or 357.805 to 357.895.

(b) The production of a videotape of a motion picture that is defined as a legislative record under ORS 171.410, in accordance with ORS 171.410 to 171.430.

(2) The provisions of ORS 164.865, 164.868, 164.869 (1) and (2) and 164.875 do not apply to the reproduction of:

(a) Any recording that is used or intended to be used only for broadcast by educational radio or television stations.

(b) A sound recording, or the production of a videotape of a motion picture, that is defined as a public record under ORS 192.005 (5), with or without charging and collecting a fee therefor, in accordance with ORS 192.005 to 192.170 or 357.805 to 357.895.

(c) A sound recording defined as a legislative record under ORS 171.410, with or without charging and collecting a fee therefor, in accordance with ORS 171.410 to 171.430. [1993 c.95 §§9,10]

Note: See note under 164.864.

164.875 Unlawful videotape recording. (1) A person commits the crime of unlawful videotape recording if the person:

(a) Produces for sale any videotape without the written consent of the owner of the motion picture imprinted thereon; or

(b) Knowingly sells or offers for sale any videotape that has been produced without the written consent of the owner of the motion picture imprinted thereon.

(2) Unlawful videotape recording is a Class B misdemeanor. [1979 c.550 §2; 1993 c.95 §4]

164.876 [1993 c.95 §12; repealed by 2001 c.666 §56]

164.877 [1989 c.1003 §§2,3; renumbered 164.886 in 2007]

164.879 [2001 c.666 §50; repealed by 2005 c.830 §48]

164.880 [Repealed by 1971 c.743 §432]

164.882 Unlawful operation of an audiovisual device. (1) A person commits the crime of unlawful operation of an audiovisual device if the person knowingly operates the audiovisual recording function of any device in a motion picture theater, while a motion picture is being exhibited, without the written consent of the motion picture theater owner.

(2) Unlawful operation of an audiovisual device is a Class B misdemeanor.

(3) The provisions of subsection (1) of this section do not apply to any activity undertaken in the course of bona fide law enforcement activity or necessary to the proper functioning of the criminal justice system. [2005 c.459 §1]

Note: 164.882 was enacted into law by the Legislative Assembly but was not added to or made a part of ORS chapter 164 or any series therein by legislative action. See Preface to Oregon Revised Statutes for further explanation.

164.885 Endangering aircraft. (1) A person commits the crime of endangering aircraft in the first degree if the person knowingly:

(a) Throws an object at, or drops an object upon, an aircraft;

(b) Discharges a bow and arrow, gun, airgun or firearm at or toward an aircraft;

(c) Tampers with an aircraft or a part, system, machine or substance used to operate an aircraft in such a manner as to impair the safety, efficiency or operation of an aircraft without the consent of the owner, operator or possessor of the aircraft; or

(d) Places, sets, arms or causes to be discharged a spring gun, trap, explosive device or explosive material with the intent of damaging, destroying or discouraging the operation of an aircraft.

(2)(a) Except as provided in paragraph (b) of this subsection, a person commits the crime of endangering aircraft in the second degree if the person knowingly possesses a firearm or deadly weapon in a restricted access area of a commercial service airport that has at least 2 million passenger boardings per calendar year.

(b) Paragraph (a) of this subsection does not apply to a person authorized under federal law or an airport security program to possess a firearm or deadly weapon in a restricted access area.

(3)(a) Endangering aircraft in the first degree is a Class C felony.

(b) Endangering aircraft in the second degree is a Class A misdemeanor.

(4) As used in this section:

(a) "Aircraft" does not include an unmanned aircraft system as defined in ORS 837.300.

(b) "Restricted access area" means an area of a commercial service airport that is:

(A) Designated as restricted in the airport security program approved by the federal Transportation Security Administration; and

(B) Marked at points of entry with signs giving notice that access to the area is restricted. [1981 c.901 §1; 2009 c.299 §1; 2016 c.72 §3]

Note: 164.885 was enacted into law by the Legislative Assembly but was not added to or made a part of ORS chapter 164 or any series therein by legislative action. See Preface to Oregon Revised Statutes for further explanation.

164.886 Unlawful tree spiking; unlawful possession of substance that can damage certain wood processing equipment. (1) A person commits the crime of unlawful tree spiking if the person knowingly drives or places in any tree or saw log, without the prior consent of the owner thereof, any iron, steel or other substance sufficiently hard to damage saws or wood manufacturing or processing equipment with intent to cause inconvenience, annoyance or alarm to any other person.

(2) Except as provided in subsection (3) of this section, unlawful tree spiking is a Class C felony.

(3) Unlawful tree spiking that results in serious physical injury to another person is a Class B felony.

(4) Any person who possesses, with the intent to use in violation of subsections (1) to (3) of this section, any iron, steel or other substance sufficiently hard to damage saws or wood manufacturing or processing equipment is guilty of a Class A misdemeanor. [Formerly 164.877]

164.887 Interference with agricultural operations. (1) Except as provided in subsection (3) of this section, a person commits the offense of interference with agricultural operations if the person, while on the property of another person who is engaged in agricultural operations, intentionally or knowingly obstructs, impairs or hinders or attempts to obstruct, impair or hinder agricultural operations.

(2) Interference with agricultural operations is a Class A misdemeanor.

(3) The provisions of subsection (1) of this section do not apply to:

(a) A person who is involved in a labor dispute as defined in ORS 662.010 with the other person; or

(b) A public employee who is performing official duties.

(4) As used in this section:

(a)(A) "Agricultural operations" means the conduct of logging and forest management, mining, farming or ranching of livestock animals or domestic farm animals;

(B) "Domestic farm animal" means an animal used to control or protect livestock animals or used in other related agricultural activities; and

(C) "Livestock animals" has the meaning given that term in ORS 164.055.

(b) "Domestic farm animal" and "livestock animals" do not include stray animals. [1999 c.694 §1]

Note: 164.887 was enacted into law by the Legislative Assembly but was not added to or made a part of ORS chapter 164 or any series therein by legislative action. See Preface to Oregon Revised Statutes for further explanation.

164.889 Interference with agricultural research. (1) A person commits the crime of interference with agricultural research if the person knowingly:

(a) Damages any property at an agricultural research facility with the intent to damage or hinder agricultural research or experimentation;

(b) Obtains any property of an agricultural research facility with the intent to damage or hinder agricultural research or experimentation;

(c) Obtains access to an agricultural research facility by misrepresentation with the intent to perform acts that would damage or hinder agricultural research or experimentation;

(d) Enters an agricultural research facility with the intent to damage, alter, duplicate or obtain unauthorized possession of records, data, materials, equipment or specimens related to agricultural research or experimentation;

(e) Without the authorization of the agricultural research facility, obtains or exercises control over records, data, materials, equipment or specimens of the agricultural research facility with the intent to destroy or conceal the records, data, materials, equipment or specimens; or

(f) Releases or steals an animal from, or causes the death, injury or loss of an animal at, an agricultural research facility.

(2) Interference with agricultural research is a Class C felony.

(3) For purposes of this section:

(a) "Agricultural research facility" means any structure or land, whether privately or publicly owned, leased or operated, that is being used for agricultural research or experimentation.

(b) "Agricultural research or experimentation" means the lawful study, analysis or testing of plants or animals, or the use of plants or animals to conduct studies, analyses, testing or teaching, for the purpose of improving farming, forestry or animal husbandry.

(4) In addition to any other penalty imposed for violation of this section, a person convicted of interference with agricultural research is liable for:

(a) Damages to real and personal property caused by acts constituting the violation; and

(b) The costs of repeating an experiment, including the replacement of the records, data, equipment, specimens, labor and materials, if acts constituting the violation cause the failure of an experiment in progress or irreparably damage completed research or experimentation. [2001 c.147 §1]

Note: 164.889 was enacted into law by the Legislative Assembly but was not added to or made a part of ORS chapter 164 or any series therein by legislative action. See Preface to Oregon Revised Statutes for further explanation.

164.890 [Repealed by 1971 c.743 §432]

164.900 [Repealed by 1971 c.743 §432]

Chapter 165 — Offenses Involving Fraud or Deception

ORS sections in this chapter were amended or repealed by the Legislative Assembly during its 2018 regular session. See the table of ORS sections amended or repealed during the 2018 regular session: 2018 A&R Tables

New sections of law were enacted by the Legislative Assembly during its 2018 regular session and pertain to or are likely to be compiled in this ORS chapter. See sections in the following 2018 Oregon Laws chapters: 2018 Session Laws 0076

FORGERY AND RELATED OFFENSES

165.002 Definitions for ORS 165.002 to 165.070. As used in ORS 165.002 to 165.027, and 165.032 to 165.070, unless the context requires otherwise:

(1) "Written instrument" means any paper, document, instrument, article or electronic record containing written or printed matter or the equivalent thereof, whether complete or incomplete, used for the purpose of reciting, embodying, conveying or recording information or constituting a symbol or evidence of value, right, privilege or identification, which is capable of being used to the advantage or disadvantage of some person.

(2) "Complete written instrument" means one which purports to be a genuine written instrument fully drawn with respect to every essential feature thereof.

(3) "Incomplete written instrument" means one which contains some matter by way of content or authentication but which requires additional matter in order to render it a complete written instrument.

(4) To "falsely make" a written instrument means to make or draw a complete written instrument in its entirety, or an incomplete written instrument which purports to be an authentic creation of its ostensible maker, but which is not, either because the ostensible maker is fictitious or because, if real, the ostensible maker did not authorize the making or drawing thereof.

(5) To "falsely complete" a written instrument means to transform, by adding, inserting or changing matter, an incomplete written instrument into a complete one, without the authority of anyone entitled to grant it, so that the complete written instrument falsely appears or purports to be in all respects an authentic creation of its ostensible maker or authorized by the ostensible maker.

(6) To "falsely alter" a written instrument means to change, without authorization by anyone entitled to grant it, a written instrument, whether complete or incomplete, by means of erasure, obliteration, deletion, insertion of new matter, transposition of matter, or in any other manner, so that the instrument so altered falsely appears or purports to be in all respects an authentic creation of its ostensible maker or authorized by the ostensible maker.

(7) To "utter" means to issue, deliver, publish, circulate, disseminate, transfer or tender a written instrument or other object to another.

(8) "Forged instrument" means a written instrument which has been falsely made, completed or altered.

(9) "Electronic record" has the meaning given that term in ORS 84.004.

(10) "Signature" includes, but is not limited to, an electronic signature, as defined in ORS 84.004. [1971 c.743 §151; 2001 c.535 §27]

165.005 [Amended by 1955 c.435 §1; repealed by 1971 c.743 §432]

165.007 Forgery in the second degree. (1) A person commits the crime of forgery in the second degree if, with intent to injure or defraud, the person:
(a) Falsely makes, completes or alters a written instrument; or
(b) Utters a written instrument which the person knows to be forged.
(2) Forgery in the second degree is a Class A misdemeanor. [1971 c.743 §152]

165.010 [Repealed by 1971 c.743 §432]

165.012 [1963 c.553 §1; repealed by 1971 c.743 §432]

165.013 Forgery in the first degree. (1) A person commits the crime of forgery in the first degree if the person violates ORS 165.007:
(a) And the written instrument is or purports to be any of the following:
(A) Part of an issue of money, securities, postage or revenue stamps, or other valuable instruments issued by a government or governmental agency;
(B) Part of an issue of stock, bonds or other instruments representing interests in or claims against any property or person;
(C) A deed, will, codicil, contract or assignment;
(D) A check for $1,000 or more, a credit card purchase slip for $1,000 or more, or a combination of checks and credit card purchase slips that, in the aggregate, total $1,000 or more, or any other commercial instrument or other document that does or may evidence, create, transfer, alter, terminate or otherwise affect a legal right, interest, obligation or status; or
(E) A public record; or
(b) By falsely making, completing or altering, or by uttering, at least 15 retail sales receipts, Universal Product Code labels, EAN-8 labels or EAN-13 labels or a combination of at least 15 retail sales receipts, Universal Product Code labels, EAN-8 labels or EAN-13 labels.
(2) The value of single check or credit card transactions may be added together under subsection (1)(a)(D) of this section if the transactions were committed:
(a) Against multiple victims within a 30-day period; or
(b) Against the same victim within a 180-day period.
(3) Forgery in the first degree is a Class C felony. [1971 c.743 §153; 1993 c.680 §25; 2005 c.761 §1]

165.015 [Repealed by 1971 c.743 §432]

165.017 Criminal possession of a forged instrument in the second degree. (1) A person commits the crime of criminal possession of a forged instrument in the second degree if, knowing it to be forged and with intent to utter same, the person possesses a forged instrument.
(2) Criminal possession of a forged instrument in the second degree is a Class A misdemeanor. [1971 c.743 §154]

165.020 [Repealed by 1971 c.743 §432]

165.022 Criminal possession of a forged instrument in the first degree. (1) A person commits the crime of criminal possession of a forged instrument in the first degree if, knowing it to be forged and with intent to utter same, the person possesses a forged instrument of the kind and in the amount specified in ORS 165.013 (1).
(2) Criminal possession of a forged instrument in the first degree is a Class C felony. [1971 c.743 §155; 2005 c.761 §2]

165.025 [Repealed by 1971 c.743 §432]

165.027 Evidence admissible to prove forgery or possession of forged instrument. (1) In any prosecution for forgery of a bank bill or note or for criminal possession of a forged bank bill or note, the testimony of any person acquainted with the signature of the officer or agent authorized to sign the bills or notes of the bank of which such bill or note is alleged to be a forgery, or who has knowledge of the difference in appearance of the true and forged bills or notes thereof, may be admitted to prove that it is a forgery.
(2) In any prosecution for forgery or for criminal possession of any note, certificate, bond, bill of credit, or other security or evidence of debt issued on behalf of the United States or any state or territory, the certificate duly sworn to of the Secretary of the Treasury, or of the Treasurer of the United States, or of the secretary or treasurer of any state or treasury on whose behalf the note, certificate, bond, bill of credit or other security or evidence of debt purports to have been issued, shall be admitted as evidence to prove that it is a forgery. [1971 c.743 §290]

165.030 [Amended by 1961 c.715 §1; repealed by 1971 c.743 §432]

165.032 Criminal possession of a forgery device. (1) A person commits the crime of criminal possession of a forgery device if:

(a) The person makes or possesses with knowledge of its character any plate, die or other device, apparatus, equipment or article specifically designed for use in counterfeiting or otherwise forging written instruments; or

(b) With intent to use, or to aid or permit another to use, the same for purposes of forgery, the person makes or possesses any device, apparatus, equipment or article capable of or adaptable to such use.

(2) Criminal possession of a forgery device is a Class C felony. [1971 c.743 §156]

165.035 [Repealed by 1971 c.743 §432]

165.037 Criminal simulation. (1) A person commits the crime of criminal simulation if:

(a) With intent to defraud, the person makes or alters any object in such a manner that it appears to have an antiquity, rarity, source or authorship that it does not in fact possess; or

(b) With knowledge of its true character and with intent to defraud, the person utters or possesses an object so simulated.

(2) Criminal simulation is a Class A misdemeanor. [1971 c.743 §157]

165.040 [Repealed by 1971 c.743 §432]

165.042 Fraudulently obtaining a signature. (1) A person commits the crime of fraudulently obtaining a signature if, with intent to defraud or injure another, the person obtains the signature of a person to a written instrument by knowingly misrepresenting any fact.

(2) Fraudulently obtaining a signature is a Class A misdemeanor. [1971 c.743 §158]

165.045 [Repealed by 1971 c.743 §432]

165.047 Unlawfully using slugs. (1) A person commits the crime of unlawfully using slugs if:

(a) With intent to defraud the supplier of property or a service sold or offered by means of a coin machine, the person inserts, deposits or otherwise uses a slug in such machine; or

(b) The person makes, possesses, offers for sale or disposes of a slug with intent to enable a person to use it fraudulently in a coin machine.

(2) As used in this section:

(a) "Coin machine" means a coin box, turnstile, vending machine, or other mechanical or electronic device or receptacle designed to receive a coin or bill of a certain denomination or a token made for such purpose, and in return for the insertion or deposit thereof, automatically to offer, provide, assist in providing or permit the acquisition or use of some property or service.

(b) "Slug" means an object, article or device which, by virtue of its size, shape or any other quality is capable of being inserted, deposited, or otherwise used in a coin machine as a fraudulent substitute for a genuine coin, bill or token.

(3) Unlawfully using slugs is a Class B misdemeanor. [1971 c.743 §159]

165.055 Fraudulent use of a credit card. (1) A person commits the crime of fraudulent use of a credit card if, with intent to injure or defraud, the person uses a credit card for the purpose of obtaining property or services with knowledge that:

(a) The card is stolen or forged;

(b) The card has been revoked or canceled; or

(c) For any other reason the use of the card is unauthorized by either the issuer or the person to whom the credit card is issued.

(2) "Credit card" means a card, booklet, credit card number or other identifying symbol or instrument evidencing an undertaking to pay for property or services delivered or rendered to or upon the order of a designated person or bearer.

(3) The value of single credit card transactions may be added together if the transactions were committed:

(a) Against multiple victims within a 30-day period; or

(b) Against the same victim within a 180-day period.

(4) Fraudulent use of a credit card is:

(a) A Class A misdemeanor if the aggregate total amount of property or services the person obtains or attempts to obtain is less than $1,000.

(b) A Class C felony if the aggregate total amount of property or services the person obtains or attempts to obtain is $1,000 or more. [1971 c.743 §160; 1973 c.133 §7; 1987 c.907 §11; 1993 c.680 §26; 2009 c.16 §7]

165.065 Negotiating a bad check. (1) A person commits the crime of negotiating a bad check if the person makes, draws or utters a check or similar sight order for the payment of money, knowing that it will not be honored by the drawee.

(2) For purposes of this section, unless the check or order is postdated, it is prima facie evidence of knowledge that the check or order would not be honored if:

(a) The drawer has no account with the drawee at the time the check or order is drawn or uttered; or

(b) Payment is refused by the drawee for lack of funds, upon presentation within 30 days after the date of utterance, and the drawer fails to make good within 10 days after receiving notice of refusal.

(3) Negotiating a bad check is:

(a) A Class A misdemeanor, except as provided in paragraph (b) of this subsection.

(b) Enhanced from a Class A misdemeanor to a Class C felony if at the time of sentencing it is established beyond a reasonable doubt that the person has been convicted in this state, within the preceding five years, of the crime of negotiating a bad check or of theft by deception by means of a bad check. [1971 c.743 §161; 1979 c.594 §1]

165.070 Possessing fraudulent communications device.

(1) A person commits the crime of possessing a fraudulent communications device if the person:

(a) Makes, possesses, sells, gives or otherwise transfers to another, or offers or advertises pictures or diagrams concerning an instrument, apparatus or device with intent that the same be used or with knowledge or reason to believe the same is intended to or may be used to avoid any lawful telephone or telegraph toll charge or to conceal the existence or place of origin or destination of any telephone or telegraph communication; or

(b) Sells, gives or otherwise transfers to another or offers, or advertises plans or instructions for making or assembling an instrument, apparatus or device described in paragraph (a) of this subsection with knowledge or reason to believe that they may be used to make or assemble such instrument, apparatus or device.

(2) An instrument, apparatus, device, plans, instructions or written publication described in subsection (1) of this section may be seized under warrant or incident to a lawful arrest, and upon the conviction of a person under subsection (1) of this section, such instrument, apparatus, device, plans, instructions or written publication may be destroyed as contraband by the sheriff of the county in which such person was convicted or turned over to the person providing telephone or telegraph service in the territory in which the same was seized.

(3) Possessing a fraudulent communications device is a Class C felony. [1973 c.133 §5]

165.072 Definitions for ORS 165.072 and 165.074. As used in this section and ORS 165.074, unless the context requires otherwise:

(1) "Cardholder" means a person to whom a payment card is issued or a person who is authorized to use the payment card.

(2) "Credit card" means a card, plate, booklet, credit card number, credit card account number or other identifying symbol, instrument or device that can be used to pay for, or to obtain on credit, goods or services.

(3) "Financial institution" means a financial institution as that term is defined in ORS 706.008.

(4) "Merchant" means:

(a) An owner or operator of a retail mercantile establishment;

(b) An agent, employee, lessee, consignee, franchisee, officer, director or independent contractor of an owner or operator of a retail mercantile establishment; and

(c) A person who receives what the person believes to be a payment card or information from a payment card from a cardholder as the instrument for obtaining something of value from the person.

(5) "Payment card" means a credit card, charge card, debit card, stored value card or any card that is issued to a person and allows the user to obtain something of value from a merchant.

(6) "Payment card transaction" means a sale or other transaction or act in which a payment card is used to pay for, or to obtain on credit, goods or services.

(7) "Payment card transaction record" means any record or evidence of a payment card transaction, including, without limitation, any paper, sales draft, instrument or other writing and any electronic or magnetic transmission or record.

(8) "Person" does not include a financial institution or its authorized employee, representative or agent.

(9) "Previous conviction" has the meaning given that term in ORS 137.712.

(10) "Reencoder" means an electronic device that places encoded information from one payment card onto another payment card.

(11) "Scanning device" means an electronic device that is used to access, read, scan, obtain, memorize or store, temporarily or permanently, information encoded on a payment card. [1991 c.398 §1; 1997 c.631 §419; 2003 c.383 §1]

165.074 Unlawful factoring of payment card transaction. (1) A person commits the crime of unlawful factoring of a payment card transaction if the person intentionally or knowingly:

(a) Presents to or deposits with, or causes another to present to or deposit with, a financial institution for payment a payment card transaction record that is not the result of a payment card transaction between the cardholder and the person;

(b) Employs, solicits or otherwise causes a merchant to present to or deposit with a financial institution for payment a payment card transaction record that is not the result of a payment card transaction between the cardholder and the merchant;

(c) Employs, solicits or otherwise causes another to become a merchant for purposes of engaging in conduct made unlawful by this section;

(d) Uses a scanning device to access, read, scan, obtain, memorize or store information encoded on a payment card:

(A) Without the permission of the cardholder; or

(B) With the intent to defraud another person; or

(e) Uses a reencoder to place encoded information from one payment card onto another payment card:

(A) Without the permission of the cardholder of the payment card from which encoded information is being taken; or

(B) With the intention to defraud another person.

(2) Unlawful factoring of a payment card transaction is a Class C felony.

(3) Notwithstanding subsection (2) of this section, unlawful factoring of a payment card transaction is a Class B felony if the person has one or more previous convictions under this section. [1991 c.398 §2; 2003 c.383 §2]

BUSINESS AND COMMERCIAL OFFENSES

165.075 Definitions. As used in chapter 743, Oregon Laws 1971, unless the context requires otherwise:

(1) "Benefit" means gain or advantage to the beneficiary or to a third person pursuant to the desire or consent of the beneficiary.

(2) "Business records" means any writing or article kept or maintained by an enterprise for the purpose of evidencing or reflecting its condition or activities.

(3) "Enterprise" means any private entity of one or more persons, corporate or otherwise, engaged in business, commercial, professional, charitable, political, industrial or organized fraternal activity.

(4) "Fiduciary" means a trustee, guardian, executor, administrator, receiver or any other person acting in a fiduciary capacity as agent or employee of an organization which is a fiduciary.

(5) "Financial institution" means a bank, insurance company, credit union, savings and loan association, investment trust or other organization held out to the public as a place of deposit of funds or medium of savings or collective investment.

(6) "Government" means the state, any political subdivision thereof, or any governmental instrumentality within the state.

(7) "Misapplies" means dealing with property contrary to law or governmental regulation governing the custody or disposition of that property; governmental regulation includes administrative and judicial rules and orders as well as statutes and ordinances.

(8) "Sports contest" means any professional or amateur sport or athletic game or contest viewed by the public.

(9) "Sports official" means any person who acts in sports contests as an umpire, referee, judge or sports contest official.

(10) "Sports participant" means any person who directly or indirectly participates in sports contests as a player, contestant, team member, coach, manager, trainer, or any other person directly associated with a player, contestant or team member in connection with a sports activity. [1971 c.743 §162]

Note: Legislative Counsel has substituted "chapter 743, Oregon Laws 1971," for the words "this Act" in section 162, chapter 743, Oregon Laws 1971, compiled as 165.075. Specific ORS references have not been substituted, pursuant to 173.160. These sections may be determined by referring to the 1971 Comparative Section Table located in Volume 20 of ORS.

165.080 Falsifying business records. (1) A person commits the crime of falsifying business records if, with intent to defraud, the person:

(a) Makes or causes a false entry in the business records of an enterprise; or

(b) Alters, erases, obliterates, deletes, removes or destroys a true entry in the business records of an enterprise; or

(c) Fails to make a true entry in the business records of an enterprise in violation of a known duty imposed upon the person by law or by the nature of the position of the person; or

(d) Prevents the making of a true entry or causes the omission thereof in the business records of an enterprise.

(2) Falsifying business records is a Class A misdemeanor. [1971 c.743 §163]

165.085 Sports bribery. (1) A person commits the crime of sports bribery if the person:

(a) Offers, confers or agrees to confer any benefit upon a sports participant with intent to influence the sports participant not to give the best effort of the sports participant in a sports contest; or

(b) Offers, confers or agrees to confer any benefit upon a sports official with intent to influence the sports official to improperly perform duties of a sports official.

(2) Sports bribery is a Class C felony. [1971 c.743 §164]

165.090 Sports bribe receiving. (1) A person commits the crime of sports bribe receiving if:

(a) As a sports participant the person solicits, accepts or agrees to accept any benefit from another person with the intent that the person will thereby be influenced not to give the best effort of the person in a sports contest; or

(b) As a sports official the person solicits, accepts or agrees to accept any benefit from another person with the intent that the person will improperly perform duties of a sports official.

(2) Sports bribe receiving is a Class C felony. [1971 c.743 §165]

165.095 Misapplication of entrusted property. (1) A person commits the crime of misapplication of entrusted property if, with knowledge that the misapplication is unlawful and that it involves a substantial risk of loss or detriment to the owner or beneficiary of such property, the person intentionally misapplies or disposes of property that has been entrusted to the person as a fiduciary or that is property of the government or a financial institution.

(2) Misapplication of entrusted property is a Class A misdemeanor. [1971 c.743 §166]

165.100 Issuing a false financial statement. (1) A person commits the crime of issuing a false financial statement if, with intent to defraud, the person:

(a) Knowingly makes or utters a written statement which purports to describe the financial condition or ability to pay of the person or some other person and which is inaccurate in some material respect; or

(b) Represents in writing that a written statement purporting to describe a person's financial condition or ability to pay as of a prior date is accurate with respect to that person's current financial condition or ability to pay, knowing the statement to be materially inaccurate in that respect.

(2) Issuing a false financial statement is a Class A misdemeanor. [1971 c.743 §167]

165.102 Obtaining execution of documents by deception.

(1) A person commits the crime of obtaining execution of documents by deception if, with intent to defraud or injure another or to acquire a substantial benefit, the person obtains by means of fraud, deceit or subterfuge the execution of a written instrument affecting or purporting to affect the pecuniary interest of any person.

(2) Obtaining execution of documents by deception is a Class A misdemeanor. [1971 c.743 §168]

165.105 [Amended by 1959 c.100 §1; repealed by 1971 c.743 §432]

165.107. [1971 c.743 §169; 1995 c.222 §1; 2007 c.475 §1; 2009 c.811 §6; 2010 c.56 §5; 2011 c.450 §1; 2011 c.597 §80; 2013 c.122 §1; renumbered 165.117 in 2013]

165.109 Failing to maintain a cedar purchase record.

(1) A person commits the offense of failing to maintain a cedar purchase record if the person buys or otherwise obtains cedar products directly from any person who has harvested the cedar without keeping a record of the products purchased or obtained.

(2) The record required by subsection (1) of this section shall be retained by the purchaser for a period of not less than one year and shall be available to any peace officer on demand.
The record shall contain:

(a) The name, address, date of sale and signature of the seller or the person making delivery;

(b) The license number of any motor vehicles used in the delivery of the cedar; and

(c) The quantity of cedar obtained and the amount paid for the cedar.

(3) The provisions of this section apply only to the first wholesale transaction involving cedar products and do not apply to retail sales of cedar.

(4) Failing to maintain a cedar purchase record is a Class B misdemeanor. [1977 c.473 §2]

165.110 [Repealed by 1971 c.743 §432]

165.114 Sale of educational assignments. (1) No person shall sell or offer to sell an assignment to another person knowing, or under the circumstances having reason to know, that the whole or a substantial part of the assignment is intended to be submitted under a student's name in fulfillment of the requirements for a degree, diploma, certificate or course of study at any post-secondary institution.

(2) No person shall sell or offer to sell to another person any assistance in the preparation of an assignment knowing, or under the circumstances having reason to know, that the whole or a substantial part of the assignment is

intended to be submitted under a student's name in fulfillment of the requirements for a degree, diploma, certificate or course of study at any post-secondary institution.

(3) Nothing in this section prohibits a person from rendering for a monetary fee:

(a) Tutorial assistance if the assistance is not intended to be submitted in whole or in substantial part as an assignment; or

(b) Service in the form of typing, transcribing, assembling, reproducing or editing an assignment if this service is not intended to make substantive changes in the assignment.

(4) A person who violates any provision of this section commits a Class A violation.

(5) A person against whom a judgment has been entered under subsection (4) of this section shall, upon conviction for any subsequent violation of this section, be subject to a fine of not more than $10,000.

(6) In addition to any fine imposed under subsections (4) and (5) of this section, a court of competent jurisdiction may grant such further relief as is necessary to enforce the provisions of this section, including the issuance of an injunction. A suit for injunction under subsections (1) to (6) of this section may be brought in the name of the State of Oregon upon the complaint of the Attorney General or any district attorney.

(7) As used in subsections (1) to (6) of this section unless the context requires otherwise:

(a) "Assignment" means any specific written, recorded, pictorial, artistic or other academic task, including but not limited to a term paper, thesis, dissertation, essay or report, intended for submission to any post-secondary institution in fulfillment of the requirements for a degree, diploma, certificate or course of study at any such institution.

(b) "Person" means any individual, partnership, corporation or association.

(c) "Post-secondary institution" means any public or private post-secondary educational institution. [1981 c.673 §§1,2; 1999 c.1051 §158]

165.115 [Repealed by 1971 c.743 §432]

165.116 Definitions for ORS 165.116 to 165.124. As used in ORS 165.116 to 165.124:

(1) "Commercial account" means an agreement or arrangement between a commercial seller and a scrap metal business for regularly or periodically selling, delivering, purchasing or receiving metal property.

(2) "Commercial metal property" means an item fabricated or containing parts made of metal or metal alloys that:

(a) Is used as, used in or used as part of:

(A) A utility access cover or a cover for a utility meter;

(B) A pole, fixture or component of a street light or traffic light;

(C) A sign or marker located, with the permission of a governmental entity, alongside a street, road or bridge for the purpose of directing or controlling traffic or providing information to motorists;

(D) A traffic safety device, including a guardrail for a highway, road or bridge;

(E) A vase, plaque, marker, tablet, plate or other sign or ornament affixed to or in proximity to a historic site, grave, statue, monument or similar property accessible to members of the public;

(F) An agricultural implement, including an irrigation wheel, sprinkler head or pipe;

(G) A forestry implement or structure, including silvicultural equipment, gates, culverts and servicing and maintenance parts or supplies; or

(H) A logging operation implement, including mechanical equipment, rigging equipment and servicing and maintenance parts or supplies;

(b) Bears the name of, or a serial or model number, logo or other device used by, a commercial seller to identify the commercial seller's property including, but not limited to, implements or equipment used by railroads and utilities that provide telephone, commercial mobile radio, cable television, electricity, water, natural gas or similar services;

(c) Consists of material used in building construction or other commercial construction, including:

(A) Copper or aluminum pipe, tubing or wiring;

(B) Aluminum gutters, downspouts, siding, decking, bleachers or risers; or

(C) Aluminum or stainless steel fence panels made of one-inch tubing 42 inches long, with four-inch gaps; or

(d) Constitutes wire of a gauge typically used by utilities to provide electrical or telecommunications service.

(3) "Commercial seller" means a business entity, as defined in ORS 60.470, nonprofit corporation or governmental entity that regularly or periodically sells or delivers metal property to a scrap metal business as part of the entity's business functions.

(4) "Electronic funds transfer" has the meaning given that term in ORS 293.525.

(5) "Law enforcement agency" has the meaning given that term in ORS 131.550.

(6) "Metal property" means commercial metal property, nonferrous metal property or private metal property.

(7)(a) "Nonferrous metal property" means an item fabricated or containing parts made of or in an alloy with copper, brass, aluminum, bronze, lead, zinc or nickel.

(b) "Nonferrous metal property" does not include gold, silver or platinum that is used in the manufacture, repair, sale or resale of jewelry.

(8) "Nonprofit corporation" means a corporation to which the Secretary of State has issued a certificate of existence or a certificate of authorization under ORS 65.027.

(9) "Private metal property" means a catalytic converter that has been removed from a vehicle and is offered for sale as an independent item, whether individually or as part of a bundle, bale or in other bulk form.

(10)(a) "Scrap metal business" means a person that:

(A) Maintains a permanent or fixed place of business at which the person:

(i) Engages in the business of purchasing or receiving metal property;

(ii) Alters or prepares metal property the person receives for use in manufacturing other products; and

(iii) Owns, leases, rents, maintains or uses a device used in metal recycling, including a hydraulic baler, metal shearer or metal shredder;

(B) Maintains a permanent or fixed place of business at which the person engages in the business of purchasing or receiving metal property for the purpose of aggregation and sale to another scrap metal business; or

(C) Does not necessarily maintain a permanent or fixed place of business in this state but engages in the business of purchasing or receiving nonferrous metal property or private metal property for the purpose of aggregation and sale to another scrap metal business.

(b) "Scrap metal business" does not include a governmental entity that accepts metal property for recycling.

(11) "Stored value device" means a debit card or other device that draws funds from an account owned or operated by the user and that allows the user to obtain something of value from a merchant.

(12)(a) "Transaction" means a sale, purchase, receipt or trade of, or a contract, agreement or pledge to sell, purchase, receive or trade, private metal property or nonferrous metal property that occurs or forms between an individual and a scrap metal business.

(b) "Transaction" does not include:

(A) A transfer of metal property made without consideration; or

(B) A sale, purchase, receipt or trade of, or a contract, agreement or pledge to sell, purchase, receive or trade, private metal property or nonferrous metal property that occurs or forms between:

(i) A commercial seller or an authorized employee or agent of the commercial seller; and

(ii) A scrap metal business or an authorized employee or agent of the scrap metal business. [2009 c.811 §1; 2010 c.56 §1; 2011 c.450 §2; 2015 c.240 §1]

165.117 Metal property transaction records; prohibited conduct; commercial sellers; penalties. (1) Before completing a transaction, a scrap metal business engaged in business in this state shall:

(a) Create a metal property record for the transaction at the time and in the location where the transaction occurs. The record must:

(A) Be accurate and written clearly and legibly in English;

(B) Be entered onto a standardized printed form or an electronic form that is securely stored and is capable of ready retrieval and printing; and

(C) Contain all of the following information:

(i) The signature of the individual with whom the scrap metal business conducts the transaction.

(ii) The time, date, location and monetary amount or other value of the transaction.

(iii) The name of the employee who conducts the transaction on behalf of the scrap metal business.

(iv) The name and telephone number of the individual with whom the scrap metal business conducts the transaction and a street address or, if a post office box is listed on the government-issued photo identification described in sub-subparagraph (vi) of this subparagraph, a post office box, to which the scrap metal business will mail payment to the individual.

(v) A description of, and the license number and issuing state shown on the license plate affixed to, the motor vehicle, if any, used to transport the individual who conducts, or the nonferrous metal property or private metal property that is the subject of, the transaction.

(vi) A photocopy of a current, valid driver license or other government-issued photo identification belonging to the individual with whom the scrap metal business conducts the transaction.

(vii) A photograph of, or video surveillance recording depicting, a recognizable facial image of the individual with whom the scrap metal business conducts the transaction.

(viii) A general description of the nonferrous metal property or private metal property that constitutes the predominant part of the transaction. The description must include any identifiable marks on the property, if readily discernible, and must specify the weight, quantity or volume of the nonferrous metal property or private metal property.

(b) Require the individual with whom the scrap metal business conducts a transaction to sign and date a declaration printed in conspicuous type, either on the record described in this subsection or on a receipt issued to the individual with whom the scrap metal business conducts the transaction, that states:

I, _____, AFFIRM UNDER PENALTY OF LAW THAT THE PROPERTY I AM SELLING IN THIS TRANSACTION IS NOT, TO THE BEST OF MY KNOWLEDGE, STOLEN PROPERTY.

(c) Require the employee of the scrap metal business who conducts the transaction on behalf of the scrap metal business to witness the individual sign the declaration, and also to sign and date the declaration in a space provided for that purpose.

(d) For one year following the date of the transaction, keep a copy of the record and the signed and dated declaration described in this subsection. If the scrap metal business uses a video surveillance recording as part of the record kept in accordance with this subsection, the scrap metal business need not keep the video surveillance recording for one year, but shall retain the video surveillance recording for a minimum of 30 days following the date of the transaction. The scrap metal business shall at all times keep the copies at the current place of business for the scrap metal business.

(2) A scrap metal business engaged in business in this state may not do any of the following:

(a) Purchase or receive kegs or similar metallic containers used to store or dispense alcoholic beverages, except from a person that manufactures the kegs or containers or from a person licensed by the Oregon Liquor Control Commission under ORS 471.155.

(b) Conduct a transaction with an individual if the individual does not at the time of the transaction consent to the creation of the record described in subsection (1) of this section and produce for inspection a valid driver license or other government-issued photo identification that belongs to the individual.

(c) Conduct a transaction with an individual in which the scrap metal business pays the individual other than by electronic funds transfer, stored value card or stored value device, or by mailing a nontransferable check, made payable to the individual, for the amount of the transaction to the street address or post office box the individual provided under subsection (1)(a)(C)(iv) of this section. Payment must be made not earlier than three business days after the date of the transaction. The check, electronic funds transfer or stored value device must be drawn on or must draw from an account that the scrap metal business maintains with a financial institution, as defined in ORS 706.008. A stored value card may be issued by a money transmission business licensed under ORS 717.200 to 717.320 or exempt from the licensing requirement under ORS 717.210.

(d) Purchase metal property from a nonprofit corporation other than by electronic funds transfer, stored value card or stored value device, or by mailing a nontransferable check, made payable to the nonprofit corporation, for the amount of the purchase price to the business address provided under subsection (4)(a)(B) of this section. Payment must be made not earlier than three business days after the date of the purchase. The check, electronic funds transfer or stored value device must be drawn on or must draw from an account that the scrap metal business maintains with a financial institution, as defined in ORS 706.008. A stored value card may be issued by a money transmission business licensed under ORS 717.200 to 717.320 or exempt from the licensing requirement under ORS 717.210.

(e) Cash or release a check issued in payment for a transaction or for a purchase described in paragraph (d) of this subsection other than as provided in this paragraph or paragraph (c) or (d) of this subsection. If a check is not delivered to the intended recipient within 10 days of the date of the transaction or the purchase, the scrap metal business may release the check directly to the individual or nonprofit corporation with the written approval of a law enforcement agency having jurisdiction over the scrap metal business. If a check is returned as undelivered or undeliverable, the scrap metal business shall:

(A) Release the check directly to the individual or nonprofit corporation with the written approval of a law enforcement agency having jurisdiction over the scrap metal business; or

(B) Retain the check until the individual or nonprofit corporation to which the check was mailed provides a valid address in accordance with subsection (1)(a)(C)(iv) or (4)(a)(B) of this section. If after 30 days following the date of the transaction or the purchase described in paragraph (d) of this subsection the individual or nonprofit corporation fails to provide a valid address, the scrap metal business may cancel the check and the individual or nonprofit corporation shall forfeit to the scrap metal business the amount due as payment.

(3) If a scrap metal business obtains the approval of a law enforcement agency under subsection (2)(e) of this section, the scrap metal business shall retain the written approval for one year following the date the approval is received.

(4) Before purchasing or receiving metal property from a commercial seller, a scrap metal business shall:

(a) Create and maintain a commercial account with the commercial seller. As part of the commercial account, the scrap metal business shall enter accurately, clearly and legibly in English onto a standardized printed form, or an electronic form that is securely stored and is capable of ready retrieval and printing, the following information:

(A) The full name of the commercial seller;

(B) The business address and telephone number of the commercial seller; and

(C) The full name of each employee, agent or other individual the commercial seller authorizes to receive payment for metal property from the scrap metal business.

(b) Record as part of the commercial account at the time the scrap metal business purchases or receives metal property from a commercial seller the following information:

(A) The time, date and location at which the commercial seller delivered the metal property for purchase or receipt;

(B) The monetary amount or other value of the metal property;

(C) A description of the type of metal property that constitutes the predominant part of the purchase or receipt; and

(D) The signature of the individual who delivered the metal property to the scrap metal business.

(5) A scrap metal business may require an individual from whom the business obtains metal property to provide the individual's thumbprint to the scrap metal business.

(6) A scrap metal business shall make all records and accounts required to be maintained under this section available to any peace officer on demand.

(7)(a) Violation of this section is a specific fine violation, and the presumptive fine for the violation is $1,000.

(b) Notwithstanding paragraph (a) of this subsection, the presumptive fine for a violation of a provision of this section is $5,000 if the scrap metal business has at least three previous convictions for violations of a provision of this section. [Formerly 165.107; 2015 c.240 §2]

165.118 Metal property offenses. (1) A person commits the offense of unlawfully altering metal property if the person, with intent to deceive a scrap metal business as to the ownership or origin of an item of metal property, knowingly removes, alters, renders unreadable or invisible or obliterates a name, logo, model or serial number, personal identification number or other mark or method that a manufacturer uses to identify the metal property.

(2) A person commits the offense of making a false statement on a metal property record if the person:

(a) Knowingly makes, causes or allows to be made a false entry or misstatement of material fact in a metal property record described in ORS 165.117; or

(b) Signs a declaration under ORS 165.117 knowing that the nonferrous metal property or private metal property that is the subject of a transaction is stolen.

(3) A person commits the offense of unlawfully purchasing or receiving metal property if the person is a scrap metal business or an agent or employee of a scrap metal business and the person fails to report any of the following to a law enforcement agency within 24 hours:

(a) The purchase or receipt of metal property that the person knows or has good reason to know was the subject of theft.

(b) The purchase or receipt of metal property that the person knows or has good reason to know has been unlawfully altered as described in subsection (1) of this section.

(c) The purchase or receipt of metallic wire from which insulation has been removed, unless the individual offering the wire for purchase or receipt can prove by appropriate documentation that the individual owns or is entitled to offer the wire for purchase or receipt and that the insulation has been removed by accident or was done by legitimate means or for a legitimate purpose. The scrap metal business shall retain a copy of the documentation provided.

(d) The purchase or receipt of commercial metal property that the person knows or has good reason to know was purchased or received from a person other than:

(A) A commercial seller that has a commercial account with the scrap metal business; or

(B) An individual who can produce written documentation or identification that proves that the individual is an employee, agent or other individual authorized by a commercial seller that has a commercial account with the scrap metal business to deliver commercial metal property for purchase or receipt.

(e) The purchase or receipt of metal property from an individual whom the person knows or has good reason to know:

(A) Is under 16 years of age; or

(B) Has, according to written or electronically transmitted information provided by a peace officer or law enforcement agency, been convicted within the past five years, as a principal, agent or accessory of a crime involving:

(i) Drugs;

(ii) Burglary, robbery or theft;

(iii) Possession or receipt of stolen property;

(iv) The manufacture, delivery or possession of, with intent to deliver, methamphetamine;

(v) The manufacture, delivery or possession of, with intent to deliver, ephedrine or a salt, isomer or salt of an isomer of ephedrine;

(vi) The manufacture, delivery or possession of, with intent to deliver, pseudoephedrine or a salt, isomer or salt of an isomer of pseudoephedrine; or

(vii) Possession of anhydrous ammonia with intent to manufacture methamphetamine.

(4) Violation of a provision of subsections (1) to (3) of this section is a Class A misdemeanor. [2009 c.811 §2; 2010 c.56 §2]

165.120 [Repealed by 1971 c.743 §432]

165.122 Compliance with subpoena for information related to metal transaction; lost or stolen metal property. (1) Not later than two business days after receiving from a peace officer or law enforcement agency a subpoena for information related to a named or specified individual, vehicle or item of metal property, a scrap metal business shall provide to the peace officer or law enforcement agency a copy of a metal property record created under ORS 165.117 or a copy of the relevant portion of a commercial account that contains the information about the individual, vehicle or item of metal property that is the subject of the subpoena. The scrap metal business shall provide the information in any form or by any method reasonably required by the peace officer or law enforcement agency.

(2) If a scrap metal business knows or has good reason to know that metal property that the scrap metal business purchased or received or possesses or controls was lost by or stolen from the metal property's owner or lawful possessor, the scrap metal business shall promptly notify an appropriate law enforcement agency and shall:

(a) Name the owner or lawful possessor of the property, if known; and

(b) Disclose the name of the person that delivered the metal property and the date on which the scrap metal business received the metal property.

(3) If a peace officer or law enforcement agency notifies a scrap metal business that an item of metal property in the possession or control of the scrap metal business is lost or stolen, the scrap metal business shall:

(a) Segregate the metal property that is the subject of the notification from other inventory kept by the scrap metal business;

(b) Protect the metal property from alteration or damage;

(c) Mark, tag or otherwise identify the metal property; and

(d) Hold the metal property for the length of time, not to exceed 10 days, that the peace officer or law enforcement agency specifies.

(4) A peace officer or law enforcement agency may not require a scrap metal business to hold metal property under subsection (3) of this section unless the peace officer or law enforcement agency reasonably suspects that the metal property was lost by or stolen from the owner or lawful possessor of the metal property. Within 10 days after notifying a scrap metal business that an item of metal property may be lost or stolen, the peace officer or law enforcement agency shall:

(a) Determine that the metal property is lost or stolen and take appropriate lawful action to impound or recover the metal property and return the metal property to the owner or lawful possessor; or

(b) Determine that the metal property is not lost or stolen and notify the scrap metal business that it is not necessary to hold the metal property any longer. [2009 c.811 §4; 2010 c.56 §3]

165.124 Application of ORS 164.857, 165.116, 165.117, 165.118 and 165.122. (1) Except as provided in subsection (2) of this section, ORS 164.857, 165.116, 165.117, 165.118 and 165.122 do not apply to:

(a) A person engaged in recycling beverage containers as defined in ORS 459A.700.

(b) A person engaged in buying or selling used or empty food containers made of metal.

(c) A person to whom a vehicle dealer certificate has been issued under ORS 822.020.

(d) A person to whom a dismantler certificate has been issued under ORS 822.110.

(e) A person to whom a towing business certificate has been issued under ORS 822.205.

(2) A person described in subsection (1)(c) to (e) of this section shall comply with and is subject to the penalty provided for violating a provision of ORS 164.857, 165.116, 165.117, 165.118 or 165.122, if the person purchases, receives or transports:

(a) Private metal property; or

(b) Commercial metal property or nonferrous metal property, that is not a motor vehicle or a part of a motor vehicle. [2009 c.811 §5]

165.125 [Repealed by 1971 c.743 §432]

165.127 County metal theft plan of action. (1) In each county in which a scrap metal business, as defined in ORS 165.116, has a place of business, the district attorney of the county shall, after consulting with representatives of the affected law enforcement agencies and the business community, create a written plan of action that ensures effective communication between law enforcement and the business community regarding the theft of metal property as defined in ORS 165.116.

(2) The written plan of action must include, but need not be limited to, a procedure for law enforcement agencies to notify scrap metal businesses of a theft of metal property within 24 hours after the receipt of the report of the theft.

(3) The district attorney shall provide a copy of the written plan of action to the local public safety coordinating council described in ORS 423.560. [2009 c.811 §11]

165.130 [Repealed by 1971 c.743 §432]

165.135 [Repealed by 1971 c.743 §432]

165.140 [Repealed by 1971 c.743 §432]

165.145 [Repealed by 1971 c.743 §432]

165.150 [Repealed by 1971 c.743 §432]

165.155 [Repealed by 1971 c.743 §432]

165.160 [Repealed by 1971 c.743 §432]

165.165 [Repealed by 1971 c.743 §432]

165.170 [Repealed by 1971 c.743 §432]

165.175 [Repealed by 1971 c.743 §432]

165.180 [Repealed by 1971 c.743 §432]

165.185 [Repealed by 1971 c.743 §432]

165.190 [Repealed by 1971 c.743 §432]

165.205 [Amended by 1971 c.290 §1; repealed by 1971 c.743 §432]

165.210 [Repealed by 1971 c.743 §432]

165.215 [Repealed by 1971 c.743 §432]

165.220 [Repealed by 1971 c.743 §432]

165.225 [Amended by 1955 c.436 §1; 1959 c.508 §1; repealed by 1971 c.743 §432]

165.230 [Repealed by 1971 c.743 §432]

165.235 [Repealed by 1971 c.743 §432]

165.240 [Repealed by 1971 c.743 §432]

165.245 [Repealed by 1971 c.743 §432]

165.250 [Repealed by 1971 c.743 §432]

165.255 [Repealed by 1971 c.743 §432]

165.260 [Repealed by 1971 c.743 §432]

165.265 [Repealed by 1971 c.743 §432]

165.270 [1957 c.369 §1; repealed by 1971 c.743 §432]

165.280 [1961 c.318 §1; repealed by 1971 c.743 §432]

165.285 [1969 c.290 §3; repealed by 1971 c.743 §432]

165.290 [1963 c.588 §2; repealed by 1971 c.743 §432]

165.295 [1963 c.588 §3; repealed by 1971 c.743 §432]

165.300 [1963 c.588 §4; repealed by 1971 c.743 §432]

165.305 [Repealed by 1971 c.743 §432]

165.310 [Repealed by 1971 c.743 §432]

165.315 [Repealed by 1971 c.743 §432]

165.320 [Repealed by 1971 c.743 §432]

165.325 [Repealed by 1971 c.743 §432]

165.330 [Repealed by 1971 c.743 §432]

165.335 [Repealed by 1971 c.743 §432]

165.340 [Amended by 1957 c.655 §1; repealed by 1971 c.743 §432]

165.345 [Repealed by 1971 c.743 §432]

165.350 [Repealed by 1971 c.743 §432]

165.352 [1961 c.454 §75(2); repealed by 1971 c.743 §432]

165.355 [Repealed by 1971 c.743 §432]

165.405 [Repealed by 1971 c.743 §432]

165.410 [Repealed by 1971 c.743 §432]

165.415 [Repealed by 1971 c.743 §432]

165.420 [Amended by 1961 c.261 §1; repealed by 1971 c.743 §432]

165.425 [Repealed by 1971 c.743 §432]

165.430 [Repealed by 1971 c.743 §432]

165.435 [Repealed by 1971 c.743 §432]

165.440 [Repealed by 1971 c.743 §432]

165.445 [Repealed by 1971 c.743 §432]

165.450 [Repealed by 1971 c.743 §432]

165.455 [Repealed by 1971 c.743 §432]

165.460 [Repealed by 1971 c.743 §432]

165.465 [Repealed by 1971 c.743 §432]

165.475 [Formerly 757.606; repealed by 2011 c.597 §309]

165.480 [Formerly 757.611; repealed by 2011 c.597 §309]

165.485 [Formerly 757.616; repealed by 2011 c.597 §309]

165.490 [Formerly 757.621; repealed by 2011 c.597 §309]

165.495 [Formerly 757.626; 2009 c.11 §13; repealed by 2011 c.597 §309]

165.505 [Repealed by 2011 c.597 §309]

165.510 [Repealed by 2011 c.597 §309]

165.515 [Repealed by 2011 c.597 §309]

165.520 [Repealed by 2011 c.597 §309]

165.525 [Repealed by 1971 c.743 §432]

165.530 [Repealed by 1971 c.743 §432]

165.532 [1961 c.428 §1; repealed by 1971 c.743 §432]

CRIMES INVOLVING COMMUNICATIONS

165.535 Definitions applicable to obtaining contents of communications. As used in ORS 41.910, 133.723, 133.724, 165.540 and 165.545:

(1) "Conversation" means the transmission between two or more persons of an oral communication which is not a telecommunication or a radio communication.

(2) "Person" has the meaning given that term in ORS 174.100 and includes:

(a) Public officials and law enforcement officers of:

(A) The state and of a county, municipal corporation or any other political subdivision of the state; and

(B) A police department established by a university under ORS 352.121 or 353.125; and

(b) Authorized tribal police officers as defined in ORS 181A.680.

(3) "Radio communication" means the transmission by radio or other wireless methods of writing, signs, signals, pictures and sounds of all kinds, including all instrumentalities, facilities, equipment and services (including, among other things, the receipt, forwarding and delivering of communications) incidental to such transmission.

(4) "Telecommunication" means the transmission of writing, signs, signals, pictures and sounds of all kinds by aid of wire, cable or other similar connection between the points of origin and reception of such transmission, including all instrumentalities, facilities, equipment and services (including, among other things, the receipt, forwarding and delivering of communications) incidental to such transmission. [1955 c.675 §1; 1959 c.681 §1; 1983 c.740 §34; 2011 c.644 §§25,67,74; 2013 c.180 §§27,28; 2015 c.174 §13]

165.540 Obtaining contents of communications. (1) Except as otherwise provided in ORS 133.724 or 133.726 or subsections (2) to (7) of this section, a person may not:

(a) Obtain or attempt to obtain the whole or any part of a telecommunication or a radio communication to which the person is not a participant, by means of any device, contrivance, machine or apparatus, whether electrical, mechanical, manual or otherwise, unless consent is given by at least one participant.

(b) Tamper with the wires, connections, boxes, fuses, circuits, lines or any other equipment or facilities of a telecommunication or radio communication company over which messages are transmitted, with the intent to obtain unlawfully the contents of a telecommunication or radio communication to which the person is not a participant.

(c) Obtain or attempt to obtain the whole or any part of a conversation by means of any device, contrivance, machine or apparatus, whether electrical, mechanical, manual or otherwise, if not all participants in the conversation are specifically informed that their conversation is being obtained.

(d) Obtain the whole or any part of a conversation, telecommunication or radio communication from any person, while knowing or having good reason to believe that the conversation, telecommunication or radio communication was initially obtained in a manner prohibited by this section.

(e) Use or attempt to use, or divulge to others, any conversation, telecommunication or radio communication obtained by any means prohibited by this section.

(2)(a) The prohibitions in subsection (1)(a), (b) and (c) of this section do not apply to:

(A) Officers, employees or agents of a telecommunication or radio communication company who perform the acts prohibited by subsection (1)(a), (b) and (c) of this section for the purpose of construction, maintenance or conducting of their telecommunication or radio communication service, facilities or equipment.

(B) Public officials in charge of and at jails, police premises, sheriffs' offices, Department of Corrections institutions and other penal or correctional institutions, except as to communications or conversations between an attorney and the client of the attorney.

(b) Officers, employees or agents of a telecommunication or radio communication company who obtain information under paragraph (a) of this subsection may not use or attempt to use, or divulge to others, the information except for the purpose of construction, maintenance, or conducting of their telecommunication or radio communication service, facilities or equipment.

(3) The prohibitions in subsection (1)(a), (b) or (c) of this section do not apply to subscribers or members of their family who perform the acts prohibited in subsection (1) of this section in their homes.

(4) The prohibitions in subsection (1)(a) of this section do not apply to the receiving or obtaining of the contents of any radio or television broadcast transmitted for the use of the general public.

(5) The prohibitions in subsection (1)(c) of this section do not apply to:

(a) A person who records a conversation during a felony that endangers human life;

(b) A person who records a conversation in which a law enforcement officer is a participant, if:

(A) The recording is made while the officer is performing official duties;

(B) The recording is made openly and in plain view of the participants in the conversation;

(C) The conversation being recorded is audible to the person by normal unaided hearing; and

(D) The person is in a place where the person lawfully may be;

(c) A person who, pursuant to ORS 133.400, records an interview conducted by a peace officer in a law enforcement facility;

(d) A law enforcement officer who is in uniform and displaying a badge and who is operating:

(A) A vehicle-mounted video camera that records the scene in front of, within or surrounding a police vehicle, unless the officer has reasonable opportunity to inform participants in the conversation that the conversation is being obtained; or

(B) A video camera worn upon the officer's person that records the officer's interactions with members of the public while the officer is on duty, unless:

(i) The officer has an opportunity to announce at the beginning of the interaction that the conversation is being obtained; and

(ii) The announcement can be accomplished without causing jeopardy to the officer or any other person and without unreasonably impairing a criminal investigation; or

(e) A law enforcement officer who, acting in the officer's official capacity, deploys an Electro-Muscular Disruption Technology device that contains a built-in monitoring system capable of recording audio or video, for the duration of that deployment.

(6) The prohibitions in subsection (1)(c) of this section do not apply to persons who intercept or attempt to intercept with an unconcealed recording device the oral communications that are part of any of the following proceedings:

(a) Public or semipublic meetings such as hearings before governmental or quasi-governmental bodies, trials, press conferences, public speeches, rallies and sporting or other events;

(b) Regularly scheduled classes or similar educational activities in public or private institutions; or

(c) Private meetings or conferences if all others involved knew or reasonably should have known that the recording was being made.

(7) The prohibitions in subsection (1)(a), (c), (d) and (e) of this section do not apply to any:

(a) Radio communication that is transmitted by a station operating on an authorized frequency within the amateur or citizens bands; or

(b) Person who intercepts a radio communication that is transmitted by any governmental, law enforcement, civil defense or public safety communications system, including police and fire, readily accessible to the general public provided that the interception is not for purposes of illegal activity.

(8) Violation of subsection (1) or (2)(b) of this section is a Class A misdemeanor.

(9) The exception described in subsection (5)(b) of this section does not authorize the person recording the law enforcement officer to engage in criminal trespass as described in ORS 164.243, 164.245, 164.255, 164.265 or 164.278 or to interfere with a peace officer as described in ORS 162.247.

(10) As used in this section:

(a) "Electro-Muscular Disruption Technology device" means a device that uses a high-voltage, low power charge of electricity to induce involuntary muscle contractions intended to cause temporary incapacitation. "Electro-Muscular Disruption Technology device" includes devices commonly known as tasers.

(b) "Law enforcement officer" has the meaning given that term in ORS 133.726. [1955 c.675 §§2,7; 1959 c.681 §2; 1961 c.460 §1; 1979 c.744 §9; 1983 c.693 §1; 1983 c.740 §35; 1983 c.824 §1; 1987 c.320 §87; 1989 c.983 §14a; 1989 c.1078 §1; 2001 c.104 §54; 2001 c.385 §4; 2003 c.14 §62; 2007 c.879 §1; 2009 c.488 §2; 2015 c.550 §2; 2015 c.553 §1]

165.542 Reports required concerning use of electronic listening device. (1) Within 30 days after the use of an electronic listening device under ORS 133.726 (7) or 165.540 (5)(a), the law enforcement agency using the device shall report to the district attorney of the county in the agency's jurisdiction:

(a) The number of uses of the device and duration of the interceptions made by the law enforcement agency;

(b) The offense investigated;

(c) The identity of the law enforcement agency intercepting the communication; and

(d) Whether the person wearing the device was a law enforcement officer or a person under the supervision of the officer and the number of persons in each category who wore the device.

(2) During January of each year, the district attorney of a county in which electronic listening devices were used under ORS 133.726 (7) or 165.540 (5)(a) shall report to the Department of Justice:

(a) The information required by subsection (1) of this section with respect to the use of electronic listening devices during the preceding calendar year; and

(b) The aggregate number of instances in which electronic listening devices have been used in the county under ORS 133.726 (7) or 165.540 (5)(a) during the preceding calendar year.

(3) The law enforcement agency shall include as part of the case file any use of electronic listening devices under ORS 133.726 (7) or 165.540 (5)(a).

(4) During April of each odd-numbered calendar year, the Department of Justice shall transmit to the Legislative Assembly a report including a summary of the information required by subsections (1) and (2) of this section.

(5) Failure to comply with the reporting requirements of this section shall not affect the admissibility of evidence. [1989 c.1078 §2; 2001 c.385 §7; 2007 c.879 §2]

165.543 Interception of communications. (1) Except as provided in ORS 133.724 or as provided in ORS 165.540 (2)(a), any person who willfully intercepts, attempts to intercept or procures any other person to intercept or attempt to intercept any wire or oral communication where such person is not a party to the communication and where none of the parties to the communication has given prior consent to the interception, is guilty of a Class A misdemeanor.

(2) As used in this section, the terms "intercept" and "wire or oral communication" have the meanings provided under ORS 133.721. [1983 c.824 §3]

165.545 Prohibitions not applicable to fire or police activities. Nothing in ORS 165.535, 165.540 and this section, shall be construed as preventing fire or police governmental entities from recording, replaying or broadcasting telecommunication or radio communication that directly concern police or fire operation at the telephone or radio operation center or centers of such governmental entity. [1959 c.681 §6; 1981 c.806 §2; 1983 c.740 §36]

165.549 Prevention of telephone communications when hostage taken; duties of telephone company; defense against liability. (1) A supervising law enforcement official having jurisdiction in a geographical area in which the official has probable cause to believe that a hostage is being held may order a telephone company security employee or alternate described in subsection (2) of this section to cut, reroute or divert telephone lines to prevent telephone communications between the individual holding the hostage and any individual other than a peace officer or an individual designated by the peace officer.

(2) The telephone company providing service within a geographical area shall notify, in writing, all law enforcement agencies having jurisdiction in that area of the address and telephone number of its security office or other office designated to provide the assistance to law enforcement officials required under this section. The telephone company shall also provide, in writing, the telephone number where the security representative or other telephone company official authorized to provide assistance under this section can be reached at any time. The telephone company shall notify the law enforcement agencies of any change in the information required under this subsection.

(3) Good faith reliance upon an order by a supervising law enforcement official is a complete defense to any civil or criminal action arising out of the cutting, rerouting or diverting of a telephone line pursuant to this section. [1979 c.605 §1]

165.550 [1967 c.109 §§1,2; repealed by 1971 c.743 §432]

165.555 Unlawful telephone solicitation of contributions for charitable purposes. (1) No person shall solicit by telephone contributions of money or any other thing of value, whether or not in exchange for a ticket or any other thing of value, for a charitable or eleemosynary purpose, whether bona fide or purported, unless the person:

(a) Has been a member in full standing for at least six months of the charitable organization conducting the solicitation and is participating in the solicitation on an uncompensated basis;

(b) Has been employed directly by the charitable organization conducting the solicitation for at least six months prior to the solicitation and is receiving a substantial salary; or

(c) And the person solicited are personally known to each other.

(2) Any violation of subsection (1) of this section is a Class C misdemeanor. [1973 c.473 §§1,4]

165.560 Application of ORS 165.555. ORS 165.555 does not apply to solicitations on behalf of hospitals or of nonprofit organizations organized and operated exclusively for religious, scientific, literary or educational purposes, or for the prevention of cruelty to children or animals. [1973 c.473 §2]

165.565 Optional local ordinances; certain existing local ordinances preserved. A city or county may enact ordinances which are more strict than ORS 165.555 to 165.565. ORS 165.555 to 165.565 do not affect any ordinances which are more strict than ORS 165.555 to 165.565 and are in effect on October 5, 1973. [1973 c.473 §3]

165.570 Improper use of emergency communications system. (1) A person commits the crime of improper use of the emergency communications system if the person knowingly:

(a) Makes an emergency call or calls the tip line for a purpose other than to report a situation that the person reasonably believes requires prompt service in order to preserve human life or property; or

(b) Allows another person to use communications equipment owned, rented or leased by or under the control of the person to make an emergency call or call the tip line for a purpose other than to report a situation that the other person reasonably believes requires prompt service in order to preserve human life or property.

(2) As used in this section:

(a) "Emergency call" has the meaning given that term in ORS 403.105.

(b) "Emergency communications system" has the meaning given that term in ORS 403.105.

(c) "Tip line" means the statewide tip line established under ORS 339.329.

(3) Improper use of the emergency communications system is a Class A misdemeanor. [1995 c.566 §1; 2001 c.619 §4; 2015 c.247 §29; 2016 c.74 §3]

165.572 Interference with making a report. (1) A person commits the crime of interference with making a report if the person, by removing, damaging or interfering with a telephone line, telephone or similar communication equipment, intentionally prevents or hinders another person from making a report to a law enforcement agency, a law enforcement official or an agency charged with the duty of taking public safety reports or from making an emergency call as defined in ORS 403.105.

(2) Interference with making a report is a Class A misdemeanor. [1999 c.946 §1; 2015 c.247 §30]

CELLULAR TELEPHONES

165.575 Definitions for ORS 165.575 to 165.583. As used in ORS 165.575 to 165.583:

(1) "Cellular telephone" means a radio telecommunications device that may be used to obtain access to the public and cellular switch telephone networks and that is programmed by the manufacturer with an electronic serial number.

(2) "Cellular telephone service" means all services and cellular telephone equipment and capabilities available from a provider to an end user for a fee.

(3) "Cloned cellular telephone" or "counterfeit cellular telephone" means a cellular telephone, the electronic serial number of which has been altered by someone other than the manufacturer.

(4) "Cloning paraphernalia" means materials that, when possessed in combination, are capable of creating a cloned cellular telephone. "Cloning paraphernalia" includes, but is not limited to:

(a) Scanners to intercept electronic serial numbers and mobile identification numbers;

(b) Cellular telephones;

(c) Cables;

(d) EPROM chips;

(e) EPROM burners;

(f) Software for programming the cellular telephone with a false electronic serial number, mobile identification number, other identifiable data or a combination thereof;

(g) Computers containing software described in paragraph (f) of this subsection; and

(h) Lists of electronic serial number and mobile identification number combinations.

(5) "Electronic serial number" means a unique number that is programmed into a cellular telephone by the manufacturer, transmitted by the cellular telephone and used by cellular telephone providers to validate radio transmissions to the system as having been made by an authorized device.

(6) "End user" is a person who pays a fee to subscribe to cellular telephone service from a provider or a person receiving a call from or sending a call to the person paying or subscribing for cellular telephone service.

(7) "Intercept" means to electronically capture, record, reveal or otherwise access the signals emitted or received during the operation of a cellular telephone by any instrument, device or equipment without the consent of the sender or receiver.

(8) "Mobile identification number" means the cellular telephone number assigned to the cellular telephone by the cellular telephone provider.

(9) "Provider" means a licensed seller of cellular telephone service or a reselling agent authorized by a licensed seller. [1995 c.524 §1]

165.577 Cellular counterfeiting in the third degree. (1) A person commits the crime of cellular counterfeiting in the third degree if the person knowingly possesses a cloned cellular telephone and knows that the telephone is unlawfully cloned.

(2) Cellular counterfeiting in the third degree is a Class A misdemeanor. [1995 c.524 §2]

165.579 Cellular counterfeiting in the second degree. (1) A person commits the crime of cellular counterfeiting in the second degree if the person knowingly possesses, and knows the unlawful nature of using, any cloning paraphernalia or any instrument capable of intercepting electronic serial numbers, mobile identification numbers, other identifiable data or a combination thereof and:

(a) Causes more than $100 in losses or damages; or

(b) Intercepts or obtains, or attempts to intercept or obtain, cellular telephone service of more than $100 in value.

(2) Cellular counterfeiting in the second degree is a Class C felony. [1995 c.524 §3]

165.581 Cellular counterfeiting in the first degree. (1) A person commits the crime of cellular counterfeiting in the first degree if the person knowingly possesses or distributes, and knows the unlawful nature of using, any cloning paraphernalia or any instrument capable of intercepting electronic serial numbers, mobile identification numbers, other identifiable data or a combination thereof and agrees with, encourages, solicits or permits one or more other persons to engage in or cause, or obtain cellular telephone service through, cellular counterfeiting and:

(a) Causes more than $100 in losses or damages; or

(b) Intercepts, obtains or causes to be obtained cellular telephone service of more than $100 in value.

(2) Cellular counterfeiting in the first degree is a Class B felony. [1995 c.524 §4]

165.583 Exemptions from ORS 165.577, 165.579 and 165.581. The provisions of ORS 165.577, 165.579 and 165.581 do not apply to:

(1) Officers, employees or agents of cellular telephone service providers who engage in conduct prohibited by ORS 165.577, 165.579 or 165.581 for the purpose of constructing, maintaining or conducting the radio telecommunication service or for law enforcement purposes;

(2) Law enforcement officers and public officials in charge of jails, police premises, sheriffs' offices, Department of Corrections institutions and other penal or correctional institutions, or any other person under the color of law, who engages in conduct prohibited by ORS 165.577, 165.579 or 165.581 for the purpose of law enforcement or in the normal course of the officer's or official's employment activities or duties; and

(3) Officers, employees or agents of federal or state agencies that are authorized to monitor or intercept cellular telephone service in the normal course of the officer's, employee's or agent's employment. [1995 c.524 §5]

165.585 [1995 c.524 §§6,7; repealed by 2001 c.666 §56]

165.586 [2001 c.666 §51; repealed by 2005 c.830 §48]

165.605 [Repealed by 1971 c.743 §432]

165.610 [Repealed by 1971 c.743 §432]

165.615 [Amended by 1965 c.454 §1; repealed by 1971 c.743 §432]

165.620 [Repealed by 1971 c.743 §432]

165.625 [Repealed by 1971 c.743 §432]

165.655 [Formerly 74.500; repealed by 1971 c.743 §432]

USE OF PEN REGISTERS AND TRAP AND TRACE DEVICES

165.657 Definitions for ORS 165.659 to 165.669. As used in ORS 165.659 to 165.669, unless the context requires otherwise:

(1) "Electronic communication" has the meaning given in ORS 133.721.

(2) "Pen register" means a device which records or decodes electronic or other impulses which identify the numbers dialed or otherwise transmitted on the telephone line to which such device is attached, but does not include any device used by a provider or customer of a provider of electronic or wire communication service for billing or recording as an incident to billing for communications services provided by such provider or any device used by a provider or customer of a wire communication service for cost accounting or other like purposes in the ordinary course of its business.

(3) "Police officer" has the meaning given in ORS 133.525.

(4) "Trap and trace device" means a device which captures the incoming electronic or other impulses which identify the originating number of an instrument or device from which a wire or electronic communication was transmitted.

(5) "Wire communication" has the meaning given in ORS 133.721. [1989 c.983 §15]

165.659 General prohibition. Except as provided in ORS 133.545, 133.575, 133.595, 133.617, 133.619, 133.721, 133.724, 133.729, 133.731, 133.735, 133.737, 133.739, 165.540 and 165.657 to 165.673, no person may install or use a pen register or trap and trace device. [1989 c.983 §16]

165.660 [Formerly 74.510; repealed by 1971 c.743 §432]

165.661 When provider of communication service may use devices. The provider of electronic or wire communication service may use a pen register or a trap and trace device:

(1) In the operation, maintenance and testing of a wire or electronic communication service or in the protection of the rights or property of such provider or in the protection of users of that service from abuse of service or unlawful use of service;

(2) To record the fact that a wire or electronic communication was initiated or completed in order to protect such provider, another provider furnishing service toward the completion of the wire communication or a user of that service, from fraudulent, unlawful or abusive use of service; or

(3) When the consent of the user of that service has been obtained. [1989 c.983 §17]

165.663 Use by police; application to court; statement required. Any police officer may apply to the circuit court in which judicial district the targeted telephone is located for an ex parte order or extension of an order authorizing the installation and use of a pen register or a trap and trace device. The application shall:

(1) Be in writing under oath;

(2) Include the identity of the applicant and the identity of the law enforcement agency conducting the investigation;

(3) Contain a statement demonstrating that there is probable cause to believe that an individual is committing, has committed or is about to commit:

(a) A particular felony of murder, kidnapping, arson, robbery, bribery, extortion or other crime dangerous to life and punishable as a felony;

(b) A crime punishable as a felony under ORS 475.752, 475.806 to 475.894 or 475.906;

(c) A crime under ORS 166.720 that includes as part of the pattern of racketeering activity at least one incident of conduct that constitutes a felony; or

(d) Any conspiracy to commit a crime described in paragraphs (a) to (c) of this subsection; and

(4) Contain a statement demonstrating that use of a pen register or trap and trace device will yield evidence relevant to the crime. [1989 c.983 §18; 2003 c.451 §1; 2005 c.708 §49]

165.665 [Formerly 74.520; repealed by 1971 c.743 §432]

165.667 Order by court; findings; contents of order. (1) Upon application made under ORS 133.545, the court shall enter an ex parte order authorizing the installation and use of a pen register or a trap and trace device if the court finds that there is probable cause to believe that:

(a) An individual is committing, has committed or is about to commit:

(A) A particular felony of murder, kidnapping, arson, robbery, bribery, extortion or other crime dangerous to life and punishable as a felony;

(B) A crime punishable as a felony under ORS 475.752, 475.806 to 475.894 or 475.906;

(C) A crime under ORS 166.720 that includes as part of the pattern of racketeering activity at least one incident of conduct that constitutes a felony; or

(D) Any conspiracy to commit a crime described in subparagraphs (A) to (C) of this paragraph; and

(b) Use of a pen register or trap and trace device will yield evidence relevant to the crime.

(2) The order shall:

(a) Specify the identity, if known, of the person to whom is leased or in whose name is listed the telephone line to which the pen register or trap and trace device is to be attached;

(b) Specify the identity, if known, of the person who is the subject of the criminal investigation;

(c) Specify the number and, if known, physical location of the telephone number to which the pen register or trap and trace device is to be attached and, in the case of a trap and trace device, the geographic limits of the trap and trace order;

(d) Contain a statement of the offense to which the information likely to be obtained by the pen register or trap and trace device relates;

(e) Direct, upon the request of the applicant, the furnishing of information, facilities and technical assistance necessary to accomplish the installation of the pen register or trap and trace device;

(f) Authorize the installation and use of a pen register or a trap and trace device for a period not to exceed 30 days, which may be extended by application and order for a period not to exceed an additional 30 days;

(g) Direct that the order and application be sealed until otherwise ordered by the court; and

(h) Direct the person owning or leasing the line to which the pen register or the trap and trace device is attached, or who has been ordered by the court to provide assistance to the applicant, not to disclose the existence of the pen register or trap and trace device or the existence of the investigation to the listed subscriber or to any other person, unless or until otherwise ordered by the court. [1989 c.983 §19; 2003 c.451 §2; 2005 c.708 §50]

165.669 Duties imposed upon certain persons upon service of order authorizing installation of pen register or trap and trace device; compensation to persons; immunity. (1) Upon service of an order issued under ORS 133.545, 133.575, 133.595, 133.617, 133.619, 133.721, 133.724, 133.729, 133.731, 133.735, 133.737, 133.739, 165.540 and 165.657 to 165.673, a provider of wire or electronic communication service, landlord, custodian or other person shall furnish the investigating law enforcement agency forthwith with all information, facilities and technical assistance necessary to accomplish the installation of the pen register unobtrusively and with a minimum of interference with the services that the person so ordered by the court accords the party with respect to whom the installation and use is to take place, if such assistance is directed by the order.

(2) Under service of an order issued under ORS 133.545, 133.575, 133.595, 133.617, 133.619, 133.721, 133.724, 133.729, 133.731, 133.735, 133.737, 133.739, 165.540 and 165.657 to 165.673, a provider of wire or electronic communication service, landlord, custodian or other person shall furnish the investigating law enforcement agency forthwith with all information, facilities and technical assistance necessary to accomplish the installation of the trap and trace device unobtrusively and with a minimum of interference with the services that the person so ordered by the court accords the party with respect to whom the installation and use is to take place, if such assistance is directed by the order. Unless otherwise ordered by the court, the results of the trap and trace device shall be furnished to the police officer designated in the order at reasonable intervals during regular business hours for the duration of the order.

(3) A provider of wire or electronic communication service, landlord, custodian or other person who furnishes facilities or technical assistance pursuant to ORS 133.545, 133.575, 133.595, 133.617, 133.619, 133.721, 133.724, 133.729, 133.731, 133.735, 133.737, 133.739, 165.540 and 165.657 to 165.673 shall be reasonably compensated for such reasonable expenses incurred in providing such facilities and assistance.

(4) No cause of action shall lie in any court against any provider of wire or electronic communication service, its officers, employees, agents or other specified persons for providing information, facilities or assistance in accordance with the terms of a court order under ORS 133.545, 133.575, 133.595, 133.617, 133.619, 133.721, 133.724, 133.729, 133.731, 133.735, 133.737, 133.739, 165.540 and 165.657 to 165.673. [1989 c.983 §§20,21,22,23]

165.670 [Formerly 74.530; repealed by 1971 c.743 §432]

165.671 Defense to civil or criminal action. A good faith reliance on a court order, a legislative authorization or a statutory authorization is a complete defense against any civil or criminal action brought under ORS 133.545, 133.575, 133.595, 133.617, 133.619, 133.721, 133.724, 133.726, 133.729, 133.731, 133.735, 133.737, 133.739, 165.540 and 165.657 to 165.673. [1989 c.983 §24; 2001 c.385 §8]

165.673 Disclosure of results prohibited; exception. No law enforcement agency shall disclose lists of telephone numbers produced by a pen register or trap and trace device except in the performance of a law enforcement function or as otherwise provided by law or order of a court. [1989 c.983 §25]

165.675 [Formerly 74.540; repealed by 1971 c.743 §432]

165.680 [Formerly 74.550; repealed by 1971 c.743 §432]

FALSE CLAIMS FOR HEALTH CARE PAYMENTS

165.690 Definitions for ORS 165.690, 165.692 and 165.694. As used in ORS 165.690, 165.692 and 165.694:

(1) "Claim for health care payment" means any request or demand for a health care payment, whether made in the form of a bill, claim form, cost report, invoice, electronic transmission or any other document. "Claim for health care payment" does not include any statement by a person on an application for coverage under a contract or certificate of health care coverage issued by an insurer, health care service contractor, health maintenance organization or other legal entity that is self-insured and provides health care benefits to its employees.

(2) "Health care payment" means money paid in compensation for the delivery of specified health care services, whether under a contract, certificate or policy of insurance, by a health care payor.

(3) "Health care payor" means:

(a) Any insurance company authorized to provide health insurance in this state;

(b) A health maintenance organization;

(c) A health care service contractor;

(d) Any legal entity that is self-insured and provides benefits for health care services to its employees;

(e) Any legal entity responsible for handling claims for health care services under a state or federal medical assistance program;

(f) The State of Oregon or any local government within this state that makes payments for health care services;

(g) Any insurer authorized under ORS chapter 731 to transact workers' compensation or casualty insurance in this state; or

(h) Any employer authorized under ORS chapter 656 to self-insure its workers' compensation risk.

(4) "Health care services" means any medical or remedial care or service, including supplies delivered in connection with the care or service, that is recognized under state law.

(5) "Person" means an individual, corporation, partnership or association that provides health care services or any other form of legal or business entity that provides health care services. [1995 c.496 §1; 2001 c.556 §1]

165.692 Making false claim for health care payment. A person commits the crime of making a false claim for health care payment when the person:

(1) Knowingly makes or causes to be made a claim for health care payment that contains any false statement or false representation of a material fact in order to receive a health care payment; or

(2) Knowingly conceals from or fails to disclose to a health care payor the occurrence of any event or the existence of any information with the intent to obtain a health care payment to which the person is not entitled, or to obtain or retain a health care payment in an amount greater than that to which the person is or was entitled. [1995 c.496 §2]

165.694 Aggregation of claims. (1) Single acts of making a false claim for health care payment may be added together into aggregated counts of making false claims for health care payments if the acts were committed:

(a) Against multiple health care payors by similar means within a 30-day period; or

(b) Against the same health care payor, or a contractor, or contractors, of the same health care payor, within a 180-day period.

(2) The charging instrument must identify those claims that are part of any aggregated counts. [1995 c.496 §3]

165.696 Who may commence prosecution. The district attorney or the Attorney General may commence a prosecution under ORS 165.692. [1995 c.496 §6]

165.698 Notice of conviction. The prosecuting attorney shall notify the Oregon Health Authority and any appropriate licensing boards of the conviction of a person under ORS 165.692. [1995 c.496 §5; 2009 c.595 §111]

IDENTITY THEFT AND RELATED OFFENSES

165.800 Identity theft. (1) A person commits the crime of identity theft if the person, with the intent to deceive or to defraud, obtains, possesses, transfers, creates, utters or converts to the person's own use the personal identification of another person.

(2) Identity theft is a Class C felony.

(3) It is an affirmative defense to violating subsection (1) of this section that the person charged with the offense:

(a) Was under 21 years of age at the time of committing the offense and the person used the personal identification of another person solely for the purpose of purchasing alcohol, tobacco products as defined in ORS 431A.175 or inhalant delivery systems as defined in ORS 431A.175; or

(b) Used the personal identification of another person solely for the purpose of misrepresenting the person's age to gain access to a:

(A) Place the access to which is restricted based on age; or

(B) Benefit based on age.

(4) As used in this section:

(a) "Another person" means an individual, whether living or deceased, an imaginary person or a firm, association, organization, partnership, business trust, company, corporation, limited liability company, professional corporation or other private or public entity.

(b) "Personal identification" includes, but is not limited to, any written document or electronic data that does, or purports to, provide information concerning:

(A) A person's name, address or telephone number;

(B) A person's driving privileges;

(C) A person's Social Security number or tax identification number;

(D) A person's citizenship status or alien identification number;

(E) A person's employment status, employer or place of employment;

(F) The identification number assigned to a person by a person's employer;

(G) The maiden name of a person or a person's mother;

(H) The identifying number of a person's depository account at a "financial institution" or "trust company," as those terms are defined in ORS 706.008, or a credit card account;

(I) A person's signature or a copy of a person's signature;

(J) A person's electronic mail name, electronic mail signature, electronic mail address or electronic mail account;

(K) A person's photograph;

(L) A person's date of birth; and

(M) A person's personal identification number. [1999 c.1022 §1; 2001 c.870 §3; 2007 c.583 §1; 2013 c.158 §34; 2015 c.158 §25; 2017 c.701 §15]

165.803 Aggravated identity theft. (1) A person commits the crime of aggravated identity theft if:

(a) The person violates ORS 165.800 in 10 or more separate incidents within a 180-day period;

(b) The person violates ORS 165.800 and the person has a previous conviction for aggravated identity theft;

(c) The person violates ORS 165.800 and the losses incurred in a single or aggregate transaction are $10,000 or more within a 180-day period; or

(d) The person violates ORS 165.800 and has in the person's custody, possession or control 10 or more pieces of personal identification from 10 or more different persons.

(2) Aggravated identity theft is a Class B felony.

(3) As used in this section, "previous conviction" includes:

(a) Convictions occurring before, on or after January 1, 2008; and

(b) Convictions entered in any other state or federal court for comparable offenses.

(4) The state shall plead in the accusatory instrument and prove beyond a reasonable doubt, as an element of the offense, the previous conviction for aggravated identity theft. [2007 c.584 §1]

165.805 Misrepresentation of age by a minor. (1) A person commits the crime of misrepresentation of age by a minor if:

(a) Being less than a certain, specified age, the person knowingly purports to be of any age other than the true age of the person with the intent of securing a right, benefit or privilege which by law is denied to persons under that certain, specified age; or

(b) Being unmarried, the person knowingly represents that the person is married with the intent of securing a right, benefit or privilege which by law is denied to unmarried persons.

(2) Misrepresentation of age by a minor is a Class C misdemeanor.

(3) In addition to and not in lieu of any other penalty established by law, a person who, using a driver permit or license or other identification issued by the Department of Transportation of this state or its equivalent in another state, commits the crime of misrepresentation of age by a minor in order to purchase or consume alcoholic liquor may be required to perform community service and the court shall order that the person's driving privileges and right to apply for driving privileges be suspended for a period not to exceed one year. If a court has issued an order suspending driving privileges under this section, the court, upon petition of the person, may withdraw the order at any time the court deems appropriate. The court notification to the department under this subsection may include a recommendation that the person be granted a hardship permit under ORS 807.240 if the person is otherwise eligible for the permit.

(4) The prohibitions of this section do not apply to any person acting under the direction of the Oregon Liquor Control Commission or a regulatory specialist or under the direction of state or local law enforcement agencies for the purpose of investigating possible violations of laws prohibiting sales of alcoholic beverages to persons who are under a certain, specified age.

(5) The prohibitions of this section do not apply to a person under the age of 21 years who is acting under the direction of a licensee for the purpose of investigating possible violations by employees of the licensee of laws prohibiting sales of alcoholic beverages to persons who are under the age of 21 years. [1971 c.743 §285; 1991 c.860 §1; 1993 c.18 §25; 2001 c.791 §3; 2011 c.355 §19; 2012 c.54 §28; 2015 c.614 §150]

165.810 Unlawful possession of a personal identification device. (1) A person commits the crime of unlawful possession of a personal identification device if the person possesses a personal identification device with the intent to use the device to commit a crime. As used in this subsection, "personal identification device" means a device that is used to manufacture or print:

(a) A driver license or permit or an identification card issued by any state or the federal government;

(b) An employee identification card issued by an employer; or

(c) A credit or debit card.

(2) Unlawful possession of a personal identification device is a Class C felony. [2003 c.632 §1]

165.813 Unlawful possession of fictitious identification. (1) A person commits the crime of unlawful possession of fictitious identification if the person possesses a personal identification card containing identification information for a fictitious person with the intent to use the personal identification card to commit a crime.

(2) Unlawful possession of fictitious identification is a Class C felony.

(3) It is an affirmative defense to violating subsection (1) of this section that the person charged with the offense was under 21 years of age at the time of committing the offense and the person possessed the personal identification card solely for the purpose of enabling the person to purchase alcohol, tobacco products as defined in ORS 431A.175 or inhalant delivery systems as defined in ORS 431A.175. [2003 c.632 §2; 2015 c.158 §26; 2017 c.701 §16]

165.815 Criminal impersonation. (1) A person commits the crime of criminal impersonation if:

(a) The person, with the intent to injure an individual, intentionally impersonates the individual in a communication to a third person without the individual's consent;

(b) The person acts with the intent to deceive the third person into believing that the third person is communicating with the individual;

(c) A reasonable person in the circumstances of the third person would believe that the third person is communicating with the individual; and

(d) The impersonation causes injury to the individual.

(2) Criminal impersonation is a Class A misdemeanor.

(3) As used in this section:

(a) "Impersonate" means to use an actual individual's name or likeness to create a representation of the individual that another person would reasonably believe was or is the actual individual being impersonated.

(b) "Injure" means to intimidate, threaten, harass or physically harm. [2016 c.22 §1]

MISCELLANEOUS

165.825 Sale of drugged horse. (1) No person shall sell or offer for sale any horse that is drugged, tranquilized or otherwise sedated without the consent of the buyer.

(2) Violation of subsection (1) of this section is a misdemeanor. [1971 c.175 §§1,2]

165.840 "Telegraphic copy" defined for ORS 165.845 and 165.850. As used in ORS 165.845 and 165.850, "telegraphic copy" means any copy of a message made or prepared for delivery at the office to which the message may have been sent by telegraph. [Formerly 757.631]

165.845 Making and drawing of checks and notes by wire.

(1) Checks, due bills, promissory notes, bills of exchange and all orders or agreements for the payment or delivery of money or other thing of value may be made or drawn by telegraph, and when so made or drawn:

(a) Have the same force and effect to charge the maker, drawer, indorser or acceptor thereof;

(b) Create the same rights and equities in favor of the payee, drawee, indorsee, acceptor, holder or bearer thereof; and

(c) Are entitled to the same days of grace, as if duly made or drawn and delivered in writing.

(2) No person other than the maker or drawer thereof shall cause any such instrument to be sent by telegraph so as to charge any person thereby.

(3) Whenever the genuineness or execution of any such instrument received by telegraph is denied on oath by the person sought to be charged thereby, it is incumbent upon the party claiming under or alleging the same to prove the existence and execution of the original writing from which the telegraphic copy was transmitted.

(4) The original message shall in all cases be preserved in the telegraph office from which it is sent. [Formerly 757.636; 1981 c.892 §91]

165.850 Manner of expressing private and official seals in telegrams. Whenever any document to be sent by telegraph bears a seal, either private or official, it is not necessary for the operator to telegraph a description of the seal, or any word or device thereon, but the seal may be expressed in the telegraphic copy by the letters "L. S.," or by the word "seal." [Formerly 757.641]

PENALTIES

165.990 Penalties. Violation of ORS 165.692 is a Class C felony. Criminal prosecution of violators of ORS 165.692 must be commenced within five years after the commission of the crime. [Formerly 757.992; subsection (4) of 1995 Edition enacted as 1995 c.496 §4; 2011 c.597 §161]

Chapter 166 — Offenses Against Public Order; Firearms and Other Weapons; Racketeering

ORS sections in this chapter were amended or repealed by the Legislative Assembly during its 2018 regular session. See the table of ORS sections amended or repealed during the 2018 regular session: 2018 A&R Tables

New sections of law were enacted by the Legislative Assembly during its 2018 regular session and pertain to or are likely to be compiled in this ORS chapter. See sections in the following 2018 Oregon Laws chapters: 2018 Session Laws 0005

RIOT, DISORDERLY CONDUCT, HARASSMENT AND RELATED OFFENSES

166.005 Treason. (1) A person commits the crime of treason if the person levies war against the State of Oregon or adheres to its enemies, giving them aid and comfort.

(2) No person shall be convicted of treason unless upon the testimony of two witnesses to the same overt act or upon confession in open court.

(3) A person convicted of treason shall be punished by imprisonment for life. [1971 c.743 §217]

166.010 [Repealed by 1971 c.743 §432]

166.015 Riot. (1) A person commits the crime of riot if while participating with five or more other persons the person engages in tumultuous and violent conduct and thereby intentionally or recklessly creates a grave risk of causing public alarm.

(2) Riot is a Class C felony. [1971 c.743 §218]

166.020 [Repealed by 1971 c.743 §432]

166.023 Disorderly conduct in the first degree. (1) A person commits the crime of disorderly conduct in the first degree if, with intent to cause public inconvenience, annoyance or alarm, or knowingly creating a risk thereof, the person initiates or circulates a report, knowing it to be false:

(a) Concerning an alleged hazardous substance or an alleged or impending fire, explosion, catastrophe or other emergency; and

(b) Stating that the hazardous substance, fire, explosion, catastrophe or other emergency is located in or upon a court facility or a public building, as those terms are defined in ORS 166.360.

(2)(a) Disorderly conduct in the first degree is a Class A misdemeanor.

(b) Notwithstanding paragraph (a) of this subsection, disorderly conduct in the first degree is a Class C felony if the defendant has at least one prior conviction for violating subsection (1) of this section. [2005 c.631 §3; 2015 c.361 §1]

166.025 Disorderly conduct in the second degree. (1) A person commits the crime of disorderly conduct in the second degree if, with intent to cause public inconvenience, annoyance or alarm, or recklessly creating a risk thereof, the person:

(a) Engages in fighting or in violent, tumultuous or threatening behavior;

(b) Makes unreasonable noise;

(c) Disturbs any lawful assembly of persons without lawful authority;

(d) Obstructs vehicular or pedestrian traffic on a public way;

(e) Initiates or circulates a report, knowing it to be false, concerning an alleged or impending fire, explosion, crime, catastrophe or other emergency; or

(f) Creates a hazardous or physically offensive condition by any act which the person is not licensed or privileged to do.

(2)(a) Disorderly conduct in the second degree is a Class B misdemeanor.

(b) Notwithstanding paragraph (a) of this subsection, disorderly conduct in the second degree is a Class A misdemeanor if the crime is committed within 200 feet of the real property on which the person knows a funeral service is being conducted.

(3) As used in this section, "funeral service" means a burial or other memorial service for a deceased person. [1971 c.743 §220; 1983 c.546 §5; 2001 c.104 §55; 2005 c.631 §1; 2012 c.35 §1]

166.030 [Repealed by 1971 c.743 §432]

166.035 [1971 c.743 §221; repealed by 1975 c.715 §2]

166.040 [Repealed by 1971 c.743 §432]

166.045 [1971 c.743 §222; repealed by 1983 c.546 §3]

166.050 [Repealed by 1971 c.743 §432]

166.060 [Amended by 1959 c.436 §1; 1961 c.503 §1; repealed by 1971 c.743 §432]

166.065 Harassment. (1) A person commits the crime of harassment if the person intentionally:

(a) Harasses or annoys another person by:

(A) Subjecting such other person to offensive physical contact;

(B) Publicly insulting such other person by abusive words or gestures in a manner intended and likely to provoke a violent response; or

(C) Distributing a visual recording, as defined in ORS 163.665, of the other person engaged in sexually explicit conduct, as defined in ORS 163.665, or in a state of nudity, as defined in ORS 163.700, when the other person is under 18 years of age at the time of the recording;

(b) Subjects another to alarm by conveying a false report, known by the conveyor to be false, concerning death or serious physical injury to a person, which report reasonably would be expected to cause alarm; or

(c) Subjects another to alarm by conveying a telephonic, electronic or written threat to inflict serious physical injury on that person or to commit a felony involving the person or property of that person or any member of that person's family, which threat reasonably would be expected to cause alarm.

(2)(a) A person is criminally liable for harassment if the person knowingly permits any telephone or electronic device under the person's control to be used in violation of subsection (1) of this section.

(b) Harassment that is committed under the circumstances described in subsection (1)(c) of this section is committed in either the county in which the communication originated or the county in which the communication was received.

(3) Harassment is a Class B misdemeanor.

(4) Notwithstanding subsection (3) of this section, harassment is a Class A misdemeanor if a person violates:

(a) Subsection (1)(a)(A) of this section by subjecting another person to offensive physical contact and:

(A) The offensive physical contact consists of touching the sexual or other intimate parts of the other person; or

(B)(i) The victim of the offense is a family or household member of the person; and

(ii) The offense is committed in the immediate presence of, or is witnessed by, the person's or the victim's minor child or stepchild or a minor child residing within the household of the person or victim;

(b) Subsection (1)(a)(C) of this section; or

(c) Subsection (1)(c) of this section and:

(A) The person has a previous conviction under subsection (1)(c) of this section and the victim of the current offense was the victim or a member of the family of the victim of the previous offense;

(B) At the time the offense was committed, the victim was protected by a stalking protective order, a restraining order as defined in ORS 24.190 or any other court order prohibiting the person from contacting the victim;

(C) At the time the offense was committed, the person reasonably believed the victim to be under 18 years of age and more than three years younger than the person; or

(D)(i) The person conveyed a threat to kill the other person or any member of the family of the other person;

(ii) The person expressed the intent to carry out the threat; and

(iii) A reasonable person would believe that the threat was likely to be followed by action.

(5) It is not a defense to a charge under subsection (1)(a)(C) of this section that the defendant did not know the age of the victim.

(6) The Oregon Criminal Justice Commission shall classify harassment as described in subsection (4)(a)(B) of this section as a person Class A misdemeanor under the rules of the commission.

(7)(a) As used in this section:

(A) "Electronic threat" means a threat conveyed by electronic mail, the Internet, a telephone text message or any other transmission of information by wire, radio, optical cable, cellular system, electromagnetic system or other similar means.

(B) "Family or household member" has the meaning given that term in ORS 135.230.

(b) For purposes of subsection (4) of this section, an offense is witnessed if the offense is seen or directly perceived in any other manner by the minor child. [1971 c.743 §223; 1981 c.468 §1; 1985 c.498 §1; 1987 c.806 §3; 1995 c.802 §1; 2001 c.870 §2; 2009 c.783 §1; 2013 c.649 §26; 2017 c.430 §1]

166.070 Aggravated harassment. (1) A person commits the crime of aggravated harassment if the person, knowing that the other person is a:

(a) Staff member, knowingly propels saliva, blood, urine, semen, feces or other dangerous substance at the staff member while the staff member is acting in the course of official duty or as a result of the staff member's official duties;

(b) Public safety officer, knowingly propels blood, urine, semen or feces at the public safety officer while the public safety officer is acting in the course of official duty or as a result of the public safety officer's official duties; or

(c) Public safety officer, intentionally propels saliva at the public safety officer, and the saliva comes into physical contact with the public safety officer, while the public safety officer is acting in the course of official duty or as a result of the public safety officer's official duties.

(2) Aggravated harassment is a Class C felony. When a person is convicted of violating subsection (1)(a) of this section, in addition to any other sentence it may impose, the court shall impose a term of incarceration in a state correctional facility.

(3) As used in this section:

(a) "Public safety officer" means an emergency medical services provider as defined in ORS 682.025, a regulatory specialist as defined in ORS 471.001 or a fire service professional, a parole and probation officer or a police officer as those terms are defined in ORS 181A.355.

(b) "Staff member" has the meaning given that term in ORS 163.165. [2009 c.783 §2; 2011 c.703 §28; 2012 c.54 §27; 2013 c.477 §1; 2015 c.614 §151]

Note: 166.070 was enacted into law by the Legislative Assembly but was not added to or made a part of ORS chapter 166 or any series therein by legislative action. See Preface to Oregon Revised Statutes for further explanation.

166.075 Abuse of venerated objects. (1) A person commits the crime of abuse of venerated objects if the person intentionally abuses a public monument or structure, a place of worship or the national or state flag.

(2) As used in this section and ORS 166.085, "abuse" means to deface, damage, defile or otherwise physically mistreat in a manner likely to outrage public sensibilities.

(3) Abuse of venerated objects is a Class C misdemeanor. [1971 c.743 §224; 1995 c.261 §2]

166.076 Abuse of a memorial to the dead. (1) A person commits the crime of abuse of a memorial to the dead if the person:

(a) Intentionally destroys, mutilates, defaces, injures or removes any:

(A) Tomb, monument, gravestone or other structure or thing placed as or designed for a memorial to the dead; or

(B) Fence, railing, curb or other thing intended for the protection or for the ornamentation of any structure or thing listed in subparagraph (A) of this paragraph;

(b) Intentionally destroys, mutilates, removes, cuts, breaks or injures any tree, shrub or plant within any structure listed in paragraph (a) of this subsection; or

(c) Buys, sells or transports any object listed in paragraph (a) of this subsection that was stolen from a historic cemetery knowing that the object is stolen.

(2) Abuse of a memorial to the dead is a Class A misdemeanor.

(3)(a) Notwithstanding ORS 161.635, the maximum fine that a court may impose for abuse of a memorial to the dead is $50,000 if:

(A) The person violates subsection (1)(a) of this section and the object destroyed, mutilated, defaced, injured or removed is or was located in a historic cemetery; or

(B) The person violates subsection (1)(c) of this section.

(b) In addition to any other sentence a court may impose, if a defendant is convicted of violating this section under the circumstances described in paragraph (a)(A) of this subsection, the court shall consider ordering the defendant to pay restitution. The court shall base the amount of restitution on the historical value of the object destroyed, mutilated, defaced, injured or removed.

(4) This section does not apply to a person who is the burial right owner or that person's representative, an heir at law of the deceased, or a person having care, custody or control of a cemetery by virtue of law, contract or other legal right, if the person is acting within the scope of the person's legal capacity and the person's actions have the effect of maintaining, protecting or improving the tomb, monument, gravestone or other structure or thing placed as or designed for a memorial to the dead.

(5) As used in this section, "historic cemetery" means a cemetery that is listed with the Oregon Commission on Historic Cemeteries under ORS 97.782. [1995 c.261 §1; 1999 c.731 §12; 2003 c.291 §1; 2005 c.22 §113]

Note: 166.076 was enacted into law by the Legislative Assembly but was not added to or made a part of ORS chapter 166 or any series therein by legislative action. See Preface to Oregon Revised Statutes for further explanation.

166.085 Abuse of corpse in the second degree. (1) A person commits the crime of abuse of corpse in the second degree if, except as otherwise authorized by law, the person intentionally:

(a) Abuses a corpse; or

(b) Disinters, removes or carries away a corpse.

(2) Abuse of corpse in the second degree is a Class C felony.

(3) As used in this section and ORS 166.087, "abuse of corpse" includes treatment of a corpse by any person in a manner not recognized by generally accepted standards of the community or treatment by a professional person in a manner not generally accepted as suitable practice by other members of the profession, as may be defined by rules applicable to the profession. [1971 c.743 §225; 1985 c.207 §2; 1993 c.294 §1]

166.087 Abuse of corpse in the first degree. (1) A person commits the crime of abuse of corpse in the first degree if the person:

(a) Engages in sexual activity with a corpse or involving a corpse; or

(b) Dismembers, mutilates, cuts or strikes a corpse.

(2) Abuse of corpse in the first degree is a Class B felony. [1993 c.294 §2]

Note: 166.087 was enacted into law by the Legislative Assembly but was not added to or made a part of ORS chapter 166 or any series therein by legislative action. See Preface to Oregon Revised Statutes for further explanation.

166.090 Telephonic harassment. (1) A telephone caller commits the crime of telephonic harassment if the caller intentionally harasses or annoys another person:

(a) By causing the telephone of the other person to ring, such caller having no communicative purpose;

(b) By causing such other person's telephone to ring, knowing that the caller has been forbidden from so doing by a person exercising lawful authority over the receiving telephone; or

(c) By sending to, or leaving at, the other person's telephone a text message, voice mail or any other message, knowing that the caller has been forbidden from so doing by a person exercising lawful authority over the receiving telephone.

(2) Telephonic harassment is a Class B misdemeanor.

(3) It is an affirmative defense to a charge of violating subsection (1) of this section that the caller is a debt collector, as defined in ORS 646.639, who engaged in the conduct proscribed by subsection (1) of this section while attempting to collect a debt. The affirmative defense created by this subsection does not apply if the debt collector committed the unlawful collection practice described in ORS 646.639 (2)(a) while engaged in the conduct proscribed by subsection (1) of this section. [1987 c.806 §2; 1999 c.115 §1; 2005 c.752 §1]

166.095 Misconduct with emergency telephone calls. (1) A person commits the crime of misconduct with emergency telephone calls if the person:

(a) Intentionally refuses to relinquish immediately a party line or public pay telephone after being informed that it is needed for an emergency call; or

(b) Requests another to relinquish a party line or public pay telephone to place an emergency call with knowledge that no such emergency exists.

(2) As used in this section:

(a) "Emergency call" means a telephone call to a police or fire department, or for medical aid or ambulance service, necessitated by a situation in which human life or property is in jeopardy and prompt summoning of aid is essential.

(b) "Party line" means a subscriber's line telephone circuit, consisting of two or more main telephone stations connected therewith, each station with a distinctive ring or telephone number.

(3) Every telephone directory that is distributed to members of the general public in this state shall contain in a prominent place a notice of the offense punishable by this section.

(4) Misconduct with emergency telephone calls is a Class B misdemeanor. [1971 c.743 §288; 2005 c.22 §114]

166.110 [Amended by 1961 c.503 §2; repealed by 1971 c.743 §432]

166.115 [1981 c.783 §3; repealed by 2001 c.851 §2 (166.116 enacted in lieu of 166.115)]

166.116 Interfering with public transportation. (1) A person commits the crime of interfering with public transportation if the person:

(a) Intentionally or knowingly enters or remains unlawfully in or on a public transit vehicle or public transit station;

(b) Intentionally or knowingly interferes with the provision or use of public transportation services by, among other things, interfering with the movement of, or access to, public transit vehicles;

(c) While in or on a public transit vehicle or public transit station, engages in disorderly conduct in the second degree as defined in ORS 166.025; or

(d) Subjects a public transportation passenger, employee, agent or security officer or transit police officer to offensive physical contact.

(2)(a)(A) Interfering with public transportation as provided in subsection (1)(a) of this section is a Class C misdemeanor.

(B) Notwithstanding subparagraph (A) of this paragraph, interfering with public transportation as provided in subsection (1)(a) of this section is a Class A misdemeanor if the person has three or more prior convictions for interfering with public transportation as provided in subsection (1)(a) of this section.

(b) Interfering with public transportation as provided in subsection (1)(b) to (d) of this section is a Class A misdemeanor.

(3) As used in this section:

(a) "Enter or remain unlawfully" has the meaning given that term in ORS 164.205.

(b) "Public transit station" includes all facilities, structures, lands and rights of way that are owned, leased, held or used for the purposes of providing public transportation services.

(c) "Public transit vehicle" means a vehicle that is used for public transportation or operated by or under contract to any public body in order to provide public transportation.

(d) "Public transportation" means transportation provided by a city, county, special district or any other political subdivision or municipal or public corporation. [2001 c.851 §3 (enacted in lieu of 166.115); 2005 c.631 §4; 2017 c.454 §1]

166.120 [Repealed by 1971 c.743 §432]

166.130 [Repealed by 1971 c.743 §432]

166.140 [Repealed by 1971 c.743 §432]

166.150 [Repealed by 1971 c.743 §432]

INTIMIDATION

166.155 Intimidation in the second degree. (1) A person commits the crime of intimidation in the second degree if the person:

(a) Tampers or interferes with property, having no right to do so nor reasonable ground to believe that the person has such right, with the intent to cause substantial inconvenience to another because of the person's perception of the other's race, color, religion, sexual orientation, disability or national origin;

(b) Intentionally subjects another to offensive physical contact because of the person's perception of the other's race, color, religion, sexual orientation, disability or national origin; or

(c) Intentionally, because of the person's perception of race, color, religion, sexual orientation, disability or national origin of another or of a member of the other's family, subjects the other person to alarm by threatening:

(A) To inflict serious physical injury upon or to commit a felony affecting the other person, or a member of the person's family; or

(B) To cause substantial damage to the property of the other person or of a member of the other person's family.

(2) Intimidation in the second degree is a Class A misdemeanor.

(3) For purposes of this section, "property" means any tangible personal property or real property. [1981 c.785 §1; 1983 c.521 §1; 1989 c.1029 §1; 2007 c.100 §18; 2011 c.421 §1]

166.160 [Repealed by 1971 c.743 §432]

166.165 Intimidation in the first degree. (1) Two or more persons acting together commit the crime of intimidation in the first degree, if the persons:

(a)(A) Intentionally, knowingly or recklessly cause physical injury to another person because of the actors' perception of that person's race, color, religion, sexual orientation, disability or national origin; or

(B) With criminal negligence cause physical injury to another person by means of a deadly weapon because of the actors' perception of that person's race, color, religion, sexual orientation, disability or national origin;

(b) Intentionally, because of the actors' perception of another person's race, color, religion, sexual orientation, disability or national origin, place another person in fear of imminent serious physical injury; or

(c) Commit such acts as would constitute the crime of intimidation in the second degree, if undertaken by one person acting alone.

(2) Intimidation in the first degree is a Class C felony. [1981 c.785 §2; 1983 c.521 §2; 1989 c.1029 §2; 1993 c.332 §1; 1995 c.79 §53; 1997 c.249 §50; 2007 c.100 §19; 2011 c.421 §2]

AUTHORITY TO REGULATE FIREARMS

166.170 State preemption. (1) Except as expressly authorized by state statute, the authority to regulate in any matter whatsoever the sale, acquisition, transfer, ownership, possession, storage, transportation or use of firearms or any element relating to firearms and components thereof, including ammunition, is vested solely in the Legislative Assembly.

(2) Except as expressly authorized by state statute, no county, city or other municipal corporation or district may enact civil or criminal ordinances, including but not limited to zoning ordinances, to regulate, restrict or prohibit the sale, acquisition, transfer, ownership, possession, storage, transportation or use of firearms or any element relating to firearms and components thereof, including ammunition. Ordinances that are contrary to this subsection are void. [1995 s.s. c.1 §1]

166.171 Authority of county to regulate discharge of firearms. (1) A county may adopt ordinances to regulate, restrict or prohibit the discharge of firearms within their boundaries.

(2) Ordinances adopted under subsection (1) of this section may not apply to or affect:

(a) A person discharging a firearm in the lawful defense of person or property.

(b) A person discharging a firearm in the course of lawful hunting.

(c) A landowner and guests of the landowner discharging a firearm, when the discharge will not endanger adjacent persons or property.

(d) A person discharging a firearm on a public or private shooting range, shooting gallery or other area designed and built for the purpose of target shooting.

(e) A person discharging a firearm in the course of target shooting on public land that is not inside an urban growth boundary or the boundary of a city, if the discharge will not endanger persons or property.

(f) An employee of the United States Department of Agriculture, acting within the scope of employment, discharging a firearm in the course of the lawful taking of wildlife. [1995 s.s. c.1 §2; 2009 c.556 §1]

166.172 Authority of city to regulate discharge of firearms. (1) A city may adopt ordinances to regulate, restrict or prohibit the discharge of firearms within the city's boundaries.

(2) Ordinances adopted under subsection (1) of this section may not apply to or affect:

(a) A person discharging a firearm in the lawful defense of person or property.

(b) A person discharging a firearm on a public or private shooting range, shooting gallery or other area designed and built for the purpose of target shooting.

(c) An employee of the United States Department of Agriculture, acting within the scope of employment, discharging a firearm in the course of the lawful taking of wildlife. [1995 s.s. c.1 §3; 2009 c.556 §2]

166.173 Authority of city or county to regulate possession of loaded firearms in public places. (1) A city or county may adopt ordinances to regulate, restrict or prohibit the possession of loaded firearms in public places as defined in ORS 161.015.

(2) Ordinances adopted under subsection (1) of this section do not apply to or affect:

(a) A law enforcement officer.

(b) A member of the military in the performance of official duty.

(c) A person licensed to carry a concealed handgun.

(d) A person authorized to possess a loaded firearm while in or on a public building or court facility under ORS 166.370.

(e) An employee of the United States Department of Agriculture, acting within the scope of employment, who possesses a loaded firearm in the course of the lawful taking of wildlife.

(f) An honorably retired law enforcement officer, unless the person who is a retired law enforcement officer has been convicted of an offense that would make the person ineligible to obtain a concealed handgun license under ORS 166.291 and 166.292. [1995 s.s. c.1 §4; 1999 c.782 §8; 2009 c.556 §3; 2015 c.709 §1]

166.174 Authority of city, county, municipal corporation or district to regulate possession or sale of firearms. Notwithstanding any other provision of law, a city, county or other municipal corporation or district may not adopt ordinances that regulate, restrict or prohibit the possession or sale of firearms in a public building that is rented or leased to a person during the term of the lease. [1995 s.s. c.1 §5]

166.175 Authority of city to regulate purchase of used firearms. (1) Notwithstanding any other provision of law, a city may continue to regulate the purchase of used firearms by pawnshops and secondhand stores.

(2) As used in this section, "secondhand store" means a store or business whose primary source of revenue is the sale of used merchandise. [1995 s.s. c.1 §6]

166.176 Exception to preemption for certain county ordinances. (1) Nothing in ORS 166.170 or 166.171 is intended to preempt, invalidate or in any way affect the operation of any provision of a county ordinance that was in effect on November 2, 1995, to the extent that the provision:

(a) Established a procedure for regulating, restricting or prohibiting the discharge of firearms; or

(b) Regulated, restricted or prohibited the discharge of firearms.

(2) Subsection (1) of this section does not apply to:

(a) Ordinances regulating, restricting or prohibiting the discharge of firearms on a shooting range or in a shooting gallery or other area designed and built for the purpose of target shooting.

(b) An employee of the United States Department of Agriculture, acting within the scope of employment, discharging a firearm in the course of the lawful taking of wildlife. [1997 c.403 §1; 2009 c.556 §4]

POSSESSION AND USE OF WEAPONS

166.180 Negligently wounding another. Any person who, as a result of failure to use ordinary care under the circumstances, wounds any other person with a bullet or shot from any firearm, or with an arrow from any bow, commits a Class B misdemeanor. In addition, any person so convicted shall forfeit any license to hunt, obtained under the laws of this state, and shall be ineligible to obtain a license to hunt for a period of 10 years following the date of conviction. [Formerly 163.310; 2011 c.597 §162]

166.190 Pointing firearm at another; courts having jurisdiction over offense. Any person over the age of 12 years who, with or without malice, purposely points or aims any loaded or empty pistol, gun, revolver or other firearm, at or toward any other person within range of the firearm, except in self-defense, shall be fined upon conviction in any sum not less than $10 nor more than $500, or be imprisoned in the county jail not less than 10 days nor more than six months, or both. Justice courts have jurisdiction concurrent with the circuit court of the trial of violations of this section. When any person is charged before a justice court with violation of this section, the court shall, upon motion of the district attorney, at any time before trial, act as a committing magistrate, and if probable cause be established, hold such person to the grand jury. [Formerly 163.320]

166.210 Definitions. As used in ORS 166.250 to 166.270, 166.291 to 166.295 and 166.410 to 166.470:

(1) "Antique firearm" means:

(a) Any firearm, including any firearm with a matchlock, flintlock, percussion cap or similar type of ignition system, manufactured in or before 1898; and

(b) Any replica of any firearm described in paragraph (a) of this subsection if the replica:

(A) Is not designed or redesigned for using rimfire or conventional centerfire fixed ammunition; or

(B) Uses rimfire or conventional centerfire fixed ammunition that is no longer manufactured in the United States and that is not readily available in the ordinary channels of commercial trade.

(2) "Corrections officer" has the meaning given that term in ORS 181A.355.

(3) "Firearm" means a weapon, by whatever name known, which is designed to expel a projectile by the action of powder.

(4) "Firearms silencer" means any device for silencing, muffling or diminishing the report of a firearm.

(5) "Handgun" means any pistol or revolver using a fixed cartridge containing a propellant charge, primer and projectile, and designed to be aimed or fired otherwise than from the shoulder.

(6) "Machine gun" means a weapon of any description by whatever name known, loaded or unloaded, which is designed or modified to allow two or more shots to be fired by a single pressure on the trigger device.

(7) "Minor" means a person under 18 years of age.

(8) "Offense" has the meaning given that term in ORS 161.505.

(9) "Parole and probation officer" has the meaning given that term in ORS 181A.355.

(10) "Peace officer" has the meaning given that term in ORS 133.005.

(11) "Short-barreled rifle" means a rifle having one or more barrels less than 16 inches in length and any weapon made from a rifle if the weapon has an overall length of less than 26 inches.

(12) "Short-barreled shotgun" means a shotgun having one or more barrels less than 18 inches in length and any weapon made from a shotgun if the weapon has an overall length of less than 26 inches. [Amended by 1977 c.769 §1; 1979 c.779 §3; 1989 c.839 §1; 1993 c.735 §14; 1995 c.670 §3; 1999 c.1040 §2; 2001 c.666 §§32,44; 2003 c.614 §7; 2007 c.368 §1; 2009 c.610 §4]

166.220 Unlawful use of weapon. (1) A person commits the crime of unlawful use of a weapon if the person:

(a) Attempts to use unlawfully against another, or carries or possesses with intent to use unlawfully against another, any dangerous or deadly weapon as defined in ORS 161.015; or

(b) Intentionally discharges a firearm, blowgun, bow and arrow, crossbow or explosive device within the city limits of any city or within residential areas within urban growth boundaries at or in the direction of any person, building, structure or vehicle within the range of the weapon without having legal authority for such discharge.

(2) This section does not apply to:

(a) Police officers or military personnel in the lawful performance of their official duties;

(b) Persons lawfully defending life or property as provided in ORS 161.219;

(c) Persons discharging firearms, blowguns, bows and arrows, crossbows or explosive devices upon public or private shooting ranges, shooting galleries or other areas designated and built for the purpose of target shooting;

(d) Persons lawfully engaged in hunting in compliance with rules and regulations adopted by the State Department of Fish and Wildlife; or

(e) An employee of the United States Department of Agriculture, acting within the scope of employment, discharging a firearm in the course of the lawful taking of wildlife.

(3) Unlawful use of a weapon is a Class C felony. [Amended by 1975 c.700 §1; 1985 c.543 §1; 1991 c.797 §1; 2009 c.556 §5]

166.230 [Repealed by 1979 c.779 §7]

166.240 Carrying of concealed weapons. (1) Except as provided in subsection (2) of this section, any person who carries concealed upon the person any knife having a blade that projects or swings into position by force of a spring or by centrifugal force, any dirk, dagger, ice pick, slungshot, metal knuckles, or any similar instrument by the use of which injury could be inflicted upon the person or property of any other person, commits a Class B misdemeanor.

(2) Nothing in subsection (1) of this section applies to any peace officer as defined in ORS 133.005, whose duty it is to serve process or make arrests. Justice courts have concurrent jurisdiction to try any person charged with violating any of the provisions of subsection (1) of this section. [Amended by 1977 c.454 §1; 1985 c.543 §2; 1989 c.839 §21; 1999 c.1040 §15]

166.245 [1989 c.839 §38; repealed by 1995 s.s. c.1 §7]

166.250 Unlawful possession of firearms. (1) Except as otherwise provided in this section or ORS 166.260, 166.270, 166.273, 166.274, 166.291, 166.292 or 166.410 to 166.470, a person commits the crime of unlawful possession of a firearm if the person knowingly:

(a) Carries any firearm concealed upon the person;

(b) Possesses a handgun that is concealed and readily accessible to the person within any vehicle; or

(c) Possesses a firearm and:

(A) Is under 18 years of age;

(B)(i) While a minor, was found to be within the jurisdiction of the juvenile court for having committed an act which, if committed by an adult, would constitute a felony or a misdemeanor involving violence, as defined in ORS 166.470; and

(ii) Was discharged from the jurisdiction of the juvenile court within four years prior to being charged under this section;

(C) Has been convicted of a felony;

(D) Was committed to the Oregon Health Authority under ORS 426.130;

(E) Was found to be a person with mental illness and subject to an order under ORS 426.130 that the person be prohibited from purchasing or possessing a firearm as a result of that mental illness;

(F) Is presently subject to an order under ORS 426.133 prohibiting the person from purchasing or possessing a firearm;

(G) Has been found guilty except for insanity under ORS 161.295 of a felony; or

(H) The possession of the firearm by the person is prohibited under ORS 166.255.

(2) This section does not prohibit:

(a) A minor, who is not otherwise prohibited under subsection (1)(c) of this section, from possessing a firearm:

(A) Other than a handgun, if the firearm was transferred to the minor by the minor's parent or guardian or by another person with the consent of the minor's parent or guardian; or

(B) Temporarily for hunting, target practice or any other lawful purpose; or

(b) Any citizen of the United States over the age of 18 years who resides in or is temporarily sojourning within this state, and who is not within the excepted classes prescribed by ORS 166.270 and subsection (1) of this section, from owning, possessing or keeping within the person's place of residence or place of business any handgun, and no permit or license to purchase, own, possess or keep any such firearm at the person's place of residence or place of business is required of any such citizen. As used in this subsection, "residence" includes a recreational vessel or recreational vehicle while used, for whatever period of time, as residential quarters.

(3) Firearms carried openly in belt holsters are not concealed within the meaning of this section.

(4)(a) Except as provided in paragraphs (b) and (c) of this subsection, a handgun is readily accessible within the meaning of this section if the handgun is within the passenger compartment of the vehicle.

(b) If a vehicle, other than a vehicle described in paragraph (c) of this subsection, has no storage location that is outside the passenger compartment of the vehicle, a handgun is not readily accessible within the meaning of this section if:

(A) The handgun is stored in a closed and locked glove compartment, center console or other container; and

(B) The key is not inserted into the lock, if the glove compartment, center console or other container unlocks with a key.

(c) If the vehicle is a motorcycle, an all-terrain vehicle or a snowmobile, a handgun is not readily accessible within the meaning of this section if:

(A) The handgun is in a locked container within or affixed to the vehicle; or

(B) The handgun is equipped with a trigger lock or other locking mechanism that prevents the discharge of the firearm.

(5) Unlawful possession of a firearm is a Class A misdemeanor. [Amended by 1979 c.779 §4; 1985 c.543 §3; 1989 c.839 §13; 1993 c.732 §1; 1993 c.735 §12; 1999 c.1040 §1; 2001 c.666 §§33,45; 2003 c.614 §8; 2009 c.499 §1; 2009 c.595 §112; 2009 c.826 §§8a,11a; 2011 c.662 §§1,2; 2013 c.360 §§6,7; 2015 c.50 §§12,13; 2015 c.201 §3; 2015 c.497 §§3,4]

166.255 Possession of firearm or ammunition by certain persons prohibited. (1) It is unlawful for a person to knowingly possess a firearm or ammunition if:

(a) The person is the subject of a court order that:

(A) Was issued or continued after a hearing for which the person had actual notice and during the course of which the person had an opportunity to be heard;

(B) Restrains the person from stalking, intimidating, molesting or menacing an intimate partner, a child of an intimate partner or a child of the person; and

(C) Includes a finding that the person represents a credible threat to the physical safety of an intimate partner, a child of an intimate partner or a child of the person; or

(b) The person has been convicted of a qualifying misdemeanor and, at the time of the offense, the person was a family member of the victim of the offense.

(2) The prohibition described in subsection (1)(a) of this section does not apply with respect to the transportation, shipment, receipt, possession or importation of any firearm or ammunition imported for, sold or shipped to or issued for the use of the United States Government or any federal department or agency, or any state or department, agency or political subdivision of a state.

(3) As used in this section:

(a) "Convicted" means:

(A) The person was represented by counsel or knowingly and intelligently waived the right to counsel;

(B) The case was tried to a jury, if the crime was one for which the person was entitled to a jury trial, or the person knowingly and intelligently waived the person's right to a jury trial; and

(C) The conviction has not been set aside or expunged, and the person has not been pardoned.

(b) "Deadly weapon" has the meaning given that term in ORS 161.015.

(c) "Family member" means, with respect to the victim, the victim's spouse, the victim's former spouse, a person with whom the victim shares a child in common, the victim's parent or guardian, a person cohabiting with or who has cohabited with the victim as a spouse, parent or guardian or a person similarly situated to a spouse, parent or guardian of the victim.

(d) "Intimate partner" means, with respect to a person, the person's spouse, the person's former spouse, a parent of the person's child or another person who has cohabited or is cohabiting with the person in a relationship akin to a spouse.

(e) "Possess" has the meaning given that term in ORS 161.015.

(f) "Qualifying misdemeanor" means a misdemeanor that has, as an element of the offense, the use or attempted use of physical force or the threatened use of a deadly weapon. [2015 c.497 §2]

166.260 Persons not affected by ORS 166.250. (1) ORS 166.250 does not apply to or affect:

(a) A parole and probation officer, police officer or reserve officer, as those terms are defined in ORS 181A.355.

(b) A federal officer, as defined in ORS 133.005, or a certified reserve officer or corrections officer, as those terms are defined in ORS 181A.355, while the federal officer, certified reserve officer or corrections officer is acting within the scope of employment.

(c) An honorably retired law enforcement officer, unless the person who is a retired law enforcement officer has been convicted of an offense that would make the person ineligible to obtain a concealed handgun license under ORS 166.291 and 166.292.

(d) Any person summoned by an officer described in paragraph (a) or (b) of this subsection to assist in making arrests or preserving the peace, while the summoned person is engaged in assisting the officer.

(e) The possession or transportation by any merchant of unloaded firearms as merchandise.

(f) Active or reserve members of:

(A) The Army, Navy, Air Force, Coast Guard or Marine Corps of the United States, or of the National Guard, when on duty;

(B) The commissioned corps of the National Oceanic and Atmospheric Administration; or

(C) The Public Health Service of the United States Department of Health and Human Services, when detailed by proper authority for duty with the Army or Navy of the United States.

(g) Organizations which are by law authorized to purchase or receive weapons described in ORS 166.250 from the United States, or from this state.

(h) Duly authorized military or civil organizations while parading, or the members thereof when going to and from the places of meeting of their organization.

(i) A person who is licensed under ORS 166.291 and 166.292 to carry a concealed handgun.

(2) It is an affirmative defense to a charge of violating ORS 166.250 (1)(c)(C) that the person has been granted relief from the disability under ORS 166.274.

(3) Except for persons who are otherwise prohibited from possessing a firearm under ORS 166.250 (1)(c) or 166.270, ORS 166.250 does not apply to or affect:

(a) Members of any club or organization, for the purpose of practicing shooting at targets upon the established target ranges, whether public or private, while such members are using any of the firearms referred to in ORS 166.250 upon such target ranges, or while going to and from such ranges.

(b) Licensed hunters or fishermen while engaged in hunting or fishing, or while going to or returning from a hunting or fishing expedition.

(4) The exceptions listed in subsection (1)(d) to (i) of this section constitute affirmative defenses to a charge of violating ORS 166.250. [Amended by 1977 c.207 §1; 1991 c.67 §36; 1993 c.735 §1; 1995 c.670 §2; 1999 c.1040 §3; 2009 c.316 §2; 2009 c.499 §4; 2012 c.106 §3; 2015 c.709 §2]

166.262 Limitation on peace officer's authority to arrest for violating ORS 166.250 or 166.370. A peace officer may not arrest or charge a person for violating ORS 166.250 (1)(a) or (b) or 166.370 (1) if the person has in the person's immediate possession:

(1) A valid license to carry a firearm as provided in ORS 166.291 and 166.292;

(2) Proof that the person is a law enforcement officer; or

(3) Proof that the person is an honorably retired law enforcement officer, unless the person has been convicted of an offense that would make the person ineligible to obtain a concealed handgun license under ORS 166.291 and 166.292. [1999 c.1040 §5; 2015 c.709 §3]

166.263 Authority of parole and probation officer to carry firearm. When authorized by the officer's employer, a parole and probation officer, as defined in ORS 181A.355, may carry a firearm while engaged in official duties if the officer has completed:

(1) A firearms training program recognized by the Board on Public Safety Standards and Training; and

(2) A psychological screening. [1995 c.670 §1]

166.270 Possession of weapons by certain felons. (1) Any person who has been convicted of a felony under the law of this state or any other state, or who has been convicted of a felony under the laws of the Government of the United States, who owns or has in the person's possession or under the person's custody or control any firearm commits the crime of felon in possession of a firearm.

(2) Any person who has been convicted of a felony under the law of this state or any other state, or who has been convicted of a felony under the laws of the Government of the United States, who owns or has in the person's possession or under the person's custody or control any instrument or weapon having a blade that projects or swings into position by force of a spring or by centrifugal force or any blackjack, slungshot, sandclub, sandbag, sap glove, metal knuckles or an Electro-Muscular Disruption Technology device as defined in ORS 165.540, or who carries a dirk, dagger or stiletto, commits the crime of felon in possession of a restricted weapon.

(3) For the purposes of this section, a person "has been convicted of a felony" if, at the time of conviction for an offense, that offense was a felony under the law of the jurisdiction in which it was committed. Such conviction shall not be deemed a conviction of a felony if:

(a) The court declared the conviction to be a misdemeanor at the time of judgment; or

(b) The offense was possession of marijuana and the conviction was prior to January 1, 1972.

(4) Subsection (1) of this section does not apply to any person who has been:

(a) Convicted of only one felony under the law of this state or any other state, or who has been convicted of only one felony under the laws of the United States, which felony did not involve criminal homicide, as defined in ORS 163.005, or the possession or use of a firearm or a weapon having a blade that projects or swings into position by force of a spring or by centrifugal force, and who has been discharged from imprisonment, parole or probation for said offense for a period of 15 years prior to the date of alleged violation of subsection (1) of this section; or

(b) Granted relief from the disability under 18 U.S.C. 925(c) or ORS 166.274 or has had the person's record expunged under the laws of this state or equivalent laws of another jurisdiction.

(5) Felon in possession of a firearm is a Class C felony. Felon in possession of a restricted weapon is a Class A misdemeanor. [Amended by 1975 c.702 §1; 1985 c.543 §4; 1985 c.709 §2; 1987 c.853 §1; 1989 c.839 §4; 1993 c.735 §2; 1995 c.518 §1; 1999 c.1040 §16; 2003 c.14 §64; 2009 c.189 §1; 2009 c.499 §3]

166.272 Unlawful possession of machine guns, certain short-barreled firearms and firearms silencers. (1) A person commits the crime of unlawful possession of a machine gun, short-barreled rifle, short-barreled shotgun or firearms silencer if the person knowingly possesses any machine gun, short-barreled rifle, short-barreled shotgun or firearms silencer.

(2) Unlawful possession of a machine gun, short-barreled rifle, short-barreled shotgun or firearms silencer is a Class B felony.

(3) A peace officer may not arrest or charge a person for violating subsection (1) of this section if the person has in the person's immediate possession documentation showing that the machine gun, short-barreled rifle, short-barreled shotgun or firearms silencer is registered as required under federal law.

(4) It is an affirmative defense to a charge of violating subsection (1) of this section that the machine gun, short-barreled rifle, short-barreled shotgun or firearms silencer was registered as required under federal law. [1989 c.839 §13a; 1997 c.749 §8; 1997 c.798 §1]

166.273 Relief from firearm prohibitions related to mental health. (1) A person barred from transporting, shipping, possessing or receiving a firearm may file a petition with the Psychiatric Security Review Board for relief from the bar if:

(a) The person is barred from possessing a firearm under ORS 166.250 (1)(c)(D) or (E);

(b) The person is barred from receiving a firearm under ORS 166.470 (1)(e) or (f) or, if the person has been found guilty except for insanity of a misdemeanor involving violence, ORS 166.470 (1)(g); or

(c) The person is barred from possessing, receiving, shipping or transporting a firearm under 18 U.S.C. 922(d)(4) or (g)(4) as the result of a state mental health determination.

(2) The petitioner shall serve a copy of the petition on:

(a) The Department of Human Services and the Oregon Health Authority; and

(b) The district attorney in each county in which:

(A) The person was committed by a court to the Oregon Health Authority, or adjudicated by a court as a person with mental illness, under ORS 426.130;

(B) The person was committed by a court to the Department of Human Services, or adjudicated by a court as in need of commitment for residential care, treatment and training, under ORS 427.290;

(C) The person was found guilty except for insanity under ORS 161.295;

(D) The person was found responsible except for insanity under ORS 419C.411; or

(E) The person was found by a court to lack fitness to proceed under ORS 161.370.

(3) Following receipt of the petition, the board shall conduct a contested case hearing, make written findings of fact and conclusions of law on the issues before the board and issue a final order. Board members from the adult panel, the juvenile panel or a combination of both panels of the board may conduct the hearings described in this section.

(4) The state and any person or entity described in subsection (2) of this section may appear and object to and present evidence relevant to the relief sought by the petitioner.

(5) The board shall grant the relief requested in the petition if the petitioner demonstrates, based on the petitioner's reputation, the petitioner's record, the circumstances surrounding the firearm disability and any other evidence in the record, that the petitioner will not be likely to act in a manner that is dangerous to public safety and that granting the relief would not be contrary to the public interest.

(6) If the board grants the relief requested in the petition, the board shall provide to the Department of State Police the minimum information necessary, as defined in ORS 181A.290, to enable the department to:

(a) Maintain the information and transmit the information to the federal government as required under federal law; and

(b) Maintain a record of the person's relief from the disqualification to possess or receive a firearm under ORS 166.250 (1)(c)(D) or (E) or 166.470 (1)(e), (f) or (g).

(7) The petitioner may petition for judicial review of a final order of the board. The petition shall be filed in the circuit court of a county described in subsection (2)(b) of this section. The review shall be conducted de novo and without a jury.

(8) A petitioner may take an appeal from the circuit court to the Court of Appeals. Review by the Court of Appeals shall be conducted in accordance with ORS 183.500.

(9) A person may file a petition for relief under this section no more than once every two years.

(10) The board shall adopt procedural rules to carry out the provisions of this section.

(11) As used in this section, "state mental health determination" means:

(a) A finding by a court that a person lacks fitness to proceed under ORS 161.370;

(b) A finding that a person is guilty except for insanity of a crime under ORS 161.295 or responsible except for insanity of an act under ORS 419C.411 or any determination by the Psychiatric Security Review Board thereafter;

(c) A commitment by a court to the Oregon Health Authority, or an adjudication by a court that a person is a person with mental illness, under ORS 426.130; or

(d) A commitment by a court to the Department of Human Services, or an adjudication by a court that a person is in need of commitment for residential care, treatment and training, under ORS 427.290. [2009 c.826 §5; 2009 c.826 §§18,18a; 2011 c.658 §32; 2013 c.360 §68; 2015 c.201 §2]

166.274 Relief from prohibition against possessing or receiving firearm; fees. (1) Except as provided in subsection (11) of this section, a person barred from possessing or receiving a firearm may file a petition for relief from the bar in accordance with subsection (2) of this section if:

(a) The person is barred from possessing a firearm under ORS 166.250 (1)(c)(A), (C) or (H) or 166.270; or

(b) The person is barred from receiving a firearm under ORS 166.470 (1)(a) or (b) or, if the person has been convicted of a misdemeanor involving violence, ORS 166.470 (1)(g).

(2) A petition for relief described in this section must be filed in the circuit court in the petitioner's county of residence.

(3) A person may apply once per calendar year for relief under the provisions of this section.

(4)(a) A person petitioning for relief under this section shall serve a copy of the petition on:

(A) The city chief of police if the court in which the petition is filed is located in a city; or

(B) The sheriff of the county in which the court is located.

(b) The copy of the petition shall be served on the chief of police or sheriff at the same time the petition is filed at the court.

(5)(a) When a petition is denied, the judge shall cause that information to be entered into the Department of State Police computerized criminal history files.

(b) When a petition is granted, the judge shall cause that information and a fingerprint card of the petitioner to be entered into the Department of State Police computerized criminal history files. If, after a petition is granted, the petitioner is arrested and convicted of a crime that would disqualify the petitioner from purchasing or possessing a firearm, the Department of State Police shall notify the court that granted relief under this section. The court shall review the order granting relief and determine whether to rescind the order. The Department of State Police may charge a reasonable fee, under ORS 192.324, for the entry and maintenance of information under this section.

(6) Notwithstanding the provisions of ORS 9.320, a party that is not a natural person, the state or any city, county, district or other political subdivision or public corporation in this state, without appearance by attorney, may appear as a party to an action under this section.

(7) If the petitioner seeks relief from the bar on possessing or purchasing a firearm, relief shall be granted when the petitioner demonstrates, by clear and convincing evidence, that the petitioner does not pose a threat to the safety of the public or the petitioner.

(8) Petitions filed under this section shall be heard and disposed of within 15 judicial days of filing or as soon as is practicable thereafter, but not more than 30 days thereafter. The judge shall then make findings and conclusions and issue a judgment based on the findings and conclusions in accordance with the requirements of law.

(9) A person filing a petition under this section must pay the filing fee established under ORS 21.135.

(10)(a) Initial appeals of petitions shall be heard de novo.

(b) Any party to a judgment under this subsection may appeal to the Court of Appeals in the same manner as for any other civil action.

(c) If the governmental entity files an appeal under this subsection and does not prevail, it shall be ordered to pay the attorney fees for the prevailing party.

(11) The court may not grant relief under this section to a person who:

(a) Has been convicted of a person felony, as that term is defined in the rules of the Oregon Criminal Justice Commission, or the statutory counterpart to a person felony in any other jurisdiction, if the offense involved the use of a firearm or a deadly weapon as defined in ORS 161.015;

(b) Has been convicted of an offense listed in ORS 137.700 or the statutory counterpart to an offense listed in ORS 137.700 in any other jurisdiction; or

(c) Is currently serving a felony sentence as defined in ORS 10.030 or has served a felony sentence in the one-year period preceding the filing of the petition. [1989 c.839 §11; 1991 c.67 §37; 1993 c.732 §§3,4; 1995 c.518 §2; 1995 c.658 §88; 2009 c.499 §2; 2009 c.826 §§19,20; 2010 c.86 §§1,2,3; 2011 c.595 §§59,60; 2011 c.662 §§3,4; 2015 c.7 §§6,7; 2015 c.201 §4; 2015 c.497 §§5,6]

166.275 Possession of weapons by inmates of institutions. Any person committed to any institution who, while under the jurisdiction of any institution or while being conveyed to or from any institution, possesses or carries upon the person, or has under the custody or control of the person any dangerous instrument, or any weapon including but not limited to any blackjack, slingshot, billy, sand club, metal knuckles, explosive substance, dirk, dagger, sharp instrument, pistol, revolver or other firearm without lawful authority, is guilty of a felony and upon conviction thereof shall be punished by imprisonment in the custody of the Department of Corrections for a term not more than 20 years. [1953 c.533 §1; 1987 c.320 §88]

166.279 Forfeiture of deadly weapons. (1) Except as provided in subsection (4) of this section, ORS 131.550 to 131.600 do not apply to the forfeiture of a firearm or other deadly weapon that was possessed, used or available for use to facilitate a criminal offense.

(2) Except as provided in subsection (3) of this section, at the time of sentencing for any criminal offense in which a firearm or other deadly weapon was possessed, used or available for use to facilitate the offense, the court shall declare the weapon to be contraband and order that the weapon be forfeited.

(3) If a firearm or other deadly weapon that was possessed, used or available for use to facilitate a criminal offense was stolen from its lawful owner and was recovered from a person other than the lawful owner, the court may not order that the weapon be forfeited but shall order that the weapon be restored to the lawful owner as soon as the weapon is no longer needed for evidentiary purposes.

(4) The court shall release a firearm or other deadly weapon forfeited under subsection (2) of this section to the law enforcement agency that seized the weapon. The law enforcement agency may destroy or sell the weapon, use the weapon as a service weapon or use the weapon for training, identification or demonstration purposes. When a weapon is sold pursuant to this subsection, the law enforcement agency shall pay the proceeds from the sale, less the costs of the sale, as provided in ORS 131.594 and 131.597.

(5) As used in this section, "deadly weapon" has the meaning given that term in ORS 161.015. [2003 c.614 §4; 2005 c.830 §24]

166.280 [Amended by 1981 c.767 §1; 1993 c.625 §2; 1997 c.480 §5; 1997 c.693 §2; repealed by 2001 c.666 §56]

166.281 [2001 c.666 §52; repealed by 2003 c.614 §13]

166.282 Sale of weapons by political subdivision; disposition of proceeds. (1) A political subdivision in this state that sells a weapon described in subsection (2) of this section shall pay the proceeds from the sale of the weapon, less the costs of the sale, to the account of the police agency that received the weapon, to be used for purposes of public safety, law enforcement and crime prevention and detection.

(2) Subsection (1) of this section applies to a weapon that is donated to the police agency. [1997 c.693 §1; 2001 c.666 §§25,37; 2003 c.614 §5]

166.290 [Amended by 1973 c.391 §1; repealed by 1989 c.839 §7 (166.291 to 166.293 enacted in lieu of 166.290)]

166.291 Issuance of concealed handgun license; application; fees; liability. (1) The sheriff of a county, upon a person's application for an Oregon concealed handgun license, upon receipt of the appropriate fees and after compliance with the procedures set out in this section, shall issue the person a concealed handgun license if the person:

(a)(A) Is a citizen of the United States; or

(B) Is a legal resident alien who can document continuous residency in the county for at least six months and has declared in writing to the United States Citizenship and Immigration Services the intent to acquire citizenship status and can present proof of the written declaration to the sheriff at the time of application for the license;

(b) Is at least 21 years of age;

(c) Is a resident of the county;

(d) Has no outstanding warrants for arrest;

(e) Is not free on any form of pretrial release;

(f) Demonstrates competence with a handgun by any one of the following:

(A) Completion of any hunter education or hunter safety course approved by the State Department of Fish and Wildlife or a similar agency of another state if handgun safety was a component of the course;

(B) Completion of any National Rifle Association firearms safety or training course if handgun safety was a component of the course;

(C) Completion of any firearms safety or training course or class available to the general public offered by law enforcement, community college, or private or public institution or organization or firearms training school utilizing instructors certified by the National Rifle Association or a law enforcement agency if handgun safety was a component of the course;

(D) Completion of any law enforcement firearms safety or training course or class offered for security guards, investigators, reserve law enforcement officers or any other law enforcement officers if handgun safety was a component of the course;

(E) Presents evidence of equivalent experience with a handgun through participation in organized shooting competition or military service;

(F) Is licensed or has been licensed to carry a firearm in this state, unless the license has been revoked; or

(G) Completion of any firearms training or safety course or class conducted by a firearms instructor certified by a law enforcement agency or the National Rifle Association if handgun safety was a component of the course;

(g) Has never been convicted of a felony or found guilty, except for insanity under ORS 161.295, of a felony;

(h) Has not been convicted of a misdemeanor or found guilty, except for insanity under ORS 161.295, of a misdemeanor within the four years prior to the application, including a misdemeanor conviction for the possession of marijuana as described in paragraph (L) of this subsection;

(i) Has not been committed to the Oregon Health Authority under ORS 426.130;

(j) Has not been found to be a person with mental illness and is not subject to an order under ORS 426.130 that the person be prohibited from purchasing or possessing a firearm as a result of that mental illness;

(k) Has been discharged from the jurisdiction of the juvenile court for more than four years if, while a minor, the person was found to be within the jurisdiction of the juvenile court for having committed an act that, if committed by an adult, would constitute a felony or a misdemeanor involving violence, as defined in ORS 166.470;

(L) Has not been convicted of an offense involving controlled substances or participated in a court-supervised drug diversion program, except this disability does not operate to exclude a person if:

(A) The person can demonstrate that the person has been convicted only once of a marijuana possession offense that constituted a misdemeanor or violation under the law of the jurisdiction of the offense, and has not completed a drug diversion program for a marijuana possession offense that constituted a misdemeanor or violation under the law of the jurisdiction of the offense; or

(B) The person can demonstrate that the person has only once completed a drug diversion program for a marijuana possession offense that constituted a misdemeanor or violation under the law of the jurisdiction of the offense, and has not been convicted of a marijuana possession offense that constituted a misdemeanor or violation under the law of the jurisdiction of the offense;

(m) Is not subject to a citation issued under ORS 163.735 or an order issued under ORS 30.866, 107.700 to 107.735 or 163.738;

(n) Has not received a dishonorable discharge from the Armed Forces of the United States;

(o) Is not required to register as a sex offender in any state; and

(p) Is not presently subject to an order under ORS 426.133 prohibiting the person from purchasing or possessing a firearm.

(2) A person who has been granted relief under ORS 166.273, 166.274 or 166.293 or 18 U.S.C. 925(c) or has had the person's record expunged under the laws of this state or equivalent laws of other jurisdictions is not subject to the disabilities in subsection (1)(g) to (L) of this section.

(3) Before the sheriff may issue a license:

(a) The application must state the applicant's legal name, current address and telephone number, date and place of birth, hair and eye color and height and weight. The application must also list the applicant's residence address or addresses for the previous three years. The application must contain a statement by the applicant that the applicant meets the requirements of subsection (1) of this section. The application may include the Social Security number of the applicant if the applicant voluntarily provides this number. The application must be signed by the applicant.

(b) The applicant must submit to fingerprinting and photographing by the sheriff. The sheriff shall fingerprint and photograph the applicant and shall conduct any investigation necessary to corroborate the requirements listed under subsection (1) of this section. If a nationwide criminal records check is necessary, the sheriff shall request the Department of State Police to conduct the check, including fingerprint identification, through the Federal Bureau of Investigation. The Federal Bureau of Investigation shall return the fingerprint cards used to conduct the criminal records check and may not keep any record of the fingerprints. The Department of State Police shall report the results of the fingerprint-based criminal records check to the sheriff. The Department of State Police shall also furnish the sheriff with any information about the applicant that the Department of State Police may have in its possession including, but not limited to, manual or computerized criminal offender information.

(4) Application forms for concealed handgun licenses shall be supplied by the sheriff upon request. The forms shall be uniform throughout this state in substantially the following form:

APPLICATION FOR LICENSE TO CARRY
CONCEALED HANDGUN

Date_____

I hereby declare as follows:

I am a citizen of the United States or a legal resident alien who can document continuous residency in the county for at least six months and have declared in writing to the United States Citizenship and Immigration Services my intention to become a citizen and can present proof of the written declaration to the sheriff at the time of this application. I am at least 21 years of age. I have been discharged from the jurisdiction of the juvenile court for more than four years if, while a minor, I was found to be within the jurisdiction of the juvenile court for having committed an act that, if committed by an adult, would constitute a felony or a misdemeanor involving violence, as defined in ORS 166.470. I have never been convicted of a felony or found guilty, except for insanity under ORS 161.295, of a felony in the State of Oregon or elsewhere. I have not, within the last four years, been convicted of a misdemeanor or found guilty, except for insanity under ORS 161.295, of a misdemeanor. Except as provided in ORS 166.291 (1)(L), I have not been convicted of an offense involving controlled substances or completed a court-supervised drug diversion program. There are no outstanding warrants for my arrest and I am not free on any form of pretrial release. I have not been committed to the Oregon Health Authority under ORS 426.130, nor have I been found to be a person with mental illness and presently subject to an order prohibiting me from purchasing or possessing a firearm because of mental illness. I am not under a court order to participate in assisted outpatient treatment that includes an order prohibiting me from purchasing or possessing a firearm. If any of the previous conditions do apply to me, I have been granted relief or wish to petition for relief from the disability under ORS 166.273, 166.274 or 166.293 or 18 U.S.C. 925(c) or have had the records expunged. I am not subject to a citation issued under ORS 163.735 or an order issued under ORS 30.866, 107.700 to 107.735 or 163.738. I have never received a dishonorable discharge from the Armed Forces of the United States. I am not required to register as a sex offender in any state. I understand I will be fingerprinted and photographed.

Legal name _____
Age _____ Date of birth _____
Place of birth _____
Social Security number _____
(Disclosure of your Social Security account number is voluntary. Solicitation of the number is authorized under ORS 166.291. It will be used only as a means of identification.)

Proof of identification (Two pieces of current identification are required, one of which must bear a photograph of the applicant. The type of identification and the number on the identification are to be filled in by the sheriff.):
    1._____
    2._____

Height _____ Weight _____
Hair color _____ Eye color _____

Current address _____

(List residence addresses for the

181

City _____ County _____ Zip _____
Phone _____

I have read the entire text of this application, and the statements therein are correct and true. (Making false statements on this application is a misdemeanor.)

_____
(Signature of Applicant)

Character references.

_____

    Name: Address

_____

    Name: Address

Approved ___ Disapproved ___ by ___

Competence with handgun demonstrated by _____ (to be filled in by sheriff)
Date _____ Fee Paid _____
License No. _____

---

    (5)(a) Fees for concealed handgun licenses are:
    (A) $15 to the Department of State Police for conducting the fingerprint check of the applicant.
    (B) $50 to the sheriff for the issuance or renewal of a concealed handgun license.
    (C) $15 to the sheriff for the duplication of a license because of loss or change of address.
    (b) The sheriff may enter into an agreement with the Department of Transportation to produce the concealed handgun license.
    (6) No civil or criminal liability shall attach to the sheriff or any authorized representative engaged in the receipt and review of, or an investigation connected with, any application for, or in the issuance, denial or revocation of, any license under ORS 166.291 to 166.295 as a result of the lawful performance of duties under those sections.
    (7) Immediately upon acceptance of an application for a concealed handgun license, the sheriff shall enter the applicant's name into the Law Enforcement Data System indicating that the person is an applicant for a concealed handgun license or is a license holder.
    (8) The county sheriff may waive the residency requirement in subsection (1)(c) of this section for a resident of a contiguous state who has a compelling business interest or other legitimate demonstrated need.
    (9) For purposes of subsection (1)(c) of this section, a person is a resident of a county if the person:
    (a) Has a current Oregon driver license issued to the person showing a residence address in the county;
    (b) Is registered to vote in the county and has a voter notification card issued to the person under ORS 247.181 showing a residence address in the county;
    (c) Has documentation showing that the person currently leases or owns real property in the county; or
    (d) Has documentation showing that the person filed an Oregon tax return for the most recent tax year showing a residence address in the county.
    (10) As used in this section, "drug diversion program" means a program in which a defendant charged with a marijuana possession offense completes a program under court supervision and in which the marijuana possession offense is dismissed upon successful completion of the diversion program. [1989 c.839 §8 (166.291 to 166.293 enacted in lieu of 166.290); 1991 c.67 §38; 1993 c.732 §2; 1993 c.735 §4; 1995 c.729 §6; 1999 c.1052 §6; 2001 c.104 §56; 2003 c.166 §1; 2005 c.22 §115; 2007 c.368 §2; 2009 c.595 §113; 2009 c.826 §§7,10; 2011 c.547 §§33,34; 2013 c.243 §§4,5; 2013 c.360 §§8,9; 2013 c.591 §§6,7; 2014 c.62 §§1,2; 2015 c.50 §§15,16; 2015 c.201 §5]

    166.292 Procedure for issuing; form of license; duration. (1) If the application for the license is approved, the sheriff shall issue and mail or otherwise deliver to the applicant at the address shown on the application, within 45 days of the application, a wallet sized license bearing the photograph of the licensee. The license must be signed by the licensee and carried whenever the licensee carries a concealed handgun.
    (2) Failure of a person who carries a concealed handgun also to carry a concealed handgun license is prima facie evidence that the person does not have such a license.
    (3) Licenses for concealed handguns shall be uniform throughout the state in substantially the following form:

OREGON CONCEALED HANDGUN
LICENSE

County_____   License Number_____
Expires_____   Date of birth_____
Height_____   Weight_____
Name_____ Address_____
Licensee's City_____ Zip___ Photograph
Signature_____
Issued by_____
Date of issue_____

(4) An Oregon concealed handgun license issued under ORS 166.291 and this section, unless revoked under ORS 166.293, is valid for a period of four years from the date on which it is issued.

(5) The sheriff shall keep a record of each license issued under ORS 166.291 and this section, or renewed pursuant to ORS 166.295.

(6) When a sheriff issues a concealed handgun license under this section, the sheriff shall provide the licensee with a list of those places where carrying concealed handguns is prohibited or restricted by state or federal law. [1989 c.839 §9 (166.291 to 166.293 enacted in lieu of 166.290); 1993 c.625 §5; 1993 c.693 §2; 1993 c.735 §5]

166.293 Denial or revocation of license; review. (1) If the application for the concealed handgun license is denied, the sheriff shall set forth in writing the reasons for the denial. The denial shall be sent to the applicant by certified mail, restricted delivery, within 45 days after the application was made. If no decision is issued within 45 days, the person may seek review under the procedures in subsection (5) of this section.

(2) Notwithstanding ORS 166.291 (1), and subject to review as provided in subsection (5) of this section, a sheriff may deny a concealed handgun license if the sheriff has reasonable grounds to believe that the applicant has been or is reasonably likely to be a danger to self or others, or to the community at large, as a result of the applicant's mental or psychological state or as demonstrated by the applicant's past pattern of behavior involving unlawful violence or threats of unlawful violence.

(3)(a) Any act or condition that would prevent the issuance of a concealed handgun license is cause for revoking a concealed handgun license.

(b) A sheriff may revoke a concealed handgun license by serving upon the licensee a notice of revocation. The notice must contain the grounds for the revocation and must be served either personally or by certified mail, restricted delivery. The notice and return of service shall be included in the file of the licensee. The revocation is effective upon the licensee's receipt of the notice.

(4) Any peace officer or corrections officer may seize a concealed handgun license and return it to the issuing sheriff if the license is held by a person who has been arrested or cited for a crime that can or would otherwise disqualify the person from being issued a concealed handgun license. The issuing sheriff shall hold the license for 30 days. If the person is not charged with a crime within the 30 days, the sheriff shall return the license unless the sheriff revokes the license as provided in subsection (3) of this section.

(5) A person denied a concealed handgun license or whose license is revoked or not renewed under ORS 166.291 to 166.295 may petition the circuit court in the petitioner's county of residence to review the denial, nonrenewal or revocation. The petition must be filed within 30 days after the receipt of the notice of denial or revocation.

(6) The judgment affirming or overturning the sheriff's decision shall be based on whether the petitioner meets the criteria that are used for issuance of a concealed handgun license and, if the petitioner was denied a concealed handgun license, whether the sheriff has reasonable grounds for denial under subsection (2) of this section. Whenever the petitioner has been previously sentenced for a crime under ORS 161.610 or for a crime of violence for which the person could have received a sentence of more than 10 years, the court shall grant relief only if the court finds that relief should be granted in the interest of justice.

(7) Notwithstanding the provisions of ORS 9.320, a party that is not a natural person, the state or any city, county, district or other political subdivision or public corporation in this state, without appearance by attorney, may appear as a party to an action under this section.

(8) Petitions filed under this section shall be heard and disposed of within 15 judicial days of filing or as soon as practicable thereafter.

(9) Filing fees for actions shall be as for any civil action filed in the court. If the petitioner prevails, the amount of the filing fee shall be paid by the respondent to the petitioner and may be incorporated into the court order.

(10) Initial appeals of petitions shall be heard de novo.

(11) Any party to a judgment under this section may appeal to the Court of Appeals in the same manner as for any other civil action.

(12) If the governmental entity files an appeal under this section and does not prevail, it shall be ordered to pay the attorney fees for the prevailing party. [1989 c.839 §9a (166.291 to 166.293 enacted in lieu of 166.290); 1993 c.735 §6; 1995 c.518 §3; 1995 c.658 §89; 1999 c.1052 §7; 2003 c.14 §65; 2007 c.202 §1; 2007 c.368 §3; 2015 c.7 §8]

166.295 Renewal of license. (1)(a) A concealed handgun license is renewable by repeating the procedures set out in ORS 166.291 and 166.292, except for the requirement to submit fingerprints and provide character references. A licensee may submit the application for renewal by mail if the licensee:

(A) Is an active member of the Armed Forces of the United States, the National Guard of the United States or the Oregon National Guard; and

(B) Submits with the application proof of the licensee's military orders and a copy of the licensee's military identification.

(b) An otherwise expired concealed handgun license continues to be valid for up to 45 days after the licensee applies for renewal if:

(A) The licensee applies for renewal before the original license expires;

(B) The licensee has proof of the application for renewal; and

(C) The application for renewal has not been denied.

(2) If a licensee changes residence, the licensee shall report the change of address and the sheriff shall issue a new license as a duplication for a change of address. The license shall expire upon the same date as would the original. [1989 c.839 §10; 1993 c.735 §7; 2007 c.368 §4]

166.297 Annual report regarding revocation of licenses. (1) The sheriff of a county shall submit annually to the Department of State Police a report containing the number of concealed handgun licenses revoked during the reporting period and the reasons for the revocations.

(2) The Department of State Police shall compile the reports submitted under subsection (1) of this section and shall submit the compilation to the Legislative Assembly biennially. [1993 c.735 §13]

166.300 Killing or injuring another with firearm as cause for loss of right to bear arms. (1) Any person who has committed, with firearms of any kind or description, murder in any degree, or manslaughter, either voluntary or involuntary, or who in a careless or reckless manner, kills or injures another with firearms, and who, at any time after committing murder or manslaughter or after said careless or reckless killing or injury of another, carries or bears firearms of any kind or description within this state, commits a Class A misdemeanor.

(2) Subsection (1) of this section does not deprive the people of this state of the right to bear arms for the defense of themselves and the state, and does not apply to any peace officer in the discharge of official duties or to a member of any regularly constituted military organization while on duty with such military organization. [Amended by 2011 c.597 §163]

166.310 [Repealed by 1985 c.709 §4]

166.320 Setting springgun or setgun. (1) Any person who places or sets any loaded springgun, setgun, or any gun, firearm or other device of any kind designed for containing or firing explosives, in any place where it may be fired, exploded or discharged by the contact of any person or animal with any string, wire, rod, stick, spring or other contrivance affixed to or connected with it, or with its trigger, commits a Class B misdemeanor.

(2) Subsection (1) of this section does not apply to any loaded springgun, setgun, firearm or other device placed for the purpose of destroying gophers, moles or other burrowing rodents, and does not prevent the use of a coyote getter by employees of county, state or federal governments engaged in cooperative predatory animal control work. [Amended by 2011 c.597 §164]

166.330 Use of firearms with other than incombustible gun wadding. Any person who uses in any firearms discharged on lands within this state, not owned by the person, anything other than incombustible gun wadding, commits a Class C misdemeanor. [Amended by 2011 c.597 §165]

166.340 [1965 c.20 §§2,3; 1969 c.351 §1; repealed by 1981 c.41 §3]

166.350 Unlawful possession of armor piercing ammunition. (1) A person commits the crime of unlawful possession of armor piercing ammunition if the person:

(a) Makes, sells, buys or possesses any handgun ammunition the bullet or projectile of which is coated with Teflon or any chemical compound with properties similar to Teflon and which is intended to penetrate soft body armor, such person having the intent that the ammunition be used in the commission of a felony; or

(b) Carries any ammunition described in paragraph (a) of this subsection while committing any felony during which the person or any accomplice of the person is armed with a firearm.

(2) As used in this section, "handgun ammunition" means ammunition principally for use in pistols or revolvers notwithstanding that the ammunition can be used in some rifles.

(3) Unlawful possession of armor piercing ammunition is a Class A misdemeanor. [1985 c.755 §2; 1987 c.158 §29]

POSSESSION OF WEAPON OR DESTRUCTIVE DEVICE IN PUBLIC BUILDING OR COURT FACILITY

166.360 Definitions for ORS 166.360 to 166.380. As used in ORS 166.360 to 166.380, unless the context requires otherwise:

(1) "Capitol building" means the Capitol, the State Office Building, the State Library Building, the Labor and Industries Building, the State Transportation Building, the Agriculture Building or the Public Service Building and includes any new buildings which may be constructed on the same grounds as an addition to the group of buildings listed in this subsection.

(2) "Court facility" means a courthouse or that portion of any other building occupied by a circuit court, the Court of Appeals, the Supreme Court or the Oregon Tax Court or occupied by personnel related to the operations of those courts, or in which activities related to the operations of those courts take place.

(3) "Judge" means a judge of a circuit court, the Court of Appeals, the Supreme Court, the Oregon Tax Court, a municipal court, a probate court or a juvenile court or a justice of the peace.

(4) "Judicial district" means a circuit court district established under ORS 3.012 or a justice of the peace district established under ORS 51.020.

(5) "Juvenile court" has the meaning given that term in ORS 419A.004.

(6) "Loaded firearm" means:

(a) A breech-loading firearm in which there is an unexpended cartridge or shell in or attached to the firearm including but not limited to, in a chamber, magazine or clip which is attached to the firearm.

(b) A muzzle-loading firearm which is capped or primed and has a powder charge and ball, shot or projectile in the barrel or cylinder.

(7) "Local court facility" means the portion of a building in which a justice court, a municipal court, a probate court or a juvenile court conducts business, during the hours in which the court operates.

(8) "Probate court" has the meaning given that term in ORS 111.005.

(9) "Public building" means a hospital, a capitol building, a public or private school, as defined in ORS 339.315, a college or university, a city hall or the residence of any state official elected by the state at large, and the grounds adjacent to each such building. The term also includes that portion of any other building occupied by an agency of the state or a municipal corporation, as defined in ORS 297.405, other than a court facility.

(10) "Weapon" means:

(a) A firearm;

(b) Any dirk, dagger, ice pick, slingshot, metal knuckles or any similar instrument or a knife, other than an ordinary pocketknife with a blade less than four inches in length, the use of which could inflict injury upon a person or property;

(c) Mace, tear gas, pepper mace or any similar deleterious agent as defined in ORS 163.211;

(d) An electrical stun gun or any similar instrument;

(e) A tear gas weapon as defined in ORS 163.211;

(f) A club, bat, baton, billy club, bludgeon, knobkerrie, nunchaku, nightstick, truncheon or any similar instrument, the use of which could inflict injury upon a person or property; or

(g) A dangerous or deadly weapon as those terms are defined in ORS 161.015. [1969 c.705 §1; 1977 c.769 §2; 1979 c.398 §1; 1989 c.982 §4; 1993 c.741 §2; 1999 c.577 §2; 1999 c.782 §6; 2001 c.201 §1; 2015 c.351 §1]

166.370 Possession of firearm or dangerous weapon in public building or court facility; exceptions; discharging firearm at school. (1) Any person who intentionally possesses a loaded or unloaded firearm or any other instrument used as a dangerous weapon, while in or on a public building, shall upon conviction be guilty of a Class C felony.

(2)(a) Except as otherwise provided in paragraph (b) of this subsection, a person who intentionally possesses:

(A) A firearm in a court facility is guilty, upon conviction, of a Class C felony. A person who intentionally possesses a firearm in a court facility shall surrender the firearm to a law enforcement officer.

(B) A weapon, other than a firearm, in a court facility may be required to surrender the weapon to a law enforcement officer or to immediately remove it from the court facility. A person who fails to comply with this subparagraph is guilty, upon conviction, of a Class C felony.

(C) A firearm in a local court facility is guilty, upon conviction, of a Class C felony if, prior to the offense, the presiding judge of the local court facility entered an order prohibiting firearms in the area in which the court conducts business and during the hours in which the court operates.

(b) The presiding judge of a judicial district or a municipal court may enter an order permitting the possession of specified weapons in a court facility.

(c) Within a shared court facility, the presiding judge of a municipal court or justice of the peace district may not enter an order concerning the possession of weapons in the court facility that is in conflict with an order entered by the presiding judge of the circuit court.

(3) Subsection (1) of this section does not apply to:

(a) A police officer or reserve officer, as those terms are defined in ORS 181A.355.

(b) A parole and probation officer, as defined in ORS 181A.355, while the parole and probation officer is acting within the scope of employment.

(c) A federal officer, as defined in ORS 133.005, or a certified reserve officer or corrections officer, as those terms are defined in ORS 181A.355, while the federal officer, certified reserve officer or corrections officer is acting within the scope of employment.

(d) A person summoned by an officer described in paragraph (a), (b) or (c) of this subsection to assist in making an arrest or preserving the peace, while the summoned person is engaged in assisting the officer.

(e) An honorably retired law enforcement officer.

(f) An active or reserve member of the military forces of this state or the United States, when engaged in the performance of duty.

(g) A person who is licensed under ORS 166.291 and 166.292 to carry a concealed handgun.

(h) A person who is authorized by the officer or agency that controls the public building to possess a firearm or dangerous weapon in that public building.

(i) An employee of the United States Department of Agriculture, acting within the scope of employment, who possesses a firearm in the course of the lawful taking of wildlife.

(j) Possession of a firearm on school property if the firearm:

(A) Is possessed by a person who is not otherwise prohibited from possessing the firearm; and

(B) Is unloaded and locked in a motor vehicle.

(4)(a) The exceptions listed in subsection (3)(d) to (j) of this section constitute affirmative defenses to a charge of violating subsection (1) of this section.

(b) A person may not use the affirmative defense described in subsection (3)(e) of this section if the person has been convicted of an offense that would make the person ineligible to obtain a concealed handgun license under ORS 166.291 and 166.292.

(5)(a) Any person who knowingly, or with reckless disregard for the safety of another, discharges or attempts to discharge a firearm at a place that the person knows is a school shall upon conviction be guilty of a Class C felony.

(b) Paragraph (a) of this subsection does not apply to the discharge of a firearm:

(A) As part of a program approved by a school in the school by an individual who is participating in the program;

(B) By a law enforcement officer acting in the officer's official capacity; or

(C) By an employee of the United States Department of Agriculture, acting within the scope of employment, in the course of the lawful taking of wildlife.

(6) Any weapon carried in violation of this section is subject to the forfeiture provisions of ORS 166.279.

(7) Notwithstanding the fact that a person's conduct in a single criminal episode constitutes a violation of both subsections (1) and (5) of this section, the district attorney may charge the person with only one of the offenses.

(8) As used in this section, "dangerous weapon" means a dangerous weapon as that term is defined in ORS 161.015. [1969 c.705 §§2,4; 1977 c.207 §2; 1979 c.398 §2; 1989 c.839 §22; 1989 c.982 §5; 1991 c.67 §39; 1993 c.625 §1; 1999 c.782 §7; 1999 c.1040 §4; 2001 c.666 §§24,36; 2003 c.614 §6; 2009 c.556 §6; 2015 c.351 §2; 2015 c.709 §4]

166.372 [1993 c.625 §3; repealed by 1996 c.16 §5]

166.373 Possession of weapon in court facility by peace officer or federal officer. (1) Notwithstanding ORS 166.370 (2) and except as provided in subsection (2) of this section, a peace officer, as defined in ORS 161.015, or a federal officer, as defined in ORS 133.005, may possess a weapon in a court facility if the officer:

(a) Is acting in an official capacity and is officially on duty;

(b) Is carrying a weapon that the employing agency of the officer has authorized the officer to carry; and

(c) Is in compliance with any security procedures established under subsections (3) and (4) of this section.

(2) A judge may prohibit a peace officer or a federal officer from possessing a weapon in a courtroom. A notice of the prohibition of the possession of a weapon by an officer in a courtroom must be posted outside the entrance to the courtroom.

(3) A presiding judge of a judicial district or a municipal court or the Chief Justice of the Supreme Court may establish procedures regulating the possession of a weapon in a court facility by a peace officer or a federal officer subject to the following:

(a) The procedures for a circuit court must be established through a plan for court security improvement, emergency preparedness and business continuity under ORS 1.177 or 1.180;

(b) The procedures for a justice court or a municipal court may only prohibit the possession of weapons within the area in which the court conducts business and during the hours in which the court operates;

(c) Within a shared court facility, the presiding judge of a municipal court or justice of the peace district may not establish procedures in conflict with the procedures established by the presiding judge of the circuit court; and

(d) Notice of the procedures must be posted at the entrance to the court facility, or at an entrance for peace officers or federal officers if the entrance is separate from the entrance to the court facility, and at a security checkpoint in the court facility.

(4) A judge may establish procedures regulating the possession of a weapon in a courtroom by a peace officer or a federal officer. A notice of the procedures regulating the possession of a weapon by an officer must be posted outside the entrance to the courtroom. [2001 c.201 §3; 2005 c.804 §7; 2015 c.351 §3]

166.375 Possession of handgun or ammunition by Department of Corrections authorized staff member; rules. (1) Notwithstanding ORS 162.135 and 162.185 or any Department of Corrections regulation, rule, policy or provision of an employment contract to the contrary, if the department has not provided a secure and locked location for the storage of personal handguns and ammunition by authorized staff, authorized staff may possess a personal handgun and ammunition in the authorized staff member's personal vehicle when the vehicle is parked in a department parking lot if the authorized staff member:

(a) Is present at a public building owned or occupied by the department;

(b) Has a valid concealed handgun license issued pursuant to ORS 166.291 and 166.292; and

(c) Has secured the personal handgun and ammunition in a closed and locked container designed for the storage of firearms inside the vehicle.

(2)(a) Authorized staff may possess and store only the amount and types of ammunition authorized by the department by written policy or rule.

(b) The department shall adopt written policies or rules to carry out the purposes of this section. The policies or rules shall include, at a minimum, procedures for and responsibilities of authorized staff when possessing and storing personal handguns and ammunition on property owned or occupied by the department under this section.

(3) As used in this section and ORS 423.045:

(a) "Authorized staff" means employees of the department and employees of the State Board of Parole and Post-Prison Supervision and Oregon Corrections Enterprises who are assigned to work in or at a public building owned or occupied by the department.

(b) "Handgun" has the meaning given that term in ORS 166.210.

(c) "Vehicle" means a vehicle that is self-propelled and that is commonly known as a passenger car, van, truck or motorcycle. [2014 c.88 §2; 2015 c.246 §1]

166.380 Examination of firearm by peace officer; presentation of concealed handgun license. (1) Except as provided in subsection (2) of this section, a peace officer may examine a firearm possessed by anyone on the person while in or on a public building to determine whether the firearm is a loaded firearm.

(2) A person who is licensed under ORS 166.291 and 166.292 to carry a concealed handgun may present a valid concealed handgun license to the peace officer instead of providing the firearm to the peace officer for examination. [1969 c.705 §3; 2015 c.605 §1]

166.382 Possession of destructive device prohibited; exceptions. (1) A person commits the crime of unlawful possession of a destructive device if the person possesses:

(a) Any of the following devices with an explosive, incendiary or poison gas component:

(A) Bomb;

(B) Grenade;

(C) Rocket having a propellant charge of more than four ounces;

(D) Missile having an explosive or incendiary charge of more than one-quarter ounce; or

(E) Mine; or

(b) Any combination of parts either designed or intended for use in converting any device into any destructive device described in paragraph (a) of this subsection and from which a destructive device may be readily assembled.

(2) As used in this section:

(a) "Destructive device" does not include any device which is designed primarily or redesigned primarily for use as a signaling, pyrotechnic, line throwing, safety or similar device.

(b) "Possess" has the meaning given that term in ORS 161.015.

(3) This section does not apply to:

(a) Persons who possess explosives as provided in ORS 480.200 to 480.290.

(b) The possession of an explosive by a member of the Armed Forces of the United States while on active duty and engaged in the performance of official duties or by a member of a regularly organized fire or police department of a public agency while engaged in the performance of official duties.

(c) The possession of an explosive in the course of transportation by way of railroad, water, highway or air while under the jurisdiction of, or in conformity with, regulations adopted by the United States Department of Transportation.

(d) The possession, sale, transfer or manufacture of an explosive by a person acting in accordance with the provisions of any applicable federal law or regulation that provides substantially the same requirements as the comparable provisions of ORS 480.200 to 480.290.

(4) Possession of a destructive device is a Class C felony. [1989 c.982 §1]

166.384 Unlawful manufacture of destructive device. (1) A person commits the crime of unlawful manufacture of a destructive device if the person assembles, produces or otherwise manufactures:

(a) A destructive device, as defined in ORS 166.382; or

(b) A pyrotechnic device containing two or more grains of pyrotechnic charge in violation of chapter 10, Title 18 of the United States Code.

(2) Unlawful manufacture of a destructive device is a Class C felony. [1989 c.982 §2]

166.385 Possession of hoax destructive device. (1) A person commits the crime of possession of a hoax destructive device if the person knowingly places another person in fear of serious physical injury by:

(a) Possessing, manufacturing, selling, delivering, placing or causing to be placed a hoax destructive device; or

(b) Sending a hoax destructive device to another person.

(2) Possession of a hoax destructive device is a Class A misdemeanor.

(3) Notwithstanding subsection (2) of this section, possession of a hoax destructive device is a Class C felony if a person possesses, or threatens to use, a hoax destructive device while the person is committing or attempting to commit a felony.

(4) As used in this section, "hoax destructive device" means an object that reasonably appears, under the circumstances:

(a) To be a destructive device, as described in ORS 166.382 (1)(a), or an explosive, as defined in ORS 166.660, but is an inoperative imitation of a destructive device or explosive; or

(b) To contain a destructive device, as described in ORS 166.382 (1)(a), or an explosive, as defined in ORS 166.660. [1997 c.749 §1]

SALE OR TRANSFER OF FIREARMS

166.410 Manufacture, importation or sale of firearms. Any person who manufactures or causes to be manufactured within this state, or who imports into this state, or offers, exposes for sale, or sells or transfers a handgun, short-barreled rifle, short-barreled shotgun, firearms silencer or machine gun, otherwise than in accordance with ORS 166.250, 166.260, 166.270, 166.291, 166.292, 166.425, 166.450, 166.460 and 166.470, is guilty of a Class B felony. [Amended by 1979 c.779 §5; 1987 c.320 §89; 1989 c.839 §23; 1995 c.729 §7; 2001 c.666 §§34,46; 2003 c.14 §§66,67; 2003 c.614 §9]

166.412 Definitions; firearms transaction record; criminal history record check; liability; rules. (1) As used in this section:

(a) "Antique firearm" has the meaning given that term in 18 U.S.C. 921;

(b) "Department" means the Department of State Police;

(c) "Firearm" has the meaning given that term in ORS 166.210, except that it does not include an antique firearm;

(d) "Firearms transaction record" means the firearms transaction record required by 18 U.S.C. 921 to 929;

(e) "Firearms transaction thumbprint form" means a form provided by the department under subsection (11) of this section;

(f) "Gun dealer" means a person engaged in the business, as defined in 18 U.S.C. 921, of selling, leasing or otherwise transferring a firearm, whether the person is a retail dealer, pawnbroker or otherwise;

(g) "Handgun" has the meaning given that term in ORS 166.210; and

(h) "Purchaser" means a person who buys, leases or otherwise receives a firearm from a gun dealer.

(2) Except as provided in subsections (3)(c) and (12) of this section, a gun dealer shall comply with the following before a handgun is delivered to a purchaser:

(a) The purchaser shall present to the dealer current identification meeting the requirements of subsection (4) of this section.

(b) The gun dealer shall complete the firearms transaction record and obtain the signature of the purchaser on the record.

(c) The gun dealer shall obtain the thumbprints of the purchaser on the firearms transaction thumbprint form and attach the form to the gun dealer's copy of the firearms transaction record to be filed with that copy.

(d) The gun dealer shall request by telephone that the department conduct a criminal history record check on the purchaser and shall provide the following information to the department:

(A) The federal firearms license number of the gun dealer;

(B) The business name of the gun dealer;

(C) The place of transfer;

(D) The name of the person making the transfer;

(E) The make, model, caliber and manufacturer's number of the handgun being transferred;

(F) The name and date of birth of the purchaser;

(G) The Social Security number of the purchaser if the purchaser voluntarily provides this number to the gun dealer; and

(H) The type, issuer and identification number of the identification presented by the purchaser.

(e) The gun dealer shall receive a unique approval number for the transfer from the department and record the approval number on the firearms transaction record and on the firearms transaction thumbprint form.

(f) The gun dealer may destroy the firearms transaction thumbprint form five years after the completion of the firearms transaction thumbprint form.

(3)(a) Upon receipt of a request of the gun dealer for a criminal history record check, the department shall immediately, during the gun dealer's telephone call or by return call:

(A) Determine, from criminal records and other information available to it, whether the purchaser is disqualified under ORS 166.470 from completing the purchase; and

(B) Notify the dealer when a purchaser is disqualified from completing the transfer or provide the dealer with a unique approval number indicating that the purchaser is qualified to complete the transfer.

(b) If the department is unable to determine if the purchaser is qualified or disqualified from completing the transfer within 30 minutes, the department shall notify the dealer and provide the dealer with an estimate of the time when the department will provide the requested information.

(c) If the department fails to provide a unique approval number to a gun dealer or to notify the gun dealer that the purchaser is disqualified under paragraph (a) of this subsection before the close of the gun dealer's next business day following the request by the dealer for a criminal history record check, the dealer may deliver the handgun to the purchaser.

(4)(a) Identification required of the purchaser under subsection (2) of this section shall include one piece of current identification bearing a photograph and the date of birth of the purchaser that:

(A) Is issued under the authority of the United States Government, a state, a political subdivision of a state, a foreign government, a political subdivision of a foreign government, an international governmental organization or an international quasi-governmental organization; and

(B) Is intended to be used for identification of an individual or is commonly accepted for the purpose of identification of an individual.

(b) If the identification presented by the purchaser under paragraph (a) of this subsection does not include the current address of the purchaser, the purchaser shall present a second piece of current identification that contains the current address of the purchaser. The Superintendent of State Police may specify by rule the type of identification that may be presented under this paragraph.

(c) The department may require that the dealer verify the identification of the purchaser if that identity is in question by sending the thumbprints of the purchaser to the department.

(5) The department shall establish a telephone number that shall be operational seven days a week between the hours of 8 a.m. and 10 p.m. for the purpose of responding to inquiries from dealers for a criminal history record check under this section.

(6) No public employee, official or agency shall be held criminally or civilly liable for performing the investigations required by this section provided the employee, official or agency acts in good faith and without malice.

(7)(a) The department may retain a record of the information obtained during a request for a criminal history record check for no more than five years.

(b) The record of the information obtained during a request for a criminal history record check by a gun dealer is exempt from disclosure under public records law.

(c) If the department determines that a purchaser is prohibited from possessing a firearm under ORS 166.250 (1)(c), as soon as practicable, the department may report the attempted transfer and the purchaser's name to the appropriate law enforcement agency.

(8) A law enforcement agency may inspect the records of a gun dealer relating to transfers of handguns with the consent of a gun dealer in the course of a reasonable inquiry during a criminal investigation or under the authority of a properly authorized subpoena or search warrant.

(9) When a handgun is delivered, it shall be unloaded.

(10) In accordance with applicable provisions of ORS chapter 183, the Superintendent of State Police may adopt rules necessary for:

(a) The design of the firearms transaction thumbprint form;

(b) The maintenance of a procedure to correct errors in the criminal records of the department;

(c) The provision of a security system to identify dealers who request a criminal history record check under subsection (2) of this section; and

(d) The creation and maintenance of a database of the business hours of gun dealers.

(11) The department shall publish the firearms transaction thumbprint form and shall furnish the form to gun dealers on application at cost.

(12) This section does not apply to transactions between persons licensed as dealers under 18 U.S.C. 923.

(13)(a) If requested by a transferor who is not a gun dealer, a gun dealer may request a criminal background check pursuant to ORS 166.435 or 166.438 and may charge a reasonable fee for providing the service.

(b) A gun dealer that requests a criminal background check under this subsection is immune from civil liability for any use of the firearm by the recipient or transferee, provided that the gun dealer requests the criminal background check as described in this section. [1995 c.729 §1; 2001 c.900 §25; 2009 c.595 §114; 2009 c.826 §17; 2015 c.50 §4]

Note: 166.412 to 166.421 were enacted into law by the Legislative Assembly but were not added to or made a part of ORS chapter 166 or any series therein by legislative action. See Preface to Oregon Revised Statutes for further explanation.

166.414 Fees for conducting criminal history record checks. (1) The Department of State Police may adopt a fee schedule for criminal history record checks required under ORS 166.412 and collect a fee for each criminal history record check requested. The fee schedule shall be calculated to recover the cost of performing criminal history record checks required under ORS 166.412, but may not exceed $10 per record check.

(2) Fees collected under this section shall be paid into the State Treasury and deposited in the General Fund to the credit of the State Police Account. [1995 c.729 §2]

Note: See note under 166.412.

166.416 Providing false information in connection with a transfer of a firearm. (1) A person commits the crime of providing false information in connection with a transfer of a firearm if the person knowingly provides a false name or false information or presents false identification in connection with a purchase or transfer of a firearm.

(2) Providing false information in connection with a transfer of a firearm is a Class A misdemeanor. [1995 c.729 §3; 2001 c.1 §9]

Note: See note under 166.412.

166.418 Improperly transferring a firearm. (1) A person commits the crime of improperly transferring a firearm if the person is a gun dealer as defined in ORS 166.412 and sells, leases or otherwise transfers a firearm and intentionally violates ORS 166.412 or 166.434.

(2) Improperly transferring a firearm is a Class A misdemeanor. [1995 c.729 §4; 2001 c.1 §10]

Note: See note under 166.412.

166.420 [Amended by 1989 c.839 §2; 1993 c.4 §1; 1993 c.594 §4; 1993 c.693 §1; repealed by 1995 c.729 §13]

166.421 Stolen firearms; determination; telephone requests. The Department of State Police may respond to a telephone request from any person requesting that the department determine if department records show that a firearm is stolen. No public employee, official or agency shall be held criminally or civilly liable for performing the investigation allowed by this section provided that the employee, official or agency acts in good faith and without malice. [1995 c.729 §5]

Note: See note under 166.412.

166.422 Enforcement of ORS 166.412. Where appropriate, a person may enforce the legal duties imposed by ORS 166.412 (7)(a) or (b), by the provisions of ORS 30.260 to 30.300 and ORS chapter 183. [1989 c.839 §12; 1995 c.729 §8; 2015 c.50 §5]

Note: 166.422 was enacted into law by the Legislative Assembly but was not added to or made a part of ORS chapter 166 or any series therein by legislative action. See Preface to Oregon Revised Statutes for further explanation.

166.425 Unlawfully purchasing a firearm. (1) A person commits the crime of unlawfully purchasing a firearm if the person, knowing that the person is prohibited by state law from owning or possessing the firearm or having the firearm under the person's custody or control, purchases or attempts to purchase the firearm.

(2) Unlawfully purchasing a firearm is a Class A misdemeanor. [1989 c.839 §15; 2011 c.662 §5]

166.427 Register of transfers of used firearms. (1) Whenever a person engaged in the business, as defined in 18 U.S.C. 921, of selling, leasing or otherwise transferring a firearm, whether the person is a retail dealer, pawnbroker or otherwise, buys or accepts in trade, a used firearm, the person shall enter in a register the time, date and place of purchase or trade, the name of the person selling or trading the firearm, the number of the identification documentation presented by the person and the make, model and manufacturer's number of the firearm. The register shall be obtained from and furnished by the Department of State Police to the dealer on application at cost.

(2) The duplicate sheet of the register shall, on the day of purchase or trade, be hand delivered or mailed to the local law enforcement authority.

(3) Violation of this section by any person engaged in the business of selling, leasing or otherwise transferring a firearm is a Class C misdemeanor. [1989 c.839 §16; 1993 c.4 §3; 2001 c.539 §12]

166.429 Firearms used in felony. Any person who, with intent to commit a felony or who knows or reasonably should know that a felony will be committed with the firearm, ships, transports, receives, sells or otherwise furnishes any firearm in the furtherance of the felony is guilty of a Class B felony. [1989 c.839 §17]

166.430 [Amended by 1971 c.464 §1; repealed by 1989 c.839 §39]

166.432 Definitions for ORS 166.412 and 166.433 to 166.441. (1) As used in ORS 166.412, 166.433, 166.434, 166.435, 166.436 and 166.438, "criminal background check" or "criminal history record check" means determining the eligibility of a person to purchase or possess a firearm by reviewing state and federal databases including, but not limited to, the:
(a) Oregon computerized criminal history system;
(b) Oregon mental health data system;
(c) Law Enforcement Data System;
(d) National Instant Criminal Background Check System; and
(e) Stolen guns system.
(2) As used in ORS 166.433, 166.434, 166.435, 166.436, 166.438 and 166.441:
(a) "Gun dealer" has the meaning given that term in ORS 166.412.
(b) "Gun show" means an event at which more than 25 firearms are on site and available for transfer. [2001 c.1 §3; 2015 c.50 §6]

Note: 166.432, 166.433 and 166.445 were made a part of 166.432 to 166.445 by law but were not added to or made a part of ORS chapter 166 or any other series therein. See Preface to Oregon Revised Statutes for further explanation.

166.433 Findings regarding transfers of firearms. The people of this state find that:
(1) The laws of Oregon regulating the sale of firearms contain a loophole that allows people other than gun dealers to sell firearms at gun shows without first conducting criminal background checks; and
(2) It is necessary for the safety of the people of Oregon that any person who transfers a firearm at a gun show be required to request a criminal background check before completing the transfer of the firearm. [2001 c.1 §1; 2015 c.50 §7]

Note: See note under 166.432.

166.434 Application of ORS 166.412 to all firearm transfers by gun dealers; fees for criminal background checks. (1) Notwithstanding the fact that ORS 166.412 requires a gun dealer to request a criminal history record check only when transferring a handgun, a gun dealer shall comply with the requirements of ORS 166.412 before transferring any firearm to a purchaser. The provisions of ORS 166.412 apply to the transfer of firearms other than handguns to the same extent that they apply to the transfer of handguns.

(2) In addition to the determination required by ORS 166.412 (3)(a)(A), in conducting a criminal background check or criminal history record check, the Department of State Police shall also determine whether the recipient is otherwise prohibited by state or federal law from possessing a firearm.

(3) Notwithstanding ORS 166.412 (5), the department is not required to operate the telephone number established under ORS 166.412 (5) on Thanksgiving Day or Christmas Day.

(4)(a) The department may charge a fee, not to exceed the amount authorized under ORS 166.414, for criminal background checks required under this section or ORS 166.435 or 166.436.

(b) The department shall establish a reduced fee for subsequent criminal background checks on the same recipient that are performed during the same day between the hours of 8 a.m. and 10 p.m. [2001 c.1 §5; 2015 c.50 §8]

166.435 Firearm transfers by unlicensed persons; requirements; exceptions; penalties. (1) As used in this section:
(a) "Transfer" means the delivery of a firearm from a transferor to a transferee, including, but not limited to, the sale, gift, loan or lease of the firearm. "Transfer" does not include the temporary provision of a firearm to a transferee if the transferor has no reason to believe the transferee is prohibited from possessing a firearm or intends to use the firearm in the commission of a crime, and the provision occurs:

(A) At a shooting range, shooting gallery or other area designed for the purpose of target shooting, for use during target practice, a firearms safety or training course or class or a similar lawful activity;

(B) For the purpose of hunting, trapping or target shooting, during the time in which the transferee is engaged in activities related to hunting, trapping or target shooting;

(C) Under circumstances in which the transferee and the firearm are in the presence of the transferor;

(D) To a transferee who is in the business of repairing firearms, for the time during which the firearm is being repaired;

(E) To a transferee who is in the business of making or repairing custom accessories for firearms, for the time during which the accessories are being made or repaired; or

(F) For the purpose of preventing imminent death or serious physical injury, and the provision lasts only as long as is necessary to prevent the death or serious physical injury.

(b) "Transferee" means a person who is not a gun dealer or licensed as a manufacturer or importer under 18 U.S.C. 923 and who intends to receive a firearm from a transferor.

(c) "Transferor" means a person who is not a gun dealer or licensed as a manufacturer or importer under 18 U.S.C. 923 and who intends to deliver a firearm to a transferee.

(2) Except as provided in ORS 166.436 and 166.438 and subsection (4) of this section, a transferor may not transfer a firearm to a transferee unless the transfer is completed through a gun dealer as described in subsection (3) of this section.

(3)(a) A transferor may transfer a firearm to a transferee only as provided in this section. Except as provided in paragraph (b) of this subsection, prior to the transfer both the transferor and the transferee must appear in person before a gun dealer, with the firearm, and request that the gun dealer perform a criminal background check on the transferee.

(b) If the transferor and the transferee reside over 40 miles from each other, the transferor may ship or deliver the firearm to a gun dealer located near the transferee or a gun dealer designated by the transferee, and the transferor need not appear before the gun dealer in person.

(c) A gun dealer who agrees to complete a transfer of a firearm under this section shall request a criminal history record check on the transferee as described in ORS 166.412 and shall comply with all requirements of federal law.

(d) If, upon completion of a criminal background check, the gun dealer:

(A) Receives a unique approval number from the Department of State Police indicating that the transferee is qualified to complete the transfer, the gun dealer shall notify the transferor, enter the firearm into the gun dealer's inventory and transfer the firearm to the transferee.

(B) Receives notification that the transferee is prohibited by state or federal law from possessing or receiving the firearm, the gun dealer shall notify the transferor and neither the transferor nor the gun dealer shall transfer the firearm to the transferee. If the transferor shipped or delivered the firearm to the gun dealer pursuant to paragraph (b) of this subsection, the gun dealer shall comply with federal law when returning the firearm to the transferor.

(e) A gun dealer may charge a reasonable fee for facilitating a firearm transfer pursuant to this section.

(4) The requirements of subsections (2) and (3) of this section do not apply to:

(a) The transfer of a firearm by or to a law enforcement agency, or by or to a law enforcement officer, private security professional or member of the Armed Forces of the United States, while that person is acting within the scope of official duties.

(b) The transfer of a firearm as part of a firearm turn-in or buyback event, in which a law enforcement agency receives or purchases firearms from members of the public.

(c) The transfer of a firearm to:

(A) A transferor's spouse or domestic partner;

(B) A transferor's parent or stepparent;

(C) A transferor's child or stepchild;

(D) A transferor's sibling;

(E) A transferor's grandparent;

(F) A transferor's grandchild;

(G) A transferor's aunt or uncle;

(H) A transferor's first cousin;

(I) A transferor's niece or nephew; or

(J) The spouse or domestic partner of a person specified in subparagraphs (B) to (I) of this paragraph.

(d) The transfer of a firearm that occurs because of the death of the firearm owner, provided that:

(A) The transfer is conducted or facilitated by a personal representative, as defined in ORS 111.005, or a trustee of a trust created in a will; and

(B) The transferee is related to the deceased firearm owner in a manner specified in paragraph (c) of this subsection.

(5)(a) A transferor who fails to comply with the requirements of this section commits a Class A misdemeanor.

(b) Notwithstanding paragraph (a) of this subsection, a transferor who fails to comply with the requirements of this section commits a Class B felony if the transferor has a previous conviction under this section at the time of the offense. [2015 c.50 §2]

Note: Section 1, chapter 50, Oregon Laws 2015, provides:

Sec. 1. Section 2 of this 2015 Act [166.435] and the amendments to ORS 166.250, 166.291, 166.412, 166.422, 166.432, 166.433, 166.434, 166.436, 166.438, 166.460, 166.470, 181.150, 181.740 and 426.133 by sections 3 to 19 of this 2015 Act shall be known and may be cited as the "Oregon Firearms Safety Act." [2015 c.50 §1]

Note: 166.435 was enacted into law by the Legislative Assembly but was not added to or made a part of ORS chapter 166 or any series therein by legislative action. See Preface to Oregon Revised Statutes for further explanation.

166.436 Department of State Police criminal background checks for gun show firearm transfers; liability. (1) The Department of State Police shall make the telephone number established under ORS 166.412 (5) available for requests for criminal background checks under this section from persons who are not gun dealers and who are transferring firearms at gun shows.

(2) Prior to transferring a firearm at a gun show, a transferor who is not a gun dealer may request by telephone that the department conduct a criminal background check on the recipient and shall provide the following information to the department:

(a) The name, address and telephone number of the transferor;

(b) The make, model, caliber and manufacturer's number of the firearm being transferred;

(c) The name, date of birth, race, sex and address of the recipient;

(d) The Social Security number of the recipient if the recipient voluntarily provides that number;

(e) The address of the place where the transfer is occurring; and

(f) The type, issuer and identification number of a current piece of identification bearing a recent photograph of the recipient presented by the recipient. The identification presented by the recipient must meet the requirements of ORS 166.412 (4)(a).

(3)(a) Upon receipt of a request for a criminal background check under this section, the department shall immediately, during the telephone call or by return call:

(A) Determine from criminal records and other information available to it whether the recipient is disqualified under ORS 166.470 from completing the transfer or is otherwise prohibited by state or federal law from possessing a firearm; and

(B) Notify the transferor when a recipient is disqualified from completing the transfer or provide the transferor with a unique approval number indicating that the recipient is qualified to complete the transfer. The unique approval number is a permit valid for 24 hours for the requested transfer. If the firearm is not transferred from the transferor to the recipient within 24 hours after receipt of the unique approval number, a new request must be made by the transferor.

(b) If the department is unable to determine whether the recipient is qualified for or disqualified from completing the transfer within 30 minutes of receiving the request, the department shall notify the transferor and provide the transferor with an estimate of the time when the department will provide the requested information.

(4) A public employee or public agency incurs no criminal or civil liability for performing the criminal background checks required by this section, provided the employee or agency acts in good faith and without malice.

(5)(a) The department may retain a record of the information obtained during a request for a criminal background check under this section for the period of time provided in ORS 166.412 (7).

(b) The record of the information obtained during a request for a criminal background check under this section is exempt from disclosure under public records law.

(c) If the department determines that a recipient is prohibited from possessing a firearm under ORS 166.250 (1)(c), as soon as practicable, the department may report the attempted transfer and the recipient's name to the appropriate law enforcement agency.

(6) The recipient of the firearm must be present when the transferor requests a criminal background check under this section.

(7)(a) Except as otherwise provided in paragraph (b) of this subsection, a transferor who receives notification under this section that the recipient is qualified to complete the transfer of a firearm, has the recipient fill out the form required by ORS 166.438 (1)(a) and retains the form as required by ORS 166.438 (2) is immune from civil liability for any use of the firearm from the time of the transfer unless the transferor knows, or reasonably should know, that the recipient is likely to commit an unlawful act involving the firearm.

(b) The immunity provided by paragraph (a) of this subsection does not apply:

(A) If the transferor knows, or reasonably should know, that the recipient of the firearm intends to deliver the firearm to a third person who the transferor knows, or reasonably should know, may not lawfully possess the firearm; or

(B) In any product liability civil action under ORS 30.900 to 30.920. [2001 c.1 §6; 2015 c.50 §3]

166.438 Transfer of firearms at gun shows; penalties.

(1) A transferor who is not a gun dealer may not transfer a firearm at a gun show unless the transferor:

(a)(A) Requests a criminal background check under ORS 166.436 prior to completing the transfer;

(B) Receives a unique approval number from the Department of State Police indicating that the recipient is qualified to complete the transfer; and

(C) Has the recipient complete the form described in ORS 166.441; or

(b) Completes the transfer through a gun dealer.

(2) The transferor shall retain the completed form referred to in subsection (1) of this section for at least five years and shall make the completed form available to law enforcement agencies for the purpose of criminal investigations.

(3) A person who organizes a gun show shall post in a prominent place at the gun show a notice explaining the requirements of subsections (1) and (2) of this section. The person shall provide the form required by subsection (1) of this section to any person transferring a firearm at the gun show.

(4) Subsection (1) of this section does not apply if the transferee is licensed as a dealer under 18 U.S.C. 923.

(5)(a) Failure to comply with the requirements of subsection (1), (2) or (3) of this section is a Class A misdemeanor.

(b) Notwithstanding paragraph (a) of this subsection, failure to comply with the requirements of subsection (1), (2) or (3) of this section is a Class C felony if the person has two or more previous convictions under this section.

(6) It is an affirmative defense to a charge of violating subsection (1) or (3) of this section that the person did not know, or reasonably could not know, that more than 25 firearms were at the site and available for transfer. [2001 c.1 §7; 2015 c.50 §9]

166.440 [Repealed by 1989 c.839 §39]

166.441 Form for transfer of firearm at gun show. (1) The Department of State Police shall develop a form to be completed by a person seeking to obtain a firearm at a gun show from a transferor other than a gun dealer. The department shall consider including in the form all of the requirements for disclosure of information that are required by federal law for over-the-counter firearms transactions.

(2) The department shall make the form available to the public at no cost. [2001 c.1 §8]

166.445 Short title. ORS 166.432 to 166.445 and the amendments to ORS 166.416, 166.418 and 166.460 by sections 9, 10 and 11, chapter 1, Oregon Laws 2001, shall be known as the Gun Violence Prevention Act. [2001 c.1 §2]

Note: See note under 166.432.

166.450 Obliteration or change of identification number on firearms. Any person who intentionally alters, removes or obliterates the identification number of any firearm for an unlawful purpose, shall be punished upon conviction by imprisonment in the custody of the Department of Corrections for not more than five years. Possession of any such firearm is presumptive evidence that the possessor has altered, removed or obliterated the identification number. [Amended by 1987 c.320 §90; 1989 c.839 §24]

166.460 Antique firearms excepted. (1) ORS 166.250, 166.260, 166.291 to 166.295, 166.410, 166.412, 166.425, 166.434, 166.438 and 166.450 do not apply to antique firearms.

(2) Notwithstanding the provisions of subsection (1) of this section, possession of an antique firearm by a person described in ORS 166.250 (1)(c)(B) to (D) or (G) constitutes a violation of ORS 166.250. [Amended by 1979 c.779 §6; 1989 c.839 §25; 1993 c.735 §8; 1995 c.729 §9; 2001 c.1 §11; 2001 c.666 §§35,47; 2003 c.614 §10; 2009 c.499 §5; 2015 c.50 §14]

166.470 Limitations and conditions for sales of firearms. (1) Unless relief has been granted under ORS 166.273 or 166.274 or 18 U.S.C. 925(c) or the expunction laws of this state or an equivalent law of another jurisdiction, a person may not intentionally sell, deliver or otherwise transfer any firearm when the transferor knows or reasonably should know that the recipient:

(a) Is under 18 years of age;

(b) Has been convicted of a felony;

(c) Has any outstanding felony warrants for arrest;

(d) Is free on any form of pretrial release for a felony;

(e) Was committed to the Oregon Health Authority under ORS 426.130;

(f) After January 1, 1990, was found to be a person with mental illness and subject to an order under ORS 426.130 that the person be prohibited from purchasing or possessing a firearm as a result of that mental illness;

(g) Has been convicted of a misdemeanor involving violence or found guilty except for insanity under ORS 161.295 of a misdemeanor involving violence within the previous four years. As used in this paragraph, "misdemeanor involving violence" means a misdemeanor described in ORS 163.160, 163.187, 163.190, 163.195 or 166.155 (1)(b);

(h) Is presently subject to an order under ORS 426.133 prohibiting the person from purchasing or possessing a firearm; or

(i) Has been found guilty except for insanity under ORS 161.295 of a felony.

(2) A person may not sell, deliver or otherwise transfer any firearm that the person knows or reasonably should know is stolen.

(3) Subsection (1)(a) of this section does not prohibit:

(a) The parent or guardian, or another person with the consent of the parent or guardian, of a minor from transferring to the minor a firearm, other than a handgun; or

(b) The temporary transfer of any firearm to a minor for hunting, target practice or any other lawful purpose.

(4) Violation of this section is a Class A misdemeanor. [Amended by 1989 c.839 §3; 1991 c.67 §40; 1993 c.735 §11; 2001 c.828 §2; 2003 c.577 §7; 2009 c.499 §6; 2009 c.595 §115; 2009 c.826 §§8,11; 2013 c.360 §§10,11; 2015 c.50 §§17,18; 2015 c.201 §6]

166.480 Sale or gift of explosives to children. Any person who sells, exchanges, barters or gives to any child, under the age of 14 years, any explosive article or substance, other than an ordinary firecracker containing not more than 10 grains of gunpowder or who sells, exchanges, barters or gives to any such child, any instrument or apparatus, the chief utility of which is the fact that it is used, or is ordinarily capable of being used, as an article or device to increase the force or intensity of any explosive, or to direct or control the discharge of any such explosive, is guilty of a misdemeanor. [Amended by 1989 c.839 §26]

166.490 Purchase of firearms in certain other states. (1) As used in this section, unless the context requires otherwise:

(a) "Contiguous state" means California, Idaho, Nevada or Washington.

(b) "Resident" includes an individual or a corporation or other business entity that maintains a place of business in this state.

(2) A resident of this state may purchase or otherwise obtain a rifle or shotgun in a contiguous state and receive in this state or transport into this state such rifle or shotgun, unless the purchase or transfer violates the law of this state, the state in which the purchase or transfer is made or the United States.

(3) This section does not apply to the purchase, receipt or transportation of rifles and shotguns by federally licensed firearms manufacturers, importers, dealers or collectors.

(4) This section expires and stands repealed upon the date that section 922(b) (3) of the Gun Control Act of 1968 (18 U.S.C. 922(b) (3)) and regulations pursuant thereto are repealed or rescinded. [1969 c.289 §§1,2,3,4]

166.510 [Amended by 1957 c.290 §1; 1973 c.746 §1; 1983 c.546 §2; repealed by 1985 c.709 §4]

166.515 [1973 c.746 §2; repealed by 1985 c.709 §4]

166.520 [Amended by 1973 c.746 §3; repealed by 1985 c.709 §4]

EXTREME RISK PROTECTION ORDERS

166.525 Definitions. As used in ORS 166.525 to 166.543:

(1) "Deadly weapon" means:

(a) Any instrument, article or substance specifically designed for and presently capable of causing death or serious physical injury; or

(b) A firearm, whether loaded or unloaded.

(2) "Family or household member" means a spouse, intimate partner, mother, father, child or sibling of the respondent, or any person living within the same household as the respondent.

(3) "Gun dealer" has the meaning given that term in ORS 166.412.

(4) "Law enforcement agency" means an agency or department of the State of Oregon or of a political subdivision of the State of Oregon whose principal function is the apprehension of criminal offenders.

(5) "Law enforcement officer" means a member of the Oregon State Police, a sheriff, a municipal police officer or an authorized tribal police officer as defined in ORS 181A.680.

(6) "Petitioner" means a person who petitions for an order under ORS 166.525 to 166.543.

(7) "Respondent" means a person against whom an order is filed under ORS 166.525 to 166.543. [2017 c.737 §1]

166.527 Petition for ex parte order; issuance and service of order; request for hearing. (1) A law enforcement officer or a family or household member of a person may file a petition requesting that the court issue an extreme risk protection order enjoining the person from having in the person's custody or control, owning, purchasing, possessing or receiving, or attempting to purchase or receive, a deadly weapon.

(2) An extreme risk protection order petition shall be heard by the court and issued or denied on the same day the petition is submitted to the court or on the judicial business day immediately following the day the petition is filed.

(3) The petition for an extreme risk protection order must be supported by a written affidavit signed by the petitioner under oath, or an oral statement taken under oath by the petitioner or any other witness the petitioner may produce.

(4) In determining whether to issue an extreme risk protection order, the court shall consider the following:

(a) A history of suicide threats or attempts or acts of violence by the respondent directed against another person;

(b) A history of use, attempted use or threatened use of physical force by the respondent against another person;

(c) A previous conviction for:

(A) A misdemeanor involving violence as defined in ORS 166.470;

(B) A stalking offense under ORS 163.732 or 163.750, or a similar offense in another jurisdiction;

(C) An offense constituting domestic violence as defined in ORS 135.230;

(D) Driving under the influence of intoxicants under ORS 813.010 or 813.011; or

(E) An offense involving cruelty or abuse of animals;

(d) Evidence of recent unlawful use of controlled substances;

(e) Previous unlawful and reckless use, display or brandishing of a deadly weapon by the respondent;

(f) A previous violation by the respondent of a court order issued pursuant to ORS 107.716 or 107.718;

(g) Evidence of an acquisition or attempted acquisition within the previous 180 days by the respondent of a deadly weapon; and

(h) Any additional information the court finds to be reliable, including a statement by the respondent.

(5)(a) The petitioner has the burden of proof at the ex parte hearing.

(b) The petitioner may appear in person or by electronic video transmission.

(c) The court may continue a hearing under this section upon a showing of good cause.

(6)(a) The court shall issue an extreme risk protection order if the court finds by clear and convincing evidence, based on the petition and supporting documentation and after considering a statement by the respondent, if provided, that the respondent presents a risk in the near future, including an imminent risk, of suicide or of causing physical injury to another person. The court may not include in the findings any mental health diagnosis or any connection between the risk presented by the respondent and mental illness.

(b) Upon making the findings described in paragraph (a) of this subsection, the court shall issue an extreme risk protection order prohibiting the respondent from having in the respondent's custody or control, owning, purchasing, possessing or receiving, or attempting to purchase or receive, a deadly weapon.

(7) An extreme risk protection order issued under this section must include:

(a) A statement of the evidence and the court's findings supporting issuance of the order;

(b) The date and time the order was issued;

(c) A description of the manner in which the respondent may request a hearing described in subsection (9) of this section;

(d) The address of the court to which a request for a hearing must be sent;

(e) A description of the requirements for surrender of deadly weapons in the respondent's possession under ORS 166.537; and

(f) A statement in substantially the following form:

To the subject of this protection order: An extreme risk protection order has been issued by the court and is now in effect. You are required to surrender all deadly weapons in your custody, control or possession. You may not have in your custody or control, purchase, possess, receive, or attempt to purchase or receive, deadly weapons while this order is in effect. You must, within 24 hours, surrender all deadly weapons in your custody, control or possession to (insert name of local law enforcement agency), a gun dealer or a third party who may lawfully possess the deadly weapons. You must, within 24 hours, surrender to (insert name of local law enforcement agency) any concealed handgun license issued to you. You may request a hearing to contest this order. If you do not request a hearing, the extreme risk protection order against you will be in effect for one year unless terminated by the court. You have the right to request one hearing to terminate this order during the 12 months that this order is in effect starting from the date of this order. You may seek the advice of an attorney as to any matter connected with this order.

---

(8)(a) The respondent shall be personally served with both a copy of the extreme risk protection order and a hearing request form described in subsection (9) of this section.

(b) Whenever an extreme risk protective order is served on a respondent, the person serving the order shall immediately deliver to the county sheriff a true copy of proof of service, on which it is stated that personal service of the order was made on the respondent, and a copy of the order. Proof of service may be made by affidavit or by declaration under penalty of perjury in the form required by ORCP 1 E.

(c) If the person serving the order cannot complete service within 10 days, the person shall notify the petitioner, at the address provided by the petitioner, that the documents have not been served. If the petitioner does not respond within 10 days, the person shall hold the order and petition for future service and file a return to the clerk of the court showing that service was not completed.

(d) Upon receipt of a copy of the order and notice of completion of service by a member of a law enforcement agency, the county sheriff shall immediately enter the order into the Law Enforcement Data System maintained by the

Department of State Police and request that the order be entered into the databases of the National Crime Information Center of the United States Department of Justice. If the order was served on the respondent by a person other than a member of a law enforcement agency, the county sheriff shall enter the order into the Law Enforcement Data System, and shall request that the information be entered into the databases of the National Crime Information Center, upon receipt of a true copy of proof of service. The sheriff shall provide the petitioner with a true copy of the proof of service. Entry into the Law Enforcement Data System constitutes notice to all law enforcement agencies of the existence of the order. Law enforcement agencies shall establish procedures adequate to ensure that an officer at the scene of an alleged violation of the order may be informed of the existence and terms of the order. The order is fully enforceable in any county in this state.

(9)(a) Within 30 days after an extreme risk protection order is served on the respondent under this section, the respondent may request a court hearing using a form prescribed by the State Court Administrator.

(b) If the respondent requests a hearing under paragraph (a) of this subsection, the clerk of the court shall notify the petitioner and the respondent of the date and time of the hearing and shall supply the petitioner with a copy of the respondent's request for a hearing. The petitioner and the respondent shall give to the clerk of the court information sufficient to allow such notification.

(c) The hearing shall occur within 21 days of the date of the respondent's request for a hearing.

(10) If the respondent fails to request a hearing within 30 days after an extreme risk protection order is served, the protection order is confirmed by operation of law and is effective for a period of one year from the date the original order was issued or until the order is terminated, whichever is sooner.

(11) A filing fee, service fee or hearing fee may not be charged for proceedings under this section or ORS 166.530 or 166.533.

(12) If the court declines to issue an extreme risk protection order under this section, the court shall state with particularity the reasons for the denial on the record. [2017 c.737 §2]

166.530 Hearing on order; continuation or termination of order. (1) At a hearing on an extreme risk protection order requested by the respondent under ORS 166.527 (9), the court may:

(a) Examine under oath the petitioner, the respondent and any witness either party may produce, including a mental health professional selected by the respondent, or, in lieu of examination, consider sworn affidavits of the petitioner, the respondent or a witness of either party; and

(b) Ensure that a reasonable search has been conducted for criminal history records related to the respondent.

(2)(a) The Oregon Evidence Code shall apply in a hearing under this section.

(b) The court may continue a hearing under this section upon a showing of good cause. If the court continues a hearing under this paragraph, the extreme risk protection order shall remain in effect until the next hearing date.

(3)(a) At the hearing, the court shall determine:

(A) Whether to terminate the extreme risk protection order or continue the order for a duration of one year; and

(B) Whether any deadly weapons surrendered to a law enforcement agency pursuant to ORS 166.537 shall be returned to the respondent or retained by the law enforcement agency.

(b) The petitioner has the burden of proving, by clear and convincing evidence, that the respondent presents a risk in the near future, including an imminent risk, of suicide or of causing physical injury to another person.

(c) If the court finds that the petitioner has met the burden of proof, the court shall:

(A) Order that the extreme risk protection order continue for the duration of one year from the date the original order was issued.

(B) Order that any deadly weapons surrendered to a law enforcement agency pursuant to ORS 166.537 remain in the custody of the law enforcement agency while the order is in effect.

(d) The court may not include in findings made under this subsection any mental health diagnosis or any connection between the risk presented by the respondent and mental illness.

(4) An extreme risk protection order continued under this section must include:

(a) A statement of the evidence and the court's findings supporting issuance of the order;

(b) The date and time the order was issued;

(c) The date and time of the expiration of the order;

(d) A description of the requirements for surrender of deadly weapons in the respondent's possession under ORS 166.537; and

(e) A statement in substantially the following form:

To the subject of this protection order: This order is valid until the date and time noted above. If you have not done so already, you are required to surrender all deadly weapons in your custody. You must immediately surrender all deadly weapons in your custody, control or possession to (insert name of local law enforcement agency), a gun dealer or a third party who may lawfully possess the deadly weapons. You must immediately surrender to (insert name of local law enforcement agency) any concealed handgun license issued to you. You may not have in your custody or control, purchase, possess, receive, or attempt to purchase or receive, a deadly weapon while this order is in effect. You have the right to request one hearing to terminate this order during the 12 months that this order is in effect starting from the date of this order. You may seek the advice of an attorney as to any matter connected with this order.

_____

(5) When the court continues an extreme risk protection order under this section, the court shall inform the respondent that the respondent is entitled to request termination of the order in the manner described in ORS 166.533. The court shall provide the respondent with a form with which to request a termination hearing.

(6) The respondent need not be served if an order of the court indicates that the respondent appeared in person before the court.

(7) If the court terminates an extreme risk protection order after a hearing under this section:

(a) The court shall state with particularity the reasons for the termination on the record.

(b) The clerk of the court shall immediately deliver a copy of the termination order to the county sheriff with whom the original order was filed. Upon receipt of the termination order, the county sheriff shall promptly remove the original order from the Law Enforcement Data System and shall request that the order be removed from the databases of the National Crime Information Center of the United States Department of Justice. [2017 c.737 §3]

166.533 Hearing to terminate order. (1) The petitioner or the respondent of an extreme risk protection order issued or continued under ORS 166.527 or 166.530 may each submit a written request once during the 12-month effective period of the order, and once during any 12-month effective period of an order renewed under ORS 166.535, for a hearing to terminate the order. A hearing under this section is in addition to any hearing requested under ORS 166.527.

(2) Upon receipt of a request described in subsection (1) of this section, the court shall schedule a termination hearing and provide notice of the hearing to both parties at least five days before the hearing.

(3)(a) The person filing the termination request has the burden of proving, by clear and convincing evidence, that the respondent no longer presents a risk in the near future, including an imminent risk, of suicide or of causing physical injury to another person.

(b) The Oregon Evidence Code shall apply in a hearing under this section.

(c) The court may continue a hearing under this section upon a showing of good cause. If the court continues a hearing under this paragraph, the extreme risk protection order shall remain in effect until the next hearing date.

(4)(a) If the court finds that the petitioner has met the burden of proof as described in subsection (3) of this section, the court shall terminate the extreme risk protection order.

(b) The court may not include in findings made under this subsection any mental health diagnosis or any connection between the risk presented by the respondent and mental illness.

(5) When an extreme risk protection order is terminated by order of the court, the clerk of the court shall immediately deliver a copy of the termination order to the county sheriff with whom the original order was filed. Upon receipt of the termination order, the county sheriff shall promptly remove the original order from the Law Enforcement Data System and shall request that the order be removed from the databases of the National Crime Information Center of the United States Department of Justice. [2017 c.737 §4]

166.535 Renewal of order. (1) A law enforcement officer or a family or household member of a respondent, including but not limited to the law enforcement officer or family or household member who petitioned the court for the original extreme risk protection order issued under ORS 166.527, may request a renewal of the order within 90 days before the expiration date of the order by filing a written request with the court.

(2) Upon receipt of the request for renewal described in subsection (1) of this section, the court shall schedule a hearing and provide notice of the hearing to both parties at least 14 days before the hearing.

(3) At a hearing to determine whether to renew an extreme risk protection order under this section, the court may:

(a) Examine under oath the petitioner, the respondent and any witness either party may produce or, in lieu of examination, consider sworn affidavits of the petitioner, the respondent or a witness of either party; and

(b) Ensure that a reasonable search has been conducted for criminal history records related to the respondent.

(4) The person requesting the renewal of the extreme risk protection order has the burden of proving, by clear and convincing evidence, that the respondent continues to present a risk in the near future, including an imminent risk, of suicide or of causing physical injury to another person.

(5)(a) The Oregon Evidence Code shall apply in a hearing under this section.

(b) The court may continue a hearing under this section upon a showing of good cause. If the court continues a hearing under this paragraph, the original extreme risk protection order shall remain in effect until the next hearing date.

(c) The petitioner may appear in person or by electronic video transmission.

(6)(a) If the court finds that the petitioner has met the burden of proof, the court may renew the extreme risk protection order for a duration of up to one year.

(b) The court may not include in findings made under this subsection any mental health diagnosis or any connection between the risk presented by the respondent and mental illness.

(7) An extreme risk protection order renewed under this section must include:

(a) A statement of the evidence and the court's findings supporting issuance of the order;

198

(b) The date and time the order was issued;

(c) The date and time of the expiration of the order;

(d) A description of the requirements for surrender of deadly weapons in the respondent's possession under ORS 166.537; and

(e) A statement in substantially the following form:

To the subject of this protection order: This renewed order is valid until the date and time noted above. If you have not done so already, you are required to surrender all deadly weapons in your custody. You must immediately surrender all deadly weapons in your custody, control or possession to (insert name of local law enforcement agency), a gun dealer or a third party who may lawfully possess the deadly weapons. You must immediately surrender to (insert name of local law enforcement agency) any concealed handgun license issued to you. You may not have in your custody or control, purchase, possess, receive, or attempt to purchase or receive, a deadly weapon while this order is in effect. You have the right to request one hearing to terminate this renewed order every 12 months that this order is in effect, starting from the date of this order. You may seek the advice of an attorney as to any matter connected with this order.

---

(8) When the court renews an extreme risk protection order, the court shall inform the respondent that the respondent is entitled to request termination of the renewed order in the manner described in ORS 166.533. The court shall provide the respondent with a form with which to request a termination hearing.

(9)(a) Service of a renewed extreme risk protective order shall be made by personal delivery of a copy of the order to the respondent. The respondent need not be served if an order of the court indicates that the respondent appeared in person before the court.

(b) Whenever a renewed extreme risk protective order is served on a respondent, the person serving the order shall immediately deliver to the county sheriff a true copy of proof of service, on which it is stated that personal service of the order was made on the respondent, and a copy of the order. Proof of service may be made by affidavit or by declaration under penalty of perjury in the form required by ORCP 1 E.

(c) If service of the order is not required under paragraph (a) of this subsection, a copy of the order must be delivered to the sheriff by the court.

(d) Upon receipt of a copy of the order and notice of completion of any required service by a member of a law enforcement agency, the county sheriff shall immediately enter the order into the Law Enforcement Data System maintained by the Department of State Police and request that the order be entered into the databases of the National Crime Information Center of the United States Department of Justice. If the order was served on the respondent by a person other than a member of a law enforcement agency, the county sheriff shall enter the order into the Law Enforcement Data System and request that the order be entered into the databases of the National Crime Information Center upon receipt of a true copy of proof of service. The sheriff shall provide the petitioner with a true copy of any required proof of service. Entry into the Law Enforcement Data System constitutes notice to all law enforcement agencies of the existence of the order. Law enforcement agencies shall establish procedures adequate to ensure that an officer at the scene of an alleged violation of the order may be informed of the existence and terms of the order. The order is fully enforceable in any county in this state.

(10) If the court declines to renew an extreme risk protection order, the court shall state with particularity the reasons for the denial on the record.

(11) A renewed extreme risk protection order may be further renewed as described in this section. [2017 c.737 §5]

166.537 Surrender of deadly weapons pursuant to order. (1) Upon issuance of an extreme risk protection order under ORS 166.527, the court shall further order that the respondent:

(a) Within 24 hours surrender all deadly weapons in the respondent's custody, control or possession to a law enforcement agency, a gun dealer or a third party who may lawfully possess the deadly weapons; and

(b) Within 24 hours surrender to a law enforcement agency any concealed handgun license issued to the respondent under ORS 166.291 and 166.292.

(2) Upon continuance of an extreme risk protection order after a hearing under ORS 166.530, or renewal of an extreme risk protection order under ORS 166.535, the court shall further order that the respondent:

(a) Immediately surrender all deadly weapons in the respondent's custody, control or possession to a law enforcement agency, a gun dealer or a third party who may lawfully possess the deadly weapons; and

(b) Immediately surrender to a law enforcement agency any concealed handgun license issued to the respondent under ORS 166.291 and 166.292.

(3)(a) A law enforcement officer serving an extreme risk protection order issued under ORS 166.527 shall request that the respondent immediately surrender to the officer all deadly weapons in the respondent's custody, control or possession and any concealed handgun license issued to the respondent under ORS 166.291 and 166.292. The law enforcement officer shall take possession of all deadly weapons appearing to be in the custody, control or possession of the respondent that are surrendered by the respondent. If the respondent indicates an intention to surrender the deadly weapons to a gun dealer or a third party, the law enforcement officer shall request that the respondent identify the gun dealer or third party.

(b) A law enforcement officer serving an extreme risk protection order continued after a hearing under ORS 166.530, or renewed under ORS 166.535, shall request that the respondent immediately surrender to the officer all deadly weapons in the respondent's custody, control or possession and any concealed handgun license issued to the respondent under ORS 166.291 and 166.292. The officer may conduct any search permitted by law for deadly weapons in the custody, control or possession of the respondent and shall take possession of all deadly weapons appearing to be in the custody, control or possession of the respondent that are surrendered, in plain sight or discovered pursuant to a lawful search.

(4) At the time of the surrender of any deadly weapons or concealed handgun licenses under subsection (3) of this section, the law enforcement officer taking possession shall issue a receipt identifying all surrendered items and provide a copy of the receipt to the respondent. Within 72 hours after service of the order, the law enforcement officer serving the order shall file the original receipt with the court and shall ensure that the law enforcement agency employing the law enforcement officer retains a copy of the receipt.

(5) If a third party claims lawful ownership or right of possession of a deadly weapon surrendered pursuant to this section, the law enforcement agency may return the deadly weapon to the third party if the third party provides proof of lawful ownership or right of possession of the deadly weapon, in a sworn affidavit, affirms that:

(a) The third party may lawfully possess the deadly weapon;

(b) The third party did not consent to the prior possession of the deadly weapon by the respondent; and

(c) The third party will prevent the respondent from accessing or possessing the deadly weapon in the future. [2017 c.737 §6]

166.540 Return of surrendered deadly weapons. (1) If an extreme risk protection order is terminated or expires without renewal, a law enforcement agency holding any deadly weapon or concealed handgun license that has been surrendered pursuant to the order shall return the surrendered items as requested by the respondent of the order only after:

(a) Confirming through a criminal background check, if the deadly weapon is a firearm, that the respondent is legally eligible to own or possess firearms under state and federal law; and

(b) Confirming that the extreme risk protection order is no longer in effect.

(2) The owner of a deadly weapon, if the deadly weapon is a firearm, in the custody of a law enforcement agency pursuant to ORS 166.537 who does not wish to have the firearm returned is entitled to sell or transfer title of any firearm to a licensed gun dealer as defined in ORS 166.412, provided that the firearm is lawful to own or possess and the person has a legal right to transfer title of the firearm.

(3) A deadly weapon surrendered by a person pursuant to ORS 166.537 that remains unclaimed by the owner shall be disposed of in accordance with the law enforcement agency's policies and procedures for the disposal of deadly weapons in the agency's custody. [2017 c.737 §7]

166.543 Criminal penalties. (1) A person commits a Class A misdemeanor if:

(a) The person knowingly possesses a deadly weapon; and

(b) The person is prohibited from possessing deadly weapons pursuant to an extreme risk protection order:

(A) Issued after notice and a hearing under ORS 166.530;

(B) Confirmed by operation of law after the person failed to request a hearing under ORS 166.527 (9); or

(C) Renewed under ORS 166.535.

(2) A person convicted under subsection (1) of this section shall be prohibited from having in the person's custody or control, owning, purchasing, possessing or receiving, or attempting to purchase or receive, any firearms for a five-year period beginning when the extreme risk protection order expires or is terminated, or the judgment of conviction is entered, whichever occurs later.

(3) A person who files a petition for any extreme risk protection order under ORS 166.525 to 166.543 with the intent to harass the respondent, or knowing that the information in the petition is false, is guilty of a Class A misdemeanor. [2017 c.737 §8]

166.560 [1965 c.118 §1; repealed by 1971 c.743 §432]

166.610 [Repealed by 1971 c.743 §432]

166.620 [Repealed by 1963 c.94 §2]

DISCHARGING WEAPONS

166.630 Discharging weapon on or across highway, ocean shore recreation area or public utility facility. (1) Except as provided in ORS 166.220, any person is guilty of a violation who discharges or attempts to discharge any blowgun, bow and arrow, crossbow, air rifle or firearm:

(a) Upon or across any highway, railroad right of way or other public road in this state, or upon or across the ocean shore within the state recreation area as defined in ORS 390.605.

(b) At any public or railroad sign or signal or an electric power, communication, petroleum or natural gas transmission or distribution facility of a public utility, telecommunications utility or railroad within range of the weapon.

(2) Any blowgun, bow and arrow, crossbow, air rifle or firearm in the possession of the person that was used in committing a violation of this section may be confiscated and forfeited to the State of Oregon. This section does not prevent:

(a) The discharge of firearms by peace officers in the performance of their duty or by military personnel within the confines of a military reservation.

(b) The discharge of firearms by an employee of the United States Department of Agriculture acting within the scope of employment in the course of the lawful taking of wildlife.

(3) The hunting license revocation provided in ORS 497.415 is in addition to and not in lieu of the penalty and forfeiture provided in subsections (1) and (2) of this section.

(4) As used in this section:

(a) "Public sign" includes all signs, signals and markings placed or erected by authority of a public body.

(b) "Public utility" has the meaning given that term in ORS 164.365 (2).

(c) "Railroad" has the meaning given that term in ORS 824.020. [Amended by 1963 c.94 §1; 1969 c.501 §2; 1969 c.511 §4; 1973 c.196 §1; 1973 c.723 §118; 1981 c.900 §1; 1987 c.447 §113; 1991 c.797 §2; 2009 c.556 §7]

166.635 Discharging weapon or throwing objects at trains. (1) A person shall not knowingly throw an object at, drop an object on, or discharge a bow and arrow, air rifle, rifle, gun, revolver or other firearm at a railroad train, a person on a railroad train or a commodity being transported on a railroad train. This subsection does not prevent a peace officer or a railroad employee from performing the duty of a peace officer or railroad employee.

(2) Violation of subsection (1) of this section is a misdemeanor. [1973 c.139 §4]

166.638 Discharging weapon across airport operational surfaces. (1) Any person who knowingly or recklessly discharges any bow and arrow, gun, air gun or other firearm upon or across any airport operational surface commits a Class A misdemeanor. Any bow and arrow, gun, air gun or other firearm in the possession of the person that was used in committing a violation of this subsection may be confiscated and forfeited to the State of Oregon, and the clear proceeds shall be deposited with the State Treasury in the Common School Fund.

(2) As used in subsection (1) of this section, "airport operational surface" means any surface of land or water developed, posted or marked so as to give an observer reasonable notice that the surface is developed for the purpose of storing, parking, taxiing or operating aircraft, or any surface of land or water when actually being used for such purpose.

(3) Subsection (1) of this section does not prohibit the discharge of firearms by peace officers in the performance of their duty or by military personnel within the confines of a military reservation, or otherwise lawful hunting, wildlife control or other discharging of firearms done with the consent of the proprietor, manager or custodian of the airport operational surface.

(4) The hunting license revocation provided in ORS 497.415 is in addition to and not in lieu of the penalty provided in subsection (1) of this section. [1981 c.901 §2; 1987 c.858 §2]

166.640 [Repealed by 1971 c.743 §432]

POSSESSION OF BODY ARMOR

166.641 Definitions for ORS 166.641 to 166.643. As used in this section and ORS 166.642 and 166.643:

(1) "Body armor" means any clothing or equipment designed in whole or in part to minimize the risk of injury from a deadly weapon.

(2) "Deadly weapon" has the meaning given that term in ORS 161.015.

(3) "Misdemeanor involving violence" has the meaning given that term in ORS 166.470. [2001 c.635 §1]

166.642 Felon in possession of body armor. (1) A person commits the crime of felon in possession of body armor if the person:

(a) Has been convicted of a felony or misdemeanor involving violence under the law of any state or the United States; and

(b) Knowingly is in possession or control of body armor.

(2) Felon in possession of body armor is a Class C felony.

(3) For purposes of subsection (1) of this section, a person who has been found to be within the jurisdiction of a juvenile court for having committed an act that would constitute a felony or misdemeanor involving violence has been convicted of a felony or misdemeanor involving violence.

(4) Subsection (1) of this section does not apply to:

(a) A person who is wearing body armor provided by a peace officer for the person's safety or protection while the person is being transported or accompanied by a peace officer; or

(b) A person who has been convicted of only one felony under the law of this state or any other state, or who has been convicted of only one felony under the law of the United States, which felony did not involve criminal homicide, as defined in ORS 163.005, and who has been discharged from imprisonment, parole or probation for the offense for a period of 15 years prior to the date of the alleged violation of subsection (1) of this section.

(5) It is an affirmative defense to a charge of violating subsection (1) of this section that a protective order or restraining order has been entered to the benefit of the person. The affirmative defense created by this subsection is not available if the person possesses the body armor while committing or attempting to commit a crime. [2001 c.635 §2]

166.643 Unlawful possession of body armor. (1) A person commits the crime of unlawful possession of body armor if the person, while committing or attempting to commit a felony or misdemeanor involving violence, knowingly:
(a) Wears body armor; and
(b) Possesses a deadly weapon.
(2) Unlawful possession of body armor is a Class B felony. [2001 c.635 §3]

MISCELLANEOUS

166.645 Hunting in cemeteries prohibited. (1) Hunting in cemeteries is prohibited.
(2) As used in subsection (1) of this section "hunting" has the meaning for that term provided in ORS 496.004.
(3) Violation of subsection (1) of this section is a misdemeanor. [1973 c.468 §2; 1987 c.158 §30]

166.649 Throwing an object off an overpass in the second degree. (1) A person commits the crime of throwing an object off an overpass in the second degree if the person:
(a) With criminal negligence throws an object off an overpass; and
(b) Knows, or reasonably should have known, that the object was of a type or size to cause damage to any person or vehicle that the object might hit.
(2) Throwing an object off an overpass in the second degree is a Class A misdemeanor.
(3) As used in this section and ORS 166.651, "overpass" means a structure carrying a roadway or pedestrian pathway over a roadway. [1993 c.731 §1]

166.650 [Repealed by 1971 c.743 §432]

166.651 Throwing an object off an overpass in the first degree. (1) A person commits the crime of throwing an object off an overpass in the first degree if the person:
(a) Recklessly throws an object off an overpass; and
(b) Knows, or reasonably should have known, that the object was of a type or size to cause damage to any person or vehicle that the object might hit.
(2) Throwing an object off an overpass in the first degree is a Class C felony. [1993 c.731 §2]

166.660 Unlawful paramilitary activity. (1) A person commits the crime of unlawful paramilitary activity if the person:
(a) Exhibits, displays or demonstrates to another person the use, application or making of any firearm, explosive or incendiary device or any technique capable of causing injury or death to persons and intends or knows that such firearm, explosive or incendiary device or technique will be unlawfully employed for use in a civil disorder; or
(b) Assembles with one or more other persons for the purpose of training with, practicing with or being instructed in the use of any firearm, explosive or incendiary device or technique capable of causing injury or death to persons with the intent to unlawfully employ such firearm, explosive or incendiary device or technique in a civil disorder.
(2)(a) Nothing in this section makes unlawful any act of any law enforcement officer performed in the otherwise lawful performance of the officer's official duties.
(b) Nothing in this section makes unlawful any activity of the State Department of Fish and Wildlife, or any activity intended to teach or practice self-defense or self-defense techniques, such as karate clubs or self-defense clinics, and similar lawful activity, or any facility, program or lawful activity related to firearms instruction and training intended to teach the safe handling and use of firearms, or any other lawful sports or activities related to the individual recreational use or possession of firearms, including but not limited to hunting activities, target shooting, self-defense, firearms collection or any organized activity including, but not limited to any hunting club, rifle club, rifle range or shooting range which does not include a conspiracy as defined in ORS 161.450 or the knowledge of or the intent to cause or further a civil disorder.
(3) Unlawful paramilitary activity is a Class C felony.
(4) As used in this section:
(a) "Civil disorder" means acts of physical violence by assemblages of three or more persons which cause damage or injury, or immediate danger thereof, to the person or property of any other individual.
(b) "Firearm" has the meaning given that term in ORS 166.210.

(c) "Explosive" means a chemical compound, mixture or device that is commonly used or intended for the purpose of producing a chemical reaction resulting in a substantially instantaneous release of gas and heat, including but not limited to dynamite, blasting powder, nitroglycerin, blasting caps and nitrojelly, but excluding fireworks as defined in ORS 480.111, black powder, smokeless powder, small arms ammunition and small arms ammunition primers.

(d) "Law enforcement officer" means any duly constituted police officer of the United States, any state, any political subdivision of a state or the District of Columbia, and also includes members of the military reserve forces or National Guard as defined in 10 U.S.C. 101 (9), members of the organized militia of any state or territory of the United States, the Commonwealth of Puerto Rico or the District of Columbia not included within the definition of National Guard as defined by 10 U.S.C. 101 (9), members of the Armed Forces of the United States and such persons as are defined in ORS 161.015 (4) when in the performance of official duties. [1983 c.792 §2; 1987 c.858 §3; 2001 c.666 §§26,38; 2005 c.830 §27; 2009 c.610 §7; 2013 c.24 §12]

166.663 Casting artificial light from vehicle while possessing certain weapons prohibited. (1) A person may not cast from a motor vehicle an artificial light while there is in the possession or in the immediate physical presence of the person a bow and arrow or a firearm.

(2) Subsection (1) of this section does not apply to a person casting an artificial light:

(a) From the headlights of a motor vehicle that is being operated on a road in the usual manner.

(b) When the bow and arrow or firearm that the person has in the possession or immediate physical presence of the person is disassembled or stored, or in the trunk or storage compartment of the motor vehicle.

(c) When the ammunition or arrows are stored separate from the weapon.

(d) On land owned or lawfully occupied by that person.

(e) On publicly owned land when that person has an agreement with the public body to use that property.

(f) When the person is a peace officer, or is a government employee engaged in the performance of official duties.

(g) When the person has been issued a license under ORS 166.291 and 166.292 to carry a concealed handgun.

(h) When the person is an honorably retired law enforcement officer, unless the person has been convicted of an offense that would make the person ineligible to obtain a concealed handgun license under ORS 166.291 and 166.292.

(3) A peace officer may issue a citation to a person for a violation of subsection (1) of this section when the violation is committed in the presence of the peace officer or when the peace officer has probable cause to believe that a violation has occurred based on a description of the vehicle or other information received from a peace officer who observed the violation.

(4) Violation of subsection (1) of this section is punishable as a Class B violation.

(5) As used in this section, "peace officer" has the meaning given that term in ORS 161.015. [1989 c.848 §2; 1999 c.1051 §159; 2005 c.22 §116; 2009 c.610 §3; 2015 c.709 §5]

166.710 [1957 c.601 §1; repealed by 1971 c.743 §432]

RACKETEERING

166.715 Definitions for ORS 166.715 to 166.735. As used in ORS 166.715 to 166.735, unless the context requires otherwise:

(1) "Documentary material" means any book, paper, document, writing, drawing, graph, chart, photograph, phonograph record, magnetic tape, computer printout, other data compilation from which information can be obtained or from which information can be translated into usable form, or other tangible item.

(2) "Enterprise" includes any individual, sole proprietorship, partnership, corporation, business trust or other profit or nonprofit legal entity, and includes any union, association or group of individuals associated in fact although not a legal entity, and both illicit and licit enterprises and governmental and nongovernmental entities.

(3) "Investigative agency" means the Department of Justice or any district attorney.

(4) "Pattern of racketeering activity" means engaging in at least two incidents of racketeering activity that have the same or similar intents, results, accomplices, victims or methods of commission or otherwise are interrelated by distinguishing characteristics, including a nexus to the same enterprise, and are not isolated incidents, provided at least one of such incidents occurred after November 1, 1981, and that the last of such incidents occurred within five years after a prior incident of racketeering activity. Notwithstanding ORS 131.505 to 131.525 or 419A.190 or any other provision of law providing that a previous prosecution is a bar to a subsequent prosecution, conduct that constitutes an incident of racketeering activity may be used to establish a pattern of racketeering activity without regard to whether the conduct previously has been the subject of a criminal prosecution or conviction or a juvenile court adjudication, unless the prosecution resulted in an acquittal or the adjudication resulted in entry of an order finding the youth not to be within the jurisdiction of the juvenile court.

(5) "Person" means any individual or entity capable of holding a legal or beneficial interest in real or personal property.

(6) "Racketeering activity" includes conduct of a person committed both before and after the person attains the age of 18 years, and means to commit, to attempt to commit, to conspire to commit, or to solicit, coerce or intimidate another person to commit:

(a) Any conduct that constitutes a crime, as defined in ORS 161.515, under any of the following provisions of the Oregon Revised Statutes:

(A) ORS 59.005 to 59.505, 59.710 to 59.830, 59.991 and 59.995, relating to securities;

(B) ORS 162.015, 162.025 and 162.065 to 162.085, relating to bribery and perjury;

(C) ORS 162.235, 162.265 to 162.305, 162.325, 162.335, 162.355 and 162.365, relating to obstructing governmental administration;

(D) ORS 162.405 to 162.425, relating to abuse of public office;

(E) ORS 162.455, relating to interference with legislative operation;

(F) ORS 163.095 to 163.115, 163.118, 163.125 and 163.145, relating to criminal homicide;

(G) ORS 163.160 to 163.205, relating to assault and related offenses;

(H) ORS 163.225 and 163.235, relating to kidnapping;

(I) ORS 163.275, relating to coercion;

(J) ORS 163.665 to 163.693, relating to sexual conduct of children;

(K) ORS 164.015, 164.043, 164.045, 164.055, 164.057, 164.075 to 164.095, 164.098, 164.125, 164.135, 164.140, 164.215, 164.225 and 164.245 to 164.270, relating to theft, burglary, criminal trespass and related offenses;

(L) ORS 164.315 to 164.335, relating to arson and related offenses;

(M) ORS 164.345 to 164.365, relating to criminal mischief;

(N) ORS 164.395 to 164.415, relating to robbery;

(O) ORS 164.865, 164.875 and 164.868 to 164.872, relating to unlawful recording or labeling of a recording;

(P) ORS 165.007 to 165.022, 165.032 to 165.042 and 165.055 to 165.070, relating to forgery and related offenses;

(Q) ORS 165.080 to 165.109, relating to business and commercial offenses;

(R) ORS 165.540 and 165.555, relating to communication crimes;

(S) ORS 166.180, 166.190, 166.220, 166.250, 166.270, 166.275, 166.410, 166.450 and 166.470, relating to firearms and other weapons;

(T) ORS 164.377 (2) to (4), as punishable under ORS 164.377 (5)(b), 167.007 to 167.017, 167.057, 167.062 to 167.080, 167.090, 167.122 to 167.137, 167.147, 167.164, 167.167, 167.212, 167.355, 167.365, 167.370, 167.428, 167.431 and 167.439, relating to prostitution, obscenity, sexual conduct, gambling, computer crimes involving the Oregon State Lottery, animal fighting, forcible recovery of a fighting bird and related offenses;

(U) ORS 171.990, relating to legislative witnesses;

(V) ORS 260.575 and 260.665, relating to election offenses;

(W) ORS 314.075, relating to income tax;

(X) ORS 180.440 (2) and 180.486 (2) and ORS chapter 323, relating to cigarette and tobacco products taxes and the directories developed under ORS 180.425 and 180.477;

(Y) ORS 411.630, 411.675, 411.690 and 411.840, relating to public assistance payments or medical assistance benefits, and ORS 411.990 (2) and (3);

(Z) ORS 462.140, 462.415 and 462.420 to 462.520, relating to racing;

(AA) ORS 463.995, relating to entertainment wrestling and unarmed combat sports, as defined in ORS 463.015;

(BB) ORS 471.305, 471.360, 471.392 to 471.400, 471.403, 471.404, 471.405, 471.425, 471.442, 471.445, 471.446, 471.485, 471.490 and 471.675, relating to alcoholic liquor, and any of the provisions of ORS chapter 471 relating to licenses issued under the Liquor Control Act;

(CC) ORS 475B.010 to 475B.545, relating to marijuana items as defined in ORS 475B.015;

(DD) ORS 475.005 to 475.285 and 475.752 to 475.980, relating to controlled substances;

(EE) ORS 480.070, 480.210, 480.215, 480.235 and 480.265, relating to explosives;

(FF) ORS 819.010, 819.040, 822.100, 822.135 and 822.150, relating to motor vehicles;

(GG) ORS 658.452 or 658.991 (2) to (4), relating to labor contractors;

(HH) ORS chapter 706, relating to banking law administration;

(II) ORS chapter 714, relating to branch banking;

(JJ) ORS chapter 716, relating to mutual savings banks;

(KK) ORS chapter 723, relating to credit unions;

(LL) ORS chapter 726, relating to pawnbrokers;

(MM) ORS 166.382 and 166.384, relating to destructive devices;

(NN) ORS 165.074;

(OO) ORS 86A.095 to 86A.198, relating to mortgage bankers and mortgage brokers;

(PP) ORS chapter 496, 497 or 498, relating to wildlife;

(QQ) ORS 163.355 to 163.427, relating to sexual offenses;

(RR) ORS 166.015, relating to riot;

(SS) ORS 166.155 and 166.165, relating to intimidation;

(TT) ORS chapter 696, relating to real estate and escrow;

(UU) ORS chapter 704, relating to outfitters and guides;

(VV) ORS 165.692, relating to making a false claim for health care payment;

(WW) ORS 162.117, relating to public investment fraud;

(XX) ORS 164.170 or 164.172;

(YY) ORS 647.140, 647.145 or 647.150, relating to trademark counterfeiting;

(ZZ) ORS 164.886;

(AAA) ORS 167.312 and 167.388;

(BBB) ORS 164.889;

(CCC) ORS 165.800; or

(DDD) ORS 163.263, 163.264 or 163.266.

(b) Any conduct defined as "racketeering activity" under 18 U.S.C. 1961 (1)(B), (C), (D) and (E).

(7) "Unlawful debt" means any money or other thing of value constituting principal or interest of a debt that is legally unenforceable in the state in whole or in part because the debt was incurred or contracted:

(a) In violation of any one of the following:

(A) ORS chapter 462, relating to racing;

(B) ORS 167.108 to 167.164, relating to gambling; or

(C) ORS 82.010 to 82.170, relating to interest and usury.

(b) In gambling activity in violation of federal law or in the business of lending money at a rate usurious under federal or state law.

(8) Notwithstanding contrary provisions in ORS 174.060, when this section references a statute in the Oregon Revised Statutes that is substantially different in the nature of its essential provisions from what the statute was when this section was enacted, the reference shall extend to and include amendments to the statute. [1981 c.769 §2; 1983 c.338 §898; 1983 c.715 §1; 1985 c.176 §5; 1985 c.557 §8; 1987 c.158 §31; 1987 c.249 §7; 1987 c.789 §20; 1987 c.907 §12; 1989 c.384 §2; 1989 c.839 §27; 1989 c.846 §13; 1989 c.982 §6; 1991 c.398 §3; 1991 c.962 §6; 1993 c.95 §13; 1993 c.215 §1; 1993 c.508 §45; 1993 c.680 §29; 1995 c.301 §35; 1995 c.440 §13; 1995 c.768 §10; 1997 c.631 §420; 1997 c.789 §1; 1997 c.867 §23; 1999 c.722 §8; 1999 c.878 §4; 2001 c.146 §1; 2001 c.147 §3; 2003 c.111 §1; 2003 c.484 §8; 2003 c.801 §15; 2003 c.804 §66; 2007 c.498 §3; 2007 c.585 §26; 2007 c.811 §7; 2007 c.869 §7; 2009 c.717 §25; 2011 c.597 §166; 2011 c.681 §6; 2013 c.584 §27; 2013 c.688 §23; 2017 c.21 §46; 2017 c.235 §21]

166.720 Racketeering activity unlawful; penalties. (1) It is unlawful for any person who has knowingly received any proceeds derived, directly or indirectly, from a pattern of racketeering activity or through the collection of an unlawful debt to use or invest, whether directly or indirectly, any part of such proceeds, or the proceeds derived from the investment or use thereof, in the acquisition of any title to, or any right, interest or equity in, real property or in the establishment or operation of any enterprise.

(2) It is unlawful for any person, through a pattern of racketeering activity or through the collection of an unlawful debt, to acquire or maintain, directly or indirectly, any interest in or control of any real property or enterprise.

(3) It is unlawful for any person employed by, or associated with, any enterprise to conduct or participate, directly or indirectly, in such enterprise through a pattern of racketeering activity or the collection of an unlawful debt.

(4) It is unlawful for any person to conspire or endeavor to violate any of the provisions of subsections (1), (2) or (3) of this section.

(5)(a) Any person convicted of engaging in activity in violation of the provisions of subsections (1) to (4) of this section is guilty of a Class A felony.

(b) In lieu of a fine otherwise authorized by law, any person convicted of engaging in conduct in violation of the provisions of subsections (1) to (4) of this section, through which the person derived a pecuniary value, or by which the person caused personal injury or property damage or other loss, may be sentenced to pay a fine that does not exceed three times the gross value gained or three times the gross loss caused, whichever is greater, plus court costs and the costs of investigation and prosecution, reasonably incurred.

(c) The court shall hold a hearing to determine the amount of the fine authorized by paragraph (b) of this subsection.

(d) For the purposes of paragraph (b) of this subsection, "pecuniary value" means:

(A) Anything of value in the form of money, a negotiable instrument, a commercial interest or anything else the primary significance of which is economic advantage; or

(B) Any other property or service that has a value in excess of $100.

(6) An allegation of a pattern of racketeering activity is sufficient if it contains substantially the following:

(a) A statement of the acts constituting each incident of racketeering activity in ordinary and concise language, and in a manner that enables a person of common understanding to know what is intended;

(b) A statement of the relation to each incident of racketeering activity that the conduct was committed on or about a designated date, or during a designated period of time;

(c) A statement, in the language of ORS 166.715 (4) or other ordinary and concise language, designating which distinguishing characteristic or characteristics interrelate the incidents of racketeering activity; and

(d) A statement that the incidents alleged were not isolated. [1981 c.769 §§3,4; 1997 c.789 §2]

166.725 Remedies for violation of ORS 166.720; time limitation. (1) Any circuit court may, after making due provision for the rights of innocent persons, enjoin violations of the provisions of ORS 166.720 (1) to (4) by issuing appropriate orders and judgments, including, but not limited to:

(a) Ordering a divestiture by the defendant of any interest in any enterprise, including real property.

(b) Imposing reasonable restrictions upon the future activities or investments of any defendant, including, but not limited to, prohibiting any defendant from engaging in the same type of endeavor as the enterprise in which the defendant was engaged in violation of the provisions of ORS 166.720 (1) to (4).

(c) Ordering the dissolution or reorganization of any enterprise.

(d) Ordering the suspension or revocation of a license, permit or prior approval granted to any enterprise by any agency of the state.

(e) Ordering the forfeiture of the charter of a corporation organized under the laws of this state, or the revocation of a certificate of authority authorizing a foreign corporation to conduct business within this state, upon finding that the board of directors or a managerial agent acting on behalf of the corporation, in conducting the affairs of the corporation, has authorized or engaged in conduct in violation of ORS 166.720 (1) to (4) and that, for the prevention of future criminal activity, the public interest requires the charter of the corporation forfeited and the corporation dissolved or the certificate of authority revoked.

(2) All property, real or personal, including money, used in the course of, derived from or realized through conduct in violation of a provision of ORS 166.715 to 166.735 is subject to civil forfeiture to the state. The state shall dispose of all forfeited property as soon as commercially feasible. If property is not exercisable or transferable for value by the state, it shall expire. All forfeitures or dispositions under this section shall be made with due provision for the rights of innocent persons. Forfeited property shall be distributed as follows:

(a)(A) All moneys and the clear proceeds of all other property forfeited shall be deposited with the State Treasurer to the credit of the Common School Fund.

(B) For purposes of subparagraph (A) of this paragraph, "clear proceeds" means proceeds of forfeited property less costs of maintaining and preserving property pending its sale or other disposition, less costs of sale or disposition and, if the Department of Justice has not otherwise recovered its costs and expenses of the investigation and prosecution leading to the forfeiture, less 30 percent of the remaining proceeds of the property which is awarded to the department as reasonable reimbursement for costs of such investigation and prosecution.

(b) Any amounts awarded to the Department of Justice pursuant to paragraph (a) of this subsection shall be deposited in the Criminal Justice Revolving Account in the State Treasury.

(3) Property subject to forfeiture under this section may be seized by a police officer, as defined in ORS 133.525 (2), upon court process. Seizure without process may be made if:

(a) The seizure is incident to a lawful arrest or search or an inspection under an administrative inspection warrant; or

(b) The property subject to seizure has been the subject of a prior judgment in favor of the state in a forfeiture proceeding based upon this section.

(4) In the event of a seizure under subsection (3) of this section, a forfeiture proceeding shall be instituted promptly. Property taken or detained under this section shall not be subject to replevin, but is deemed to be in the custody of the police officer making the seizure, subject only to the order of the court. When property is seized under this section, pending forfeiture and final disposition, the police officer may:

(a) Place the property under seal;

(b) Remove the property to a place designated by the court; or

(c) Require another agency authorized by law to take custody of the property and remove it to an appropriate location.

(5) The Attorney General, any district attorney or any state agency having jurisdiction over conduct in violation of a provision of ORS 166.715 to 166.735 may institute civil proceedings under this section. In any action brought under this section, the circuit court shall give priority to the hearing and determination. Pending final determination, the circuit court may at any time enter such injunctions, prohibitions or restraining orders, or take such actions, including the acceptance of satisfactory performance bonds, as the court may deem proper. The Attorney General, district attorney or state agency bringing an action under this section may be awarded, upon entry of a judgment in favor of the state, costs of investigation and litigation, reasonably incurred. Amounts recovered may include costs and expenses of state and local governmental departments and agencies incurred in connection with the investigation or litigation.

(6)(a) Any aggrieved person may institute a proceeding under subsection (1) of this section:

(A) If the proceeding is based upon racketeering activity for which a criminal conviction has been obtained, any rights of appeal have expired and the action is against the individual convicted of the racketeering activity; or

(B) If the person is entitled to pursue a cause of action under subsection (7)(a)(B) of this section.

(b) In such proceeding, relief shall be granted in conformity with the principles that govern the granting of injunctive relief from threatened loss or damage in other civil cases, except that no showing of special or irreparable damage to the person shall have to be made. Upon the execution of proper bond against damages for an injunction improvidently granted and a showing of immediate danger of significant loss or damage, a temporary restraining order and a preliminary injunction may be issued in any such action before a final determination on the merits.

(7)(a) Any person who is injured by reason of any violation of the provisions of ORS 166.720 (1) to (4) shall have a cause of action for three-fold the actual damages sustained and, when appropriate, punitive damages:

(A) If a criminal conviction for the racketeering activity that is the basis of the violation has been obtained, any rights of appeal have expired and the action is against the individual convicted of the racketeering activity; or

(B) If the violation is based on racketeering activity as defined in ORS 166.715 (6)(a)(B) to (J), (K) as it relates to burglary and criminal trespass, (L) to (P), (S), (T), (U), (V), (X) to (Z), (AA) to (EE), (LL), (MM) or (PP) to (WW).

(b) The defendant or any injured person may demand a trial by jury in any civil action brought pursuant to this subsection.

(c) Any injured person shall have a right or claim to forfeited property or to the proceeds derived therefrom superior to any right or claim the state has in the same property or proceeds.

(8) An investigative agency may bring an action for civil penalties for any violation of ORS 166.720 (1) to (4). Upon proof of any such violation, the court shall impose a civil penalty of not more than $250,000.

(9) A judgment rendered in favor of the state in any criminal proceeding under ORS 166.715 to 166.735 shall estop the defendant in any subsequent civil action or proceeding brought by the state or any other person as to all matters as to which such judgment would be an estoppel as between the state and the defendant.

(10) The Attorney General may, upon timely application, intervene in any civil action or proceeding brought under subsection (6) or (7) of this section if the Attorney General certifies that, in the opinion of the Attorney General, the action or proceeding is of general public importance. In such action or proceeding, the state shall be entitled to the same relief as if the Attorney General instituted the action or proceeding.

(11)(a) Notwithstanding any other provision of law, a criminal or civil action or proceeding under ORS 166.715 to 166.735 may be commenced at any time within five years after the conduct in violation of a provision of ORS 166.715 to 166.735 terminates or the cause of action accrues. If a criminal prosecution or civil action or other proceeding is brought, or intervened in, to punish, prevent or restrain any violation of the provisions of ORS 166.715 to 166.735, the running of the period of limitations prescribed by this section with respect to any cause of action arising under subsection (6) or (7) of this section which is based in whole or in part upon any matter complained of in any such prosecution, action or proceeding shall be suspended during the pendency of such prosecution, action or proceeding and for two years following its termination.

(b) A cause of action arising under subsection (6)(a)(A) or (7)(a)(A) of this section accrues when the criminal conviction for the underlying activity is obtained. In addition to any suspension of the running of the period of limitations provided for in paragraph (a) of this subsection, the period of limitations prescribed by paragraph (a) of this subsection is suspended during any appeal from the criminal conviction for the underlying activity.

(12) The application of one civil remedy under any provision of ORS 166.715 to 166.735 shall not preclude the application of any other remedy, civil or criminal, under ORS 166.715 to 166.735 or any other provision of law. Civil remedies under ORS 166.715 to 166.735 are supplemental and not mutually exclusive.

(13) Notwithstanding subsection (6) or (7) of this section, a person may not institute a proceeding under subsection (6) of this section and does not have a cause of action under subsection (7) of this section if the conduct that is the basis of the proceeding or action could also be the basis of a claim of discrimination because of sex that constitutes sexual harassment.

(14) In an action brought under the provisions of this section by a person other than the Attorney General, a district attorney or a state agency, the court may award reasonable attorney fees to the prevailing party. In a civil action brought under the provisions of this section by the Attorney General, a district attorney or a state agency:

(a) The court may award reasonable attorney fees to the Attorney General, district attorney or state agency if the Attorney General, district attorney or state agency prevails in the action; and

(b) The court may award reasonable attorney fees to a defendant who prevails in an action under this section if the court determines that the Attorney General, district attorney or state agency had no objectively reasonable basis for asserting the claim or no reasonable basis for appealing an adverse decision of the trial court. [1981 c.769 §5; 1983 c.715 §2; 1995 c.79 §54; 1995 c.618 §58a; 1995 c.619 §1; 1995 c.696 §17; 1997 c.249 §51; 1997 c.789 §3; 2003 c.576 §390; 2007 c.869 §8; 2017 c.21 §101]

166.730 Authority of investigative agency; compelling compliance with subpoena. (1) If, pursuant to the civil enforcement provisions of ORS 166.725, an investigative agency has reason to believe that a person or other enterprise has engaged in, or is engaging in, activity in violation of ORS 166.715 to 166.735, the investigative agency may administer oaths or affirmations, subpoena witnesses or documents or other material, and collect evidence pursuant to the Oregon Rules of Civil Procedure.

(2) If matter that the investigative agency seeks to obtain by the subpoena is located outside the state, the person or enterprise subpoenaed may make such matter available to the investigative agency or its representative for examination at the place where such matter is located. The investigative agency may designate representatives, including officials of the jurisdiction in which the matter is located, to inspect the matter on its behalf and may respond to similar requests from officials of other jurisdictions.

(3) Upon failure of a person or enterprise, without lawful excuse, to obey a subpoena, and after reasonable notice to such person or enterprise, the investigative agency may apply to the circuit court for the judicial district in which

such person or enterprise resides, is found or transacts business for an order compelling compliance. [1981 c.769 §6; 1983 c.715 §3]

166.735 Short title; construction. (1) ORS 166.715 to 166.735 may be cited as the Oregon Racketeer Influenced and Corrupt Organization Act.

(2) The provisions of ORS 166.715 to 166.735 shall be liberally construed to effectuate its remedial purposes. [1981 c.769 §§1,7; 1983 c.715 §4]

Chapter 167 — Offenses Against General Welfare and Animals

PROSTITUTION AND RELATED OFFENSES

167.002 Definitions for ORS 167.002 to 167.027. As used in ORS 167.002 to 167.027, unless the context requires otherwise:

(1) "Place of prostitution" means any place where prostitution is practiced.

(2) "Prostitute" means a male or female person who engages in sexual conduct or sexual contact for a fee.

(3) "Prostitution enterprise" means an arrangement whereby two or more prostitutes are organized to conduct prostitution activities.

(4) "Sexual conduct" means sexual intercourse or oral or anal sexual intercourse.

(5) "Sexual contact" means any touching of the sexual organs or other intimate parts of a person not married to the actor for the purpose of arousing or gratifying the sexual desire of either party. [1971 c.743 §249; 1973 c.699 §5; 2017 c.318 §14]

167.005 [Repealed by 1971 c.743 §432]

167.007 Prostitution. (1) A person commits the crime of prostitution if the person engages in, or offers or agrees to engage in, sexual conduct or sexual contact in return for a fee.

(2) Prostitution is a Class A misdemeanor.

(3) It is an affirmative defense to prosecution under this section that the defendant, at the time of the alleged offense, was a victim of the crime of trafficking in persons as described in ORS 163.266 (1)(b) or (c). [1971 c.743 §250; 1973 c.52 §1; 1973 c.699 §6; 2011 c.151 §1; 2017 c.246 §1]

167.008 Commercial sexual solicitation. (1) A person commits the crime of commercial sexual solicitation if the person pays, or offers or agrees to pay, a fee to engage in sexual conduct or sexual contact.

(2) Commercial sexual solicitation is a Class A misdemeanor. [2011 c.151 §3; 2013 c.720 §2; 2015 c.98 §1]

167.010 [Repealed by 1971 c.743 §432]

167.012 Promoting prostitution. (1) A person commits the crime of promoting prostitution if, with intent to promote prostitution, the person knowingly:

(a) Owns, controls, manages, supervises or otherwise maintains a place of prostitution or a prostitution enterprise;

(b) Induces or causes a person to engage in prostitution or to remain in a place of prostitution;

(c) Receives or agrees to receive money, goods, property, services or something else of value, other than as a prostitute being compensated for personally rendered prostitution services, pursuant to an agreement or understanding that the money, goods, property, services or something else of value is derived from a prostitution activity; or

(d) Engages in any conduct that institutes, aids or facilitates an act or enterprise of prostitution.

(2) Promoting prostitution is a Class C felony. [1971 c.743 §251; 2016 c.10 §1]

167.015 [Repealed by 1971 c.743 §432]

167.017 Compelling prostitution. (1) A person commits the crime of compelling prostitution if the person knowingly:

(a) Uses force or intimidation to compel another to engage in prostitution or attempted prostitution;

(b) Induces or causes a person under 18 years of age to engage in prostitution;

(c) Aids or facilitates the commission of prostitution or attempted prostitution by a person under 18 years of age; or

(d) Induces or causes the spouse, child or stepchild of the person to engage in prostitution.

(2) Compelling prostitution is a Class B felony.

(3) In a prosecution under subsection (1)(b) or (c) of this section, the state is not required to prove that the defendant knew the other person was under 18 years of age and it is no defense that the defendant did not know the person's age or that the defendant reasonably believed the person to be older than 18 years of age. [1971 c.743 §252; 2011 c.334 §1; 2013 c.271 §1]

167.020 [Repealed by 1971 c.743 §432]

167.022 [1971 c.743 §253; repealed by 1979 c.248 §1]

167.025 [Repealed by 1971 c.743 §432]

167.027 Evidence required to show place of prostitution. (1) On the issue of whether a place is a place of prostitution as defined in ORS 167.002, its general repute and repute of persons who reside in or frequent the place shall be competent evidence.

(2) Notwithstanding ORS 136.655, in any prosecution under ORS 167.012 and 167.017, spouses are competent and compellable witnesses for or against either party. [1971 c.743 §254]

167.030 [Repealed by 1971 c.743 §432]

167.035 [Repealed by 1971 c.743 §432]

167.040 [Repealed by 1971 c.743 §432]

167.045 [1953 c.641 §§1,7; 1955 c.636 §6; repealed by 1971 c.743 §432]

167.050 [1953 c.641 §7; 1955 c.636 §7; 1963 c.353 §1; repealed by 1971 c.743 §432]

OBSCENITY AND RELATED OFFENSES

167.051 Definitions for ORS 167.057. As used in ORS 167.057:
(1) "Furnishes" means to sell, give, rent, loan or otherwise provide.
(2) "Minor" means a person under 18 years of age.
(3) "Sexual conduct" means:
(a) Human masturbation or sexual intercourse;
(b) Genital-genital, oral-genital, anal-genital or oral-anal contact, whether between persons of the same or opposite sex or between humans and animals;
(c) Penetration of the vagina or rectum by any object other than as part of a medical diagnosis or as part of a personal hygiene practice; or
(d) Touching of the genitals, pubic areas or buttocks of the human male or female or of the breasts of the human female. [2007 c.869 §1; 2011 c.681 §1]

Note: 167.051 and 167.057 were enacted into law by the Legislative Assembly but were not added to or made a part of ORS chapter 167 or any series therein by legislative action. See Preface to Oregon Revised Statutes for further explanation.

167.054 [2007 c.869 §2; repealed by 2011 c.681 §10]

167.055 [1955 c.636 §9; 1963 c.513 §1; repealed by 1971 c.743 §432]

167.057 Luring a minor. (1) A person commits the crime of luring a minor if the person furnishes to, or uses with, a minor, a police officer posing as a minor or an agent of a police officer posing as a minor, a visual representation or explicit verbal description or narrative account of sexual conduct for the purpose of inducing the minor or purported minor to engage in sexual conduct.

(2) A person is not liable to prosecution for violating subsection (1) of this section if the person furnishes or uses a representation, description or account of sexual conduct that forms merely an incidental part of an otherwise nonoffending whole and serves some purpose other than titillation.

(3) In a prosecution under subsection (1) of this section, it is an affirmative defense:
(a) That the representation, description or account was furnished or used for the purpose of psychological or medical treatment and was furnished by a treatment provider or by another person acting on behalf of the treatment provider;

(b) That the defendant had reasonable cause to believe that the person to whom the representation, description or account was furnished or with whom the representation, description or account was used was not a minor; or

(c) That the defendant was less than three years older than the minor or, in the case of a police officer or agent of a police officer posing as a minor, the age of the purported minor as reported to the defendant at the time of the alleged offense.

(4) Luring a minor is a Class C felony.

(5)(a) The court may designate luring a minor as a sex crime under ORS 163A.005 if the court determines that:

(A) The offender reasonably believed the minor or, in the case of a police officer or agent of a police officer posing as a minor, the purported minor to be more than five years younger than the offender or under 16 years of age; and

(B) Given the nature of the offense, the age of the minor or purported minor as reported to the defendant and the person's criminal history, designation of the offense as a sex crime is necessary for the safety of the community.

(b) The court shall indicate the designation and the findings supporting the designation in the judgment.

(6) As used in this section, "police officer" has the meaning given that term in ORS 181A.355. [2007 c.869 §3; 2011 c.681 §2; 2013 c.293 §1; 2015 c.101 §1]

Note: See note under 167.051.

167.060 Definitions for ORS 167.060 to 167.095. As used in ORS 167.060 to 167.095, unless the context requires otherwise:

(1) "Advertising purposes" means purposes of propagandizing in connection with the commercial sale of a product or type of product, the commercial offering of a service, or the commercial exhibition of an entertainment.

(2) "Displays publicly" means the exposing, placing, posting, exhibiting, or in any fashion displaying in any location, whether public or private, an item in such a manner that it may be readily seen and its content or character distinguished by normal unaided vision viewing it from a public thoroughfare, depot or vehicle.

(3) "Furnishes" means to sell, give, rent, loan or otherwise provide.

(4) "Minor" means an unmarried person under 18 years of age.

(5) "Nudity" means uncovered, or less than opaquely covered, post-pubertal human genitals, pubic areas, the post-pubertal human female breast below a point immediately above the top of the areola, or the covered human male genitals in a discernibly turgid state. For purposes of this definition, a female breast is considered uncovered if the nipple only or the nipple and areola only are covered.

(6) "Obscene performance" means a play, motion picture, dance, show or other presentation, whether pictured, animated or live, performed before an audience and which in whole or in part depicts or reveals nudity, sexual conduct, sexual excitement or sadomasochistic abuse, or which includes obscenities or explicit verbal descriptions or narrative accounts of sexual conduct.

(7) "Obscenities" means those slang words currently generally rejected for regular use in mixed society, that are used to refer to genitals, female breasts, sexual conduct or excretory functions or products, either that have no other meaning or that in context are clearly used for their bodily, sexual or excretory meaning.

(8) "Public thoroughfare, depot or vehicle" means any street, highway, park, depot or transportation platform, or other place, whether indoors or out, or any vehicle for public transportation, owned or operated by government, either directly or through a public corporation or authority, or owned or operated by any agency of public transportation that is designed for the use, enjoyment or transportation of the general public.

(9) "Sadomasochistic abuse" means flagellation or torture by or upon a person who is nude or clad in undergarments or in revealing or bizarre costume, or the condition of being fettered, bound or otherwise physically restrained on the part of one so clothed.

(10) "Sexual conduct" means human masturbation, sexual intercourse, or any touching of the genitals, pubic areas or buttocks of the human male or female, or the breasts of the female, whether alone or between members of the same or opposite sex or between humans and animals in an act of apparent sexual stimulation or gratification.

(11) "Sexual excitement" means the condition of human male or female genitals or the breasts of the female when in a state of sexual stimulation, or the sensual experiences of humans engaging in or witnessing sexual conduct or nudity. [1971 c.743 §255]

167.062 Sadomasochistic abuse or sexual conduct in live show. (1) It is unlawful for any person to knowingly engage in sadomasochistic abuse or sexual conduct in a live public show.

(2) Violation of subsection (1) of this section is a Class A misdemeanor.

(3) It is unlawful for any person to knowingly direct, manage, finance or present a live public show in which the participants engage in sadomasochistic abuse or sexual conduct.

(4) Violation of subsection (3) of this section is a Class C felony.

(5) As used in ORS 167.002, 167.007 and this section unless the context requires otherwise:

(a) "Live public show" means a public show in which human beings, animals, or both appear bodily before spectators or customers.

(b) "Public show" means any entertainment or exhibition advertised or in some other fashion held out to be accessible to the public or member of a club, whether or not an admission or other charge is levied or collected and whether or not minors are admitted or excluded. [1973 c.699 §§2,3; 2007 c.869 §9]

167.065 [1971 c.743 §256; repealed by 2007 c.869 §11]

167.070 [1971 c.743 §257; repealed by 2007 c.869 §11]

167.075 Exhibiting an obscene performance to a minor.
(1) A person commits the crime of exhibiting an obscene performance to a minor if the minor is unaccompanied by the parent or lawful guardian of the minor, and for a monetary consideration or other valuable commodity or service, the person knowingly or recklessly:
(a) Exhibits an obscene performance to the minor; or
(b) Sells an admission ticket or other means to gain entrance to an obscene performance to the minor; or
(c) Permits the admission of the minor to premises whereon there is exhibited an obscene performance.
(2) No employee is liable to prosecution under this section or under any city or home-rule county ordinance for exhibiting or possessing with intent to exhibit any obscene motion picture provided the employee is acting within the scope of regular employment at a showing open to the public.
(3) As used in this section, "employee" means any person regularly employed by the owner or operator of a motion picture theater if the person has no financial interest other than salary or wages in the ownership or operation of the motion picture theater, no financial interest in or control over the selection of the motion pictures shown in the theater, and is working within the motion picture theater where the person is regularly employed, but does not include a manager of the motion picture theater.
(4) Exhibiting an obscene performance to a minor is a Class A misdemeanor. Notwithstanding ORS 161.635 and 161.655, a person convicted under this section may be sentenced to pay a fine, fixed by the court, not exceeding $10,000. [1971 c.743 §258]

167.080 Displaying obscene materials to minors. (1) A person commits the crime of displaying obscene materials to minors if, being the owner, operator or manager of a business or acting in a managerial capacity, the person knowingly or recklessly permits a minor who is not accompanied by the parent or lawful guardian of the minor to enter or remain on the premises, if in that part of the premises where the minor is so permitted to be, there is visibly displayed:
(a) Any picture, photograph, drawing, sculpture or other visual representation or image of a person or portion of the human body that depicts nudity, sexual conduct, sexual excitement or sadomasochistic abuse; or
(b) Any book, magazine, paperback, pamphlet or other written or printed matter, however reproduced, that reveals a person or portion of the human body that depicts nudity, sexual conduct, sexual excitement or sadomasochistic abuse.
(2) Displaying obscene materials to minors is a Class A misdemeanor. Notwithstanding ORS 161.635 and 161.655, a person convicted under this section may be sentenced to pay a fine, fixed by the court, not exceeding $10,000. [1971 c.743 §259]

167.085 Defenses in prosecutions under ORS 167.075 and 167.080. In any prosecution under ORS 167.075 and 167.080, it is an affirmative defense for the defendant to prove:
(1) That the defendant was in a parental or guardianship relationship with the minor;
(2) That the defendant was a bona fide school, museum or public library, or was acting in the course of employment as an employee of such organization or of a retail outlet affiliated with and serving the educational purpose of such organization;
(3) That the defendant was charged with furnishing, showing, exhibiting or displaying an item, those portions of which might otherwise be contraband forming merely an incidental part of an otherwise nonoffending whole, and serving some purpose therein other than titillation; or
(4) That the defendant had reasonable cause to believe that the person involved was not a minor. [1971 c.743 §260; 1993 c.18 §27; 2001 c.607 §1]

167.087 [1973 c.699 §4; repealed by 2007 c.869 §11]

167.089 [1975 c.272 §2; repealed by 2007 c.869 §11]

167.090 Publicly displaying nudity or sex for advertising purposes. (1) A person commits the crime of publicly displaying nudity or sex for advertising purposes if, for advertising purposes, the person knowingly:
(a) Displays publicly or causes to be displayed publicly a picture, photograph, drawing, sculpture or other visual representation or image of a person or portion of the human body that depicts nudity, sadomasochistic abuse, sexual

conduct or sexual excitement, or any page, poster or other written or printed matter bearing such representation or a verbal description or narrative account of such items or activities, or any obscenities; or

(b) Permits any display described in this section on premises owned, rented or operated by the person.

(2) Publicly displaying nudity or sex for advertising purposes is a Class A misdemeanor. [1971 c.743 §261]

167.095 Defenses in prosecutions under ORS 167.090. In any prosecution for violation of ORS 167.090, it shall be an affirmative defense for the defendant to prove:

(1) That the public display, even though in connection with a commercial venture, was primarily for artistic purposes or as a public service; or

(2) That the public display was of nudity, exhibited by a bona fide art, antique or similar gallery or exhibition, and visible in a normal display setting. [1971 c.743 §262]

167.100 Application of ORS 167.060 to 167.100. ORS 167.060 to 167.100 shall be applicable and uniform throughout the state and all political subdivisions and municipalities therein, and no local authority shall enact any ordinances, rules or regulations in conflict with the provisions thereof. [1971 c.743 §262a]

167.105 [Repealed by 1971 c.743 §432]

GAMBLING OFFENSES

167.108 Definitions for ORS 167.109 and 167.112. As used in ORS 167.109 and 167.112:

(1) "Credit" and "credit card" have the meaning given those terms under the federal Consumer Credit Protection Act (P.L. 90-321, 82 Stat. 146, 15 U.S.C. 1601).

(2) "Electronic funds transfer" has the meaning given that term in ORS 293.525.

(3) "Financial institution" has the meaning given that term in ORS 706.008.

(4) "Money transmission" has the meaning given that term in ORS 717.200. [2001 c.502 §4]

167.109 Internet gambling. (1) A person engaged in an Internet gambling business may not knowingly accept, in connection with the participation of another person in unlawful gambling using the Internet:

(a) Credit, or the proceeds of credit, extended to or on behalf of such other person, including credit extended through the use of a credit card;

(b) An electronic funds transfer or funds transmitted by or through a money transmission business, or the proceeds of an electronic funds transfer or money transmission service, from or on behalf of the other person;

(c) Any check, draft or similar instrument that is drawn by or on behalf of the other person and is drawn on or payable at or through any financial institution; or

(d) The proceeds of any other form of financial transaction that involves a financial institution as a payor or financial intermediary on behalf of or for the benefit of the other person.

(2) Violation of subsection (1) of this section is a Class C felony. [2001 c.502 §2]

167.110 [Repealed by 1971 c.743 §432]

167.112 Liability of certain entities engaged in certain financial transactions. Notwithstanding any other provision of law, a creditor, credit card issuer, financial institution, operator of a terminal at which an electronic funds transfer may be initiated, money transmission business or any national, regional or local network utilized to effect a credit transaction, electronic funds transfer or money transmission service that is not liable under ORS 167.109:

(1) May collect on any debt arising out of activities that are illegal under ORS 167.109;

(2) Shall not be deemed to be participating in any activities that are illegal under ORS 167.109 by reason of their processing transactions arising out of such activities or collecting debts arising out of such activities; and

(3) Shall not be liable under any provision of ORS 166.715 to 166.735, 336.184 or 646.605 to 646.652 by reason of their processing transactions arising out of activities that are illegal under ORS 167.109 or collecting debts arising out of such activities. [2001 c.502 §3]

167.114 Application of ORS 167.109 and 167.112 to Oregon Racing Commission. ORS 167.109 and 167.112 do not apply to activities licensed and regulated by the Oregon Racing Commission under ORS chapter 462. [2001 c.502 §5]

167.115 [Repealed by 1971 c.743 §432]

167.116 Rulemaking for certain exceptions under ORS 167.117. (1) The Oregon State Lottery Commission shall adopt rules to carry out the provisions of ORS 167.117 (9)(c)(E) and (20)(b).

(2) Devices authorized by the Oregon State Lottery Commission for the purposes described in ORS 167.117 (9)(c)(E) and (20)(b) are exempted from the provisions of 15 U.S.C. 1172. [1999 c.193 §2; 2001 c.502 §6]

Note: 167.116 was enacted into law by the Legislative Assembly but was not added to or made a part of ORS chapter 167 or any series therein by legislative action. See Preface to Oregon Revised Statutes for further explanation.

167.117 Definitions for ORS 167.108 to 167.164 and 464.270 to 464.530. As used in ORS 167.108 to 167.164 and 464.270 to 464.530, unless the context requires otherwise:

(1) "Bingo or lotto" means a game, played with cards bearing lines of numbers, in which a player covers or uncovers a number selected from a container, and which is won by a player who is present during the game and who first covers or uncovers the selected numbers in a designated combination, sequence or pattern.

(2) "Bookmaker" means a person who unlawfully accepts a bet from a member of the public upon the outcome of a future contingent event and who charges or accepts a percentage, fee or vigorish on the wager.

(3) "Bookmaking" means promoting gambling by unlawfully accepting bets from members of the public as a business, rather than in a casual or personal fashion, upon the outcomes of future contingent events.

(4) "Casino game" means any of the traditional gambling-based games commonly known as dice, faro, monte, roulette, fan-tan, twenty-one, blackjack, Texas hold-'em, seven-and-a-half, big injun, klondike, craps, poker, chuck-a-luck, Chinese chuck-a-luck (dai shu), wheel of fortune, chemin de fer, baccarat, pai gow, beat the banker, panquinqui, red dog, acey-deucey, or any other gambling-based game similar in form or content.

(5)(a) "Charitable, fraternal or religious organization" means any person that is:

(A) Organized and existing for charitable, benevolent, eleemosynary, humane, patriotic, religious, philanthropic, recreational, social, educational, civic, fraternal or other nonprofit purposes; and

(B) Exempt from payment of federal income taxes because of its charitable, fraternal or religious purposes.

(b) The fact that contributions to an organization profiting from a contest of chance do not qualify for a charitable deduction for tax purposes or that the organization is not otherwise exempt from payment of federal income taxes pursuant to the Internal Revenue Code of 1986, as amended, constitutes prima facie evidence that the organization is not a bona fide charitable, fraternal or religious organization.

(6) "Contest of chance" means any contest, game, gaming scheme or gaming device in which the outcome depends in a material degree upon an element of chance, notwithstanding that skill of the contestants may also be a factor therein.

(7) "Gambling" means that a person stakes or risks something of value upon the outcome of a contest of chance or a future contingent event not under the control or influence of the person, upon an agreement or understanding that the person or someone else will receive something of value in the event of a certain outcome. "Gambling" does not include:

(a) Bona fide business transactions valid under the law of contracts for the purchase or sale at a future date of securities or commodities, and agreements to compensate for loss caused by the happening of chance, including but not limited to contracts of indemnity or guaranty and life, health or accident insurance.

(b) Engaging in contests of chance under the following conditions:

(A) The contest is played for some token other than money;

(B) An individual contestant may not purchase more than $100 worth of tokens for use in the contest during any 24-hour period;

(C) The tokens may be exchanged only for property other than money;

(D) Except when the tokens are exchanged for a beverage or merchandise to be consumed on the premises, the tokens are not redeemable on the premises where the contest is conducted or within 50 miles thereof; and

(E) Except for charitable, fraternal or religious organizations, no person who conducts the contest as owner, agent or employee profits in any manner from operation of the contest.

(c) Social games.

(d) Bingo, lotto or raffle games or Monte Carlo events operated in compliance with ORS 167.118, by a charitable, fraternal or religious organization licensed pursuant to ORS 167.118, 464.250 to 464.380 and 464.420 to 464.530 to operate such games.

(e) Savings promotion raffles, as defined in ORS 708A.660.

(8) "Gambling device" means any device, machine, paraphernalia or equipment that is used or usable in the playing phases of unlawful gambling, whether it consists of gambling between persons or gambling by a person involving the playing of a machine. Lottery tickets, policy slips and other items used in the playing phases of lottery and policy schemes are not gambling devices within this definition. Amusement devices other than gray machines, that do not return to the operator or player thereof anything but free additional games or plays, shall not be considered to be gambling devices.

(9)(a) "Gray machine" means any electrical or electromechanical device, whether or not it is in working order or some act of manipulation, repair, adjustment or modification is required to render it operational, that:

(A) Awards credits or contains or is readily adaptable to contain, a circuit, meter or switch capable of removing or recording the removal of credits earned by a player, other than removal during the course of continuous play; or

(B) Plays, emulates or simulates a casino game, bingo or keno.

(b) A device is no less a gray machine because, apart from its use or adaptability as such, it may also sell or deliver something of value on the basis other than chance.

(c) "Gray machine" does not include:

(A) Any device commonly known as a personal computer, including any device designed and marketed solely for home entertainment, when used privately and not for a fee and not used to facilitate any form of gambling;

(B) Any device operated under the authority of the Oregon State Lottery;

(C) Any device manufactured or serviced but not operated in Oregon by a manufacturer who has been approved under rules adopted by the Oregon State Lottery Commission;

(D) A slot machine;

(E) Any device authorized by the Oregon State Lottery Commission for:

(i) Display and demonstration purposes only at trade shows; or

(ii) Training and testing purposes by the Department of State Police; or

(F) Any device used to operate bingo in compliance with ORS 167.118 by a charitable, fraternal or religious organization licensed to operate bingo pursuant to ORS 167.118, 464.250 to 464.380 and 464.420 to 464.530.

(10) "Handle" means the total amount of money and other things of value bet on the bingo, lotto or raffle games, the value of raffle chances sold or the total amount collected from the sale of imitation money during Monte Carlo events.

(11) "Internet" means an interactive computer service or system or an information service, system or access software provider that provides or enables computer access by multiple users to a computer server and includes, but is not limited to, an information service, system or access software provider that provides access to a network system commonly known as the Internet, or any comparable system or service and also includes, but is not limited to a World Wide Web page, newsgroup, message board, mailing list or chat area on any interactive computer service or system or other online service.

(12) "Lottery" or "policy" means an unlawful gambling scheme in which:

(a) The players pay or agree to pay something of value for chances, represented and differentiated by numbers or by combinations of numbers or by some other medium, one or more of which chances are to be designated the winning ones;

(b) The winning chances are to be determined by a drawing or by some other method; and

(c) The holders of the winning chances are to receive something of value.

(13) "Monte Carlo event" means a gambling event at which wagers are placed with imitation money upon contests of chance in which players compete against other players or against the house. As used in this subsection, "imitation money" includes imitation currency, chips or tokens.

(14) "Numbers scheme or enterprise" means a form of lottery in which the winning chances or plays are not determined upon the basis of a drawing or other act on the part of persons conducting or connected with the scheme, but upon the basis of the outcome of a future contingent event otherwise unrelated to the particular scheme.

(15) "Operating expenses" means those expenses incurred in the operation of a bingo, lotto or raffle game, including only the following:

(a) Salaries, employee benefits, workers' compensation coverage and state and federal employee taxes;

(b) Security services;

(c) Legal and accounting services;

(d) Supplies and inventory;

(e) Rent, repairs, utilities, water, sewer and garbage;

(f) Insurance;

(g) Equipment;

(h) Printing and promotions;

(i) Postage and shipping;

(j) Janitorial services and supplies; and

(k) Leasehold improvements.

(16) "Player" means a person who engages in any form of gambling solely as a contestant or bettor, without receiving or becoming entitled to receive any profit therefrom other than personal gambling winnings, and without otherwise rendering any material assistance to the establishment, conduct or operation of the particular gambling activity. A person who gambles at a social game of chance on equal terms with the other participants therein is a person who does not otherwise render material assistance to the establishment, conduct or operation thereof by performing, without fee or remuneration, acts directed toward the arrangement or facilitation of the game, such as inviting persons to play, permitting the use of premises therefor and supplying cards or other equipment used therein. A person who engages in bookmaking is not a player.

(17) "Profits from unlawful gambling" means that a person, acting other than solely as a player, accepts or receives money or other property pursuant to an agreement or understanding with another person whereby the person participates or is to participate in the proceeds of unlawful gambling.

(18) "Promotes unlawful gambling" means that a person, acting other than solely as a player, engages in conduct that materially aids any form of unlawful gambling. Conduct of this nature includes, but is not limited to, conduct

directed toward the creation or establishment of the particular game, contest, scheme, device or activity involved, toward the acquisition or maintenance of premises, paraphernalia, equipment or apparatus therefor, toward the solicitation or inducement of persons to participate therein, toward the conduct of the playing phases thereof, toward the arrangement of any of its financial or recording phases or toward any other phase of its operation. A person promotes unlawful gambling if, having control or right of control over premises being used with the knowledge of the person for purposes of unlawful gambling, the person permits the unlawful gambling to occur or continue or makes no effort to prevent its occurrence or continuation.

(19) "Raffle" means a lottery operated by a charitable, fraternal or religious organization wherein the players pay something of value for chances, represented by numbers or combinations thereof or by some other medium, one or more of which chances are to be designated the winning ones or determined by a drawing and the player holding the winning chance is to receive something of value.

(20)(a) "Slot machine" means a gambling device that as a result of the insertion of a coin or other object operates, either completely automatically, or with the aid of some physical act by the player, in such a manner that, depending upon elements of chance, it may eject something of value or otherwise entitle the player to something of value. A device so constructed or readily adaptable or convertible to such use is no less a slot machine because it is not in working order or because some mechanical act of manipulation or repair is required to accomplish its adaptation, conversion or workability. Nor is it any less a slot machine because apart from its use or adaptability as such it may also sell or deliver something of value on the basis other than chance.

(b) "Slot machine" does not include any device authorized by the Oregon State Lottery Commission for:

(A) Display and demonstration purposes only at trade shows; or

(B) Training and testing purposes by the Department of State Police.

(21) "Social game" means:

(a) A game, other than a lottery, between players in a private home where no house player, house bank or house odds exist and there is no house income from the operation of the social game; and

(b) If authorized pursuant to ORS 167.121, a game, other than a lottery, between players in a private business, private club or place of public accommodation where no house player, house bank or house odds exist and there is no house income from the operation of the social game.

(22) "Something of value" means any money or property, any token, object or article exchangeable for money or property, or any form of credit or promise directly or indirectly contemplating transfer of money or property or of any interest therein.

(23) "Trade show" means an exhibit of products and services that is:

(a) Not open to the public; and

(b) Of limited duration.

(24) "Unlawful" means not specifically authorized by law. [1971 c.669 §3a; 1971 c.743 §263; 1973 c.788 §1; 1974 c.7 §1; 1975 c.421 §1; 1977 c.850 §1; 1983 c.813 §1; 1987 c.914 §1; 1991 c.962 §7; 1995 c.577 §2; 1997 c.867 §1; 1999 c.193 §1; 2001 c.228 §1; 2001 c.502 §7; 2005 c.57 §1; 2005 c.355 §2; 2015 c.137 §3]

167.118 Certain games or events conducted by charitable, fraternal or religious organizations; rules. (1) When a charitable, fraternal or religious organization is licensed by the Department of Justice to conduct bingo, lotto or raffle games or Monte Carlo events, only the organization or an employee of the organization authorized by the department may receive money or property or otherwise directly profit from the operation of the games, except that:

(a) The organization operating the games may present a prize of money or other property to any player not involved in the administration or management of the games.

(b) An organization licensed to conduct Monte Carlo events may contract with a licensed supplier of Monte Carlo event equipment to operate the event, including the provision of equipment, supplies and personnel, provided that the licensed supplier is paid a fixed fee to conduct the event and the imitation money is sold to players by employees or volunteers of the licensed charitable, fraternal or religious organization.

(c) A person may sell, rent or lease equipment, including electronic equipment, proprietary computer software and real property to a licensed charitable, fraternal or religious organization. Rent or lease payments must be made in compliance with the provisions of ORS 464.510.

(d) An organization licensed by the department may act as an escrow agent to receive money or property to be awarded as prizes.

(2) A charitable, fraternal or religious organization may not operate bingo, lotto or raffle games or Monte Carlo events except at locations and upon days and for periods of time as the department authorizes pursuant to this section and ORS 464.250 to 464.380, 464.420 and 464.450 to 464.530.

(3)(a) An organization licensed by the department to operate bingo or lotto games may not award a prize exceeding $5,000 in value in any one game. An organization licensed by the department to operate a Monte Carlo event may not present any prize of money, or a cash equivalent, to any player.

(b) Notwithstanding any provision of ORS 167.108 to 167.164 and 464.270 to 464.530 to the contrary, a bingo licensee may operate two games per year with a prize not to exceed $10,000 per game and, if approved by the department, may also participate in a linked progressive game involving only Oregon licensees, without regard to the number of games or the size of the prize awarded.

(4) Each charitable, fraternal or religious organization that maintains, conducts or operates any bingo, lotto or raffle game or Monte Carlo event under license of the department must operate the game or event in accordance with rules adopted by the department.

(5) It is unlawful for a licensee to permit the operating expenses of the games to exceed 22 percent of the annual handle of its bingo, lotto and raffle operation.

(6) It is unlawful for a charitable, fraternal or religious organization licensed by the department to operate bingo, lotto or raffle games if:

(a) The handle of the games and events exceeds $250,000 in a year; and

(b) The games and events do not generate for the organization's purposes, after the cost of prizes and operating expenses are deducted from the handle, an amount that equals or exceeds five percent of the handle. [1987 c.914 §3; 1991 c.274 §2; 1995 c.331 §1; 1997 c.867 §2; 1999 c.218 §1; 2001 c.228 §2; 2003 c.417 §1; 2017 c.60 §1]

167.119 [1973 c.788 §3; repealed by 1974 c.7 §2]

167.120 [Amended by 1955 c.514 §1; 1969 c.404 §1; repealed by 1971 c.743 §432]

167.121 Local authorization of social games. Counties and cities may, by ordinance, authorize the playing or conducting of a social game in a private business, private club or in a place of public accommodation. Such ordinances may provide for regulation or licensing of the social games authorized. [1974 c.7 §3]

Note: 167.121 was enacted into law by the Legislative Assembly but was not added to or made a part of ORS chapter 167 or any series therein by legislative action. See Preface to Oregon Revised Statutes for further explanation.

167.122 Unlawful gambling in the second degree. (1) A person commits the crime of unlawful gambling in the second degree if the person knowingly:

(a) Places a bet with a bookmaker; or

(b) Participates or engages in unlawful gambling as a player.

(2) Unlawful gambling in the second degree is a Class A misdemeanor. [1971 c.743 §264; 1997 c.867 §21]

167.125 [Amended by 1969 c.404 §2; repealed by 1971 c.743 §432]

167.127 Unlawful gambling in the first degree. (1) A person commits the crime of unlawful gambling in the first degree if the person knowingly promotes or profits from unlawful gambling.

(2) Unlawful gambling in the first degree is a Class C felony. [1971 c.743 §265; 1997 c.867 §22]

167.130 [Repealed by 1971 c.743 §432]

167.132 Possession of gambling records in the second degree. (1) A person commits the crime of possession of gambling records in the second degree if, with knowledge of the contents thereof, the person possesses any writing, paper, instrument or article:

(a) Of a kind commonly used in the operation or promotion of a bookmaking scheme or enterprise; or

(b) Of a kind commonly used in the operation, promotion or playing of a lottery or numbers scheme or enterprise.

(2) Possession of gambling records in the second degree is a Class A misdemeanor. [1971 c.743 §266]

167.135 [Repealed by 1971 c.743 §432]

167.137 Possession of gambling records in the first degree. (1) A person commits the crime of possession of gambling records in the first degree if, with knowledge of the contents thereof, the person possesses any writing, paper, instrument or article:

(a) Of a kind commonly used in the operation or promotion of a bookmaking scheme or enterprise, and constituting, reflecting or representing more than five bets totaling more than $500; or

(b) Of a kind commonly used in the operation, promotion or playing of a lottery or numbers scheme or enterprise, and constituting, reflecting or representing more than 500 plays or chances therein.

(2) Possession of gambling records in the first degree is a Class C felony. [1971 c.743 §267]

167.140 [Repealed by 1971 c.743 §432]

167.142 Defense to possession of gambling records. In any prosecution under ORS 167.132 or 167.137 it is a defense if the writing, paper, instrument or article possessed by the defendant is neither used nor intended to be used in the operation or promotion of a bookmaking scheme or enterprise, or in the operation, promotion or playing of a lottery or numbers scheme or enterprise. [1971 c.743 §268]

167.145 [Repealed by 1971 c.743 §432]

167.147 Possession of a gambling device; defense. (1) A person commits the crime of possession of a gambling device if, with knowledge of the character thereof, the person manufactures, sells, transports, places or possesses, or conducts or negotiates a transaction affecting or designed to affect ownership, custody or use of:
(a) A slot machine; or
(b) Any other gambling device, believing that the device is to be used in promoting unlawful gambling activity.
(2) Possession of a gambling device is a Class A misdemeanor.
(3) It is a defense to a charge of possession of a gambling device if the slot machine or gambling device that caused the charge to be brought was manufactured:
(a) Prior to 1900 and is not operated for purposes of unlawful gambling; or
(b) More than 25 years before the date on which the charge was brought and:
(A) Is located in a private residence;
(B) Is not operated for the purposes of unlawful gambling; and
(C) Has permanently affixed to it by the manufacturer, the manufacturer's name and either the date of manufacture or the serial number. [1971 c.743 §269; 1977 c.264 §1; 1983 c.403 §1; 1993 c.781 §1; 1995 c.577 §1]

167.150 [Repealed by 1961 c.579 §2]

167.151 [1961 c.579 §1; 1963 c.480 §1; repealed by 1971 c.743 §432]

167.152 [1955 c.494 §1; repealed by 1971 c.743 §432]

167.153 Proving occurrence of sporting event in prosecutions of gambling offenses. In any prosecution under ORS 167.117 and 167.122 to 167.147 in which it is necessary to prove the occurrence of a sporting event, the following shall be admissible in evidence and shall be prima facie evidence of the occurrence of the event:
(1) A published report of its occurrence in a daily newspaper, magazine or other periodically printed publication of general circulation; or
(2) Evidence that a description of some aspect of the event was written, printed or otherwise noted at the place in which a violation of ORS 167.117 and 167.122 to 167.147 is alleged to have been committed. [1971 c.743 §270]

167.155 [Repealed by 1961 c.503 §3]

167.157 [1969 c.169 §1; repealed by 1971 c.743 §432]

167.158 Lottery prizes forfeited to county; exception; action by county to recover. (1) Except for bingo or lotto operated by a charitable, fraternal or religious organization, all sums of money and every other valuable thing drawn as a prize in any lottery or pretended lottery, by any person within this state, are forfeited to the use of the county in which it is found, and may be sued for and recovered by a civil action.
(2) Nothing contained in ORS 105.550 to 105.600 shall interfere with the duty of officers to take possession of property as provided by subsection (1) of this section. [1971 c.743 §271; 1977 c.850 §3; 1989 c.846 §14]

167.160 [Repealed by 1961 c.503 §3]

167.162 Gambling device as public nuisance; defense; seizure and destruction. (1) A gambling device is a public nuisance. Any peace officer shall summarily seize any such device that the peace officer finds and deliver it to the custody of the law enforcement agency that employs the officer, which shall hold it subject to the order of the court having jurisdiction.
(2) Whenever it appears to the court that the gambling device has been possessed in violation of ORS 167.147, the court shall adjudge forfeiture thereof and shall order the law enforcement agency holding the gambling device to destroy the device and to deliver any coins taken therefrom to the county treasurer, who shall deposit them to the general fund of the county. However, when the defense provided by ORS 167.147 (3) is raised by the defendant, the gambling device or slot machine shall not be forfeited or destroyed until after a final judicial determination that the defense is not applicable. If the defense is applicable, the gambling device or slot machine shall be returned to its owner.
(3) The seizure of the gambling device or operating part thereof constitutes sufficient notice to the owner or person in possession thereof. The law enforcement agency shall make return to the court showing that the law enforcement agency has complied with the court's order.

(4) Whenever, in any proceeding in court for the forfeiture of any gambling device except a slot machine seized for a violation of ORS 167.147, a judgment for forfeiture is entered, the court shall have exclusive jurisdiction to remit or mitigate the forfeiture.

(5) In any such proceeding the court shall not allow the claim of any claimant for remission or mitigation unless and until the claimant proves that the claimant:

(a) Has an interest in the gambling device, as owner or otherwise, that the claimant acquired in good faith.

(b) At no time had any knowledge or reason to believe that it was being or would be used in violation of law relating to gambling.

(6) In any proceeding in court for the forfeiture of any gambling device except a slot machine seized for a violation of law relating to gambling, the court may in its discretion order delivery thereof to any claimant who shall establish the right to the immediate possession thereof, and shall execute, with one or more sureties, or by a surety company, approved by the court, and deliver to the court, a bond in such sum as the court shall determine, running to the State of Oregon, and conditioned to return such gambling device at the time of trial, and conditioned further that, if the gambling device be not returned at the time of trial, the bond may in the discretion of the court stand in lieu of and be forfeited in the same manner as such gambling device. [1971 c.743 §272; 1977 c.264 §2; 1999 c.59 §32; 2003 c.576 §391; 2005 c.22 §117; 2009 c.835 §9]

167.164 Possession of a gray machine; disposition of machine; defense. (1) A person commits the crime of possession of a gray machine if the person manufactures, sells, leases, transports, places, possesses or services a gray machine or conducts or negotiates a transaction affecting or designed to affect the ownership, custody or use of a gray machine.

(2) Possession of a gray machine is a Class C felony.

(3) If any device is seized by a law enforcement agency based on a contention that the device is a gray machine, and a motion for return or restoration of the device is filed under ORS 133.633, the burden of proof is on the state to establish that the device is in fact a gray machine.

(4) Violation of, solicitation to violate, attempt to violate or conspiracy to violate subsection (1) of this section constitutes prohibited conduct for purposes of ORS chapter 131A. A device that is claimed to be a gray machine may be destroyed or otherwise disposed of only if a judgment of forfeiture has been entered under ORS 131.550 to 131.600 or ORS chapter 131A.

(5) It is a defense to a charge of possession of a gray machine if the machine that caused the charge to be brought was manufactured prior to 1958 and was not operated for purposes of unlawful gambling. [1991 c.962 §5; 1999 c.59 §33; 2009 c.78 §58; 2013 c.128 §1]

167.165 [Repealed by 1963 c.340 §1 (167.170 enacted in lieu of 167.165)]

167.166 Removal of unauthorized video lottery game terminal.
On and after December 1, 1991, any video lottery game terminal that is not authorized by the Oregon State Lottery Commission must be removed from the State of Oregon. [1991 c.962 §8]

Note: 167.166 was enacted into law by the Legislative Assembly but was not added to or made a part of ORS chapter 167 or any series therein by legislative action. See Preface to Oregon Revised Statutes for further explanation.

167.167 Cheating. (1) A person commits the crime of cheating if the person, while in the course of participating or attempting to participate in any legal or illegal gambling activity, directly or indirectly:

(a) Employs or attempts to employ any device, scheme or artifice to defraud any other participant or any operator;

(b) Engages in any act, practice or course of operation that operates or would operate as a fraud or deceit upon any other participant or any operator;

(c) Engages in any act, practice or course of operation with the intent of cheating any other participant or the operator to gain an advantage in the game over the other participant or operator; or

(d) Causes, aids, abets or conspires with another person to cause any other person to violate paragraphs (a) to (c) of this subsection.

(2) As used in this section, "deceit," "defraud" and "fraud" are not limited to common law deceit or fraud.

(3) Cheating is a Class C felony. [1997 c.867 §20]

167.170 [1963 c.340 §2 (enacted in lieu of 167.165); repealed by 1971 c.743 §432]

167.202 [1971 c.743 §273; 1974 s.s. c.67 §1; repealed by 1977 c.745 §3 (167.203 enacted in lieu of 167.202)]

OFFENSES INVOLVING CONTROLLED SUBSTANCES

167.203 Definitions for ORS 167.212 to 167.252. As used in ORS 167.212 to 167.252, unless the context requires otherwise:

(1) "Apothecary" means a pharmacist, as defined by ORS 689.005, and where the context so requires, the owner of a store or other place of business where controlled substances are compounded or dispensed by a licensed pharmacist.

(2) "Controlled substance" and "manufacture" have the meaning given those terms by ORS 475.005.

(3) "Official written order" means an order written on a form provided for that purpose by the United States Commissioner of Internal Revenue, under any laws of the United States making provision therefor, if such order form is not provided, then on an official form provided for that purpose by the State Board of Pharmacy.

(4) "Practitioner" has the meaning given that term by ORS 475.005.

(5) "Wholesaler" means a person who supplies controlled substances that the wholesaler has not produced or prepared, on official written orders, but not on prescriptions.

(6) "Unlawfully" means in violation of any provision of ORS 475.005 to 475.285 and 475.752 to 475.980. [1977 c.745 §33 (enacted in lieu of 167.202); 1979 c.777 §44; 1995 c.440 §14]

167.205 [Amended by 1961 c.333 §1; repealed by 1971 c.743 §432]

167.207 [1971 c.743 §274; 1973 c.680 §1; 1974 c.67 §2; repealed by 1977 c.745 §54]

167.210 [Repealed by 1971 c.743 §432]

167.212 Tampering with drug records. (1) A person commits the crime of tampering with drug records if the person knowingly:

(a) Alters, defaces or removes a controlled substance label affixed by a manufacturer, wholesaler or apothecary, except that it shall not be unlawful for an apothecary to remove or deface such a label for the purpose of filling prescriptions;

(b) Affixes a false or forged label to a package or receptacle containing controlled substances;

(c) Makes or utters a false or forged prescription or false or forged official written order for controlled substances; or

(d) Makes a false statement in any controlled substance prescription, order, report or record required by ORS 475.005 to 475.285 and 475.752 to 475.980.

(2) Tampering with drug records is a Class C felony. [1971 c.743 §275; 1977 c.745 §34; 1995 c.440 §15]

167.215 [Repealed by 1971 c.743 §432]

167.217 [1971 c.743 §276; 1973 c.680 §2; 1974 c.67 §3; repealed by 1977 c.745 §54]

167.220 [Amended by 1957 c.403 §8; 1961 c.261 §2; repealed by 1971 c.743 §432]

167.222 Frequenting a place where controlled substances are used. (1) A person commits the offense of frequenting a place where controlled substances are used if the person keeps, maintains, frequents, or remains at a place, while knowingly permitting persons to use controlled substances in such place or to keep or sell them in violation of ORS 475.005 to 475.285 and 475.752 to 475.980.

(2) Frequenting a place where controlled substances are used is a Class A misdemeanor.

(3) As used in this section, "frequents" means repeatedly or habitually visits, goes to or resorts to. [1971 c.743 §277; 1974 c.43 §1; 1977 c.745 §35; 1979 c.641 §1; 1991 c.67 §41; 1993 c.469 §3; 1995 c.440 §16; 1999 c.1051 §160; 2017 c.21 §47]

167.225 [Repealed by 1971 c.743 §432]

167.227 [1969 c.655 §2; repealed by 1971 c.743 §432]

167.228 [1971 c.743 §278; repealed by 1977 c.745 §54]

167.230 [Repealed by 1971 c.743 §432]

167.232 [1971 c.743 §278a; repealed by 1977 c.745 §54]

167.235 [Amended by 1967 c.527 §1; repealed by 1971 c.743 §432]

167.237 [1967 c.527 §2; repealed by 1971 c.743 §432]

167.238 Prima facie evidence permitted in prosecutions of drug offenses. (1) Proof of unlawful manufacture, cultivation, transportation or possession of a controlled substance is prima facie evidence of knowledge of its character.

(2) Proof of possession of a controlled substance not in the container in which it was originally delivered, sold or dispensed, when a prescription or order of a practitioner is required under the provisions of ORS 475.005 to 475.285 and 475.752 to 475.980, is prima facie evidence that the possession is unlawful unless the possessor also has in possession a label prepared by the pharmacist for the drug dispensed or the possessor is authorized by ORS 475.005 to 475.285 and 475.752 to 475.980 to possess the controlled substance. [1971 c.743 §279; 1977 c.745 §36; 1995 c.440 §17]

167.240 [Repealed by 1971 c.743 §432]

167.242 [1971 c.743 §280; 1977 c.745 §37; 1995 c.440 §18; repealed by 1997 c.592 §6 (167.243 enacted in lieu of 167.242)]

167.243 Exemption contained in drug laws as defense to drug offenses. In any prosecution under ORS 167.212 and 167.222, any exception, excuse, proviso or exemption contained in ORS 475.005 to 475.285 and 475.752 to 475.980 shall be an affirmative defense. [1989 c.791 §16; 1995 c.440 §19; enacted in lieu of 167.242 in 1997]

167.245 [Amended by 1955 c.504 §1; 1959 c.322 §1; repealed by 1971 c.743 §432]

167.247 [1971 c.743 §281; 1977 c.745 §38; 1995 c.440 §20; repealed by 1997 c.592 §6 (167.248 enacted in lieu of 167.247)]

167.248 Search and seizure of conveyance in which drugs unlawfully transported or possessed. A district attorney or peace officer charged with the enforcement of ORS 167.212 and 167.222, having personal knowledge or reasonable information that controlled substances are being unlawfully transported or possessed in any boat, vehicle or other conveyance, may search the same without warrant and without an affidavit being filed. If controlled substances are found in or upon such conveyance, the district attorney or peace officer may seize them, arrest any person in charge of the conveyance and as soon as possible take the arrested person and the seized controlled substances before any court in the county in which the seizure is made. The district attorney or peace officer shall also, without delay, make and file a complaint for any crime justified by the evidence obtained. [1989 c.791 §17; enacted in lieu of 167.247 in 1997]

167.250 [Amended by 1959 c.322 §2; repealed by 1971 c.743 §432]

167.252 Preclusion of state prosecution. No person shall be prosecuted under ORS 167.203 to 167.222 if the person has been acquitted or convicted under the federal narcotic laws of the same act or omission which it is alleged constitutes a violation of ORS 167.203 to 167.222. [1971 c.743 §282]

167.255 [Repealed by 1959 c.322 §3]

167.260 [Repealed by 1959 c.322 §3]

167.262 Use of minor in controlled substance or marijuana item offense. (1) It is unlawful for an adult to knowingly use as an aider or abettor or to knowingly solicit, force, compel, coerce or employ a minor, with or without compensation to the minor:

(a) To manufacture a controlled substance or a marijuana item as defined in ORS 475B.015; or

(b) To transport, carry, sell, give away, prepare for sale or otherwise distribute a controlled substance or a marijuana item as defined in ORS 475B.015.

(2)(a) Except as otherwise provided in paragraph (b) of this subsection, violation of this section is a Class A felony.

(b) Violation of this section is a Class A misdemeanor if the violation involves delivery for no consideration of less than one ounce of usable marijuana as defined in ORS 475B.015. [1991 c.834 §1; 2017 c.21 §48]

Note: 167.262 was enacted into law by the Legislative Assembly but was not added to or made a part of ORS chapter 167 by legislative action. See Preface to Oregon Revised Statutes for further explanation.

167.265 [Repealed by 1959 c.322 §3]

167.270 [Repealed by 1959 c.322 §3]

167.275 [Repealed by 1959 c.322 §3]

167.280 [Repealed by 1959 c.322 §3]

167.285 [Repealed by 1959 c.322 §3]

167.290 [Repealed by 1959 c.322 §3]

167.295 [Amended by 1963 c.314 §1; repealed by 1971 c.743 §432]

167.300 [Repealed by 1971 c.743 §432]

OFFENSES AGAINST ANIMALS

167.305 Legislative findings. The Legislative Assembly finds and declares that:
(1) Animals are sentient beings capable of experiencing pain, stress and fear;
(2) Animals should be cared for in ways that minimize pain, stress, fear and suffering;
(3) The suffering of animals can be mitigated by expediting the disposition of abused animals that would otherwise languish in cages while their defendant owners await trial;
(4) The suffering of animals at the hands of unlicensed animal rescue organizations that are unable to provide sufficient food and care for the animals can be reduced by requiring such organizations to comply with regulations;
(5) The State of Oregon has an interest in facilitating the mitigation of costs of care incurred by a government agency, a humane investigation agency or its agent or a person that provides treatment for impounded animals;
(6) A government agency, a humane investigation agency or its agent or a person that provides care and treatment for impounded or seized animals:
(a) Has an interest in mitigating the costs of the care and treatment in order to ensure the swift and thorough rehabilitation of the animals; and
(b) May mitigate the costs of the care and treatment through funding that is separate from, and in addition to, any recovery of reasonable costs that a court orders a defendant to pay while a forfeiture proceeding is pending or subsequent to a conviction;
(7) Use of preconviction civil remedies is not an affront to the presumption of innocence; and
(8) Amendments to current law are needed to ensure that interested parties are afforded adequate notice and an opportunity to be heard and thus cannot unduly delay or impede animal lien foreclosure and preconviction forfeiture processes through unfounded due process claims. [2013 c.719 §1; 2017 c.677 §1]

Note: 167.305 was enacted into law by the Legislative Assembly but was not added to or made a part of ORS chapter 167 or any series therein by legislative action. See Preface to Oregon Revised Statutes for further explanation.

167.310 Definitions for ORS 167.310 to 167.351. As used in ORS 167.310 to 167.351:
(1) "Adequate bedding" means bedding of sufficient quantity and quality to permit a domestic animal to remain dry and reasonably clean and maintain a normal body temperature.
(2)(a) "Adequate shelter" includes a barn, doghouse or other enclosed structure sufficient to protect a domestic animal from wind, rain, snow or sun, that has adequate bedding to protect against cold and dampness and that is maintained to protect the domestic animal from weather and physical injury.
(b) "Adequate shelter" does not include:
(A) Crawl spaces under buildings or parts of buildings, such as steps, decks or stoops;
(B) The space under a vehicle;
(C) The inside of a vehicle if the domestic animal is kept in the vehicle in a manner or for a length of time that is likely to be detrimental to the domestic animal's health or safety;
(D) Shelters made from cardboard or other materials that are easily degraded by the elements;
(E) Animal carriers or crates that are designed to provide temporary housing;
(F) Shelters with wire or chain-link floors, unless the domestic animal is a bird; or
(G) Shelters surrounded by waste, debris, obstructions or impediments that could adversely affect an animal's health.
(3) "Animal" means any nonhuman mammal, bird, reptile, amphibian or fish.
(4) "Domestic animal" means an animal, other than livestock or equines, that is owned or possessed by a person.
(5) "Equine" means a horse, pony, donkey, mule, hinny, zebra or a hybrid of any of these animals.

(6) "Good animal husbandry" includes, but is not limited to, the dehorning of cattle, the docking of horses, sheep or swine, and the castration or neutering of livestock, according to accepted practices of veterinary medicine or animal husbandry.

(7) "Law enforcement animal" means a dog or horse used in law enforcement work under the control of a corrections officer, parole and probation officer, police officer or youth correction officer, as those terms are defined in ORS 181A.355, who has successfully completed at least 360 hours of training in the care and use of a law enforcement animal, or who has passed the demonstration of minimum standards established by the Oregon Police Canine Association or other accredited and recognized animal handling organization.

(8)(a) "Livestock," except as provided in paragraph (b) of this subsection, has the meaning provided in ORS 609.125.

(b) "Livestock" does not include psittacines.

(9) "Minimum care" means care sufficient to preserve the health and well-being of an animal and, except for emergencies or circumstances beyond the reasonable control of the owner, includes, but is not limited to, the following requirements:

(a) Food of sufficient quantity and quality to allow for normal growth or maintenance of body weight.

(b) Open or adequate access to potable water in sufficient quantity to satisfy the animal's needs. Access to snow or ice is not adequate access to potable water.

(c) For a domestic animal other than a dog engaged in herding or protecting livestock, access to adequate shelter.

(d) Veterinary care deemed necessary by a reasonably prudent person to relieve distress from injury, neglect or disease.

(e) For a domestic animal, continuous access to an area:

(A) With adequate space for exercise necessary for the health of the animal;

(B) With air temperature suitable for the animal; and

(C) Kept reasonably clean and free from excess waste or other contaminants that could affect the animal's health.

(f) For a livestock animal that cannot walk or stand without assistance:

(A) Humane euthanasia; or

(B) The provision of immediate and ongoing care to restore the animal to an ambulatory state.

(10) "Physical injury" means physical trauma, impairment of physical condition or substantial pain.

(11) "Physical trauma" means fractures, cuts, punctures, bruises, burns or other wounds.

(12) "Possess" has the meaning provided in ORS 161.015.

(13) "Serious physical injury" means physical injury that creates a substantial risk of death or that causes protracted disfigurement, protracted impairment of health or protracted loss or impairment of the function of a limb or bodily organ.

(14)(a) "Tethering" means to restrain a domestic animal by tying the domestic animal to any object or structure by any means.

(b) "Tethering" does not include using a handheld leash for the purpose of walking a domestic animal. [1985 c.662 §1; 1995 c.663 §3; 1999 c.756 §13; 2001 c.926 §7; 2003 c.543 §6; 2003 c.549 §1; 2005 c.264 §18; 2009 c.233 §2; 2013 c.382 §3; 2017 c.677 §2]

167.312 Research and animal interference. (1) A person commits the crime of research and animal interference if the person:

(a) With the intent to interfere with research, releases, steals or otherwise causes the death, injury or loss of any animal at or from an animal research facility.

(b) With the intent to interfere with research, damages, vandalizes or steals any property in or on an animal research facility.

(c) With the intent to interfere with research, obtains access to an animal research facility to perform acts not authorized by that facility.

(d) Obtains or exerts unauthorized control over records, data, materials, equipment or animals of any animal research facility with the intent to interfere with research by concealing, abandoning or destroying such records, data, materials, equipment or animals.

(e) With the intent to interfere with research, possesses or uses equipment or animals that the person reasonably believes have been obtained by theft or deception from an animal research facility or without the authorization of an animal research facility.

(2) For the purposes of this section, "animal research facility" means any facility engaging in legal scientific research or teaching involving the use of animals.

(3) Research and animal interference is a:

(a) Class C felony if damage to the animal research facility is $2,500 or more; or

(b) Class A misdemeanor if there is no damage to the facility or if damage to the animal research facility is less than $2,500.

(4) Determination of damages to an animal research facility shall be made by the court. In making its determination, the court shall consider the reasonable costs of:

(a) Replacing lost, injured or destroyed animals;

(b) Restoring the animal research facility to the approximate condition of the facility before the damage occurred; and

(c) Replacing damaged or missing records, data, material or equipment.

(5) In addition to any other penalty imposed for violation of this section, a person convicted of such violation is liable:

(a) To the owner of the animal for damages, including the costs of restoring the animal to confinement and to its health condition prior to commission of the acts constituting the violation;

(b) For damages to real and personal property caused by acts constituting the violation; and

(c) For the costs of repeating an experiment, including the replacement of the animals, labor and materials, if acts constituting the violation cause the failure of an experiment. [1991 c.843 §2; 2001 c.147 §2; 2001 c.554 §1]

167.315 Animal abuse in the second degree. (1) A person commits the crime of animal abuse in the second degree if, except as otherwise authorized by law, the person intentionally, knowingly or recklessly causes physical injury to an animal.

(2) Any practice of good animal husbandry is not a violation of this section.

(3) Animal abuse in the second degree is a Class B misdemeanor. [1985 c.662 §2]

167.320 Animal abuse in the first degree. (1) A person commits the crime of animal abuse in the first degree if, except as otherwise authorized by law, the person intentionally, knowingly or recklessly:

(a) Causes serious physical injury to an animal; or

(b) Cruelly causes the death of an animal.

(2) Any practice of good animal husbandry is not a violation of this section.

(3) Animal abuse in the first degree is a Class A misdemeanor.

(4) Notwithstanding subsection (3) of this section, animal abuse in the first degree is a Class C felony if:

(a) The person committing the animal abuse has previously been convicted of one or more of the following offenses:

(A) Any offense under ORS 163.160, 163.165, 163.175, 163.185 or 163.187 or the equivalent laws of another jurisdiction, if the offense involved domestic violence as defined in ORS 135.230 or the offense was committed against a minor child; or

(B) Any offense under this section or ORS 167.322, or the equivalent laws of another jurisdiction; or

(b) The person knowingly commits the animal abuse in the immediate presence of a minor child. For purposes of this paragraph, a minor child is in the immediate presence of animal abuse if the abuse is seen or directly perceived in any other manner by the minor child.

(5) When animal abuse in the first degree is a felony, the Oregon Criminal Justice Commission shall classify the offense as crime category 6 of the sentencing guidelines grid. [1985 c.662 §3; 2001 c.926 §8; 2003 c.577 §8; 2013 c.719 §2]

167.322 Aggravated animal abuse in the first degree. (1) A person commits the crime of aggravated animal abuse in the first degree if the person:

(a) Maliciously kills an animal; or

(b) Intentionally or knowingly tortures an animal.

(2) Aggravated animal abuse in the first degree is a Class C felony and the Oregon Criminal Justice Commission shall classify the offense as crime category 6 of the sentencing guidelines grid.

(3) As used in this section:

(a) "Maliciously" means intentionally acting with a depravity of mind and reckless and wanton disregard of life.

(b) "Torture" means an action taken for the primary purpose of inflicting pain. [1995 c.663 §2; 2001 c.926 §9; 2013 c.719 §3]

167.325 Animal neglect in the second degree. (1) A person commits the crime of animal neglect in the second degree if, except as otherwise authorized by law, the person intentionally, knowingly, recklessly or with criminal negligence:

(a) Fails to provide minimum care for an animal in such person's custody or control; or

(b) Tethers a domestic animal in the person's custody or control and the tethering results in physical injury to the domestic animal.

(2) Animal neglect in the second degree is a Class B misdemeanor.

(3) Notwithstanding subsection (2) of this section, animal neglect in the second degree is a Class C felony if:

(a) The person committing the offense has previously been convicted of two or more offenses under this section, ORS 167.330 or the equivalent laws of another jurisdiction;

(b) The offense was part of a criminal episode involving 11 or more animals; or

(c) The person knowingly commits the offense in the immediate presence of a minor child and the person has one or more previous convictions for an offense involving domestic violence as defined in ORS 135.230. For purposes of this paragraph, a minor child is in the immediate presence of animal neglect if the neglect is seen or directly perceived in any other manner by the minor child.

(4) The Oregon Criminal Justice Commission shall classify animal neglect in the second degree under subsection (3) of this section:

(a) As crime category 6 if 11 to 40 animals were the subject of the neglect.

(b) As crime category 7 if more than 40 animals were the subject of the neglect or if the offense is a felony because of circumstances described in subsection (3)(a) or (c) of this section. [1985 c.662 §4; 2013 c.382 §5; 2013 c.719 §4]

167.330 Animal neglect in the first degree. (1) A person commits the crime of animal neglect in the first degree if, except as otherwise authorized by law, the person intentionally, knowingly, recklessly or with criminal negligence:

(a) Fails to provide minimum care for an animal in the person's custody or control and the failure to provide care results in serious physical injury or death to the animal; or

(b) Tethers a domestic animal in the person's custody or control and the tethering results in serious physical injury or death to the domestic animal.

(2) Animal neglect in the first degree is a Class A misdemeanor.

(3) Notwithstanding subsection (2) of this section, animal neglect in the first degree is a Class C felony if:

(a) The person committing the offense has previously been convicted of one or more offenses under this section, ORS 167.325 or the equivalent laws of another jurisdiction;

(b) The offense was part of a criminal episode involving 10 or more animals; or

(c) The person knowingly commits the offense in the immediate presence of a minor child. For purposes of this paragraph, a minor child is in the immediate presence of animal neglect if the neglect is seen or directly perceived in any other manner by the minor child.

(4) The Oregon Criminal Justice Commission shall classify animal neglect in the first degree under subsection (3) of this section:

(a) As crime category 6 if 10 to 40 animals were the subject of the neglect.

(b) As crime category 7 if more than 40 animals were the subject of the neglect or if the offense is a felony because of circumstances described in subsection (3)(a) or (c) of this section. [1985 c.662 §5; 2001 c.926 §10; 2013 c.382 §4; 2013 c.719 §5]

167.332 Prohibition against possession of same genus or domestic animal; prohibition period reduction; waiver procedure. (1) Except as provided in subsections (3) and (4) of this section:

(a) In addition to any other penalty imposed by law, a person convicted of violating ORS 167.315, 167.340 or 167.355 or of a misdemeanor under ORS 167.320, 167.325 or 167.330 may not possess any animal of the same genus against which the crime was committed or any domestic animal for a period of five years following entry of the conviction.

(b) In addition to any other penalty imposed by law, a person convicted of violating ORS 167.322, 167.333, 167.365 or 167.428 or of a felony under ORS 167.320, 167.325 or 167.330 may not possess any animal of the same genus against which the crime was committed or any domestic animal for a period of 15 years following entry of the conviction. However, the sentencing court may reduce the prohibition period if the person successfully completes mental health treatment approved by the court.

(2) A person who possesses an animal in violation of this section commits a Class C misdemeanor. When a person is convicted of possessing an animal in violation of this section, as part of the sentence the court may order the removal of that animal from the person's residence and as a condition of the person's probation may prohibit the person from possessing any animal of the same genus that the person unlawfully possessed under this section or against which the underlying violation of ORS 167.315, 167.320, 167.322, 167.325, 167.330, 167.333, 167.340, 167.355, 167.365 or 167.428 was committed.

(3) The animal possession prohibition described in subsection (1) of this section does not apply to a person's first conviction if the person is the owner of a commercial livestock operation and the underlying violation of ORS 167.315, 167.320, 167.322, 167.325, 167.330, 167.333, 167.340, 167.355, 167.365 or 167.428 was committed against livestock.

(4)(a) A person subject to an animal possession prohibition described in subsection (1) of this section may file a motion with the sentencing court requesting a waiver of the prohibition. The person must file a sworn affidavit in support of the motion stating that:

(A) The person's conviction leading to the possession prohibition involved only livestock;

(B) During the two years before the conviction triggering the prohibition, the person was the owner of a commercial livestock operation;

(C) The person has not been convicted, in the previous five years, of a crime involving animals or domestic violence or a crime where the victim was under 18 years of age; and

(D) The person's conviction was the result of:

(i) Criminal liability for the conduct of another person under ORS 161.155 (2)(c);

(ii) Criminal liability of a corporation as described in ORS 161.170, and the person is a corporation; or

224

(iii) Animal neglect as described in ORS 167.325 or 167.330 and the person's criminal conduct was not knowing or intentional.

(b) When a person files a motion and affidavit described in paragraph (a) of this subsection, the sentencing court shall hold a hearing. At the hearing, the sentencing court shall grant the motion if the person proves by clear and convincing evidence that:

(A) Continued enforcement of the prohibition against possessing livestock would result in substantial economic hardship that cannot otherwise be mitigated;

(B) The person no longer poses any risk to animals; and

(C) The person is capable of providing and willing to provide necessary, adequate and appropriate levels of care for all livestock that would come within the person's custody or control if the petition is granted.

(c) When deciding a motion filed under this subsection, the sentencing court may consider the person's financial circumstances and mental health in determining whether the person is capable of adequately caring for livestock.

(d) If the sentencing court grants the motion described in this subsection, the waiver of the prohibition against possessing animals shall apply only to livestock. The sentencing court shall further order that for five years the person must consent to reasonable inspections by law enforcement and the United States Department of Agriculture to ensure the welfare of the livestock under the person's custody or control. A refusal to consent to a reasonable inspection described in this paragraph is contempt of court and, if the person is found in contempt, shall result in the sentencing court revoking the waiver of the possession prohibition.

(e) As used in this subsection, "commercial livestock operation" means a business engaged in the raising, breeding or selling of livestock for profit. [2001 c.926 §3; 2009 c.486 §1; 2013 c.719 §6; 2015 c.324 §4; 2017 c.677 §3]

167.333 Sexual assault of an animal. (1) A person commits the crime of sexual assault of an animal if the person:

(a) Touches or contacts, or causes an object or another person to touch or contact, the mouth, anus or sex organs of an animal or animal carcass for the purpose of arousing or gratifying the sexual desire of a person; or

(b) Causes an animal or animal carcass to touch or contact the mouth, anus or sex organs of a person for the purpose of arousing or gratifying the sexual desire of a person.

(2) Subsection (1) of this section does not apply to the use of products derived from animals.

(3) Sexual assault of an animal is a Class C felony. [2001 c.926 §5b; 2003 c.428 §1; 2015 c.324 §3]

167.334 Evaluation of person convicted of violating ORS 167.333. Upon the conviction of a defendant for violation of ORS 167.333, the court may order a psychiatric or psychological evaluation of the defendant for inclusion in the presentence report as described in ORS 137.077. [2001 c.926 §5c]

Note: 167.334 was enacted into law by the Legislative Assembly but was not added to or made a part of ORS chapter 167 or any series therein by legislative action. See Preface to Oregon Revised Statutes for further explanation.

167.335 Exemption from ORS 167.315 to 167.333. Unless gross negligence can be shown, the provisions of ORS 167.315 to 167.333 do not apply to:

(1) The treatment of livestock being transported by owner or common carrier;

(2) Animals involved in rodeos or similar exhibitions;

(3) Commercially grown poultry;

(4) Animals subject to good animal husbandry practices;

(5) The killing of livestock according to the provisions of ORS 603.065;

(6) Animals subject to good veterinary practices as described in ORS 686.030;

(7) Lawful fishing, hunting and trapping activities;

(8) Wildlife management practices under color of law;

(9) Lawful scientific or agricultural research or teaching that involves the use of animals;

(10) Reasonable activities undertaken in connection with the control of vermin or pests; and

(11) Reasonable handling and training techniques. [1985 c.662 §6; 1995 c.663 §4; 2001 c.926 §10a]

167.337 Interfering with law enforcement animal. (1) A person commits the crime of interfering with a law enforcement animal if the person intentionally or knowingly injures or attempts to injure an animal the person knows or reasonably should know is a law enforcement animal while the law enforcement animal is being used in the lawful discharge of its duty.

(2) Interfering with a law enforcement animal is a Class A misdemeanor. [Formerly 164.369; 2009 c.555 §1; 2011 c.597 §167]

167.339 Assaulting a law enforcement animal. (1) A person commits the crime of assaulting a law enforcement animal if:

(a) The person knowingly causes serious physical injury to or the death of a law enforcement animal, knowing that the animal is a law enforcement animal; and

(b) The injury or death occurs while the law enforcement animal is being used in the lawful discharge of the animal's duties.

(2) Assaulting a law enforcement animal is a Class C felony. [2003 c.543 §3; 2009 c.555 §2; 2011 c.597 §168]

167.340 Animal abandonment. (1) A person commits the crime of animal abandonment if the person intentionally, knowingly, recklessly or with criminal negligence leaves a domestic animal or an equine at a location without providing minimum care.

(2) It is no defense to the crime defined in subsection (1) of this section that the defendant abandoned the animal at or near an animal shelter, veterinary clinic or other place of shelter if the defendant did not make reasonable arrangements for the care of the animal.

(3) Animal abandonment is a Class B misdemeanor. [1985 c.662 §8; 2001 c.926 §11; 2009 c.233 §1]

167.341 Encouraging sexual assault of an animal. (1) A person commits the crime of encouraging sexual assault of an animal if the person:

(a) Knowingly possesses or controls, for the purpose of arousing or satisfying the sexual desires of the person or another person, a visual recording of a person engaged in sexual conduct with an animal; and

(b) Knows or is aware of and consciously disregards the fact that the creation of the visual recording involved the sexual assault of an animal as described in ORS 167.333.

(2) Encouraging sexual assault of an animal is a Class A misdemeanor.

(3) As used in this section:

(a) "Sexual conduct" means touching or contacting the mouth, anus or sex organs of an animal or animal carcass, or causing an animal or animal carcass to touch or contact the mouth, anus or sex organs of a person, for the purpose of arousing or gratifying the sexual desire of a person.

(b) "Visual recording" includes, but is not limited to, photographs, films, videotapes and computer and other digital pictures, regardless of the manner in which the recording is stored. [2015 c.324 §2]

167.343 Unlawful tethering. (1) A person commits the offense of unlawful tethering if the person tethers a domestic animal in the person's custody or control:

(a) With a tether that is not a reasonable length given the size of the domestic animal and available space and that allows the domestic animal to become entangled in a manner that risks the health or safety of the domestic animal;

(b) With a collar that pinches or chokes the domestic animal when pulled;

(c) For more than 10 hours in a 24-hour period; or

(d) For more than 15 hours in a 24-hour period if the tether is attached to a running line, pulley or trolley system.

(2) A person does not violate this section if the person tethers a domestic animal:

(a) While the domestic animal remains in the physical presence of the person who owns, possesses, controls or otherwise has charge of the domestic animal;

(b) Pursuant to the requirements of a campground or other recreational area;

(c) For the purpose of engaging in an activity that requires licensure in this state, including but not limited to hunting;

(d) To allow the person to transport the domestic animal; or

(e) That is a dog kept for herding, protecting livestock or dogsledding.

(3) Unlawful tethering is a Class B violation. [2013 c.382 §2]

167.345 Authority to enter premises or motor vehicle; search warrant; notice of impoundment of animal; damage resulting from entry. (1) As used in this section, "peace officer" has the meaning given that term in ORS 161.015.

(2) If there is probable cause to believe that any animal is being subjected to treatment in violation of ORS 167.315 to 167.333, 167.340, 167.355, 167.365 or 167.428, a peace officer, after obtaining a search warrant or in any other manner authorized by law, may enter the premises or motor vehicle where the animal is located to provide the animal with food, water and emergency medical treatment and may impound the animal. If after reasonable effort the owner or person having custody of the animal cannot be found and notified of the impoundment, the notice shall be conspicuously posted on the premises or motor vehicle and within 72 hours after the impoundment the notice shall be sent by certified mail to the address, if any, where the animal was impounded.

(3) A peace officer is not liable for any damages for an entry under subsection (2) of this section, unless the damages were caused by the unnecessary actions of the peace officer that were intentional or reckless.

(4)(a) A court may order an animal impounded under subsection (2) of this section to be held at any animal care facility in the state. A facility receiving the animal shall provide adequate food and water and may provide veterinary care.

(b) A court may order a fighting bird impounded under subsection (2) of this section to be held on the property of the owner, possessor or keeper of the fighting bird in accordance with ORS 167.433. [Formerly 167.860; 1993 c.519 §1; 1995 c.663 §5; 2001 c.926 §12; 2009 c.550 §1; 2015 c.177 §1]

167.347 Forfeiture of animal to animal care agency prior to disposition of criminal action. (1)(a) If an animal is impounded pursuant to ORS 167.345 and is being held by a county animal shelter or other animal care agency pending outcome of a criminal action charging a violation of ORS 167.315 to 167.333, 167.340, 167.355, 167.365 or 167.428, prior to the final disposition of the criminal action, the county or other animal care agency or, on behalf of the county or other animal care agency, the district attorney, may file a petition in the criminal action requesting that the court issue an order forfeiting the animal to the county or other animal care agency prior to the final disposition of the criminal action. The petitioner shall serve a true copy of the petition upon the defendant and, unless the district attorney has filed the petition on behalf of the county or other animal care agency, the district attorney.

(b) A petition may be filed in the criminal action under paragraph (a) of this subsection concerning any animal impounded under ORS 167.345 and held pending the outcome of the criminal action, regardless of whether the specific animal is the subject of a criminal charge, or named in the charging instrument, in the criminal action.

(2)(a) Upon receipt of a petition pursuant to subsection (1) of this section, the court shall set a hearing on the petition. The hearing shall be conducted within 14 days after the filing of the petition, or as soon as practicable.

(b) To provide notice on any potential claimant who may have an interest in any animals impounded pursuant to ORS 167.345 and as an alternate form of service upon a defendant who cannot be personally served as required in subsection (1) of this section, a petitioner may publish notice of the filing of the petition, printed twice weekly for up to 14 consecutive days in a daily or weekly newspaper, as defined in ORS 193.010, published in the county in which the hearing is to be held or, if there is none, in a daily or weekly newspaper, as defined in ORS 193.010, generally circulated in the county in which the hearing is to be held. The notice of the filing of the petition required under this subsection shall contain a description of the impounded animal or animals, the name of the owner or reputed owner thereof, the location from which the animal or animals were impounded and the time and place of the hearing if the hearing has been set at the time of publication, or otherwise the name, address and phone number for the attorney for the petitioner, who shall upon request provide further details on the hearing date, place and time.

(3) At a hearing conducted pursuant to subsection (2) of this section, the petitioner shall have the burden of establishing probable cause to believe that the animal was subjected to a violation of ORS 167.315 to 167.333, 167.340, 167.355, 167.365 or 167.428. The defendant or any other claimant shall have an opportunity to be heard before the court makes its final finding. If the court finds that probable cause exists, the court shall order immediate forfeiture of the animal to the petitioner, unless the defendant or any other claimant, within 72 hours of the hearing, posts a security deposit or bond with the court clerk in an amount determined by the court to be sufficient to repay all reasonable costs incurred, and anticipated to be incurred, by the petitioner in caring for the animal from the date of initial impoundment to the date of trial.

(4) If a security deposit or bond has been posted in accordance with subsection (3) of this section, and the trial in the action is continued at a later date, any order of continuance shall require the defendant or any other claimant to post an additional security deposit or bond in an amount determined by the court that shall be sufficient to repay all additional reasonable costs anticipated to be incurred by the petitioner in caring for the animal until the new date of trial.

(5) If a security deposit or bond has been posted in accordance with subsection (4) of this section, the petitioner may draw from that security deposit or bond the actual reasonable costs incurred by the petitioner in caring for any impounded animal from the date of initial impoundment to the date of final disposition of the animal in the related criminal action.

(6) The provisions of this section are in addition to, and not in lieu of, the provisions of ORS 167.350 and 167.435 and ORS chapters 87 and 88. [1995 c.369 §2; 2001 c.926 §13; 2009 c.550 §2; 2011 c.455 §1; 2013 c.719 §7; 2017 c.279 §1]

167.348 Placement of forfeited animal. (1) If an animal is forfeited according to the provisions of ORS 167.347 or 167.350, the agency to which the animal was forfeited may place the animal with a new owner. The agency may give placement preference to any person or persons who had prior contact with the animal, including but not limited to family members and friends of the former owner whom the agency determines are capable of providing necessary, adequate and appropriate levels of care for the animal. The agency may not, however, place the animal with family members or friends of the former owner who aided or abetted the criminal conduct underlying the forfeiture or had knowledge of the criminal conduct and failed to intervene. As a condition of placement, the agency shall require the new owner to execute an agreement to provide minimum care to the animal. The agreement must indicate that allowing the former owner to possess the animal constitutes a crime.

(2) Notwithstanding subsection (1) of this section, the agency may not place the animal with any person who resides with the former owner. [1995 c.369 §3; 2009 c.273 §1; 2013 c.719 §8]

167.349 Encouraging animal abuse. (1) A person commits the crime of encouraging animal abuse if the person:

(a) Obtains a previously abused, neglected or abandoned animal from an animal care agency under ORS 167.348 or the court under ORS 167.350; and

(b) Knowingly allows the person from whom the animal was forfeited to possess the animal.

(2) Encouraging animal abuse is a Class C misdemeanor. [2009 c.273 §3]

167.350 Forfeiture of rights in mistreated animal; costs; disposition of animal. (1)(a) In addition to and not in lieu of any other sentence it may impose, a court may require a defendant convicted under ORS 167.315 to 167.333, 167.340, 167.355 or 167.365 to forfeit any rights of the defendant in the animal subjected to the violation, and to repay the reasonable costs incurred by a government agency, a humane investigation agency or its agent or a person prior to judgment in caring for each animal associated with the criminal proceeding.

(b) If a government agency or a humane investigation agency or its agent provides care and treatment for impounded or seized animals, a court that orders a defendant to repay reasonable costs of care under paragraph (a) of this subsection may not reduce the incurred cost amount based on the agency having received donations or other funding for the care.

(2)(a) When the court orders the defendant's rights in the animal to be forfeited, the court may further order that those rights be given over to an appropriate person or agency demonstrating a willingness to accept and care for the animal or to the county or an appropriate animal care agency for further disposition in accordance with accepted practices for humane treatment of animals. The court may not transfer the defendant's rights in the animal to any person who resides with the defendant.

(b) This subsection does not limit the right of the person or agency to whom rights are granted to resell or otherwise make disposition of the animal. A transfer of rights under this subsection constitutes a transfer of ownership. The court shall require a person to whom rights are granted to execute an agreement to provide minimum care to the animal. The agreement must indicate that allowing the defendant to possess the animal constitutes a crime.

(3) In addition to and not in lieu of any other sentence it may impose, a court may order the owner or person having custody of an animal to repay any reasonable costs incurred by a government agency, a humane investigation agency or its agent or a person in providing minimum care to the animal that are not included in a repayment order under subsection (1) of this section.

(4) A court may order a person convicted under ORS 167.315 to 167.333, 167.340, 167.355, 167.365 or 167.428 to participate in available animal cruelty prevention programs or education programs, or both, or to obtain psychological counseling for treatment of mental health disorders that, in the court's judgment, contributed to the commission of the crime. The person shall bear any costs incurred by the person for participation in counseling or treatment programs under this subsection.

(5) ORS 131.550 to 131.600 do not apply to the forfeiture of an animal subjected to a violation of ORS 167.315 to 167.333, 167.340, 167.355, 167.365 or 167.428. Any such animal is subject to forfeiture as provided in subsections (1) to (3) of this section or, if the animal is a fighting bird, as provided in ORS 167.435. [Formerly 167.862; 1993 c.519 §2; 1995 c.663 §6; 2001 c.666 §29; 2001 c.926 §§14a,14b; 2005 c.830 §28; 2009 c.273 §2; 2009 c.550 §3; 2017 c.677 §4]

167.351 Trading in nonambulatory livestock. (1) As used in this section:

(a) "Nonambulatory" means unable to stand or walk unassisted.

(b) "Livestock auction market" has the meaning given that term in ORS 599.205.

(2) A person commits the crime of trading in nonambulatory livestock if the person knowingly delivers or accepts delivery of a nonambulatory livestock animal at a livestock auction market. This subsection does not apply to the delivery to, or acceptance by, a licensed veterinarian at a livestock auction market for the purpose of humanely euthanizing or providing appropriate medical care to the animal.

(3) The crime of trading in nonambulatory livestock is a Class A misdemeanor. [2003 c.287 §2]

167.352 Interfering with an assistance, a search and rescue or a therapy animal. (1) A person commits the crime of interfering with an assistance, a search and rescue or a therapy animal if the person intentionally or knowingly:

(a) Injures or attempts to injure an animal the person knows or reasonably should know is an assistance animal, a search and rescue animal or a therapy animal;

(b) Interferes with an assistance animal while the assistance animal is being used to provide assistance to a person with a disability; or

(c) Interferes with a search and rescue animal or a therapy animal while the animal is being used for search and rescue or therapy purposes.

(2) As used in this section, "assistance animal" has the meaning given that term in ORS 659A.143.

(3) As used in this section and ORS 30.822:

(a) "Search and rescue animal" means that the animal has been professionally trained for, and is actively used for, search and rescue purposes.

(b) "Therapy animal" means an animal other than an assistance animal that has been professionally trained for, and is actively used for, therapy purposes.

(4) Interfering with an assistance, a search and rescue or a therapy animal is a Class A misdemeanor. [1993 c.312 §3; 2007 c.70 §37; 2013 c.530 §6]

167.355 Involvement in animal fighting. (1) A person commits the crime of involvement in animal fighting if the person:

(a) Owns or trains an animal with the intention that the animal engage in an exhibition of fighting;

(b) Promotes, conducts, participates in or is present as a spectator at an exhibition of fighting or preparations thereto;

(c) Keeps or uses, or in any way is connected with or interested in the management of, or receives money for the admission of any person to any place kept or used for the purpose of an exhibition of fighting; or

(d) Knowingly suffers or permits any place over which the person has possession or control to be occupied, kept or used for the purpose of an exhibition of fighting.

(2) For purposes of this section:

(a) "Animal" means any bird, reptile, amphibian, fish or nonhuman mammal, other than a dog or a fighting bird as defined in ORS 167.426.

(b) "Exhibition of fighting" means a public or private display of combat between two or more animals in which the fighting, killing, maiming or injuring of animals is a significant feature. "Exhibition of fighting" does not include demonstrations of the hunting or tracking skills of an animal or the lawful use of animals for hunting, tracking or self-protection.

(3) Involvement in animal fighting is a Class C felony. [Formerly 167.865; 1987 c.249 §6; 2003 c.484 §9; 2009 c.796 §2]

167.360 Definitions for ORS 167.360 to 167.372. As used in ORS 167.360 to 167.372:

(1) "Breaking stick" means a device designed for insertion behind the molars of a dog for the purpose of breaking the dog's grip on another animal or object.

(2) "Cat mill" means a device that rotates around a central support with one arm designed to secure a dog and one arm designed to secure a cat, rabbit or other small animal beyond the grasp of the dog.

(3) "Dogfight" means a fight, arranged by any person, between two or more dogs the purpose or probable result of which fight is the infliction of injury by one dog upon another.

(4) "Dogfighting paraphernalia" means:

(a) A breaking stick;

(b) A springpole;

(c) A cat mill;

(d) A treadmill;

(e) A fighting pit;

(f) A leather or mesh collar with a strap more than two inches in width;

(g) A weighted or unweighted chain collar weighing 10 pounds or more; or

(h) An unprescribed veterinary medicine that is a prescription drug as defined in ORS 689.005.

(5) "Fighting dog" means a dog that is intentionally bred or trained to be used in, or that is actually used in, a dogfight. A dog does not constitute a fighting dog solely on account of its breed.

(6) "Fighting pit" means a walled area designed to contain a dogfight.

(7) "Springpole" means a biting surface attached to a stretchable device, suspended at a height sufficient to prevent a dog from reaching the biting surface while touching the ground.

(8) "Treadmill" means:

(a) A carpet mill made of narrow sections of carpet;

(b) A modified electric treadmill for the purpose of conditioning dogs; or

(c) A slat mill with a running surface constructed of slats made of wood, fiberglass, plastic or other similar material. [1987 c.249 §1; 2005 c.467 §1; 2008 c.42 §3]

167.365 Dogfighting. (1) A person commits the crime of dogfighting if the person knowingly does any of the following:

(a) Owns, possesses, keeps, breeds, trains, buys, sells or offers to sell a fighting dog, including but not limited to any advertisement by the person to sell such a dog.

(b) Promotes, conducts or participates in, or performs any service in the furtherance of, an exhibition of dogfighting, including but not limited to refereeing of a dogfight, handling of dogs at a dogfight, transportation of spectators to a dogfight, organizing a dogfight, advertising a dogfight, providing or serving as a stakes holder for any money wagered on a fight.

(c) Keeps, uses or manages, or accepts payment of admission to, any place kept or used for the purpose of dogfighting.

(d) Suffers or permits any place over which the person has possession or control to be occupied, kept or used for the purpose of an exhibition of dogfighting.

(2) Dogfighting is a Class C felony. [1987 c.249 §2]

167.370 Participation in dogfighting. (1) A person commits the crime of participation in dogfighting if the person knowingly:

(a) Attends or has paid admission at any place for the purpose of viewing or betting upon a dogfight.

(b) Advertises or otherwise offers to sell equipment that the person knows or reasonably should know will be used for the purpose of training and handling a fighting dog.

(2) Participation in dogfighting is a Class C felony. [1987 c.249 §3; 2008 c.42 §1]

167.372 Possessing dogfighting paraphernalia. (1) A person commits the crime of possessing dogfighting paraphernalia if the person owns or possesses dogfighting paraphernalia with the intent that the paraphernalia be used to train a dog as a fighting dog or be used in the furtherance of a dogfight.

(2) Possessing dogfighting paraphernalia is a Class C felony. [2005 c.467 §3; 2008 c.42 §2]

167.374 Possession or control of dogs for purpose of reproduction; records; exceptions. (1) As used in this section:

(a) "Boarding kennel" means a facility that provides care for a fee to dogs that stay at the facility an average of less than 30 days.

(b) "Dog" means a member of the subspecies Canis lupus familiaris or a hybrid of that subspecies.

(c) "Litter" means one or more dogs, sold individually or together, that are all or part of a group of dogs born to the same mother at the same time.

(2) A person may not possess, control or otherwise have charge of at the same time more than 50 sexually intact dogs that are two years of age or older for the primary purpose of reproduction. It is prima facie evidence that a person possesses dogs for the primary purpose of reproduction if during a 12-month period the person sells, offers for sale, barters or exchanges more than three litters of dogs that are less than eight months of age.

(3) A person that possesses, controls or otherwise has charge of 50 or more sexually intact dogs that are eight months of age or older shall maintain a record for each of those dogs that identifies:

(a) The date of birth for the dog or, if the date of birth is unknown, the date the person acquired possession, control or charge of the dog and the source of the dog;

(b) The dates on which the dog has been bred;

(c) For a female, the number of dogs in each litter produced; and

(d) The disposition the person makes of each dog possessed by, controlled by or in the charge of the person, including the date of disposition, manner of disposition and the name and address information for any person taking possession, control or charge of a dog.

(4) A person shall retain a record required under subsection (3) of this section for a period of three years following the death of the dog or a date on which the person permanently ceased to have possession, control or charge of the dog.

(5) Subsections (2) to (4) of this section do not apply to:

(a) An animal control agency, humane society or animal shelter;

(b) A person who provides care for dogs at the request of a unit of government, government agency, humane society or animal shelter;

(c) A veterinary facility;

(d) A person that is transporting dogs; or

(e) A boarding kennel.

(6) A violation of this section is a Class B misdemeanor. However, a court shall suspend sentence under this subsection for a violation of subsection (2) of this section if the person agrees to have a sufficient number of dogs spayed or neutered to remedy the violation. [2009 c.297 §1]

167.375 [1987 c.249 §4; repealed by 2009 c.550 §7]

167.376 Standards of care applicable to dog breeders; records; exceptions. (1) As used in this section:

(a) "Boarding kennel" means a facility that provides care for a fee to dogs that stay at the facility an average of less than 30 days.

(b) "Dog" means a member of the subspecies Canis lupus familiaris or a hybrid of that subspecies.

(c) "Litter" means one or more dogs, sold individually or together, that are all or part of a group of dogs born to the same mother at the same time.

(d) "Regular exercise" means the removal of the dog from the dog's primary enclosure and:

(A) Walking the dog on a leash;

(B) Allowing the dog to move about freely within a building or an outdoor space at least one hour per day; or

(C) Allowing the dog to walk on a treadmill, jenny mill, slat mill or similar device, if use of the device is prescribed for the dog by a veterinarian to accommodate a specific medical condition.

(2) A person that possesses, controls or otherwise has charge of at the same time 10 or more sexually intact dogs that are eight months of age or older shall, in addition to providing minimum care as defined in ORS 167.310:

(a) Provide each dog with sufficient space to turn about freely, stand and sit and to lie down without the head, face, tail, legs or feet of the dog touching the sides of the enclosure or touching any other dog.

(b) Provide each dog with an enclosure that:

(A) Has a solid floor without slats or gaps;

(B) Is six inches higher than the head of the tallest dog in that enclosure when the tallest dog is in a normal standing position;

(C) If elevated above the floor of a room, is placed so that the floor of the enclosure is no more than 42 inches above the floor of the room; and

(D) Is not stacked or otherwise placed above or below any other dog enclosure.

(c) Provide each dog that is more than four months of age with at least one hour of regular exercise each day, unless a veterinarian has certified that the dog is medically precluded from exercise.

(d) Remove waste and contaminants from the enclosure at least once each day.

(e) Remove the dog from the enclosure when cleaning the enclosure of waste and contaminants.

(f) Maintain a record for each sexually intact dog that is eight months of age or older that identifies:

(A) The date of birth for the dog or, if the date of birth is unknown, the date on which the person acquired possession, control or charge of the dog and the source of the dog;

(B) Any veterinary care provided for the dog; and

(C) The disposition the person makes of each dog possessed by, controlled by or in the charge of the person, including the date of disposition, manner of disposition and the name and address information for any person taking possession, control or charge of a dog.

(3) A person shall retain a record required under subsection (2) of this section for a period of three years following the death of the dog or a date on which the person permanently ceased to have possession, control or charge of the dog.

(4) Subsections (2) and (3) of this section do not apply to:

(a) An animal control agency, humane society or animal shelter;

(b) A person who provides care for dogs at the request of a unit of government, government agency, humane society or animal shelter;

(c) A veterinary facility;

(d) A person that is transporting dogs; or

(e) A boarding kennel.

(5) A violation of this section is a Class B misdemeanor. [2009 c.297 §2]

167.379 [2001 c.666 §54; repealed by 2005 c.830 §48]

167.380 [1987 c.249 §5; repealed by 2001 c.666 §56]

167.383 Equine tripping. (1) As used in this section, "equine" means any member of the family Equidae.

(2) Except as provided in subsection (3) of this section, a person commits the offense of equine tripping if, for purposes of a rodeo, contest, exhibition, entertainment or sport or as practice for a rodeo, contest, exhibition, entertainment or sport, the person intentionally ropes or lassos the legs of an equine, intentionally causing the equine to trip or fall.

(3) Subsection (2) of this section does not apply to a person who causes an equine to trip or fall for the purpose of allowing veterinary care for the equine.

(4) The offense of equine tripping is a Class B misdemeanor. [2013 c.616 §2]

Note: 167.383 was enacted into law by the Legislative Assembly but was not added to or made a part of ORS chapter 167 or any series therein by legislative action. See Preface to Oregon Revised Statutes for further explanation.

167.385 Unauthorized use of a livestock animal. (1) A person commits the crime of unauthorized use of a livestock animal when the person knowingly:

(a) Takes, appropriates, obtains or withholds a livestock animal from the owner thereof or derives benefit from a livestock animal without the consent of the owner of the animal; or

(b) Takes or holds a livestock animal and thereby obtains the use of the animal to breed, bear or raise offspring without the consent of the owner of the animal.

(2) Except as otherwise provided by law, offspring born to a female livestock animal or hatched from the egg of a female livestock animal belong to the owner of the female livestock animal until the owner transfers ownership of the offspring.

(3) As used in this section, "livestock animal" has the same meaning given that term in ORS 164.055.

(4) Unauthorized use of a livestock animal is a Class A misdemeanor.

(5) In addition to any criminal sanctions, if a defendant is convicted of the crime of unauthorized use of a livestock animal under this section, the court shall order the defendant to pay restitution to the owner of the animal. [1993 c.252 §1]

167.387 Definitions for ORS 167.387 and 167.388. As used in this section and ORS 167.388:
(1) "Livestock" has the meaning given in ORS 609.125.
(2) "Livestock production facility" means:
(a) Any facility or organization engaged in animal breeding, production or processing; or
(b) Any facility or institution whose primary purpose is to impound estray animals, as that term is defined in ORS 607.007. [1993 c.252 §4; 1999 c.756 §14]

167.388 Interference with livestock production. (1) A person commits the crime of interference with livestock production when the person, with the intent to interfere with livestock production:
(a) Takes, appropriates, obtains or withholds livestock from the owner thereof, or causes the loss, death or injury of any livestock maintained at a livestock production facility;
(b) Damages, vandalizes or steals any property located on a livestock production facility; or
(c) Obtains access to a livestock production facility to perform any act contained in this subsection or any other act not authorized by the livestock production facility.
(2) The crime of interference with livestock production is:
(a) A Class C felony if damage to the livestock production facility is $2,500 or more; or
(b) A Class A misdemeanor if there is no damage to the livestock production facility or if damage to the facility is less than $2,500.
(3) Determination of damages to a livestock production facility shall be made by the court. In making its determination, the court shall consider the reasonable costs of:
(a) Replacing lost, injured or destroyed livestock;
(b) Restoring the livestock production facility to the approximate condition of the facility before the damage occurred; and
(c) Replacing damaged or missing records, data, material, equipment or substances used in the breeding and production of livestock.
(4) In addition to any criminal sanctions, if a defendant is convicted of the crime of interference with livestock production under subsection (1) of this section, the court shall order the defendant to pay restitution to the owner of the animal or the owner of the livestock production facility. [1993 c.252 §§2,3; 2001 c.554 §2]

167.390 Commerce in fur of domestic cats and dogs prohibited; exception. (1) A person may not take, buy, sell, barter or otherwise exchange for commerce in fur purposes the raw fur or products that include the fur of a domestic cat or dog if the fur is obtained through a process that kills or maims the cat or dog. As used in this section, "domestic cat or dog" does not include coyote, fox, lynx, bobcat or any other wild or commercially raised wild feline or wild canine species or a hybrid thereof that is not recognized as an endangered species by the United States Fish and Wildlife Service.
(2) Violation of subsection (1) of this section, or any rule promulgated pursuant thereto, is a Class A misdemeanor when the offense is committed with a culpable mental state as defined in ORS 161.085. [1999 c.995 §§1,2]

167.400 [1991 c.970 §1; 1999 c.1051 §161; 2015 c.158 §7; 2017 c.701 §9; renumbered 167.785 in 2017]

167.401 [1999 c.1077 §8; 2011 c.355 §20; 2011 c.597 §168a; 2015 c.158 §8; repealed by 2017 c.701 §27]

167.402 [1991 c.970 §2; 1999 c.1051 §162; 2009 c.600 §1; 2015 c.158 §9; 2017 c.701 §6; renumbered 167.780 in 2017]

167.404 [1991 c.970 §3; 2015 c.158 §10; 2017 c.701 §7; renumbered 167.775 in 2017]

167.405 [Repealed by 1971 c.743 §432]

167.407 [2003 c.804 §84; 2015 c.158 §11; 2017 c.701 §8; renumbered 167.765 in 2017]

167.410 [Repealed by 1971 c.743 §432]

167.415 [Repealed by 1971 c.743 §432]

167.420 [Repealed by 1971 c.743 §432]

167.425 [Repealed by 1971 c.743 §432]

OFFENSES INVOLVING FIGHTING BIRDS

167.426 Definitions for ORS 167.426 to 167.439. As used in ORS 167.426 to 167.439:

(1) "Cockfight" means a fight between two or more birds that is arranged by a person and that has the purpose or probable result of one bird inflicting injury to another bird.

(2) "Constructive possession" means an exercise of dominion and control over the location and treatment of property without taking physical possession of the property.

(3) "Fighting bird" means a bird that is intentionally reared or trained for use in, or that actually is used in, a cockfight.

(4) "Gaff" means an artificial steel spur designed for attachment to the leg of a fighting bird in replacement of the bird's natural spurs.

(5) "Slasher" means a steel weapon resembling a curved knife blade designed for attachment to the foot of a fighting bird.

(6) "Source bird" means:

(a) A hen used to produce one or more chicks intended for eventual use as fighting birds; or

(b) A chick being reared with the intent that the chick eventually be used as a fighting bird or as a hen described in paragraph (a) of this subsection. [2003 c.484 §1; 2017 c.276 §1]

Note: 167.426 to 167.439 were enacted into law by the Legislative Assembly but were not added to or made a part of ORS chapter 167 or any series therein by legislative action. See Preface to Oregon Revised Statutes for further explanation.

167.428 Cockfighting. (1) A person commits the crime of cockfighting if the person knowingly:

(a) Owns, possesses, keeps, rears, trains, buys, sells or advertises or otherwise offers to sell a fighting bird.

(b) Promotes or participates in, or performs services in furtherance of, the conducting of a cockfight. As used in this paragraph, "services in furtherance" includes, but is not limited to, transporting spectators to a cockfight, handling fighting birds, organizing, advertising or refereeing a cockfight and providing, or acting as stakeholder for, money wagered on a cockfight.

(c) Keeps, uses or manages, or accepts payment of admission to, a place for the conducting of a cockfight.

(d) Suffers or permits a place in the possession or control of the person to be occupied, kept or used for the conducting of a cockfight.

(e) Manufactures, buys, sells, barters, exchanges, possesses, advertises or otherwise offers to sell a gaff, slasher or other sharp implement designed for attachment to a fighting bird with the intent that the gaff, slasher or other sharp implement be used in cockfighting.

(2) Subsection (1)(a) of this section does not apply to the owning, possessing, keeping, rearing, buying, selling, advertising or otherwise offering for sale of a bird for purposes other than training the bird as a fighting bird, using or intending to use the bird in cockfighting or supplying the bird knowing that the bird is intended to be used in cockfighting.

(3) Cockfighting is a Class C felony. [2003 c.484 §2]

Note: See note under 167.426.

167.430 [Amended by 1961 c.648 §8; repealed by 1971 c.743 §432]

167.431 Participation in cockfighting. (1) A person commits the crime of participation in cockfighting if the person knowingly:

(a) Attends a cockfight or pays admission at any location to view or bet on a cockfight; or

(b) Manufactures, buys, sells, barters, exchanges, possesses, advertises or otherwise offers to sell equipment with the intent that the equipment be used in training or handling a fighting bird or for enhancing the fighting ability of a fighting bird. This paragraph does not apply to a gaff, slasher or other sharp implement designed for attachment to a fighting bird.

(2) Participation in cockfighting is a Class C felony. [2003 c.484 §3; 2009 c.796 §1]

Note: See note under 167.426.

167.433 Seizure of fighting birds or source birds; procedure. (1) Pursuant to ORS 133.525 to 133.703, a judge may order the seizure of an alleged fighting bird or source bird owned, possessed or kept by any person.

(2) A judge ordering the seizure of an alleged fighting bird or source bird under subsection (1) of this section may order that the bird be impounded on the property of the owner, possessor or keeper of the bird. If a judge orders an alleged fighting bird or source bird impounded on the property of the owner, possessor or keeper of the bird, the court

shall order the owner, possessor or keeper to provide all necessary care for the bird and to allow regular and continuing inspection of the bird by a person designated by the court, or the agent of a person designated by the court. The owner, possessor or keeper shall pay the costs of conducting the inspections. The court shall further order the owner, possessor or keeper not to sell or otherwise dispose of the bird unless the court authorizes the sale or disposition, or until the seized bird is forfeited pursuant to an order under ORS 167.435 or restored to the person pursuant to an order under ORS 133.643. [2003 c.484 §4; 2017 c.276 §2]

Note: See note under 167.426.

167.435 Forfeiture of rights in fighting birds, source birds or property; public nuisance. (1) In addition to and not in lieu of any other penalty the court may impose upon a person convicted of cockfighting under ORS 167.428 or participation in cockfighting under ORS 167.431, the court shall include in the judgment an order for forfeiture to the city or county where the crime occurred of the person's rights in any property proved to have been used by the person as an instrumentality in the commission of the crime, including any fighting bird or source bird. This subsection does not limit the ability of the court to dispose of a fighting bird or source bird as provided under subsection (2) of this section.

(2) A fighting bird is a public nuisance, regardless of whether a person has been convicted of cockfighting or participation in cockfighting. If a fighting bird is ordered forfeited under subsection (1) of this section or is proved by a preponderance of the evidence in a forfeiture proceeding to be a fighting bird, the court shall order that the bird be destroyed or be otherwise disposed of. Upon the conviction of the person charged, the court shall adjudge all of the seized property of the person to be forfeited and shall order that the property be destroyed or otherwise disposed of. The court shall provide for a humane disposition of any source birds included in the forfeited property. [2003 c.484 §5; 2017 c.276 §3]

Note: See note under 167.426.

167.437 Constructive possession of fighting birds or source birds; procedure. (1) A peace officer having jurisdiction may, upon probable cause to believe that a bird is a fighting bird or source bird, take constructive possession of the bird on behalf of the law enforcement agency employing the officer.

(2) A peace officer who takes constructive possession of an alleged fighting bird or source bird pursuant to this section must do the following:

(a) Place a tag or other device approved by the law enforcement agency on the cage or other enclosure where the alleged fighting bird or source bird is located. The tag or other device must clearly state that it is unlawful to conceal, remove or release the bird for purposes of interfering with law enforcement agency control over the bird.

(b) Notify the owner, possessor or keeper of the bird that the bird has been seized by the law enforcement agency and may not be concealed, removed or released until authorized by a court or as provided in this section.

(c) Promptly apply to an appropriate court for an order described in ORS 167.433.

(3) If a law enforcement agency takes constructive possession of an alleged fighting bird or source bird under this section, the owner, possessor or keeper of the bird shall provide all necessary care for the bird.

(4) Constructive possession of an alleged fighting bird or source bird pursuant to this section terminates when a court order described in ORS 167.433 is served on the owner, possessor or keeper of the bird, or after 24 hours, whichever occurs first. [2003 c.484 §6; 2017 c.276 §4]

Note: See note under 167.426.

167.439 Forcible recovery of a fighting bird. (1) A person commits the crime of forcible recovery of a fighting bird if the person knowingly dispossesses, or knowingly attempts to dispossess, a law enforcement agency of constructive possession of a fighting bird, a source bird or an alleged fighting bird or source bird.

(2) Forcible recovery of a fighting bird is a Class C felony. [2003 c.484 §7; 2017 c.276 §5]

Note: See note under 167.426.

OFFENSES INVOLVING UNUSED PROPERTY MARKETS

167.500 Definitions for ORS 167.502, 167.506 and 167.508. As used in ORS 167.502, 167.506 and 167.508:

(1) "Baby food" or "infant formula" means food manufactured, packaged and labeled specifically for sale for consumption by a child under the age of two years.

(2) "Medical device" means an object or substance that is:

(a) Required under federal law to bear the label "Caution: Federal law requires dispensing by or on the order of a physician"; or

(b) Defined by federal law as a medical device and is intended:

(A) For use in the diagnosis of disease or other conditions in humans or animals;

(B) For use in the cure, mitigation, treatment or prevention of disease in humans or animals; or

(C) To affect the structure or a function of the bodies of humans or animals without achieving any of its principal intended purposes through metabolism or through chemical action within or on the bodies of humans or animals.

(3) "New and unused property" means tangible personal property:

(a) That was acquired by a person directly from a producer, manufacturer, wholesaler or retailer in the ordinary course of business and has not been used since its production or manufacture; or

(b) That was packaged when it was originally produced or manufactured and the property is in its original and unopened package.

(4)(a) "Nonprescription drugs" means drugs that may be sold without a prescription and that, in accordance with the requirements of the statutes and regulations of this state and the federal government, are:

(A) Prepackaged for use by a consumer;

(B) Prepared by a manufacturer or producer for use by a consumer; and

(C) Labeled and unadulterated.

(b) "Nonprescription drugs" does not include herbal products, dietary supplements, botanical extracts or vitamins.

(5) "Prior conviction" means a conviction that was entered prior to imposing sentence on the current crime, provided that the prior conviction is based on a crime committed in a separate criminal episode.

(6) "Unused property market" means an event:

(a) Where at least two persons offer new and unused property for sale or exchange and the person organizing or conducting the event charges a fee upon the sale or exchange of the new and unused property;

(b) Where at least two persons offer new and unused property for sale or exchange and a prospective buyer must pay a fee for admission to an area where new and unused property is offered for sale or exchange; or

(c) Where new and unused property is offered for sale or exchange for more than 12 days in one 12-month period. [2003 c.338 §1]

Note: 167.500, 167.502, 167.506 and 167.508 were enacted into law by the Legislative Assembly but were not added to or made a part of ORS chapter 167 or any series therein by legislative action. See Preface to Oregon Revised Statutes for further explanation.

167.502 Sale of certain items at unused property market prohibited; exceptions. (1) Except as provided in subsection (2) of this section, a person may not offer for sale or exchange or knowingly permit the sale or exchange of baby food, infant formula, cosmetics, personal care products, nonprescription drugs or medical devices at an unused property market.

(2) A person may sell or exchange the items listed in subsection (1) of this section if the person:

(a) Has a written authorization that identifies the person as an authorized representative of the manufacturer or distributor of those items; and

(b) Makes the written authorization available for public inspection.

(3)(a) A person who violates this section commits a Class C misdemeanor.

(b) A person who violates this section and who has one prior conviction under this section that was entered within the last 10 years commits a Class B misdemeanor.

(c) A person who violates this section and who has two or more prior convictions under this section that were entered within the last 10 years commits a Class A misdemeanor. [2003 c.338 §2]

Note: See note under 167.500.

167.505 [Amended by 1959 c.530 §3; repealed by 1971 c.743 §432]

167.506 Recordkeeping requirements. (1) When a person purchases more than 10 items of new and unused property for resale at an unused property market, the person shall maintain a record for two years after the date of purchase.

(2) The record required in subsection (1) of this section must contain:

(a) The date of the purchase of the new and unused property;

(b) The name and address of the person from which the new and unused property was purchased;

(c) A description and identification of the new and unused property; and

(d) The price paid for the new and unused property.

(3) A person shall, upon request, provide the record described in subsection (2) of this section for the purpose of inspection within a reasonable time.

(4)(a) A person who violates this section commits a Class C misdemeanor.

(b) A person who violates this section and who has one prior conviction under this section that was entered within the last 10 years commits a Class B misdemeanor.

(c) A person who violates this section and who has two or more prior convictions under this section that were entered within the last 10 years commits a Class A misdemeanor. [2003 c.338 §3]

Note: See note under 167.500.

167.508 Exemptions from ORS 167.502 and 167.506. (1) ORS 167.502 and 167.506 do not apply to a person who:

(a) Sells or exchanges new and unused property that was not produced or manufactured within the last five years as indicated by the style of the packaging or of the material itself;

(b) Sells by sample, catalog or brochure for future delivery; or

(c) Makes a sales presentation to a consumer who received an individualized invitation to attend the sales presentation prior to the sales presentation from an owner or legal occupant of the premises where the sales presentation takes place.

(2) The recordkeeping requirements in ORS 167.506 do not apply to:

(a) A person who sells or exchanges new and unused property at an event that is organized and operated:

(A) For the exclusive benefit of a community chest, a fund, a foundation, an association or a corporation; and

(B) For religious, educational or charitable purposes.

(b) A person who sells or exchanges motor vehicles or trailers that are subject to state vehicle registration requirements.

(c) A person who sells or exchanges new and unused property at a gun show as defined in ORS 166.432.

(d) A person who sells or exchanges new and unused property at a livestock auction market as defined in ORS 599.205. [2003 c.338 §4]

Note: See note under 167.500.

167.510 [Amended by 1959 c.530 §4; repealed by 1971 c.743 §432]

167.515 [Repealed by 1971 c.743 §432]

167.520 [Repealed by 1971 c.743 §432]

167.525 [Repealed by 1971 c.743 §432]

167.530 [Repealed by 1971 c.743 §432]

167.535 [Amended by 1959 c.530 §5; repealed by 1971 c.743 §432]

167.540 [Repealed by 1971 c.743 §432]

167.545 [Repealed by 1971 c.743 §432]

167.550 [Amended by 1959 c.426 §8; repealed by 1971 c.743 §432]

167.555 [Repealed by 1971 c.743 §432]

167.605 [Amended by 1963 c.201 §1; repealed by 1971 c.743 §432]

167.610 [Repealed by 1971 c.743 §432]

167.615 [Repealed by 1971 c.743 §432]

167.620 [Repealed by 1971 c.743 §432]

167.625 [Repealed by 1971 c.743 §432]

167.630 [Repealed by 1971 c.743 §432]

167.635 [Repealed by 1971 c.743 §432]

167.640 [Repealed by 1971 c.743 §432]

167.645 [Repealed by 1971 c.743 §432]

167.705 [Amended by 1959 c.503 §6; repealed by 1971 c.743 §432]

167.710 [Repealed by 1971 c.743 §432]

167.715 [Repealed by 1971 c.743 §432]

167.720 [Repealed by 1971 c.743 §432]

167.725 [Repealed by 1971 c.743 §432]

167.730 [Repealed by 1971 c.743 §432]

167.735 [Repealed by 1971 c.743 §432]

167.740 [Amended by 1965 c.370 §1; repealed by 1971 c.743 §432]

167.745 [1959 c.200 §1; repealed by 1971 c.743 §432]

OFFENSES INVOLVING TOBACCO PRODUCTS AND INHALANT DELIVERY SYSTEMS

167.747 Definitions for ORS 167.750 to 167.785. As used in ORS 167.750 to 167.785:
(1) "Inhalant delivery system" has the meaning given that term in ORS 431A.175.
(2) "Tobacco products" has the meaning given that term in ORS 431A.175. [2017 c.701 §1]

Note: 167.747 to 167.785 were enacted into law by the Legislative Assembly but were not added to or made a part of ORS chapter 167 or any series therein by legislative action. See Preface to Oregon Revised Statutes for further explanation.

167.750 Definition for ORS 167.755 and 431A.175. For purposes of ORS 167.755 and 431A.175, "allows to be sold" includes the negligent omission of an act by a manager or other person who supervises the retail sale of tobacco products or inhalant delivery systems, the commission of which would have prevented the distribution or sale of the tobacco products or inhalant delivery system. [2017 c.701 §5]

Note: See note under 167.747.

167.755 Selling tobacco products or inhalant delivery systems to person under 21 years of age; penalties. (1) A person commits the offense of selling tobacco products or inhalant delivery systems to a person under 21 years of age upon the occurrence of one of the following:
(a) The person knowingly distributes or sells, or allows to be sold, to a person under 21 years of age, tobacco products;
(b) The person knowingly distributes or sells, or allows to be sold, to a person under 21 years of age, an inhalant delivery system;
(c) If the person is a manager or other person who supervises the retail sale of tobacco products or inhalant delivery systems, the person is acting within the course and scope of the person's employment and the person has supervisory authority over a person who violates paragraph (a) or (b) of this subsection; or
(d) If the person is an owner of a business that sells tobacco products or inhalant delivery systems at retail, a violation of paragraph (a) or (b) of this subsection occurs at the business.
(2)(a) Violation of subsection (1)(a) or (b) of this section is a specific fine violation punishable by a fine not to exceed $50.
(b) Violation of subsection (1)(c) of this section is a specific fine violation punishable by a fine not to exceed:
(A) $250 for the first or second violation; or
(B) $500 for the third or subsequent violation.
(c) Violation of subsection (1)(d) of this section is a specific fine violation punishable by a fine not to exceed:
(A) $500 for the first or second violation; or
(B) $1,000 for the third or subsequent violation. [2017 c.701 §2]

Note: See note under 167.747.

167.760 Purchase or attempted purchase of tobacco products or inhalant delivery system by person under 21 years of age. (1) Except as provided in subsection (2) of this section, a person under 21 years of age may not purchase or attempt to purchase tobacco products or an inhalant delivery system.

(2) A person under 21 years of age who is acting under the supervision of a person 21 years of age or older may purchase or attempt to purchase tobacco products or an inhalant delivery system for the purpose of testing compliance with a federal law, state law, local law or retailer policy limiting or regulating the distribution or sale of tobacco products or inhalant delivery systems to persons who are under the legal minimum purchase age. [2017 c.701 §4]

Note: See note under 167.747.

167.765 Retail store location of tobacco products or inhalant delivery systems; penalty. (1) A person having authority over the location of tobacco products or inhalant delivery systems in a retail store may not locate the tobacco products or inhalant delivery systems in a location in the store where the tobacco products or inhalant delivery systems are accessible by store customers without assistance by a store employee.

(2) Violation of this section is a Class B violation. Each day that the person commits the violation constitutes a separate offense.

(3) This section does not apply to a person if the location at which the tobacco products or inhalant delivery systems are sold is a store or other establishment that prohibits persons under 21 years of age from entering the store or establishment. [Formerly 167.407]

Note: See note under 167.747.

167.770 Display of sign; penalty. (1) A person who sells tobacco products or inhalant delivery systems shall display a sign clearly stating that the sale of the tobacco products or inhalant delivery systems to persons under 21 years of age is prohibited by law.

(2) Failure to display a sign required by this section is a Class A violation. [2017 c.701 §3]

Note: See note under 167.747.

167.775 Local regulation of vending machines. Cities and counties by ordinance or resolution may not regulate vending machines that dispense tobacco products or inhalant delivery systems and that are in any manner accessible to persons under 21 years of age. [Formerly 167.404]

Note: See note under 167.747.

167.780 Sale or dispensing of tobacco products or inhalant delivery systems by vending machine. (1) As used in this section and ORS 167.775, "vending machine" means a device that, upon the insertion of tokens, money or another form of payment, dispenses tobacco products or inhalant delivery systems.

(2) A person may not sell or dispense tobacco products or inhalant delivery systems from a vending machine, except in an establishment where the premises are permanently and entirely off-limits to persons under 21 years of age as required by rules adopted by the Oregon Liquor Control Commission.

(3) A person who violates this section commits a Class B violation. Each day that the person commits the violation constitutes a separate offense. [Formerly 167.402]

Note: See note under 167.747.

167.785 Possession of tobacco products or inhalant delivery systems by person under 18 years of age; penalty. (1) It is unlawful for a person under 18 years of age to possess tobacco products or inhalant delivery systems.

(2) A person who violates this section commits a Class D violation. [Formerly 167.400]

Note: See note under 167.747.

MISCELLANEOUS

167.808 Unlawful possession of inhalants. (1) For the purposes of this section:

(a) "Inhalant" means any glue, cement or other substance that is capable of causing intoxication and that contains one or more of the following chemical compounds:

(A) Acetone;

(B) Amyl acetate;

(C) Benzol or benzene;

(D) Butane;

(E) Butyl acetate;

(F) Butyl alcohol;

(G) Carbon tetrachloride;

(H) Chloroform;

(I) Cyclohexanone;

(J) Difluoroethane;

(K) Ethanol or ethyl alcohol;

(L) Ethyl acetate;

(M) Hexane;

(N) Isopropanol or isopropyl alcohol;

(O) Isopropyl acetate;

(P) Methyl cellosolve acetate;

(Q) Methyl ethyl ketone;

(R) Methyl isobutyl ketone;

(S) Nitrous oxide;

(T) Toluol or toluene;

(U) Trichloroethylene;

(V) Tricresyl phosphate;

(W) Xylol or xylene; or

(X) Any other solvent, material, substance, chemical or combination thereof having the property of releasing toxic vapors or fumes.

(b) "Intoxication" means any mental or physical impairment or incapacity.

(2) It is unlawful for a person to possess any inhalant if the person intends to use the inhalant for the purpose of inducing intoxication in the person who possesses the inhalant or for the purpose of inducing intoxication in any other person.

(3) A person may not use any inhalant for the purpose of inducing intoxication in the person using the inhalant or for the purpose of inducing intoxication in any other person.

(4) The prohibitions of this section do not apply to any substance that:

(a) Has been prescribed by a health practitioner, as described in ORS 31.740, and that is used in the manner prescribed by the health practitioner; or

(b) Is administered or used under the supervision of a health practitioner, as described in ORS 31.740.

(5)(a) Any person who violates this section commits a violation. Violation of this section is a Class C violation. In addition to or in lieu of a fine, a juvenile court may require that a minor who engages in conduct prohibited by this section be provided with treatment and counseling.

(b) Notwithstanding paragraph (a) of this subsection, a second or subsequent violation of this section by a person is a Class B misdemeanor. If a juvenile court finds that a minor has engaged in conduct prohibited by this section on a second or subsequent occasion, the court shall require that the minor receive treatment and counseling. [1999 c.229 §1; 1999 c.1051 §322f; 2011 c.597 §81]

Note: 167.808 was enacted into law by the Legislative Assembly but was not added to or made a part of ORS chapter 167 or any series therein by legislative action. See Preface to Oregon Revised Statutes for further explanation.

167.810 Creating a hazard. (1) A person commits the crime of creating a hazard if:

(a) The person intentionally maintains or leaves in a place accessible to children a container with a compartment of more than one and one-half cubic feet capacity and a door or lid which locks or fastens automatically when closed and which cannot easily be opened from the inside; or

(b) Being the owner or otherwise having possession of property upon which there is a well, cistern, cesspool, excavation or other hole of a depth of four feet or more and a top width of 12 inches or more, the owner intentionally fails or refuses to cover or fence it with a suitable protective construction.

(2) Creating a hazard is a Class B misdemeanor. [1971 c.743 §284]

167.820 Concealing the birth of an infant. (1) A person commits the crime of concealing the birth of an infant if the person conceals the corpse of a newborn child with intent to conceal the fact of its birth or to prevent a determination of whether it was born dead or alive.

(2) Concealing the birth of an infant is a Class A misdemeanor. [1971 c.743 §286]

167.822 Improper repair of a vehicle inflatable restraint system. (1) A person commits the crime of improper repair of a vehicle inflatable restraint system if the person knowingly:

(a) Installs as part of a vehicle inflatable restraint system an object that is not designed in accordance with federal safety regulations for the make, model and year of the motor vehicle; or

(b) If requested to repair or replace a vehicle inflatable restraint system, fails to install an object that is required to make a vehicle inflatable restraint system comply with federal safety regulations for the make, model and year of the motor vehicle.

(2) Improper repair of a vehicle inflatable restraint system is a Class A misdemeanor. [2001 c.439 §1]

Note: 167.822 was enacted into law by the Legislative Assembly but was not added to or made a part of ORS chapter 167 or any series therein by legislative action. See Preface to Oregon Revised Statutes for further explanation.

167.824 Unlawful possession of undeployed air bags or air bag canisters. (1) A person may not possess more than two undeployed air bags or air bag canisters containing sodium azide that have been removed from a vehicle. This subsection does not apply to motor vehicle dealers, automobile repair facilities or dismantlers certified under ORS 822.110.

(2) A violation of subsection (1) of this section is a Class C misdemeanor. [2005 c.514 §2; 2005 c.654 §13b]

Note: 167.824 was enacted into law by the Legislative Assembly but was not added to or made a part of ORS chapter 167 or any series therein by legislative action. See Preface to Oregon Revised Statutes for further explanation.

167.830 Employment of minors in place of public entertainment. Except as provided in ORS 167.840, any person operating or conducting a place of public amusement or entertainment, who employs or allows a child under the age of 18 years to conduct or assist in conducting any public dance, including but not limited to dancing by the child as a public performance, or to assist in or furnish music for public dancing, commits a Class D violation. [1971 c.743 §292; 1987 c.905 §18; 1999 c.1051 §163]

167.840 Application of ORS 167.830 limited. (1) ORS 167.830 does not apply if:
(a) Alcoholic beverages are not permitted to be dispensed or consumed in the place of public amusement or entertainment open to the individuals attending the public dance;
(b) Alcoholic beverages are not permitted to be dispensed or consumed in any place connected by an entrance to the place of public amusement or entertainment;
(c) Applicable laws, regulations and ordinances for the protection of children under the age of 18 years are observed in the conduct of the dance; and
(d) At least one responsible adult is present at all times during the public dance to see that applicable laws, regulations and ordinances for the protection of children under 18 years of age are observed.
(2) ORS 167.830 does not apply if the child has the written permission of the judge of the juvenile court, for the county in which the child resides, to conduct or assist in conducting the public dance. The judge of the juvenile court shall grant such permission only if:
(a) The parents or legal guardians of the child have consented to the child's participation in such activity; and
(b) The judge has found that participation in such activity will not be inconsistent with the health, safety and morals of the child.
(3) This section is not intended to make lawful any activity that is prohibited within a political subdivision of this state by ordinance or other regulation of the political subdivision.
(4) The requirements of this section are in addition to, and not in lieu of, the requirements of ORS 653.315. [1971 c.743 §293]

167.850 [1971 c.743 §226; repealed by 1985 c.662 §15]

167.860 [1971 c.596 §1; 1973 c.836 §345; 1985 c.662 §7; renumbered 167.345]

167.862 [1983 c.648 §1; 1985 c.662 §9; renumbered 167.350]

167.865 [1977 c.539 §2; renumbered 167.355]

167.870 [1973 c.316 §1; repealed by 1999 c.729 §1]

Chapter 168 (Former Provisions) Habitual Criminals

HABITUAL CRIMINALS

CRIMES AND PUNISHMENTS

168.010 [Repealed by 1955 c.663 §1 (168.011, 168.021 and 168.031 enacted in lieu of 168.010, 168.020 and 168.030)]

168.011 [1955 c.663 §2 (168.011, 168.021 and 168.031 enacted in lieu of 168.010, 168.020 and 168.030); repealed by 1961 c.648 §13]

168.015 [1961 c.648 §1; repealed by 1971 c.743 §432]

168.020 [Repealed by 1955 c.663 §1 (168.011, 168.021 and 168.031 enacted in lieu of 168.010, 168.020 and 168.030)]

168.021 [1955 c.663 §3 (168.011, 168.021 and 168.031 enacted in lieu of 168.010, 168.020 and 168.030); repealed by 1961 c.648 §13]

168.025 [1961 c.648 §§2, 14; repealed by 1971 c.743 §432]

168.030 [Repealed by 1955 c.663 §1 (168.011, 168.021 and 168.031 enacted in lieu of 168.010, 168.020 and 168.030)]

168.031 [1955 c.663 §4 (168.011, 168.021 and 168.031 enacted in lieu of 168.010, 168.020 and 168.030); repealed by 1961 c.648 §13]

168.040 [Amended by 1955 c.663 §5; repealed by 1961 c.648 §13]

168.050 [Amended by 1955 c.663 §6; 1961 c.648 §9; 1963 c.245 §1; 1969 c.502 §5; repealed by 1971 c.743 §432]

168.055 [1961 c.648 §3; repealed by 1971 c.743 §432]

168.060 [Amended by 1955 c.663 §7; 1961 c.648 §10; renumbered 168.090]

168.065 [1961 c.648 §4; repealed by 1971 c.743 §432]

168.070 [1955 c.660 §4; repealed by 1959 c.550 §4]

168.075 [1961 c.648 §6; repealed by 1971 c.743 §432]

168.080 [1961 c.648 §5; repealed by 1971 c.743 §432]

168.085 [1961 c.648 §7; 1967 c.358 §1; repealed by 1971 c.743 §432]

168.090 [Formerly 168.060; 1969 c.198 §75; repealed by 1971 c.743 §432]

168.210 [1957 c.577 §1; repealed by 1961 c.648 §13]

Chapter 169 — Local and Regional Correctional Facilities; Prisoners; Juvenile Facilities

169.005 Definitions for ORS 169.005 to 169.677 and 169.730 to 169.800. As used in ORS 169.005 to 169.677 and 169.730 to 169.800, unless the context requires otherwise:
(1) "Detainee" means a person held with no criminal charges.
(2) "Forced release" means temporary freedom of an inmate from lawful custody before judgment of conviction due to a county jail population emergency under ORS 169.046.
(3) "Juvenile detention facility" means a facility as described in ORS 419A.050 and 419A.052.
(4) "Local correctional facility" means a jail or prison for the reception and confinement of prisoners that is provided, maintained and operated by a county or city and holds persons for more than 36 hours.
(5) "Lockup" means a facility for the temporary detention of arrested persons held up to 36 hours, excluding holidays, Saturdays and Sundays, but the period in lockup shall not exceed 96 hours after booking.
(6) "Month" means a period of 30 days.

(7) "Prisoner" means a person held with criminal charges or sentenced to the facility.

(8) "Temporary hold" means a facility, the principal purpose of which is the temporary detention of a prisoner for four or less hours while awaiting court appearance or transportation to a local correctional facility. [1973 c.740 §1; 1979 c.487 §1; 1985 c.499 §4; 1993 c.33 §309; 2001 c.517 §1]

169.010 [Amended by 1963 c.236 §1; 1973 c.740 §8; repealed by 1983 c.327 §16]

169.020 [Amended by 1973 c.740 §9; repealed by 1983 c.327 §16]

LOCAL CORRECTIONAL FACILITIES

169.030 Construction, maintenance and use of local correctional facilities by county and city; renting suitable structure; provision of facilities by another county or city. (1) Every county and city in this state shall provide, keep and maintain within or without the county or city, as the case may be, a local correctional facility for the reception and confinement of prisoners committed thereto. The local correctional facility shall be constructed of fireproof materials and should have fire exits in sufficient number and suitably located for the removal of prisoners.

(2) Any county, or incorporated city may rent or lease any structure answering the requirements of subsection (1) of this section, either in connection with or separately from any other county or city building.

(3) Any county and any incorporated city may, by agreement, provide, maintain, and use for their separate requirements, such a local correctional facility as is required by this section.

(4) Any county or incorporated city may, by agreement with any other county or incorporated city, provide for one such county or city to furnish local correctional facility accommodations for the imprisonment of prisoners of the other such county or city. Pursuant to such agreement, an Oregon county or city may secure the use of jail accommodations outside the state, but only in a county that adjoins the Oregon county or the county in which the Oregon city is located.

(5) The jail accommodations provided by or furnished to a county under this section shall be considered to be jail accommodations of the county for purposes of ORS 135.215, 137.167 and 137.330. [Amended by 1963 c.236 §2; 1973 c.740 §10; 1987 c.550 §1]

169.040 Inspection of local correctional facilities. (1) The county court or board of county commissioners of each county is the inspector of the local correctional facilities in the county. The court or board shall visit local correctional facilities operated by the county at least once in each regular term and may visit local correctional facilities within the county that are not operated by the county. When the court or board visits a local correctional facility, it shall examine fully into the local correctional facility, including, but not limited to, the cleanliness of the facility and the health and discipline of the persons confined. If it appears to the court or board that any provisions of law have been violated or neglected, it shall immediately give notice of the violation or neglect to the district attorney of the district.

(2) The local health officer or the representative of the local health officer may conduct health and sanitation inspections of local correctional facilities on a semiannual basis. If the local health officer determines that the facility is in an insanitary condition or unfit for habitation for health reasons, the officer may notify the appropriate local governmental agency in writing of the required health and sanitation conditions or practices necessary to ensure the health and sanitation of the facility. If the local governmental agency does not comply with the required health and sanitation conditions or practices within an appropriate length of time, the local health officer may recommend the suspension of the operation of the local correctional facility to the local public health authority, as defined in ORS 431.003. If after a hearing the local public health authority finds that the local correctional facility is in an insanitary or unhealthful condition, it may suspend the operation of the facility until such time as the local correctional facility complies with the recommended health and sanitation conditions and practices. [Amended by 1973 c.740 §11; 2005 c.286 §1; 2015 c.736 §52]

169.042 Maximum facility population; recommendation. The county court or board of commissioners of a county may institute an examination of the county's local correctional facility for the purpose of obtaining a recommendation regarding the maximum number of inmates that should be held in the facility. This recommendation shall be based on consideration of the following:

(1) The advice of the district attorney, county counsel and sheriff concerning prevailing constitutional standards relating to conditions of incarceration;

(2) The design capacity of the local correctional facility;

(3) The physical condition of the local correctional facility; and

(4) The programs provided for inmates of the local correctional facility. [1989 c.884 §2]

169.044 Action on recommendation. When the county court or board has received a recommendation pursuant to ORS 169.042, it shall either:

(1) Reject the recommendation and decline to adopt a limit on the number of inmates that may be held in the local correctional facility; or

(2) Adopt the recommendation and, after consultation with the officials listed in ORS 169.046 (1), issue an order establishing the maximum allowable number of inmates that may be held in the local correctional facility. This shall include specific standards for determining a county jail population emergency and a specific plan for resolving the emergency. [1989 c.884 §3]

169.046 Notice of county jail population emergency; action to be taken; notification if release of inmates likely; forced release. (1) If a county court or board adopts a jail capacity limit under ORS 169.044 and the number of inmates in its local correctional facility exceeds that capacity limit so that a county jail population emergency exists, the sheriff shall notify the presiding circuit judge, each municipal court judge and justice of the peace in the county, the district attorney for the county, the county counsel, the chief law enforcement officer for each city located in the county and the county court or board of commissioners that the number of inmates in the local correctional facility has exceeded capacity and that a county jail population emergency exists.

(2) If the county court or board has adopted a jail capacity limit and action plan under ORS 169.044 and if a county jail population emergency occurs under the terms of the plan, the county court or board and the county sheriff may carry out the steps of the plan. This includes any authorization, under the plan, for the sheriff to order inmates released in order to reduce the jail population. A sheriff shall be immune from criminal or civil liability for any good faith release of inmates under ORS 169.042 to 169.046.

(3) If it becomes necessary to order inmates released under ORS 169.042 to 169.046, or if it appears to the sheriff that release of inmates is likely to become necessary in the near future, the sheriff shall immediately notify all police agencies in the county to make maximum use of citations in lieu of custody pursuant to ORS 133.055 to 133.076 until further notice.

(4) If it becomes necessary to order the release of inmates under ORS 169.042 to 169.046, the sheriff may place inmates on forced release subject to a forced release agreement. A forced release agreement must be in writing and be signed by the sheriff and the inmate and must include:

(a) The date of the next court appearance of the inmate;

(b) A statement that the inmate is required to appear at the next court appearance; and

(c) A statement that failure of the inmate to appear at the next court appearance is subject to prosecution under ORS 162.195 or 162.205. [1989 c.884 §§4,5,6; 1999 c.1051 §71; 2001 c.517 §2]

169.050 Contracts for boarding of prisoners. The county court or board of county commissioners of each county in this state, not having more than 300,000 inhabitants, shall advertise for bids for boarding of prisoners confined in the county local correctional facilities of the county, and may award the contract for boarding them to the lowest responsible bidder. If any responsible bidder, other than the sheriff, receives the contract from the county for the boarding of prisoners, such bidder shall receive compensation for boarding such prisoners rather than the sheriff, and the sheriff shall afford to such bidder all facilities for carrying out the county's contract for boarding prisoners. [Amended by 1973 c.740 §12]

169.053 Agreements with other counties or Department of Corrections for confinement and detention of offenders. (1) A county may enter into an agreement with one or more other counties of this state under ORS 190.010 for the confinement and detention of offenders subject to the legal and physical custody of the county. The agreement may provide for the reception, detention, care and maintenance, and work assignment of:

(a) Pretrial detainees;

(b) Offenders convicted of a misdemeanor; and

(c) Offenders convicted of a felony who are:

(A) Sentenced, on or after January 1, 1997, to 12 months or less incarceration; or

(B) Sanctioned, on or after January 1, 1997, by a court or the State Board of Parole and Post-Prison Supervision to 12 months or less incarceration for a violation of a condition of parole, probation or post-prison supervision.

(2) A county may enter into an agreement with the Department of Corrections under ORS 190.110 for the confinement and detention of offenders subject to the legal and physical custody of the county. The agreement may provide for the reception, detention, care and maintenance, and work assignment of:

(a) Offenders convicted of a misdemeanor; and

(b) Offenders convicted of a felony who are:

(A) Sentenced, on or after January 1, 1997, to 12 months or less incarceration; or

(B) Sanctioned, on or after January 1, 1997, by a court or the State Board of Parole and Post-Prison Supervision to 12 months or less incarceration for a violation of a condition of parole, probation or post-prison supervision.

(3) An agreement entered into under ORS 190.110 and subsection (2) of this section shall include a provision that the county reimburse the Department of Corrections for its costs incurred in confining the county inmate. Reimbursement shall be made on a per diem basis at a rate determined by the department to be its average daily incarceration cost per inmate. In lieu of reimbursement, the department and county may enter into an agreement providing for the comparable exchange of inmates as determined by the department. [1996 c.4 §1]

169.055 Contracts with Department of Corrections for county prisoners awaiting sentencing. (1) The Department of Corrections may enter into contracts or arrangements with the authorities of any county in this state to provide for the reception, detention, care, maintenance and employment of county prisoners convicted of a felony in the courts of this state who are awaiting sentencing and who, in the judgment of the sentencing court, pose an unusual security risk if they were to remain incarcerated in a local correctional facility pending sentencing.

(2) Nothing in this section requires the Department of Corrections to incarcerate a county prisoner in a Department of Corrections facility.

(3) A county prisoner poses an unusual security risk under this section if the prisoner poses a level of risk of violence or escape that exceeds the security level of the county facility. The risk of violence or escape may result from or be manifested by:

(a) A history of violence against law enforcement or corrections employees;

(b) A history of escape attempts;

(c) Documented enemies in the county facility; or

(d) A charge of aggravated murder. [1997 c.369 §1]

169.060 [Repealed by 1983 c.327 §16]

169.070 Coordination of state services by Department of Corrections; inspections to determine compliance with standards. (1) The Department of Corrections shall provide and coordinate state services to local governments with respect to local correctional facilities and juvenile detention facilities. The Director of the Department of Corrections shall designate staff to provide technical assistance to local governmental agencies in the planning and operation of local correctional facilities, lockups, temporary holds and juvenile detention facilities, and advice on provisions of state law applicable to these facilities. The department shall inspect local correctional facilities, lockups, temporary holds and juvenile detention facilities, to ensure compliance with the standards established in ORS 169.076 to 169.078, 169.740, 419A.059 and 419B.180.

(2) In carrying out its duties under subsection (1) of this section, the department may enter into agreements with public or private entities to conduct inspections of local correctional facilities, lockups, temporary holds and juvenile detention facilities.

(3) When a county that operates a local correctional facility has conducted, or caused a public or private entity to conduct, an inspection of the local correctional facility within 24 months before an inspection would be conducted under subsection (1) of this section, the department is not required to conduct the next inspection required under subsection (1) of this section if:

(a) The standards meet or exceed the standards established in ORS 169.076;

(b) The inspection is conducted in a manner that allows the county to satisfy the requirement of paragraph (c) of this subsection; and

(c) Within 45 days after the inspection is completed, the county provides to the department:

(A) A statement or copy of the standards used to conduct the inspection and the date the standards were adopted; and

(B) A portion of the findings and recommendations of the inspection that is the equivalent of the information that would have been obtained in an inspection conducted under subsection (1) of this section.

(4) The information provided to the department under subsection (3) of this section is a public record for the purposes of ORS 192.311 to 192.478 and is subject to the same disclosure requirements and retention schedule that applies to an inspection conducted under subsection (1) of this section. [1973 c.740 §2; 1979 c.338 §2; 1979 c.487 §2; 1987 c.320 §91; 1993 c.33 §310; 2003 c.475 §1; 2013 c.63 §1]

169.072 Provision of services or assistance by Department of Corrections through arrangements with local governments. (1) The Department of Corrections may enter into arrangements, contracts or agreements with local governments to provide services or other assistance to local governments with respect to local correctional facilities and juvenile detention facilities. Services and assistance provided to local governments under this section may include health care services and assistance, including providing pharmaceuticals, treatment services, transport services, training assistance, security assistance and tactical assistance.

(2) An arrangement, contract or agreement entered into under subsection (1) of this section may authorize the use of department facilities, personnel, supplies, equipment or material in providing services or other assistance to local governments. [2001 c.194 §2]

169.075 [1973 c.740 §3; repealed by 1979 c.487 §5 (169.076, 169.077, 169.078 and 169.740 enacted in lieu of 169.075)]

169.076 Standards for local correctional facilities. Each local correctional facility shall:

(1) Provide sufficient staff to perform all audio and visual functions involving security, control, custody and supervision of all confined detainees and prisoners, with personal inspection at least once each hour. The supervision may include the use of electronic monitoring equipment when approved by the Department of Corrections and the governing body of the jurisdiction in which the facility is located.

(2) Have a comprehensive written policy with respect to:

(a) Legal confinement authority.

(b) Denial of admission.

(c) Telephone calls.

(d) Admission and release medical procedures.

(e) Medication and prescriptions.

(f) Personal property accountability which complies with ORS 133.455.

(g) Vermin and communicable disease control.

(h) Release process to include authority, identification and return of personal property.

(i) Rules of the facility governing correspondence and visitations.

(3) Formulate and publish plans to meet emergencies involving escape, riots, assaults, fires, rebellions and other types of emergencies; and regulations for the operation of the facility.

(4) Not administer any physical punishment to any prisoner at any time.

(5) Provide for emergency medical and dental health, having written policies providing for:

(a) Review of the facility's medical and dental plans by a licensed physician, physician assistant, naturopathic physician or nurse practitioner.

(b) The security of medication and medical supplies.

(c) A medical and dental record system to include request for medical and dental attention, treatment prescribed, prescriptions, special diets and other services provided.

(d) First aid supplies and staff first aid training.

(6) Prohibit firearms from the security area of the facility except in times of emergency as determined by the administrator of the facility.

(7) Ensure that confined detainees and prisoners:

(a) Will be fed daily at least three meals served at regular times, with no more than 14 hours between meals except when routinely absent from the facility for work or other purposes.

(b) Will be fed nutritionally adequate meals in accordance with a plan reviewed by a registered dietitian or the Oregon Health Authority.

(c) Be provided special diets as prescribed by the facility's designated physician, physician assistant, naturopathic physician or nurse practitioner.

(d) Shall have food procured, stored, prepared, distributed and served under sanitary conditions, as defined by the authority under ORS 624.041.

(8) Ensure that the facility be clean, and provide each confined detainee or prisoner:

(a) Materials to maintain personal hygiene.

(b) Clean clothing twice weekly.

(c) Mattresses and blankets that are clean and fire-retardant.

(9) Require each prisoner to shower at least twice weekly.

(10) Forward, without examination or censorship, each prisoner's outgoing written communications to the Governor, jail administrator, Attorney General, judge, Department of Corrections or the attorney of the prisoner.

(11) Keep the facility safe and secure in accordance with the State of Oregon Structural Specialty Code and Fire and Life Safety Code.

(12) Have and provide each prisoner with written rules for inmate conduct and disciplinary procedures. If a prisoner cannot read or is unable to understand the written rules, the information shall be conveyed to the prisoner orally.

(13) Not restrict the free exercise of religion unless failure to impose the restriction will cause a threat to facility or order.

(14) Safeguard and ensure that the prisoner's legal rights to access to legal materials are protected. [1979 c.487 §6 (enacted in lieu of 169.075); 1987 c.320 §92; 2005 c.471 §6; 2009 c.595 §116; 2013 c.63 §2; 2014 c.45 §29; 2017 c.356 §20]

169.077 Standards for lockup facilities. Each lockup facility shall:

(1) Maintain 24-hour supervision when persons are confined. The supervision may include the use of electronic monitoring equipment when approved by the Department of Corrections and the governing body of the jurisdiction in which the facility is located.

(2) Make a personal inspection of each person confined at least once each hour.

(3) Prohibit firearms from the security area of the facility except in times of emergency as determined by the administrator of the facility.

(4) Ensure that confined detainees and prisoners will be fed daily at least three nutritionally adequate meals served at regular times, with no more than 14 hours between meals except when routinely absent from the facility for work or other such purposes.

(5) Forward, without examination or censorship, each prisoner's outgoing written communications to the Governor, jail administrator, Attorney General, judge, Department of Corrections or the attorney of the prisoner.

(6) Provide rules of the facility governing correspondence and visitations.

(7) Keep the facility safe and secure in accordance with the State of Oregon Structural Specialty Code and Fire and Life Safety Code.

(8) Formulate and publish plans to meet emergencies involving escape, riots, assaults, fires, rebellions and other types of emergencies; and policies and regulations for the operation of the facility.

(9) Ensure that the facility be clean, provide mattresses and blankets that are clean and fire-retardant, and furnish materials to maintain personal hygiene.

(10) Provide for emergency medical and dental health, having written policies providing for review of the facility's medical and dental plans by a licensed physician, physician assistant, naturopathic physician or nurse practitioner. [1979 c.487 §7 (enacted in lieu of 169.075); 1987 c.320 §93; 2013 c.63 §3; 2014 c.45 §30; 2017 c.356 §21]

169.078 Standards for temporary hold facilities. Each temporary hold shall:

(1) Provide access to sanitation facilities.

(2) Provide adequate seating.

(3) Maintain supervision of prisoners or detainees when confined. The supervision may include the use of electronic monitoring equipment when approved by the Department of Corrections and the governing body of the jurisdiction in which the facility is located.

(4) Prohibit firearms from the secure area except in times of emergency.

(5) Keep the facility safe and secure in accordance with the State of Oregon Structural Specialty Code and Fire and Life Safety Code. [1979 c.487 §8 (enacted in lieu of 169.075); 1987 c.320 §94; 2013 c.63 §4]

169.079 [1979 c.487 §9 (enacted in lieu of 169.075); 1981 c.869 §1; renumbered 169.740]

ENFORCEMENT OF STANDARDS FOR LOCAL CORRECTIONAL AND JUVENILE DETENTION FACILITIES

169.080 Effect of failure to comply with standards; enforcement by Attorney General; private action. (1) If the condition or treatment of prisoners in a local correctional facility, lockup or temporary hold or juvenile detention facility is not in accordance with the standards established in ORS 169.076 to 169.078, 169.740, 419A.059 or 419B.180, the staff of the Department of Corrections may notify in writing the appropriate local governmental agency of the standards which are not being met and specific recommendations for the agency to comply with the standards. Corrective measures shall be taken by the local governmental agency to insure compliance with all standards within a reasonable length of time jointly agreed upon by the agency and the Department of Corrections.

(2) The provisions of ORS 169.076 to 169.078, 169.740, 419A.059, 419B.160, 419B.180 and 419C.130 shall be enforceable by the Attorney General of the State of Oregon. The Attorney General, at the request of the Department of Corrections, may bring suit or action and may seek declaratory judgment as provided in ORS chapter 28 as well as pursue any other form of suit or action provided under Oregon law. Nothing in this section shall preclude a private right of suit or action. [1973 c.740 §4; 1979 c.338 §3; 1979 c.487 §3; 1987 c.320 §95; 1993 c.33 §311]

169.085 Submission of construction or renovation plans to Department of Corrections; recommendations by department. All plans of new construction or major renovation of local correctional facilities, lockups and juvenile detention facilities shall be submitted to the Department of Corrections for review and advisory recommendations to assist local governmental agencies to provide a safe and secure facility. The recommendations of the Department of Corrections shall be advisory and not binding upon the local governmental agency with the exception of those standards established in ORS 169.076 to 169.078, 169.740, 419A.059 and 419B.180. The Department of Corrections must notify the respective local governmental agency 45 days after submission of the plans of its recommendations on the proposed construction or major renovation of the local correctional facility. [1973 c.740 §5; 1979 c.487 §4; 1987 c.320 §96; 1993 c.33 §312]

169.090 Manual of guidelines for local correctional facility operation; guidelines for juvenile detention facility operation. (1) The Director of the Department of Corrections shall publish and distribute a manual of recommended guidelines for the operation of local correctional facilities and lockups as developed by a jail standards committee appointed by the director. This manual shall be revised when appropriate with consultation and advice of the Oregon State Sheriffs' Association, the Oregon Association Chiefs of Police, Association of Oregon Counties, the League of Oregon Cities and other appropriate groups and agencies and will be redistributed upon the approval of the Governor.

(2) The Youth Development Council established by ORS 417.847 and the Department of Corrections shall develop guidelines pertaining to the operation of juvenile detention facilities, as defined in ORS 169.005. Guidelines shall be revised by the Youth Development Council and the Department of Corrections, whenever appropriate. The guidelines shall be included in the manual published and distributed under subsection (1) of this section. However, the Youth Development Council may choose to publish and distribute the guidelines independently. [1973 c.740 §6; 1981 c.869 §7; 1987 c.320 §97; 1993 c.18 §28; 1993 c.676 §40; 2001 c.517 §5; 2001 c.904 §1; 2001 c.905 §2; 2003 c.14 §68; 2012 c.37 §108]

TREATMENT OF PRISONERS

169.105 Unconscious person not to be admitted to custody in facility. No person who is unconscious shall be admitted to custody in a facility described in ORS 169.005, but shall instead be taken immediately to the nearest appropriate medical facility for medical diagnosis, care and treatment. [1983 c.547 §2]

169.110 Time credit for good behavior. (1) Each prisoner convicted of an offense against the laws of this state, who is confined, in execution of the judgment or sentence upon conviction, including confinement imposed as a condition of probation pursuant to ORS 137.540, in a county local correctional facility in this state for a definite term, whose record of conduct shows that the prisoner has faithfully observed all the rules of the facility, is entitled, in the discretion of the sheriff or other officer having custody of such prisoner, to a deduction from the term of the sentence of the prisoner to be calculated as follows, commencing on the first day of the arrival of the prisoner at the facility to serve the sentence of the prisoner:

(a) Upon a sentence of not less than 10 or more than 30 days, one day for each 10 days.

(b) Upon a sentence of more than 30 days but not more than 90 days, three days for each 30-day period.

(c) Upon a sentence of more than 90 days but not more than 180 days, four days for each 30-day period.

(d) Upon a sentence of more than 180 days but not more than 270 days, five days for each 30-day period.

(e) Upon a sentence of more than 270 days, six days for each 30-day period.

(2)(a) Deductions under this section may be allowed for time served in an alternative sentencing facility operated pursuant to a community corrections plan if the county governing body authorizes the allowing of deductions.

(b) For purposes of calculating deductions allowable under paragraph (a) of this subsection, each day served in the facility is counted as a day of confinement. [Amended by 1965 c.346 §3; 1971 c.196 §1; 1973 c.740 §13; 1979 c.487 §11; 2011 c.203 §1]

169.115 Temporary leave; rules. (1) Any prisoner serving a sentence in a county jail may be eligible for temporary leave for a period not to exceed 10 days for the purpose of visiting a seriously ill relative, attending the funeral of a relative, or obtaining medical services not otherwise available.

(2) All requests for temporary leave must be presented to the sheriff for examination. Exemptions shall be restricted to those prisoners who are considered a possible threat to society, or those who pose a risk of not returning at the termination of such leave.

(3) Upon determining that circumstances are suitable for a prisoner to be granted temporary leave, the sheriff may grant leave to the prisoner and fix the duration and conditions of the leave.

(4) In adopting rules governing temporary leave, the sheriff shall consult with the Department of Corrections in an effort to establish statewide uniform rules governing temporary leave for county jail prisoners. [1973 c.499 §1; 1979 c.487 §12; 1987 c.320 §98]

169.120 Credit for work. (1)(a) In addition to the allowances provided for in ORS 169.110, all prisoners in a county local correctional facility who are engaged in work either inside or outside the facility are entitled to an allowance of credits in time or compensation, or both, for the work.

(b) The allowances under paragraph (a) of this subsection may not be inconsistent with ORS 169.170 to 169.210.

(2)(a) The credits provided by this section may not be in excess of 10 days for a period of 30 days and shall be set by the county court, board of county commissioners or local correctional facility supervisor.

(b) Notwithstanding paragraph (a) of this subsection, in the case of a sentence of not less than 10 or more than 30 days the credits provided by this section are one day of credit for each 10 days of sentence.

(3)(a) Credits under this section may be allowed for time served in an alternative sentencing facility operated pursuant to a community corrections plan if the county governing body authorizes the allowing of credits.

(b) For purposes of calculating credits allowable under paragraph (a) of this subsection, each day served in the facility is counted as a day of confinement. [Amended by 1967 c.284 §1; 1971 c.196 §2; 1973 c.740 §14; 1979 c.487 §13; 2011 c.203 §2]

169.130 [Amended by 1959 c.533 §1; repealed by 1971 c.743 §432]

169.140 Furnishing prisoners food, clothing and necessary medical aid. The keeper of each local correctional facility shall furnish and keep clean the necessary bedding and clothing for all prisoners in the custody of the keeper, and shall supply them with wholesome food, fuel and necessary medical aid. [Amended by 1973 c.740 §15]

169.150 Payment of expenses of keeping prisoners; health care fees. (1) The charges and expenses for safekeeping and maintaining all persons duly committed to the local correctional facility of the county for trial, sentenced to imprisonment in the county local correctional facility, or committed for the nonpayment of any fine or for any contempt, shall, unless otherwise provided by law, be paid out of the treasury of the county. The account of the keeper shall be first allowed by the county court or board of county commissioners of the county from which the prisoner was committed.

(2) A city or, notwithstanding subsection (1) of this section or any other provision of law, the county may charge persons committed to the local correctional facility of the county or city a reasonable health care fee for any health care services, medications and equipment provided to the person while committed if the county or city:

(a) Provides necessary medical care regardless of the person's ability to pay;

(b) Provides equal treatment to all persons committed to the local correctional facility regardless of a person's ability to pay;

(c) Establishes a system that notifies the person of the fees and what services are covered; and

(d) Establishes a grievance system that allows a person to challenge the deduction of a fee from the person's account. [Amended by 1973 c.740 §16; 1995 c.523 §1; 1999 c.801 §1]

169.151 Expenses of keeping prisoners; reimbursement from prisoners; amounts; procedures. (1) A city or, notwithstanding ORS 169.150 (1), a county may seek reimbursement from a person who is or was committed to the local correctional facility of the county or city upon conviction of a crime for any expenses incurred by the county or city in safekeeping and maintaining the person. The county or city may seek reimbursement:

(a) At a rate of $60 per day or its actual daily cost of safekeeping and maintaining the person, whichever is less, multiplied by the total number of days the person was confined to the local correctional facility, including, but not limited to, any period of pretrial detention; and

(b) For any other charges or expenses that the county or city is entitled to recover under ORS 169.150.

(2) The county or city may seek reimbursement for expenses as provided in subsection (1) of this section by filing a civil action no later than six years after the person from whom reimbursement is sought is released from the local correctional facility.

(3) When a person is found liable for expenses described in subsection (1) of this section and an amount is determined, the court shall, before entering a judgment against the person, allow the person to present evidence on the issue of the person's ability to pay. When a person presents such evidence, the court shall determine the person's ability to pay taking into consideration:

(a) The financial resources of the person and the burden that payment will impose on the person in providing basic economic necessities to the person or the person's dependent family; and

(b) Any other monetary obligations imposed upon the person by the court as a result of the conviction for which the person was committed to the local correctional facility.

(4) The court, and not a jury, shall determine the defendant's ability to pay under subsection (3) of this section.

(5) Upon the conclusion of a proceeding under subsection (3) of this section, the court may enter a judgment:

(a) Of dismissal if the court finds that the person lacks the ability to pay;

(b) For less than the full amount determined if the court finds that the person has the ability to pay a portion of the amount; or

(c) For the full amount determined, plus costs and disbursements, if the court determines the person has the ability to pay.

(6) Any reimbursements collected under this section must be credited to the general fund of the county or city to be available for general fund purposes. [1997 c.349 §2; 1999 c.801 §2; 2009 c.783 §15]

169.152 Liability for costs of medical care for persons in county facility. Notwithstanding ORS 169.140, 169.150 and 169.220, when a person is lawfully confined in a county local correctional facility for violation of a city ordinance, for nonpayment of a fine imposed by a municipal court or as a result of a warrant of arrest issued by a magistrate in another county, the county in which the warrant was issued or the city shall be liable for the costs of medical care provided to the person while confined in the county local correctional facility. The keeper of the local correctional facility shall bill the other county or city for the actual cost of the medical care provided, and the other county or city shall pay the charges within 60 days after receiving the cost statement from the keeper. [1985 c.530 §2]

169.153 Liability of public agency for costs of medical care provided to persons in transport. (1) Subject to ORS 30.260 to 30.300 and 414.805, payment of the costs of medical care provided to a person who becomes ill or is injured while being lawfully transported in the custody of a law enforcement officer at the request of a public agency other than the public agency by which the officer is employed is the responsibility of the public agency that requested the transportation of the person.

(2) As used in this section, "law enforcement officer" and "public agency" have the meanings given those terms by ORS 414.805. [1985 c.530 §3; 1993 c.196 §5]

169.155 Definitions for ORS 169.155 and 169.166. As used in ORS 169.166 and this section:

(1) "Local correctional facility" includes lockups and temporary hold facilities.

(2) "Reasonable efforts to collect the charges and expenses" means that the provider has billed the individual to whom the emergency medical services were provided or the insurer or health care service contractor of the individual before seeking to collect from the keeper of the local correctional facility. [1979 c.530 §4; 1993 c.196 §6]

169.160 [Repealed by 1971 c.743 §432]

169.165 [1979 c.530 §2; 1981 c.690 §1; repealed by 1993 c.196 §12]

169.166 Liability for costs of medical services. Notwithstanding ORS 169.140 and 169.150 and except as otherwise provided in ORS 414.805 and 414.807:

(1) An individual who receives medical services not provided by the county or city while in the custody of a local correctional facility or juvenile detention facility is liable:

(a) To the provider of the medical services not provided by the county or city for the charges and expenses therefor; and

(b) To the keeper of the local correctional facility for any charges or expenses paid by the keeper of the facility for the medical services not provided by the county or city.

(2) A person providing medical services not provided by the county or city to an individual described in subsection (1)(a) of this section shall first make reasonable efforts to collect the charges and expenses thereof from the individual before seeking to collect them from the keeper of the local correctional facility.

(3)(a) Except as otherwise provided in subsection (4) of this section, if the provider has not been paid within 45 days of the date of the billing, the provider may bill the keeper of the local correctional facility who shall pay the account in accordance with ORS 169.140 and 169.150.

(b) A bill submitted to the keeper of a local correctional facility under this subsection must be accompanied by evidence documenting that:

(A) The provider has billed the individual or the individual's insurer or health care service contractor for the charges or expenses owed to the provider; and

(B) The provider has made a reasonable effort to collect from the individual or the individual's insurer or health care service contractor the charges and expenses owed to the provider.

(c) If the provider receives payment from the individual or the insurer or health care service contractor after receiving payment from the keeper of the facility, the provider shall repay the keeper the amount received from the keeper less any difference between payment received from the individual, insurer or contractor and the amount of the billing.

(4) Except as otherwise provided by ORS 30.260 to 30.300 and federal civil rights laws, upon release of the individual from the actual physical custody of the local correctional facility, the keeper of the local correctional facility is not liable for the payment of charges and expenses for medical services provided to the individual. [1991 c.778 §6; 1999 c.801 §3; 2007 c.71 §53]

Note: 169.166 was enacted into law by the Legislative Assembly but was not added to or made a part of ORS chapter 169 or any series therein by legislative action. See Preface to Oregon Revised Statutes for further explanation.

169.170 Assignment of county prisoners to public works; rules. All convicts sentenced by any court or legal authority, whether in default of the payment of a fine, or committed for a definite number of days to serve sentence in a county local correctional facility, during the period of such sentence, for the purposes of ORS 169.120 and 169.170 to 169.210, are under the exclusive and absolute control of the county court or board of county commissioners of the county in which the crime was committed for which the convict was sentenced. The court or board has full power to place such convicts under the control of any road supervisor or other person appointed to take charge of them, and to cause them to work upon the public roads of the county, or such other work of a public nature as said court or board may direct. All such convicts shall be delivered to the supervisor or other person appointed to take charge of them, upon the written request of the court or board. The sheriff shall obtain a receipt from the person to whom such convicts are delivered for each of the convicts, and thereupon the sheriff's liability ceases. The county court may at any time return any convict, taken under the provisions of this section, to the sheriff, who shall thereupon take charge of the convict. The court or board is authorized and directed to provide rules and regulations in regard to the employment of said convicts not inconsistent with ORS 169.170 to 169.210. [Amended by 1959 c.530 §7; 1973 c.740 §17]

169.180 Assignment of city prisoners to public works. All convicts sentenced by any court or legal authority in any city, whether in default of the payment of a fine or committed for a definite number of days to serve sentence in any local correctional facility, during the period of the sentence shall, with the consent of the proper city authorities and for the purposes of ORS 169.120 and 169.170 to 169.210, be under the absolute and exclusive control of the county court or board of county commissioners of the county in which said city is located. Such city convicts shall be delivered to the county court by any officer having custody thereof in the same manner as county prisoners, and may be returned to the officer from whom they are received in the same manner, and shall be subject to the same rules and regulations as provided in ORS 169.170 for county prisoners. [Amended by 1973 c.740 §18]

169.190 Transfer of prisoners to another county for public work. Any county court or board of county commissioners may transfer to the county court or board of county commissioners of any other county any of the convicts committed to its control, under ORS 169.170 or 169.180. The court or board to which such convicts are so transferred has the same power and authority respecting such convicts as if they had been sentenced to serve in that county. The transfer of convicts from one county to another shall be made upon such terms and conditions as may be agreed upon by the county courts or boards concerned in the transfer.

169.200 [Repealed by 1973 c.740 §28]

169.210 Contracts for private employment of prisoners; agencies having power to work prisoners. (1) Except for work release programs, no county or city shall enter into any agreement or contract with any private person, firm or corporation for the employment of any convict.

(2) If any board or tribunal is created which has charge and management of the public roads of the county, such board or tribunal shall have the same power and authority as is conferred upon the county court or board of county commissioners by ORS 169.120 and 169.170 to 169.210. [Amended by 1973 c.740 §19]

169.220 Care of county prisoners. All persons lawfully confined in a county local correctional facility, or as prisoners engaged in work under the custody and jurisdiction of a county, shall be fed and maintained at actual cost to the county. All persons confined in a county local correctional facility shall be given three meals per day. An accurate account of each meal furnished to others than inmates of local correctional facilities, together with the names of the recipients thereof, whether facility employees or otherwise, shall be kept and reported by the sheriff each month to the county court or board of county commissioners. The county court or board of county commissioners shall furnish the sheriff with adequate equipment and supplies for carrying out the provisions of this section. The sheriff has authority to employ such assistance therefor as may be necessary. All supplies and equipment needed to feed and maintain such persons as provided in this section shall be purchased by the county court or board of county commissioners upon requisitions duly verified and presented by the sheriff to the county court or board of county commissioners. All supplies so purchased shall be paid for by warrant drawn upon the general fund of the county, upon presentation of vouchers containing itemized statements of all supplies so furnished, duly verified by the sheriff and by the person selling the same, each of whom shall certify that the supplies were actually furnished and received in the quantities represented and were of good quality, and that the price charged therefor was reasonable and just. [Amended by 1957 c.698 §1; 1973 c.740 §20]

169.310 [Repealed by 1957 c.698 §2]

DUTIES AND LIABILITIES OF SHERIFF

169.320 Control over prisoners; work by prisoners. (1) Except as otherwise provided in ORS 169.170 to 169.210, each county sheriff has custody and control of all persons legally committed or confined in the county local correctional facility of the county of the sheriff during the period of the commitment or confinement. Under the direction of the county court or board of county commissioners of the county, the sheriff may cause the prisoners in the county local correctional facility to engage in any work that is otherwise authorized by law. The work shall be performed at the places and times and in the manner as the court or board may direct. The sheriff may retain and put to work any prisoners as may be required to perform necessary services in and about the facility.

(2)(a) If the county is located within an intergovernmental corrections entity formed under ORS 190.265, the county sheriff of the county in which the facility is located is responsible for the physical custody and control of all persons legally committed to or confined in the facility during the period of the commitment or confinement and as provided in the intergovernmental agreement. The county sheriff may cause the prisoners in the local correctional facility to engage in any work that is otherwise authorized by law. The work shall be performed at the places and times and in the manner as the governing body of the intergovernmental corrections entity may direct. The sheriff may retain and put to work any prisoners as may be required to perform necessary services in and about the facility.

(b) Notwithstanding paragraph (a) of this subsection, a sheriff oversight committee has the responsibilities described in paragraph (a) of this subsection if the following requirements have been met:

(A) The agreement establishing the intergovernmental corrections entity provides for the formation and operation of a sheriff oversight committee;

(B) A sheriff oversight committee consisting of the sheriff of each county that is a member of the intergovernmental corrections entity has been formed; and

(C) Each sheriff has an equal vote on the sheriff oversight committee.

(c) A sheriff oversight committee formed as described in this subsection has all the duties and liabilities regarding the management of the local correctional facility and the physical custody and control of all persons legally committed to or confined in the facility as described in ORS 169.320 to 169.360 and 169.610 to 169.677. [Amended by 1973 c.740 §21; 1996 c.4 §5; 1999 c.801 §4]

169.330 Civil liability for release of prisoner. When a prisoner has been committed to the county local correctional facility to be held until the prisoner has paid a sum of money to a private party, or a fine or penalty to the state, and is permitted to depart the facility without legal order or process, the private party or the state may recover in a civil action against the sheriff, the damages sustained by reason of the prisoner's departure. [Amended by 1961 c.649 §8; 1973 c.740 §22]

169.340 Liability for escape of defendant in a civil action. (1) A sheriff who suffers the escape of a prisoner, arrested or in a local correctional facility, without the consent or connivance of the party on whose behalf the arrest or imprisonment was made, is liable to an action by such party, as follows:

(a) When the arrest is upon an order of arrest in a civil action, suit or proceeding; when the presence of the defendant at the return of the summons is necessary to enable the plaintiff to proceed therein, and the defendant does not appear at the time and place specified in the summons.

(b) When the arrest or imprisonment is upon an order of arrest in any other civil action, suit or proceeding, or upon a surrender in exoneration of the sheriff or security release, and the defendant is not found upon an execution against the person of the defendant issued to the proper county on a judgment in such action, suit, or proceeding.

(c) When the arrest is on an execution or commitment to enforce the payment of money, and the party interested is not recaptured or surrendered into custody at the expiration of the time limited for the service thereof, or legally discharged therefrom.

(d) When a person is imprisoned on an execution or commitment to enforce the payment of money, and the person escapes after the time limited for the service, and is not recaptured or surrendered before an action is commenced for the escape.

(2) The measure of damages in an action brought under subsection (1) of this section, is as follows:

(a) For the escape mentioned in subsection (1)(a) of this section, the actual damages sustained.

(b) In any other case, the amount expressed in the execution or commitment. [Amended by 1973 c.740 §23; 1999 c.1051 §259; 2003 c.576 §392]

169.350 Liability for failing to serve papers. When a sheriff or the officer of the sheriff, upon whom is served a paper in a judicial proceeding directed to a prisoner in the custody of the sheriff or officer, fails to forthwith deliver it to the prisoner, with a note thereon of the time of its service, the sheriff is liable to the prisoner for all damages occasioned thereby, and if the sheriff or officer willfully fails to so act, such sheriff or officer is guilty of a misdemeanor.

169.360 Appointment of keeper of local correctional facility. The sheriff may appoint a keeper of the county local correctional facility, to be denominated the jailer, for whose acts as such the sheriff is responsible. The appointment shall be in writing, and the sheriff shall file a certified copy thereof in the office of the county clerk. [Amended by 1973 c.740 §24]

169.370 [Repealed by 1961 c.22 §1]

169.380 [Amended by 1973 c.740 §25; repealed by 1981 c.41 §3]

169.510 [Repealed by 1963 c.547 §11]

169.520 [Amended by 1959 c.687 §4; repealed by 1963 c.547 §11]

FEDERAL PRISONERS

169.530 Duty to receive federal prisoners. The sheriff shall receive and keep in the county local correctional facility every prisoner who is committed thereto under civil or criminal process issued by a court of the United States, until the prisoner is discharged according to the laws thereof, as if the prisoner had been committed under process issued by the authority of this state. The prisoner shall receive all sums payable by the United States for the use of the facility, and remit such sums to the county treasurer not later than the first day of the month succeeding their receipt. A sheriff or jailer to whose custody such prisoner is committed is answerable for the safekeeping of the prisoner in the courts of the United States, according to the laws thereof. [Amended by 1973 c.740 §26]

169.540 Liability for expenses of keeping federal prisoners. The United States shall pay for the support and keeping of prisoners committed by virtue of legal process issued by or under its authority, the same charges and allowance provided for the support or keeping of prisoners committed under the laws of this state.

REGIONAL FACILITIES

169.610 Policy. It is the policy of the Legislative Assembly to encourage better rehabilitative care to misdemeanants by encouraging the establishment of regional correctional facilities that can effectively provide a program that not only includes better custodial facilities than can be provided by cities or counties individually, but also that can provide work release, educational and other types of leave, and parole supervision by the Department of Corrections. [1971 c.636 §1; 1987 c.320 §99]

169.620 "Regional correctional facility" defined. As used in ORS 169.610 to 169.677, "regional correctional facility" means a correctional facility operated pursuant to agreement as described in ORS 169.630 and used to house prisoners of the parties to the agreement, such prisoners having either pretrial or post-trial status. [1971 c.636 §2; 1985 c.708 §2]

169.630 Joint establishment or operation of facilities; agreement. (1) Two or more counties, two or more cities, any combination of them, or the State of Oregon in combination with one or more cities or counties or both, may by agreement entered into pursuant to ORS 190.003 to 190.620, construct, acquire or equip, or may by such agreement operate, a regional correctional facility.
(2) An agreement pursuant to this section shall set forth at least:
(a) The party or combination of parties to the agreement that shall be responsible for the operation and administration of the facility;
(b) The amount of funding to be contributed by each party toward the construction or acquisition and equipping of the facility, or toward the operation of the facility, or toward both, as the case may be; and
(c) The number of beds to be reserved to the use of each party to the agreement. [1971 c.636 §3; 1985 c.708 §3]

169.640 Status of facility for custody of misdemeanants and violators. (1) For purposes of sentencing and custody of a misdemeanant, a regional correctional facility shall be considered a county local correctional facility.
(2) For purposes of sentencing or custody of a person for violating a city ordinance, the regional correctional facility shall be considered a city local correctional facility. [1971 c.636 §4; 1973 c.740 §27]

169.650 Status of facility operated by Department of Corrections. A regional correctional facility operated under agreement by the Department of Corrections is not a state institution but it may be located in the same buildings as are used for a facility authorized by ORS 421.805. [1971 c.636 §7; 1987 c.320 §100]

169.660 Status of persons confined in facility operated by Department of Corrections; assignment to regional facility. (1) Persons confined in a regional correctional facility operated by the Department of Corrections shall be considered to be in the custody of the department and shall be subject to such rules as the department may prescribe.
(2) Persons committed to the custody of the Department of Corrections may be assigned to Department of Corrections bedspace at a regional correctional facility when the department is a party to the operation of the facility. Prisoners so assigned are subject to such rules as the department may prescribe and shall be considered to remain in the custody of the department regardless of whether, pursuant to agreement, the regional correctional facility is or is not under the actual administration of the department. [1971 c.636 §5; 1985 c.708 §4; 1987 c.320 §101]

169.670 Transfer of persons to facility operated by Department of Corrections; costs; return; exception. Whenever the governing body of a county or city transfers a misdemeanant or violator or a person with pretrial or post-trial status to a regional correctional facility operated by the Department of Corrections, the county or city shall pay the cost of transportation to and from the facility and other expenses incidental thereto, including the expenses of law enforcement officers accompanying the misdemeanant, violator or person with pretrial or post-trial status. The Department of Corrections shall cause at the expense of the county or city, each misdemeanant, violator or person with pretrial or post-trial status transferred to its custody under ORS 169.660 to be returned upon request of the governing body of the county or city. However, such return is not required when the release is pursuant to work release or parole where other arrangements have been made for the placement of the misdemeanant, violator or person with pretrial or post-trial status. [1971 c.636 §6; 1987 c.320 §102]

169.673 Conversion of state correctional institutions into regional correctional facilities. (1) The Department of Corrections shall negotiate with Marion County and Umatilla County, respectively, the conversion of Oregon State Correctional Institution and Eastern Oregon Correctional Institution into regional correctional facilities to house both state and county prisoners. The department shall include in the negotiations any other nearby counties desiring to participate in the operation of the regional correctional facility.

(2) If agreement is reached with Marion County, in the case of the Oregon State Correctional Institution, and with Umatilla County, in the case of Eastern Oregon Correctional Institution, the department shall proceed to operate those institutions, or either of them as to which agreement is negotiated, as regional correctional facilities according to the terms of the agreement. [1985 c.708 §6; 1987 c.320 §103]

169.677 Converted facilities to house felony or misdemeanant prisoners. If a Department of Corrections institution is made to operate as a regional correctional facility pursuant to agreement under ORS 169.673, the purposes of the institution shall include the imprisonment of either felony or misdemeanant prisoners, or both, of the parties to the agreement under which the facility is operated. [1985 c.708 §7; 1987 c.320 §104]

169.680 [1971 c.636 §8; repealed by 1985 c.708 §9]

HALFWAY HOUSES

169.690 Establishment of halfway houses and other facilities; advice of facility advisory subcommittee of local public safety coordinating council. (1)(a) Before the Department of Corrections, Department of Human Services, Oregon Health Authority, Oregon Youth Authority or any city, county or other public agency establishes a facility described in paragraph (b) of this subsection, the city, county, department, authority or agency shall fully inform the local public safety coordinating council convened under ORS 423.560 of the following:

(A) The proposed location, estimated population size and use of the facility;

(B) The proposed number and qualifications of resident professional staff at the facility;

(C) The proposed rules of conduct for residents of the facility; and

(D) Other relevant information that the city, county, department, authority or agency responsible for establishing the facility considers appropriate or that the council requests. Nothing in this subparagraph authorizes the disclosure of information that is protected under state or federal law.

(b) The facilities to which paragraph (a) of this subsection applies are:

(A) Halfway houses, work release centers or any other domiciliary facilities for persons released from any penal or correctional facility but still in the custody of the city, county or public agency;

(B) Youth care centers or other facilities authorized to accept youth offenders under ORS 419C.478; and

(C) Residential treatment homes and residential treatment facilities, as those terms are defined in ORS 443.400, for persons who, as a condition of release under ORS 161.315 to 161.351, are required to live in a secure home or facility.

(2) The facility advisory subcommittee of the local public safety coordinating council shall advise the city, county, department, authority or agency responsible for establishing the facility as to the suitability of the proposed facility and may suggest changes in the proposal submitted under subsection (1) of this section. The advice shall:

(a) Be in writing;

(b) Represent the view of the majority of the subcommittee; and

(c) Be provided to the city, county, department, authority or agency no more than 60 days after receiving the information described in subsection (1) of this section.

(3) If the city, county, department, authority or agency responsible for establishing the facility rejects any of the advice of the facility advisory subcommittee, it must submit its reasons in writing to the subcommittee.

(4) This section does not apply if a board of county commissioners has failed to convene a local public safety coordinating council.

(5) As used in this section:

(a) "Establishes" includes entering into a contract to provide for the operation of a facility described in subsection (1)(b) of this section.

(b) "Secure home or facility" has the meaning given that term in rules adopted by the Oregon Health Authority. [1975 c.367 §1; 1977 c.381 §1; 1987 c.320 §105; 1999 c.763 §1; 2009 c.595 §117; 2009 c.828 §38]

JUVENILE DETENTION FACILITIES

169.730 Definitions for ORS 169.740 to 169.760. As used in ORS 169.740 to 169.760:

(1) "Isolation" means confinement of a juvenile in any room which lacks toilet facilities, furniture, reading and recreation materials or access to light and air comparable to that in other rooms used for the detention of juveniles.

(2) "Roomlock" means confinement of a juvenile in any sleeping room, other than an isolation room, except during regular sleeping periods; except that, in the case of facilities serving counties with a population less than 70,000,

based on the 1980 census, "roomlock" does not include confining a juvenile in a sleeping room when all detained juveniles of the same sex are similarly confined due solely to the limitations of physical facilities or staff. [1981 c.869 §1a]

169.740 Standards for juvenile detention facilities. (1) The standards established in ORS 169.076 to 169.078 apply to juveniles detained in juvenile detention facilities.

(2) In addition, juvenile detention facilities shall:

(a) Provide for personal inspection of each juvenile at least once each hour unless a particular situation requires more frequent inspection;

(b) Provide for personal or electronically monitored supervision on each floor where juveniles are detained;

(c) Provide for separation of detained juveniles from the sight and sound of detained adults. Juveniles may not be placed in facilities that are designated for isolation of adult prisoners in order to meet this standard;

(d) Provide for unrestricted contact between 8 a.m. and 5 p.m. for a period of not less than five hours per day between detained juveniles and their attorneys and unrestricted attorney access to the facility for private attorney-client consultation;

(e) Unless otherwise ordered by the juvenile court following a hearing, provide for the private and unrestricted receipt of and sending of mail; except that incoming mail may be opened in the presence of the juvenile upon reasonable suspicion to believe that the mail contains contraband as defined in ORS 162.135 (1) and that incoming packages shall be opened in the presence of the juvenile and their contents may be held until the juvenile is released. The juvenile shall be informed of any confiscated contraband;

(f) Provide for the payment of postage for the juvenile's mail to an attorney or to federal, state, county or municipal government officials;

(g) Provide for nondispositional counseling and physical exercise of any juvenile held in excess of five judicial days and cause access to the juvenile held in excess of five judicial days for education pursuant to ORS 336.585;

(h) Provide for the free exercise of religion by a detained juvenile, unless such provision will cause a threat to the security of the facility or a threat of disorderly conduct within the facility;

(i) Make a written report, one copy of which shall be maintained in a general log, of each use of physical force, restraint, isolation, roomlock or internal search, setting forth in detail the reason such action was taken and the name of the staff person taking such action;

(j) Notify the attorney and the parent or guardian of the detained juvenile after the use of any physical force, restraint, isolation or internal search upon the juvenile both:

(A) As soon as reasonable after the use thereof; and

(B) By mailing a copy of the written report within 24 hours after the use thereof;

(k) For juveniles detained in an adult correctional facility, provide for in-person contact by juvenile department staff within 24 hours of the juvenile's admission and on a daily basis for as long as the juvenile shall remain in the facility; and

(L) Provide for counseling of any detained juvenile found to be within the jurisdiction of the court.

(3) As used in this section:

(a) "Adult" does not include a person who is 18 years of age or older and is alleged to be, or has been found to be, within the jurisdiction of the juvenile court under ORS 419C.005.

(b) "Juvenile" means a person alleged to be within the jurisdiction of the juvenile court under ORS 419C.005 and a youth offender. [Formerly 169.079; 1991 c.833 §2; 2003 c.442 §5]

169.750 Restrictions on operation of juvenile detention facilities. A juvenile detention facility may not:

(1) Impose upon a detained juvenile for purposes of discipline or punishment any infliction of or threat of physical injury or pain, deliberate humiliation, physical restraint, withholding of meals, or isolation, or detention under conditions that violate the provisions of subsections (2) to (8) of this section or ORS 169.076 (7) to (11), (13) or (14) or 169.740;

(2) Use any physical force, other means of physical control or isolation upon a detained juvenile except as reasonably necessary and justified to prevent escape from the facility, physical injury to another person, to protect a detained juvenile from physical self-injury or to prevent destruction of property, or to effectuate the confinement of the juvenile in roomlock or isolation as provided for in ORS 169.090, 169.730 to 169.800, 419A.050 and 419A.052, and for only so long as it appears that the danger exists. A use of force or other physical means of control may not employ:

(a) The use of restraining devices for a purpose other than to prevent physical injury or escape, or, in any case, for a period in excess of six hours. However, the time during which a detained juvenile is being transported to another facility pursuant to court order shall not be counted within the six hours; or

(b) Isolation for a period in excess of six hours;

(3) Use roomlock except for the discipline and punishment of a detained juvenile for violation of a rule of conduct or behavior of the facility as provided for in ORS 169.076 (12) or for conduct that constitutes a crime under the laws of this state or that would justify physical force, control or isolation under subsection (2) of this section;

(4) Cause to be made an internal examination of a detained juvenile's anus or vagina, except upon probable cause that contraband, as defined in ORS 162.135 (1), will be found upon such examination and then only by a

physician licensed under ORS chapter 677, naturopathic physician licensed under ORS chapter 685, physician assistant licensed under ORS 677.505 to 677.525 or nurse licensed under ORS chapter 678;

(5)(a) Administer to any detained juvenile medication, except upon the informed consent of the juvenile or in the case of an imminent threat to the life of the juvenile or where the juvenile has a contagious or communicable disease that poses an imminent threat to the health of other persons in the facility. However, prescription medication may not be administered except upon a written prescription or written order by a physician licensed under ORS chapter 677, physician assistant licensed under ORS 677.505 to 677.525, nurse practitioner licensed under ORS 678.375 to 678.390, naturopathic physician licensed under ORS chapter 685 or dentist licensed under ORS chapter 679, and administered by a person authorized under ORS chapter 677, 678 or 679 to administer medication. Facility staff not otherwise authorized by law to administer medications may administer noninjectable medications in accordance with rules adopted by the Oregon State Board of Nursing pursuant to ORS 678.150 (8);

(b) Nonmedical personnel shall receive training for administering medications, including recognition of and response to drug reactions and unanticipated side effects, from the responsible physician, physician assistant, naturopathic physician or nurse and the official responsible for the facility. All personnel shall be responsible for administering the dosage medications according to orders and for recording the administrations of the dosage in a manner and on a form approved by the responsible physician, physician assistant, naturopathic physician or nurse practitioner; and

(c) Notwithstanding any other provision of law, medication may not be administered unless a physician, physician assistant licensed under ORS 677.505 to 677.525, naturopathic physician licensed under ORS chapter 685 or nurse licensed under ORS chapter 678 is either physically on the premises or readily available by telephone and within 30 minutes travel time of the patient;

(6) Administer to any detained juvenile any medication or medical procedure for purposes of experimentation;

(7) Discipline or punish any juvenile for conduct or behavior by roomlock, for a period in excess of 12 hours, or by denial of any privilege, regularly awarded other detained adults or juveniles, for more than one day, except after:

(a) Advising the juvenile in writing of the alleged offensive conduct or behavior;

(b) Providing the juvenile the opportunity to a hearing before a staff member who was not a witness to the alleged offensive conduct or behavior;

(c) Providing the juvenile the opportunity to produce witnesses and evidence and to cross-examine witnesses;

(d) Providing the detained juvenile the opportunity to testify, at the sole option of the juvenile; and

(e) A finding that the alleged conduct or behavior was proven by a preponderance of the evidence and that it violated a rule of conduct or behavior of the facility as provided for in ORS 169.076 (12) or constituted a crime under the laws of this state; and

(8) Detain juveniles with emotional disturbances, mental retardation or physical disabilities on the same charges and circumstances for which other juveniles would have been released or provided with another alternative. [1981 c.869 §3; 1983 c.598 §1; 1993 c.33 §313; 1997 c.765 §1; 2007 c.70 §38; 2009 c.535 §32; 2014 c.45 §31; 2017 c.356 §22]

169.760 Juvenile detention facilities to establish written policy. All juvenile detention facilities, within six months following November 1, 1981, shall have established comprehensive written policies providing for the least restrictive alternative consistent with the safety and security of the facility, ORS 169.076, 169.078, 169.740 and 169.750, with respect to:

(1) The admission and release of juveniles to and from the facility and proper notification of the juvenile's parent, guardian or other person responsible for the juvenile;

(2) The use of physical restraints, physical force, chemical agents, internal searches and isolation of or upon a detained juvenile;

(3) A detained juvenile's access to medical and dental treatment, education, counseling and exercise;

(4) Access to the facility by the public and news media;

(5) Access to reading materials for detained juveniles;

(6) Dress and groom code which will allow for individual identity of detained juveniles;

(7) Access to visitation and telephone calls for a detained juvenile with family and friends;

(8) Sanctions for violating rules of inmate conduct made pursuant to ORS 169.076 (12) and procedures for fact-finding and imposition of discipline or punishment; and

(9) Access to records and grievance procedures for complaints by the detained juvenile, the attorney of the detained juvenile, parent or guardian or other interested person as provided for in ORS 419A.255. [1981 c.869 §5; 1993 c.33 §314]

169.770 Release of detained juvenile when detention facility violates standards. Notwithstanding the procedures set out in ORS 169.080 and 419A.061, the juvenile court in which venue lies pursuant to 419B.100 or 419C.005 shall, upon motion of any party or on its own motion, and after prompt hearing, release any juvenile detained in a facility which violates ORS 169.076 (7) to (11), (13) or (14), 169.740 or 169.750, unless the court finds that such violation is not likely to reoccur. The court may comply with the release provisions of this section by transferring a detained juvenile to an available juvenile detention facility which it finds complies with ORS 169.076 (7) to (11), (13) or (14), 169.740 and 169.750, or by placing the juvenile in shelter care, or by releasing the juvenile to the custody of a responsible adult under terms and conditions specified by the court, or by releasing the juvenile on personal recognizance under terms and conditions specified by the court. The appeal of a final order under this section does not suspend the jurisdiction of the juvenile court while the appeal is pending. No subsequent order of the juvenile court shall moot the appeal. [1981 c.869 §4; 1985 c.499 §8; 1985 c.618 §11; 1993 c.33 §315; 2001 c.480 §12]

MISCELLANEOUS

169.800 Detention of juveniles before conviction and execution of sentence. Notwithstanding a waiver order under ORS 419C.349, 419C.352, 419C.364 or 419C.370, if a person under 16 years of age is detained prior to conviction or after conviction but prior to execution of sentence, such detention shall be in a facility used by the county for detention of juveniles. [1985 c.631 §3; 1993 c.33 §316; 1993 c.546 §120]

169.810 Assumption of duties by regional correctional facility constitutes assumption by public employer; rights of transferred employees. (1) Assumption by the regional correctional facility of those custodial duties formerly performed by a county or city jail constitutes an assumption of duties by a public employer subject to ORS 236.610 to 236.640.

(2) An employee who transfers from employment at a county or city jail to employment at a regional correctional facility operated by the county or city by which the employee has been employed shall be accorded the following rights:

(a) If a trial or probationary service period is required for employment at the county or city jail, the period of county or city employment of the employee shall apply to that requirement.

(b) An employee who transfers from employment at a county or city jail to employment at the regional correctional facility shall retain accumulated unused sick leave with pay and the accumulated unused vacation with pay to which the employee was entitled under county or city employment on the day before the transfer that are supported by written records of accumulation and use pursuant to a plan formally adopted and applicable to the employee under county or city employment.

(c) Notwithstanding any other provision of law applicable to a retirement system for county employees or city employees, an employee who transfers from employment at a county or city jail to employment at the regional correctional facility who was participating in a retirement system under county or city employment may elect, not later than the first day of the month following the month in which the employee transfers, to continue under the retirement system in which participating and not to become, if eligible, a member of another retirement system. The election shall be made in writing and shall be submitted to the regional correctional facility administrator, the Public Employees Retirement Board and the governing body of the counties and cities that operate the regional correctional facility.

(d) If an employee elects to continue under the retirement system in which participating under county or city employment, the employee shall continue to make required contributions to that system and the administration of the regional correctional facility shall make contributions on behalf of the employee required of an employer participating in that system.

(e) If an employee fails to elect to continue under the retirement system in which participating under county or city employment as provided in paragraph (c) of this subsection or was not participating in a retirement system under county or city employment, the employee shall become, if eligible, a member of the Public Employees Retirement System. If the employee is eligible to become a member of the Public Employees Retirement System, the period of continuous service of the employee under county or city employment immediately before the transfer of the employee shall apply to the six months' service requirement of ORS 238.015, 238A.100 or 238A.300 (1).

(3) The county or city employment records, or a copy thereof, applicable to an employee transferred under subsection (2) of this section shall be provided by the person having custody of the records to the regional correctional facility administrator. [1985 c.708 §8; 2003 c.733 §48; 2011 c.722 §20]

CHAPTER 170 [Reserved for expansion]

Made in the USA
Monee, IL
21 December 2019